MILITARY COMMUNICATIONS

MILITARY COMMUNICATIONS

From Ancient Times to the 21st Century

Christopher H. Sterling

Editor

A B C ⬢ C L I O

Santa Barbara, California   Denver, Colorado   Oxford, England

Copyright 2008 by ABC-CLIO, Inc.

Library of Congress Cataloging-in-Publication Data
Military communications : from ancient times to the 21st century / Christopher H. Sterling, Editor.
   p. cm.
  Includes bibliographical references and index.
  ISBN 978-1-85109-732-6 (hard copy : alk. paper) — ISBN 978-1-85109-737-1 (ebook) 1. Armed Forces—Communication systems—Encyclopedias. I. Sterling, Christopher H., 1943–

UG590.M56 2008
358′.2403—dc22

2007018160

12 11 10 09 08   1 2 3 4 5 6 7 8 9 10

This book is also available on the World Wide Web as an ebook. Visit www.abc-clio.com for details.

ABC-CLIO, Inc.
130 Cremona Drive, P.O. Box 1911
Santa Barbara, California 93116-1911

Senior Production Editor: Cami Cacciatore
Editorial Assistant: Sara Springer
Production Manager: Don Schmidt
Media Manager: Caroline Price
Media Editor: Ellen Rasmussen
File Manager: Paula Gerard

This book is printed on acid-free paper. ∞
Manufactured in the United States of America

CONTENTS

Contributors, xi
Preface, xv
Acknowledgments, xix
Introduction, xxiii

A

Air Force Communications Agency
  (AFCA, 1991–2006), 1
Air Force Communications Service (AFCS),
  Air Force Communications Command
  (AFCC) (1961–1991), 3
Air Force Research Laboratory,
  (Rome, New York), 6
Airborne Warning and Control System
  (AWACS), 7
Airmobile Communications, 8
Airplanes, 10
Airships and Balloons, 13
Alaska Communications System,
  15
Aldis Lamp, 17
Alexander, Edward Porter (1835–1910), 18
American Civil War (1861–1865), 19
American Telephone & Telegraph Co.
  (AT&T), 21
American Wars to 1860, 23
Ancient Signals, 24
Appalachian, USS, 26
Ardois Light, 27
Arlington Hall, 28
Armed Forces Communications &
  Electronics Association (AFCEA), 30
Armstrong, Edwin Howard
  (1890–1954), 31
Army Airways Communications System,
  Airways and Air Communications
  Service (AACS, 1938–1961), 32

Army Battle Command System (ABCS), 34
Army Signal Corps, 35
Artillery / Gunfire, 40
Association of Old Crows (AOC), 41
Atlantic, Battle of the (1939–1945), 42
Atlantic Wall, 44
Australia: Royal Australian Corps of
  Signals, 45
Automatic Digital Network
  (AUTODIN), 47
Automatic Secure Voice Communications
  (AUTOSEVOCOM), 48

B

Bain, Alexander (1811–1877), 51
Baltic Nations, 52
Banker, Grace (1892–1960), 54
Beardslee Telegraph, 55
Bell, Alexander Graham (1847–1922), 57
Bell Telephone Laboratories (BTL), 58
Berlin Airlift (1948–1949), 60
Blair, William Richards (1874–1962), 61
Blandford Camp, 62
Bletchley Park, 63
Boer War Wireless (1899–1902), 65
Britain, Battle of (1940), 66
Bull Run, Battle of (1861), 68
Bush, Vannevar (1890–1974), 69

C

Camp Crowder, Missouri, 71
Canada, 72

Canada: Communications Security
    Establishment (CSE), 75
Chappe, Claude (1763–1805), 76
Cher Ami and the "Lost Battalion," 77
Chicksands, 78
China, People's Republic of, 79
Coast Defense, 82
Code, Codebook, 84
Code Breaking, 86
Code Talkers, 87
Color, 89
Combat Information Center (CIC), 90
Combat Information Transport System
    (CITS), 91
Commonwealth Communications Army
    Network (COMCAN), 92
Communication Satellites, 92
Communications Security (COMSEC), 96
Computer, 98
Computer Security (COMPUSEC), 101
Confederate Army Signal Corps, 102
Coston Signals, 103
Couriers, 105
Cuban Missile Crisis (1962), 106

D
DARPANET, 109
de Forest, Lee (1873–1961), 110
Deception, 111
Defence Communications Service Agency
    (DCSA), 113
Defence Fixed Telecommunications System
    (DFTS), 114
Defense Advanced Research Projects
    Agency (DARPA), 115
Defense Communications Agency (DCA,
    1960–1991), 117
Defense Communications Board/Board of
    War Communications (1940–1947), 117
Defense Communications System
    (DCS), 118
Defense Information Systems Agency
    (DISA), 119
Defense Message System (DMS), 120

Defense Switched Network (DSN), 121
Defiance, HMS, 122
Diego Garcia, 123
Dogs, 124
Driscoll, Agnes Meyer (1889–1971), 126

E
Eastern Europe, 129
Edelcrantz, Abraham (1754–1821), 130
Edison, Thomas A. (1847–1931), 131
Egypt, 132
Electric Cipher Machine (ECM Mark II,
    "SIGABA"), 134
Electromagnetic Pulse (EMP), 136
Electronic Countermeasures/Electronic
    Warfare (ECM/EW), 137
E-Mail Systems, 139
Enigma, 140
European Late Nineteenth-Century Wars,
    142

F
Facsimile/Fax, 145
Falklands Conflict (1982), 146
Fateful Day—25 June 1876, 147
Ferrié, Gustave-Auguste (1868–1932),
    148
Fessenden, Reginald A. (1866–1932), 149
Fiber Optics, 151
Field, Cyrus W. (1819–1892), 152
Field Wire and Cable, 153
Fire/Flame/Torch, 154
Fiske, Bradley A. (1854–1942), 155
Flaghoist, 156
Flags, 158
Flagship, 161
Fleming, John Ambrose (1849–1945), 161
Fort Gordon, Georgia, 163
Fort Huachuca, Arizona, 164
Fort Meade, Maryland, 165
Fort Monmouth, New Jersey, 166
Fort Myer, Virginia, 167
France: Air Force (*Armée de l'Air*), 168
France: Army, 169

France: Navy (*Marine Nationale*), 172
Friedman, William F. (1891–1969), 174
Fullerphone, 176
Future Combat Systems (FCS), 177

G

German "Fish" Codes, 179
Germany: Air Force, 181
Germany: Army, 182
Germany: Military Communications
    School, 186
Germany: Naval Intelligence (*B-Dienst*), 187
Germany: Navy, 189
Global Command and Control System
    (GCCS), 190
Global Information Grid (GIG), 192
Global Positioning System (GPS), 193
Golden Arrow Sections, 195
Government Code & Cipher School
    (GC&CS, 1919–1946), 196
Great Wall of China, 197
Greece, 198
Greely, Adolphus W. (1844–1935), 199
Ground Radio, 200
Gulf War (1990–1991), 201

H

Hadrian's Wall, 207
Heliograph and Mirrors, 208
Hello Girls, 211
Heraldry/Insignia, 213
High-Frequency Direction Finding
    (HF DF), 215
High-Speed Morse, 217
Hooper, Stanford C. (1884–1955), 218
Horses and Mules, 219
Hotline/Direct Communications Link
    (DCL), 221
Howe, Admiral Lord Richard
    (1726–1799), 222
Human Signaling, 223

I

Identification, Friend or Foe (IFF), 225

India, 226
Information Revolution in Military Affairs
    (IRMA), 228
Infrared Signal Systems, 229
Institute of Electrical and Electronic
    Engineers (IEEE), 230
Institution of Electrical Engineers (IEE), 232
Intelligence Ships, 233
International Code of Signals (ICS), 234
International Telecommunication Union
    (ITU), 236
Internet, 237
Iraq War (2003–Present), 240
Israel, 244

J

Jackson, Henry B. (1855–1929), 247
Jamming, 248
Japan: Air Force, 250
Japan: Army, 251
Japan: Navy (*Nippon Teikoku Kaigun*), 254
Joint Assault Signal Company
    (JASCO), 255
Joint Tactical Information Distribution
    System (JTIDS), 256
Joint Tactical Radio System (JTRS), 258
Joint Task Force–Global Network
    Operations (JTF-GNO), 259
"Jungle Telegraph", 260
Jutland, Battle of (1916), 261

K

Kilby, Jack St. Clair (1923–2005) and Noyce,
    Robert Norton (1927–1990), 263
Korean War (1950–1953), 264

L

Lamarr, Hedy (1913–2000), 267
Language Translation, 268
Laser, 269
Lights and Beacons, 270
Lincoln in the Telegraph Office
    271
Lowe, Thaddeus S. C. (1832–1913), 273

M

Magic, 275

Maginot Line, 277

Maori Signaling, 278

Marconi, Guglielmo (1874–1937), 279

Marne, Battle of (September 1914), 281

Mauborgne, Joseph Oswald
(1881–1971), 282

Medal of Honor Winners, Signal Corps,
284

Medieval Military Signaling
(500–1500 CE), 286

Mercury, HMS, 287

Meteor Burst Communications
(MBC), 288

Mexican Punitive Expedition
(1916–1917), 289

Microwave, 290

Midway, Battle of (3–6 June 1942), 291

Military Affiliate Radio System
(MARS), 292

Military Communications-Electronics
Board (MCEB), 294

Military Roads, 295

Miniaturization, 296

Missile Range Communications, 297

Mobile Communications, 298

Modulation, 302

Morse Code, 303

Morse, Samuel F. B. (1791–1872), 305

Music Signals, 306

Myer, Albert James (1828–1880), 308

N

Napoleonic Wars (1795–1815), 311

National Bureau of Standards (NBS),
National Institute of Standards and
Technology (NIST), 313

National Communications System
(NCS), 314

National Defense Research Committee
(NDRC), 315

National Reconnaissance Office (NRO),
316

National Research Council (NRC), 318

National Security Agency (NSA), 319

National Telecommunications and
Information Administration
(NTIA), 321

Native American Signaling, 322

Naval Radio Stations/Service, 323

Naval Research Laboratory (NRL), 326

Naval Security Group (NSG), 328

Naval Tactical Data System (NTDS), 329

Navy Commands and Systems, 330

Navy Radio Laboratory, 332

Nebraska Avenue, Washington DC, 333

Network Enterprise Technology Command
(NETCOM), 334

New Zealand: Royal New Zealand Corps
of Signals, 336

Night Signals, 337

North Atlantic Treaty Organization
(NATO) Communications &
Information Systems Agency, 338

O

Office of Strategic Services (OSS), 341

Ohio, USS, 342

OP-20-G, 343

P

Pearl Harbor, Hawaii, 347

Philippines, 348

Phonetic Alphabet, 350

Photography, 352

Phu Lam, Vietnam (1961–1972), 354

Pigeons, 355

Polish Code Breaking, 357

Popham, Home Riggs (1762–1820), 360

Postal Services, 361

Propaganda and Psychological
Warfare, 363

Q

Quartz Crystal for Radio Control, 367

R

Radio, 369

Radio Silence, 374

Reber, Samuel (1864–1933), 375
Renaissance and Early Modern Military Signals (1450–1800), 376
Robison, Samuel Shelburne (1867–1952), 378
Rogers, James Harris (1850–1929), 379
Room 40, 380
Rowlett, Frank B. (1908–1998), 381
Russia/Soviet Union: Air Force, 382
Russia/Soviet Union: Army, 383
Russia/Soviet Union: Navy, 386

S

Safford, Laurance F. (1890–1973), 389
Satellite Communications, 390
Scott Air Force Base, Illinois, 394
Searchlights/Signal Blinkers, 395
Semaphore (Mechanical Telegraphs), 397
Semi-Automatic Ground Environment (SAGE), 399
Signal Book, 400
Signal Rockets, 401
Signal Security Agency (SSA, 1943–1949), 402
Signals Intelligence (SIGINT), 404
Signals Research and Development Establishment (SRDE), 407
SIGSALY, 409
Silicon Valley, California, 410
Single Channel Ground and Airborne Radio System (SINCGARS), 412
Single Sideband (SSB), 413
Site R, 413
Smoke, 415
Solid State Electronics, 416
South Africa, 417
Spanish-American War (1898), 418
Spectrum Frequencies, 420
Spectrum Management, 422
Spies, 425
Spread Spectrum, 427
Squier, George Owen (1865–1934), 428
Stager, Anson (1825–1885), 429
Strategic Communications Command (STRATCOM), 430

Submarine Communications, 431
Suez Crisis (1956), 432
"System of Systems," 433

T

Talk Between Ships (TBS), 437
Tannenberg, Battle of (1914), 438
TELCOM Mobile Wireless Units, 439
Telegraph, 440
Telephone, 444
Teleprinter/Teletype, 447
Television, 449
Tesla, Nikola (1856–1943), 451
Tiltman, John Hessell (1894–1982), 452
Trafalgar, Battle of (21 October 1805), 453
Transistor, 455
Tri-Service Tactical Communications Program (TRI-TAC), 456
Tropospheric Scatter, 457
Truxton, Thomas (1755–1822), 458
Tsushima, Battle of (27–28 May 1905), 459
Turing, Alan Mathison (1912–1954), 460

U

Ultra, 463
Underground Communication Centers, 464
Undersea Cables, 467
United Kingdom: Royal Air Force, 470
United Kingdom: Royal Corps of Signals, 473
United Kingdom: Royal Navy, 476
U.S. Marine Corps, 480
U.S. Military Telegraph Service (USMTS), 481
U.S. Navy, 483

V

V-Mail, 489
Vacuum Tube, 490
Van Deman, Ralph Henry (1865–1952), 491
Vehicles and Transport, 492
Vietnam War (1959–1975), 494
Voice over Internet Protocol (VoIP), 499
Voice Relay, 500

W

Walkie-Talkie, 503
War Department Radio Net, 505
War on Terrorism, 507
Warfighter Information Network–Tactical
    (WIN-T), 509
Warsaw Pact (1955–1991), 510
Waterloo, Battle of (18 June 1815), 511
Weapons Data Link Network (WDLN), 513
Welchman, Gordon (1906–1985), 513
White House Communications Agency
    (WHCA), 514

Wireless Telegraph Board, 515
World War I, 516
World War II, 519
World Wide Military Command and
    Control System (WWMCCS), 522

Y

Y Service, 525
Yardley, Herbert O. (1889–1958), 527

Z

Zossen, Germany, 529

Military Communications Museums, 531
Military Communications Conferences, 537
Glossary of Acronyms, 539
Further Reading: A Basic Bibliography, 543
Index, 553

CONTRIBUTORS

William H. Brown is editor of *Governors' Documentaries* with the historical publications section of the North Carolina Office of Archives and History in Raleigh.

Colin Burke is an independent historian who has been a research fellow at Yale University and with the Chemical Heritage Foundation.

Laura M. Calkins is an oral historian and assistant archivist at the Vietnam Archive at Texas Tech University in Lubbock.

Kathryn Roe Coker is with the Office of Army Reserve History at Fort McPherson, Georgia.

Ralph Erskine is a retired barrister in Northern Ireland who has published extensively on World War II signals intelligence.

Peter Freeman was a retired British civil servant.

David Alan Grier is associate dean of the Elliott School of International Affairs at the George Washington University and edits the quarterly *IEEE Annals of the History of Computing*.

Michael R. Hall teaches history at Armstrong Atlantic State University in Savannah, Georgia.

Robert Hanyok is a historian with the Center for Cryptologic History, National Security Agency, Fort Mead, Maryland, and has published extensively on cryptology history.

Daniel Harrington is a historian in the Office of History, Headquarters Air Combat Command, Langley Air Force Base, Virginia.

Kerric S. Harvey is an associate professor of media and public affairs at George Washington University with a particular interest in communications technology.

Kathleen Hitt is an independent historian living in Burbank, California.

Arthur M. Holst teaches government and politics at Widener University in Chester, Pennsylvania.

Danny Johnson is with the U.S. Army's 5th Signal Command in Mannheim, Germany, and was formerly command historian for the U.S. Army Signal Command at Fort Huachuca, Arizona.

Łukasz Kamieński is completing a doctor of philosophy degree in international and political studies, Jagiellonian University, Krakow, Poland.

Zdzislaw J. Kapera is a librarian at the Institute of Oriental Philology at Jagiellonian University in Krakow, Poland, and edits the twice-yearly *Enigma Bulletin*.

Melissa S. Kozlowski is with the historical office, U.S. Army Communications-Electronics Command, at Fort Monmouth, New Jersey.

John Laprise is a doctoral candidate in communication at Northwestern University, Evanston, Illinois.

Karl G. Larew is an emeritus professor of history at Towson State University in Maryland, now living in Pennsylvania.

Cliff Lord is a telecommunications specialist who serves as historian of the Royal New Zealand Corps of Signals, and is author of several books on Commonwealth signals organizations.

Wendy A. Maier is a lecturer in history at Oakton Community College in Des Plains, Illinois.

Larry R. Morrison has been a U.S. Air Force historian for nearly a quarter-century, working at the various communications commands that have been headquartered at Scott Air Force Base, Illinois.

James A. ("Al") Moyers is chief of the historical office of the U.S. Air Force Weather Agency at Offutt Air Force Base in Omaha, Nebraska.

Jaime Olivares teaches history at Houston Community College—Central.

Douglas Penisten is a professor and associate dean at the Oklahoma College of Optometry, Northeastern State University, Tahlequah, Oklahoma. Among his avocations is researching and writing about the early history of wireless telegraphy.

Rebecca Robbins Raines authored the official history of the U.S. Army Signal Corps and is chief of the Force Structure and Unit History Branch of the Army's Center of Military History in Washington DC.

Steven J. Rauch is command historian of the U.S. Army Signal Center, Fort Gordon, Georgia.

Wendy A. Réjàn is command historian of the U.S. Army Communications-Electronics Life Cycle Management Command, Fort Monmouth, New Jersey.

Margaret Sankey teaches history at Minnesota State University in Moorhead.

Marc L. Schwartz teaches history at the University of New Hampshire in Durham.

Kent G. Sieg is with the office of history of the U.S. Army Corps of Engineers, Alexandria, Virginia.

Bolling W. Smith is a retired captain with the Washington DC Police Department and edits the quarterly *Coast Defense Journal* from his Maryland home.

Thomas S. Snyder is the former chief historian of the Air Force Communications Agency at Scott Air Force Base, Illinois.

Robert Stacy edits the H-Levant listserv and is manager of customer documentation for a medical software company in Massachusetts.

Christopher H. Sterling (editor) teaches media and public affairs courses at George Washington University and has authored or edited twenty other books on media and telecommunication.

Keir B. Sterling is command historian for the U.S. Army Combined Arms Support Command, based in Fort Lee, Virginia.

Charles A. Swann was a fire direction control specialist in the Army National Guard and will receive his bachelor of science degree in history from Utah State University in fall 2007.

Ronald R. Thomas is a communication specialist in Atlanta. In the 1960s, he served as the U.S. Air Force communications electronics officer at Cape Canaveral in support of the missile and space program.

Richard J. Thompson, Jr., is dean of mathematics and science at the College of Saint Rose, Albany, New York.

Thomas W. Thompson is an independent scholar.

Lionel E. ("Timm") Timmerman is chief of the Air Force Communications and Information Office of History at Scott Air Force Base, Illinois.

Matthew Wahlert is a doctoral candidate in political science at Miami University in Oxford, Ohio, where he has begun publishing papers about homeland security and terrorism.

Andrew J. ("Jack") Waskey, Jr., teaches in the social sciences division of Dalton State College in Georgia.

Timothy Wolters is commanding officer, Pacific Submarine Strike Group Operations Detachment D, and teaches history at Utah State University in Logan.

Brett F. Woods is an independent historical writer living in Santa Fe, New Mexico.

David L. Woods is a captain in the U.S. Naval Reserve (ret.) and has written widely on early military and naval communications. He lives in West Virginia.

Tommy R. Young II is a consultant and a retired command historian, Air Force Communications Command, Scott Air Force Base, Illinois.

PREFACE

This volume is the result of a concerted effort by nearly fifty scholars to assemble a historical reference on a topic that stretches over thousands of years. While huge amounts of ink have been devoted to just about every other aspect of military history (commanders, battles, weapons, even fortification), for some reason communications has not been one of them. Yet without effective communication, little can be accomplished, regardless of the scale of the military event. What follows is an attempt to rectify that hole in the military literature.

Taken together, the 322 entries contained in this volume provide an introduction to the vast and fascinating topic of communications in a military context. More specifically, our concern on these pages is with both the tactical and strategic applications of communication technology (and sometimes, as in selected battles, with the impact of those applications) in military organizations in war and peace. The scope is purposely broad rather than deep. Entries range from ancient times and the use of fire, smoke, and couriers, up to present-day digital integrated systems. To the extent that information is available, coverage includes as wide a variety of countries as possible over the years, though our emphasis is on the English-speaking world (material on other countries or regions has been limited by availability of the source material and volunteers to write relevant entries).

As is made clear in the introduction, communication has been central to the process of fighting throughout history. But to a great extent, it seems to have become part of the background context of hostilities—always there, even if not always well applied. Whether we are talking about the use of human runners as couriers or the use of fire or smoke signals—surely the earliest modes of military communication—communications has been vital to victory even if it has rarely been able to stave off defeat. The effective use of modes of communication, of course, is subject to all the limitations of any other human endeavor.

We have provided entries on specific battles where communication played a central part (e.g., the Battle of Midway in 1942), general periods of military history (e.g., Napoleonic), key individuals (military and civilian), commands and other military organizations, specific locations (e.g., chiefly important command headquarters), and—most relevant and the largest category—the specific modes and means of message transmission. These range from the natural (e.g., birds, animals, human runners) to the latest technologies (e.g., the growing variety of digital systems).

Each entry places its subject topic within a historical context, is linked to related materials by "see also" suggestions, and includes references for further reading. Some of the latter are Web based, always a risky business as Web sites all too often come and go without notice. We have leaned toward print sources whenever possible as they will—presumably—last.

Brevity and concise writing are a hallmark of any encyclopedia project. We are not telling the whole story here by a long shot. Rather, we have attempted to survey a huge field (both as to historical time covered and breadth of means and modes) in what must be considered an introductory survey.

Any project including current military information naturally must work within the confines of security concerns and classified information restrictions. Put another way, as coverage in these pages gets more current (say, in the period since Vietnam, and especially since about 1990), we are writing entries based on information that is publicly available—not classified. There are doubtless many other organizations, processes, and systems not yet known in the open literature. And doubtless the conclusions drawn here will become outdated with time as more is learned.

You will find little information here on specific equipment types or models. That is a huge subject in itself, as epitomized, for example, by Louis Muelstee's substantial (three volumes with another in preparation) directory of British signals equipment. We focus here on overall developments and provide some equipment examples. Numerous Web sites offer detailed equipment information.

Save for minor exceptions, this volume does not deal with the mass media (radio, television, the press) and their coverage of military affairs. Nor does it generally include the broadcasting operations of the military, operated chiefly as moral support for fighting forces. We are not concerned here with international diplomacy, except when those efforts fail and military action results.

A few topics are dealt with briefly but not extensively—code breaking is a good example. Many of the historical efforts at code breaking were not inherently military (but were diplomatic or even religious, for example), nor did they have direct military impact. Most importantly, however, excellent code breaking reference material already fills several books the size of this one.

Less information is available on countries other than Britain and the United States than the editor would have liked to include. Likewise, fewer "foreign" people, sites, and organizations are listed here than we would have liked. This is due primarily to a lack of authors with the background to write about the host of nations not represented on these pages, or adequate material in English on which to base entries. Sadly, the information on British military communications suffers from a lack of participation in the project by the impressive Royal Corps of Signals Museum in Blandford Camp, England, one of the world centers of artifacts and research in this field. We tried on numerous occasions to interest them in our project, to no avail.

There is no intended bias in these pages. We are not touting a particular point of view—save that communication links are vital to military operations—nor any particular mode to accomplish military needs. As a group of authors, we do not adhere to any single point of view, political or otherwise.

Christopher H. Sterling
Washington DC

ACKNOWLEDGMENTS

As with any multiauthor project, this one has benefited from many invaluable contributors who have brought it to fruition. Thanks go first to prolific series editor **Spencer C. Tucker** who accepted my proposal to edit the book, despite my own lack of any military background. I had first worked with him as a contributor to his multivolume encyclopedias on the two world wars. At numerous points along the way, he lent a hand, and sometimes a needed word of encouragement when things looked a mite bleak. Editor of a perfectly amazing shelf (more like a bookcase) of encyclopedia references himself, Spence has set the model by which the rest of military encyclopedia makers abide.

The project's advisory board has been essential in shaping the original list of likely entries, writing a number of them and suggesting other authors. This project relied especially heavily on its editorial board, given the breadth of this subject matter and the fact that the book's editor was an admitted amateur on its many aspects. Made up of civilian historians, former military officers, and expert others both here and abroad, the board was vital to the project. I am especially grateful to those members who not only advised but also agreed to take on the writing of some entries themselves. Among the advisory group, several individuals proved especially helpful.

Dave Woods and I go back the farthest—to a late-1970s publishing project that reprinted important contemporary reports and articles on military and naval communications. These included his own path-breaking *History of Tactical Communication Techniques* (reprinted by Arno, 1974) and his edited two-volume anthology, *Signaling and Communication at Sea* (Arno, 1980), both of which helped greatly to inform the present project. I am grateful for his positive outlook and advice all along the way. **Paul J. Scheips**, another of our colleagues on that project who unfortunately died a year before we began this one, edited a matching anthology, *Military Signal Communications* (Arno, 1980), which has provided another valuable guidepost for work on this volume.

Cliff Lord of New Zealand came to the project thanks to our Web page, about 18 months after we had begun the process that has led to this book. He provided a valuable freshness of perspective, numerous good ideas, much helpful information, and many entries, all of which helped to broaden the scope of the volume from being more U.S.-centric than it has turned out to be. Conquering distance and time zones, he added considerable authority to much of what you read on these pages. Likewise, **Danny Johnson**, a retired U.S. Army signals officer now living in Germany, came to us via the Web site and helped greatly with a number of entries, both domestic and those covering European nations. And he kept volunteering to do more. **Łukasz Kamieński**, a graduate student in Poland, also came to the project thanks to the Web site and took on a number of central entries about recent technologies and wars.

Army Signal Corps Command Historian **Steven Rauch** has been hugely helpful, not just for specific Signal Corps entries and ideas but also in putting me on the straight and narrow editorial path. Like me, he had contributed entries for other encyclopedias (most edited by the ubiquitous Spence Tucker) and helped me get organized early to keep better track of who was doing what and when. He was a continuing source of good ideas, needed corrections, and solid advice. The Air Force communications historians at Scott Air Force Base in Illinois, most especially **Lionel Timmerman**, also provided encouragement, good advice, and numerous relevant publications to help launch this project. **Dennis Reader** was most kind to share chapters of his in-progress work on post–World War II Royal Air Force signals development.

Toward the end of the project, **Ralph Erskine** in Northern Ireland came across our Web page and contacted me. An acknowledged authority on wartime signals intelligence, he very kindly volunteered to vet our relevant entries—an offer I accepted with alacrity before he could change his mind. His extensive efforts were invaluable and saved the project from mistakes that might otherwise have made it through the editing process.

At ABC-CLIO, several people have demonstrated considerable patience in the three-year process of getting this book published. **Alicia Merritt** was my original editor and she was positive and encouraging whenever I raised a question. She is now retired, and I hope she gets to see the result of her help. **Alex Mikaberidze** helped shepherd the project through to publication. I've very much enjoyed working with both **Cami Cacciatore** and **Ellen Rasmussen** in the production process that led to the book you now hold. They each have a good sense of humor which goes a long way with any author.

I am especially pleased to thank several family members for specific roles. My brother **Keir Sterling,** a member of the advisory board as well as a contributor, helped me better understand the intricacies of military commands and structure from his role as a command historian at Fort Lee, Virginia. My elder daughter, **Jennifer A. Sterling,** pushed me into accepting the idea of creating a Web site for this project (and others). She then designed it and got it up and running online. It has since grown into a more general professional and a vocational site (www.ChrisSterling.com). She continues to assist in keeping it current. It has proved invaluable in attracting many of our authors and communicating with all of them. My younger daughter, **Robin B. Sterling**, being the one member of the family involved in the military-industrial complex (she is a consultant to the U.S. Navy), was very helpful in providing ideas and links to people—and solving occasional computer crises.

And, as always, my spouse **Ellen** was a great sounding board, good relief, and strong booster in those moments in any project when things seemed not to be going well. I would not get half as much done without her continued support—now for more than four decades.

INTRODUCTION

It has often been said that armies travel on their stomach. Even truer is that armies (and navies, and more recently air forces) travel—and fight—by relying strongly on their modes of communication. This survey introduces the history of military communications, in part by placing the entries that follow in a larger context, with the intent of providing a brief chronological overview of major trends in both the relevant technologies and their many applications. It suggests at least three revolutions have occurred in military communications since the first, around 1850—the coming of the electric telegraph, of wireless a half-century later, and of the digital era of today.

In the vast and growing literature on all aspects of military history on land, at sea, and in the air, a common omission in most cases is any description or analysis of the role of communications. (The relatively few exceptions are found in the Further Reading section at the end of this book, as well as in the references for individual entries within the text.) The numbers of general wartime histories, assessments of specific battles, reviews of weapons development, and biographies of key figures are countless—but precious little is mentioned of the actual communication links that often made the difference between victory and defeat. While exceptions to this dearth can be found (the literature describing the 1942 Battle of Midway comes to mind, as do other studies of World War II code breaking), several reasons underlie this missing history.

Central to the "missing in action" status of communications history is that modes of communicating (whether military or in general) changed little over most of the span of human conflict. Human couriers, messages sent by pigeons or dogs, signaling with fire, smoke, drums, or horns—all of these were well known to the ancient Greeks and even earlier populations. While technology gradually transformed weapons (artillery and small guns, for example, by the early Renaissance), fortification (from castles of the Middle Ages to underground defenses by the eighteenth century), transport (steam rail and ships by the nineteenth century), and medical care for the wounded, comparatively little progress was evident in communications.

Considering communications technology went unchanged until about 1850, how orders were sent or received was seen (if noted at all) as part of the background to confrontation, sometimes acknowledged by historians, but more usually ignored—or merely presumed, thus requiring no comment. As one British Royal Navy officer said about the role of military communications nearly a hundred years ago, "Considering the amount of attention bestowed to the art of war by the ancients, it is strange that so little information regarding the methods of transmitting orders amongst the armies and fleets can have filtered down to modern times" (Shore 1915).

Though perhaps not immediately evident, the entries in this encyclopedia demonstrate that military communication history can be divided into several distinct periods.

Pre-Electric Era (to 1850)

Prior to the last two centuries, military communication was generally restricted to the distance a man could see or the speed at which he could travel. Couriers, or messengers—on foot, horseback, wagon, or stagecoach, or aboard a ship—defined the speed of sending and receiving messages. Likewise, communication distances were severely limited. The twenty-six-mile marathons run today honor a Greek courier who in 490 BCE ran that distance to tell Athens of a military victory—and promptly dropped dead from the exertion.

From those days down to the famous 1776 lamp-in-the-steeple signal ("one if by land, two if by sea"), sent to Paul Revere and bringing about his famous ride of warning, means of signaling saw remarkably little change, let alone improvement. A Roman commander would have readily understood most communication methods used nearly two millennia later. Yet the need for effective communication grew with the size of armies committed to battle. From the late sixteenth to the late eighteenth centuries, fighting forces became both better trained and more professional—and expanded by a factor of ten—making coordination and signaling that much more important.

From the earliest times, fire beacons or smoke signals were used for simple, unidirectional, prearranged messages, such as reporting a victory or the sighting of enemy forces. Elizabethan England, for example, used a system of fire beacons to warn of the progress of the Spanish Armada through the English Channel in 1588. Signaling modes through history also included sound—drums and other music signals in addition to simple shouting. Pigeons and dogs, and sometimes couriers, were often used to carry messages over greater distances. Maori signaling, in what is now modern New Zealand, and the study of Native American signaling help to demonstrate the innovative communication used by various native populations. Indeed, during the French and Indian War in North America (1756–1763), both sides used traditional modes of Native American signaling often not that much different from those of the European powers, which had changed so little over time.

In late twelfth-century China, Genghis Khan used homing pigeons as couriers, establishing pigeon messenger posts and relay sites from his Mongol capital, extending to Europe and Asia. A pigeon carried messages at speeds of up to 50 miles per hour and flew over mountains, rivers, and enemy territory, while a mounted courier could only travel a few miles per hour. Using pigeons as messengers, Genghis Khan was able to send expedited commands to his various armies and distant sovereignties.

Architecture also played a part in early modes of communication. Surviving evidence indicates, for example, that means of communication (chiefly signal towers) were included as an integral part of both the Great Wall of China and of Hadrian's Wall, among other Roman works. Signal station remains clutter the British Isles, some dating from before Rome's occupation. The military roads of the Roman and later empires, including the British in the eighteenth and nineteenth centuries, were an important means of both transport and communications.

Only by the seventeenth and eighteenth centuries did important innovations in military communications first begin to appear. In the late 1700s, the United Kingdom's Royal Navy introduced a standard system of signal flags, developed by Admiral Lord Howe and improved by Home Riggs Popham during Britain's constant wars with France. These soon facilitated the sending of unplanned messages in both directions. Admiral Nelson made good use of Popham's flag system to control his ships at the 1805 Battle of Trafalgar (sending the iconic "England expects that every man will do his duty" message just as the fighting began), resulting in his defeating the French and Spanish fleets.

Changes were evident ashore as well. The invention of the telescope in 1608 helped to initiate the use of visual signaling methods and prompted several early semaphore systems. In 1684, Robert Hook offered a semaphore system that used various suspended shapes in the daytime and torches at night. Irishman Richard Lovell Edgeworth, in the late 1760s, proposed his "tellograph," a series of windmill sails of specific shapes and colors for which he proposed a system of towers and trained operators—one of the first proposals for a complete signaling system.

In France, Claude Chappe began building mechanical semaphore stations at various high points around the country in 1794. Each one used a system of flexible rods that, by setting different patterns, could indicate different words or messages. Reserved for senior military officials and government users, his complex network eventually linked Paris to important French towns and, during the Napoleonic Wars, even reached Amsterdam and

Milan. Napoleon's Military Telegraph Service operated the Chappe semaphore system and could achieve message transmission speeds as high as 120 miles per hour in ideal conditions. It was used for tactical field signals on occasion, but was generally more helpful on logistic and strategic levels. The semaphore networks that had so aided Napoleon's armies were also used to report his final defeat at Waterloo in 1815.

The British Admiralty also built a system of fixed semaphore stations to communicate between London and its bases along the south coast, though it operated on different principles. Similar, though shorter, systems built in Sweden by Abraham Edelcrantz, by Germany, and around some East Coast harbors of the United States (using two- or three-armed metal semaphores) could provide early notice of ship arrivals—and gave rise to the many "telegraph hill" or "signal hill" locations that survive still. Semaphore stations, however, were expensive to build, staff (they required well-trained operators), and maintain and were abandoned to fall into disrepair as soon as the immediate emergency passed. And as more countries became allied in larger wars, language differences often slowed message communication. In the meantime, military forces continued to rely on postal services (their own and those more generally available) to serve the needs of both commanders and common soldiers to stay in touch with their families.

Telegraph and Telephone (1850–1900)

The first important revolution in military signaling came in the mid-nineteenth century with the invention of electric telegraphy. This was an era of electrifying change—in the sense of the technologies introduced as well as their transforming impact. For the first time, messages could be sent considerable distances (eventually thousands of miles) in a matter of minutes. While many inventors worked on the telegraph, the system most widely adopted eventually was that developed by Samuel F. B. Morse, which ultimately used a standard Morse code made up of patterns of dots and dashes to represent letters and numbers.

The military potential of telegraphy soon led to its application. The first military test of telegraphy came during the Crimean War (1854–1856) in which Britain and France sought to stop Russian expansion into Ottoman (Turkish) territory. An extensive Russian electric telegraph system provided a vital link from north of St. Petersburg (then the capital) through Moscow and south to Sevastopol on the Black Sea (site of a long siege) as well as east to Warsaw. On the other side, British Royal Engineers built and operated 21 miles of telegraph line between British headquarters at Balaclava and those of the French in Kamiesch. In 1855, a private firm under military direction constructed an undersea cable of 340 miles (by far the longest ever built to that point) to connect Balaclava across the Black Sea with Varna in present-day Bulgaria and then connect with existing continental telegraph lines. Thus commanders in the field were for the first time interfered with (they felt) by constant questions and suggestions (and sometimes orders) from distant military headquarters in London and Paris. Cyrus Field spearheaded the many expeditions to create a successful undersea cable across the Atlantic.

During the 1861–1865 American Civil War, the key communications organizations included the competing Union Army's Army Signal Corps (established in 1860), headed by Albert Myer, and the U.S. Military Telegraph Corps (formed in 1863), directed by Anson Stager, as well as the Confederate Signal Corps. Construction and operation (let alone protection) of telegraph lines became an increasingly central military function. Indeed, development of mobile telegraph units was needed to keep up with fast-moving troop formations, as were older and more traditional methods such as the use of couriers. The news of President Abraham Lincoln's death in April 1865 was sent around Washington DC's guard posts by flag and lantern signals, but reached the world by electric telegraph.

The Army Signal Corps also pioneered aerial reconnaissance and communication when Thaddeus Lowe used hot air balloons to survey above Confederate lines. Simple means of signaling (waving arms or white rags, or dropping messages tied to a rock) allowed those who were carried in the balloons' baskets to indicate what they saw back to forces on the ground. For the first time, common modes of visual (flag and torch) communication were taught at both Annapolis and West Point, a sure indicator of the growing importance of communications in the American military. Balloons and pigeons were used to communicate messages in and out of Paris during the 1871 siege by the Germans.

Use of both the telegraph and the heliograph mirror device greatly aided military forces (some of which would soon become the Royal Corps of Signals in 1920) during British colonial military signaling efforts in India, Africa (including the Boer War), and the Middle East. These technologies were also valuable to U.S. Army detachments during the post–Civil War expeditions in the American West to suppress Indian uprisings. Effective communication and thus coordination of often thinly spread military forces frequently proved essential to success. The short Spanish-American War saw similar applications, along with use of some field telephones.

At the same time, naval communication was greatly improved by the development of several types of night signals that used prearranged patterns of colored lights mounted high on a ship's mast. Heretofore, naval signaling had been largely limited to daytime hours when ships could see signal flags flown by other vessels.

The telephone, developed in the late 1870s, largely by Alexander Graham Bell, had a slower initial acceptance than had its wired forebear, telegraphy. It did not strike most observers as being as revolutionary as the earlier telegraph.

Bell demonstrated his talking device to fascinated people at the Centennial Exhibition in Philadelphia on a fateful day in June 1876. But for several decades (until the early 1900s), the telephone remained an expensive device and service (few could afford to subscribe), it could only communicate short distances, and it left no physical record of the communicated message. The telegraph readily overcame these shortcomings, though it required well-trained operators who could present security problems. Thus the full potential of the telephone was only slowly realized. The first military telephone switchboard was not installed by Britain until 1896. While telephones were quickly adopted in headquarters, tactical or strategic use would await improved technology in the twentieth century. Only in 1915, for example, did the American Telephone & Telegraph Co. (AT&T) open the first coast-to-coast telephone link—and telephone undersea cables did not appear until 1956.

Britain demonstrated what diplomatic and military needs—melded with vision and planning—could accomplish as it developed its "All Red" network of telegraph undersea cables to link its empire posts. (The term "all red" was a reference to maps, sometimes on postage stamps, that often showed the British Empire and its colonies in red.) Combined with land telegraph lines, that network allowed for quicker military response when needed, for example, to quell colonial uprisings. By the late nineteenth century, Britain effectively controlled most world communication networks.

Propelled by the 1898 Spanish-American War, the United States also expanded its own networks, constructing military telegraph cable connections with Cuba (which could sometimes get messages to Washington in twenty minutes, though communications with naval commanders often took far longer), out to the Philippines, and up to and within Alaska (which by 1900 included a 150-mile wireless telegraph link across a bay), all of which were eventually turned over to commercial operators. The United States also integrated wired modes of communication into its extensive system of turn-of-the-century coast defense installations built to protect major harbor cities and naval bases. These concrete structures included sometimes complex means of fire control to enable large guns to hit targets miles off shore. Telephone links tied commanders both to individual gun batteries and to central headquarters. The Army Signal Corps first provided extensive combat photography during this conflict.

Wireless (1895–1914)

Development of wireless telegraphy or radio took military communications another huge step forward—a second revolution in communications barely a half-century after the first. Now signals could be sent rapidly beyond the reach of sight or travel distances, anywhere, in fact, and not just where wires reached. British army and Royal Navy officers such as Henry Jackson were among those who pioneered research on the military potential of wireless telegraphy, applying crude systems to experimental field conditions. The French installed wireless on a gunboat in 1899. German military units were assisted by the work of their countrymen Adolph Slaby and George von Arco in the 1890s. Generally merchant ships were quicker to adopt wireless than their military counterparts. Marconi's work was closely monitored by the Royal Navy and the British army while de Forest sold radio equipment to the American military. Fessenden had a fractious relationship with the U.S. Navy, which often used his devices without any patent payments. Armstrong made one of his key innovations while serving with the Signal Corps in France and, in World War II, allowed the free use by the military of his frequency modulation (FM) invention. Radio opportunities for "remote control" of land forces were exceeded only by what wireless promised for naval fleets.

For the first time, wireless allowed naval commanders to keep in touch with vessels and whole fleets sailing far from land. It fell to Japan, in the Battle of Tsushima in 1905, to first demonstrate the vital importance of effective use of wireless to control a battle fleet. The opposing Russian force was nearly wiped out. The Royal Navy and, only slightly more slowly, the U.S. Navy, adapted the benefits of radio to fleet operations, expanding their installations as radio equipment improved. The U.S. Navy, designated by the Wireless Telegraph Board of 1904 to lead American efforts in the new medium, established an expanding number of naval radio stations to improve fleet communications. Indeed, the Navy played a dominant role in all technical and policy-related American radio developments prior to and during World War I. The Naval Radio Laboratory and the Naval Research Laboratory would become centers of communication technology development and application testing. Ships could now call for help in emergencies—most spectacularly in the case of the White Star ocean liner Titanic in 1912.

Invented in 1904, improved in 1906, and fully understood by about 1912, the vacuum tube (or "valve" in British usage) became central to wireless communication from about 1920 until superseded by the transistor in the 1960s. For a half-century fragile vacuum tubes formed the core of most military electronic equipment.

Britain enhanced its existing telegraph cables by developing (with Marconi) an imperial chain of All Red wireless transmitters early in the twentieth century. It also made limited use of wireless in South Africa during the Boer War.

World War I (1914–1918)

Both wired and wireless communication saw their first real military testing during the bloody World War I, especially on the long-stalemated Western

Front. The early battles of the Marne in the west and Tannenberg in the east underscored the importance of good communications. But after the war of movement ended in September 1914, armies limited their use of tactical radio, the equipment for which was still cumbersome to use. Only late in the war did forward units obtain field radio equipment. Germany experimented with radios for its airship fleet, as did both sides, late in the war, with airplanes, first sending messages from ground to air, and then both ways.

Military radio in 1914 was crude on both sides of the conflict. Antennas were obvious targets, and equipment was fragile, cumbersome, and vulnerable to weather or enemy action. There were few trained operators and never enough radios available (a U.S. Army division of 20,000 men rarely had more than six radios even in 1918). But radio's biggest drawback was the lack of senior commanders willing to use or trust it in battlefield conditions. Poorly organized at first, Army radio users also suffered from security breaches such as sending vital messages in the clear rather than in code. One concern was that all radio signals were subject to being heard by the enemy and thus required effective systems of message coding. To allow short-range telephony with little chance of being overheard, the British introduced the use of the Fullerphone in trench warfare.

While all sides sought to "listen in," the British most effectively developed the direction-finding receivers and careful traffic analysis essential to successful code breaking. German undersea cables were cut by the British in the early days of the war, forcing the enemy to use radio transmissions to which the British could tune—and eventually understand as their code-breaking expertise expanded. With the help of codebooks seized from captured German naval vessels, the Royal Navy Intelligence, or Room 40 cryptanalysis staff, was able to decrypt many German naval signals—including the infamous "Zimmermann telegram" urging Mexico to declare war on the United States, which finally brought the United States into the war in early 1917. Until the end of the war, however, cryptography remained poorly integrated with operational practice. American efforts, for example, some under the Army's Herbert O. Yardley, were only partially successful.

World War I naval forces also made extensive use of radio to control widely dispersed fleets. In the 1916 battle of Jutland (and in many other battles), admirals often failed to make the best use of radio information, relying on flag signals that might be misread in battle conditions. As spark-gap equipment was replaced (1916–1917) by better arc and then (1918) vacuum tube–powered equipment, naval radio's value increased further. Wartime needs and growing equipment procurement greatly accelerated the pace of radio's technical development. Vacuum tube–based equipment, rare in 1914 (when obsolete spark-gap wireless telegraphy was still widespread), was becoming standard by 1918, vastly increasing radio's capabilities by adding voice to code communication. Until 1916, German U-boats, too cramped to carry bulky long-wave radio equipment, were limited to shorter-range (200–300 miles) radio links. As vacuum tube technology made possible longer-distance sending and receiving, submarines shifted their attacks farther into the Atlantic. Not all ships' captains appreciated their loss of independent action with the development of wireless.

More than radio, telegraph and telephone lines linked fighting units down to the battalion level. Some of the 38,000-mile telephone service by 1918 was designed and operated by AT&T on behalf of the military; Army Signal Corps personnel operated the remainder. Hello Girls acted as operators to allow more men to be assigned to military duties. Because lines could be so easily broken in the fighting, however, effective command and control often depended on the use of couriers (frequently mounted on horses, bicycles, motorcycles, or small motor vehicles) or message-carrying pigeons or dogs, as in the past. One carrier pigeon, for example, Cher Ami, helped to get messages through that led to the rescue of the famous "Lost Battalion." Static trench warfare on the Western Front also required widespread use of pyrotechnic signals (such as signal rockets) and whistles to shift troops into or out of trenches or warn of gas attacks.

A new element in military communications and fighting first appeared in this war—propaganda and psychological warfare. "Propaganda" is a type of military communication designed to weaken an enemy before and during operations. It seeks military gains without, or more usually in support of, military force. While used well before nineteenth-century warfare (there are many historical references to propaganda-like combat efforts, and both sides in the American Civil War made use of propaganda), propaganda and psychological warfare really came into their own during the two world wars. Drawing on growing understanding of persuasive techniques—and fear—propagandists for both the Central Powers and the Allies used a variety of communication media to soften up enemy forces and countries. In past times as well as more recent wars, propaganda has drawn on occult themes. These would be greatly expanded in World War II—as would jamming of enemy radio transmitters to try to obliterate their messages.

The Army Signal Corps expanded fiftyfold as it served growing American forces in Europe. This growth created a huge need for trained personnel as well as a formal research and development establishment, so the corps created what would become Fort Monmouth, New Jersey, which remained the country's chief signal school until 1974. Extensive training programs were established in most countries that introduced principles of wireless (and wired systems) to thousands of men. These trained personnel would play an important role in helping to push radio developments in the years to come.

Between the Wars (1918–1939)

During the interwar period, innovation continued at both commercial and military laboratories (despite draconian budget cuts at the latter), which further aided military communications. Vacuum tube radios would reign supreme for several decades, despite their fragility. By 1922 improved means of tube manufacture and cooling led to vastly more powerful tubes. But vacuum tubes, like the light bulbs they resembled, were fragile, threw off heat, and needed constant replacement. Radio equipment had to "warm up" (their tubes) before being used. Development of four-element vacuum tubes in 1929 was the last fundamental improvement in basic tube technology. By the late 1930s considerable progress had been made in miniaturization of vacuum tubes to develop smaller electrical devices.

Radar was developed that would help save the day for the Royal Air Force in the forthcoming Battle of Britain. Microwave transmission was developed and perfected. Shortwave radio could communicate at great distances, yet equipment remained small enough to fit into submarines, aircraft, and tanks. Armstrong developed FM radio, which would enjoy widespread tactical use during the coming war. With new radio services, military commanders could more easily control naval fleets (including submarines), fast-moving armored divisions, or bombers spread over enormous areas.

And of huge importance in the coming conflict, electric cipher machines to encode radio transmissions (of which the German Enigma device is the best known) appeared in several countries, allowing for faster coding of longer messages. Their use made enemy decoding far more difficult (some of the Enigma and German "Fish" codes were never broken). William F. Friedman became a central figure in developing American methods of military code breaking, as did his colleague Frank B. Rowlett.

Improved modes of facsimile and teleprinter equipment allowed military forces to more readily and rapidly exchange maps and other graphic material. The growing importance of aviation radio led to the 1938 formation of the Army Airways Communications Service, the first of a succession of Air Force communications commands.

World War II (1939–1945)

Even more than the previous world war, World War II demonstrated the value of a host of both old and new communications technologies. Communication links, both wired and wireless, were made a central part of massive defensive fortifications, including American coast defenses, the French Maginot Line of the 1930s, and the German-built Atlantic Wall of the early 1940s.

In a global war in which air power and mobility were dominant factors in the fighting, all countries made extensive use of radio traffic, for the need to effectively command and control forces took precedence over the risks of interception. The U.S. Army's Command and Administrative Network connected Washington DC with all major field commands at home and overseas. Newly developed FM radio was used for local communication on land and sea, as, for instance, between merchant ships and their naval escorts in a convoy. By the end of the war, virtually every Allied military vehicle and aircraft carried a transceiver. Walkie-talkies allowed infantry to stay in constant communication with headquarters—one of the first demonstrations of small-scale mobile communications in wartime.

Improved communications allowed political or military leaders to micromanage distant battles, a temptation to which Hitler increasingly succumbed as the war turned against Germany. His orders were sent through the huge underground Zossen site near Berlin, all of them coded by the Enigma or more advanced devices—and by the end of the war, most were being read in real time (as Ultra) by the Allies. Although all sides relied on machine encryption to protect their communications, the British Government Code & Cipher School at Bletchley Park and American cryptanalysts at Arlington Hall and Nebraska Avenue developed techniques to break codes (aided by captured codebooks) and thus read enemy messages almost as quickly as their intended recipients. Alan Turing, John Tiltman, Gordon Welchman, and others worked at Bletchley Park to develop early analog computers to assist in the growing code-breaking task. The ability to read enemy codes helped in several highly successful Allied deception efforts to mislead enemy commanders.

Indeed, the code-breaking advantage of the Allies (in one of the closest-held secrets during, and for decades after, the war) had a huge impact on the course of the war, from the eventual winning of the Battle of the Atlantic against German U-boats to placing American forces in the right place to defeat the Japanese navy at the Battle of Midway. Careful monitoring and analysis of enemy radio transmissions, or signals intelligence, brought vital information to the Allies. On the other hand, the American and British electric cipher machine (SIGABA and Typex) equipment and the SIGSALY system used by Prime Minister Churchill and President Roosevelt to talk by telephone across the Atlantic, each of them perfected during the war, could be operated by hastily trained personnel and proved invulnerable to enemy code-breaking efforts. Code-breaking abilities were very closely held, and many field commanders did not know the derivation of information provided to them (which did not help them believe what they were told).

Essential radio security was sometimes achieved by requiring total radio silence, but another approach was the U.S. Army's use of Native American code talkers communicating messages by simply speaking their own languages, which were totally unknown to the Germans or Japanese.

All sides learned propaganda lessons from World War I to apply to World War II. Of all the fighting powers, Germany's propaganda was clearly the best synchronized with its military effort. Film and radio (broadcasting was new to this war) helped promote the mighty power of German arms, as did bright poster art and printed media. Propaganda and psychological warfare on the tactical level were first used on a large scale in World War II. By late in the war, psychological warfare units often operated at the small-unit level. The most successful Allied military efforts were carefully designed leaflets intended to lower enemy soldier morale and/or induce desertion or surrender. They emphasized the decent treatment a prisoner would receive as well as bad conditions back home, and that officers were getting better food and shelter than frontline soldiers. These were particularly effective in Europe, less so in the Pacific because of cultural differences. Many millions of leaflets were dropped by German aircraft.

As in World War I, communication needs again led to extensive programs devoted to training of the thousands of radio operators needed on land, at sea, and in the air. The variety of more sophisticated communication systems, including those for air and naval forces, required longer and more specialized training efforts.

The Korean and Vietnam Wars (1945–1975)

Research to improve military communication continued apace following World War II. Many government entities including the National Bureau of Standards contributed to research, as did many corporations seeking government contracts, including David Sarnoff's RCA. Effective radio communication was essential in the year-long Berlin Airlift that involved both military and civilian pilots flying cargo along narrow flight paths.

Korean War (1950–1953) communications generally used equipment from and followed patterns set in World War II, though television brought a delayed view of the war to home viewers. Much World War II communications equipment had been properly moth-balled and stockpiled in Japan in 1949 to 1950. American forces lived off this equipment during the early, desperate months of the Korean War. Korea's climatic extremes, mountainous terrain, and lack of good roads greatly complicated communications. The Army Signal Corps depended heavily on very high frequency (VHF) radios to span the long distances, while on the ground signal soldiers often used water buffalo to string wire. After truce talks began in mid-1951, the front became largely static, and wire and radio operations more routine. Paradoxically, the Army Signal Corps also tried carrier pigeons, though they proved vulnerable to Korean hawks.

Seeds of the third military communications revolution were laid in this period. Development of the transistor at the Bell Telephone Laboratories in the late 1940s began what would become the solid state electronics revolution in communications. The notion of solid state electronics had been suggested in principle in the early 1950s and was of central interest to the armed services. If workable, such systems promised huge benefits of special value to military applications—robustness, lower weight and power requirements, and far greater capacity. The U.S. Air Force contracted with Westinghouse in 1959 to experiment with "molecular electronics." The Signal Corps was already developing a "micro-module" project to shrink component size across a variety of military needs. Research and development work was underway at many companies, usually funded by Air Force or Navy contracts. Over the next dozen years reliance on fragile vacuum tubes was swept away in the face of more durable transistor circuits.

That revolution was substantially boosted with the integrated circuit invented independently by Jack Kilby and Robert Noyce in 1959. They both determined that squeezing all elements of an electrical circuit—transistors, connections, and other electronic devices—onto a tiny silicon chip could be accomplished and would save considerable space while speeding up signal processing speed. Eliminating the need for individually hand-wired connections between the transistors and other elements would also greatly increase circuit reliability. The potential was huge. These tiny means of powering electronic devices aided the drive to component miniaturization that lay behind the development of ballistic missiles and computers. By the 1960s, Silicon Valley was fast developing, funded in part by growing military procurement of information technology (IT).

Working with the U.S. Air Force, the Army Signal Corps launched the world's first communications satellite in December 1958. Two years later it cooperated with the Weather Bureau and others to develop the first weather satellite.

Communication links proved vital in the short but intense 1962 Cuban Missile Crisis. By the late 1960s, communications satellites had begun to allow instantaneous communication from central military commands to remote parts of the world. For more local areas, intelligence ships bristled with communication antennas of all sorts, but as the Liberty affair proved, they were vulnerable to attack or takeover. China, India, and Pakistan developed increasingly sophisticated systems of military communications, as did such smaller countries as the Netherlands. British Commonwealth nations including Canada, Australia, New Zealand, and South Africa all honed their communications systems, many of which dated to before World War I.

In 1960 the U.S. Department of Defense put its various communication systems under unified control to become a single Defense Communications System, managed by the Defense Communications Agency. In October 1962, a concept of operations for a World Wide Military Command and Control

System (WWMCCS) sought to integrate all of these systems. Operating from 1963 to 1996, the WWMCCS was a centralized system to access information and communicate directives to American military forces. Labeled a "loosely knit confederation" of systems, WWMCCS lacked the centralized design, procurement, and operations needed to perform its mission successfully on a consistent basis. In 1967, the packet-switched DARPANET began to connect a growing number of academic and defense research establishments—it would operate for more than two decades. DARPANET (which would evolve into the Internet in the mid-1990s) used computer protocols to interconnect different types of equipment and software.

The Vietnam War (1959–1975) saw the peak of analog military communications potential. Airmobile communications closely tied ground troops to their air support. For the first time, high-quality commercial communications became available to the soldier in the field. On the tactical level, new transistorized combat radios enabled infantry, armor, and artillery to communicate directly with each other. For strategic purposes, the Signal Corps employed such sophisticated techniques as microwave relay and tropospheric scatter. The American Phu Lam communications hub in South Vietnam processed growing amounts of military information by the early 1970s.

Priority access over all systems—including the first communication satellite links—was assigned to command-and-control and intelligence users, while logistics, personnel, and other less urgent matters were carried on slower radio-teletype links until the introduction of first-generation digital communications (the automatic digital network, or AUTODIN, system) in 1968. After American withdrawal from Vietnam in 1973, shortages of skilled technicians and spare parts rendered some 40 percent of the U.S.-supplied communications equipment held by South Vietnam forces inoperable. As a result, increasing quantities of their classified messages were also carried by courier until the war's end in 1975.

North Vietnamese and Viet Cong forces relied on a combination of old and newer means of communication, primarily paper orders carried by couriers as well as Chinese and Soviet radio equipment. U.S. intelligence estimates showed that signals personnel comprised less than 5 percent of total enemy unit strength, compared with up to 20 percent in American ground forces. Security protocols included use of prearranged transmission times, spectrum frequency changes, concise messaging, and one-way communications. During large operations, minimal use was made of radios; troops relied instead on traditional couriers, fire and flame, lights and beacons, and music signals (whistles and the like).

Unlike in earlier wars, tactical military and larger political concerns were very closely intertwined, often confusing propaganda messages and effects. Broadcasts, loudspeaker announcements, and leaflets were the primary means of transmitting messages against the Viet Cong and North Vietnamese throughout the fighting areas. But both enemy forces were far more complex targets (they were more committed to their fighting role than earlier opponents) in what many considered a civil war. The way in which the war ended in Vietnam had a debilitating impact on the practice of military propaganda and psychological warfare, and their importance sharply declined in the American military services for several years.

Throughout the 1945–1990 Cold War, both the United States and the Soviet Union spent enormous sums on weapons, communications security, and counterintelligence efforts, though often with only limited result. As but two examples of expensive means of air defense communications, the Airborne Warning and Control System (AWACS) and Semi-Automatic Ground Environment (SAGE) system pushed analog technology to the edge of what was attainable. Security of American military transmissions fell to the Signals Security Agency, soon to become the huge National Security Agency based at Fort Meade, located north of Washington.

Digital Era (since 1975)

The third revolution, development of computer-controlled digital means of communication, has again transformed military communications, creating dramatic new information war capabilities. Navigation and global positioning satellites allow small units to fix their (or an enemy's) position within a few yards—although, of course, only the richest nations can afford such technologies.

Terror organizations and guerrilla fighters rely (once again) on less expensive human messengers rather than electronic communications, which can be so easily read by sophisticated snooping systems.

In its constant quest for the best and latest systems of IT, the U.S. Department of Defense's Defense Information Systems Agency moved to replace its WWMCCS with the Global Command and Control System in 1996. For much of the period after Vietnam, technology could not support all of the missions that the Joint Chiefs of Staff wanted performed. WWMCCS was also a collection of systems that had never been designed or built with interoperability in mind: They could often work well individually, but not together. Further, the military culture in the 1980s and 1990s was hostile to interservice cooperation, and thus systems were procured without reference to overall defense needs because centralized objectives were seen as secondary. Increasing integration of formerly separate systems led in the twenty-first century to U.S. pursuit of the Global Information Grid (GIG) at a huge cost but offering considerable potential. When fully operational after 2010, the GIG will allow widespread and secure military use of both e-mail and Voice over Internet Protocol (VoIP) technologies.

The expansion and continued importance of these and other technologies are evident in the growing number of military communications conferences that provide a useful interface between commercial contractors and military procurement officials. Additionally a host of military communications museums help to preserve what has gone before—and attest to a growing fascination with the three revolutions that have transformed the field. The Association of Old Crows and many other veterans' groups also seek to preserve the older systems and what it was like "to be there."

The first network-centric wars were the Gulf War (1990–1991) and the Iraq War (starting in 2003 and ongoing at the time of publication). The first made use of more than sixty communication satellites while the second used more than a hundred. During the Gulf War, the global positioning system (GPS) was invaluable on often featureless desert fighting areas. AWACS aircraft helped support a variety of joint land, sea, and air operations. The Iraqi high command's ability to communicate and control its forces was destroyed early in the war, giving the coalition forces tactical superiority. Ironically, this was accomplished by sophisticated weapons systems, which themselves were completely dependent on communication systems. The overall coalition communication system was impressive, consisting of 2,300 personnel, 7,000 radio frequencies, and 59 communication centers. During the war 29 million phone calls were made. Yet the Gulf War also demonstrated limitations in military communication due to poor interservice compatibility.

A dozen years later, the Iraq War was the first to be overwhelmingly dominated by computerized and digital communications. Indeed, IT was the cornerstone of military communication. Based on the Iraq War experience, modern military communication appears to be more about communication among machines (computers, systems, and networks) than among humans. Communication has become real time, automatic, digitized, netlike, multilevel, multiservice, and dependent on commercial IT innovations. For example, improvement in GPS accuracy by more than 20 percent since the 1990s increased the effectiveness of thousands of GPS-guided munitions used during the Iraq conflict. Digital communications and networks gave coalition forces unprecedented air-land-naval operations coordination and near-perfect battlespace awareness. The Army Battle Command System (ABCS) enabled commanders to transmit orders, intelligence, logistics information, and other useful data. On a more personal level, VoIP allowed instant messaging from 180 Internet kiosks set up throughout Iraq. Virtually all soldiers used e-mail and instant messaging to stay connected with home.

Summing Up

Several trends underlie the development of military communications. First, communication innovations almost never originate within military or naval organizations. With few exceptions, new ideas for improved (faster, more capable) tactical and strategic communication come from individuals and (increasingly) private companies. In the United States, for example, most of the initiative has come from the private sector, with only occasional government innovation. Where government plays a vital role, of course, is in its procurement decisions that have often speeded telecommunications development, especially in wartime.

Second, and all too often, senior officials rejected seminal ideas—perhaps most classically illustrated by the Italian navy's disinterest in Marconi's wireless system in the mid-1890s. Many cases are seen where military leaders have their heads in the last war (or century) and ignore breakthrough ideas for improving communications, only to adopt them after their opponents do. This occurred on several levels—running through this history are examples of commanders distrusting that which they could not see for themselves, and thus ignoring communicated messages. Nelson's famous "blind eye" to an order he did not wish to "see" is but one example.

Third, in every conflict each side seeks information about the other while hiding its own. Yet such information is especially vulnerable while it is being communicated, and thus military forces have always been concerned about maintaining secrecy as well as promoting intelligence efforts. Security concerns can slow the pace of military message sending, but countless cases in history demonstrate how security lapses have resulted in military reversals. Allied code-breaking success in both world wars resulted, in part, from such lapses.

Fourth, military communications' development is made up of systems carrying ever-more complex messages. For centuries the limited means of signaling meant that only the most simple and preplanned communication signals could be sent any distance. Only around 1800 did that situation begin to change as both land and sea systems of communication allowed for the sending of more complex signals, including limited two-way messaging. Another half-century would pass before the first electrical system (the telegraph) opened up even more opportunities.

Fifth, an organizational trend evident here is that armies generally set up separate communications arms while navies often do not. The military signals process can be organized in a variety of ways. A centralized and specialized signal corps has often been created for armies, but most naval and air services seem to have preferred a more dispersed role for communications.

Increasingly, military communication needs and operations have become a central part of electronics research and development. This is partially a factor of scale—government procurement contracts have underwritten much of the IT industry—and partially a matter of parallel interests. The business world seeks greater speed and message integrity, for example, just as military authorities do. Indeed, the cross-fertilization between the civilian and military economies seems to grow closer by the day. Cold War needs, for example, pushed the miniaturization needed to fit electronic equipment into ballistic missiles—and those electronics capabilities now see widespread use in civilian markets. Flat-screen technology, faster computer chips, GPS navigation, higher definition television, and improved means of weather reporting have all benefited from military procurement that has helped pay the costs of development. Indeed, the list of civilian spin-offs from military communications projects is virtually endless.

Perhaps the most important trend is the continuing search for military communication systems with greater speed and capacity. Military needs have almost always exceeded the means available—as with concern about sufficient spectrum frequencies, despite use of single-sideband, spread spectrum, and tropospheric scatter systems. Digital systems and compression have greatly aided the capacity problem, as have the use of laser and fiber optic links.

Finally, while communication technologies have largely resolved how to get information to and from commanders and fighting forces, they have also contributed to the information overload that can slow or confuse any military action. Less attention has been paid to how to help humans prioritize the flow of information on which they must act. Communicating information is a vital part of military decision making, but so is the ability to parse what is most vital from that which is only potentially useful.

Source

Shore, Henry N. 1915. "Signalling Methods Among the Ancients." *United Service Magazine* 52 (November): 166–174.

A

Air Force Communications Agency (AFCA, 1991–2006)

The end of the Cold War prompted a major reorganization of U.S. Air Force communications. The Air Force Communications Command (AFCC) transferred more than 600 subordinate units and some 47,000 personnel to Air Force service commands. AFCC was downgraded to field operating agency (FOA) status in 1991, though Illinois congressional delegation intervention delayed this action until 28 May 1993, when it became the Air Force Command, Control, Communications and Computer Agency (AFC4A). An Air Force–wide integration of communication/computer and information functions prompted yet another name change—to the Air Force Communications Agency (AFCA)—on 13 June 1996.

During the 1990s, the FOA transferred responsibility for frequency management to the Air Force Frequency Management Center (October 1991); operational test and evaluation to the Air Force Operational Test and Evaluation Center (June 1992); acquisition, most software support, and engineering and installation functions to Air Force Materiel Command (July 1992); and air traffic services to the Air Force Flight Standards Agency (October 1992). Two further FOA units were reassigned in 1994: The Air Force Telecommunications Certification Office was inactivated, with most functions transferring to the Defense Information Systems Agency (May), and a training squadron was transferred to Air Education and Training Command (October). Now a small, technically oriented headquarters with two specialized communications functions—Hammer ACE (a mobile communications element) and the Air Force Protective Services Support Team (supporting the U.S. Secret Service)—the FOA acted as an extension of the Air Staff, assisting in the development of architectures, policies, procedures, requirements, standards, and technical solutions for Air Force command, control, communications, and computer (C4) systems; ensuring integration and interoperability among all such systems; and overseeing the professional development of relevant personnel.

In late 1993, the FOA began to acquire new responsibilities as the Air Force assigned a

1

lead command or agency for each weapon system and those associated programs operated by more than one major command. The communications community established a similar program for its C4 systems, and the Air Staff designated the agency as executive agent to advocate Air Force–wide planning, testing, training, implementation, and life-cycle management for designated programs. Initially designated as the lead command for the Base Information Infrastructure (the Air Force portion of the Defense Information Infrastructure), the redesignated AFCA gradually gained responsibility for leading Air Force efforts including secure voice, electronic messaging, electronic data interchange, wireless communication, information assurance, high-frequency radio, integrating National Airborne Operations Center communications modifications, the Executive Airlift communications network, and Internet protocol applications. The list varied through the years, with the agency serving as lead command for an average of eighteen programs between 1997 and 2006.

As the FOA gained new missions, its commanders reorganized the agency to mirror Air Force headquarters and major commands to better support both. Prior to the 1996 designation of the agency as AFCA, commanders stressed the support of major commands and units in the field. Since then, AFCA has been designated as lead agency for common-user communications infrastructure systems connecting to the network and developing architectures that people in the field could quickly implement. This included standardization of equipment, processes, and training that had existed before the AFCC command dissolved. AFCA resources were focused on operational support, aligning them closely to the major commands and units in the field.

George W. Bush's administration (2001–2009) initiated a substantial transformation of the military to develop joint, network-centric, and distributed forces capable of rapid decisions and massed effect as needed. With existing battlefield networks composed of disparate systems operating in discrete data enclaves, often unable to share information, the seamless integration of systems, activities, and expertise across all manned, unmanned, and space capabilities became the Air Force's key aim. This prompted the creation of a new deputy chief of staff for Warfighting Integration (AF/XI) in April 2002 to modernize and integrate Air Force manned, unmanned, and space information systems by integrating command, control, communications, computer, intelligence, surveillance, and reconnaissance (C4ISR) capabilities. As AF/XI's technical arm, AFCA became responsible for maintaining information superiority by ensuring Air Force communications and information systems were both integrated and interoperable.

AFCA commanders after 2000 realigned AFCA resources to better serve the ever-expanding Air Force network, while leading efforts to provide seamless connectivity for command and control of air and space forces by optimizing and integrating Air Force data, voice, video, imagery, and information services. This included developing and validating progressive architectures, technical standards, requirements, policies, and technical solutions; serving as the Air Force focal point for obtaining and managing commercial and government-owned long-haul communications services and equipment; deploying technical teams and network assessment capabilities to ensure communications and information combat power; and maintaining quick reaction communications capabilities to respond to worldwide emergencies.

Development of a centralized and integrated operation and architecture proved essential for integrating manned, unmanned, and space platforms and their communications infrastructure. It was also vital for assessing how well planned programs actually delivered capabilities and finding the gaps and seams in C4ISR capabilities; further, it comprised a key element in managing budget decisions. Lacking the in-house capability to create an accurate "infostructure" architecture, in March 2003 AF/XI designated AFCA as chief architect for Air Force networks, responsible for developing architecture, standards, and policies for information transport. This included computing and security as well as network operations planning, programming, and acquisition. AFCA developed the first Air Force–wide network architecture (dubbed "Constellation Net"). It also became the lead agency for network-centric airborne communications, and developing and maintaining both terrestrial and airborne architectures to support Air Staff capabilities.

AFCA influenced the development and use of key air and space communications and information technologies. The agency played a crucial role in the construction of forward-based coalition air operations centers for combat operations in the Middle East, U.S.-based operations support centers aiding those operations, and network operations and security centers providing both management and security for network links among vital centers. AFCA designed a secure network providing coalition partners access to critical command-and-control (C2) systems and information, and immeasurably aided problem analysis by accurately assessing application performance and impact on Air Force networks, resolving battlefield performance issues, and validating

network combat readiness. Its communication programs accelerated integration of advanced beyond-line-of-sight terminals on "Global Hawk" platforms. AFCA increased Air Force efficiency with plans to integrate air-, ground-, and space-based assets by extending network capabilities to aircraft cockpits. It has developed standards for collaborative tools linking warfighting concepts and capabilities with support systems and networks, security testing, and evaluation of systems that mitigated vulnerabilities prior to use in the field.

Lionel E. Timmerman and Larry R. Morrison

See also Air Force Communications Service (AFCS), Air Force Communications Command (AFCC) (1961–1991); Air Force Research Laboratory, Rome, New York; Airborne Warning and Control System (AWACS); Army Airways Communications System, Airways and Air Communications Service (AACS, 1938–1961); Defense Information Systems Agency (DISA); Global Command and Control System (GCCS); Gulf War (1990–1991); Iraq War (2003–Present)

Source
Air Force Communications Agency (AFCA). Home page. [Online information; retrieved December 2006.] http://public.afca.af.mil/.

Air Force Communications Service (AFCS), Air Force Communications Command (AFCC) (1961–1991)

By the early 1960s, U.S. Air Force leaders generally agreed that the importance of communications in command and control dictated that Air Force communications required a single manager. On 1 July 1961, the Air Force relieved the Airways and Air Communications Service (AACS) from assignment to the Military Air Transport Service, redesignated

AACS as the Air Force Communications Service (AFCS), and made it a major air command. AFCS headquarters was located at Scott Air Force Base, Illinois (just east of St. Louis), where it remained except for 1970–1977 when it was relocated to Richards-Gebaur Air Force Base, Missouri.

Given its mission of being the sole manager of air traffic control, on-base communications, long-haul communications, and emergency mission support, AFCS soon assumed those roles for most of the major air commands with the notable exceptions of Strategic Air Command and Air Defense Command, whose communications infrastructures did not come under AFCS until the late 1970s. In 1962, the Department of Defense also transferred the Alaska Communication System (ACS), which supported both military and civilian telecommunications needs, from the U.S. Army Signal Corps to AFCS. AFCS operated the Alaska system until its sale to private owners in 1971.

Air Force communications in the 1960s responded to the development of electronic computers with improvements. In the first half of the 1960s, AFCS personnel oversaw the installation and operation of large data transfer systems, such as the Air Force Data Communications System, at that time the world's largest. This system was the first increment of what eventually became the Automatic Digital Network (AUTODIN). AFCS personnel installed, operated, and maintained the defense long-haul, nonsecure voice system, the Automatic Voice Network (AUTOVON), at air bases beginning in the early 1960s.

The Air Force increased its emphasis on the advancement of quick reaction communications capabilities. In the 1960s, AFCS planners developed Talking Bird, an air-transportable communications package designed to be loaded in a C-130 transport airplane and operated from within the aircraft after landing. Air Force communicators continued development of long-haul communications systems during the 1960s, such as tropospheric scatter communications systems with installations in Europe; the Automated Weather Network, which passed meteorological data around the globe; and the first base distribution system, a computerized storage and forwarding data communications network.

War in Southeast Asia created new demands on Air Force communicators for a broad spectrum of intra- and intertheater capabilities. In 1966, AFCC personnel installed the first satellite communications terminal in South Vietnam using a synchronous communications satellite to provide one voice and one record circuit between Saigon and Hawaii.

Air Force communicators worked on hundreds of communications projects throughout the 1970s. These included microwave and cable modernization programs, improved tropospheric scatter transmission systems, high-frequency transmission upgrades, solid-state electronics equipment renewal, and continued satellite communications development. In 1977, the first operational use was made of the global Air Force Satellite Communications System, designed to carry Air Force communications into the 1990s.

In 1978 AFCS was given increased responsibilities for the design, acquisition, operation, and maintenance of Air Force automatic data processing systems. Soon thereafter, Air Force leadership became concerned that the service was falling behind in the employment of information technology. In 1984, the Air Force chief of staff directed the integration of the communications, data automation, and office automation disciplines across the Air

Force to take advantage of the merger of these technologies. AFCC became the single manager for the Air Force's information systems. AFCC undertook major data automation efforts in the 1980s to replace older computers and provide standardized computer systems. For example, the Phase IV program brought the overhaul effort to all Air Force installations to support base functions including supply, maintenance, personnel, and finance.

The development of local area networks and office information systems in the 1980s marked a new period in Air Force communications. With their installation, members of the Air Force were able to directly communicate with other Air Force personnel on base and across the service; the necessity to employ centralized base communications centers diminished. Among other modification efforts, in 1981 AFCC contracted for the upgrade to digital telephone switching systems. AFCC began meteor burst communications testing in 1986 and had a system in operation in 1987. The design of the Defense Switched Network, the AUTOVON's replacement, was authorized at the same time, and an improved weather data distribution system, the Automated Weather Distribution System, became operational.

Technological advancements—such as fiber optics, T-carriers (broadband cable connections), and digital transmission and switching systems—were exploited within the Base Information Digital Distribution System program to modernize base communications, providing increased capacity and more reliable circuits for both voice and data transmission. Members of AFCC were also increasingly involved in joint service communications programs such as Mystic Star, the worldwide, high-frequency communications network that supported U.S. government and military officials with voice

and data communications while aboard special mission aircraft anywhere in the world. The need for secure, rapid-response communications continued. AFCC developed a small, quickly deployable communications team, Hammer ACE, in the 1980s to provide secure communications support for emergencies and contingencies.

Changes in the Cold War climate caused Air Force leadership to reconsider AFCC's single manager role in the late 1980s. Portions of the command's mission were returned to the major air commands. In the early 1990s the Air Force dramatically restructured, and AFCC was one of several function-oriented organizations to be divested of most of its field operations, which were returned to the major air commands. AFCC was realigned as a field operating agency of Headquarters United States Air Force on 1 July 1991, though the organization retained its name for several more years.

James A. Moyers

See also Air Force Communications Agency (AFCA, 1991–2006); Alaska Communications System; Army Airways Communications System, Airways and Air Communications Service (AACS, 1938–1961); Automatic Digital Network (AUTODIN); Fiber Optics; Meteor Burst Communications (MBC); Satellite Communications; Tropospheric Scatter; Vietnam War (1959–1975)

Sources

Miller, Linda G., and Cora J. Holt. 1989. *Window to the Future: Air Force Communications Command Chronology, 1938–1988*. Scott Air Force Base, IL: Air Force Communications Command Office of History.

Morrison, Larry R. 1997. *From Flares to Satellites: A Brief History of Air Force Communications*. Scott Air Force Base, IL: Air Force Communications Command Office of History.

Snyder, Thomas S., ed. 1991. *Air Force Communications Command, 1938–1991: An Illustrated History*, 3rd ed. Scott Air Force Base, IL: Air

Force Communications Command Office of History.

Air Force Research Laboratory (Rome, New York)

Technology using the electromagnetic spectrum to disseminate and process information ranks among the most critical to U.S. Air Force needs. The 900 military and civilian employees of what is now called the Air Force Research Laboratory Information Directorate, Rome (New York) Research Site aim to advance information technology.

The historical roots of the Rome site stretch back to World War I. In 1917 the U.S. Army Signal Corps set up a radio laboratory at Fort Monmouth, New Jersey, consolidating all its electronics laboratories there in 1929. On 1 February 1945, the Signal Corps, concluding that aviation electronics required special emphasis, created Watson Laboratories from parts of the Fort Monmouth laboratory complex. Rome became the site of part of this research and development tradition when the Air Force, wanting to consolidate its electronics work, moved Watson Laboratories to Rome in order to establish an electronics and upper atmospheric research center.

The Cold War rivalry with the Soviet Union had begun, and electronically generated information formed a key piece of the emerging strategy of nuclear deterrence, giving the move to Rome special significance. Watson Laboratories personnel and equipment began moving to Rome in November 1950, and by 12 June 1951 the new organization, Rome Air Development Center (RADC), was operating on the grounds of Griffiss Air Force Base.

The tradition of technology development soon thrived in Rome. Out of research conducted there came tropospheric scatter and high-frequency radios, satellite communications, and standards for electronic reliability. The first intercontinental satellite communication transmission took place on 12 August 1960 when RADC scientists and engineers transmitted radio and radar signals between Trinidad in the British West Indies and Floyd, New York, via the Echo I passive communication satellite. Rome researchers have contributed to such aerospace systems as the Ballistic Missile Early Warning System, the Distant Early Warning Line, the Semi-Automated Ground Environment system, the Airborne Warning and Control System, the first Air Force telephone switching facility, and the first operational Russian-to-English translator. The Internet and related technology owes much to Rome too, as RADC served as one of the sites for DARPANET, a forerunner to the Internet. Phased array radars, computer memories, machine language translation, and photonics became synonymous with Rome as well.

In 1990, RADC was renamed Rome Laboratory, and it became the Information Directorate in 1997 upon the consolidation of Air Force laboratories into the single Air Force Research Laboratory. Recent research has emphasized "information fusion," principally as a means for improving combat awareness, decision making, and targeting.

Thomas W. Thompson

See also Airborne Warning and Control System (AWACS); Communication Satellites; DARPANET; Internet; Language Translation; Satellite Communications; Semi-Automatic Ground Environment (SAGE); Spectrum Frequencies; Tropospheric Scatter

Source
Information Directorate, Air Force Research Laboratory. Home page. [Online information;

retrieved April 2007.] http://www.rl
.af.mil/.

Airborne Warning and Control System (AWACS)

The Airborne Warning and Control System (AWACS) allows controllers to monitor all aircraft flying within a 200-mile radius. Further, these controllers can manage an air battle by communicating to friendly aircraft where targets are located and plotting their interception routes so they can destroy the targets. Its intrinsic worth as a military system has also given it an importance in diplomatic relations and in the important area of arms sales.

The origins of the AWACS can be traced back to World War II. Radar operated from ships could pick up enemy aircraft approaching but only within a fairly short range. By 1944 it was determined that the best solution would be to mount a radar on aircraft, and by the end of the war some planes had been developed for this capability. It took years of research and development before a dependable and effective system was created.

In essence, the AWACS is an airborne electronic command-and-control (C2) system based around a radar. That radar allows the crew of the plane to track and identify friendly and hostile aircraft, ships, and ground targets. Onboard crew can identify potential targets, be alerted to direct attacks, and communicate with other aircraft or organizations on the ground. Depending on the specific model, it can defeat electronic countermeasures (antijamming) or apply its own.

The United States has more than thirty AWACS aircraft in its inventory. Several other nations have an AWACS that was bought from the United States, developed on their own, or purchased from other nations. These include Britain, France, and Saudi Arabia. An improved AWACS version has been developed by the North Atlantic Treaty Organization. Israel manufactured its own version (the Phalcon), which it has used and sold to other nations including India and Chile. Both Russia and China developed AWACS. Sweden, Mexico, and Brazil have their own smaller versions. Australia and Turkey contracted for a related airborne radar and communication system mounted in a twin-engine Boeing 737, and the first entered service in 2006. The British, Italian, and Indian air forces have smaller helicopter-based airborne early-warning systems for tactical application.

The American AWACS development began in 1975, and the first AWACS-enabled aircraft was deployed two years later. Typically the radar is mounted on a large air transport such as the Boeing 707 (used by the United States), 737, or 767. Other nations have used the Russian Ilyushin Il-76 or Gulfstream aircraft. They are usually characterized by a rotating radar dome mounted atop the aircraft. A crew of four flies the aircraft, which carries from thirteen to eighteen systems operators. Range depends on not only the equipment but the height at which the aircraft is flying. The range for the U.S. AWACS is between 200 and 250 miles with the ability to track up to 250 aircraft simultaneously and to plot intercepts for up to 15 friendly aircraft.

Although American AWACS aircraft are based in the continental United States, they have been used throughout the world. Early on they were used in Europe to monitor aircraft activity in East Germany, Poland, and Czechoslovakia. The Israelis have used them extensively, beginning with monitoring the conflict in Lebanon in 1982. AWACS aircraft supported American military efforts in Grenada (1983), Panama (1989), the Gulf War (1990–1991), and Iraq (since 2003). In 1990, they were used extensively to monitor air traffic in South America as part of the antidrug effort. They were also used in the Balkans, most notably during the NATO air campaign against Serbia in 1999.

Because the AWACS provides its users with the abilities to coordinate and control air warfare, it has acquired an importance beyond its usefulness over a battlefield. Possession of the AWACS (or denial by refusing sales) is the product of and can affect foreign relations. In the early 1980s, the sale of AWACS aircraft by the United States to Saudi Arabia created a controversy with Israelis. The sale eventually went through, much to the benefit of the United States and its allies in the Gulf War a decade later. In 1982 Britain sought the loan of the AWACS to assist in its efforts to retake the Falkland Islands from Argentina. Concerned with its relationships in Latin America, the United States turned down that request. While the British won that conflict, AWACS capability might have prevented loss of a British warship to Argentine Exocet missiles. More recently, the United States opposed the Israelis' selling the AWACS to China because of its possible use against Taiwan. The Chinese obtained a Russian system and then replaced it with one of their own.

Robert Stacy

See also Airmobile Communications; Airplanes; Australia: Royal Australian Corps of Signals; China, People's Republic of; Computer; Electronic Countermeasures / Electronic Warfare (ECM / EW); Falklands Conflict (1982); Identification, Friend or Foe (IFF); Israel; North Atlantic Treaty Organization (NATO) Communications & Information Systems Agency; Russia / Soviet Union: Air Force; United Kingdom: Royal Air Force

Sources
Armistead, Leigh. 2002. *AWACS and Hawkeyes: The Complete History of Airborne Early Warning Aircraft*. Osceola, WI: Motorbooks International.
Benson, J., and T. Holmes. 1996. *USAF for the 21st Century*. Botley, Oxford, UK: Osprey.
Boeing. "E-3 AWACS Overview." [Online information; retrieved December 2006.] http://www.boeing.com/defense-space/ic/awacs/index.html.
Gordon, Yefim. 2006. *Soviet/Russian AWACS Aircraft*. Hersham, Surrey, UK: Midland Publishing.
Laham, Nicholas. 2002. *Selling AWACS to Saudi Arabia: The Reagan Administration and the Balancing of America's Competing Interests in the Middle East*. Westport, CT: Praeger.
Tessmer, Arnold Lee. 1998. *Politics of Compromise: NATO and AWACS*. Washington, DC: National Defense University Press.

Airmobile Communications

During military operations in South Vietnam in the early 1960s, command and control of tactical forces assumed new importance. Military operations conducted by the Viet Cong were mainly hit-and-run tactics against small advisory American units and the South Vietnamese army in jungle areas. Command and control necessitated an aerial command post from which a Vietnamese commander, together with his American adviser and a limited staff, could get quickly to an area under attack.

That procedure often meant briefing reaction forces en route to the objective, coordinating with other friendly forces, and providing additional support as needed—in short, using several radios at the same time. The commander and his staff had to compete with the high noise level in the cabin to talk to each other and to crew members. An early attempt to meet these needs was made by lashing three FM radios together in the aircraft passenger compartment and mounting the antennas at a 45-degree angle on the landing skids. Although successful, the scheme was awkward and lacked the needed very high frequency (VHF) and high-frequency single-sideband radios. And the rigged method failed to provide for communications within the helicopter.

In early 1963, the Army Concept Team in South Vietnam defined requirements for an aerial command post for command control of ground and air operations. The plan was approved by higher authority, and four command post communications system consoles for UH-1B Huey helicopters were built. Each included an operations table and a compact five-position interphone system independent of the aircraft interphone but capable of entry into that system. Each console also provided equipment for two different FM radio channels.

The first consoles arrived in South Vietnam in December 1963 and were issued to two Army aviation units for evaluation. These units found the original design to be too ambitious. Because of the size and weight of the console, two single seats normally occupied by the aerial door gunners had to be removed, and the additional weight upset the helicopter's center of gravity. Nevertheless, when the map board and table were eliminated and the single-sideband radio relocated, the console performed so well that in July 1964 the U.S. Military Assistance Command, Vietnam put in an urgent request for a helicopter command post for each Vietnamese division and one corps.

While improvements in air mobility operations were being tested and evaluated in

Vietnam, the 11th Air Assault Division was activated at Fort Benning, Georgia, on 15 February 1963 and given a high priority on personnel and equipment to develop new airmobile concepts and procedures. When the question of air versus ground radios arose, the division chose ground radios like those used by ground maneuver units in the helicopter command consoles. It permitted rapid replacement of damaged or inoperative radios at almost any supply point or battalion maintenance facility. It also eased the problem of obtaining spare parts. There were greater operational advantages over the aircraft radios in that ground radios were compatible and had a greater range.

The U.S. Army Electronics Research and Development Laboratories at Fort Monmouth, New Jersey, built the first prototype to division specifications. It was delivered in March 1964 and, after testing and modification, was finally designated the Airborne Communications Control AN/ASC-5. Fifteen more were built for the division (which became the 1st Cavalry Division in South Vietnam). Adaptations placed this specialized equipment in fixed wing aircraft as well.

The unique airborne equipment ensured communication with all support units and permitted planning and execution of tactical troop moves and, most importantly, the ability to have immediate surveillance of the battle area so that entire operations could be directed from airborne command posts. The use of an airborne tactical operations center was new to command and control on the battlefield but would become part of the scheme of maneuver for U.S. forces. The idea that grew out of operational needs in South Vietnam remains today a big part of commanding and controlling military operations on the battlefield.

During the short 1990–1991 Gulf War, aerial command and control used the UH-60 Black Hawk helicopter, though with communications technology designed during the Vietnam War. The command-and-control suite only provided line-of-sight single-frequency voice communications, so aircrews had to rely on maps and other devices to navigate and obtain battlefield intelligence. The system was cumbersome, incompatible with the current generation of frequency-hopping tactical radios, and lacked provision for receiving or transmitting digital data.

For the Iraq War, beginning in 2003, the deep airborne assault by the 101st Airborne Division featured a jump (mobile tactical) command post that provided communications support. Known as the C2 (for command and control), the UH-60 helicopter provided ultra-high frequency communications, high-frequency radio, single-channel tactical satellite links, and FM communications—the same as ground forces. These helicopters were key conduits between the leading edge of the division's operations and main headquarters, depending on which was in charge at different times. The C2 aircraft is more than a communications relay as it can also serve as a flying command post capable of carrying senior commanders.

Danny Johnson

See also Airplanes; Fort Monmouth, New Jersey; Gulf War (1990–1991); Iraq War (2003—Present); Radio; Vietnam War (1959–1975)

Sources

Ackerman, Robert K. 2003. "Information Technology Drives Tip of Airborne Spear." *Signal* (June). [Online article; retrieved February 2006.] http://www.afcea.org/signal/articles/anmviewer.asp?a=204&z=40.

Bergen, John D. 1986. *Military Communications: A Test for Technology*. Washington, DC: Government Printing Office, Center for Military History Publication 91-12.
Myer, Charles R. 1982. *Division-Level Communications, 1962–1973*. Washington, DC: Government Printing Office, Center for Military History Publication 90-11.
Reinzi, Thomas M. 1972. *Communications-Electronics, 1962–1970*. Washington, DC: Government Printing Office, Center for Military History Publication 90-9-1.

Airplanes

The value of aircraft for military communications became obvious almost from the start of flying. In particular, the needs of the two world wars and the long Cold War pushed the speed of technological development.

Late in 1907 the U.S. Army Signal Corps issued a specification for a heavier-than-air machine for testing. Within a year, the corps experimented with Wright brothers' aircraft at Fort Myer, Virginia, outside Washington. An airfield and training program were established at College Park, Maryland, north of Washington. Until 1911, however, the U.S. Army had but one pilot and aircraft at any given time. Early work was also undertaken by the major European powers, especially Britain, Germany, and France. The communications problem, of course, was how to get what information a pilot could gather to the ground rapidly.

In World War I aircraft were used for observation, flying dispatches (and couriers), scouting duties—and soon spotting targets for artillery. Communication from ground to air at first was limited to symbols based on white cloth panels laid out on the ground. The airplane could send signals to the ground by means of colored lights, or simply by dropping weighted notes. Experimental use of aircraft wireless telegraphy took place by both the Royal Naval Air Service and the Royal Flying Corps on the eve of war, but heavy radio equipment limited its application. By 1915, extensive British artillery spotting was made possible by lighter-weight spark-gap wireless transmitters. Within two years, British aircraft were carrying much improved vacuum tube wireless and undertook some wireless telephony (voice) signaling as well. Radio signals were difficult to discern in the noisy open aircraft of the period, and at first, some pilots feared being electrocuted. German aircraft wireless technology exceeded that of the Allies early in the war, then lagged badly, but its largely Telefunken-made equipment was the equal of the Allies by at least 1917.

Despite budget limitations in all countries, the interwar years saw continued improvement of aircraft radio systems, though interference from their growing number was a serious issue throughout the 1920s. This was partially resolved by growing use of short-wave frequencies and, by the late 1930s, the VHF band as well. Antenna design was another focus of concern, as trailing out 150 to 200 feet of antenna wire behind an airplane had obvious operational shortcomings. Two-way radios were added to Army aircraft when the service flew U.S. domestic mails in early 1934. A squadron of ten Martin bombers flew from Washington to Alaska in summer 1934 and, thanks to developing radio facilities, was never out of touch with ground controllers. This precedent led in November 1938 to the creation of the Army Airways Communications System to centralize development and operation of military air communications. The Signal Corps retained responsibility for improving the radios themselves. Aircraft radios grew steadily more proficient (gaining greater range and more interference control) and aided navigation as well as communication.

By 1939, the major fighting powers had all improved their aircraft radio communication systems and capabilities, despite budget limitations. To a far greater degree than during World War I in 1914–1918, fighting aircraft were directed from the ground. Both the United States and Britain involved scientists in steadily improving their aircraft radio equipment while Germany froze its standardized designs early in the war and was thus increasingly outclassed. As in the earlier world war, aircraft helped in artillery spotting as well as other communication and courier duties. The U.S. Army Artillery developed its own aerial eyes after 1942. Germany made extensive use of radio beam technology to guide its night bombers toward British targets. Unlike American (and Japanese) practice, German radios were not mounted on shock-absorbing bases but directly on aircraft bulkheads. They were among the first radios to make use of ribbon interconnecting cables (similar to those in modern computers) and were both compact and usually well constructed. To protect their radio designs from capture, Luftwaffe equipment housings often included externally mounted explosives for emergency self-destruction. By 1944, Allied bombing of German and Japanese air control facilities went a long way toward destroying the enemy's ability to effectively communicate with defending fighter aircraft.

The successful 1948–1949 Berlin Airlift was made possible by what had been learned during the war about effective radio communication and air traffic control. Increasing jet speeds of military aircraft after the war made radio communications even more vital, as were radio-based navigation and command structures. The pace of technological change made systems obsolete much faster than before. Application of the transistor in the 1950s as well as growing use of mainframe computers in all electronic systems helped keep pace. The Semi-Automatic Ground Environment (SAGE) radar and control centers, installed from 1957 on, were among the first to try to tie much of this together. During the Vietnam War, regular updating of modes of communication was central to extensive air operations. So was increasing awareness that aircraft radio signals could be intercepted and read, forcing greater attention to the use of coded communication or radio silence.

A special Cold War application of aircraft was their use as airborne communication centers. For nearly four decades, the Airborne Command Post, also called "Looking Glass," was always ready to direct bombers and missiles from the air should ground-based command centers become inoperable. The Looking Glass (so named because the mission mirrored ground-based command, control, and communications) began 3 February 1961, and for nearly thirty years (until 24 July 1990), a Looking Glass aircraft was in flight twenty-four hours a day. For another eight years (until 1 October 1998) it remained on ground or airborne alert at all times. The aircraft used was an EC-135 (a modified Boeing 707) jammed with the latest communication equipment. When airborne, Looking Glass was commanded by an Air Force general or Navy admiral. E-6 aircraft (based on the same airframe) have somewhat replaced the Looking Glass aircraft, serving as airborne means of launching land or submarine missiles.

Over the past two decades, aircraft communications have been increasingly based on solid-state technology, automation, and data-supplemented voice channels. Drone (unpiloted) aircraft were used for reconnaissance and communications in several Middle East wars. Thanks largely to developments in the missile and space field, aircraft radios became both smaller and more proficient. By the 1980s digital services and equipment were steadily replacing their analog forbears. Computers and information technology became a central driver in military aviation planning around the world.

Christopher H. Sterling

See also Air Force Communications Agency (AFCA, 1991–2006); Air Force Communications Service (AFCS), Air Force Communications Command (AFCC) (1961–1991); Airborne Warning and Control System (AWACS); Airmobile Communications; Airships and Balloons; Army Airways Communications System, Airways and Air Communications Service (AACS, 1938–1961); Berlin Airlift (1948–1949); Germany: Air Force; Global Positioning System (GPS); Identification, Friend or Foe (IFF); Radio Silence; Semi-Automatic Ground Environment (SAGE); Solid State Electronics; United Kingdom: Royal Air Force; Vietnam War (1959–1975)

Sources

Anonymous. 1916. "Wireless Equipped Aeroplanes in Warfare." *The Wireless Age* III: 6 (March): 409–421.

Beauchamp, Ken. 2001. "Military Telegraphy in the Air." In *History of Telegraphy*, chap. 10, 348–388. London: Institution of Electrical Engineers.

Edwards, C. P. 1944. "Enemy Airborne Radio Equipment." *Journal of the Institution of Electrical Engineers* 91 (3A): 44–66.

Johnson, T., Jr. 1920. "Naval Aircraft Radio." *Proceedings of the Institute of Radio Engineers* 8 (February): 32–38.

Lansford, Willis R. 1943. "Aircraft Communication in World War I." *Radio News* 29 (June): 50–54, 208–216.

Mikesh, Robert C. 2004. "Radios." In *Japanese Aircraft Equipment: 1940–1945*. Atglen, PA: Schiffer Publishing.

Morrison, Larry R. 1997. *From Flares to Satellites: A Brief History of Air Force Communications.* Scott Air Force Base, IL: Air Force Communications Agency Office of History.

Orme, Robert. 1920. "Radiotelegraphy and Aviation." In *The Yearbook of Wireless Telegraphy and Telephony: 1920*, 988–994. London: Wireless Press.

Raines, Edgar F., Jr. 2000. *Eyes of Artillery: The Origins of Modern U.S. Army Aviation in World War II.* Army History Series. Washington, DC: Center of Military History.

Roberts, Henry W. 1945. *Aviation Radio.* New York: Morrow.

Airships and Balloons

Theorizing about and experimenting with large aerial balloons for military communication dates at least to the 1790s. Tethered and free balloons were used extensively by both sides during the American Civil War for artillery spotting and intelligence gathering. During and between both world wars, airships, or dirigibles, of several nations used radio as a prime means of communication with ground commanders and (in the case of the U.S. Navy) with scouting airplanes carried aboard.

Benjamin Franklin was among those who predicted the military use of the man-carrying balloons first demonstrated in France in the 1780s. The French first applied tethered balloons to gather military intelligence in mid-1794 (messages were dropped to the ground) and with varying degrees of success operated two balloon companies for five years. Similar applications were proposed for U.S. Army operations in the Indian wars of the 1830s and 1840s and the United States' siege of Veracruz, Mexico, in 1846, though no action was taken.

Several pioneers offered use of balloons to Union forces in the American Civil War for observation and intelligence, a task most successfully taken up by Thaddeus Lowe from mid-1861 to 1863. Both the Union and Confederate armies made extensive use of observation balloons early in the Civil War but activity stopped for various reasons in 1863. During the Franco-Prussian War (1870–1871), nearly sixty-five balloons were used to carry messages, people, and pigeons (who would return with messages from outside) out of Paris during the siege of the city. The French reopened their balloon school in 1871, as did the British two decades later. Indeed, balloons were standard equipment in both the British and German armies by the late 1890s. Many of the world's navies also experimented with the use of balloons for scouting.

The Army Signal Corps created its first balloon section in 1892. A balloon was briefly used by the U.S. Army to signal intelligence during the Spanish-American War's Battle of San Juan Hill in 1898. Signal Corps balloon activity, based at Fort Omaha, Nebraska, was revived in 1907 when two balloons were purchased. By 1918 the Army had two balloon companies operating aerial telephones on the Western Front, providing general intelligence and artillery spotting. The balloons made more than 1,600 ascensions and spent more than 3,000 hours in the air.

Based on their extensive early twentieth-century experiments, from the inception of World War I in 1914, German Zeppelins made use of both spark-gap (despite the danger of causing a fire in the hydrogen-filled airship) low and medium frequency radios and radio direction-finding aids on their raids over England. Many of the Telefunken radios (which used five different frequency bands) were converted Navy thousand-watt transmitters housed in soundproof operating rooms or sharing the forward control gondola.

During World War II, dirigible airships were used in antisubmarine warfare along the coast and escorting convoys. They could destroy German U-boats by matching their slow surface speed and then bombarding them with depth charges. The dirigible USS Casablanca *is seen on escort duty in 1943. (National Archives)*

Not long before World War II, Germany's nominally civilian *Hindenburg* (LZ-129) carried two military radios in 1936–1937. One, called a "bread bin" because of its shape, was made from a very light alloy (probably zinc) and weighed just under 20 kilograms. The E 318S was an all-wave Telefunken receiver ranging more than 15 kHz to 20 MHz and ten bands. The second *Graf Zeppelin* (LZ-130, the last rigid airship) carried extensive radio equipment on its August 1939 flights along the British east coast, seeking transmissions from English radar installations.

The British began experimenting with wireless aboard army balloons as early as 1908. By 1911 the British army's *Beta* airship carried a Marconi spark wireless apparatus (apparently the first airship so equipped) that could transmit up to 30 miles. Over the next two years, several wireless-equipped airships were used for observation on army maneuvers. Most carried carrier pigeons in case the wireless unit failed. By the time fighting began in World War I, transmission distances were up to 130 miles, and two airships were radio equipped. By 1917 British rigid airships carried radios using vacuum tubes, not the earlier and more dangerous spark-gap transmitters, as well as pigeons to communicate with the ground. The British R.34 rigid airship maintained wireless contact throughout its transatlantic round-trip flight of mid-1919 (the first double crossing), sending or receiving some 20,000 words and reaching or hearing from receivers a thousand miles distant.

After operating radio-equipped blimps on convoy and antisubmarine patrols beginning in 1917, the U.S. Navy used radio aboard its several rigid airships from 1924 to 1935. *Los Angeles* (ZRS-3) had a well-equipped radio facility and used telephone links for onboard communication.

Akron (ZRS-4) and *Macon* (ZRS-5), the ultimate Navy rigid airships of the early 1930s, used air-to-ground Westinghouse radios in a radio room built into the hull above the external control room. Both experimented with radio communication and direction finding with the handful of scouting airplanes each carried. Portable ultra-high frequency radio was used to communicate with the ground in mooring operations.

The U.S. Navy's extensive World War II fleet of smaller nonrigid blimps were all radio equipped to aid in their scouting, antisubmarine, and convoy protection roles. Radio transmitting and receiving equipment was constantly updated as some of these served until 1962 as off-shore early-warning radar and antisubmarine platforms.

Christopher H. Sterling

See also Airplanes; Army Signal Corps; Lowe, Thaddeus, S. C. (1832–1913)

Sources

Althorpe, William F. 1990. *Sky Ships: A History of the Airship in the United States Navy*. New York: Orion Books.

Beauchamp, Ken. 2001. "Military Telegraphy in the Air: The Dirigible." In *History of Telegraphy*, 348–350. London: Institution of Electrical Engineers.

Christopher, John. 2004. *Balloons at War: Gasbags, Flying Bombs, and Cold War Secrets*. Stroud, UK: Tempus.

Ege, Lennart. 1974. *Balloons and Airships*. New York: Macmillan.

Maitland, E. M. 1920. "Wireless Log of H.M.A. R.34." In *The Log of H.M.A. R.34: Journey to America and Back*, 143–166. London: Hodder & Stoughton.

Popular Science Monthly. 1918. "How the Zeppelin Raiders Are Guided by Radio Signals." *Popular Science Monthly* (April): 632–634.

Tierney, R. K. 1965. "Offspring of the Signal Corps—The Balloon, Dirigible, and Airplane." In *The Story of the U.S. Army Signal Corps*, edited by Max L. Marshall, 127–135. New York: Franklin Watts.

Woods, David L. 1965. "The Military Balloon," In *A History of Tactical Communications Techniques*, chap. X. Orlando, FL: Martin-Marietta.

Alaska Communications System

Communications in the vast reaches of Alaska began with indigenous people thousands of years ago. Russian settlers in the nineteenth century brought European means of connecting their coastal communities. Little changed with the American purchase of the territory in 1867 as there were few settlers and thus little military need. The rush for gold at the end of the nineteenth century rapidly changed Alaska's outlook.

Organized American military communications in Alaska began in May 1900 when Congress appropriated a half-million dollars for the establishment of a military telegraph system and cable lines in the then territory. The system would come to be known as the Washington Alaska Military Cable and Telegraph System (WAMCATS). By June 1903, the U.S. Army completed the first trans-Alaska telegraph line from Eagle to Nome, a project headed by then Lieutenant Billy Mitchell, who declared that Alaska was thus open to civilization. WAMCATS was operated by soldiers assigned to signal depot companies at forts in the territory. From the start, however, the system served a broad variety of users. Of the 300,000 messages being handled by 1906, only about one-fifth were military in nature. The "talking wire" was linked to a submarine cable that eventually connected Seattle with Juneau, Sitka, and Valdez.

Overland lines soon stretched from Seward to Anchorage and north into the interior, following the Alaskan Railroad. Repairmen traveled by dogsled as they checked on the lines. The WAMCATS commander reported directly to the Army's chief signal officer, but little technical improvement in or expansion of the system took place during the tight-budget interwar years. In 1936 WAMCATS was redesignated as the Alaska Communications System (ACS). Most of the major telegraph land lines had been replaced by radio due to the high cost of maintaining cable systems over the vast, inhospitable expanse of Alaska. However, a short resurgence arose in the use of cable systems for security purposes during World War II. It was during this time that the first full duplex teletype system was established between Seattle and Alaska. In 1942, the wartime Alaska-Canada Highway (now the Alaska Highway) was built in record time (despite appalling conditions of weather and terrain) to ferry war materiel to Alaska, with construction sites connected by the ACS. By 1950, the ACS operated thirty-two sites across the territory and civilian use of the system continued to expand.

Three years after Alaska became a state, the ACS was transferred to the U.S. Air Force (1 July 1962). The Air Force completed an upgrade to the ACS to include both microwave and tropospheric radio links. Originally designed to connect several lines of early warning radar systems to the lower forty-eight states, the system was known as WHITE Alaska Integrated Communications and Electronics (WHITE ALICE or WACS), a tropospheric and microwave communications system used throughout Alaska from May 1958 until 1979 (when it was replaced by satellite links). The twenty-five WACS tropospheric stations (ultimately there would be twice as many, covering much of the state and the Aleutian Islands) were built for $140 million by Western Electric and took 3,500 people about three years to complete.

Recognizing the growing commercial value of the network as the state expanded and population grew, the system was purchased by RCA in 1971. As RCA Alascom, the network's capacity was greatly expanded thanks to RCA's major involvement in television. The first intrastate satellite television links became available, and Alascom provided communication links for the construction and operation of the Alaska oil pipeline from the North Shore south 800 miles to Valdez. In 1979, Pacific Telecom purchased Alascom and soon placed three communication satellites, the "Aurora" series, into orbit in 1982, 1991, and 2000. All three are dedicated solely to providing telecommunications services to the state—the first such network. An extensive system of rural telecommunications soon developed, with some satellite earth stations serving communities of as few as twenty-five people. Digital switching was introduced in 1989, and four years later the last telegraph office was closed. AT&T purchased Alascom in 1994 and, a decade later, operated a backbone of microwave links and more than a hundred earth satellite stations.

Danny Johnson

See also American Telephone & Telegraph Co. (AT&T); Communication Satellites; Meteor Burst Communications (MBC); Television; Tropospheric Scatter

Sources

59th Signal Battalion. 2003. "Voice of the Arctic: Signal Corps Lineage in Alaska." [Online information; retrieved January 2006.] http://www.usarak.army.mil/59internet/Lineage.htm.

Allen, June. 2005. "ACS Bids for KPU Telecom: ACS a Longtime Presence." *Sitnews, Stories in the News* (Ketchikan). [Online article; retrieved January 2006.] http://www.sitnews.us/JuneAllen/ACSKPU/010505_acs_kpu.html.

AT&T Alascom. 2005. "Who We Are." [Online information; retrieved January 2006.] http://www.attalascom.com/about/profile.html.

Geocities.com. "The White Alice Communications System." [Online information; retrieved January 2006.] http://www.geocities.com/~billev/wacs/main.html.

Signal Corps. 1911. *Manual No. 2: Regulations for United States Military Telegraph Lines, Alaskan Cables, and Wireless Telegraph Stations*, chaps. 9 and 10. Washington, DC: Government Printing Office.

Stokes, Carol. 1995. "Alaska: New Challenges on Old Ground." *Army Communicator* (November). [Online article; retrieved January 2006.] http://www.gordon.army.mil/AC/WWII/alaska.htm.

A British naval signalman uses an Aldis lamp to communicate with a nearby vessel in the North Atlantic in 1941. This short-range mode of visual signaling allowed convoy ships to maintain radio silence, making it harder for enemy submarines to find them. (Hulton-Deutsch Collection/Corbis)

Aldis Lamp

The signaling, or "Aldis," lamp was a visual signaling device for optical communication (typically using Morse code) between ships. The Aldis was a focused lamp that could produce intermittent bursts of light.

The idea of flashing dots and dashes from a shipboard lantern was first put into practice by British Royal Navy Captain (later Vice Admiral) Philip Colomb in 1867. His original code (used by the Royal Navy for seven years) differed from Morse's, but Morse code was eventually adopted with the addition of several special signals from Colomb's code. Such flashing lights made up the second generation of signaling in the Royal Navy (after the use of flag signals).

Named after its inventor, A. C. W. Aldis, who died in 1953, the electric Aldis lamp could flash intervals (or "pulses") of light by rapidly opening and closing metal shutters mounted in front of the lamp. These operated either manually or, in later versions, automatically. The lamps were usually equipped with some form of optical sight. They were normally mounted on the mastheads of vessels; smaller, handheld versions were also used. Power was usually provided by the vessel's emergency generator, and the lamps were powerful enough to be used during daylight hours. They had a secondary function as simple spotlights.

Aldis lamps were used for more than a hundred years. They provided secure communications, especially valuable during periods of radio silence, such as with convoys operating during both world wars across the Atlantic. Aldis lamps were also commonly used in early airport control towers in addition to or in lieu of radio signaling. Signaling to aircraft used red, green, or white lights in either a steady or flashing form.

The Royal Navy phased out active use of Aldis lamps in 1997 (along with the Morse code), although by that time the devices had become largely ceremonial. They still appear on many naval vessels and are sometimes used in merchant shipping. Other modern naval forces have followed suit as technological advances in digital and infrared communications have made the device obsolete.

Aldis lamps are perhaps the most publicly seen mode of naval communications, showing up (often in the background) constantly in both documentary and dramatic movies about wartime convoys and naval action.

Christopher H. Sterling

See also Atlantic, Battle of the (1939–1945); Infrared Signal Systems; Morse Code; Night Signals; Radio Silence; Searchlights/Signal Blinkers; Talk Between Ships (TBS); United Kingdom: Royal Navy

Sources

Aldis, A. C. W. 1920. "The Optical Theory of Portable Daylight Signalling Lamps." *Transactions of the Optical Society* 21 (March): 113–126.

Kent, Captain Barrie. 1993. *Signal! A History of Signalling in the Royal Navy.* London: Hydon House.

Nalder, Major General R. F.. H. 1956. *The Royal Corps of Signals,* London: Royal Signals Institution.

Royal Navy Signal Division. 1918. *Handbook of Signalling.* London: Royal Navy Signal Division.

Alexander, Edward Porter (1835–1910)

Edward Porter Alexander was the first signal officer of the Confederate Army and founder of the Confederate Signal Corps. He also served the Confederacy as an ordnance officer but achieved fame as an artillery commander, ending the war with the rank of brigadier general of artillery.

Alexander was born 26 May 1835 in Wilkes County, Georgia. At an early age, he determined to become a professional soldier and achieved that goal in 1853 when he entered West Point. He graduated third in the class of 1857 and was commissioned an engineer. In 1859 he was assigned to work with army surgeon Albert J. Myer, who had invented a new communication system using flags called the "wig-wag" system. Myer and Alexander conducted experiments near New York City to refine the system, which was eventually adopted by the U.S. Army as the first tactical communications system.

During the secession crisis Alexander sought appointment in the Confederate Army, where Jefferson Davis assigned him to P. G. T. Beauregard's staff to provide the commander with signal capability. Alexander quickly trained a detachment of signalmen and built signal towers throughout the area of operations. His efforts paid off on 21 July 1861 during the Battle of Bull Run when, while atop one of the signal towers, Alexander discovered Union columns attempting to turn the Confederate left flank and notified Beauregard using the wig-wag system. For the first time in U.S. history tactical information had been transmitted more rapidly than a courier could ride and contributed to the Confederate victory in that battle.

After Bull Run, Alexander maintained control of signal operations and assumed the duties as Joseph E. Johnston's chief of ordnance. He took part in every battle in 1862 and provided Robert E. Lee, general of the Confederate Army, with supplies of ammunition throughout the so-called Seven Days engagements. In April 1862 the Confederate Signal Corps was formally established but Alexander turned down the position of chief signal officer. He did, however, take charge of the short-lived Confederate Air Force, consisting of an observation balloon, often tethered to a river boat on the James River from which he reconnoitered the enemy line. In effect, in addition to his other accomplishments, Alexander had used the first aircraft carrier in military operations.

Alexander constantly sought a field command, which he obtained in November 1862 when Lee appointed him to command an artillery battalion. Alexander perhaps achieved his greatest fame at Gettysburg when he was put in command of all First Corps artillery by General James Longstreet to prepare the way for 15,000 infantrymen to attack the Union line on 3 July 1863. Alexander was promoted to brigadier general on 26 February 1864 and in June was wounded in the shoulder by a sharpshooter at Petersburg. He continued to fight with the Confederate Army until the surrender at Appomattox in April 1865.

After the war, Alexander became involved in the expanding railroad industry and eventually became president of the Central of Georgia Railroad, earning the reputation as "the young Napoleon of the Railways." Alexander devoted his remaining years to writing and at age sixty-five wrote of his war experiences in *Military Memoirs of a Confederate*. In 1909 he suffered a stroke, which left him partially paralyzed, and on 28 April 1910, he died in Savannah, Georgia. Alexander is remembered at the U.S. Army Signal Center, Fort Gordon, Georgia, where the post auditorium is named in his honor.

Steven J. Rauch

See also Airships and Balloons; American Civil War (1861–1865); Bull Run, Battle of (1861); Confederate Army Signal Corps; Myer, Albert James (1828–1880)

Sources
Alexander, E. Porter. 1989. *Fighting for the Confederacy*, edited by Gary W. Gallagher. Chapel Hill: University of North Carolina Press.
Alexander, E. Porter. 1907 (reprinted 1993). *Military Memoirs of a Confederate*. New York: Da Capo.
Klein, Maury. 1971. *Edward Porter Alexander*. Athens: University of Georgia Press.

American Civil War (1861–1865)

Military communications during the American Civil War reflected a merging of existing communications technologies with military organizational structures that enabled more effective command and control of armies at the strategic, operational, and tactical levels of war. Prior to the Civil War, little thought had been expended on the problems of communicating on the battlefield. One who did study this issue was Albert James Myer, an assistant Army surgeon who sought the acceptance of both new technology and commitment of organizational resources to ensure information could be passed in a more timely manner to commanders on the battlefield. Myer had developed a system of visual communication derived from the sign language for the deaf that he had devised while a medical student. This "wig-wag" system used a single flag by day or a torch at night with the motion of the staff to the left, right, and vertical to indicate numbers, which substituted for the dots and dashes of the electric telegraph.

This system could overcome the limitations of mounted messengers by sending messages as events were occurring with a visual range up to fifteen miles. By June 1860, the U.S. Army had adopted the wig-wag system, signaling the initial step in the establishment of American military communications as an identifiable career. In addition to the wig-wag system, an extensive existing civilian electric telegraph system was adapted to the needs of war. In April 1861, with the cooperation of the telegraph companies, the U.S. government assumed control of all telegraph lines leading into Washington DC. Edward S. Sanford, president of the American Telegraph Company, helped organize a unit in the War Department to operate and control the lines. Following the Union's disastrous defeat at Bull Run, more effective efforts were made to harness the existing communications structure by establishing the U.S. Military Telegraph Service (USMTS), an organization staffed by civilians from the commercial telegraph industry. Anson Stager of the Western Union Telegraph Company was selected as the chief of the service and appointed a colonel. He developed a plan for telegraph lines to reach from Washington DC to the headquarters of every major independent army command.

Unlike the Union Army, the Confederate States organized the first independent branch of signalmen in history. A deciding factor was the great success of the wig-wag system under control of Captain Edward Porter Alexander during the Battle of Bull Run in July 1861. On 19 April 1862 the Con-federate States Signal Corps was formed as a distinct organization. When Alexander declined to serve as a chief signal officer, William Norris was selected with control over a branch of ten officers, ten sergeants, and any additional soldiers required to perform signal duties. The Confederate Army took a wider view than the Union Army regarding the duties of its Signal Corps, which included electrical telegraphy, military intelligence, espionage networks, naval communications for blockade runners, and experimentation with hot air balloons.

The relationship between the Signal Corps under Myer and the USMTS under Stager was both complementary and contentious. The USMTS telegraph capability reached army- and corps-level commanders, but did not reach down to the tactical units on the battlefield. To fill this gap, Myer established a small "flying telegraph" or field system using the Beardslee magneto telegraph that employed an alphabet dial and did not require a skilled telegrapher. He wanted this system to be light, rugged, and as simple as possible to ensure tactical mobility and ease of operation. This highly mobile field train carried flags, night signals, rockets, the Beardslee telegraph, and ten miles of wire for use in the combat zone, usually a distance of five to eight miles. As the Union armies moved forward, the field telegraph was employed to establish forward communications back to the more permanent installations of the USMTS.

The complementary aspect ended in 1863 when Myer challenged the status of the USMTS, arguing that the Signal Corps should have control of all military communications from the strategic to tactical level. When he sought to recruit trained telegraphers, Myer incurred the wrath of Secretary of War Edwin Stanton and was relieved as chief signal officer. Stager was put in charge of all military telegraphy, which then consisted of more than 950 civilians who operated 5,326 miles of telegraph line. Before Myer was relieved, he did achieve the goal of getting the Army to authorize a separate Signal Corps branch in March 1863 to replace the detail system and allow men to specialize in communications without concern of being recalled to a combat regiment.

During the course of the war, signal soldiers from both sides were deployed on high ground, in tree tops, on roof tops, and on signal towers to locate enemy troop movements and help adjust friendly artillery fire. They served as intelligence gatherers who could often intercept and read each other's messages. Signalmen were dispatched on reconnaissance missions to inspect enemy locations. Both also employed their communications personnel and systems in joint operations with their navy. In the Union Army it became routine to station signal officers and men aboard naval vessels operating along the rivers and coasts in support of ground operations.

By the end of the Civil War, commanders on both sides and at all levels had grown to depend on the military communications systems in whatever form they took. The war had proven that specially trained signal soldiers were required to harness the ever-growing communications technology that allowed military leaders to effectively command and control armies over vast distances and in a timely manner.

Steven J. Rauch

See also Alexander, Edward Porter (1835–1910); Beardslee Telegraph; Bull Run, Battle of (1861); Confederate Army Signal Corps; Lincoln in the Telegraph Office; Myer, Albert James (1828–1880); Stager, Anson (1825–1885); U.S. Military Telegraph Service (USMTS)

Sources

Brown, J. Willard. 1896. *The Signal Corps, USA in the War of the Rebellion*. Boston: U.S. Veteran Signal Corps Association (reprinted by Arno Press, 1974).

Plum, William R. 1882. *The Military Telegraph During the Civil War in the United States*. Chicago: Jansen, McClurg & Company (reprinted by Arno Press, 1974).

Raines, Rebecca Robbins. 1996. *Getting the Message Through: A Branch History of the U.S. Army Signal Corps*. Washington, DC: U.S. Army Center of Military History.

American Telephone & Telegraph Co. (AT&T)

For most of the twentieth century AT&T served as the primary American telephone service and manufacturing company. AT&T's long distance, local service, Western Electric manufacturing, and Bell Telephone Lab divisions all worked closely with government and military entities, especially in wartime.

After America's entry into World War I on 6 April 1917, the U.S. Postal Service was assigned supervisory control over domestic telephone and telegraph operations (31 July 1918–1 August 1919). Given the small pre-war size of the Army Signal Corps, AT&T and independent telephone personnel played a substantial role in the buildup of people and facilities in both Europe and the United States in 1917–1918. Eventually fourteen Signal Corps "Bell Battalions" were made up entirely of Bell System employees, organized according to their prewar local operating companies. By the end of hostilities, their new European telephone network utilized 100,000 miles of wire, some 100 switchboards, and more than 3,000 local stations.

Manufacturing subsidiary Western Electric supplied the first ship-to-shore radio telephone equipment for new destroyers being built for the U.S. Navy. More than 2,000 radios were installed on United States and British naval vessels and some remained in use until 1930. Beginning in mid-1917, Western also developed small airborne radiotelephone sets that worked by wind-driven generators, allowing voice communication with aircraft. By the end of 1918, the company was also producing 25,000 vacuum tubes a week and had shipped 15,000 telephones, including wires and switches, for use on the Western Front. Two battalions of Signal Corps personnel were made up of Western's technical employees.

AT&T played an even more central role in World War II military communications. While the company's domestic operations were not placed under governmental supervision, AT&T limited civilian use of its facilities to keep lines open for priority military use; for the same reason civilian telephone manufacture and installation was all but banned from late 1942 to the end of the war. An underground transcontinental telephone cable was opened for service in late 1942, allowing more secure communication links. By 1943 some 3,000 Bell operators ran 300 Army switchboards in military facilities.

Western Electric built communication links along the developing Alaska Highway. From 1942 to 1945, the firm made five million military telephones including 300,000 sound-powered phones, more than a half-million aircraft radio receivers, 1.4 million microphones, thousands of teletypewriters, thousands of switchboards, and about seventy different types of radar (between 30 and 40 percent of all U.S. radar manufactured during the war). Most products were radio and wire communications equipment for war use at Army and Navy bases and defense contractors across the United States. Western

also created the communications nerve center used to direct the entire defense effort, installing the world's largest private branch exchange (PBX) at the Pentagon in 1942, with 13,000 lines of dial PBX equipment and 125 operator positions. By 1944 roughly 85 percent of contracts came from the federal government—indeed, Western Electric provided more than 30 percent of all wartime electronic equipment. The scale of World War II is evident in that by 1944, Western was supplying in two weeks communication equipment equivalent to that supplied during all of World War I.

When the Department of Justice brought suit in 1949 to break up AT&T, action on the case was delayed when the Department of Defense intervened during the Korean crisis (1950–1953), arguing the integrated Bell System was vital to national security. AT&T remained intact in the settlement of the case in 1956. Cold War efforts by Western Electric included elements of the Nike missile air defense system and construction (starting at the end of 1954) and operation of the Distant Early Warning (DEW) Line radar line in Arctic Canada. The DEW Line's electronics and communications were completed across the Arctic in mid-1957, extended west through to the Aleutian Islands two years later, and east to Iceland by late 1961. Western was also a key contractor in the Air Force Semi-Automatic Ground Environment system of computer-assisted air defense centers. By the end of the 1950s, about 18,000 Western Electric employees were engaged in defense work alone. During the 1962 Cuban missile crisis, Western installed emergency switchboards and long-distance channels in Florida.

Western turned increasingly to microwave and coaxial cable installation by the 1960s and began developing digital switching and other devices the next decade, while at the same time downsizing its workforce. With the forced breakup of AT&T in 1984, Western became AT&T Technologies, which was spun off as Lucent Technologies in 1996. In 2005, AT&T, by then a much smaller firm than it had once been, was taken over by one of its former regional telephone companies, SBC, which later took on the better-known name of its one-time parent, AT&T. When AT&T took over Bell South in late 2006 (leaving only Verizon and Qwest as regional independent telephone companies), it reassembled much of the old AT&T dominance of domestic telecommunication.

Christopher H. Sterling

See also Army Signal Corps; Bell Telephone Laboratories (BTL); Cuban Missile Crisis (1962); Microwave; Semi-Automatic Ground Environment (SAGE); SIGSALY; Telephone; Vacuum Tube; World War I; World War II

Sources

AT&T. 1993. *Events in Telcommunications History.* New York: AT&T.

Adams, Stephen B., and Orville R. Butler. 1999. *Manufacturing the Future: A History of Western Electric,* chap 5. New York: Cambridge University Press.

Bolling, George. 1983. *AT&T: Aftermath of Antitrust.* Washington, DC: National Defense University Press.

Brooks, John. 1976. *Telephone: The First Hundred Years,* chaps. 7, 9. New York: Harper & Row.

Lavine, A. Lincoln. 1921. *Circuits of Victory.* Garden City, NY: Country Life/Doubleday.

Young, W. Russell. 1982. *The Origin of the AT&T National Defense Policy and Its Relations with the Federal Government.* Arlington, VA: SRI International.

American Wars to 1860

From the American Revolution (1776–1781) to just before the Civil War (1861–1865), American military forces campaigned against both foreign armies and Native Americans. During that time communications technology advanced dramatically and was accompanied by gradual, and sometimes halting, practical implementation. These changes, however, primarily affected strategic, not tactical, communications.

The Revolutionary Army's means of communications were not essentially different from those used by other armies. In May 1776, George Washington established a communications network of couriers from Long Island to New York City (Manhattan) to Staten Island. Its purpose, which it fulfilled successfully, was to let him know when and where the British would land. On the tactical level, a year later at Saratoga, American riflemen used turkey calls to communicate with one another. The defeat at Germantown, Pennsylvania, that same year, however, underscored the communication problems, chiefly the lack of standard signaling practices, encountered by the Revolutionary Army. Though several factors contributed to the loss, the breakdown of communications and, subsequently, cohesion, played a part.

In the winter of 1777, when Washington's army trained at Valley Forge, one result was to develop standardized tactical communications. These practices, eventually codified in the drill manual of Friedrich von Steuben, a German (Hessian) general working with Washington, increased the effectiveness of the Continental Army's operations. Drummers signaled troops to gather, advance, or retreat. The role and duties of the ensign, who carried the regimental flag, were defined. By his position and the manner in which he carried the flag, he indicated a regiment's location, its changes of direction, or when it halted.

Communications technology advanced little between the American Revolution and the War of 1812, but the terrain over which communications were sent expanded, creating difficulties. Communications to such separate areas as Michigan, Canada, and New Orleans could be interrupted by hostile Indians who occupied the center of the continent. Even without overt interference, there was little infrastructure to support rapid and dependable transmission of messages from the government in Washington DC to distant outposts and battlefields. The British Royal Navy restricted the use of sea lanes and could interdict efforts at maritime communications. As a classic example of the slowness of communications, an exchange of letters between General Andrew Jackson in New Orleans and his superiors in Washington took six weeks. The Battle of New Orleans in late 1814 was itself a symptom of slow communications: the participants had not yet learned that a treaty ending the war had been signed.

By the time the Mexican War began in 1846, the number of steamboats in use for purposes of military communications had increased. Couriers traveling by steamboat relayed instructions and information. Railroads were also used to some extent. Most important, telegraph lines now connected Army offices in Washington, Baltimore, Philadelphia, and New York. The Army used the telegraph extensively, though letters were also sent to ensure vital communications were received. Though faster and more secure than before, communication problems continued. After Zachary Taylor's army entered Mexico, it lacked communication links back to Washington. To allow resupply from the Rio Grande, Taylor sent a force to bring supplies and ensure that the lines were safe. Though generally successful, this force was involved in some heavy fighting. A report reached Matamoras, Texas (as noted in the local newspaper on 3 March 1847), that Taylor's force

had suffered a major defeat. This news was carried to New Orleans and from there to Washington, arriving on 25 March. This was a good example of the slowness and precarious nature of communications, relying on hearsay rather than communication directly from the commander.

In 1860 the American Union Army became the first in the world to organize a separate signals department. Experience using new technologies during the Mexican War resulted in advances in organization and implementation to match technological developments.

Robert Stacy

See also American Civil War (1861–1865); European Late Nineteenth-Century Wars; Fire/Flame/Torch; Lights and Beacons; Morse Code; Morse, Samuel F. B. (1791–1872); Music Signals; Telegraph.

Sources
Quimby, Robert S. 1997. *The U.S. Army in the War of 1812: An Operational and Command Study.* East Lansing: Michigan State University Press.
Raines, Rebecca Robbins. 1996. *Getting the Message Through: A Branch History of the U.S. Army Signal Corps.* Washington, DC: U.S. Army Center of Military History.
Von Steuben, Frederick William. 1985. *Baron von Steuben's Revolutionary War Drill Manual.* New York: Dover (reprint).
Winders, Richard Bruce. 1997. *Mr. Polk's Army: The American Military Experience in the Mexican War.* College Station: Texas A&M University Press.

Ancient Signals

Military and nautical writings prior to 500 CE refer to signals, though mostly by obscure hints about one-way signals: "charge," "attack," "commence firing," or "commence shooting" (for longbows and/or crossbows). Seldom were any more complex than "entry of cavalry" or "release warship vanguard." Signal towers by Hannibal, Tiberius's flashing sunbeams between Capri and the mainland, drums in both Persia and Africa, smoke in North America, and pigeons from Egyptian ships are also chronicled. Save for some Roman and Chinese Great Wall signal station locations, precious few physical artifacts survive. Many early military historians, including Homer, Herodotus, and Thucydides, mention the use of fire signals. Plutarch, Livy, and Vegetius all cite various visual "telegraphs" in use by all Roman generals. Marcellinus reports flags, steamers, fires, lights, and sounds (trumpets or similar instruments). Yet few descriptions of actual signals or signal systems exist. As British Royal Navy Commander Henry N. Shore noted in 1915, "Considering the amount of attention bestowed to the art of war by the ancients, it is strange that so little information regarding the methods of transmitting orders amongst the armies and fleets can have filtered down to modern times." Assuming that modern motion pictures, such as *Braveheart*, present a reasonable replication of pregunfire battlefields, the absence of ordered signals seems logical. Most ancient land battles were fought on large flat terrain amid constant noise. Even had tactical signals existed, how could they be seen or heard amid a battle's confusion, dust, and noise?

Only two ancient European signal systems have been described sufficiently to render them replicable. One was devised by Aneas the Tactician about 341 BCE whereby two large, identical cylindrical pots—one at each signal point—were filled with water and a large cork floated on the surface of each pot. In the middle of each cork was a stick carved flat on one side. Various battle situations were carved on both sticks in iden-

tical fashion. Two torches waved and acknowledged provided warning of a message to come. At sight of the second torch, taps were opened to allow water out of each jug. When the correct battle situation reached the top of the water, a third torch signaled "close taps." Each jug now showed the same situation, thus transmitting the message, though not very quickly.

Polybius, the Greek slave tutor/scholar in Rome, who wrote of Aneas's system in about 230 BCE, described the second ancient system, "which was more 'precise,' as invented by Cleoxones or Democritus but perfected by myself," in chapter 46 of his tenth history book. The Greek or Roman alphabet was to be laid out into five vertical and five horizontal sections. Two large tablets were set at least 10 feet apart at each of two signal stations. The twenty-five letters on each tablet were displayed identically. Messages were spelled by a series of three signals per letter: One or two torches signified the table, one to five torches indicated a letter's vertical division, and one to five torches indicated a letter's horizontal division. The system was indeed precise, but it was also very slow, cumbersome, and is not known to have ever been used.

David L. Woods

See also Couriers; Fire/Flame/Torch; Flags; Great Wall of China; Hadrian's Wall; Horses and Mules; Lights and Beacons; Maori Signaling; Military Roads; Music Signals; Native American Signaling; Pigeons; Smoke

Sources

Burns, Russell W. 2004. "Communication Among the Ancients" In *Communications: An International History of the Formative Years*, 1–27. Stevanage, England: Institution of Electrical Engineers.

Shore, Henry N. 1915. "Signalling Methods Among the Ancients." *United Service Magazine* 52 (November): 166–174.

Warre, Edmund. 1876. "Ancient Naval Tactics." *Royal United Service Institution Journal* 28: 593–605.

Woods, David L. 1965. "The First Three Thousand Years." In *A History of Tactical Communication Techniques,* 1–11. Orlando, FL: Martin-Marietta (reprinted by Arno Press, 1974).

Woolliscroft, D. J. 2001. *Roman Military Signalling.* Stroud, UK: Tempus.

Yadin, Yigael. 1963. *The Art of Warfare in Biblical Lands in the Light of Archaeological Discovery.* London: Weidenfeld & Nicolson.

Appalachian, USS

The USS *Appalachian* (AGC-1) was the first in a class of four 14,000-ton, 460-foot amphibious force flagships built beginning in 1943. This was a new type of naval auxiliary, a specially equipped command and communications ship. The increasing complexity of communications in modern amphibious warfare and the growing number of officers and enlisted sailors necessary to staff amphibious force headquarters necessitated these ships. A landing force commander with his staff and their unique equipment simply took up more room than was available, even on a battleship or cruiser of the day.

Amphibious force flagships were designed to provide ample space for the large command staffs needed to plan and direct the many phases of a landing operation. Their special communications facilities would help to ensure proper coordination of troop movement, naval gunfire, and supporting air strikes. Commanders of land, sea, and air forces would have all relevant data before them in a war-room setting in order to coordinate tactics. This type of operational setting would require hundreds of available radio circuits, as well as complete photo labs to process photographs, a map-making plant to draw and print battle maps, and complete cryptography capability for rapid coding and decoding of communications.

The *Appalachian* was commissioned in October 1943 and served in the Pacific Theater. She served as a command ship for the invasion of Kwajalein in January–February 1944 and subsequently supported amphibious assaults at Guam in July 1944, Leyte in October 1944, and Lingayen Gulf in January 1945. Following a West Coast overhaul, *Appalachian* returned to the combat zone just as the war against Japan was drawing to a close. In September–November 1945, she participated in the occupation of Japan.

Early in 1946 she was assigned to Joint Task Force 1, established for Operation Crossroads, a series of atomic bomb tests to be carried out at Bikini Atoll in the Pacific. From May to July 1946, *Appalachian* served as a headquarters ship for media reporters covering the tests. During the second, or "Baker," detonation, the broadcast ship *Spindle Eye* was moved to Hawaii to improve radio transmission to the United States by acting as a relay between the *Appalachian* and another AGC, the *Mount McKinley,* to the U.S. mainland. *Appalachian* became the flagship of the Fifth Fleet and also served the Pacific Fleet in a similar role until 30 January 1947, operating out of San Diego. She was decommissioned there in May 1947 and sold for scrap after a dozen years in the reserve fleet.

Spurred by the success of these flagships of World War II as well as the continuing desire to remove major tactical force commanders and their staffs from excessively crowded combat ships, the postwar Navy converted an incomplete heavy cruiser, *Northampton* (CA-125), to become a tactical command ship. She was redesignated CLC-1 in 1947, completed in 1953, and became CC-1 in 1961, when the role of National Emergency Command Post Afloat was added to her mission. The "AGC" designation used during the war became "LCC," or amphibious command ship, on 14 August 1968. These are the only ships to be designed for such an amphibious command ship role (earlier amphibious command ships lacked sufficient speed to keep up with a 20-knot amphibious force). Subsequently, the *Appalachian* and the *Northampton* became fleet flagships (LCC). USS *Blue Ridge* became the Seventh Fleet flagship in 1979, and USS *Mount Whitney* became the Second Fleet flagship in 1981.

Danny Johnson

See also Flagship; U.S. Navy

Sources
Mooney, James L., ed. 1991. *Dictionary of American Naval Fighting Ships*. Washington, DC: Government Printing Office (Naval Historical Center).
Radio News. 1946. "The Broadcasting Fleet, A Survey of All Radio Ships and Artificial Structures." *Radio News* (September). [Online article; retrieved April 2007.] http://www.offshore-radio.de/fleet/appalachian.htm.

Ardois Light

Ardois lights were a widely used French system of double electric red and white lamps, usually arranged vertically on a naval vessel's mast and used for coded night signaling.

In 1875 the U.S. Navy began experimenting with the use of electric lights for signaling. Two years later, Lieutenant W. N. Wood perfected an electric system for visually transmitting the English Morse telegraphic code, which had been adopted for naval use the previous year. This electric system was installed in U.S. naval vessels in 1878 and extended signaling distances from six to sixteen miles.

In 1891 the U.S. Navy experimentally installed the Ardois system of electric lights in some squadrons. Initially eight systems were ordered at the then considerable cost of more than $1,000 each. The first order was followed a year later by one for six more Ardois systems. Each apparatus used a series of eight double lamps (four red and four white) placed vertically and read down (if mounted horizontally, they were read from the sender's right to the left). Each system came equipped with an Ardois-devised code, but the systems could be used with other codes as well. The Ardois system was intended to be mounted on a mast and operated from a keyboard on a convenient deck below.

Whatever code was utilized, Ardois red lights indicated the "dots" and white lights the "dashes" used in Morse code. For example, in English Morse code, the letter "A" became red-white (dot-dash) and "B" was white-red-red-red (dash-dot-dot-dot). Used in this way, the Ardois light system could be considered the first "allied" signal system with French lights carrying an American telegraph code as modified by the British army and Royal Navy.

In 1891–1892, the U.S. Navy compared the Ardois system with the Sellner system of lights developed in Austria. While not as well made as the Ardois system, the Sellner system cost only $700 for each apparatus. The Ardois system was retained, however, until finally supplanted in 1897 by adding an improved keyboard, know as the "Telephotos."

Some reports suggest the U.S. Army also made use of Ardois lights for night signaling. With the innovation of wireless, signal lights became of secondary importance, save in conditions of radio silence.

Christopher H. Sterling

See also Coston Signals; Night Signals; Radio Silence

Source
Niblack, A. P. 1892. "Naval Signaling." *U.S. Naval Institute Proceedings* 18: 431–505.

Arlington Hall

Located just west of Washington DC in northern Virginia, Arlington Hall, a former young women's finishing school, became the center of U.S. Army code-breaking operations during and after World War II.

From 1927 to 1942, the leafy suburban site was the home of Arlington Hall Junior College. After the December 1941 attack on Pearl Harbor, the Army's Signal Intelligence Service (SIS) (renamed the Signal Security Service by mid-1942, and Signal Security Agency in 1943) found its duties in breaking Japan's naval and military codes greatly expanding. While seeking space for military needs, several officers surveyed the school's grounds in April 1942. After the college's final graduation, the War Department purchased it for a court-imposed settlement of $650,000 (which barely paid off the mortgage on the existing buildings). In August 1942, SIS's growing operation and increased number of personnel moved from the downtown Washington DC Munitions Building on Constitution Avenue to the grounds of what was now called Arlington Hall Station.

There SIS operations continued to expand for the duration of the war. Over the next three years, construction was undertaken to meet the operational and support needs of the expanding workforce, which by 1945 had reached 5,700 civilians and 2,250 military personnel (including, perhaps fittingly given the location's former role, a thousand members of the Women's Army Corps). Two large, multistory operations buildings plus troop support facilities (barracks, post exchange, theater, recreational center) were ultimately built.

Among other machine devices installed to help the code-breaking process were more than seventy Western Electric–built "bombes" added in 1943 and built to British designs (though slower because they used standard telephone switching equipment). Researchers at Arlington Hall also developed the "auto-scritcher," "super-scritcher," and "dudbuster" electrical devices to assist in breaking German and Japanese army codes. The super-scritcher, for example, used some 3,500 vacuum tubes and may have been the first application of digital technology to the code-breaking process. The dudbuster was used, as its name suggested, to help recover partially garbled Enigma messages. All of these machines were needed, for while Arlington Hall was handling 15,000 messages a month in 1942, the quantity soared to more than 700,000 per month two years later. With assistance from these machines, the human code breakers could usually break into a new enemy code within a couple of months.

Following World War II the army combined all of its signals intelligence and communications missions and resources into one unit, the Army Security Agency, on 15 September 1945. For the next thirty-two years, Arlington Hall Station served as the headquarters of the Army Security Agency and its worldwide command. It was also the home of the top-secret "Venona" project to read Soviet codes, a project closed in 1980 and first revealed fifteen years later. In 1977 the agency became the U.S. Army Intelligence and Security Command.

Arlington Hall near Washington DC was headquarters for the U.S. Army's Signal Intelligence Service cryptography operation during World War II. It became part of the National Security Agency in 1952. (National Security Agency)

Through the years Arlington Hall Station served as a temporary home to a number of major tenants, including the Armed Forces Security Service, the then-new National Security Agency, the Air Force Intelligence Command, the Army's Signal Communications Security Command, and both the Defense Intelligence Agency and Defense Communications Agency.

Following relocation of the last Army unit to Fort Belvoir, Virginia, Arlington Hall Station was officially closed on 30 September 1989. The facility now serves (in new buildings, though the old white-columned dormitory hall of the women's school survives) as the home of the State Department's Foreign Service Training Center and the National Guard Bureau.

Christopher H. Sterling

See also Bletchley Park; Defense Communications Agency (DCA, 1960–1991); Driscoll, Agnes Meyer (1889–1971); Enigma; Friedman, William F. (1891–1969); Magic; National Security Agency (NSA); Rowlett, Frank B. (1908–1998); Ultra

Sources

Crawford, D. J., and P. E. Fox. 1992. "The Autoscritcher and Superscritcher: Aids to Cryptanalysis of the German Enigma Cipher Machines." *IEEE Annals of the History of Computing* 14 (3): 9–22.

Robertson, Laurie. 2004. "Arlington Hall Station: The U.S. Army's World War II Cryptanalytic Center." *IEEE Annals of the History of Computing* 26 (2): 86–89.

Armed Forces Communications & Electronics Association (AFCEA)

Although AFCEA officially began in 1946, it enjoys a heritage dating back to a handful of Union Signal Corps veterans who banded together after the American Civil War—probably more for sociability than professional development. There are few not-for-profit professional associations more influential in military communications than AFCEA.

AFCEA began as the Army Signal Association in 1946, was renamed the Armed Forces Communication Association a year later, and added "Electronics" to its name in 1954. In 1979, a European office was opened in Brussels, Belgium. AFCEA offers numerous programs with educational, professional, and intellectual goals for civilian and military communications and electronics in most major nations. The European office of AFCEA International was established in Brussels to serve European members. Currently about 30 European chapters and sub-chapters in 22 countries, with more than 4,000 members, communicate in 19 different languages.

AFCEA's monthly publication, *Signal*, is sixty years old as of this writing. Its Source Book issue, published each January, contains company profiles and contacts of AFCEA's corporate members. While most defense-oriented magazines have shrunk during the past one or two decades as defense budgets decline in the United States and abroad, *Signal* remains at least the same size, if not larger. Likewise, the AFCEA publishing organization continues to grow and includes published conference proceedings and collections of articles from the monthly magazine. AFCEA publishes (and makes available online) several directories.

Perhaps the most unusual AFCEA feature is that its membership includes communications and electronics experts from each of the American armed services as well as those from allied countries along with many people in the private sector. As of the early 2000s, AFCEA had some 31,000 members (20,000 individual and 11,000 corporate associates) arranged into more than thirty regions around the world, and 1,300 corporate members. Two-thirds of the individual members are with private industry. The total number of AFCEA chapters in the United States and abroad is 134.

AFCEA, in partnership with its Educational Foundation (formed in 1979) and chapters, presents $1.4 million annually in scholarships, grants, and awards to students in the mathematical and physical sciences attending the five service academies, Reserve Officer Training Corps (ROTC) programs, graduate schools, and other educational institutions. The awards program began in 1964. The AFCEA Professional Development Center complements the association's educational efforts by providing a wide-ranging program of continuing education and technical training courses.

AFCEA is headquartered in Fairfax, Virginia, outside Washington DC.

David L. Woods

See also Institute of Electrical and Electronic Engineers (IEEE)

Source
Armed Forces Communications & Electronics
    Association (AFCEA). "About AFCEA."
    [Online information; retrieved August 2006.]
    http://www.afcea.org/about/.

Armstrong, Edwin Howard (1890–1954)

Edwin Howard Armstrong was one of radio's more prolific inventors, developing the regenerative, superheterodyne, and frequency modulation (FM) circuits. On active service in World War I, he made his several patents freely available for American military use in both world wars.

Born in New York City on 18 December 1890, Armstrong was attracted to radio as a boy. He had built sophisticated receivers by the time he graduated from high school in 1909. He studied electricity with Michael Pupin at Columbia University, graduating in 1913 (the same institution awarded him an honorary doctorate of science degree in 1929). In 1912 he developed the radio regenerative, or "feedback," circuit for signal amplification using three-element vacuum tubes. This initiated two decades of patent litigation with inventor Lee de Forest, which ended with the Supreme Court finding for de Forest in 1934. Despite the ruling, most engineers concluded then and since that the invention was clearly Armstrong's.

During World War I, Armstrong served in the Army Signal Corps, beginning as a captain in mid-1917 and promoted to major early in 1919. He was stationed in France, working on intelligence and aircraft radio. Just prior to the armistice of 1918, he invented and later patented what became known as the superheterodyne circuit to tune high frequency spectrum bands. For each of his key inventions, Armstrong conducted countless laboratory experiments to work out the kinks in his circuits. He strongly favored physical evidence over mathematical theory.

In 1920 Armstrong invented the superregenerative circuit that would make two-way mobile radio systems possible. During the late 1920s and through the 1930s, Armstrong developed a system of FM radio, patented in 1933 and first offered to the Radio Corporation of America (RCA) for further development. When RCA focused instead on television, Armstrong and a small band of followers experimented with and perfected FM (thanks to his considerable income from his earlier invention royalties and his dividends as the largest RCA individual shareholder). Commercial FM broadcast service began in the United States in 1941.

Armstrong began work for the Signal Corps again in 1939, developing an FM mobile radio. He undertook further projects at no salary in 1940–1941. With America's entry into World War II, Armstrong waived royalties on his inventions for any equipment manufactured for military use. He continued to work on FM two-way radio systems and radar research during and after the war. Armstrong's research helped to develop and perfect circuits and equipment to help in detection and identification; strategic and tactical ship, short, and air communications systems; and weapons control and guidance systems.

In the early 1950s he perfected a system of FM multiplex communications. During his career Armstrong published a score of technical and many general audience papers on all aspects of radio communication. But despite a lifetime of awards and honors,

The innovations in electrical engineering that Edwin Howard Armstrong created were so essential that several of his inventions are still used in radar and radio equipment. His most important achievement was the invention of wide-band frequency modulation (FM) radio. (Library of Congress)

frustrated by the costs of an extended patent battle (chiefly with RCA) over rights to FM circuits, Armstrong took his own life in New York City on 31 January 1954.

Christopher H. Sterling

See also Army Signal Corps; de Forest, Lee (1873–1961); Modulation; Vacuum Tube; World War I

Sources

Armstrong, Edwin H. 1940. "Evolution of Frequency Modulation." *Electrical Engineering* (December): 485–493.
Lessing, Lawrence. 1956. *Edwin Howard Armstrong: Man of High Fidelity*. Philadelphia: J. P. Lippincott.
Lewis, Tom. 1991. *Empire of the Air: The Men Who Invented Radio*. New York: HarperCollins.
Morrisey, John W., ed. 1990. *The Legacies of Edwin Howard Armstrong*. New York: Radio Club of America.
Ragazzini, John R. 1954. "Creativity in Radio: Contributions of Major Edwin H. Armstrong." *Journal of Engineering Education* 45 (October): 112–119.

Army Airways Communications System, Airways and Air Communications Service (AACS, 1938–1961)

The U.S. Army transmitted the first radio message from an aircraft in 1910, and by the decade's end the Aviation Section of the Army Signal Corps was actively experimenting with air-to-ground and ground-to-air communications. In 1923 the Air Service established its first radio stations for air-to-ground and point-to-point communications and to disseminate weather data. But by 1938 only thirty-three stations had been established, and flying was still usually undertaken only in good weather and during daylight hours. When an aircraft left the ground, its whereabouts often remained in doubt until it landed.

To overcome these restrictions on its complex operations, the War Department established the Army Airways Communications System (AACS) on 15 November 1938 to operate all fixed Air Corps radio facilities that aided air traffic between Army flying fields in the continental United States. Major Wallace G. Smith became the Air Corps communications control officer. To operate the system, Smith divided the United States into three regions, each with a squadron. Authorized staffing for the entire system consisted of three officers and 300 enlisted men.

As the United States moved toward war, AACS expanded its operations. In May 1941 it established its first foreign station at Goose Bay, Labrador, to support ferry routes to Britain and made possible the Bolero Project, the mass movement of aircraft to Britain between July and September 1942. Starting a tradition of being in the thick of every operation, AACS personnel were in the Hickam Airfield control towers on Oahu when Japan attacked Pearl Harbor on 7 December 1941. AACS men were also involved in the battle at Dutch Harbor, Alaska, in early 1942, and later used its sites in Alaska to establish a ferry route to the Soviet Union. As the U.S. war effort expanded around the globe, AACS went with it, establishing a worldwide network of stations providing "highways in the sky." The success of the AACS airways communication network revolutionized the entire science of logistics. Among its achievements, it made possible the resupply of the British at El Alamein and served the China-Burma-India supply line.

AACS mobile units reached Normandy, France, on 12 June 1944, just six days after D-Day, and raced with Patton's army for the Rhine. AACS men were consistently the first Army/Air Force personnel to appear in overrun territory, winning a proud reputation of being first in and last out. Though technically noncombatants, AACS troops often had to take up arms to defend themselves because control towers were prime targets during an enemy attack.

AACS played a key role in the surrender of the Japanese. After General Douglas MacArthur tried unsuccessfully to contact the Japanese with surrender terms, AACS sent MacArthur's instructions to the Japanese on 15 August 1945 using the frequency over which AACS had been broadcasting uncoded weather information. Within two hours, Tokyo replied. This represented the first direct communications between the Allies and Japan. On 28 August 1945, Colonel Gordon Blake and his AACS contingent flew to Atsugi Airfield as part of a task force to provide advance support for American troops.

When World War II ended, AACS was a major military command with a worldwide mission. Eight wings, 21 groups, 55 squadrons, and more than 700 detachments comprised its ranks. Its 49,000 military men and women operated 819 stations throughout the world. Thirty-eight allied nations, including the Soviet Union, used AACS facilities. AACS operated in all theaters and in all campaigns of the war. Communications made a quantum leap as military planners reacted to conditions and needs imposed by war. AACS had steadily introduced new equipment and new techniques such as radio teletype, facsimile, automatic high speed transmissions, and ground-controlled approach radar.

The war's end and demobilization brought rapid changes to AACS. In March 1946 it lost its status as an independent command, became a subordinate field unit of Air Transport Command, and was redesignated Airways and Air Communications Service (AACS), an association that lasted until June 1961. In December 1946, AACS had only 8,635 military personnel, which seriously affected its ability to meet its occupation duties and maintain its worldwide air networks. The Berlin Airlift crisis in 1948 initially swamped AACS air traffic operators in Berlin, but quick augmentation and improvisation allowed AACS to provide the airways navigation, air traffic control, and communications that made the airlift possible. No aircraft were lost while under AACS ground-controlled approach radar control.

The Korean War soon followed the Berlin Airlift, and as in World War II, AACS personnel were among the first to deploy. AACS detachments were operating at Pusan, Taegu, and Pohang, South Korea, a week after President Truman authorized U.S. military involvement in July 1950. By the end of the war, traffic volume at several South Korean airfields often exceeded traffic at Tempelhof Airport during the height of the Berlin Airlift.

Communications technology expanded during the 1950s to keep pace with changes in aviation technology and the world political situation. By 1960, AACS air-to-ground communications used the electronic spectrum from low to ultra-high frequencies. Modulation techniques included amplitude modulation (AM), frequency modulation (FM), single sideband, data link, and digitized command. Navigation aids used operational radio, radar, stellar, and inertial guidance systems. AACS also played an important role in the fielding of ballistic missile early warning systems and pioneered improvements in point-to-point, computer, and satellite communications. The AACS mission also included flight check and engineering and installation.

The importance of communications for the effective use of airpower in a stressed world prompted the establishment of AACS as a major air command on 1 July 1961, and its simultaneous redesignation as the Air Force Communications Service. The decision to organize Air Force communications on a global scale under a single manager was the result of AACS's twenty-three years of experience in developing communications specifically responsive to the needs of airpower. The new command continued to provide basic services of air traffic control and long-haul communications and added on-base communications systems, cable systems plants, and maintenance networks previously assigned to other major commands.

Thomas S. Snyder

See also Airplanes; Army Signal Corps; Berlin Airlift; Computer; Facsimile/Fax; Modulation; Satellite Communications; Single Sideband; Spectrum Frequencies; Teleprinter/Teletype

Sources

Miller, Linda G., and Cora J. Holt. 1988. *Air Force Communications Command Chronology, 1938–1988.* Scott Air Force Base, IL: Air Force Communications Command Office of History.

Shores, Louis. 1947. *Highways in the Sky: The Story of the AACS.* New York: Barnes & Noble.

Snyder, Thomas S., ed. 1981. *Air Force Communications Command: An Illustrated History.* Scott Air Force Base, IL: Air Force Communications Command Office of History.

Army Battle Command System (ABCS)

An automated command-and-control (C2) system, the U.S. Army Battle Command System (ABCS) employs a mix of fixed and mobile networks and is designed to be interoperable with theater, joint, and combined command systems. Put another way, ABCS is the new overarching "system of systems" intended to coordinate and standardize nearly a dozen existing Army networks.

In 1988 an effort was initiated to integrate those systems into a family (or system) of systems operating out of command centers called Army Tactical Command and Control Systems. The U.S. Army began a set of formal experiments in harnessing military information in 1994 with its advanced warfighter experiments using computer and information technology networks to increase the speed and agility of combat power. ABCS was first identified as such in 1995. While constant updating and enhancement of the system was initially planned, with the war on terrorism, the Army chief of staff directed that the effort should be refocused to deliver those capabilities most desired by commanders for use in current operations.

ABCS was first deployed during operations in Afghanistan and the Iraq War, though it was often underutilized due to limited training. Sometimes referred to as a "good enough" system, the idea behind ABCS is not necessarily to include all possible bells and whistles at the top command level, but rather to standardize software, integrating only those capabilities essential to ensure joint interoperability, and distribute this standardized capability to all Army combat units. The "good enough" approach saves development time and money and ensures all levels of the service will see the same information at the same time. ABCS provides more data communications, for while voice communications will always be important on a battlefield, a visual image can be far more useful.

The ABCS system is tested at the Army's Central Technical Support Facility at Fort Hood, Texas (the largest Army post in the United States), before it is fielded. Under the consolidated structure of ABCS, a user is able to log on to the network from a "ruggedized" Army laptop computer. ABCS will enhance training, improve field operation, and reduce communications support requirements while improving the functionality and effectiveness of the Army's command system.

Christopher H. Sterling

See also Future Combat Systems; Iraq War (2003–Present); Single Channel Ground and Airborne Radio System (SINCGARS); "System of Systems"; Warfighter Information Network–Tactical (WIN-T); World Wide Military Command and Control System (WWMCCS)

Sources
Chisholm, Patrick. 2004. "'Good Enough' Battle Command," [Online article; retrieved January 2007.] *Military Information Technology* 8 (August 17): 6. http://www .military -information-technology.com/article.cfm ?DocID=576.
Federation of American Scientists. 1999. "Army Battle Command System." [Online article; retrieved January 2007.] http://www.fas .org/man/dod-101/sys/land/abcs.htm.
Rider, Tim. n.d. "Digital Dreams: A Concise History of Army Battle Command Systems." [Online article; retrieved January 2007.] http://www.monmouth.army.mil/ monmessg/newmonmsg/jun162006/ m24tim.htm.

Army Signal Corps

The U.S. Army's communications branch was established by Congress in June 1860 as the first American military organization dedicated solely to communications.

The Army Signal Corps' creation coincided with technological advances that extended the battlefield and made it more deadly. The situation called for new methods of signaling beyond voice commands and mounted messengers. Major Albert J. Myer became the Army's first chief signal officer. He had earlier devised the wig-wag system of signaling using flags by day and torches at night to rapidly send messages over long distances. With the outbreak of the American Civil War early in 1861, Myer organized a separate wartime corps of soldiers trained in signaling and assigned them to the various field armies. He ordered construction of a "field train" to enable telegraph equipment to be carried onto the battlefield.

The Signal Corps' use of electrical telegraphy, however, put it in competition with Secretary of War Edwin M. Stanton's own telegraph corps, known as the United States Military Telegraph. Consequently, in 1863 Stanton dismissed Myer as chief and removed electrical telegraphy from the Signal Corps' auspices. Nevertheless, signal soldiers continued to provide visual communications for the duration of the Civil War. Although the Signal Corps did not contribute decisively to the outcome of the conflict, it did play an important role in such battles as Fredericksburg (1862) and Gettysburg (1863) and in the fighting around Atlanta (1864).

In the postwar period, Myer regained his position as chief signal officer and worked to establish the branch on a permanent basis. Some respected army leaders, among them General William T. Sherman, questioned the necessity for such a branch. Myer accomplished his goal by assuming responsibility for the nation's weather service. Using existing telegraph lines and building others in remote locations not served by commercial systems, the Signal Corps organized a nationwide weather reporting network. It issued daily forecasts and began publishing *Monthly Weather Review*, which continues in print today. The Army ran the U.S. Weather Bureau until 1891 when Congress transferred it to the Department of Agriculture.

While the signaling aspect of the corps' mission received less emphasis during this period, it did not disappear altogether. The corps began using the telephone soon after its commercial introduction in 1877 and incorporated it into its wire network. The field telegraph train received some improvements, and the corps adopted a standard heliograph for use in the late nineteenth-century Indian campaigns in the southwestern United States.

Electrical communications came to the forefront during the 1898 war with Spain, when the Signal Corps found itself facing unprecedented challenges of time and space. Moreover, the branch was too small (then just eight officers and fifty enlisted men) to cover necessary signaling duties. Congress responded by authorizing a volunteer Signal Corps for the duration of the conflict. Signal soldiers established land and undersea communications systems in Cuba, Puerto Rico, and the Philippines and connected those distant shores with the United States. The corps succeeded in transmitting messages between Cuba and Washington DC in as little as twenty minutes. This conflict also marked the corps' first significant practice of combat photography, a function with which it would become closely associated.

Toward the end of the nineteenth century, the Army Signal Corps explored the use of aerial communications, employing captive balloons as portable observation platforms. The anchor rope carried a telephone line to transmit the information obtained aloft. The balloon's most notable use occurred during the battle of Santiago, Cuba, in 1898 when observers located a previously unknown trail that hastened the deployment of troops to San Juan Hill. In 1909 the Signal Corps purchased the Army's first airplane from the Wright brothers, the origins of today's U.S. Air Force. The corps' involvement with airplanes stemmed from the perception that they represented a more sophisticated form of aerial observation.

The twentieth century saw the advent of electronic communications. The Signal Corps experimented with wireless technology as early as 1899. In 1900 the corps began constructing the Washington-Alaska Military Cable and Telegraph System (WAMCATS), which included a wireless link across Norton Sound, a distance of 107 miles. The corps established a laboratory in the basement of the Signal Corps office in Washington, where signal personnel built and tested new equipment. The corps also set up a radio lab in the newly established Bureau of Standards where the U.S. Navy carried out similar experimentation. As the United States moved toward entering the war in Europe in 1917, military communications stood at a crossroads between the past and the future, using pigeons as well as electricity to carry the Army's messages.

World War I proved to be a significant milestone in the Army Signal Corps' history. From fewer than 2,000 officers and men, the branch mushroomed by war's end to approximately 55,000 members. Moreover, the corps made substantial investments in research and development. Outgrowing its existing space in Washington, the corps opened training and laboratory facilities at Camp Alfred Vail, New Jersey (later renamed Fort Monmouth, it remained the site of the Army Signal Corps school until 1974). Consulting with experts in the private sector, such as John J. Carty of AT&T, and recruiting others from the communications industry, the branch gathered the resources it needed. The corps also called upon civilian scientists, such as Edwin Howard Armstrong, who developed the superheterodyne circuit while serving in the Army Signal Corps in France. Despite these efforts, the United States depended largely

on its allies for radio equipment. In Europe, the corps installed a strategic wire network that ultimately extended some 38,000 miles. Because radios were still large and cumbersome, field telephony carried the backbone of wartime tactical communications. Although the branch lost its aviation section in the war's waning months, it retained responsibility for aerial radio. The Signal Corps' contribution to victory can be measured in its casualty rate, second only to the Infantry's. Its role on the battlefield was now beyond doubt.

Despite meager budgets and greatly reduced staffing, the corps devoted its efforts during the interwar years to developing such critical items as radar and FM radio. In addition, the teletypewriter proved faster and more versatile than older Morse code–based systems. On the tactical level, the walkie-talkie provided soldiers with portable battlefield communications.

The 1941 surprise attack at Pearl Harbor by the Japanese, however, highlighted the limitations of the Army's communications. Although the Signal Corps had installed radar sets on Oahu, they were not yet fully operational in December 1941. Once again the corps underwent an enormous expansion to meet the demands of a global conflict. One of its most daunting tasks was to establish a worldwide military communications system. Known as the Army Command and Administrative Network (ACAN), it connected Washington with all major field commands at home and overseas. The Army Signal Corps joined forces once again with the commercial communications industry, and the fruits of this effort—in particular, improvements in radar technology—were critical to winning the war. On the battlefield, the walkie-talkie and the handie-talkie

Signal Corps soldiers use a radar plotting board at an aircraft warning information center on New Caledonia in 1943. Radio-based radar was a crucial technology in all theaters of World War II and such centers proved invaluable in directing battles on land, sea, and in the air. (Library of Congress)

put radios in soldiers' hands. Radio relay—the marriage of wire and radio—allowed communications to keep up with fast-moving operations.

But the growing reliance on electronic communications came with a price: increased susceptibility to enemy jamming and interception. Consequently signal security and intelligence assumed critical importance. The Signal Intelligence Service had been created in 1929 to control all Army cryptology. William Friedman, an Army Signal Corps cryptologist, had supervised the team that broke the Japanese PURPLE code prior to Pearl Harbor, but it was the Poles and British who succeeded in cracking the German Enigma machine.

After 1945, peace proved short lived, and the Cold War era began. The Signal Corps soon found itself fighting in Korea using its World War II–vintage equipment. That country's climatic extremes, mountainous terrain, and lack of good roads greatly complicated communications. The corps depended heavily on very high frequency (VHF) radios to span the long distances, while on the ground signal soldiers often used water buffalo to string wire.

Meanwhile, communications entered the space age. The Signal Corps had successfully bounced radar signals off the moon in 1946. In response to the Soviet Union's launch of Sputnik in 1957, the corps participated in America's nascent space program. With the creation of the National Aeronautics and Space Administration in 1958, military dominance of the space program ended, but not its participation in it. Working with the Air Force, the Signal Corps launched the world's first communications satellite in December 1958. Two years later it cooperated with the Weather Bureau and other agencies to develop the first weather satellite.

In its laboratories at Fort Monmouth, New Jersey, the Signal Corps continued the trend toward miniaturization that had begun with the walkie-talkie. The development of the transistor and the integrated circuit launched the digital revolution. In 1954 the Army established an electronic proving ground at Fort Huachuca, Arizona, to conduct experimentation free from the interference associated with Monmouth's increasingly urban location. The Army made the arrival of this new era official by replacing the office of the chief signal officer with the chief of communications–electronics in 1964.

The prolonged Vietnam conflict (1959–1975) witnessed the culmination of a century of progress in military signaling. For the first time, high-quality commercial communications became available to the soldier in the field. On the tactical level, new transistorized combat radios enabled infantry, armored divisions, and artillery troops to communicate directly with each other. For strategic purposes, the Signal Corps employed such sophisticated techniques as microwave relay

and tropospheric scatter. While communications satellites proved disappointing in their combat zone debut, they held great promise for future strategic applications.

In 1974 the signal school moved from Fort Monmouth to Fort Gordon, Georgia. Fort Monmouth retained its research and development role as home of the Communications and Electronics Command. The branch reached another milestone with the opening of many of its occupational specialties to women. By 1976 the corps included 7,000 enlisted women distributed among all but six of its sixty-one communications specialties. In 2002 Brigadier General Janet E. A. Hicks became the first female commander of the Signal Center and School at Fort Gordon. Since 1986 the commandant has also carried the title of chief of signal.

The closing decades of the twentieth century saw the Army engaged in a number of small-scale conflicts. As joint operations became more commonplace, communications interoperability among the services took on increasing importance. The lack of interoperability posed particular problems during an invasion of Grenada in 1983. By the time the United States and an allied coalition battled Iraq in the Gulf War in 1990–1991, many of these difficulties had been resolved. Moreover, computers and satellites greatly enhanced the ability of commanders to coordinate their forces. Army modernization since 1991 has concentrated on the digitization of command and control.

As the Signal Corps approaches its sesquicentennial in 2010, its basic mission remains the same: to get the message through in peace and war. It is one of the Army's largest branches and its military value is undeniable. Wherever they are being worn around the world, the crossed flags and torches of the Army Signal Corps' insignia are visible reminders of the branch's rich heritage as it carries military communications into the twenty-first century.

Rebecca Robbins Raines

See also Airplanes; Alaska Communications System; American Civil War (1861–1865); Armstrong, Edwin Howard (1890–1954); Fort Gordon, Georgia; Fort Huachuca, Arizona; Fort Monmouth, New Jersey; Greely, Adolphus W. (1844–1935); Gulf War (1990–1991); Heliograph and Mirrors; Korean War (1950–1953); Myer, Albert James (1828–1880); Signals Intelligence (SIGINT); Squier, George Owen (1865–1934); Telegraph; U.S. Military Telegraph Service (USMTS); Vietnam War (1959–1975); World War I; World War II

Sources

Bergen, John D. 1986. *Military Communications: A Test for Technology*. United States Army in Vietnam Series. Washington, DC: Government Printing Office.

Brown, J. Willard. 1896. *The Signal Corps, U.S.A. in the War of the Rebellion*. Boston: U.S. Army Veteran Signal Corps Association (reprinted by Arno Press, 1974).

Glassford, William A. 1896. "The Signal Corps." In *The Army of the United States*, edited by Theophilus F. Rodenbough and William L. Haskin. New York: Maynard, Merrill, and Co.

Marshall, Max L., ed. 1965. *The Story of the U.S. Army Signal Corps*. New York: Franklin Watts.

Raines, Rebecca Robbins. 1996. *Getting the Message Through: A Branch History of the U.S. Army Signal Corps*. Washington, DC: Government Printing Office.

Scheips, Paul J., ed. 1980. *Military Signal Communications*. 2 vols. New York: Arno Press.

Artillery/Gunfire

Gunfire and artillery have often served as means of communicating in addition to their more usual ordnance function. Not only can gunshots be used for crude aural signaling but also artillery shells can be loaded with messages or propaganda leaflets, much like bombs. Both world wars saw numerous instances of the latter, but the earliest recorded use dates to the late nineteenth century.

Gunfire can be used as a simple means of communications in wartime conditions, with the number of shots, for example, indicating a certain prearranged message. Gunfire, or even a recording of gunfire, can readily be used to attract (or distract) attention of an enemy force. It can be useful in helping to locate isolated forces. Gunfire can be an effective means of signaling day or night and under any weather conditions. Under carefully controlled circumstances, artillery can fire shells containing messages to allied forces, albeit with the danger that such "airborne" communication may be intercepted.

Artillery has been more widely used for communicating propaganda than messages. Sometimes called "carrier shells," an artillery shell can be simply a hollow carrier equipped with a fuse that ejects the contents at a calculated time. The contents are most often propaganda leaflets but can be anything that meets the weight limit and is able to withstand the shock of firing. Famously, on Christmas Day 1899 during the Boer War siege of Ladysmith, the Boers fired into surrounded British forces a carrier shell without a fuse that contained a Christmas pudding, two Union Jack flags, and the message, "Compliments of the season."

During World War I, Italy and Britain used "rocket sticks" as message carriers. A map or message was contained in a metal tube shot from a mortar and attached to a smoke bomb to make finding the message easier. Germans made use of four types of pistol signal cartridges with different-colored charges.

In World War II, British forces used smoke shells for propaganda, removing the smoke-generating devices and inserting sometimes hundreds of propaganda leaflets, which would then be shot into German or Italian lines. This was done in both North Africa and, after D-Day, in western Europe. The Americans used 105- and 155-mm howitzer shells in a similar way. The Germans designed one 105-mm artillery shell specifically for spreading leaflets. It was called "Weiss-Rot Geschoss" after the red color coding applied to it. In field operations, grenades could serve a similar purpose, though obviously carrying fewer and smaller leaflets. Army cartoonist Bill Mauldin made light of the process with one of his famous "Willy and Joe" drawings suggesting the Germans had no time to read the messages being shot over their lines.

Artillery or grenades used for leaflet distribution used a time fuse that fired a small explosive charge to expel the leaflets in air over enemy trenches. The firing of the gun often compacted the leaflets in the grenade in such a way that caused a characteristic folding pattern on the leaflets. Indeed, the expelling charge often burned parts of the leaflets. Artillery shells were also used for sending propaganda leaflets in later wars, including Vietnam.

Christopher H. Sterling

See also Propaganda and Psychological Warfare

Sources

Alexander, David J. "The Propaganda Shell." [Online article; retrieved February 2006.] http://www.psywar.org/psywar/reproductions/pshell.pdf.

Erdmann, James M. 1969. *Leaflet Operations in the Second World War.* Denver, CO: James Erdmann.

Margolin, Leo J. 1946. *Paper Bullets: A Brief Story of Psychological Warfare in World War II.* New York: Froben Press.

Propaganda Leaflets of the Second World War. "Falling from the Sky." [Online article; retrieved February 2006.] http://members.home.nl/ww2propaganda/spread5.htm.

Woods, David L. 1965. "Pyrotechnic Signals." In *A History of Tactical Communication Techniques,* chap. 6. Orlando, FL: Martin-Marietta (reprinted by Arno Press, 1974).

Association of Old Crows (AOC)

The Association of Old Crows (AOC), nearly 15,000 strong in the early 2000s, is a tax-exempt organization of those who work or once worked in electronic countermeasures (ECM) for one of the American military services or supporting companies.

What would become AOC grew out of the work of one man. In early 1942, Mel Jackson was the first officer assigned to ECM duties in the U.S. Army Air Force. He decided to form an association of former ECM personnel, and around 1953, while marketing ECM equipment, Jackson had membership certificates and identifying coins made, passing them out to the military personnel he was dealing with, as a sort of honorarium from his company. He adopted a logo that appeared on coffee mugs and other memorabilia. Some carried the motto *Non Videbunt,* which translates to "They Shall Not See." The next step was an informal gathering of men who had served in the Strategic Air Command (SAC) as ECM officers. By September 1964, the reunion idea had taken hold, and 360 people gathered for a banquet at the Washington DC Shoreham Hotel. They included people from all three military services, as well as many from industry and universities engaged in ECM research. Of that group of attendees, many joined to form the new AOC.

The group's name always attracts questions. During World War II Allied ECM officers, assigned to disrupt enemy communications and radar (the first were in May 1942), were given the code name "Raven." After the war, a group of Raven operators were directed to establish a SAC flying course in ECM operations at McGuire Air Force Base, New Jersey. According to those present, the students changed the name "Raven" to "Crows" and those engaged in the profession became known as Old Crows. The unofficial action soon became widely accepted.

By 1966 AOC had grown to 2,300 members and was publishing a regular magazine, *Crow Caws*, which later became the quarterly and more formal *Electronic Warfare* in 1968. AOC annual conventions began to attract industry exhibitions. By 1968, 8,000 members organized into fifty local chapters. An educational foundation was formed in 1974 and has spearheaded substantial scholarship funding. A national full-time office was set up in Washington in 1970—by the late 1980s, AOC operated out of its own building in Alexandria, Virginia. AOC funded a long-term project by Alfred Price to document and publish the history of United States electronic warfare (EW), and three volumes appeared in 1984, 1989, and 2000. A three-part video series, *The Invisible War*, aired on cable television in 1996 and was made available on video.

By the early 2000s, AOC had become a professional association with an annual budget of approximately $2.4 million, ten staff members, and more than 14,500 members organized into sixty-five chapters from nineteen countries (comprising 29 percent government and active duty military and 49 percent defense electronics industry personnel).

Membership peaked at 25,000 in 1988 but has declined almost 40 percent in the two decades since. This is the result of several factors, including reduced defense spending on EW since the end of the Cold War; reduced threat research by the Department of Defense; changes in service missions; and downsizing, consolidations, and mergers within the defense industry. Despite the decline, AOC provides twelve to fifteen professional development courses each year, attended by ten to twenty-five students and focused on advanced technology topics related to EW and information operations. AOC annually cosponsors (with defense agencies or related organizations) about a dozen two-day technology conferences attended by from 75 to 450 conferees. AOC is also continually active in several ECM informational campaigns in both government and industry.

Christopher H. Sterling

See also Armed Forces Communications & Electronics Association (AFCEA); Electronic Countermeasures/Electronic Warfare (ECM/EW)

Sources

Association of Old Crows. Home page. [Online information; retrieved April 2007.] www.crows.org.

Bartlow, Gene. "A Brief History of the Association of Old Crows (AOC)." [Online article; retrieved September 2005.] https://www.myaoc.org/eweb/dynamicpage.aspx?webcode=history.

Price, Alfred. 1984–2000. *The History of U.S. Electronic Warfare*. 3 vols. Alexandria, VA: Association of Old Crows.

Atlantic, Battle of the (1939–1945)

Winston Churchill dubbed the Battle of the Atlantic the most important of World War II. It was certainly the longest, lasting nearly seventy months. With substantial losses of ships and men on both sides, the Atlantic struggle became a long conflict—really a series of individual actions—of attrition and steadily improving technologies. Though essentially won by 1943 thanks largely to more effective Allied use of code breaking, radar, and aircraft, actual fighting ranged over the whole six years of World War II.

While the Allies sought to protect vital military trade routes, the aim of the German submarine effort (with the occasional aid of surface raiders and long-range bombers) under Admiral Karl Dönitz was to sink sufficient shipping so as to force Britain out of the war. As the war began, Dönitz had fifty-seven U-boats and only twenty-seven fit for long-range Atlantic service. Though he claimed to need 300 to do the job, he achieved initial successes, including the 3 September 1939 sinking of the British passenger liner *Athenia*.

The U-boat menace in the Atlantic expanded after the German occupation of Norway and France in early 1940, which gave the submarines new coastal bases closer to major shipping lanes. U-boats could now make speedy entry into the Atlantic and interrupt Allied convoy lanes. This inaugurated the so-called happy time when Dönitz utilized Enigma-coded radio communications to direct U-boat wolf packs to more effectively attack the convoys. As the number of Atlantic U-boats increased in 1941, the monthly tonnage of lost Allied ships soared— to a total of more than two million tons in the Atlantic over the course of the war. Some early convoys lost two-thirds of their ships.

The British hoped to deal with the U-boat problem through the use of convoy escorts equipped with depth charges directed toward targeted U-boats by the Allied Submarine Detection Investigating Committee (ASDIC) device or sonar. But ASDIC was not a reliable means of identifying enemy vessels on or under the sea. The convoy system, initiated slowly in the first months of the war, was hampered until 1943 by a lack of sufficient escort vessels and long-range patrol aircraft.

With ASDIC failing to thwart the German U-boats, the British began to devote intensive effort to solve the Enigma codes. In the spring of 1941, Enigma code machinery and codebooks were captured from several German vessels, giving British code breakers a huge leap forward. When the Germans changed their codes in February 1942, however, conditions in the Atlantic deteriorated for the British once again and losses rose as Britain could not read German communications for the rest of the year. U-boats enjoyed another happy time, made worse for the Allies when the U.S. Navy initially resisted convoying ships. Further, for the first six months of 1942, American seaboard cities did not adopt evening blackouts, thus silhouetting vessels against the shore and making them easy targets. German code breakers were also able to read some Allied convoy codes. Resulting shipping losses in the western Atlantic rose to record levels and the U-boat fleet peaked at over 200.

The eventual demise of the German submarine threat began after March 1943. Britain once again penetrated the improved German codes and as a result could reroute convoys around known submarine wolf packs. Also contributing were the more effective application of radar and ASDIC, the improvement of antisubmarine vessels (and more of them), more reliable depth charges, and the growing use of patrolling aircraft that could read all areas of the Atlantic. In addition, Allied bombing of U-boat construction sites and bases became more effective. In the end the Allies' ability to replace losses faster than Germany could destroy ships tipped the scales.

Germany's use of acoustic torpedoes, better radar detection, and antiaircraft weaponry made little overall difference. Nor did, in the final year of the war, snorkel breathing apparatus allowing submarines to stay submerged for extended periods of time. Despite their responsibility for 70 percent of Allied ship losses, Germany's own submarine losses rose sharply in 1943–1944, and by the end of the war more than 500 U-boats had been sunk during the Atlantic engagement.

Marc L. Schwartz and Christopher H. Sterling

See also Aldis Lamp; Bletchley Park; Enigma; Germany: Naval Intelligence (*B-Dienst*); Nebraska Avenue, Washington DC; Signals Intelligence (SIGINT); Submarine Communications; Ultra

Sources

Blair, Clay. 1996, 1998. *Hitler's U-Boat War.* 2 vols. New York: Random House.

Kahn, David. 1991. *Seizing the Enigma: The Race to Break the German U-Boat Codes, 1939–1943.* Boston: Houghton-Mifflin.

Sarty, Roger. 1997. "The Limits of Ultra: The Schnorkel U-Boat Offensive Against North America, November 1944–January 1945." *Intelligence and National Security* 12 (2): 44–68.

Showell, Jak P. Mallmann. 2000. *Enigma U-Boats: Breaking the Code.* Annapolis, MD: Naval Institute Press.

Syrett, David. 1994. *The Defeat of the German U-Boats: The Battle of the Atlantic.* Columbia: University of South Carolina Press.

Williams, Andrew. 2003. *The Battle of the Atlantic.* New York, Basic Books.

Atlantic Wall

From 1942 to 1944, after it became clear that Germany would not invade Britain, the German military construction entity, the *Organization Todt*, employed an army of conscript labor to construct a massive (though never fully completed) string of 15,000 coastal defense installations along the Atlantic coast of France, the Low Countries, and Norway. Much of the effort was concentrated on the long Norwegian coastline and in the Channel Islands off Brittany. Consisting of thousands of artillery bunkers and some extensive multi-bunker fortified sites, the majority of which were built to a series of standardized designs, the huge venture was designed to make an Allied invasion of German-occupied Europe excessively costly.

The effectiveness of the line as a mode of defense depended, in considerable part, on secure communications. As with the earlier French Maginot Line, radio was but one means of communication along the Atlantic Wall fortifications and from them to various military headquarters behind the coast. Communication within strong points of the wall line was nearly always by voice tube within individual bunkers, or by telephone (connected with buried cables) between bunkers of larger strong points. The system used was similar to German field telephones, with hand-cranked end-user equipment and switchboards powered from batteries.

Radio was used only in the most important buildings of larger complexes and rarely within individual bunkers. The problem was that radio needed external antennas as the steel-reinforced concrete of bunker construction otherwise blocked radio signals. Further, the housings for such antennas required openings in bunker walls or ceilings that could be exploited by an enemy force, especially one using gas. Those radio antennas that were required usually were telescopic, being raised only when actually in use.

A few specialized communication bunkers (*nachrichtenstände*), about 2 percent of all structures, were constructed at key sites, usually combining both radio and telephone

Radio and telephone facilities linked gun batteries like this one on the Atlantic Wall fortifications, built by the Germans along the European coast from 1941 to 1944 in an attempt to ward off Allied invasion. (LAPI/Roger Viollet/Getty Images)

links. Air and naval bases also had their own communications bunkers, some of them extensive, which combined telegraphic connections and often radar installations as well. Timely use of radar required rapid radio communications to other units.

The massive construction effort, which had been accelerated after mid-1942, continued until the Allied invasion on D-Day, 6 June 1944. The Allied bombing effort that preceded their landings concentrated on destroying communication links between the Atlantic Wall and inland German command centers. The Norwegian and Channel Island elements of the Atlantic Wall fortifi-

cations remained fully manned to the end of the war nearly a year later. Numerous museums now operate within former Atlantic Wall installations, some of them featuring the wall's communication links.

Christopher H. Sterling

See also Coast Defense; Maginot Line; Radio; Telephone; World War II

Source
Chazette, Alain, et al. 1995. "La Transmission." In *Atlantikwall: Le Mur de L'Atlantique en France 1940–1944*, 38–39, 58–70. Paris: Editions Heimdal.

Australia: Royal Australian Corps of Signals

Military signaling has been vital to the development and protection of the expansive Australian continent for at least 150 years. Australia played a part in the British Empire and Commonwealth and its signal forces served widely in both world wars and in many peacekeeping efforts since.

The provinces of Victoria and New South Wales both had their own torpedo and signaling corps from 1869 until 1882, when the units were disbanded. South Australia had a signaling corps from 1885 until 1901. These units used electric telegraph and visual signaling methods.

The Australian Corps of Signallers was formed on 12 January 1906 and consisted of nine companies located at Sydney, Newcastle, Melbourne, Brisbane, Rockhampton, Adelaide, Perth, Freemantle, Hobart, and Launceston. In some cases a company was spread over two cities. Signaling also existed within the engineer corps, the artillery, a naval brigade, administrative and instructional staff, scouting units, the intelligence corps, cycle sections, and regimental signalers. The Corps of Signallers was merged into the Royal Australian Engineers on 12 July 1912 as Signal Engineers.

The Divisional Signal Company was formed at Broadmeadows, Victoria (close to Melbourne), on the outbreak of World War I in 1914, and on 19 October, with three Light Horse Brigade Signal Troops, it sailed for the Middle East. The Signal Engineers served at Gallipoli and in Egypt, Palestine, Mesopotamia, and France. During the course of the war, five Divisional Signal Engineer companies, a Mounted Division Squadron, a Corps Company, and the ANZAC (Australian and New Zealand forces) Wireless Squadron were formed. Wireless sets were at first Marconi pack equipment and were used by the Light Horse Signal Troops. The subsequent wireless sets and equipment were of British manufacture as used by all the empire signal units.

After World War I, compulsory military training was instituted, and five infantry and two cavalry divisions were formed, each with a divisional signal regiment. All signal units in the Royal Australian Engineers became the Australian Corps of Signals on 14 February 1925. With the termination of compulsory service in 1929, the corps' ranks were reduced, and military signaling was maintained by a small number of dedicated enthusiasts until preparations were made for World War II.

During World War II the corps grew to 24,000 strong. Australian signals personnel served in North Africa, Greece, and Palestine before being recalled to Australia in 1942 to meet the Japanese threat. Signals units participated in the defense of Malaya and Singapore and the hardships of the New Guinea campaign. Australian signal intercept units played an important role in the Pacific monitoring of Japanese military communications as part of a huge Allied signals intelligence network.

King George VI recognized the achievements of the Corps of Signals by granting a Royal Warrant to the corps on 10 November 1948, at which time the organization became known as the Royal Australian Corps of Signals. The corps served in the Korean War (1950–1953) and during the uprisings in Malaya and Singapore in the 1950s. A major contribution by the corps was in the Vietnam War, and at its peak comprised 16 percent of all Australian forces there.

Australian signal units also served in many United Nations (UN) peacekeeping missions in the second half of the twentieth century and in 1992–1993 provided the bulk of the force communications unit in Cambodia with the UN authority there, a task shared with the Royal New Zealand Corps of Signals.

Cliff Lord

See also New Zealand: Royal New Zealand Corps of Signals; World War I; World War II

Sources

Australia Corps of Signals. 1949. *Signals: Story of the Australian Corps of Signals.* Sydney: Australian Corps of Signals.

Barker, Theo. 1987. *Signals: A History of the Royal Australian Corps of Signals 1788–1947.* Canberra: Royal Australian Corps of Signals.

Blaxland, J. 1998. *A History of the Royal Australian Corps of Signals 1947 to 1972.* Canberra: Royal Australian Corps of Signals Corps Committee.

Burke, Keast, 1927. *With Horse and Morse in Mesopotamia.* Sydney: no publisher indicated.

Thyer, Brigadier J. H. *Royal Australian Corps of Signals, Corps History, 1906–1918.* Manuscript, Royal Australian Signals Archives.

Automatic Digital Network (AUTODIN)

A program of the U.S. Department of Defense, the Automatic Digital Network (AUTODIN) evolved from two earlier Air Force systems, the Air Force Data Communications (AFDATACOM) system, which was an expansion of the manual Combat Logistics Network (COMLOGNET). The original concept for upgrading COM-LOGNET was to create an automatic, fully electronic, transistorized, high-speed data network that used automatic switching techniques. Although initially intended for Air Force use, the system soon became the primary record communications system for the Department of Defense.

In 1961, the Air Force demonstrated a prototype of the COMLOGNET that would eventually link 450 bases, air stations, and civilian suppliers. Western Union leased five large switching centers and connecting terminals to the Air Force for this purpose. By November 1962 the first AFDATACOM station opened at Norton Air Force Base, California, replacing the COMLOGNET station. AFDATACOM enabled users to send messages from punched cards, accounting machines, paper tapes, magnetic tape drives, and teletypewriters. Automatic electronic switching centers converted formats, speeds, and differences in codes before the data were transmitted on the system. The system became fully operational on 4 February 1963, and AFDATACOM became a part of the Defense Communications System.

The primary purpose of AUTODIN was to provide a single long-haul system that could utilize all available circuits by integrating automatic switching technology. AUTODIN was a fully transistorized communications system that initially linked defense organizations (such as bases, supply depots, and major air commands) into a single network using high-speed data and teletype communications. Initially, the AUTODIN system consisted of five automatic switching centers (ASCs) located around the United States. These five centers, which could handle seven million punched cards a day or 100 million words, were saturated by the end of the first year. The secretary of defense approved fourteen new switching centers to increase the capacity of the network and extend it around the world.

In more than thirty years of operations, the AUTODIN switching centers provided the U.S. Air Force, Navy, Army, Coast Guard, other government agencies, and industrial contractors with a worldwide, high-speed, automatic, electronic data communications system. The AUTODIN system provided for the transmission of narrative and data traffic on a store-and-forward basis. The Defense Communications Agency (DCA) had overall responsibility for the AUTODIN system.

The AUTODIN switching centers (ASCs) were the heart of the system. They were connected by trunk lines to form a digital network and local lines connected them to individual subscriber communications center terminals. All messages entered the AUTODIN system through the subscriber terminals and passed through to the ASC. When the message was accepted by the ASC, the classification and precedence of the message was determined and the message was relayed to the addressee.

The AUTODIN system, based on mainframe technology, was highly manpower intensive and could not be easily upgraded to meet the growing demands for additional types of information. The inability of AUTO-DIN to meet expanding requirements combined with the high cost of operating and maintaining the system spelled the eventual end of AUTODIN. Although the system was frequently upgraded, efforts to replace AUTODIN failed because of cost and operational considerations. Consequently, the Department of Defense was using a system that was limited in its capabilities and ever more costly to maintain.

The AUTODIN system was eventually replaced by the Defense Message System.

Tommy R. Young II

See also Computer; Defense Communications Agency (DCA, 1960–1991); Defense Message System (DMS)

Sources
Department of Defense, Office of Inspector General. 2003. *Information Technology Management: Transition from the Automatic Digital Network to the Defense Message System.* [Online report; retrieved December 2006.] http://www.fas.org/nuke/guide/usa/c3i/igautodin.pdf.
Hall, Jared. 2005. "AUTODIN (Automatic Digital Network)." [Online article; retrieved December 2006.] http://jproc.ca/crypto/autodin.html.
Thomas S. Snyder, et al. 1986. *The Air Force Communications Command: 1938–1986 An Illustrated History.* [Online information; retrieved December 2006.] http://coldwar-c4i.net/COMLOGNET/fact _sheet_1.jpg through /fact_sheet_7.jpg; http://massis.lcs.mit.edu/archives/history/western.union.

Automatic Secure Voice Communications (AUTOSEVOCOM)

Automatic Secure Voice Communications (AUTOSEVOCOM) provided authorized Department of Defense and other users with a secure worldwide switched telephone network. In use for three decades, the system was closely related to the Automatic Voice Network system, which carried only unclassified conversations.

The U.S. Department of Defense began implementing the AUTOSEVOCOM system in the mid-1960s. It consisted of a large suite of equipment: a secure voice cryptographic device that was enclosed in a safe; equipment that converted analog voice into a clear text digital stream; a key generator that mixed the code key with clear text digital stream and interfaced with a modem and conditioned line; a secure cord board desk-mounted patch panel, which was manually operated; and an automatic telephone switch and "red telephone" switches located at secure and classified locations. The AUTOSEVOCOM network included narrowband subscriber terminals that were installed and used within a communications center; wideband subscriber terminals, which allowed local secure communications by interconnecting one of the automatic switches; and a narrowband trunking unit, which allowed long distance secure telephone calls.

When designing the system, engineers accepted a number of limitations in the interest of getting it operational quickly. These included insufficient capacity, the lack of voice recognition capabilities, poor voice quality, the inability to hold conference calls, and its need for continual maintenance accompanied by ever-increasing costs. Efforts to improve the system began almost as soon as it was implemented.

By 1980, defense officials decided to implement an improved system, AUTOSEVOCOM II, that worked to improve existing equipment and acquire new equipment that used new technologies. But despite the best efforts to update and upgrade AUTOSEVO-COM, the system continued to be costly to maintain and cumbersome to use. Technological advances in areas such as keying of cryptographic devices and system miniaturization offered the opportunity to implement an entirely new secure voice system.

The replacement for AUTOSEVOCOM was the secure telephone unit—generation III (STU-III). The STU-III combined ordinary and secure telephone service over dial-up public switch telephone networks. Using a crypto-ignition key to switch the telephone from a nonclassified to a secure instrument while using public telephone networks, STU-III eliminated many of the problems associated with AUTOSEVOCOM. (It was an STU-III device that President George W. Bush used to make and receive calls from a Florida public school classroom after the ter-

rorist attacks of 11 September 2001.) The last AUTOSEVOCOM secure voice switch was deactivated at the Pentagon in 1994.

Tommy R. Young II

See also Communications Security (COMSEC); Miniaturization; Telephone

Sources

Mace, George. 2005. "AUTOSEVOCOM I and II." [Online information; retrieved December 2006.] http://www.jproc.ca/crypto/autosevocom.html.

Proc, Jerry. 2004. "STU III (Secure Telephone and KSD-64)." [Online article; retrieved December 2004.] http://www.jproc.ca/crypto/stuiii.html.

Snyder, Thomas S., et al. 1986. *The Air Force Communications Command: 1938–1986—An Illustrated History*. Scott Air Force Base, IL: Air Force Communications Command Office of History.

Bain, Alexander (1811–1877)

Despite a chronic lack of financial backing, Alexander Bain invented some of the basics of both facsimile and telegraph systems during the 1840s in Britain. Both modes of communication proved to have important military applications in the nineteenth and twentieth centuries.

Born in Watten, Scotland, in October 1811, Bain received little formal education, but hearing a science lecture at about age twelve helped to set the course of his life. He became a clock and instrument maker, or to use the term of the day, a "mechanic" or "mechanist," working in Wick, Scotland. He had an inventive mind and was most active in telegraphy developments during the 1840s after moving to London.

Bain proposed what we would today call a facsimile telegraph system in 1842 based on the earlier work of the French inventor Edmond Becquerel. In November 1843 he received a British patent for an electrochemical recording telegraph that includes some of the basic principles of the fax machine.

Bain's contributions to eventual facsimile capabilities included three critical elements.

First was the notion of scanning an image (usually printed words) so it could be transmitted one bit at a time. Second was the use of special chemically treated paper to show the resulting image (almost always letters and words). Third was the synchronization of sending and receiving equipment. As effective electric motors did not yet exist, his system was run by a series of clockwork "motors" actuated either by springs or falling weights (pendulums). Bain attempted to use these mechanisms in a master-slave system (one clock controlling another, or many others) to aid transmission of graphic messages, but this never worked satisfactorily and was soon superseded by the work of others, especially Giovanni Caselli, in the 1860s.

Bain became the chief competitor of British telegraph pioneers William Cooke and Charles Wheatstone. The conflict concerned their relative primacy in the invention of the electric clock and the printing telegraph. Cooke and Wheatstone's Electric Telegraph Company purchased patent rights after Bain successfully defended his own priority.

Bain's system was patented in December 1849 in Britain and the United States and was used in experiments in 1848–1849 on lines between Washington, New York, and Boston and between Glasgow and Edinburgh, Scotland, as late as 1852. The tests used Morse code but were abandoned as no consistently useful means existed of perforating the paper tape. On the other hand, Bain's automatic (chemical) telegraph recorder device offered a dramatic increase in the words-per-minute rate of sending—upward of 300 or more. It was used for years by the General Post Office, Britain's postal system and telecommunications carrier.

Bain's health began to fail in the 1870s and he was struck with paralysis in his legs. He became mentally impaired and was moved to a "home for incurables" at Broomhill, Kirkintilloch, Glasgow, where he died on 2 January 1877.

Christopher H. Sterling

See also Facsimile/Fax; Morse Code; Morse, Samuel F. B. (1791–1872); Telegraph

Sources

Bain, Alexander. 1844. "Bain's Printing Telegraph." *Journal of the Franklin Institute* 38: 61.
Bain, Alexander. 1852. *A Short History of Electric Clocks*. London: Chapman & Hall.
Bain, Alexander. 1866. "Automatic Telegraphy." *English Mechanic and Mirror of Science* 2 (February 9): 273–274.
Marland, E. A. 1964. *Early Electrical Communication*. London: Abelard-Schuman.
Schaffner, Tal. P. 1859. "Bain's Printing Telegraph." In *The Telegraph Manual: A Complete History and Description*, chap. 17. New York: Pudney & Russell.

Baltic Nations

The Baltic states of Estonia, Latvia, and Lithuania emerged as independent nations after World War I. Swallowed by the Soviet Union in 1940 and then occupied by Germany in 1941–1944 during World War II, each nation suffered tremendous losses. Dominated again by the Soviets from 1945 to 1991, they once again became independent.

Estonia

An engineer company was formed in Tallin, Estonia, on 15 December 1917 comprising combat engineer and signal units with thirty officers and about 400 men. By February 1918, amid the confusion of the retreating Germans and the Bolshevik Revolution in Russia, Estonian forces assumed control over the country. On 24 February the Rescue Committee proclaimed the country's independence, and by 1920 Estonia was officially an independent state. The new army had 50,000 soldiers. In November 1918, the provisional government declared the voluntary mobilization of soldiers (and compulsory mobilization of officers) to face advancing Russian troops. On 15 March 1924, the engineering battalion was split into separate signal and engineer groups.

After decades of Soviet and German occupation, on 3 September 1991, the newly independent state of Estonia established its defense forces. Professional training began in June 1992 (including a radio-technical air defense battalion) and a separate signal battalion was formed on 29 October 1993. Considerable military equipment was imported from both Israel and the United States.

Latvia

On 6 February 1919, a small telephone section was formed in Liepaja, Latvia, and was immediately sent to the front lines as Latvia was fighting remnants of the German army and an invasion from the new Soviet Union. The section was under the command of

Colonel Oskars Kalpaks, Latvia's most famous war hero. The section established communications between combat units at the front and became known as 1 Independent Battalion, Signal Group. Just a month later the battalion expanded to a brigade. It was popularly called the South Latvian Brigade to distinguish it from the new combat units appearing in northern Latvia and Estonia. On 15 July 1919 the south and north brigades joined to form the Latvian Army Command Headquarters Signal Unit, assigned to maintain communications between headquarters and combat units as well as the Allied nations. The first telegraph line was built in mid-1919 between Riga and two smaller towns about 140 miles away. At the same time, the Latvian army conscripted all civilians in Riga who were known to have had wireless communications experience in the Russian army during World War I. They were assigned to the Army Engineer Company, which had one wireless station that had been abandoned after the German occupation. They also operated an old Russian naval 10-kilowatt wireless station in Riga and maintained wireless communications with British warships in the Baltic Sea and with Warsaw. During October and November 1919, when Latvia was invaded by a Soviet force, this station directed artillery fire from the British warships supporting the Latvian army. Later the wireless station broadcast news and maintained contact among divisions.

To meet the growing demand for army communications, a separate telegraph and telephone company was formed on 4 October 1919 with telegraph, telephone, and construction sections. This company maintained line communications between Latvian headquarters and Latvia's allies, Estonia and Poland, and eventually was used to conduct peace talks with the Soviet Union. The company also established postal and telegraph communications in liberated Latvian territories before regular service was established. A signals equipment repair shop was set up to repair, replace, and update equipment. In 1920, the telegraph and telephone company became part of Army Ordnance. Later, the commander of the Chief Communications Department established a substantial headquarters, and many other signal units were formed.

On 9 September 1921 some communications units were combined to become the Electrotechnical Battalion as a training institution for future signalers. The unit was reorganized on 15 May 1935 into the Signal Battalion (*Sakaru Bataljons*). Administratively the battalion was assigned to the Technical Division, but operationally it functioned under the army's chief of staff. The Signal Battalion consisted of a headquarters company, two companies for training noncommissioned officers in signaling, and a supply company. An operations company also worked directly with army headquarters to train personnel in wireless and telegraphy for the army.

With the occupation of Latvia by the Soviet Union in June 1940, the army became the Latvian Peoples Army and in September a part of the Red Army. Germany and Russia (each with Latvian partisans) fought over the country from 1941 to 1944, and the population declined by one-third. The limited signals capability was based on Russian equipment during the Cold War.

An independent Latvia reemerged in 1991. On 29 March 2004, Latvia joined the North Atlantic Treaty Organization, which protects the country's airspace. The army stopped conscription in 2005 and by 2007 had converted to a volunteer professional force. Latvia cooperates with Estonia and Lithuania in a joint infantry battalion and a naval squadron, which are available for international peacekeeping operations.

Lithuania

In January 1919 a sapper (engineering) company was formed in Lithuania and grew in strength, eventually becoming an engineer battalion. Signal specialists were incorporated within the battalion. Later a signal corps was formed, but it did not become fully independent from the engineers. Lithuania's air force had its genesis in the army signal corps and was formally established in 1920.

Occupied by the Soviets from 1920 to 1941, by Germany from 1941 to 1944, and again by the Soviet Union from 1945 to 1991, the country's military relied totally on Soviet equipment, systems, and training. Only with final withdrawal of Soviet troops in 1993 did Lithuania turn to the West for military supplies and advice. Equipment came from Germany and France, and training took place in those countries as well.

Cliff Lord

See also Germany: Army; North Atlantic Treaty Organization (NATO) Communications & Information Systems Agency; Russia/Soviet Union: Army; Warsaw Pact (1955–1991)

Sources

Estonian Defence Forces. "Chronology of the Defence Forces." [Online information; retrieved January 2007.] http://www.mil.ee/index_eng.php?s=ajalugu.

Indylatvians.com. 2005. "Latvia Facts: A Brief History of Latvia." [Online information; retrieved December 2006.] http://www.indylatvians.com/latvia%20facts.htm.

Library of Congress. 1995. "Lithuania: National Security." [Online article; retrieved January 2007.] http://lcweb2.loc.gov/cgi-bin/query/r?frd/cstdy:@field(DOCID+lt0028).

Banker, Grace (1892–1960)

Grace Banker served the U.S. Army Signal Corps as a civilian telephone operator of the American Expeditionary Forces (AEF) during World War I. Her role as chief operator for First Army headquarters during the St. Mihiel and Meuse-Argonne offensives earned her the Distinguished Service Medal, the only woman to receive that honor during the war.

Born 25 October 1892 in Passaic, New Jersey, Grace Banker was among the first group of women (commonly called the "Hello Girls") sent to France to operate telephone switchboards to support AEF. Because of her previous experience as a switchboard instructor with AT&T, Banker was placed in charge of thirty-three women of Telephone Unit No.1, which sailed from New Jersey on 6 March 1918. Upon arrival in Paris, Banker was assigned to the headquarters of the Advance Section in Chaumont sur Haute Marne, which served as General John J. Pershing's headquarters.

Banker spent almost five months at Chaumont until 25 August 1918, when she was ordered to the First Army headquarters at Ligny-en-Barrois, about five miles south of St. Mihiel. With only six operators working in shifts at this forward location, Banker and her team were immersed in supporting the planning for the upcoming offensive operation. When the St. Mihiel offensive began, Banker and the other women operated the switchboards during the opening artillery bombardment at the front. When First Army headquarters moved to Bar-le-Duc on 20 September, Banker and her operators displaced their operations to a facility that had

Grace Banker, chief telephone operator, First U.S. Army Headquarters, American Expeditionary Forces during World War I was awarded the Distinguished Service Medal. (U.S. Army Signal Center Command History Office, Fort Gordon, Georgia)

be assigned to the Army of Occupation at Coblenz, Germany, Banker accepted and left Paris. While at Coblenz, Banker was presented with the Distinguished Service Medal during a ceremony recognizing her with a citation for "exceptional ability . . . [and] untiring devotion to her exacting duties under trying conditions . . . to assure the success of the telephone service during the operations of the First Army against the Saint Mihiel salient and the operations to the north of Verdun."

In September 1919, Banker and the other women sailed for home after almost twenty months of service, which had been described as "indispensable" by General Edgar Russel, chief signal officer of AEF. Upon return from the war, women such as Grace Banker, who were considered civilian volunteers and not members of the military, did not receive a formal discharge or even a certificate of service. In 1977 Congress finally passed legislation that recognized their accomplishments and granted them status as veterans. Grace Banker did not live to receive this recognition, as she died on 17 December 1960 in Scarsdale, New York.

Steven J. Rauch

See also Hello Girls; Telephone; World War I

Sources
"I Remember." 1954. *Signal Magazine* January–February: 26–27.
Paddock, Grace Banker. 1979. "I Was a Hello Girl." *Yankee* March: 66–71, 102–107.
Schneider, Dorothy, and Carl Schneider. 1991. *Into the Breach: American Women Overseas in World War I.* New York: Viking Press.

been greatly damaged from the fighting. While there, Banker and the others endured aerial bombardment from German planes, but none incurred injury. They also suffered during a cold, wet autumn in leaky barracks that often greeted them with no heat after long hours at the switchboards. Banker and the others suffered more challenges on 30 October when fire destroyed those barracks.

After the armistice ended combat operations on 11 November 1918, Banker was sent back to Paris, where she was assigned to work at President Woodrow Wilson's temporary residence, a duty she described as "not particularly exciting" as she greatly missed the camaraderie and hard work of the front. When offered the choice to remain in Paris or

Beardslee Telegraph

An innovation of the American Civil War (1861–1865), the Beardslee telegraph was designed to operate on magneto-electric power and be usable by operators who did not understand Morse code. While it was only partially successful, replacing it became central in the conflict between the Army Signal Corps and the U.S. Military Telegraph Service in 1863.

The Union Army sought a portable source of electricity to power its field telegraphs so communications could readily keep up with shifts in military positions. George W. Beardslee's 1859 invention of a magneto-electric generator seemed to make that possible. Early in 1862, at the request of the Signal Corps, Beardslee combined his hand-cranked magneto device with a dial telegraph device developed by Henry J. Rogers to create a portable telegraph wagon "train" suitable for field work. The magnetos (rather than heavy batteries) generated the power necessary to send electricity over a telegraph wire. The operator moved a lever to a point on Rogers's dial matching the letter he wished to send. On the receiving end, a similar dial would move to the corresponding position. Thus the signal was sent without either operator having to know Morse code, as the receiving operator needed only to copy down the characters he saw dialed.

Initial operations of the Beardslee-equipped telegraph trains at the Battle of Fredericksburg in mid-1862—commanded by the inventor's son Frederick (a captain in the Signal Corps)—seemed to suggest that the device did what it promised. Beardslee's firm assembled about thirty telegraph trains and sixty telegraph sets for use by various Union armies. A year later at Chancellorsville, however, the Beardslee devices performed poorly under battlefield conditions. Operators had to follow a complex set of procedures for Beardslee operation. Trained operators using a conventional Morse telegraph system could send messages faster than those using a Beardslee

The Beardslee magneto-electric telegraph was used by Union forces early in the American Civil War. It did not require batteries and could be operated by men with little training, but it required considerable maintenance and offered limited range and was thus removed from service by early 1864. (U.S. Army Signal Center Command History Office, Fort Gordon, Georgia)

device. This was partially due to the tendency of the Beardslee/Rogers dials to get out of synchronization with one another, resulting in garbled messages (and the need to send the machines back for repair). Beardslee operators also never gained the same level of familiarity with their equipment as did conventional telegraph operators. Furthermore, the Beardslee device lacked the power to send a message more than about five to eight miles, often far less than that needed to maintain control over shifting military forces.

These accumulating Beardslee drawbacks forced the Signal Corps to revert to traditional Morse operation, and thus to recruit more trained Morse operators. This fanned the existing competition between Albert

Myers's Signal Corps and Anson Stager's U.S. Military Telegraph Service (USMTS). Beardslee machines were removed from service by 1863, though their ancillary poles, insulated wire, wire reels, and wire-laying methods were used by USMTs for the duration of the Civil War. Late in the war both the Army and the Navy adopted Beardslee's device for electric detonation of subterranean and submarine explosives.

The Beardslee/Rogers dial device was only one of several different types of dial telegraph machines. Dial telegraph equipment was neither new nor unique to this period. Werner Siemens, for example, had developed one as early as 1847. The Beardslee device was unique, however, in combining the dial feature with magneto-electric operation.

Christopher H. Sterling

See also American Civil War (1861–1865); Army Signal Corps; Morse Code; Myer, Albert James (1828–1880); Stager, Anson (1825–1885); Telegraph; U.S. Military Telegraph Service (USMTS)

Sources

Robbins Raines, Rebecca. 1996. *Getting the Message Through: A Branch History of the US Army Signal Corps.* Washington, DC: Center of Military History.

Signal Corps Civil War. "Beardslee Telegraph Machine." [Online information; retrieved November 2004.] http://www.beardslee telegraph.org/.

Thompson, George Raynor. 1954. "Civil War Signals." *Military Affairs* 18 (Winter): 188–201.

Thompson, George Raynor. 1958. "Development of the Sig C. Field Telegraph." *Signal* July: 28–31, 34.

Bell, Alexander Graham (1847–1922)

Inventor of the telephone in the mid-1870s, Alexander Graham Bell created the basis for an industry with great impact on all aspects of communication.

Bell was born on 3 March 1847 in Edinburgh, Scotland, the second of three sons. He added the name Graham in 1858 after a family friend. In the 1860s, he attended both the University of Edinburgh and University College in London. He followed his father by 1868 in teaching the deaf to speak. Two years later the family immigrated to Canada, settling in Ontario. Bell moved to Boston to teach the next year.

While on a family visit in Brantford, Ontario, in the summer of 1874, Bell first sketched out his idea of what would become the telephone. He also met skilled electrician Thomas Watson who would work closely with him in the years to come. On 14 February 1876, Bell filed for his first telephone patent, which was granted three weeks later—it is often called the single most valuable patent ever issued (though at the time Bell lacked a working telephone model). On 10 March 1876 Bell called Watson in a nearby room for assistance and said the first intelligible words spoken over a telephone.

Bell had not been seeking what we think of as the telephone, but rather an improved form of telegraphy that might prove helpful in training the deaf to speak, possibly by visibly recording sound. After all, he lacked formal training and practical experience in electricity (one reason he hired Watson to assist). His developmental effort in that Boston garret in the mid-1870s was more a matter of trial-and-error tinkering than pursuit of clear, scientifically based research. As with any inventor, luck played a big part in this story.

Bell's telephone device was publicly demonstrated at the Centennial Exhibition in Philadelphia in the summer of 1876. After that began a series of demonstrations in the United States and abroad as Bell and a small

American inventor Alexander Graham Bell invented the telephone, which he demonstrated to the public at the 1876 Exposition in Philadelphia. Telephones became vitally important in military headquarters and operations by the turn of the twentieth century. (Library of Congress)

group of backers sought more support. The telephone was competing with entrenched telegraph interests, which offered service everywhere while the telephone was limited in its first decades only to local service. Nor could a telephone provide a permanent record as the telegraph did, making it less useful to government or business. Multiple patent battles developed beginning in 1878 as the value of the telephone slowly became

apparent, ending up in a victory for Bell before the Supreme Court in 1887.

Bell became an American citizen in late 1882. He took part in the opening of long distance services from New York to Chicago (1892) and across the country (1915). After about 1885, he had little to do with further development of the telephone device or business, essentially retiring on his royalty income. He focused on other areas of interest such as teaching the deaf, medical electronics, recording, the National Geographic Society, kites and early airplanes, and fast motorboats. Bell died on 2 August 1922 at his home at Beinn Bhreagh, Nova Scotia, Canada.

Christopher H. Sterling

See also American Telephone & Telegraph Co. (AT&T); Telephone

Sources

Bruce, Robert V. 1973. *Bell: Alexander Graham Bell and the Conquest of Solitude*. Boston: Little, Brown.

Deposition of Alexander Graham Bell in the Suit Brought by the United States to Annul the Bell Patents, The. 1908. Boston: American Bell Telephone Co. (reprinted by Arno Press, 1974).

Grosvenor, Edwin S., and Morgan Wesson. 1997. *Alexander Graham Bell: The Life and Times of the Man Who Invented the Telephone*. New York: Abrams.

Library of Congress. 2000. "The Alexander Graham Bell Family Papers at the Library of Congress: 1862–1939." [Online information; retrieved April 2007.] http://memory.loc.gov/ammem/bellhtml/bellhome.html.

Bell Telephone Laboratories (BTL)

A subsidiary of American Telephone & Telegraph Co. (AT&T) until 1995, Bell Telephone Laboratories (BTL) was formed in late 1925 to merge the research operations of AT&T

and its Western Electric manufacturing subsidiary, which then shared ownership. Based primarily around Murray Hill, New Jersey, after 1941, for decades BTL formed America's premier commercial research organization and included many Nobel Prize winners among its staff.

Soon after America's entry into World War II, four-fifths of BTL work was focused on military communications and weapons control systems, including extensive work with radar. BTL had already begun developmental work in microwave and coaxial cable systems, which had extensive military and civilian applications. From 1941 to 1945, BTL personnel worked on approximately 1,200 military projects. These typically involved BTL design and development for devices produced by Western Electric. Most were shrouded in secrecy at the time, including the "Project X," or SIGSALY, system initiated for the Signal Corps in late 1940 that by 1943 scrambled the transatlantic telephone connection linking Britain and U.S. political and military leaders. Teletypewriter circuits were constantly upgraded in both their capacity and security. BTL developed airplane-laid wire systems for rapid expansion of combat telecommunications links. Mobile radio systems included a rugged "tank set," including a version for aircraft. BTL produced numerous communications training manuals for both Army and Navy use.

Certainly best known of all BTL inventions was the transistor, announced in 1948, which heralded the beginnings of the solid state revolution that would sweep electronics. In the quest for military miniaturization, transistorized products led the way by the late 1950s. Development of communication links for several Arctic and Alaskan missile defense systems (including WHITE ALICE) was one application; communication aspects of the Semi-Automatic Ground Environment warning network were another. A digital data system developed for the Navy allowed an aircraft carrier to maintain simultaneous two-way links with up to a hundred airplanes at a time. A variety of surface and underwater surveillance systems were also designed for the Navy. BTL was the prime designer of the switching and transmission elements of the Automatic Voice Network communication system for the Department of Defense.

All of BTL's military communications efforts were hugely expensive and were funded by AT&T's long monopoly on domestic voice communications. BTL's organization was first divided when AT&T was broken up in 1984, with about half of the employees going to Bell Communication Research or the regional operating companies and half remaining with AT&T. The whole regulatory economics sector (including a respected scholarly quarterly) was transferred to non-Bell organizations. A decade later, most of the remaining lab personnel and facilities were spun off as part of Lucent Technologies, with only a small portion remaining with AT&T. With the decline of the telecommunications business after 2000, as well as outsourcing of most military equipment purchases, most BTL lab personnel and facilities were terminated, with a few converted to working on short-term product or service development.

Christopher H. Sterling

See also Alaska Communications System; American Telephone & Telegraph Co. (AT&T); Microwave; Semi-Automatic Ground Environment (SAGE); SIGSALY; Teleprinter/Teletype; Transistor

Sources
Buckley, Oliver E. 1944–1945. "Bell Laboratories and the War." *Bell Telephone Magazine* 23 (Winter): 227–240.

Fagen, M. D., ed. 1978. *A History of Science and Technology in the Bell System: National Service in War and Peace, 1925–1975*, chaps. 5, 12. New York: Bell Telephone Laboratories.

Ingles, Harry C. 1945. "Electrical Communications in World-Wide Warfare." *Bell Telephone Magazine* 24 (Summer): 54–100.

Berlin Airlift (1948–1949)

Communications, especially air traffic control, made the Berlin Airlift possible. Arrangements made by the Allies during World War II for the occupation of Germany assigned sectors of Berlin to the British, French, and Americans without guaranteeing access to those sectors across the Soviet zone of occupation. When the Soviets closed surface transportation routes on 24 June 1948, British and American aircraft supplied the Western sectors for nearly a year. Coordination of aircraft routes, landings, and takeoffs depended on reliable air and radar links, while an extensive ground support network was tied together by telephone, telegraph, and teletype. Initially a makeshift affair intended to deal with a temporary emergency, the airlift evolved into a complex effort. From 78 aircraft at the start, it expanded to nearly 400 at its peak.

Planners calculated the city's need at 4,500 tons a day (later increased to 5,620), an enormous number in light of the technological limits of the time. No operation on this scale had been attempted before, and the odds looked very long. Western air transports could use three narrow air corridors to the city, each 20 miles wide, and land at two airfields (later four—Gatow, Tempelhof, Tegel, and—for flying boats—Havelsee) in the city. Peak efficiency required standardization, but the British flew a dozen different aircraft types and the Americans five. All were military versions of passenger airliners or converted bombers; none had been designed to carry cargo. The weather was usually stormy with dense clouds, rain, and wind, forcing pilots to fly on instrument flight rules (relying on cockpit instruments rather than visual flight rules) 70 to 80 percent of the time in winter. Navigational aids were few, communications offices were short-handed, and many of those available for duty were inexperienced. Overshadowing the operation was an ever-present possibility of Soviet interference.

British and American controllers at the Berlin Air Traffic Control Center served as the brains of the airlift, orchestrating arrivals and departures. Flight plans were standardized down to the smallest detail. During the flight, pilots and controllers relied on radar and radio to adjust timing and intervals between aircraft. Twenty-one low-frequency beacons, three low-frequency radio ranges, and six very high frequency ranges were installed at critical spots along the flight paths. Ground control approach (GCA) radar units were diverted from U.S. airports and military bases. Starting in December, radar at Tempelhof spaced all aircraft in the corridors. Its operators guided pilots until they were close to the city, then turned them over to GCA controllers, who talked them down to a safe landing.

An American after-action report hailed GCA as "possibly the greatest contributing factor to the success of the airlift," an assessment echoed by the Royal Air Force. U.S. controllers in Berlin averaged 7,700 radio contacts a month before the blockade, and more than 127,000 during it. Pilots filed 1,767 flight plans with Berlin air traffic control in April 1948, and 42,054 a year later. The highest one-day total was the famous "Easter Parade," 15–16 April 1949: 1,398 flights landed and took off from Berlin, delivering 12,941 tons of supplies. The airlift continued after the Russians lifted the blockade 12 May 1949, as the Allies stockpiled supplies against any renewed blockage. The airlift ended 30 September 1949.

Daniel Harrington

See also Army Airways Communications System, Airways and Air Communications Service (AACS, 1938–1961)

Sources

Pearcy, Arthur. 1997. *Berlin Airlift.* Shrewsbury, UK: Airlife.

Snyder, Thomas S., et al. 1991. *Air Force Communications Command: 1938–1991, An Illustrated History,* 3d ed., 49–58. Scott Air Force Base, IL: Air Force Communications Command Office of History.

"A Special Study of Operation 'Vittles.'" 1949. *Aviation Operations Magazine* April (Special issue): 33–46.

U.S. Air Force. 1949. *Berlin Airlift: A USAFE Summary,* 39–50. Wiesbaden, Germany: Headquarters, United States Air Forces in Europe.

Blair, William Richards (1874–1962)

Considered the father of American radar, William Richards Blair's inventions and their military uses have included the detection of aircraft, the detection of anti-aircraft fire, detection and location of ships, and air and ocean navigation. Commercial uses have included aircraft and ship navigation and flight control. He held eleven patents, which, in addition to radar, included a "radiometeorograph," a forerunner to the radiosonde that was carried by a balloon to transmit weather data back to earth.

Blair was born in County Derry, Ireland, on 7 November 1874 and immigrated to the United States with his parents at the age of nine. He graduated from the University of Chicago with a doctor of philosophy degree in 1906 and went to work for the U.S. Weather Bureau. Blair joined the Army on 3 September 1917 and was commissioned as a major in the Aviation Section of the Signal Officers' Reserve Corps. During World War I, he served in France as officer in charge of the Meteorological Section, Signal Corps, American Expeditionary Force. Immediately following the war, he served as a member of the technical subcommittee of the Aeronautical Committee at the Paris Peace Conference (1919). He was then assigned as officer in charge of the Meteorological Section, Office of the Chief Signal Officer. One of his assignments was forecasting the weather for the first around-the-world flight, conducted by Army aircraft in 1924. Blair graduated from the Signal School at Camp Alfred Vail (which became Fort Monmouth in 1925) and then from the Command and General Staff School at Fort Leavenworth, Kansas, in 1926.

Blair took charge of the Engineering and Research Division in the Office of the Chief Signal Officer that same year. He served as director of the Signal Corps Laboratories at Fort Monmouth from 1930 until his promotion to colonel and then his retirement on 31 October 1938. While acting as director of the laboratories, Blair pioneered the work of radio direction finding on meteorological balloons and encouraged experimental work in infrared, heat detection, radio detection, and pulse equipment.

In the late 1920s, Blair had outlined a need for radio detection as a means of identifying hostile aircraft. Under his leadership, a complete workable radar set had been developed at Fort Monmouth and demonstrated for the secretary of war and Congress by

1937. Locating and tracking targets by radio echoes is commonly regarded as one of the most important contributing factors to the Allied victory in World War II.

A top secret security classification restricted Blair from applying for a patent for his radar pulse echo technique until June 1945. When he finally applied, the U.S. Navy, AT&T, Raytheon, the Radio Corporation of America, and other companies contested his claim. He was not officially credited with the invention of radar until 20 August 1957 when he received patent number 2,803,819, entitled "Object Locating System." The government was given a royalty-free license.

Blair died in Fair Haven, New Jersey, on 2 September 1962 at eighty-seven years of age.

Melissa S. Kozlowski

See also Fort Monmouth, New Jersey

Sources

Clark, Ernie. 1997. "Blair Hall Honors Past Hero." *Monmouth Message* (11 July).
"Father of Radar—It's Official." 1957. *Electronic Week* August: 5–6.
"Fort Monmouth's Guest House Dedicated in Honor of Late Col. William R. Blair." 1969. *Monmouth Message*, 6 March.
"Retirement of Col. William R. Blair." 1939. *Signal Corps Bulletin* January–May: 86–88.

Blandford Camp

Since the mid-1960s Blandford Camp has been home to the British Royal Corps of Signals and its historical museum. Located near the Georgian market town of Blandford Forum in the south of England, Blandford Camp owes its name to the races, wrestling, and jumping contests that were held in the area annually during the seventeenth century. The area was also the site of many skirmishes during the English Civil War in the 1640s.

A Royal Navy shutter telegraph relay station was built in 1806 near the racecourse on the site now known as Telegraph Clump. The Admiralty shutter telegraph was designed to convey messages from London to the Naval Dockyards of both Portsmouth and Plymouth. The relay station was operated by a team of three men and remained in use until 1825. Yeomanry and volunteer units of Dorsetshire continued to use Blandford Race Down as a training ground during the first half of the nineteenth century. In August 1872, a large army exercise was held in southern England and C Telegraph Troop of the Royal Engineers—the forebears of today's Royal Signals—sent personnel (2 officers, 108 men, and 80 troop horses) to provide the communications for the field army.

At the start of World War I in 1914, a hutted camp was built at Blandford. A large number of reservists were called for full-time service with the outbreak of war. As the Royal Navy had an excess of volunteers, a Royal Naval Division was formed at Blandford. A base depot and training camp were established in November 1914, and a German prisoner of war camp was soon established nearby.

Rapid development of the camp was something of an engineering feat. All materials were brought to the Blandford Forum railway station, from which steam tractors and horses hauled them three miles to the camp site. When finished it was a small community with churches, a hospital, canteens, and a railway line and station. The navy moved out in 1918 and was briefly replaced by Royal Air Force administrative units. At the end of 1919, the camp closed and the wooden huts and camp's railway line were sold and the site returned to agricultural use.

In 1939 the camp was reactivated and a new hutted camp built as a mobilization and training center for reservists called up to meet the threat from Nazi Germany. Later, Royal Artillery anti-aircraft units trained on the site and it became a battle training camp. With the large buildup of Allied forces in Britain during 1943–1944, the training camp was converted for use by U.S. Army general hospital personnel. After having treated some 20,000 patients, the facility was closed (it is commemorated by Roosevelt Memorial Park, located alongside the Royal Signals Headquarters Mess). After World War II, the camp was converted to its original use as a training site for the Royal Artillery and Royal Army Service Corps (later to become the Royal Corps of Transport) and other units.

In 1960, a signal regiment was the first Royal Corps of Signals unit to move into the facility. Four years later, Blandford Camp was selected to be the home of the School of Signals, construction for which was completed in September 1971, though the school had moved to Blandford in 1967. The location permitted its engineering officers to be close to the centers of research and development. The school (now the Royal School of Signals) was responsible for management and technical courses for Royal Signals officers and noncommissioned officers.

In the early 1990s, the face of Blandford Camp changed considerably with new construction from 1992 to 1996 to accommodate soldier training requirements that resulted from the closure of several other bases. The Royal School of Signals was placed under command of the Army Individual Training Organization in 1996, which became the Army Training and Recruiting Agency a year later. The headquarters of the corps also moved to the site from London. The 11 Signal Regiment based at Blandford is the administrative unit for the Royal School of Signals and carries out basic training and promotion courses for potential noncommissioned officers as well as basic training for the Territorial Army soldiers of the Royal Signals. The camp is also the home to several other military entities.

Danny Johnson

See also Semaphore (Mechanical Telegraphs); United Kingdom: Royal Corps of Signals

Sources

Bridge, Maureen, and John Pegg. 2001. *Call to Arms: A History of Military Communications from the Crimean War to the Present Day.* Tavistock, UK: Focus Publishing.

Lord, Cliff, and Graham Watson. 2003. *The Royal Corps of Signals. Unit Histories of the Corps (1920–2001), and its Antecedents.* Solihull, UK: Helion.

Warner, Philip. 1989. *The Vital Link: The Story of Royal Signals, 1945–1985.* London: Leo Cooper.

Bletchley Park

Bletchley Park (BP to everyone involved) was a large Victorian mansion on a country estate located about 50 miles northwest of London. It was secretly purchased in 1938 by the Government Code & Cipher School (GC&CS) to become the center of British military code-breaking efforts during World War II. Bletchley's wartime function was highly secret during the war and remained so for three decades afterward. Only in the mid-1970s did the story of code breaking and Bletchley's development of proto-computers used in the code-breaking process (particularly the Colossus) begin to come out. Parts of the surviving site now form a museum open to the public.

After operating in a downtown London location for many years, in the late summer of 1939 the GC&CS relocated away from the city, to a 600-acre Victorian estate, Bletchley Park. BP was located near several rail and road links roughly equidistant between Oxford and Cambridge, which would supply many of its mathematical and other experts. The move got the GC&CS out into the countryside, thus achieving two goals: shifting the code-breaking operation away from likely London bombing and making it more isolated for improved security. Initial code breakers, many of them academics from the two universities, occupied rooms in the mansion or its outbuildings.

As the number of employees rapidly expanded, however, a series of quickly constructed wood-and-asbestos, one-story buildings began to cover the estate's grounds, each such "hut" assigned a specific function. "Hut 6," for example, helped to break German army and Luftwaffe coded messages transmitted with the Enigma machine. Decoding was initially a slow process, but soon hundreds and then thousands of messages flowed in daily, necessitating a dramatically increased pace for decoding. In 1942 Bletchley's huts were supplemented by the first permanent multistory, blast-proof buildings (though they were still called huts, the names of which designated specific roles rather than locations). By the end of the war, BP had expanded from employing a few dozen people to more than 10,000 workers of all types. BP saw the development of increasingly sophisticated means of breaking Enigma and other coded messages, from electro-mechanical "bombe" devices to the sophisticated Colossus vacuum tube–powered computers (nearly a dozen by 1945) that greatly speeded up the process of reading messages.

BP, also called Station X, operated at the apex of an immense code-breaking effort that depended on dozens of "Y Service" wireless listening posts located around Britain. By 1944 a large number of Special Liaison Units controlled Bletchley's distribution of the "Top Secret Ultra" decrypts to selected senior military and naval officials. Decrypts also went to only a handful of the most senior government officials, including Prime Minister Winston Churchill. Very few people ever saw the actual decrypted messages (save for the naval decrypts, all of which were sent to the Admiralty), which were usually restated to disguise their origin. By 1942, a few Americans joined the British effort at BP, guided after mid-1943 by an agreement between the two countries to cooperate in the code-breaking process. Americans then worked in Huts 3 and 6 and staffed some of the bombes.

The GC&CS moved out of crowded Bletchley after World War II (first to Eastcote and later to Cheltenham), and the site was used primarily for training by government agencies devoted to aviation and telecommunications. British Telecom moved out of BP in the early 1980s and the site was nearly turned over to developers for housing, but it was preserved by the efforts of dedicated volunteers.

Christopher H. Sterling

See also Arlington Hall; Code Breaking; Computer; Enigma; German "Fish" Codes; Government Code & Cipher School (GC&CS, 1919–1946); Magic; Tiltman, John Hessell (1894–1982); Turing; Alan Mathison (1912–1954); Ultra; Welchman, Gordon (1906–1985); Y Service

Sources

Bletchley Park National Codes Centre. Home page. [Online information; retrieved January 2004.] http://www.bletchleypark .org.uk/.

Enever, Ted. 1999. *Britain's Best-Kept Secret: Ultra's Base at Bletchley Park*. 3rd ed. Stroud, UK: Alan Sutton.

Hinsley, F. H., and Alan Stripp, eds. 1993. *Codebreakers: The Inside Story of Bletchley Park.* London: Oxford University Press.

Smith, Michael. 1998. *Station X: The Codebreakers of Bletchley Park.* London: Channel 4 Books.

Smith, Michael, and Ralph Erskine, eds. 2001. *Action this Day.* London: Bantam.

Boer War Wireless (1899–1902)

During the years 1899–1902, war raged on the southern tip of the African continent. The conflict between Britain and the Afrikaners (Boers) of South Africa struck a major blow to Pax Britannica, resulting in the most devastating military losses for Britain since the Napoleonic Wars. The war is remembered for the refinement of several military tactics including guerrilla warfare by the Boers, the infamous civilian concentration camps established by the British—and the first use of wireless telegraphy by an army and navy on active service in a military operational area. The potential benefits of using wireless technology for military purposes was appreciated by both the Boers and the British, but the timing and manner in which this application evolved, and the final outcome, was very different for the two sides.

In February 1898, C. K. van Trotsenburg, general manager of telegraphs in the South African Republic, initiated confidential correspondence with Siemens Brothers in London to explore purchasing wireless telegraphic equipment. He had researched the new technology, and with tensions building with the British in South Africa, he sought a more secure communications network by installing wireless links between the Boer military headquarters in Pretoria, five forts surrounding the city, and a further fort in Johannesburg. He traveled to Europe in June 1899 and visited companies manufacturing wireless equipment in London, Paris, and Berlin. As a result of his evaluations, he placed an order on 24 August 1899 through the Siemens agent in Johannesburg for three Siemens and Halske wireless stations. If satisfied with their performance, he planned to order three more. The equipment, however, never reached the Boers. War broke out in October and the British traced the customs paperwork. The equipment was confiscated in Cape Town, and some of the instruments were cannibalized by the British army for its own use.

In contrast, British army use of wireless during the war was prompted by Guglielmo Marconi. Always the entrepreneur, Marconi saw an opportunity to promote his wireless telegraph system and offered to send wireless equipment and company engineers with the British troops shipping out to South Africa. On 24 November 1899, equipment for erecting five portable wireless stations and six Marconi engineers arrived in Cape Town. The equipment first provided ship-to-shore communications during troop disembarkation. Wireless equipment was successfully demonstrated on 4 December at Cape Town Castle in front of the military staff and invited dignitaries. In mid-December, the equipment was carried into the field by two separate units going to the relief of the besieged towns of Kimberly and Ladysmith. Over the next two months, however, events took an expected turn for the British as the wireless equipment was moved inland for the army's use.

British army field trials of the Marconi equipment were soon considered a failure as communication between the portable field stations was irregular at best. The causes for the failure have since been variously attributed to equipment design, meteorological conditions, and poor grounding conductivity in the South African soil. Whatever the cause, finger-pointing started between the army and Marconi, and on 12 February 1900 the director of Army Telegraphs ordered the equipment dismantled and removed.

The army's failure, however, became a Royal Navy success. By March 1900, the five Marconi wireless sets were installed on five cruisers in Delagoa Bay off the coast of Lourenco Marques (now Maputo, Mozambique). Wireless was used successfully for communications among the five ships, which were securing a blockade against supplies being landed and delivered to Boer forces in the Transvaal. In addition, by connecting a land telegraph line to one of the wireless-equipped ships anchored near shore, the remaining four Royal Navy cruisers were able to communicate with the distant navy headquarters in Simonstown, Cape Colony, while at sea up to 100 kilometers away.

The Royal Navy's success in utilizing wireless in the Boer War theater greatly aided the rapid development and implementation of wireless throughout the navy. The British army did not pursue wireless as vigorously. As a result, by the advent of World War I, the Royal Navy was much more advanced in its use of wireless than the British army.

Doug Penisten

See also Marconi, Guglielmo (1874–1937);
    United Kingdom: Royal Corps of Signals;
    United Kingdom: Royal Navy

Sources

Baker, Duncan. 2006. "Wireless Telegraphy in South Africa at the Turn of the Twentieth Century." In *History of Wireless*, edited by Tapan Sarkar et al. New York: John Wiley.

Baker, William. 1970. *A History of the Marconi Company*. London: Methuen.

Beauchamp, Ken. 2001. *History of Telegraphy*. London: Institution of Electrical Engineers.

Burns, Russell. 2004. *Communications: An International History of the Formative Years*. London: Institution of Electrical Engineers.

Hezlet, Arthur. 1975. *The Electron and Sea Power*. London: P. Davies.

Pakenham, Thomas. *The Boer War*. New York: Random House.

Britain, Battle of (1940)

The aerial Battle of Britain turned back a threatened German invasion in the fall of 1940. In addition to the aircraft, two integrated technologies played a large part—radar and the effective use of radio and ground telephone links. The British Royal Air Force (RAF) system of command and control made the difference in what some termed the "narrow margin" of victory.

Initially developed in the 1930s by Robert Watson-Watt and others, the first radar station was operational by 1937. By 1940, the RAF had in place fourteen Chain Home radio direction finding (RDF) stations, most equipped with four 350-foot transmitting towers holding a curtain aerial array. Incoming attacking aircraft could be located 100 miles away up to a height of 10,000 feet. Information about incoming German air raids from the Chain Home stations as well as ground observer reports were transferred to Fighter Command headquarters at Bentley Priory and to British fighter squadrons sent up to do battle. Low-flying aircraft could sometimes get in underneath the radar curtain until "low" RDF stations were added to the network.

The radar system was but one part of the extensive RAF control network that made British victory possible. Large regions of the country were assigned to groups that were subdivided into sectors. Local control rooms

This Chain Home radar antenna, mounted on a 185-foot tower, was a central part of the Royal Air Force's technological defense against the German air attack in the Battle of Britain. Multiple similar radar facilities were tied to RAF central command by telephone links enabling rapid fighter defense response to oncoming German aircraft. (Bettmann/Corbis)

were linked by telephone to group and Fighter Command group headquarters in Uxbridge, west of London. A filter room would take in all the information (which after April 1940 could include Ultra decodes of German Lufwaffe signals), which was organized for display on large table maps with both British squadrons and German air fleets assigned codes. British aircraft carried "pip-squeak" radar that allowed their positions to be plotted from the ground.

They also carried a secret identification, friend or foe device, code named "Parrot," so ground controllers could tell British from German fighters. The instruction to switch it on was therefore "Squawk your Parrot" (that term is still used today as modern transponder codes are known as "squawks"). Anti-aircraft guns and searchlights were an integrated part of the system. Night fighting became possible with airborne ground control interception radar in November 1940, which, along with special training, allowed British fighter units to take on attacking German aircraft.

The Germans soon caught up with radar of their own. They also used a special radio navigational system called "crooked leg" (*knickebein*), first used in August–September 1940. This was a blind-bombing system that utilized radio direction to assist aerial navigation. Operating on 30 MHz, it was based on the Lorenz blind-landing system that had been pioneered in the 1930s. Pilots flew along one beam, dropping their bombs when they crossed a second beam. The British developed means of locating the two *knickebein* transmitters in France and either jammed their signals or knocked them out from the air.

In his soon-to-be-immortal words about the British fighter pilots, British Prime Minister Winston Churchill told the House of Commons early in the battle (20 August 1940) that "Never in the field of human conflict was so much owed by so many to so few."

Christopher H. Sterling

See also Airplanes; Bletchley Park; Enigma; Germany: Air Force; Identification, Friend or Foe (IFF); Signals Intelligence (SIGINT); Ultra; United Kingdom: Royal Air Force; World War II

Sources

Dempster, Derek, and Derek Wood. 1961. *The Narrow Margin: The Battle of Britain and the Rise of Air Power 1930–1940.* New York: McGraw-Hill.

His Majesty's Stationery Office. 1941. *The Battle of Britain: An Air Ministry Account of the Great Days from 8th August–31st October 1940.* London: HMSO.

Overy, Richard. 2002. *The Battle of Britain: The Myth and the Reality.* New York: Norton.

Royal Air Force Museum. 1990. *Against the Odds: The Battle of Britain Experience.* London: Royal Air Force Museum.

Bull Run, Battle of (1861)

On 21 July 1861 the first great battle of the American Civil War occurred near Manassas Junction and Bull Run Creek in northern Virginia, about 25 miles from Washington DC. There a 35,000-man Union Army under the command of Irvin McDowell fought two Confederate armies of about 33,000 men under P. G. T. Beauregard and Joseph Johnston. Both sides anticipated a decisive battle, perhaps ending the war quickly. What neither side anticipated, however, was that application of a new communications concept would prove decisive in the Confederate victory.

Beauregard decided to apply economy of force measures by positioning several brigades on his left flank to guard key crossing points south of Bull Run Creek while at the same time massing the bulk of his force on his right to attack north toward Centerville. What he did not know was that McDowell had much the same plan and had massed his army for a wide-turning maneuver west of Centerville to hit the Confederates at their weakest points in the area of Sudley's Ford, cross Bull Run, and then destroy Beauregard's left flank near Matthews Hill.

In preparation for battle, Beauregard allowed Captain E. Porter Alexander to set up a newly invented visual communications system called "wig-wag" signal flags and codes to pass messages quickly. Alexander had trained on the method while serving as assistant to U.S. Army Major Albert J. Myer, who invented the concept, equipment, and codes that entered Union Army use in 1860. Alexander, convinced of the system's viability despite many skeptics, recruited and trained signal personnel, reconnoitered the ground, and selected sites for four elevated signal stations to support Confederate positions.

On the morning of 21 July, Alexander was at the signal station on the Wilcoxen farm, east of Manassas. With the sun behind him in the east, at about 8:30 a.m. Alexander observed a sudden flash of light as he looked toward his signal station near the Van Ness house on the left. Alexander later reported, "It was about 8 miles from me, a faint gleam, but I had a fine glass & well trained eyes, & I knew at once what it was." He had sighted the glitter of muskets, bayonets, and cannon of McDowell's flanking movement to cross Bull Run at Sudley's Ford. He quickly wig-wagged the station nearest Nathan Evans's Confederate brigade, the closest unit at the far left of the line, with a warning message: "Look out for your left. You are flanked." Evans quickly repositioned his force to block the Union threat until reinforcements could arrive. Alexander also notified Beauregard, who began to funnel forces to his threatened flank. The delaying forces (about 2,800 men) held off Union troops for about ninety minutes until a stronger defense could blunt the Union attack.

Ironically, while Alexander was proving the value of the wig-wag system against the very army it was designed for, Myer was frustrated in an attempt to apply another new technology in the fight. He backed use of an observation balloon that he hoped to use for reconnaissance and communication to McDowell's headquarters. To move it quickly to the battle, Myer ordered the balloon tethered to a wagon. However, in his haste to not miss the action, Myer moved too quickly and the balloon was soon tangled in low-hanging trees and torn to shreds. Thus he found himself without a wig-wag system or any other unique signal capability for the battle. By the end of the day, the Union Army retreated back across Bull Run Creek and the Confederates celebrated a decisive tactical victory.

The Confederate victory at Bull Run can be directly attributed to the success of Alexander's signal stations. This success would lead to early Confederate adoption of a separate signal corps as an important battlefield arm. Myer must have felt a bitter satisfaction that he had been correct about the value of such a tactical communication system, though it was employed by an enemy against his own army.

Steven J. Rauch

See also Airships and Balloons; Alexander, Edward Porter (1835–1910); American Civil War (1861–1865); Confederate Army Signal Corps; Flags; Myer, Albert James (1828–1880); Stager, Anson (1825–1885)

Sources

Alexander, E. Porter. 1989. *Fighting for the Confederacy*. Chapel Hill: University of North Carolina Press.

Alexander, E. Porter. 1907. *Military Memoirs of a Confederate*. New York: Da Capo (reprint).

Davis, William C. 1977. *Battle at Bull Run*. Baton Rouge: Louisiana State University Press.

Hennessy, Juliette A. 1985. *The United States Army Air Arm: April 1861 to April 1917*. Washington, DC: Office of Air Force History.

Raines, Rebecca Robbins. 1996. *Getting the Message Through: A Branch History of the US Army Signal Corps*. Washington, DC: U.S. Army Center of Military History.

Bush, Vannevar (1890–1974)

One of America's scientific and engineering leaders in the first half of the twentieth century, Vannevar Bush developed an early analog computing device useful in code breaking and promoted development of radar and the atomic bomb. He was a strong advocate of both wartime and Cold War university-based scientific work for the defense establishment.

Born 11 March 1890 in Everett, Massachusetts, Bush graduated from Tufts College with undergraduate and master's engineering degrees (1913). After a brief stint as a U.S. Navy inspector, he earned a doctorate of English degree from both Harvard University and Massachusetts Institute of Technology (MIT) (1917). During World War I he worked on magnetic methods of submarine detection for the Navy, though the device he developed for that purpose was not properly employed at the time. After the war he served on the faculty and administration (rising to become dean of the School of Engineering) of MIT for twenty years. He was a cofounder of what became Raytheon in the early 1920s. Bush also became president of the Carnegie Institution in Washington DC in 1938, serving as head of the research funding entity until 1955.

As he sought methods of automating human thinking and memory, Bush became a pioneer in the analog era of computing. In the early 1930s he devised what he termed the "differential analyzer," which was a large and complex analog computing device that never emerged from the experimental stage. His "rapid selector" would scan microfilm records to retrieve needed information, making it easier for researchers to keep track of the exponential expansion of human knowledge. Four of the desk-size instruments were built. Perhaps most importantly he conceived of a "memex," which was a prototype for what we now think of as an individual computer—in this case a microfilm-based device to allow for rapid storage and retrieval of information. Much of his own experimental work was soon superseded by the rapid post–World War II development of digital computing devices. His "As We May Think" article in *Atlantic* (July 1945) was prophetic of the advent of today's hypertext.

During World War II, Bush created (1940) and headed the National Defense Research Committee, which was soon subsumed in the larger, congressionally funded Office of Scientific Research and Development, which he also directed from 1941 to 1947. He thus managed the activities of approximately 6,000 scientists involved in military research (including many working with the Manhattan Project) during the war. He became the first director of the National Science Foundation in 1950. In all of these positions, he fostered a new respect for science and scientists.

In his extensive publications and drawing on his many academic and government positions, Bush became a persuasive and popular spokesman for what science could accomplish. His *Science, the Endless Frontier* (1945) promoted the need for continuing government support so that technology could continue to help the United States. He helped to create the government-university-business connections that would help to apply scientific research to defense needs during the Cold War. Bush saw government agencies, and especially the military services, as the key patrons of scientific research work. Eventually the holder of forty-nine patents, Bush died 28 June 1974 in Belmont, Massachusetts.

Christopher H. Sterling

See also Computer; National Defense Research
Committee (NDRC)

Sources
Burke, Colin. 1994. *Information and Secrecy: Vannevar Bush, Ultra, and the Other Memex.* Lanham, MD: Scarecrow Press.
Bush, Vannevar. 1970. *Pieces of the Action.* New York: Morrow.
Nyce, James M., and Paul Kahn, eds. 1991. *From Memex to Hypertext: Vannevar Bush and the Mind's Machine.* San Diego, CA: Academic Press.
Zachary, G. Pascal. 1997. *Endless Frontier: Vannevar Bush, Engineer of the American Century.* New York: Free Press.

C

Camp Crowder, Missouri

Camp Crowder was the largest U.S. Army Signal Corps training post during World War II. Located in the foothills of the Ozark Mountains, ground was broken for the base on 30 August 1941, and the first troops moved in five days before the Pearl Harbor attack by the Japanese. The post was named for Major General Enoch H. Crowder, a native Missourian who authored the Selective Service [draft] Act of World War I.

Camp Crowder occupied some 75 square miles. It had not been intended for signals use but rather for infantry training. With changing requirements, Crowder was largely turned over to signals training. Although 350 buildings were built initially, more construction was needed within six months. Army signal recruits spent three weeks learning the basics of soldiering as well as defense against chemical attack, articles of war, and basic signal communication. In July 1942, the Midwestern Signal Corps School opened its doors with a capacity of 6,000 students, and the following month the corps' first unit training center opened. The headquarters established in October 1942 to administer this group of schools was designated the Central Signal Corps Training Center. The center provided technical training in radio operations, radio repair, and high-power station operation and maintenance. By 1943, Camp Crowder had expanded to 43,000 acres.

Camp Crowder activated signal units by the hundreds as well as aircraft-warning units (for radar-warning services to the Army's air forces). Crowder also trained numerous radio intelligence and signal information and monitoring companies as well as joint-assault signal companies to meet the amphibious assault communications needs of joint Army/Navy operations. Force requirements were so pressing, and often arose so suddenly, that students were taken out of school with their course work incomplete to fill requirements in new signal companies and battalions. These units continued training while in their overseas assignments. The Pigeon Breeding and Training Center moved from Fort Monmouth, New Jersey, to Camp Crowder in October 1942, though it returned to Monmouth at the end of World War II.

Camp Crowder was closed as a basic training site (and prisoner of war camp for Germans and Italians) in 1946. It remained active as soldiers were mustered out of the service. In 1947, 29,000 acres were sold for agricultural use, though the Missouri National Guard retained about 4,000 acres for training. During the Korean conflict, the camp saw a small bump in activity, but Missouri already had Fort Leonard Wood and no need was seen for two active Army training facilities in the same state. Crowder's mission was changed again in 1953 when it became a branch of the disciplinary barracks until 1958. The Air Force took over a portion of the camp in 1956 to manufacture rocket engines.

Most of Camp Crowder was closed in 1958 and declared surplus four years later. The land reverted to agricultural use, and Crowder College was formed in 1963, which continues to use some of the buildings constructed for the military in the early 1940s. With the growth of the war on terror, however, the training facility has seen a revival for the state's National Guard units.

Danny Johnson

See also Army Signal Corps; Fort Monmouth, New Jersey; Pigeons; War on Terrorism; World War II

Source
GlobalSecurity.org. "Camp Crowder." [Online information; retrieved January 2007.] http:// www.globalsecurity.org/military/facility/ camp-crowder.htm.

Canada

Following extensive colonial semaphore and telegraph development, Canada's military communications efforts operated as separate service-defined functions. These were merged in 1968.

Origins
Early European signaling in Canada originated from the eighteenth-century efforts of competing companies and colonizers of the British and French. Where possible in the sparsely populated colonies, methods approximated those used in Britain and Europe at the same time. By 1705, St. Johns, Newfoundland, used cannon fire and signal flags to denote any trouble approaching by sea. By the end of the century, Halifax was using an extensive system of flags, pennants, and large colored balls (supplemented with use of its lighthouse at night). Several of the signaling masts were located in the city's citadel, which was on high ground overlooking the British naval port. These semaphore telegraph systems were soon extended to Nova Scotia and the shore of New Brunswick, and plans were laid to extend the system to Quebec, Montreal, and farther west.

With the War of 1812 and American threats to Canada, the telegraph system was renewed and fully staffed. Inland sites made more use of direction poles and signal fires. The system around Quebec, Montreal, and Kingston, Ontario, was maintained after the war, but most of it was abandoned by the late 1820s due to the cost of continued operation in the face of no obvious military threat.

Commercial electric telegraphy arrived in Halifax by the late 1850s, and the city kept in touch with Montreal to the west and Boston to the south. But revived tension with the United States in the 1860s led the military to adopt the technology to supplement (not replace) its semaphore systems. On Canada's confederation in 1867, British military forces began to pull out, leaving their facilities for Canadian forces. By the 1880s, telephone links were in use within major military posts and to connect nearby outliers.

In 1903 the Canadian Signalling Corps was created largely due to the efforts of Captain Bruce Carruthers, now considered the father of Canadian army signals. A school of signaling was established at Petawawa in 1912, with its own instructional staff. Signal companies were provided for divisions and signal troops for mounted brigades along with a signaling staff for instruction. Line telegraphy and wireless remained in the hands of the engineers. In line with other British Empire signal services, the Canadians used British equipment to maintain a continuity of quality communication throughout British and Dominion armies.

Army Signals

A Canadian divisional signal company was mobilized on 20 August 1914 from a nucleus of permanent force signal personnel. During World War I, six signal companies were raised for Canadian divisions in addition to other signal units. In the early stages of fighting, pigeons were used, and the pigeon service became a special branch of signals. Signaling by lamp was used at night, and the Hucks and Aldis signaling lamps were replaced by the superior Lucas lamp in 1916. The Lucas lamp was lighter, was more mobile, and had a narrower beam of light. It was at this time that the telephone came into its own as the main means of communications at the front.

The Canadian Corps Wireless Section was formed in 1916 and operated large spark-gap sets. Improved wireless equipment gradually replaced the earlier spark-gap wireless sets. Continuous wave, made possible by the invention of the vacuum tube, rapidly superseded them. Notable was the trench set, a 50-watt, spark-gap, low-frequency wireless using a 50-foot antenna with a 3-foot aerial. The Wilson wireless set, if used in conjunction with trench sets, could double the range of the wireless net. One drawback of early wireless was its visibility—the Wilson set

required a 60-yard aerial standing 12 feet high to reach an effective range of 4,000 yards. As the aerial attracted enemy artillery fire, it was an unpopular addition to any location.

By July 1917, wireless communication between corps and divisions was common. Power buzzers provided useful communications in the trenches. Ranges of up to 3,000 yards between stations were achieved. Listening sets or amplifiers became available in February 1916 for eavesdropping on enemy telephone conversations monitoring Allied telephone security. A major breakthrough in signals security came with adoption of the Fullerphone in 1917.

Only on 1 April 1919 did signals fully separate from the engineers as the Canadian Signalling Instructional Staff became a unit of the permanent force. On 15 December 1920, the Canadian Permanent Signal Corps was authorized. King George V honored the corps on 15 June 1921, when it became the Royal Canadian Corps of Signals. Royal Canadian Engineers Defence and Electric Light detachments continued to provide communications at the coastal defenses at Halifax and elsewhere. In the early1920s signal training was centralized at a depot opened at Camp Borden, Ontario. The Permanent Force Signal Corps supervised the signal training program of the nonpermanent active militia. In 1937, the Corps School of Signals moved to Vimy Barracks at Kingston, Ontario.

In 1923, the corps provided radio stations for the Yukon mining communities of Mayo Landing and Dawson City, heralding the beginning of the Northwest Territories and Yukon Radio System. The network eventually grew to twenty-eight stations as it became a vital link in the development of Canada's northern frontier, providing reliable communications for mining companies, aircraft, trading posts, and prospectors. Weather information was another important task provided by the network. Regular weather reports from these systems formed the basis for national forecasts from the Dominion Observatory. (In 1957, the corps began turning over all of these stations to the federal Department of Transport and by 1965 had relinquished its responsibilities.)

During World War II, the Royal Canadian Corps of Signals provided five divisional, two corps, and many smaller signals units including interception sections. Canadian signalers served many theaters, including northwest Europe, Sicily and Italy, and Hong Kong, and provided an intercept unit in northern Australia. The Canadian Signals Research and Development Establishment was created at Ottawa.

An infantry brigade signal squadron and an artillery signal troop served in the 1950–1953 Korean conflict. The corps also provided a brigade signal squadron for Canadian North Atlantic Treaty Organization forces in Germany from the early 1950s until it was withdrawn in 1994. Canadian signals operated the army component of the National Defence Communications System, a country-wide teletype network. Throughout the last half of the twentieth century the corps has served in many United Nations peacekeeping operations including in Indochina, Korea, the Congo, Middle East, and Cyprus.

Air Force Signals

When airmail postage was introduced in Canada during 1927, the Royal Canadian Corps of Signals was given responsibility for a nationwide system of radio beacons, required to guide the mail planes. The corps also supplied communications for the first transatlantic airmail from a radio station at Red Bay, Labrador, to mail ships at sea and aircraft of the Royal Canadian Air Force

A Canadian signaler, seen with a pile of artillery shells, receives orders in France in 1944. Canadian signals personnel served with distinction in both world wars. (Corel)

(RCAF). Most of these responsibilities were handed over to the RCAF by 1934.

The Royal Canadian Air Force Signals Branch, later to evolve into the Telecommunications Branch, was formed in 1935. This supported operations of the RCAF in Canada and overseas during World War II. RCAF Station Clinton trained more than 6,000 radar personnel for service in Canada's coastal defense, the United Kingdom's home radar chain, and many other areas of Allied operations.

Navy Signals

The Royal Canadian Navy operated the Supplementary Radio System with some 800 sailors who worked in high-frequency radio direction finding and communications research, primarily in the north. "Supplementary" was a euphemism for interception of enemy signals. The headquarters and school were at HMCS *Gloucester*, Ottawa, which also became the center for communications research in 1947. The Communications Special Branch was created to perform the interception work, though its title varied. A number of naval radio stations (NRSs) were activated including HMCS *Churchill* in 1948, and NRS Gander in 1949. Later stations included HMCS *Coverdale*, HMCS *Inuvik*, and naval radio stations in Aklavik, Masset, Frobisher Bay, Chimo, and Bermuda.

Merger

The Canadian Forces Reorganisation Act of 1968 brought the signal organizations of the army, navy, and air force together. The new Communications and Electronics Branch became responsible for all communications and electronics matters in the Canadian Forces. Its components included the Royal Canadian Corps of Signals, the Royal Canadian Air Force Telecommunications Branch, the Royal Canadian Navy Communications Research Branch, and some elements of the Royal Canadian Electrical and Mechanical Engineers. In theory these disparate groups became one, with the same badge and uniform. At first all three services continued to operate their own trans-Canadian message networks, and the air force also retained a ground-to-air communication system.

Integration brought them all under the Canadian Forces Communication System, renamed the Canadian Forces Communications Command in 1970. In the mid-1990s, communications became a direct responsibility of National Defence Headquarters, Defence Information Services Organization with the closure of Communications Com-

mand. The navy and air force schools also closed after integration. From that point on, training was conducted at the Canadian Forces School of Communications and Electronics in Kingston, Ontario.

Cliff Lord

See also Aldis Lamp; Fullerphone; Pigeons; United Kingdom: Royal Corps of Signals; World War I; World War II

Sources

Lord, Cliff, and Graham Watson. 2003. "Canada." In *The Royal Corps of Signals: Unit Histories of the Corps (1920–2001) and its Antecedents.* Solihall, UK: Helion.

Moir, John S. 1962. *History of the Royal Canadian Corps of Signals: 1903–1961.* Ottawa: Corps Committee, Royal Canadian Corps of Signals.

Morrison, James. H. 1982. *Wave to Whisper: British Military Communications in Halifax and the Empire, 1780–1880.* Ottawa: Parks Canada.

Proc, Jerry. 2005. "Radio Communications and Signals Intelligence in the RCN." [Online information; retrieved August 2005.] http://jproc.ca/rrp/index.html.

Royal Canadian Corps of Signals. "Northwest Territories and Yukon Radio System." [Online information; retrieved November 2004.] http://www.nwtandy.rcsigs.ca/index.htm.

Weir, A. Norman. 1986. *Special Wireless Edition 446.* Ottawa: Canadian Forces Communications and Electronics Newsletter.

Canada: Communications Security Establishment (CSE)

The Communications Security Establishment (CSE) is Canada's national signals intelligence (SIGINT) organization. A civilian agency of the Department of National Defence, CSE processes SIGINT and disseminates reports to Canadian and allied (British, U.S., Australian, and New Zealand) agencies.

CSE began on 3 September 1946 as the Communications Branch of the National Research Council. It was the direct descendant of Canada's wartime military and civilian SIGINT processing operations, which also had worked in close cooperation with its American and British counterparts. The next year, the branch took on the additional responsibility of communications and electronic security (prior to this Canadian government encryption systems and keys had been provided by Britain). On 1 April 1975, the operation was transferred to the Department of National Defence and took its present name. At the time of its transfer, CSE had nearly 600 personnel. It expanded by 50 percent by the mid-1990s.

Actual collection of SIGINT is conducted by the Canadian Forces Supplementary Radio System (SRS), which operates under the direction of CSE. Small-scale SIGINT collection for the British Royal Navy began in 1925, but collection for Canadian processing began during World War II. All three services operated SIGINT collection facilities during the war, and continued to do so after 1945. The unified collection organization, SRS, was created in 1966 as part of the unification of the Canadian Armed Forces.

During the Cold War, the primary target of CSE and SRS was the Soviet Union, and the SRS intercept stations were sited accordingly, often in far northern parts of Canada to better "read" Soviet communications. Over the past fifteen years, some monitoring sites have been converted to operation by remote control, while new ones have opened to exploit changing targets of opportunity including communication satellites in the Western Hemisphere.

Since 1996 when Canadian security law was substantially revised, CSE operations have been monitored and reported by the Office of the Communications Security Establishment Commissioner, which issues occasional public and many more frequent classified reports.

Christopher H. Sterling

See also Canada; Code Breaking; Government Code & Cipher School (GC&CS, 1919–1946); National Security Agency (NSA); Signals Intelligence (SIGINT)

Sources
Bryden, John. 1993. *Best-Kept Secret: Canadian Secret Intelligence in the Second World War.* Toronto: Lester Publishing.
Communications Security Establishment. 2002. "Canada's Signals Intelligence Agency." [Online information; retrieved April 2006.] http://www.tscm.com/cse.html.
Communications Security Establishment. 2002. "Chronology of Canada's Postwar SIGINT Activities." [Online information; retrieved April 2006.] http://www.tscm.com/csechron.html.
Communications Security Establishment. 2006. "Welcome to the Communications Security Establishment." [Online information; retrieved April 2006.] http://www.cse-cst.gc.ca/index-e.html.

Chappe, Claude (1763–1805)

Developer of a widely used mechanical or optical semaphore system, Claude Chappe lived long enough only to see its original success, though his invention was used for more than four decades in France and elsewhere in Europe. Chappe was born on Christmas Day of 1763 in Brûlon, France, one of five brothers, several of whom were raised to become priests. Chappe also had an interest in science from an early age and by 1790 was working on various mechanical means of rapid distance communication, which he dubbed the *télégraphe.* He first demonstrated a model of his optical system in 1791 between two towns a dozen miles apart.

Chappe's perfected system used two vertical 30-foot wooden poles or masts, each with a 15-foot transverse arm, or "regulator," to which were attached two articulated arms, or "indicators." Worked by a system of weights and two levers, the movable arms could be shifted into nearly 200 positions to indicate different words, phrases, or (most likely) numbers in a table of signals. This code was revised several times. Half of the coded signals were used for actual messages while the other half were used to regulate and police the process of communicating up and down the line (start of messages, weather difficulties, etc.).

Chappe needed government help to test his system over a longer distance. His brother Ignace (1760–1829), newly elected to the revolutionary Legislative Assembly, helped gain the needed funding. Thus the French government funded the construction of fifteen telegraph stations (ranging from wooden houses to stone towers) on hilltops from Paris north to Lille, each about 10 to 20 miles apart and equipped with telescopes, covering an overall distance of about 120 miles. It was placed into service in mid-1794 and rapidly showed its ability to carry messages far faster than any means of transport. Soon other lines were developed, including east to Strasbourg (1798) and west to Brest and the English Channel. Amsterdam, Milan, and Venice (which could get a signal from Paris in about six hours) were all reached by 1810.

Many claimed at least partial credit for the Chappe system, and hounded by such claimants, Chappe committed suicide in Paris on 23 January 1805. His brothers and others in the family remained active in managing the telegraph lines for years to follow. Four years earlier brother Abraham Chappe developed a field telegraph system and a dozen were made for Napoleon's army.

Mounted on carts with hand-operated signaling arms, the Chappe field telegraphs were used as late as the Crimean War (1853–1865). Chappe's system remained in use for decades, expanding to provide some 3,000 miles of telegraph "line" serviced by more than 530 signaling stations serving nearly thirty of Europe's largest cities. Night operations with lanterns were attempted, but these did not work. Though Chappe had proposed the system be extended to commercial use, the telegraph, built and retained by the French government as a monopoly, was generally restricted to military or diplomatic messages until the 1820s. The system was widely copied by other countries until replaced by electric telegraphy after 1844.

Christopher H. Sterling

See also France: Army; Napoleonic Wars (1795–1815); Semaphore (Mechanical Telegraphs)

Sources
Chappe, Ignace V. J. 1840. *Histoire de la Telegraphie.* AuMans, France: Ch. Richelet.
Holtzmann, Gerard J., and Björn Pehrson. 1995. *The Early History of Data Networks.* Los Alamitos, CA: IEEE Computer Society Press.
Koenig, Duane. 1944. "Telegraphs and Telegrams in Revolutionary France." *The Scientific Monthly* LIX (December): 431–437.
Mallinson, Howard. 2005. *Send it by Semaphore: The Old Telegraphs During the Wars with France.* Ramsbury, UK: Crowood Press.
Wilson, Geoffrey. 1976. "France." In *The Old Telegraphs,* 120–130. Totowa, NJ: Rowman & Littlefield.

Cher Ami and the "Lost Battalion"

Among the most famous of the 600 carrier pigeons donated by British pigeon fanciers that served American forces on the Western Front in late 1918 was Cher Ami ("dear friend"). He flew at least a dozen message missions, most importantly one to assist the famous "Lost Battalion."

On 3 October 1918 more than 500 men of the U.S. Army's 77th Infantry Division became trapped behind German lines during the Battle of the Meuse-Argonne. By the second day only 200 men were still unwounded. Their commanding officer, Major Charles S. Whittlesey, sent out three pigeons (their radios had been destroyed) to tell American forces where his unit was, but they appear to have been shot down. When American artillery shells began to fall among the surrounded U.S. troops, Whittlesey wrote a quick note and placed it in the message canister on the left leg of his last pigeon, Cher Ami. It said, "We are along the road parallel to 276.4. Our own artillery is dropping a barrage directly on us. For heaven's sake, stop it." As Cher Ami began to fly back home to the main American line, the Germans opened fire. Cher Ami managed to climb higher, beyond the range of enemy guns, and flew 25 miles in only 25 minutes to deliver his message. The shelling was halted and more than 200 American lives were saved.

But Cher Ami had been hit—when he reached his coop, he was lying on his back, covered in blood. He had been blinded in one eye, and a bullet had hit his breastbone, making a hole the size of a quarter. Hanging by just a few tendons was the pigeon's almost severed leg with the canister holding the all-important message. Though dedicated medics saved Cher Ami's life, they could not save his leg. The men of the division took care of the little bird that had saved 200 of their friends, and even carved a small wooden leg for him. When Cher Ami was well enough to travel, the one-legged hero (and forty other message-carrying pigeons) was put on a ship back to the United States.

The bird's role was soon filling stories in newspapers and magazines. Cher Ami died of his multiple war wounds at Fort Monmouth, New Jersey, on 13 June 1919—less than a year after he had completed his service to the U.S. Army Signal Corps. A few years later a fifteen-stanza poem was written in the bird's honor. Visitors to the National Museum of American History in Washington DC can see Cher Ami, preserved for history alongside the French medal that the bird earned.

Christopher H. Sterling

See also Pigeons

Sources

Fairfield County Pigeon Fanciers Association. "Pigeons During the Two World Wars." [Online information; retrieved September 2005.] http://www.pigeonclubsusa .com/faircount_facts_info_world_war.htm.
Farrington, Harry Web. 1926. "Cher Ami." [Online poem; retrieved September 2005.] http://iml.jou.ufl.edu/projects/Fall03/Working/Bird.html.

Chicksands

Chicksands was the primary center of the British Y Service (radio detecting and listening) operations, which during World War II supported the code-breaking functions of Bletchley Park. Since 1997 it has housed the British army's Intelligence Corps and a related museum.

The history of Chicksands is a long one, dating back before the Norman Conquest of 1066. Located just southwest of the town of Bedford in central England, for four centuries Chicksands Priory was a Gilbertine monastery serving the needs of resident monks and nuns (one of nine such locations in the country). After the dissolution of the monasteries in 1538 by Henry VIII, Chicksands became the home of the Osborn family for 400 years. The priory and surrounding grounds were sold to the Air Ministry in 1936, for use as a radio signals station because of its relatively high ground location.

Five 240-foot radio antennas (one remains today) and many additional one-story buildings (dubbed blocks) were constructed in 1940–1941. Radio listening activities began in 1940 with three squadrons of Women's Auxiliary Air Force and Royal Air Force (RAF) personnel operating twenty-four hours a day, recording Luftwaffe Enigma machine-coded messages for relay to and decoding by Bletchley Park. In early 1941, navy and RAF operators helped to locate the German battleship *Bismark* by her radio signals. For the duration of the war, Y operators intercepted Enigma's five-letter code group radio messages, which were carefully copied down in pencil on special forms for transmission to Bletchley. Few had much idea of the value of what they were doing, but all struggled with weak signals and external noise while trying to extract the all-important messages. Soon operators could recognize individual German transmitters by their mode of transmission.

An area just a few hundred feet west of the priory and listening blocks served as an RAF radio transmission site, operating as the hub of a high frequency radio network. The site was also used for clandestine radio communications to European resistance groups.

With the end of World War II, RAF Chicksands reverted to caretaker status for five years. In 1950 the priory became a primary U.S. Air Force communications security base, continuing its role as a radio intercept station (for voice, code, and later radioteletype and facsimile services), now directed against the Soviet Union and states allied with it. The RAF left the base in 1961, and considerable construction of new and expanded buildings soon followed as the U.S. Air Force expanded operations. The base continued to be operated by the U.S. Air Force until 30 September 1995, when the combination of modern technology and the lessening of East-West tensions made the function redundant. A large circular radio antenna constructed in the 1960s and covering some 35 acres (known locally as the "Elephant Cage") was dismantled during 1996.

After budget and other considerations, in 1997 the largely deserted RAF Chicksands became the home of the Ministry of Defence Intelligence and Security Centre and a museum of defense intelligence. The priory serves as the home of the British Army Intelligence Corps. All training for the intelligence corps and for RAF intelligence officers and analysts is carried out at Chicksands.

Christopher H. Sterling

See also Bletchley Park; Code Breaking; Enigma; Signals Intelligence (SIGINT); Ultra; Y Service

Sources
Grayson, William C. 1999. *Chicksands: A Millennium of History.* 3rd ed. Crofton, MD: Shefford Press.
Intelligence Corps. "Chicksands." [Online information; retrieved August 2005.] http://www.army.mod.uk/intelligence corps/chicksands.htm.

China, People's Republic of

China originated paper, printing, gunpowder, and rocketry, to name but four technologies useful in military communication. For much of the eighteenth to early twentieth centuries, China was a technically backward region, exploited by numerous other powers.

By the early twenty-first century, the People's Republic of China had the world's largest standing military and its defense spending was second only to the United States. Modern military communications are increasingly central to the operation of Chinese forces.

Modern signal troops first appeared in the early 1920s with the National Revolutionary Forces in south China. Special signal courses were held in Whampoa Military Academy in 1925, and signal engineers were established the next year under the National Revolution Army. In 1928, the Signal Corps became semi-independent from the engineers and joined with transport troops to become a new branch of the Nationalist Army, the Transport and Signal Branch. The Signals Technical School was established early in 1928 (and soon received some technical assistance from Germany), and by the fall, a signal regiment was formed at army headquarters with thirty-seven radio stations under its control. Radio was tactically employed during 1929 in the northern provinces. The Signal Regiment became two regiments, and in 1931, a battalion was formed. The Signal Corps was formally established in 1934.

The Signal Corps expanded rapidly. In January 1938, the Signal Command was established under the Ministry of Military Operations. Many new regiments and subunits were raised. The Directorate of Signals was established in March 1939. China suffered hugely in its 1931–1945 war with Japan, in part due to the ongoing strife between the Communists and the Nationalist government. After four years (1945–1949) of civil war, the People's Republic of China was founded in October 1949.

Chinese electronic warfare equipment currently includes a combination of 1950s to 1980s technologies, with only a few select military units receiving the most modern components. China has an extensive network of hardened, underground shelters and command-and-control facilities. Fear of possible war with the former Soviet Union in the 1960s and 1970s prompted China to construct extensive national command posts and associated communications while increasing the pace of modernization. Over the past two decades, the country has largely completed a shift from reliance on analog to more secure digital military communication links.

China's military communications network is separate from the civil telecommunications network, although the two would be linked in any crisis. China's military national-level command-and-control communications are carried over multiple transmission systems in order to create a system that is survivable, secure, flexible, mobile, and less vulnerable to exploitation, destruction, or electronic attack. China's communications networks are capable of supporting People's Liberation Army (PLA) military operations within China's borders; while they might be damaged, they are unlikely to be completely destroyed.

Communication and information modernization and automation has been a top Chinese priority since at least 1979. This effort has produced a command automation data network capable of rapidly passing operational orders down the chain of command and moving information to national- and theater-level decision makers. However, China's communications infrastructure, including the command automation data network portions, appears not yet capable of controlling or directing military forces in a sophisticated, Western-style joint operating environment. The command automation data network can support domestic operations and conventional attack options along

China's borders. China still lags behind Western standards for controlling complex joint operations and lacks the robust architecture required to meet the demands of the modern battlefield.

Microwave communications equipment is present at PLA installations. Cellular telephone service has only recently become another element of PLA military communications, and China has shown interest in establishing dedicated military cellular systems for PLA use. The explosive growth of cellular communications in the civilian sector probably aids military adoption of cellular technology for PLA operations.

Chinese networks are composed largely of commercial, off-the-shelf technology. Europe, Japan, and Israel, among others, compete to sell telecommunications technology, as well as related hardware and software, to China. China is procuring state-of-the-art technology to improve its intercept, direction-finding, and jamming capabilities. In addition to providing extended imagery reconnaissance and surveillance and electronic intelligence collection, China's unmanned aerial vehicle programs probably will provide platforms for improved radio and radar jammers. Existing earth stations can be modified to interfere with satellite communications. PLA also is developing an electronic countermeasures (ECM) doctrine and has performed structured training in an ECM environment. Chinese military communication satellites entered service in the early 2000s.

China increasingly sees information warfare as a strategic weapon outside traditional operational boundaries. China's capacities include those in combat secrecy, military deception, psychological warfare, electronic warfare, and physical destruction of enemy capacities. The country's expanding manufacture of sophisticated electronic devices has hastened improvements. China currently focuses on understanding information warfare as a military threat, developing effective countermeasures, and studying offensive employment of information warfare against foreign economic, logistics, and command, control, communications, and computer information (C4I) systems. Driven by the perception that China's information systems are vulnerable, the highest priority has been assigned to defensive programs and indigenous information technology development. Some technologies could provide enhanced defensive or offensive capabilities against foreign military and civilian information infrastructure systems. Computer antivirus solutions, network security, and advanced data communications technologies are a few examples. Over the last few years, the Communication Command Academy in Wuhan has emerged as one of the major PLA centers in information warfare research.

China appears interested in researching methods to insert computer viruses into foreign networks as part of its overall information strategy. China reportedly has adequate hardware and software tools and possesses a strong and growing understanding of the technologies involved. However, China's strategic use of advanced information technologies in the short to mid-term likely will lack depth and sophistication; however, as it develops more expertise in defending its own networks against enemy attack, it is likely to step up attempts to penetrate foreign information systems.

Open source articles claim that PLA has incorporated information warfare–related scenarios into its operational exercises. Efforts reportedly have focused on increasing PLA's proficiency in defensive measures, especially against computer viruses. This anti-access strategy is centered on targeting operational centers of gravity, including C4I centers, airbases, and aircraft carrier battle groups located around the periphery of China.

Christopher H. Sterling and Cliff Lord

See also Electronic Countermeasures/ Electronic Warfare (ECM/EW); Information Revolution in Military Affairs (IRMA); Jamming; Microwave; Mobile Communications

Sources
Federation of American Scientists. 2000. "Command and Control." [Online information; retrieved June 2006.] http://www.fas .org/nuke/guide/china/c3i/index.html.
U.S. Department of Defense. 2000. *Annual Report on the Military Power of the People's Republic of China*. [Online report; retrieved November 2004.] http://www.defenselink .mil/news/Jun2000/china06222000.htm.
U.S. Department of Defense. 2003. *Annual Report on the Military Power of the People's Republic of China*. [Online report; retrieved March 2006.] http://www.globalsecurity .org/military/library/report/2003/20030730 chinaex.pdf.

Coast Defense

American coast defense communications technology was unique and grew in complexity from 1890 through 1945. In the nineteenth century, need for and means of coast defense communication were minimal as ballistic calculations were done at the guns, which were so concentrated that officers could personally direct their fire. Any further communication used voice, runners, flags, or rockets.

In the 1890s, however, introduction of new weapons with greatly increased range demanded improved communication to operate at their full potential. In addition to normal post-telephone systems, coast artillery required communication to identify and locate targets (especially moving warships) and control the battery's guns. Complicating the need, the new guns could fire at targets unseen by their gunners, as coastal mortars always did.

Target location required observers distant from the guns to communicate their observations rapidly to plotting rooms. These messages were converted into predicted target positions and then into specific aiming data and transmitted to the guns. Submarine mines (a key element of coast defense) had essentially the same fire control requirements as gun batteries. A growing number of searchlights also had to be directed by officers not located near them, while the tactical command structure had to direct the fire of subordinate elements. As two base end stations for each coastal battery had to take observations of the same target simultaneously, and since the plotting rooms calculated the firing data for a specific firing instant, time-interval apparatus was necessary to simultaneously operate bells at the observing stations, plotting rooms, and guns.

Improved tactical, or fire control (FC), communication was clearly necessary. The question was how to tie all these elements together in an effective system of communications. Telegraphy was slow and required expensive specialists. The telephone was promising but in the late nineteenth century was still too inefficient to be relied upon, especially during the noise of battle. One partial solution was the speaking tube. Concrete coastal batteries were crisscrossed with metal speaking tubes, connecting battery commanders, plotting rooms, ammunition magazines, and the guns. Despite some interference from rumbling ammunition carts, these tubes were an effective means of communication within batteries through World War I.

The more difficult problem of communication with distant coastal stations led to the development of the "telautograph." A remarkably modern device introduced around 1904, it could transmit writing over wires and duplicate it at a distant receiver. Despite some initial troubles with bringing it online for practical use, a reliable system evolved. Although expensive and complicated, it minimized miscommunication while preserving a written record. Though not installed at all harbor defenses, the telautograph was widely used in the early twentieth century, as was the "aeroscope," a device for transmitting tide and meteorological data to the various plotting rooms.

No sooner had the installation of these modern devices begun, however, than the efforts of the U.S. Army Signal Corps to develop telephones suitable for FC communication began to bear fruit. The first generation, introduced around 1905, were "composite" phones, powered by either local dry-cell batteries or a common battery power supply. Inside models were housed in wooden cases, while outdoor telephones were mounted in heavy iron boxes; telephone booths soon became common in gun and mortar emplacements. Within less than a decade, use of local battery power had been eliminated in favor of "common battery" telephones, which operated more efficiently on the common power supply. Experience in tropical territory soon resulted in replacement of wooden with metal cases to better protect against dampness and insects. Development of efficient telephone communications doomed the much more expensive and complicated telautograph and aeroscope, and both were phased out after 1910.

Fully developed before World War I, this FC system as installed in most harbor defenses and remained the basis for coast artillery communication until World War II. Extensive networks of massive armored cables, both terrestrial and submarine, connected stations, batteries, and forts. These FC telephones had neither dials nor switchboard operators as they were essentially hardwired point to point, with operators assigned to each instrument. Commanders' stations contained numerous booths for telephone operators. Telephones came in several versions: battery commander's sets, gun telephones, wall sets, plotting-room sets, and desk instruments. These differed largely in their containers and in the inclusion or omission of ringing apparatus and bells. The telephones did not include the talking set—a headset with speaking tube was the most common type—but handsets and standard commercial "candlestick" phones were also used. The nerve center of the system was the FC switchboard room, which contained not only the connections between telephones and the time-interval apparatus but also the motor generators that supplied the 30 volts necessary to operate the entire system.

Within mortar batteries, zone signal systems with lights and bells in the powder magazines indicated the zone (size) charges needed for subsequent shots. Mechanical data transmission systems, an integral part of batteries constructed before and immediately after World War I, displayed plotting room firing data at the guns.

Between the wars, as need arose for communicating with mobile tractor-drawn and railway artillery, standard army portable field phones were used. After considerable effort, the Signal Corps developed a portable time-interval system for mobile batteries not connected to a switchboard room. Acknowledging that FC telephones had not kept pace with technical advancements, the

Signal Corps developed a new telephone by the eve of World War II, and during that war these largely replaced the variety of older FC telephones. Interwar experiments aimed at increasing the versatility of FC systems resulted in new switchboards that improved interconnections, allowing stations to observe for more than one gun battery.

Radio steadily grew in importance. Used early in the twentieth century primarily in place of signal flags and lights for communicating with ships, by World War II radio had become another important link, providing communication with remote stations and tying coastal defenses together, though the telephone remained the primary means of data transmission. Shortly after World War II, however, coast defense batteries and their accompanying communications systems were declared obsolete and all were disposed of.

Bolling W. Smith

See also Atlantic Wall; Maginot Line

Sources
Coast Artillery School. 1936, 1940. *Signal Communication: Coast Artillery*. Army Extension Courses, Special Text No. 39. Prepared under the direction of the Chief of Coast Artillery. Fort Monroe, VA: Coast Artillery School.
Office of the Chief Signal Officer. 1904. *General Instructions for Fire Control Installations of the United States Signal Corps in Force April 30, 1904: Memorandum No. 3*. Washington, DC: Government Printing Office.
Office of the Chief Signal Officer. 1914. *Installation and Maintenance of Fire Control Systems at Seacoast Fortifications: Manual No. 8*. Washington, DC: Government Printing Office.
Scriven, George P. 1908. "The Signal Corps and the Coast Defense; The Coast Patrol; The Relation of the Signal Corps to the Coast Artillery." In *The Transmission of Military Information*. Governors Island, NY: Journal of the Military Service Institution of the United States.
War Department. 1900–1918. "Report of the Chief Signal Officer." In *Annual Report of the Secretary of War*. Washington, DC: Government Printing Office.

Code, Codebook

Some modes of transmitting messages over a distance make use of lights (e.g., "one if by land, and two if by sea"), flags or other visual signals, or audible signs (e.g., gunfire, bugles, whistles) that are clearly understood by both sender and receiver. Such signals are usually used more for efficiency than secrecy, but they also form a kind of code. More complex codes and codebooks have been used for many years both to save message transmission time and cost and to ensure confidentiality.

A code is a communication system in which a word, number, letter, symbol, or phrase is substituted for (or represents) plain text words or phrases. It differs from a cipher, which substitutes or transposes one letter (or a pair) for another. Codes are more widely used and are often superenciphered with added numbers or letters to make it harder for code breakers to discern patterns. Such a code is often transmitted in long lists of four- or five-digit number groups. A code breaker must seek the plain code "behind" the superenciphered material. There are literally hundreds of types of codes, though most are now generated (and broken) with the use of computers.

Confidentiality of codes used by military forces is obviously vital. Limited access to codes and constant monitoring of their use as well as code changes over time help to impede code-breaking activity. But virtually no code is unbreakable, save the "one-time pad" method where a specific code combination is used only once and then discarded.

In its most basic form, any codebook is designed to encode or decode messages. It is usually in the form of a printed volume with columns of alphabetically arranged words or phrases and their brief code letter or word representation. During the electric telegraph era (used from the mid-nineteenth to the early twentieth century), these large commercially issued volumes were designed more to save money (by reducing the number of words, letters, or numbers transmitted) rather than ensure secrecy of transmission. Some were trade specific, and others were sold to the public. Hundreds were published—there are more than a thousand of them in the Library of Congress.

Codebooks are of two general types. One-part codes have both the words and phrases and their equivalent codes listed in alphabetical or numerical sequence, requiring only a single publication for both encoding and decoding. The eighty-eight-page 1871 Chief Signal Officer's Code, used by both the U.S. Army and State Department, was of this type. It offered alternate code words for common words or terms, thus reducing repetition (which is often used to help break into codes). So were far more complex (upward of 1,500 pages) "color" codes of the State Department that followed at regular intervals. The American Trench Code and Front-Line Code used in World War I were also one-part codes, but simplified for portability. The former could encode words using either numbers or a short lettered code word.

Two-part codebooks, on the other hand, applied coded terms (either numbers or letters) in a random sequence, thus requiring a second list or book with the codes shown in alphabetical or numerical order. This complexity adds to the time and cost of making a code, but can greatly increase message security. The "river" and "lake" series of Army codes, beginning with "Potomac" in 1918, for example, were two-part codes used at the battalion level and up. The "Huron" lake code of late 1918 was designed for use with telephone communication to allow encoding of entire telephone exchanges. It also included a two-letter brief "emergency code" for use on the front lines. A radio code was also developed that year. These codebooks were all created by the very small (eight people) Code Compilation Section of the Signal Corps that was formed in 1917.

A severe drawback to any military codebook is the danger of capture (as happened on numerous occasions in both world wars), and thus of fatally opening the relevant code to prying eyes. They were usually printed in very limited numbers and guarded closely. Still, distribution of multiple copies over great distances and to multiple locations was a highly risky activity. Codebooks used by naval forces were often printed with ink that would run if wet so they could be thrown overboard in weighted bags to prevent capture.

Christopher H. Sterling

See also Ardois Light; Code Breaking; Communications Security (COMSEC); Coston Signals; Fire/Flame/Torch; Flags; Heliograph and Mirrors; Lights and Beacons; Morse Code; Music Signals; Night Signals; Semaphore (Mechanical Telegraphs); Smoke

Sources

Barker, Wayne G., ed. 1978. *The History of Codes and Ciphers in the United States Prior to World War I*. Laguna Hills, CA: Aegean Park Press.

Friedman, William F. 1928. *Report on the History of the Use of Codes and Code Language, the International Telegraph Regulations Pertaining Thereto, and the Bearing of this History on the*

Cortina Report. Washington, DC: Government Printing Office.

Kahn, David. 1967. *The Codebreakers: The Story of Secret Writing.* New York: Macmillan.

Singh, Simon. 1999. *The Code Book: The Science of Secrecy from Ancient Egypt to Quantum Cryptography.* Garden City, NY: Doubleday.

Weber, Ralph E. 2002. *Masked Dispatches: Cryptograms and Cryptography in American History, 1775–1900.* Fort Meade, MD: National Security Agency, Center for Cryptologic History.

Wrixton, Fred B. 1998. *Codes, Ciphers & Other Cryptic and Clandestine Communication.* New York: Black Dog & Leventhal.

Code Breaking

Creation of codes and ciphers (sometimes spelled "cyphers") naturally created the need to find ways to read protected signal content. Code breaking, more recently termed cryptanalysis, means to create the means to read (to "break") the code or cipher communications of an opposing entity, whether a commercial company, military force, or nation. Other closely related terms include "decode," "decipher," and "decrypt," though these each have slightly different meanings. Author David Kahn calls code breaking the most important kind of secret intelligence today.

The basic principles of code breaking as well as many of its methods are ages old (some date back at least 4,000 years to Egyptian hieroglyphs). Many methods were mechanized during the early twentieth century and then substantially computerized and digitized in the past few decades. Not surprisingly, code breaking in one form or another has played an important part in military campaigns since ancient times. The ability to determine details about the makeup and strength of an opposing force and its plans—especially if the enemy is unaware you have gained this information—has often proven decisive to the outcome of a battle or campaign.

Secrecy is essential to success in such endeavors, and among the best-kept secrets of World War II (and in some cases for decades longer) was the success of the Allies in breaking German, Japanese, and other countries' military and diplomatic codes.

The growing complexity of the code-breaking process has increasingly centered such activity on those government and military specialized agencies best able to support the budget, equipment, and personnel needed. Development of the Internet has created a whole new subset of code-breaking activity in the fight against terrorism.

Little coordination of code-breaking activities took place in government or military agencies for much of American history. The Military Intelligence Division section (created in 1903) of the General Staff, often referred to as G-2, was at least nominally responsible for most cryptographic activities of the military for much of the twentieth century, though it was ill equipped to do so at the inception of either world war. Parker Hitt's 1916 monograph summarized all that was known by that time. Herbert Yardley's famous New York City operation (known as the "Black Chamber") focused Army and diplomatic code-breaking efforts from World War I until its closure in 1929. In the early 1930s, William F. Friedman began to build the code-breaking team for the Army that would perform so well in World War II.

The Army and Navy ran totally separate operations before and during that war: the Army Signal Intelligence Service based at Arlington Hall, Virginia, and the Navy's Op-20-G at Nebraska Avenue in Washington DC. Both maintained numerous overseas posts as well. These activities were merged in 1949 but their lackluster performance during the Korean War resulted in the formation of the National Security Agency (NSA) in 1952. Two decades later the Central Security Service was established within NSA to centralize Pentagon code-breaking activities across the services.

Christopher H. Sterling

See also Arlington Hall; Atlantic, Battle of the (1939–1945); Bletchley Park; Code, Codebook; Code Talkers; Communications Security (COMSEC); Driscoll, Agnes Meyer (1889–1971); Electric Cipher Machine (ECM Mark II, "SIGABA"); Enigma; Friedman, William F. (1891–1969); Germany: Naval Intelligence (*B-Dienst*); Government Code & Cipher School (GC&CS, 1919–1946); Magic; Mauborgne, Joseph Oswald (1881–1971); Midway, Battle of (3–6 June 1942); National Security Agency (NSA); Nebraska Avenue, Washington DC; OP-20-G; Polish Code Breaking; Room 40; Rowlett, Frank B. (1908–1998); Signal Security Agency (SSA, 1943–1949); Signals Intelligence (SIGINT); SIGSALY; Tannenberg, Battle of (1914); Tiltman, John Hessell (1894–1982); Ultra; Y Service; Yardley, Herbert O. (1889–1958)

Sources

Hitt, Parker. 1916. *Manual for the Solution of Military Ciphers*. Washington, DC: Government Printing Office.

Kahn, David. 1967. *The Codebreakers: The Story of Secret Writing*. New York: Macmillan.

Kippenhahn, Rudolf. 1999. *Code Breaking: A History and Exploration*. Woodstock, NY: Overlook.

Newton, David E. 1997. *Encyclopedia of Cryptology*. Santa Barbara, CA: ABC-CLIO.

Singh, Simon. 1999. *The Code Book: The Science of Secrecy from Ancient Egypt to Quantum Cryptography*. New York: Doubleday.

Smith, Derek J. 2003. "Codes and Ciphers in History." [Online information; retrieved October 2004.] http://www.smithsrisca.demon.co.uk/crypto-ancient.html.

Wrixton, Fred B. 1998. *Codes, Ciphers & Other Cryptic and Clandestine Communication*. New York: Black Dog & Leventhal.

Code Talkers

Native Americans provided a unique means of communication during both world wars, but especially in World War II's Pacific island campaigns from 1942 to 1945. Drawn from many tribes, chiefly the Navajo of the American Southwest, these U.S. Marines were able to use their own language to communicate military information by radio or telephone links without fear that the Japanese could understand what was being said.

Native American "code talkers" (then primarily Choctaw, though five other tribes also served as code talkers) were first employed at the end of World War I on the Western Front. Germany had broken many American codes, and a new approach was needed quickly. More than a dozen Choctaw served during the battle of the Meuse-Argonne in October–November 1918. They translated Choctaw telephone messages into English on several occasions in the final two weeks of the war.

Recalling this earlier use of the Choctaw, Philip Johnston, a missionary's son who had grown up on a Navajo reservation and spoke the language, suggested a way to meet the military's 1942 need for "unbreakable" communication. Johnston believed Navajo answered the requirement because it is an unwritten language of extreme complexity. Its syntax and tonal qualities, not to mention dialects, make it unintelligible without extensive exposure and training. It has no alphabet or symbols and is spoken only on the Navajo lands. Probably fewer than thirty non-Navajos could understand the language

Two U.S. Marine Navajo "code talkers" signalmen use their native language to send a radio message during the fighting on Bougainville in the Solomon Islands in 1943. The Japanese were never able to break signals sent in several different Native American languages. (Bettmann/Corbis)

at the outbreak of the war. With five Navajo, Johnston conducted a demonstration for Marine officers who agreed to try the idea.

By mid-1942, a small group ("the first 29") of Navajo underwent Marine training and developed a dictionary of native terms to cover military needs. This was memorized (printed codebooks could not be taken into combat) and included Navajo terms used to indicate more than 400 military terms that did not exist in the Navajo tongue. The Navajo were then deployed to the Pacific as others joined the training process. All told, some 400 Navajo code talkers became an

invaluable part of many Marine island invasions, able to communicate far faster and with greater security than many other means of transmitting coded messages.

Fourteen Comanche also served as code talkers with the Army's Fourth Division in Europe (their language also lacked a written version at the time). Members of at least a dozen other tribes served in a similar fashion, but have received comparatively less attention. Because of the continuing value of the code talkers, little was revealed of what they had accomplished until decades after the war. A 2002 feature motion picture,

Windtalkers, featured a highly fictional view of the Navajo role in World War II.

Christopher H. Sterling

See also U.S. Marine Corps; World War II

Sources

McClain, Sally. 2002. *Navajo Weapon: The Navajo Code Talkers*. Tucson, AZ: Rio Nuevo Publishers.

Meadows, William C. 2002. *The Comanche Code Talkers of World War II*. Austin: University of Texas Press.

Paul, Doris A. 1973. *The Navajo Code Talkers*. Pittsburgh, PA: Dorrance.

Color

The use of one or more colors is often a critical part of military communications. For example, waving a white flag (no color) is widely understood to indicate surrender. The main consideration is to select colors that will be readily apparent at some distance and that carry a predetermined meaning.

The use of colors in signal flags is especially important when the flag is hanging limply without wind. To increase legibility, most designs are chosen as if they were in black and white. Color is added to brighten each flag, and thus make it more visible against the sky. Most signaling flags use only one or two colors. Half a dozen have three colors (most commonly red, white, and blue). Several have four colors (yellow, blue, red, and black, for example). Modern flag designs were improved over many years of application in the field and all multicolored flags are assumed to be readable while flying as well as while hanging during an absence of wind. Green is deemed a poorer color selection, and now most codes use it in only two designs. The most common colors are yellow, red, and blue.

Flag color patterns are chosen carefully and may include vertical and horizontal patterns of two to ten colors, crosses from the flag middle or flag corners, quartered squares, sixteen squares, four triangles, a colored circle or square in the center, two colored squares in the center, or a small triangle or square in the center of a pennant, among others. Pennants often have slight variations of flag design. To find examples of poorly chosen colors, shapes, or design one merely need scan the many flaghoist systems proposed during the period from 1650 to about 1875. For decades, almost every admiral in every navy in the world had his own set of flags and codebook—and few could really accomplish the job their navy needed done without them. But the multiplicity of systems contributed to confusion in their use and the eventual drive for standardization.

Colors have also been used with signaling lights and rockets. Use of color signals sent at predetermined intervals could signal fairly complex messages. The modern Very pistol is a descendant of such rocket signals. Very night signals using balls of red and green fire shot from a pistol first appeared in 1877, their arrangement having a prearranged code significance. Star shells of different colors, as well as rockets to carry tactical messages, were widely used in World War I. After 1917 signal rockets came into more general use. Some made use of colors to communicate Morse code, with red indicating a dot and white or green a dash. Lights dropped from aircraft also used colors to send signals.

David L. Woods

See also Aldis Lamp; Coston Signals; Flags; Flaghoist; Lights and Beacons; Night Signals; Semaphore (Mechanical Telegraphs); Signal Book; Signal Rockets

Source

Woods, David L. 1965. *A History of Tactical Communications Techniques.* Orlando, FL: Martin-Marietta (reprinted by Arno Press in *Telecommunications*, 1974).

Combat Information Center (CIC)

A combat information center (CIC, or "combat" for short), is the communications and electronics hub of any modern naval vessel. The multipurpose CIC developed from World War II radar plotting rooms (plots), mounted in dark internal spaces on American combat ships beginning with capital vessels (battleships and aircraft carriers), and eventually down to destroyers.

The concept was first developed during World War II (CICs were fitted into the *Iowa*-class battleships under construction, for example, though the vessels were not originally designed with such a facility). A CIC is usually an internal and protected (armored) space located near the bridge to allow for coordinated continuity of action while under attack. The CIC is always manned when a naval ship is at sea. Equipped with radar scopes, wax plotter boards (or today, more often their electronic equivalent), and extensive multimode communications links, the CIC compartment is restricted space in both size and access.

During normal operations, the CIC supports the commander on the bridge by tracking and identifying surface and air contacts,

The combat information center (CIC) directs operations onboard the USS George Washington *while underway in the Arabian Sea in 1998. (Department of Defense)*

coordinating with onshore command centers via satellite communications links, and communicating with other vessels via maritime radio traffic. The CIC operates a variety of encrypted communications systems; surface search and fire control radars; and an identification, friend or foe system. The CIC personnel also maintain the Shipboard Command-and-Control System and the Joint Operational Tactical System, which provide real-time navigation and tactical information to personnel in the CIC on the bridge. CIC personnel also have a secure data link to onshore computer networks from which they can gather information about potential targets or threats.

The CIC's primary purpose, however, is to assume tactical coordinated control of the ship and its various weapons and defense systems during combat operations. When a ship goes to battle stations (referred to as going to "general quarters"), the captain will monitor events, direct the ship's maneuvering, and order the appropriate use of weapons from the CIC. Some may be fired directly from the CIC, while orders to others are relayed via sound-powered phones to gun crews, who then fire the weapons.

A version of the CIC can also be found on board Airborne Warning and Control System aircraft specially equipped to collect, display, evaluate, and disseminate tactical information for the use of the commanding officer or ground control agencies. Such a CIC can serve as air traffic control, providing communications and navigation information to other aircraft. It can also serve as an aerial command post.

Christopher H. Sterling

See also Airborne Warning and Control System (AWACS); Communication Satellites; Identification, Friend or Foe (IFF)

Sources

Storming Media. Combat Information Centers search results. [Online search engine; retrieved September 2004.] http://www.stormingmedia.us/keywords/combat_information_centers.html.

U.S. Navy. 2005. "Division Officer Training." [Online information; retrieved September 2005.] http://www.fas.org/man/dod-101/navy/docs/swos/stu2/STU01.html.

Combat Information Transport System (CITS)

The Combat Information Transport System (CITS) is a multiyear U.S. Air Force program managing the life cycle of the service's many communications and information systems. The CITS program is designed to provide a high speed, broadband, digital information transport system responsible for integrating existing data systems and providing the capability to integrate all existing and planned voice, video, imagery, and sensor systems, including those that are classified.

The CITS program, based at the Air Force's Electronic Systems Center at Hanscom Air Force Base, Massachusetts, is intended to modernize the information transport capability at each Air Force base, replace obsolete copper cable with the latest fiber technology, improve network management, and upgrade voice phone service with new digital switches.

The CITS includes several interconnected parts. The Information Transport System includes everything that relates to the physical pathways that information passes through, network defense concerns security, and network management provides the control. The Network Operations/Information Assurance, Telecommunications Management System, and Voice Switching System combine to provide connectivity throughout the Air Force to link in-garrison command-and-control and combat-support systems to the Defense Information System Network. Network connectivity, information assurance, asset management, interoperability, and standard interfaces to joint service networks form the core concerns for this program.

Christopher H. Sterling

See also Air Force Communications Service (AFCS), Air Force Communications Command (AFCC) (1961–1991); Defense Communications System (DCS); Fiber . Optics; Global Information Grid (GIG)

Sources

General Dynamics Network Systems. "Programs & Contracts: CITS." [Online information; retrieved March 2006.] http:// www.gd-ns.com/cits/.

Mondro, Mitchell J. "Combat Information Transport System: Reliability and Availability Performance." [Online article; retrieved April 2006.] http://www.mitre.org/work/ tech_papers/tech_papers_00/mondro _cits/mondro.pdf.

Commonwealth Communications Army Network (COMCAN)

The Commonwealth Communications Army Network (COMCAN) was a teleprinter-based system that connected British military bases and the military establishments of various commonwealth countries. The network interfaced with the North Atlantic Treaty Organization and the United States.

COMCAN evolved from the British Army's strategic Army Chain, a worldwide wireless network linking British military bases. During World War II a choice of replacing hand-speed Morse with high-speed Morse or teleprinters had to be made. Due to production difficulties with teleprint-

ers, high-speed Morse was chosen. After the war, availability of teleprinters increased and they gradually replaced the high-speed Morse circuits.

In the early 1950s, torn tape relay became common. Instead of point-to-point teleprinter circuits, a destination would use reperforator equipment, which punched out a five-unit tape. The tape could then be manually inserted into an auto head (tape reader), which would transmit the tape on to a selected circuit.

During the following decade, COMCAN introduced the Signal Transmit Receive and Distribution system and its associated Telegraph Automatic Relay Equipment, which provided message switching facilities at primary sites throughout the British Commonwealth, thus providing a fast automatic tape relay network. Taken over by the Royal Air Force in the late 1960s, the COMCAN system survived until the 1980s.

Cliff Lord

See also High-Speed Morse; Morse Code; Teleprinter/Teletype; United Kingdom: Royal Air Force

Sources

Blaxland, John. 1998. *Swift and Sure, A History of the Royal Australian Corps of Signals 1947–1972.* Canberra: Royal Australian Corps of Signals Corps Committee.

Nalder, R. F. H. 1958. *The Royal Corps of Signals: A History of its Antecedents and Development (circa 1800–1955)*, 479–481. London: Royal Signals Institution.

Communication Satellites

Military satellites are usually strategic or tactical. Strategic satellites are typically networked through fixed ground stations. They allow communications between stations served by the same satellite using any number of routes. Tactical satellite systems, on the other hand, utilize mobile earth stations. Military users have traditionally avoided commercial satellites because of security concerns, though increased use of encryption eases that worry.

A communication satellite must have a receiver and a transmitter, antennas for both functions, a method to convert the received message at the transmitter, and a source of electrical power. The ground portion of a satellite system consists of a transmitter, a receiver, antennas, and a means of connecting the station to end users. The most obvious difference between a satellite ground station and a point-to-point microwave station is that the satellite high-gain antenna is able to track the satellite.

Origins

The U.S. Army and Navy experimented with reflecting radio signals off the moon in the 1940s and 1950s; the Army did so for the first time on 11 January 1946. On 24 July 1954, as a part of the Navy's Communication Moon Relay Project (CMR), James H. Trexler, an engineer at the Naval Research Laboratory, became the first person to transmit his voice into space and have it returned to earth. The CMR was first tested and publicly revealed in January 1960 and operated between Hawaii and Maryland with sixteen teleprinter channels at the rate of sixty words per minute. Within two years, the system had been expanded to include ship-to-shore communications. The CMR was the only operational satellite communications relay system in the world until the Defense Satellite Communications System began operation on 16 June 1966.

All of these experiments were intended to use the theoretical advantages that satellite communications offer over the traditional methods of long-haul communications such as underwater cables, land lines, microwave transmission, and television signals. Submarine cables are expensive to lay and lack the large capacity necessary to meet the continual demand for more circuits. Because microwave transmissions travel in a straight line, relay stations have to be constructed about every thirty-five miles. The relay stations must receive, amplify, and retransmit the signal. Normal radio transmissions are subject to atmospheric disturbances, such as sun spots. The optimum altitude for a communication satellite is 22,300 miles above the equator, where the satellite appears to be stationary because it is in a geosynchronous orbit. A constellation of three such satellites, positioned 120 degrees from each other, with the capability of relaying communications between the satellites, provides communications to virtually every part of the earth except the North and South poles.

On 4 October 1957, military and civilian communications changed with the launch of the Soviet Union's Sputnik 1. On 18 December 1958, the United States Signal Communications by Orbiting Relay Equipment (SCORE) was launched and a taped Christmas message from President Dwight Eisenhower was broadcast from orbit. SCORE was also used to transmit messages between Arizona, Texas, and Georgia. SCORE was a store-and-forward satellite, receiving a message from earth, storing it on a tape, and then retransmitting it on command from an earth station. On 12 August 1960, the ECHO 1 satellite, a passive aluminized Mylar balloon, was launched, and experiments with radio and television transmission began in earnest. The first geosynchronous satellite, Syncom III, launched in August 1964. The Syncom series was a joint project of the U.S. Department of Defense and the National Aeronautics and Space Administration to demonstrate the economic viability of satellite communications.

Spreading Use

The Soviet Union followed its initial Sputnik by launching more satellites than any other nation. The Soviet space program ranked second only to the United States in the resources devoted to its efforts. Most Soviet military satellites, regardless of type, were named Cosmos. In addition, "civilian" satellites, the use of which the Soviets did not want to explain, also received the Cosmos designation. In the three decades leading to 1990, most, if not all, satellites launched by the Soviets had some military functions. In the post-Soviet era, Russian military satellites are identified as such, but still receive the Cosmos identifier.

Development of military satellite communications had drawn heavily upon advancements in the construction of commercial satellites. The fact that the Intelsat IV satellite had more than 4,000 two-way voice channels was a powerful incentive for developers of high-capacity military communications systems. The number of nations providing domestic satellite service has increased dramatically since Canada started the service in 1972 and the United States launched its first in 1974.

Planners at the Department of Defense increasingly realized that a specialized architecture for military satellite communications (MILSATCOM) was necessary. The first MILSATCOM architecture was published in 1976 and has been refined numerous times to meet changing requirements and advances in technology. The architecture has three parts: mobile and tactical, wideband, and protected systems. Users are grouped together according to their requirements that can be met by a common satellite system.

Development of more sophisticated electronics has increased the capability of satellite communication. Its importance to military operations during the Gulf War

(1990–1991) was summarized by Lieutenant General James Cassity, Joint Staff Directorate for C3 Systems, who said, "From day one, satellite communications have been our bread and butter. From first deployment through today, military and commercial satellite communications systems have been vital in providing essential command and control. . . . In 90 days, we established more military communications connectivity to the Persian Gulf than we have in Europe after 40 years." The essential role played by satellites in that conflict was noted by military planners around the world.

Present U.S. Military Satellites

Current U.S. MILSATCOM architecture has three basic systems: the Fleet Satellite Communications system (FLTSATCOM), the Defense Satellite Communications System (DSCS), and Milstar. The satellites of each system operate in the geosynchronous orbit (22,300 miles high), and each system utilizes specific frequency ranges. FLTSATCOM satellites operate in the ultra-high frequencies at 225–400 MHz; DSCS satellites operate in the super-high frequencies at 7250–8400 MHz; and Milstar satellites operate in the extremely high frequencies at 22–44 GHz. A fourth system, the Air Force Satellite Communications System (AFSATCOM), is supported by the three basic systems. AFSATCOM has no dedicated satellites but uses channels or transponders on the satellites of the MILSATCOM system. The AFSATCOM is used to transmit Emergency Action Messages and Single Integrated Operation Plan messages.

The U.S. Navy's FLTSATCOM system provided near worldwide coverage through its constellation of geosynchronous satellites. The FLTSATCOM system was the first operational system fielded by the Department of Defense to support tactical operations. The first FLTSATCOM satellite was launched in

1978 and the last in 1989. The system was used by naval aircraft, ships, submarines, and ground stations. In addition, the system supported communications between the National Command Authority and high-priority users, such as the White House Communications Agency.

In an effort to increase the use of leased commercial satellites, Congress directed that the follow-on system for FLTSATCOM be leased. The LEASAT program primarily served the Navy, the Air Force, and mobile ground forces. The LEASAT program used FLTSATCOM terminals, and its communications channels were very similar to FLTSATCOM. The first LEASAT was launched in 1984 and the last in 1990. By 1999, all of the FLTSATCOM satellites had been removed from service.

FLTSATCOM and LEASAT satellite systems were both replaced by UHF Follow-On (UHF F/O) satellites. The Navy's requirements for additional UHF capacity had increased dramatically after the FLTSATCOM system was initiated. The UHF F/O constellation of satellites was implemented to meet the increased demand for more capacity. The first successful launch was in 1993 and the last in 1999. Two UHF F/O satellites are located at each of the FLTSATCOM locations. The new satellites more than double the capacity of the system. All of the UHF F/O satellites are electromagnetic pulse protected. The satellites carry transponders for use by the Milstar ground terminals and the Global Broadcast Service (GBS). The enhanced capability of the satellites has allowed a reduction in the size of terminals; for example, the Army's Enhanced Manpack UHF terminal can be carried, set up, and used by individual soldiers to communicate using the UHF F/O satellites.

The GBS utilizes technology from commercial television to broadcast large streams of data to numerous small antennas. The system broadcasts only one way and resembles the system used for home satellite television reception. The need for the GBS system grew out of the Gulf War when service-operated and commercial leased communication channels were overloaded and essential information had to be moved to fighting units by airlift assets. Since the GBS can transmit to small, phased-array antennas on mobile platforms, data can be transmitted to forces while they are in motion. Commercial off-the-shelf and government off-the-shelf technology were used to quickly acquire and field the GBS capability.

The DSCS provides secure voice, teletype, television, facsimile, and digital data services. The primary users of the DSCS are the Global Command and Control System, White House Communications Agency, Defense Information Systems Network, Defense Switched Network, Defense Message System, Ground Mobile Forces, the Diplomatic Telecommunications Service, and several allied nations. The DSCS evolved through three phases: DSCSI, or the Initial Defense Satellite Communications System (IDSCS), began in 1967; DSCSII began in 1971 with the launch of two satellites; and DSCSIII began in 1982 when its first satellite was launched. The five DSCSIII satellites allow most earth terminals to access two satellites. The Ground Mobile Forces (GMF) operate on a subnetwork using the DSCS satellites. The GMF subnetwork requires use of a gateway terminal as it is not compatible with the DSCS network's strategic terminal.

The Milstar Satellite Communications System is the most advanced satellite communications system. It provides secure, jam-resistant, worldwide communications to meet joint service requirements. The Milstar system consists of five satellites in geosynchronous orbits, the first of which was launched 7 February 1994. Milstar terminals allow a user to transmit encrypted voice, data, teletype, or facsimile communications. The satellite functions as a switchboard by routing traffic from terminal to terminal anywhere on earth. The system has reduced requirements for ground-controlled switching because the satellite processes the communications signal and can link with other satellites in the constellation through crosslinks. One of the driving factors behind the Milstar program is to provide interoperable communications between Army, Navy, and Air Force Milstar users.

The capability of the Milstar system to operate under adverse conditions, such as jamming and nuclear attack, is achieved by frequency hopping, extensive on-board processing, and crosslinks. The flexibility of the Milstar system is improved by multiple uplink and downlink channels operating at different rates; multiple uplink and downlink beams; and routing of individual signals between uplinks, downlinks, and crosslinks.

Tommy R. Young II

See also Defense Information Systems Agency (DISA); Defense Message System (DMS); Electromagnetic Pulse (EMP); Global Command and Control System (GCCS); Gulf War (1990–1991); Spectrum Frequencies; White House Communications Agency (WHCA)

Sources

Butricia, Andrew J., ed. 1997. *Beyond the Ionosphere: Fifty Years of Satellite Communication.* NASA History Series SP-4217. Washington, DC: Government Printing Office.

Cassity, James. 1991. "Operation Desert Storm—The J-6 Perspective." *AFCEA News* February.

Chun, Clayton K. S. 2006. *Defending Space: U.S. Anti-Satellite Warfare and Space Weaponry.* Oxford: Osprey Publishing.

Elfers, Glen, and Stephen B. Miller. 2001. "Future U.S. Military Satellite Communication Systems." [Online article; retrieved December 2006.] www.aero.org/publications/crosslink/winter2002/08.html.

Federici, Gary. 1997. "From the Sea to the Stars: A History of U.S. Navy Space and Space-Related Activities." [Online article; retrieved December 2006.] http://www.history.navy.mil/books/space/index.htm.

Martin, Donald H. 2001. "A History of U.S. Military Satellite Communication Systems." [Online article; retrieved December 2006.] www.aero.org/publications/crosslink/winter2002/01.html.

National Aeronautics and Space Administration. "DSCS (Defense Satellite Communications System)." [Online information; retrieved December 2006.] http://msl.jpl.nasa.gov/Programs/dscs.html.

RussianSpaceWeb.com. 2006. "Spacecraft: Military." [Online information; retrieved December 2006.] http://www.russianspaceweb.com/spacecraft_military.html.

Communications Security (COMSEC)

Communications security measures, along with computer security, are a vital subcomponent of information security. Communications security covers a range of measures taken to prevent unauthorized individuals from gaining information from the interception and study of telecommunications or to mislead unauthorized individuals in the use and study of the information. COMSEC includes security of transmission, physical facilities, emissions, and cryptography.

Transmission security is designed to protect information transmissions from interception, analysis, imitative deception, and any type of disruption other than by cryptographic means. Physical security relates to the protection of cryptographic materials, information, and equipment from unauthorized individuals. Emission security involves procedures to prevent emanations from telecommunications systems, computers and their networks, and cryptographic equipment. Cryptographic security is the proper use of cryptosystems. To ensure that military communications are secure, all four elements must be considered in the development and use of communications systems.

Rapid technological developments in both telecommunications and computers have increased the COMSEC challenge. The ability to transmit vast amounts of information and data through numerous communications systems means that opportunities for compromising integrity of both the system and its data have increased dramatically. To meet this concern, older systems have been replaced by better ones utilizing newer technologies. Examples include the Secure Telephone Units–III, which have replaced the Automatic Secure Voice Communications System; the Automatic Digital Network, which has been replaced by the Defense Message System; and the Secret Internet Protocol Router Network, which provides secure networking for computers. Improvements within these and other systems have raised the security of communications by reducing the possibility of intercepting or disrupting transmissions; these include meteor burst communications, packet switching, frequency hopping, multiple security levels, firewalls, encryption programs, and system and machine passwords.

One of the most important items in ensuring the security of American military communications is the use of the FORTEZZA card. The card was developed using specifications and requirements of the National Security Agency's Multi-level Information System Security Initiative. The credit card–size FORTEZZA card plugs into the user's PCMCIA (or PC card) reader. The card contains the capstone cryptographic engine, the user's private key that will provide cryptographic services—the encryption and decryption of messages. Each card is prepared for the individual user, and the user is required to authenticate before accessing the system. The card also contains the user's privileges and what precedence information he or she can access.

Communications security is essential to the military and is gaining additional importance in the civilian community. The explosion of communications and computer technology has had a significant impact on all organizations that handle sensitive information, such as financial, medical, and personnel data. The development of personal communications devices, laptops, personal digital assistants, and cell phones with text messaging capability means that large databases of sensitive information have become portable. The development of wireless communications for computers has increased the possibility that sensitive information will pass through a nonsecure system. As the equipment for personal communications continues to improve, the requirement to adhere to the basic rules of COMSEC will remain essential to successful military and civilian operations.

Tommy R. Young II

See also Automatic Digital Network (AUTODIN); Automatic Secure Voice Communications (AUTOSEVOCOM); Code Breaking; Computer; Computer Security (COMPUSEC); Defense Message System (DMS); Internet; Meteor Burst Communications (MBC); National Security Agency (NSA); Signals Intelligence (SIGINT)

Sources
Information Warfare website. "Security Awareness Toolbox." [Online information;

retrieved April 2007.] http://iwar.org.uk/comsec/resources/sa-tools/.

National Security Agency Central Security Service. "COMSEC Evaluation Programs." [Online information; retrieved April 2007.] http://www.nsa.gov/ia/industry/cep.cfm.

Computer

The effort to produce a machine capable of carrying out numerous complex calculations was a goal of researchers for hundreds of years. Initially the term "computer" was applied to human clerks who did calculations in an effective manner. By the early twentieth century, the term "computing machines" was applied to machines that did the calculations performed by the human computers. Eventually the term was shortened to computer.

Charles Babbage (1791–1871) proposed one of the earliest devices that offered the possibility of producing a computing machine. His "difference engine" was a digital computing machine intended to automatically produce mathematical tables and was constructed from mechanical components. Babbage never completed his full-scale engine, but he did complete a small model, which was used for mathematical calculations. Babbage also proposed a second machine, known as the "analytical engine," which was to have been a general-purpose mechanical digital computer. The analytical engine was to have a memory store and a central processing unit and would have been controlled by a program of instructions contained on punched cards. The work done by Babbage would spur others to continue to design and attempt to build a computing machine.

During World War I (1914–1918), mechanical analog machines were used for gunnery calculations. In 1931 Massachusetts Institute of Technology researcher Vannevar Bush (1890–1974) built the first large-scale automatic general purpose mechanical analog computer, called the "differential analyzer." Over the years, Bush replaced mechanical parts with electromechanical and then electronic devices. In 1935 British mathematician Alan Turing (1912–1954) advanced his theory for the modern computer. Known as the "universal machine," it would have limitless memory and a scanner that would move through the memory reading symbols and writing additional symbols. The scanner's activities were dictated by instructions stored in the machine's memory. Though he worked with electromechanical devices for code breaking during World War II, Turing would have to wait until after the war to build a stored program computing machine.

The war effort hastened programs to develop a functional electronic digital computer. The need to decipher German radio communications led to the development of the Colossus computer at Bletchley Park. The first of nearly a dozen of the large machines was installed on 8 December 1943. A faster version with greater capabilities was operational six months later. Colossus lacked two features of modern computers: internally stored programs and application to general purposes. As it was designed for a specific code-breaking task, the operator had to alter the machine's wiring when a new task was to be executed. Eight of the machines were destroyed at the end of the war to maintain their secrecy, while two were retained by the British code-breaking office for training, ceasing operation only in 1960. Existence of the Colossus was covered by the British Official Secrets Act, and it was not until the 1970s that any knowledge of the machines became public. Operational details were revealed only in the late 1990s.

In the United States, the U.S. Army Ordnance Department was overwhelmed by requests for the preparation of firing and bombing tables. The repetitive work was performed at the Ballistic Research Laboratory at Aberdeen Proving Ground, Maryland, by civilian "computers." At the beginning of the war, the workers used desk calculators and a differential analyzer to prepare the tables. By early 1942, it was apparent that the human computers could not keep up with the workload. A contract was made with the Moore School of Electrical Engineering of the University of Pennsylvania to use its differential analyzer. A number of talented scientists and engineers at the Moore School, such as physicist John W. Mauchly (1907–1980) and engineer J. Presper Eckert, Jr. (1919–1995), began work on an electronic numerical integrator and computer (ENIAC) under a contract with the Ordnance Department. The ENIAC's component assembly began in June 1944. The computer was dedicated on 15 February 1946 and accepted by the Ordnance Department in July. The room-size computer was dismantled in the winter of 1946–1947 and moved to Aberdeen where, by August 1947, it was again operational.

The ENIAC was a huge machine. It consisted of thirty separate floor units, plus power supply and a forced air cooling unit— it weighed more than 30 tons and occupied 1,800 square feet. It included some 19,000 vacuum tubes; 1,500 relays; and thousands of resistors, capacitors, and inductors. During its decade of active use, the ENIAC operated for 80,223 hours performing the computation of all ballistic tables for the Army and Air

Force. In addition to ballistic computations, the ENIAC performed weather predictions, atomic energy calculations, wind tunnel design, and other scientific calculations. Despite various efforts to modernize the ENIAC, operating costs were high and the workload was shifted to other machines. On 2 October 1955, power to the ENIAC was turned off.

Advances in mainframe computers came rapidly following the conclusion of World War II. In 1949, the first practical stored program computer, EDSAC, was developed at Cambridge University. The same year, Engineering Research Associates of Minneapolis built the ERA-101, the first commercially produced computer. The first customer for the ERA-101 was the U.S. Navy. In 1951, the first UNIVAC was built by Remington Rand and delivered to the U.S. Census Bureau. International Business Machines (IBM) shipped its first electronic computer, the 701 in 1953. The following year, the IBM 650, the first mass-produced computer to use magnetic data storage drums, was introduced.

The military was among the initial customers for these expensive mainframe computers. They were used for stand-alone operations and were for the most part designed for specific jobs, such as logistics management systems, personnel, and financial management. The Semi-Automatic Ground Environment system, implemented in 1958, which linked hundreds of radar stations in the United States and Canada, was the first large-scale communications network. The dedicated computer systems were usually located in large data processing or communications centers that were built specifically to house the computers and their associated peripherals, data entry terminals, tape drives, card readers, card punch machines, and various pieces of communications equipment.

For three decades, most computing by the military was done in the batch mode or from terminals directly connected to the large mainframe computers. With the introduction of the desktop personal computer in the early 1980s, military computing changed dramatically. The military began to develop dedicated networks to allow users to communicate information across the various services. The primary issue that slowed the growth of computer networks was the requirement to protect sensitive information. The development and application of computer security (COMPUSEC) measures allowed users of military systems to take advantage of the tremendous advances in computer and network technology in the 1980s and 1990s. Firewalls, passwords, and other measures were implemented to provide security for the information passing through and stored on the numerous military systems. One factor that increased the speed of the acquisition of the new technology was the directive issued by the secretary of defense in June 1994 requiring that the military purchase products and components from commercial sources. This new policy of buying commercial off-the-shelf devices meant that the products would not have to be built to military specifications.

The first Secret Internet Protocol Router Network (SIPRNet) backbone router went online on 3 March 1994. The SIPRNet is the largest Department of Defense command-and-control data network. Unclassified applications, as well as controlled access to the Internet, are handled by the nonsecure Internet Protocol Router Network. Programs and systems implemented to protect defense information have allowed the military to take full advantage of all the resources of the Information Age. The ability to utilize commercial communications technology combined with COMPUSEC has brought laptop computers, personal communications systems, personal digital assistants, satellite telephones, and transmission of streaming video to the battlefield. Computers have become central and essential to military communications.

A prediction in the March 1949 issue of *Popular Mechanics* sixty years ago makes clear just how far the revolution in information management has come: "Where a computer like the ENIAC is equipped with 18,000 vacuum tubes and weighs 30 tons, computers in the future may have only 1,000 vacuum tubes and weigh only 1½ tons."

Tommy R. Young II

See also Bletchley Park; Bush, Vannevar (1890–1974); Computer Security (COMPUSEC); Information Revolution in Military Affairs (IRMA); Semi-Automatic Ground Environment (SAGE); Signals Intelligence (SIGINT); Solid State Electronics; Turing, Alan Mathison (1912–1954); Vacuum Tube

Sources

Goldstine, Herman H. 1991. "Computers at the University of Pennsylvania's Moore School, 1943–1946." [Online article; retrieved April 2007.] http://ftp.arl.mil/~mike/comphist/91moore/index.html.

Hamilton, Andrew. 1949. "Brains That Click." *Popular Mechanics*, March: 162.

Kempf, Karl. 1961. "Electronic Computers Within the Ordnance Corps." [Online article; retrieved April 2007.] http://ftp.arl.mil/~mike/comphist/61ordnance/index.html.

Kopplin, John. 2002. "An Illustrated History of Computers: Part 1." [Online article; retrieved April 2007.] http://www.computersciencelab.com/computerhistory/history.htm.

Moye, William T. 1996. "ENIAC: The Army-Sponsored Revolution." [Online article; retrieved December 2006.] http://

ftp.arl.mil/~mike/comphist/96summary/
index.html.

Sale, Tony. 2006. "Lorenz Ciphers and the
Colossus." [Online article; retrieved
December 2006. http://www.codesand
ciphers.org.uk/lorenz/index.htm.

Weik, Martin H. 1961. "The ENIAC Story."
[Online article; retrieved April 2007.]
http://ftp.arl.mil/~mike/comphist/
eniac-story.html.

Williams, Michael. 1997. *A History of Computing
Technology.* 2nd ed. Los Alamitos, CA: IEEE
Computer Society Press.

Computer Security (COMPUSEC)

Computer security is the application of measures and controls that will ensure the confidentiality, integrity, and availability of the information processed and stored by a computer. The problems of maintaining security and integrity of military computer systems have grown dramatically with the rise of networks, personal computers, and the Internet. When automated data processing was done on large mainframe computers, the machines were located in secure data processing or communications facilities. The printed products and data tapes produced by the systems were treated according to the classification of the information. Data were communicated between the large data processing centers over secure communications lines that complied with communications security (COMSEC) standards. Taken together, COMPUSEC and COMSEC are the two subcomponents of information security.

The arrival of personal computers around 1980 raised new problems. Some of the issues about data security had been addressed when word processing equipment using magnetic disks to store information was introduced. The disks had to be removed from the machines and stored in accordance with the classification of the information stored on the disk, just as were the ribbons on typewriters that produced classified materials. In addition, the system had to be TEMPEST (a code name referring to investigations and studies of compromising emanations) tested to ensure that the word processor was not emanating electronic signals that could be monitored by those unauthorized to access the information.

Early word processing equipment could be confined to specific areas that could be controlled, as the equipment was not located on every desk. Two of the earliest solutions to the processing of classified information on personal computers (PCs) were the use of a removable hard drive or a dedicated machine. With the removable hard drive, programs and data were stored on the hard drive, which was removed and stored in a security container when the classified processing was completed. The classified drive would be replaced by an unclassified drive for routine data processing. In order to transfer classified data from one PC to another, specially marked floppy disks were used. The dedicated machine would only be used for classified processing and had to be secured from access by unauthorized users.

Once efforts to create local area networks began, the problems of protecting information stored and processed by PCs increased dramatically. Requirements to link PCs over wide area networks and the Internet presented even more challenges. One possible solution was simply not to connect the PCs to a network, but that defeated the rapid sharing of information. Closed networks were implemented in operations centers where access was controlled. These measures, combined with firewalls and individual and systems passwords, were implemented to protect the information contained on the systems. It very quickly became apparent that to take full advantage of the opportunities offered by the computing revolution, additional measures were required.

By the 1990s, the Department of Defense had created two networks and the National Security Agency had developed and trademarked a number of security products, the most important of which was the FORTEZZA card. The nonsecure Internet Protocol Router Network provides a seamless interoperability for unclassified applications and controlled access to the Internet. The Secret Internet Protocol Router Network (SIPRNet) is the Department of Defense's largest interoperable command-and-control data network. The SIPRNet supports the Global Command and Control System, the Defense Message System, and other classified systems. The FORTEZZA card is prepared for the individual user who must authenticate before accessing the system. The card also contains the user's privileges and what precedence messages that user can originate. With these measures in place, the military has been able to take full and safe advantage of new information technology. Security of the information is dependent on the user, however. If rules and procedures are not followed and equipment is used improperly, COMPUSEC measures are useless.

Tommy R. Young II

See also Communications Security (COMSEC); Computer; DARPANET; Defense Message System (DMS); Global Command and Control System (GCCS); Internet; National Security Agency (NSA)

Sources

Anderson, Ross J. 2001. *Security Engineering: A Guide to Building Dependable Distributed Systems.* New York: Wiley.

Schneier, Bruce. 2000. *Secrets & Lies: Digital Security in a Networked World.* New York: Wiley.

Stoll, Clifford. 1989. *Cuckoo's Egg: Tracking a Spy Through the Maze of Computer Espionage.* Garden City, NY: Doubleday.

Confederate Army Signal Corps

At the beginning of the American Civil War both North and South recognized that a tactical communications system could provide timely information across the ever-growing distances of the battlefield. But that capability required having dedicated soldiers to undertake these tasks and the resources to equip and supply such an arm. Though Union Army Major Albert J. Myer, the first signal officer in either army, had convinced the U.S. Congress of the need to invest in such a branch, it was the Confederate States that organized the first independent branch of signalmen in history.

The Confederates quickly embraced the new signal capability during the first great battle fought at Bull Run in July 1861. Former Myer protege Captain Edward Porter Alexander was charged with organizing a small signal element with four men hastily trained in the use of the wig-wag system. This investment of manpower paid off on 21 July 1861 when Alexander, while atop one of the signal towers, discovered Union columns attempting to turn the Confederate left flank. He used the wig-wag system to get a message to General P. G. T. Beauregard, and, for the first time in U.S. history, tactical information had been transmitted more rapidly than a courier could ride.

While Alexander was performing his duties another officer, Captain William Norris, had developed his own signal system employing flags and balls on poles based on his experience in naval operations. Another officer who had adopted the Myer system was Captain James F. Milligan, who operated along the James River. In order to provide standardization of the various signaling activities the Confederate government authorized the formation of a Signal Corps, which fell under the Adjutant and Inspector's General Department for staff control. On 19 April 1862 the Confederate States Signal Corps was formed as a distinct organization. However, unity was not entirely achieved as Milligan's unit continued to serve as an independent signal corps, which caused some friction throughout the war.

Since Alexander desired field command duties, Norris was selected to be the chief signal officer with the rank of major. The branch was initially authorized ten officers, ten sergeants, and any additional soldiers required to perform signal duties. Norris lobbied for more men and had the law amended on 27 September 1862 to one major, ten captains, twenty lieutenants, and twenty sergeants, with soldiers assigned as needed. In addition Special Order Number 40 directed every officer in the Adjutant General's Corps, all staff officers, and all aides-de-camp to be knowledgeable in the use of wig-wags and signals. The equipment they used was based on Myer's system and included the use of a cipher system to encode messages, though the Union was frequently able to break those codes.

The Confederate Army had a wide view regarding the duties of the Signal Corps. By the end of the war it was responsible for electrical telegraphy, military intelligence, espionage networks, naval communications for blockade runners, and experimentation with hot air balloons. Many of the activities of the branch are still shrouded in secrecy as many records were destroyed to shield clan-

destine activities, and a fire destroyed all of Norris's personal papers. Throughout the Civil War Confederate signalmen relayed critical intelligence and orders to leaders in all theaters of war. By the end of the Civil War, more than 1,500 men had served in the Confederate Army as signal soldiers.

Steven J. Rauch

See also Airships and Balloons; Alexander, Edward Porter (1835–1910); American Civil War (1861–1865); Bull Run, Battle of (1861); Myer, Albert James (1828–1880)

Sources
Alexander, E. Porter. 1989. *Fighting for the Confederacy*, edited by Gary W. Gallagher. Chapel Hill: University of North Carolina Press.

Gaddy, David Winfred. 1975. "William Norris and the Confederate Signal and Secret Service." *Maryland Historical Magazine* 70 (Summer): 167–188.

Raines, Rebecca Robbins. 1996. *Getting the Message Through: A Branch History of the US Army Signal Corps*. Washington, DC: U.S. Army Center of Military History.

Coston Signals

Utilized by the U.S. Navy during the American Civil War (1861–1865), Coston, or night, signals were a system of pyrotechnical signal flares (semaphore) for use in nighttime communication between ships and from ships to land. The Coston system of bright, long-lasting signal flares revolutionized naval communication and continued in use (especially by lifesaving services) for decades.

A former naval scientist, Benjamin Franklin Coston had died in 1848, leaving behind only a rough sketch in his diary of plans for pyrotechnic signaling flares. In need of funds to support her two surviving children, and with considerable effort, his twenty-one-year-old widow, Martha J. Coston (1829–1904), developed the idea into an elaborate system of night signal flares allowing ships to communicate after dark. She received a patent (in her husband's name) in 1859.

Coston's challenge had been to develop a flame that would burn long enough and used a coded combination of colors. She worked for a decade with chemists before finally achieving her first patent for the "pyrotechnic night signal" system. Her system was based on the use of both colors and patterns. Three cartridges of different colors (white, red, and green—an attempt to use a patriotic blue color had failed) were flashed or burned in combinations representing the numbers zero through nine and letters A through P, for a total of twenty-seven possible combinations. "P" indicated a message was coming while "A" was a "yes" response that the receiver was ready, or had received the message sent. Other words were sent by standard code of different number combinations. The flare was produced by burning a specific chemical composition for each desired color. A handle was used to hold the color cartridge to be burned.

In 1859 a panel of three Navy officers carefully tested the Coston system and recommended its adoption to the secretary of the Navy. Hundreds of sets of the flares were sold to the Navy, and in 1861, Coston sold her U.S. patent rights for the equipment and the related code to the Navy for $20,000 under the provisions of an act of Congress. Coston signals were widely used by the naval squadrons blockading the Confederacy and seeking to capture or sink Southern vessels attempting to run the blockade. Some operations developed their own special codes for terms used in stopping blockade runners. Coston signals were one means of coordinating the ships involved in the reduction of Fort Fisher (North Carolina) early in 1865.

Coston established the Coston Supply Company in 1859 to manufacture the night signals, manufacturing more than 100,000 during the Civil War years alone. The Coston system was patented abroad and adopted by numerous governments including those of France, Italy, Denmark, the Netherlands, and Brazil. Coston patented improvements in the system in 1871 (this time in her own name), and secured patents in European countries as well. Her two surviving sons were brought into the business and inherited the company from her. The U.S. Coast Guard and the Lifesaving Service made use of Coston signals well into the twentieth century. The Coston company remained in business at least into the 1980s.

Christopher H. Sterling

See also American Civil War (1861–1865); Code, Codebook; Lights and Beacons; Night Signals; Semaphore (Mechanical Telegraphs)

Sources
Coston, Martha J. 1886. *Signal Success: The Work and Travels of Mrs. Martha J. Coston.* Philadelphia: J. B. Lippincott.
Coston, Martha J. "Night Signals (Coston Flares)." [Online article; retrieved November 2004.] http://scard.buffnet.net/pages/signal/signalpages/flare/coston.html.
Pilato, Denise E. 2002. "Martha Coston: A Woman, a War, and a Signal to the World." [Online article; retrieved November 2004.] http://www.ijnhonline.org/volume1_number1_Apr02/pdf_april02/pdf_pilato.pdf.
U.S. Army Signal Corps. 1910. *Visual Signaling.* Washington, DC: War Department, Office of the Chief Signal Officer.

Couriers

The use of couriers to send military messages includes the use of runners, messengers, dispatch carriers (or riders), and relays, whether on foot or traveling by other means. This is one of the world's oldest means of communication, limited in speed only by the pace of a human runner or his mode of transport. Use of couriers depends most on people and least on technology.

Pheidippides, who died of exhaustion after running 26 miles from Marathon to Athens in 490 BCE, is the earliest known runner carrying military information (in this case of a victory of Athens over a Persian force). For centuries, messages were verbally received and delivered. Only much later were messages carried in more permanent form. The relay was an organized system of multiple couriers/runners allowing the carrying of messages over greater distances. British kings developed a regular courier/messenger service by the late twelfth century and much of its role concerned the constant military campaigns afflicting the country.

Couriers began to use horses at some time in antiquity. As other modes of transport (e.g., ships powered by oars, sails, and eventually steam) became available, couriers could travel ever faster and much farther. Military roads and the later military railway were critically important to couriers. The British army introduced courier use of the military bicycle in 1881; the French did likewise in 1896. French examination boards required a courier to be able to ride 40 miles through hilly country in no more than six hours—and the ability to repair the bicycle. U.S. Army units were also equipped with bicycle couriers by at least the 1890s. Such couriers were usually armed. Adolf Hitler served for a time as a courier for his Bavarian regiment on the Western Front early in World War I.

As motorized and then air transport became available, couriers could travel still faster and farther—and sometimes with greater safety. Traveling out of uniform and with many others, they often melted into the background, making capture less likely. The use of multiple couriers using different routes also helped them elude capture. Yet conditions on battlefields (including crowded roadways) have always required human couriers on foot, including numerous instances in both world wars. Military use of couriers has always suffered a crucial potential drawback—capture of the courier by enemy forces, which at least would prevent a message getting through and at worst would give away the content of the message carried.

U.S. military courier corps have been reorganized many times. The Defense Postal Express Service became the Army Security Service, and in 1946 the Security Courier Service. After 1953 the Department of Defense operated the Armed Forces Courier Service, which in 1987 became simply the Defense Courier Service (DCS) under the direction of the Army's chief of staff. DCS headquarters and training are based at Fort Meade, Maryland. DCS has about 300 personnel to serve some 6,500 users through thirty-six stations around the world. They make use of both military and civilian modes of transport. The British Forces Post Office provides a parallel function for the British army.

Christopher H. Sterling

See also Fort Meade, Maryland; Horses and Mules; Military Roads; Mobile Communications; Native American Signaling; Postal Services

Sources

Department of Defense. "Defense Courier Service (DCS)." [Online directive; retrieved October 2004.] http://www.fas.org/irp/doddir/dod/d5200_33.htm.

Harfield, Alan. 1989. *Pigeon to Packhorse: The Illustrated Story of Animals in Army Communication.* Chippenham, UK: Picton Publishing.

Hill, Mary C. 1961. *The King's Messengers 1199–1377: A Contribution to the History of the Royal Household.* London: Edward Arnold.

Wheeler-Holohan, V. 1934. *The History of the King's Messengers.* New York: Dutton.

Woods, David L. 1965. "Messengers: Men, Horses and Dogs." In *A History of Tactical Communication Techniques*, chap IV. Orlando, FL: Martin-Marietta (reprinted by Arno Press, 1974).

Cuban Missile Crisis (1962)

The tense military and political face-off between the United States and the Soviet Union in October 1962 was probably the most dangerous moment in the long Cold War. Signals and other intelligence played a central part on both sides of the conflict.

When Fidel Castro took power in Cuba in 1959, he was hailed as a liberator by the Cuban people and became a hero to many Americans as well. Castro soon publicly aligned his country with the Soviet Union. In Havana, one of the consequences of this change was the fear that the United States might intervene against the new Cuban government. That concern was strengthened in April 1961, when Cuban exiles, trained by America's Central Intelligence Agency (CIA), staged a botched invasion at Cuba's Bay of Pigs.

Agreements with the Soviet Union were followed by a secret Soviet arms buildup in Cuba in the summer of 1962. The first indications of that buildup came from signals intelligence (SIGINT) when American intercept operators began to hear Spanish along with the usual mix of Slavic coming from airfields in Czechoslovakia, where Cuban pilots were being trained. In response, U.S. intelligence began a closer focus on Cuban information, including U-2 aircraft overflights and radio intercepts. It soon became apparent that the Soviet Union was building nine intermediate range ballistic missile (IRBM) launch facilities in western Cuba for missiles that could carry nuclear warheads. The sites were about a hundred miles from Florida, and the missiles' potential range (over 2,000 miles) would take in much of the eastern United States. The National Security Agency deployed a considerable capability around Cuba, including SIGINT from ground-based stations and aircraft circling the periphery of the island, just outside Cuban territorial waters. The USS *Oxford*, a specially configured SIGINT collection ship, sailed close to the Cuban coastline intercepting radio communications.

On 16 October the CIA produced for President John F. Kennedy hundreds of detailed aerial photographs clearly identifying IRBM sites and anti-aircraft missile support facilities (despite attempts to camouflage them), all nearing completion. Regular aerial photography showed four sites were operational just days later. After a week of intense analysis and policy debate (including bombing or invasion options), Kennedy went public on 22 October with a nationally televised address and announced the placing of a naval quarantine (essentially a blockade) in a ring 500 miles from Cuba to prevent Soviet ships from carrying further missile equipment to the island. U.S. Navy surface and submarine units moved into place to attack any ship crossing the declared line. A week of intensive face-off and direct communica-

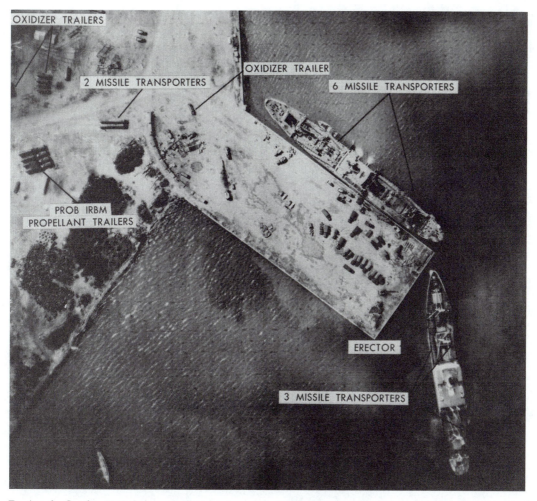

During the October 1962 Cuban missile crisis, many modes of communication informed American political and military actions. Photographs from U-2 and other reconnaissance aircraft (here a view of Mariel Bay, Cuba) provided clear evidence of Soviet missile equipment and arriving transport ships. (Library of Congress)

tions between President Kennedy and Soviet leader Nikita Khrushchev followed. On 28 October, the Soviets turned their ships back, a fact first learned from SIGINT from radio messages, and soon dismantled and withdrew the missiles.

The crisis did not immediately end with the Soviet decision to remove its missiles. For three more weeks, tensions between the United States, Cuba, and the Soviet Union ran high over several unresolved issues. Negotiations held in November 1962 finally resolved verification of the missile withdrawal, the U.S. noninvasion "guarantee," and the question of Soviet jet bombers and troops remaining on the island. The quarantine ended on 20 November.

One later result of the face-off was installation of the soon-famous "hotline" between Moscow and Washington to allow rapid crisis resolution. With the end of the Cold War, some information on both Soviet and Cuban intelligence gathering has also become available. The crisis has become one of the most studied events of the Cold War era.

Christopher H. Sterling

See also Airplanes; Deception; Hotline/Direct Communications Link (DCL); Intelligence Ships; National Security Agency (NSA); Signals Intelligence (SIGINT)

Sources

Cuban Missile Crisis (various documents). http://www.mtholyoke.edu/acad/intrel/cuba.htm.

Federation of American Scientists. "Cuban Missile Crisis." [Online photographs; retrieved July 2005.] http://www.fas.org/irp/imint/cuba.htm.

Johnson, Thomas R., and David A. Hatch. 1998. "NSA and the Cuban Missile Crisis." [Online article; retrieved July 2005.] http://www.nsa.gov/cuba/.

Leighton, Richard M. 1978. *The Cuban Missile Crisis of 1962: A Case in National Security Crisis Management.* Washington, DC: National Defense University.

National Security Archive. "The Cuban Missile Crisis, 1962." [Online information; retrieved July 2005.] http://www.gwu.edu/~nsarchiv/nsa/publications/cmc/cmc.html.

Welch, David A., and James G. Blight, eds. 1998. *Intelligence and the Cuban Missile Crisis.* London: Routledge.

DARPANET

DARPANET, developed under the supervision of the Defense Advanced Research Projects Agency (DARPA), is a predecessor of the modern Internet. Initially connecting the Stanford Research Institute and the University of California, Los Angeles in 1967, DARPANET was retired in 1989 after being supplanted by NSFNET, which was the immediate predecessor to the Internet.

DARPANET's theoretical foundations can be traced to the work of three individuals working independently toward different ends but relying on the concept of packet switching. Paul Baran, a RAND researcher, sought to build a communications network that was resilient to a nuclear attack. Donald Watts Davies, a researcher at the British National Physical Laboratory, was seeking to create a new type of communications network that took advantage of the advances in digital technology. Robert Taylor, the director of the Information Processing Techniques Office (IPTO) at DARPA from 1966 through 1970, was looking for a way to allow the steadily growing number of computer systems that DARPA managed to communicate with each other. These differing problems were solved with very similar solutions and the result was the basic computer network architecture of DARPANET. Packet switching allowed computers to break down unique large data fields into small uniform pieces or packets that could be reassembled by a receiving computer.

Packet switching networks offered computer users two key new features, of which the first was decentralization. Unlike telephone or postal networks, message routing was not handled at central nodes, but was kept at the edge of the network using dynamic routing tables. This design feature ensured that the collapse of any individual node would not compromise the integrity of the network. The dynamic nature of the tables would allow the network to adjust to problems in other parts of the network and reroute messages. Furthermore, lost or missing packets would be re-sent if an acknowledgment of receipt was not received. Thus, DARPANET was highly resilient to disruption.

The second key feature of the network was its use of computer protocols. These enabled computers of differing specifications and employing different operating systems to interconnect and communicate with one another. Telnet allowed computers to communicate over telephone lines, while file transfer protocol allowed computers to interact by exchanging data.

These features met the needs of the defense research community and the defense establishment because they made the network simultaneously highly resilient and easy to integrate. By the mid-1970s, the U.S. Department of Defense was increasingly interested in the military potential of DARPANET as a communications medium. In 1975 the Defense Communications Agency took over management of DARPANET from IPTO with disruptive results. No longer a network of largely academic users managed by academics, DARPANET's new management began rigorously enforcing security rules and limiting the exchange of information among users. This shift spurred the development of the civilian NSFNET, which would, in turn, become the Internet. DARPANET continued to operate until 1989 serving as one of many computer networks operated by DARPA.

John Laprise

See also Computer; Defense Advanced Research Projects Agency (DARPA); Defense Communications Agency (DCA, 1960–1991); Internet; Semi-Automatic Ground Environment (SAGE)

Sources

Abbate, Janet. 2000. *Inventing the Internet.* Cambridge, MA: MIT Press.
Ceruzzi, Paul E. 2003. *A History of Modern Computing.* Cambridge, MA: MIT Press.
Hafner, Katie, and Matthew Lyon. 1998. *Where Wizards Stay Up Late: The Origins of the Internet.* New York: Simon & Schuster.

de Forest, Lee (1873–1961)

Radio engineer and inventor Lee de Forest developed the three-element vacuum tube that made continuous wave transmissions possible, and he widely promoted early radio. His wireless career often intersected with military and naval communication needs, but he had limited success in serving those needs.

Lee de Forest was born 26 August 1873 in Council Bluffs, Iowa, growing up there and (after 1879) in Talladega, Alabama. He earned a bachelor of science degree from Yale University's Sheffield Scientific School in 1896 and a doctor of philosophy degree in physics in 1899. His was one of the first American dissertations based on Hertzian waves—an experimental form of what became wireless. He was involved with many different companies and stock schemes in the early twentieth century as he actively promoted wireless while seeking funds to continue his developmental wireless work.

In 1902 the U.S. Signal Corps compared de Forest, Fessenden, and Marconi equipment, and decided to order de Forest's. Based on this decision, the U.S. Navy extensively tested and compared European and American wireless equipment, including that of de Forest, finally deciding to buy German Slaby-Arco devices. A year later, the Army installed de Forest apparatus as part of its Alaskan telegraph service. In 1907 the Navy purchased twenty-six sets of de Forest equipment to furnish its "Great White Fleet" of battleships, about to undertake a world voyage. But the equipment was hastily manufactured, was not well understood, and did not operate properly, and was thus taken out save for the installation aboard U.S.S *Ohio*, which continued experimentation. The Signal Corps purchased de Forest radiotele-

Inventor of the three-element vacuum tube (1906) which revolutionized radio communications, Lee de Forest eventually held more than 200 patents. He was a prolific inventor and business promoter, though not always successful. (Library of Congress)

phones for use in artillery spotting at Fort Monroe, Virginia.

De Forest sought to develop an improved means of detecting wireless signals, which led in 1906 to his discovery of what he called the "audion," or three-element vacuum tube—by far his most important contribution. Later development of vacuum tubes and long-distance telephony (in 1913 AT&T bought partial rights to use the audion) were based on his device. But development was slow due both to lack of funds and his poor understanding of what the improved tube could accomplish. The Navy purchased ten de Forest vacuum tube amplifiers for testing in 1913. During World War I, de Forest developed vacuum tube radiotelephone (voice)

equipment for the Navy, which became the first installed in an airplane in 1916. These sets were later transferred to the Army Signal Corps for Army Air Corps use.

De Forest worked on motion picture sound systems and tinkered with television in the 1930s, publishing a book on the latter in 1941. During World War II, de Forest received patents on various aviation, radar, and bomb projects, but lacking corporate support, few were developed. But while he endlessly promoted himself as the "father" of radio, he contributed little more to that field. De Forest fought more than 120 patent battles with other inventors, one with Edwin Armstrong dragging on until 1934, including two Supreme Court decisions in his favor. He held 216 patents at his death. De Forest operated a small radio and film laboratory in California in his final decades and died in Hollywood on 30 June 1961.

Christopher H. Sterling

See also Alaska Communications System; Armstrong, Edwin Howard (1890–1954); Fessenden, Reginald A. (1866–1932); *Ohio, USS*; Radio

Sources
Carneal, Georgette. 1930. *Conqueror of Space: The Life of Lee De Forest.* New York: Horace Liveright.
de Forest, Lee. 1950. *Father of Radio: The Autobiography of Lee De Forest.* Chicago: Wilcox & Follett.
Hijiya, James A. 1992. *Lee De Forest and the Fatherhood of Radio.* Bethlehem, PA: Lehigh University Press.
Lewis, Tom. 1991. *Empire of the Air: The Men Who Made Radio.* New York: HarperCollins.

Deception

Modes of communication can be used to deceive an enemy, as has been often demonstrated. Deception can be accomplished with false messages (to suggest false military plans, for example), no messages at all (as with radio silence), or partially misleading messages. Related terms are "disinformation" and "information warfare."

Several of the most pertinent examples occurred during World War II. Operation Mincemeat was the stuff on which adventure fiction is built, creating a "man who never was." To mislead the Italians and Germans into thinking the Allies intended to invade the island of Sardinia (rather than the real target of Sicily), the British concocted an elaborate plan involving a dead man, using the submarine *Seraph* to deliver the body off the coast of Spain. The corpse carried a variety of documents identifying him as Major William Martin of the Royal Marines with other papers suggesting detailed Allied plans for an impending invasion of Sardinia. The "drop" of the body took place on 30 April 1943. The British knew that after the body washed ashore (seemingly from a plane crash), officials in Francisco Franco's Spain would turn over the documents to the Germans. Analysis of Enigma machine radio traffic confirmed the delivery of the false materials. (Only decades later was it revealed that the body used was that of a thirty-four-year-old Welsh alcoholic suicide.)

In Operation Fortitude, General George S. Patton was established as commander of the First U.S. Army Group (FUSAG), a fictitious army that was seemingly based in southeast England, giving the impression that the Allies were going to invade France via the Pas de Calais (at the narrowest part of the English Channel) sometime in early 1944. The deception was made stronger by the fact that it seemed to support the already-existing German strategic thinking that Calais was the obvious landing point for the Allied invasion. The imaginary FUSAG included radio operators who steadily broadcast "orders" to troops that did not exist, this for the benefit of German radio intercept stations (Allied abilities to read German Enigma machine-based radio traffic confirmed the success of the deception). Small numbers of soldiers wandered through London wearing shoulder patches of nonexistent units for the benefit of possible German spies. The deceptionists also sought to mislead German intelligence with visual displays of mock equipment, fake port facilities and military installations, gossip in neutral embassies, deliberate leakage of seemingly confidential information, and double agents. The Germans fell for the bait and retained forces in the Calais region, thus easing the eventual June Allied landings in Normandy (well south and west of Calais). To the Allies' surprise, the deception (which included another imaginary army in Scotland intending to invade Norway) lasted longer than six weeks after the real landings, misleading German planners for some months.

In 1943 Britain began to use turned enemy agents against Germany (Britain's ability to decode German radio traffic helped to identify the agents). Within the British security organization MI-5, the Twenty Committee (XX) directed by Oxford don John Masterman, created the "double cross" (XX again) system of using turned double agents. The Twenty Committee decided what information could be safely conveyed to the Germans by the double agents. The goal was to build up the double agents' credibility by feeding the Germans plausible falsehoods as well as accurate information they either had or would obtain anyway, while giving away nothing vital. The committee ran "the man who never was" ploy in 1943. The double agents (of whom the most famous was Juan Pujol, known as "Garbo") communicated with their Abwehr (German Intelligence) controllers by radio telegraphy, courier, mail, or personal contact. The double-cross system contributed to the seeming validity of Operation Fortitude as well.

Deception continued in use during the Korean and Vietnam wars, as well as in various Middle East wars from the 1950s to the 1970s. In the early 2000s, the Department of Defense engaged in bitter, high-level debate over how far it could or should go in managing or manipulating information to influence opinion abroad. Defense Secretary Donald Rumsfeld, under intense criticism, closed the Pentagon's Office of Strategic Influence in 2002, a short-lived operation to provide news items, possibly including false ones, to foreign journalists in an effort to influence overseas opinion. Before the 2003 Iraq War, the military's electronic warfare arsenal was used to single out certain members of Saddam Hussein's inner circle with e-mail messages and cell phone calls in an effort to persuade them to the American cause. Deceptive communications have also been employed in the ongoing war on terrorism.

Christopher H. Sterling

See also Electronic Countermeasures/ Electronic Warfare (ECM/EW); Propaganda and Psychological Warfare; Radio Silence; Signals Intelligence (SIGINT); Ultra; War on Terrorism

Sources

Glantz, David M. 1989. *Soviet Military Deception in the Second World War*. London: Frank Cass.

Hatfield, Thomas. 1997. "The Crucial Deception." [Online article; retrieved September 2005.] http://www.utexas.edu/ opa/pubs/discovery/disc1997v14n2/ disc-deception.html.

Hesketh, Roger. 2000. *Fortitude: The D-Day Deception Campaign*. Woodstock, NY: Overlook Press.

Howard, Michael. 1990. *British Intelligence in the Second World War: Volume 5, Strategic Deception*. London: Her Majesty's Stationery Office.

Masterman, John C. 1972. *The Double-Cross System in the War of 1939–45*. New Haven, CT: Yale University Press.

Montagu, Ewan. 1953. *The Man Who Never Was*. Philadelphia: Lippincott.

Pujol, Juan, with Nigel West. 1985. *Garbo: The Personal Story of the Most Successful Agent of World War II*. New York: Random House.

Shanker, Thom, and Eric Schmidt. 2004. "Pentagon Weighs Use of Deception in a Broad Arena," *Seattle Post-Intelligencer* (13 December).

Defence Communications Service Agency (DCSA)

Formed in April 1998 and with an annual budget of about £1.2 billion, the British Defence Communications Service Agency (DCSA) is responsible for information and communication services across the Ministry of Defence (MOD). These range from fixed and mobile telephones to satellite communication links and from computers and associated networks/infrastructures to airfield support. The 5,000-person agency is a mix of military and civilian staff, based throughout Britain and around the world. DCSA's mission is to shift away from technology-centric planning to a focus on services, regardless of the technologies used.

DCSA operates with six directorates (Technology, Information Services Delivery, Operations, Procurement, Resources, and Strategic Transition) and sixteen integrated project teams. The latter deal with such matters as Air Defence Ground Based Systems, Airfield Operations Support, Defence Corporate Business Applications, Defence Fixed Networks, Defence Information Infrastructure, and tactical and logistic operations, both terrestrial and satellite based. DCSA is the liaison with British Telecommunications for operation of the Defence Fixed Telecommunications System.

DCSA is working to better understand interoperability requirements as a service provider. This encompasses each of the three British military services as well as international operations in both peacekeeping and wartime missions (as in Iraq). With most military operations combining elements of all services, the army, navy, and air force provide their own personnel and platforms. The trade-off between system capability and security is constantly in play.

Early in 2000, DCSA became a part (about 10 percent in terms of personnel) of the Defence Logistics Organisation. At that time, DCSA added several functions such as the Directorate of Communications and Information Systems for Fleet Support and the Royal Air Force Signals and Engineering Establishment. DCSA also assumed responsibility for the corporate office technology system, which links 30,000 people at MOD headquarters locations.

The DCSA is located at RAF Brampton. Maintenance and repair of ground radio and radar equipment is carried out by the Ground Radio Servicing Centre based at RAF Sealand. This includes radars, radio navigation aids, and point-to-point and ground-to-air communications. DCSA provides support to technician training facilities located at RAF Cosford and RAF Sealand. The agency provides an antenna systems maintenance service on a worldwide basis, embracing the fields of communications, radar, and navigation aids. The personnel required for this highly specialized work are trained at the Aerial Erector School at RAF Digby.

Christopher H. Sterling

See also Defence Fixed Telecommunications System (DFTS); United Kingdom: Royal Air Force

Sources

Defence Communications Service Agency. 2005. *Annual Report and Accounts.* London: The Stationery Office.

Defence Communications Service Agency website: *http://www.mod.uk/dcsa/* (accessed December 2005).

Defence Fixed Telecommunications System (DFTS)

The Defence Fixed Telecommunications System (DFTS) was developed in the mid-1990s to integrate and digitize British army, Royal Navy, and Royal Air Force communication links. Supplied by British Telecommunications (BT), the system was designed to serve through the early part of the twenty-first century.

Signed on 25 July 1996 after a competitive bidding process, the contract from the Ministry of Defence (MOD) with BT (which already operated most MOD fixed systems) signed over military communication links within the United Kingdom for private ownership and operation for the first time. The contract provided for "turnkey" service for (and maintenance and updating of) communications rather than the traditional purchase of equipment. Rationalization and elimination of overlapping and aging technologies were projected to save the government £100 million over the decade-long life of the contract. All told, forty-six different networks operated by the three services and MOD were taken over and integrated. The new system is operated, as of April 1998, by the Defence Communications Service

MILITARY COMMUNICATIONS
Defense Advanced Research Projects Agency

Agency. The DFTS is based in Basil Hill Barracks in Corsham, Wiltshire.

After a period of transition and migration (from 1997 to 2000), DFTS began to supply and manage two data services (one packet switched, the other a local area network interconnect service), circuit-switched telephone links, a point-to-point voice and data service, e-mail and Internet access, and videoconferencing. A new numbering system allowed for more rapid internal MOD and service dialing. Various levels of security are available for all services, and each is upgraded as needed.

By 2005, DFTS was serving some 200,000 users making 2.5 million daily calls among nearly 2,500 sites across Britain. On 1 April 2005, the original decade-long contract with BT was extended for five more years, to July 2012, for a total contract value of about £3 billion over fifteen years.

Christopher H. Sterling

See also Defence Communications Service Agency (DCSA); United Kingdom: Royal Corps of Signals

Sources

Bridge, Maureen, and John Pegg. 2001. "Defence Fixed Telecommunications System." In *Call to Arms: A History of Military Communications from the Crimean War to the Present Day*, 169–182. Tavistock, UK: Focus.
Comptroller and Auditor General. 2000. *The Private Finance Initiative: The Contract for the Defence Fixed Telecommunications Network*. London: The Stationery Office.

Defense Advanced Research Projects Agency (DARPA)

The Defense Advanced Research Projects Agency (DARPA) is part of the U.S. Department of Defense. It was established in 1958 in response to the Soviet launching of its Sputnik satellite the year before, to prevent adversaries from technologically surprising the United States. Over time its mission broadened to secure future American technological superiority by directing long-term research and development for military application. DARPA is the "technological engine" for development of new weapons and communication systems. Its original name—Advanced Research Projects Agency—was changed in 1972 to Defense Advanced Research Projects Agency (in 1993 it was renamed ARPA, only to be changed back three years later).

DARPA's projects usually run from three to five years. Program managers work for up to six years so new people can bring fresh ideas, making the agency more responsive to changing security challenges, scientific developments, and technological opportunities. Changing personnel and the lack of dedicated laboratories or facilities (DARPA invests 98 percent of its funds with universities and industry) limit personal or institutional interests that might undermine the agency's purpose. Structurally, DARPA is divided into (as of 2006) these technical offices: Defense Science Office, Microsystems Technology Office, Information Processing Technology Office, Tactical Technology Office, and Strategic Technology Office.

The agency's priorities have changed over time. Set up in the shadow of Sputnik, it was initially concerned with space; in the 1960s and 1970s that focus shifted to intercontinental ballistic missile technology. Since then conventional technologies have developed as part of the American information-driven revolution in military affairs. Major DARPA accomplishments include stealth technology (Have Blue program), unmanned aerial vehicles (Teal Rain program), the Internet

(ARPANet), space-based communication and surveillance (such as global positioning systems [GPS]), and advanced air surveillance (e.g., the E-8C Joint Surveillance Target Attack Radar System, or Joint STARS).

The eight major concerns in DARPA's early twenty-first century agenda are (1) detection, precision identification, tracking, and destruction of elusive surface targets; (2) robust, secure, self-forming tactical networks; (3) networked manned and unmanned systems; (4) urban area operations; (5) detection, characterization, and assessment of underground structures; (6) assured use of space; (7) cognitive computing; and (8) the bio-revolution. Developments in military communication techniques are vitally important as access to accurate information has become a condition sine qua non of a successful military engagement.

New DARPA research programs not only focus on "traditional" communication (between units and command centers) but also develop new warfare requirements. Central to its concerns is military communication among weapons, platforms, and networks for the twenty-first century Army. Connecting sensors, data processing computer centers, and weapons through numerous communication links enables the development of more precision weapons. Traditional interpersonal communication is slowly giving way to communication between humans and weapons and among weapons systems themselves. DARPA projects design new software tools to merge a variety of data gathered by the "army of sensors" and translate it into battlefield knowledge.

The modern American way of war is network-centric. This requires development of new methods, channels, and techniques for communication between small (modular) units of various services. Conducting such operations depends on networks that quickly and effectively distribute huge amounts of data. The basic challenge is how best to build the strong communication networks required for network-centric warfare. At the same time antijamming defensive means are developed to make communication secure. One challenge that DARPA deals with is providing each human and machine with a common clock time. GPS, which provides one means now, cannot be relied on because enemy jamming could disable the entire network. Thus DARPA has developed a chip-scale atomic clock to overcome this vulnerability. New tools for protecting the network against computer worms are another example of ongoing activities. The neXt Generation (XG) Communications program is aimed at enhancing spectrum availability for the U.S. military by a factor of ten to twenty by dynamically allocating spectrum across frequency, time, and space. The Networking in Extreme Environments program creates ultra wideband wireless networks for effective military communications. Another major area of DARPA's focus is building defensive means for protecting satellite systems and other military communication space-based devices.

Łukasz Kamieński

See also Communication Satellites; Communications Security (COMSEC); Computer; DARPANET; Global Positioning System (GPS); Information Revolution in Military Affairs (IRMA); Jamming; Spectrum Frequencies; Spectrum Management

Sources

Defense Advanced Research Projects Agency. 2005. *Bridging the Gap: DARPA Powered by Ideas*. Washington, DC: Defense Advanced Research Projects Agency.

Defense Advanced Research Projects Agency. "Welcome." [Online information; retrieved November 2006.] http://www.darpa.mil.

Van Atta, Richard H., et al. 2003. *Transformation and Transition: DARPA's Role in Fostering an Emerging Revolution in Military Affairs.* Alexandria, VA: Institute for Defense Analyses.

Defense Communications Agency (DCA, 1960–1991)

The Defense Communications Agency (DCA) was established at the end of the Eisenhower administration and operated for three decades. It was formed on 12 May 1960 by Secretary of Defense Thomas Gates. The mission of its 450 employees was to manage the Defense Communications System (DCS), itself a consolidation of the independent long-haul communications functions of the Army, Navy, and Air Force. Later in the decade, DCA moved its headquarters to Arlington Hall, west of Washington DC, in the Virginia suburbs.

Over the next three decades, DCA took over a variety of related functions and periodically reorganized. The Air Force Office of Commercial Communications Management (now the Defense Information Technology Contracting Organization), White House Signal Agency (now the White House Communications Agency), and Department of Defense (DoD) Damage Assessment Center (now the Joint Staff Support Center) all became a part of DCA. DCA also established six regional communications control centers and two area centers for operational control of DCS. In the 1970s, DCA took control of the Minimum Essential Emergency Communications Network and the Military Satellite Communications Systems Office. It also became responsible for engineering and operating the World Wide Military Command and Control System. Early in the decade, it also began conversion of analog DCS systems to digital technology.

In the 1980s, DCA absorbed the Joint Tactical Command, Control, and Communications Agency, improving its ability to manage and enhance the interoperability of command, control, and communications systems. The Joint Interoperability Test Command was formed within DCA to provide interoperability compliance testing and certification.

On 25 June 1991, DCA was renamed the Defense Information Systems Agency to better reflect its role in providing total information systems management for DoD.

Christopher H. Sterling

See also Arlington Hall; Defense Communications System (DCS); Defense Information Systems Agency (DISA); White House Communications Agency (WHCA)

Source
Defense Information Systems Agency. "History of DISA." [Online information; retrieved April 2005.] http://www.disa.mil/main/about/history.html.

Defense Communications Board/ Board of War Communications (1940–1947)

The Defense Communications Board, which changed its name in mid-1942 to the Board of War Communications, was created as a means of providing overall national policy for wartime applications of the domestic telecommunications infrastructure. The board helped to create priorities for use of wired and wireless networks.

The Defense Communications Board was established by President Franklin Roosevelt with Executive Order 8046 on 24 September 1940. Its stated function was to plan for the wartime use and control of American radio, telephone, telegraph, and cable communications. During World War II, the board controlled (through the Office for Emergency Management and thence to the president) the use of radio and wire communications, directed the closing of some transmitters and other facilities, and established national defense communication priorities. In two further executive orders, the board was given the president's wartime authority to "direct that communications essential to the national defense and security shall have preference or priority." In its first year or so it provided contingency plans for wartime loss of communication links and civil defense. The board recommended (and the Federal Communications Commission [FCC] established in 1941) the Foreign Broadcast Monitoring Service, which continues to this day as the Foreign Broadcast Information Service.

The board was headed by the chairman of the FCC (James Lawrence Fly until 1944, then Paul Porter) and included the chief signal officer of the Army, director of Naval Communications, assistant secretary of state in charge of the Office of Transportation and Communications, assistant secretary of the treasury in charge of Treasury Enforcement Activities, and chief of Communications (Coast Guard) as members. The board operated out of FCC offices, which provided administrative support.

With the entry of the United States into World War II, the board was renamed the Board of War Communications on 15 June 1942 (Executive Order 9183). During the next three years it was concerned with such matters as the speed of the domestic telegraph service (then used extensively by the War and Navy departments), closed or monitored a number of international radio telegraph circuits, and established priorities for

long-distance telephone service. It was finally abolished by President Harry Truman in Executive Order 9831 on 24 February 1947.

Christopher H. Sterling

See also World War II

Sources

Federal Communications Commission. 1941–1945. "Defense Communications Board / Board of War Communications." In *Annual Report*. Washington, DC: Government Printing Office.

National Archives and Record Service. "Records of the Board of War Communications." [Online information; retrieved April 2006.] http://www.archives.gov/research/guide-fed-records/groups/259.html.

Paschal, Leo, and Robert E. Webb, comps. 1965. "Preliminary Inventory of the Records of the Board of War Communications." NC 133. Washington, DC: National Archives.

Defense Communications System (DCS)

The Defense Communications System (DCS) combines several U.S. Department of Defense communications systems and networks, including government and commercially operated facilities. Together, these provide long-haul, point-to-point, and switched-network telecommunications.

The Defense Switched Network (DSN) is the principal switched voice communications DCS network. It consists of a worldwide network made up of many different commercial leased and government-owned facilities. The Defense Information Systems Network integrates the Defense Data Network packet-switching networks to provide worldwide packet-switched data communications through four physically separate networks, including the Military Network, which is unclassified, and three additional DSNs of increasing levels of classification. These are being transferred increasingly to Internet-based systems under the Global Information Grid program.

The Automatic Digital Network (AUTO-DIN) was for two decades the Department of Defense's common user store-and-forward message switching network for all record (physical) message traffic. It consisted of a network of fixed and mobile switching centers and communications centers. AUTO-DIN evolved from the consolidation of the Defense Special Security Communications System with the General Services Administration (GSA) system in the mid-1970s. Though the two systems merged, each retained its own identity and function. The former GSA system (referred to as the "R" side) handled unclassified though top secret record traffic. The former defense system (referred to as the "Y" side) handled record message traffic containing highly secure information. By the late 1990s, however, the aging and increasingly inefficient AUTODIN was being replaced with the modern e-mail–based Defense Message System (DMS) which, in turn, was by late 2000 giving way to the GIG.

The DMS has components that provide message services and will continue to be the composite result of many coordinated projects. DMS supports two classes of messages: organizational (formal records) and individual (informal e-mail). Its distributed message system supports online message preparation, coordination, and release of organizational messages.

DCS also operates the extensive Defense Satellite Communications System.

Christopher H. Sterling

See also Automatic Digital Network (AUTODIN); Communication Satellites;

Defense Advanced Research Projects Agency (DARPA); Defense Information Systems Agency (DISA); Defense Message Service (DMS); Defense Switched Network (DSN); Global Information Grid (GIG)

Source
Pike, John. 1997. "Defense Communications System (DCS)." [Online article; retrieved April 2006.] http://www.fas.org/irp/program/disseminate/dcs.htm.

Defense Information Systems Agency (DISA)

The Defense Information Systems Agency (DISA) was established in May 1960 as the Defense Communications Agency (DCA), based in Washington DC with 450 personnel. Its initial charter was to manage and direct the Defense Communications System (DCS), which consolidated the long-haul communications functions of the Army, Navy, and Air Force's independently operated communications systems.

DCA experienced rapid growth through its first two decades, incorporating as part of its mission the White House Signal Agency (later the White House Communications Agency) as well as space and ground elements of the Defense Communications Satellite System. DCA also provided engineering and technical support for the National Military Command System and, in the late 1970s, the World Wide Military Command and Control System. In January 1987, DCA merged with the Joint Tactical Command, Control, and Communications Agency. The Joint Interoperability Test Command was later created for interoperability and compliance and testing and certification. In 1989, DCA was assigned to lead the Department of

Defense (DoD) command, control, communications, and intelligence support on the national counternarcotics operations.

On 25 June 1991, DCA was redesignated DISA to reflect its expanded role and to clearly identify it as a combat support agency. DISA is responsible for planning, developing, fielding, operating, and supporting command, control, communications, and information systems that serve the needs of the highest levels of the federal government including the White House, secretary of defense, Joint Chiefs of Staff, combat commanders, and other DoD components under all conditions. DISA functions under a director (appointed by the secretary of defense) who is a three-star flag-rank officer responsible for coordinating communications of the three military services. DISA gives operational direction to DCS, ensuring that the system is operated and improved so as to meet continual long-haul, point-to-point requirements. The director also commands the Joint Task Force–Global Network Operations and is the deputy commander for global network operations and defense, U.S. Strategic Command, Joint Forces Headquarters–Information Operations. As such, he or she is responsible for directing the operation and defense of the Global Information Grid to ensure timely and secure network capabilities across strategic, operational, and tactical boundaries in support of DoD's varied missions.

Besides its headquarters in Arlington, Virginia, DISA has twenty-seven offices worldwide, more than 7,500 military and civilian employees, and an annual budget estimated at more than $1 billion. DISA's core operations include the Global Command and Control System, Defense Information System Network, Defense Message System, Global Combat Support System, Defense Information Infrastructure Common Operating Environment, and Information Assurance. The Defense Technical Information Center and the Joint Spectrum Center are now aligned under DISA.

DISA provides seamless, end-to-end, integrated information services intended to give a complete picture of any battle situation. The agency is responsible for planning, developing, and supporting command, control, communications, computers, intelligence, and information systems that serve national authorities in both peace and war.

Danny Johnson

See also Defense Communications Agency (DCA, 1960–1991); Defense Communications System (DCS); Global Command and Control System (GCCS); Joint Task Force–Global Network Operations (JTF-GNO); White House Communications Agency (WHCA); World Wide Military Command and Control System (WWMCCS)

Sources

Defense Information Systems Agency. Home page. [Online information; retrieved November 2005.] http://www.disa.mil/.

Department of Defense. 1991. *Defense Information Systems Agency (DISA) Directive 5105.19* June 25. Washington, DC: Department of Defense.

Donnelly, Harrison, ed. 2005. "Network Commander: Interview with USAF Lt. Gen. Charles E. Croom Jr., Director, Defense Information Systems Agency." [Online article; retrieved April 2007.] http://www.military-information-technology.com/article.cfm?DocID=1150.

Seffers, George I. 2001. "At a Glance." *Federal Computer Week*, April 16.

Defense Message System (DMS)

The Defense Message System (DMS) is the replacement for the AUTODIN system, which was the primary message system for the U.S. Department of Defense for more than thirty years.

Development of the DMS began in 1988 with the creation of the Defense Message System Working Group at the direction of the assistant secretary of defense for Command, Control, Communications and Intelligence. The basic requirements for the DMS were extensive and presented a complex developmental effort in the areas of connectivity and interoperability, guaranteed and timely delivery, confidentiality and security, sender authentication, integrity, survivability, availability and reliability, ease of use, identification of recipients, preparation support, storage and retrieval support, and distribution determination and delivery. The transition from AUTODIN to the DMS was completed on 30 September 2003.

The DMS provides a fully integrated, supportable, secure, accountable, and completely commercial off-the-shelf capability for e-mail and organizational (official) messages for the Department of Defense. The fact that commercial off-the-shelf capabilities are used ensures that technological advances can be incorporated as they occur for years to come. Three main components make up the DMS: the message handling system, directory services, and a management system. The DMS is not a network, but rather an application system. Messages are moved between various parts of the system using existing and planned communications networks of the Defense Information Systems Network.

The message handling system of DMS is defined by the X.400 standard recommended by the International Telecommunication Union–Telecommunication Sector (ITU-T). By mandating X.400 compliance, the Department of Defense has standardized its mail system and retained the various features and capabilities of commercial e-mail systems. The directory services, containing addresses, security information, and the information required to provide individual and organizational mes-

saging in a worldwide system, are defined by the X.500 standard of the ITU-T.

Security on the DMS is implemented through the use of a FORTEZZA card, the user's private key that will provide access to cryptographic services for the encryption and decryption of messages. The card was developed according to specifications and requirements of the National Security Agency's Multi-level Information System Security Initiative. Each card is prepared for the individual user, and the user is required to authenticate before accessing the DMS. The card also contains the specific user's privileges and what precedence messages he or she can originate.

Tommy R. Young II

See also Automatic Digital Network (AUTODIN); Defense Information Systems Agency (DISA); E-mail Systems; International Telecommunication Union (ITU); National Security Agency (NSA)

Sources

Department of the Army. "Defense Message System (DMS)." [Online information; retrieved December 2006.] http://www .redstone.army.mil/documents/dmswhite .html.

Joint Operability Test Command. 2005. "Defense Messaging Service (DMS)." [Online information; retrieved December 2006.] http://jitc .fhu.disa.mil/washops/jtca/dms.html.

Sheldon, Tom. 2001. *The Encyclopedia of Networking and Telecommunications.* New York: McGraw Hill.

Defense Switched Network (DSN)

The Defense Switched Network (DSN) is a telephone interconnected network used by the Department of Defense and other federal installations in the United States and overseas. The DSN is the switched circuit telecommunications system of the Defense Information System Network.

In 1982, the secretary of defense designated the DSN to be the provider of long-distance communications service for the Department of Defense. By 1990, in a series of planned stages, it had replaced the earlier Automatic Voice Network (AUTOVON) system, adding automatic callback, call forwarding, call transfer, and call waiting capabilities. DSN was designed to support command-and-control traffic with the robustness to provide service under all conditions. It interfaces with foreign national tactical networks as well as public telephone and administrative private line networks—indeed, and where possible, the DSN must use commercial links. The DSN was engineered to provide precedence to military users, providing them with secure and reliable communications without compromising the quality of service to others. It is designed for the most essential elements of command and agency operations requiring long-distance telephone communications.

The DSN system interface, when added to a private branch exchange, allows dial service attendants and other users of the system to enter the military network by dialing an access code. Users can get assistance on outgoing DSN calls by dialing an operator assistance code. Calls taking precedence are routed over special trunks and can be routed through the network without operator assistance. The DSN encompasses inter- and intrabase, secure or nonsecure command-and-control telecommunications systems that provide end-to-end common use and dedicated telephone services. DSN services include traditional long-haul switched voice, facsimile, data, and videoconference calling. One of the primary responsibilities that DSN meets is for a nonsecure dial-up voice (tele-

phone) service. The DSN covers the United States and a large portion of the rest of the world.

The DSN is managed by the Defense Information Systems Agency (DISA), and its switched voice service allows calls to be connected to any DISA location. Its use overseas is negotiated country by country. The DSN incorporates the former AUTOVON and classified systems, as well as several other defense systems here and abroad.

Danny Johnson

See also Automatic Voice Network (Autovon);
 Defense Information Systems Agency (DISA)

Sources
Chairman, Joint Chiefs of Staff. 1995. *Policy for the Defense Switched Network*. Washington, DC: Department of Defense.
Defense Information Systems Agency. "The Defense Switched Network (DSN)." [Online information; retrieved December 2005.] http://www.disa.mil/gs/dsn/index.html.
Department of Defense. 2005. *DOD Telecommunications and Defense Switched Network, Security Technical Implementation Guide* (June 30). Washington, DC: Defense Information Systems Agency.
Department of Defense Voice Networks. 2004. Instruction 8100.3 (16 January). Washington, DC: Department of Defense.

Defiance, HMS

This now-obsolete British Royal Navy sailing vessel was the site of important pioneering experiments with maritime wireless telegraphy from 1895 to 1898.

HMS *Defiance* was originally launched at Pembroke Dock in 1861 as a full-rigged wooden sailing ship of the line carrying ninety-one guns and weighing 5,270 tons. She was built at the end of the era of the fighting ship powered by sails—indeed, just the year before the Royal Navy placed HMS *Warrior* in service as the first ironclad screw-driven fighting vessel. Serving with the fleet for a comparatively brief period because of her rapid obsolescence, *Defiance* had been laid up for many years when she was recommissioned at Devonport in 1884 to become the Royal Navy Torpedo School. Her main masts were removed and her deck was taken over by a continuous barrack structure. Though in commission, the ship served as a stationary training facility.

From 1895 to 1897, *Defiance* and the torpedo school aboard her were commanded by Captain Henry Jackson. He had developed considerable interest in applications of science to the navy and had become interested in the possibilities of wireless communication. Unaware of the work of Guglielmo Marconi, Jackson began his experiments from the decks of *Defiance* early in 1896, at first succeeding in sending a wireless signal across the after-cabin of the ship, and then the length of the vessel and ringing a signal bell. This was the first use of wireless aboard any ship. Jackson reported that the wireless signals passed through the wooden bulkheads of the ship with no ill effect or loss of power.

The next year, *Defiance* was one of two ships Jackson used as he increased the coverage of his wireless apparatus. HMS *Scourge* acted as tender for the larger training ship and in early 1897 held Jackson's wireless transmitter. Using aerials upward of 70 feet long, Jackson managed to extend his wireless reach to 1,200 yards. For officially observed trials of Jackson's apparatus a few months later, the receiver was on *Defiance* while the transmitter was on *Scourge*. While the former remained at her moorings, *Scourge* demonstrated wireless telegraphy

transmission from various distances and compass bearings. These trials extended out more than 5,000 yards. An October test pushed that distance to 6,000 yards when *Defiance* communicated with the Admiral's House in Plymouth Harbor. Wireless experiments on *Defiance* continued through 1898 under the command of another officer.

At that point, further experiments took place on modern vessels at sea. HMS *Defiance* had served the purpose of providing a suitable location for the beginnings of Royal Navy wireless telegraphy—the first application of radio by any of the world's navies.

Christopher H. Sterling

See also Jackson, Henry B. (1855–1929); Radio; United Kingdom: Royal Navy

Source
Pocock, R. F., and G. R. M. Garratt. 1972. *The Origins of Maritime Radio: The Story of the Introduction of Wireless Telegraphy in the Royal Navy Between 1896 and 1900.* London: Science Museum/HMSO.

Diego Garcia

Diego Garcia is a major American military base in the Indian Ocean. Its development began in the early 1970s as a naval communications facility.

The island was discovered by Portuguese explorers in the early 1500s. It is the largest of fifty-two islands that form the Chagos Archipelago in the midst of the Indian Ocean. A footprint-shaped island just 7 degrees south of the equator, Diego Garcia covers about 11 square miles with an average elevation of 4 feet above sea level. The shoreline is about 40 miles long and the island encloses a lagoon 6.5 miles wide and 13 miles long. The island is a part of the British Indian Ocean Territory administered by the British Foreign Office. During roughly 170 years of plantation life, coconut harvests dominated life on the island. Colonial workers, a native population of 1,200 to 2,000 members of the Ilois, were moved off the island in the late 1960s by the British (they now live 1,200 miles away on the isle of Mauritius). U.S. and British government texts refer to them as temporary workers, not indigenous inhabitants. When the present U.S. lease on the island expires in 2016, the Ilois plan to turn the place into a sugarcane and fishing enterprise.

The U.S. presence began on 23 January 1971 when a naval advance party landed to survey beach landing areas. Seabees (construction battalions) marked underwater obstructions, installed temporary navigational aids, and cleared beach areas for landing additional personnel and materials. Two months later construction of the U.S. Naval Communication Facility Diego Garcia began, including radio transmitter and receiver buildings and an airfield. The communications facility became the Naval Computer and Telecommunication Station (NCTS) in October 1991. Its mission is to provide quality assurance evaluation and management of Naval telecommunication facilities; communications security and Defense Information Systems Agency assets; and tactical and strategic support to the fleet, national consumers, allied forces in the Indian Ocean theater, and all commands and activities on Diego Garcia.

Facilities were expanded in 1975, 1976, and 1978. Following the overthrow of the Iranian government in 1979, Diego Garcia saw the most dramatic military buildup of any location since the Vietnam War era. In 1986, it became fully operational with the completion of a $500 million construction program. By the early 2000s, the island's occupants were all Naval Support Facility personnel and tenants—most of the approximately 3,500 people are third-country nationals working under contract. The NCTS, which began all this development, continues in operation, and the Air Force and Army also maintain support elements on the island. Diego Garcia was the only U.S. Navy base that launched offensive air operations during the Gulf War (1990–1991), and the island played a central role in air attacks during the Afghan and Iraq wars of 2002 to the present when the United States built special shelters for four to six B-2 stealth bombers.

Christopher H. Sterling

See also Defense Information Systems Agency (DISA)

Source

GlobalSecurity.org. "Diego Garcia 'Camp Justice' 7ß20'S 72ß25'E." [Online information; retrieved September 2005.] http://www.globalsecurity.org/military/facility/diego-garcia.htm.

Dogs

The use of dogs to carry military messages extends at least to Egypt about 4,000 BCE. Plutarch and Pliny mention war dogs, and Agesilaus used them in his siege of Mantinea. Many military commanders, such as Attila and Pling (king of the Garamantes), used dogs to guard military camps at night. An early British war dog authority, E. H. Richardson, reported use of dogs in the American Civil War and suggests that this success got Germany interested in their use in wartime.

Dogs were active in the Franco-Prussian (1870–1871) and Russo-Turkish (1877–1878) wars. By the early 1900s, the Germans had established many dog training schools. They expanded the use of dogs in military actions to include searching for wounded on the battlefield, sentry duty, scout missions, and as message carriers—a role Richardson belittled at the time he wrote about war dogs. Nonetheless, the Imperial German Army used approximately 30,000 dogs during World War I, mostly as sentries and messengers. By 1930 Germany had begun to rebuild her military dog strength. A central training school in Frankfurt housed 2,000 dogs. Within ten years, more than 200,000 were trained—mostly German Shepherds—for sentry, scout, and messenger duties. In the 1939 invasion of Poland, these dogs were as ready and well trained as the Luftwaffe. Germany used dogs in virtually all of its other World War II campaigns.

Some 10,000 to 25,000 dogs were sent by Germany to Japan several years before Japan's attack on Pearl Harbor. These dogs were retrained in Japan and China to obey Japanese commands and were used in the Malay campaign of 1941–1942. The Russians had trained about 40,000 dogs before Germany's 1941 attack on Russian soil, specializing in white-coated dogs, which are difficult to see against a snowy background.

Richardson developed a British dog training school before World War I. Dogs were trained to return to their handler and to ignore the loud sounds of battle. British engineers developed a small backpack that permitted a trained dog to lay signal wire for a telephone or telegraph, though only over fairly short distances. Alternatively, the containers could hold messages. One drawback was that British soldiers were often more apt to retain the dogs as pets than as messengers. Though the British restarted a guard dog training school in 1941, there is appar-

For centuries dogs were used for scouting and running messages. Here U.S. Marines and their dogs start off for the jungle front lines on Bougainville in the Solomon Islands in 1943. (National Archives)

ently no record of their use as messengers in World War II.

In August 1918, a U.S. Army field signal battalion used a group of trained messenger dogs over ground that was impassible (usually because of enemy action) to men. Two decades later, civilians began Dogs for Defense, Inc., which provided the Army K-9 Corps with 30,000 trained, healthy dogs at a cost of less than $7.00 each. Many breeds were used and six schools were established. At the school, set in a tropical location, 150 Japanese Americans loyal to the United States wore captured Japanese uniforms and served as live targets for war dogs to hunt and attack. Dogs learned to carry messages, string wire, transport two carrier pigeons in a special basket, and (depending on the dog species) carry up to thirty pounds of supplies. The most famous Marine Corps dog was Caesar, who landed within the first two hours of the Bougainville invasion in November 1943. He provided the only mode of communication for the battalion command post until telephone line was laid. After installation, the line was damaged and Caesar took over again. He was credited with nine runs carrying messages, overlays, and captured Japanese papers—doing so more than three times under fire.

The primary value of dogs—in addition to their speed and endurance—is their acute senses of smell and hearing and superior night vision, all of which assisted in getting messages through. The average dog's sense of smell is 50 to 100 times better than a human's, and a dog can remember specific smells and detect one from another with ease. Dogs can hear up to 35,000 cycles per second (humans hear only 20,000 at best). Dogs with ears that stand up hear better than floppy-eared breeds. While dogs are nearsighted and thus do not see as well as humans, the fact that their eyes contain more rods than cones allows them to see better in dim light.

David L. Woods

See also Horses and Mules; Pigeons

Sources

Going, Clayton G. 1944. *Dogs at War*. New York: Macmillan.

Hamer, Blythe. 2001. *Dogs at War*. London: Carlton.

Harfield, Alan. 1989. "Messenger Dogs." In *Pigeon to Packhorse: The Illustrated Story of Animals in Army Communications*, 83–89. Chippenham, UK: Picton Publishing.

Richardson, E. H. 1910. *War, Police, and Watch Dogs*. Edinburgh: William Blackwood.

Woods, David L. 1965. "Messengers: Men, Horses, and Dogs," In *A History of Tactical Communications Techniques*, chap. 4. Orlando, FL: Martin-Marietta (reprinted by Arno Press, 1974).

Driscoll, Agnes Meyer (1889–1971)

A senior cryptanalyst for the U.S. Navy in the 1920s and 1930s, Agnes Driscoll also designed cryptographic systems for the Navy.

Agnes Driscoll (born Meyer) was born in Genesco, Illinois, on 24 July 1889, and graduated from Ohio State University in 1911. After several years of teaching in Texas, she joined the U.S. Navy as a chief yeoman in 1918 and worked in censorship in Washington DC. After World War I, Driscoll was assigned to the Code and Signal Section for the Navy's director of Naval Communications. In 1919 she was discharged but remained as a civilian code clerk.

Over the next few years, she moved through a number of positions. In early 1920, she trained with the Department of Ciphers at George Fabyan's Riverbank Laboratory and then spent about three months at Herbert Yardley's Black Chamber in New York City. She spent two years developing cryptographic systems for the Navy—one of which, the "CM" (or code machine), became the main naval cryptographic system for the next decade. In 1923, Edward Hebern hired her to help develop a cipher wheel coding device. She married Michael Driscoll the next year.

With Driscoll's return to the Navy in 1924, naval cryptologic activity coalesced around the newly formed Research Desk where she worked under Laurance Safford. One of her duties was to train future naval cryptologists; such officers as Joseph Rochefort and Joseph Wenger graduated from this program. The operation's first major success was to break the Japanese navy's operational/ administrative code known as Red to the Americans. A copy had been stolen by naval intelligence, and she broke the overlaying transposition cipher in 1926. For the next four years, intelligence from this breakthrough allowed Americans to follow Japanese technical naval advances and tactics.

In 1930 the Japanese replaced Red with a new code, called Blue by the Americans. Driscoll broke this code, which contained 85,000 values further encrypted with a transposition cipher. Because she had no codebook to work from, Safford considered this feat the equal of the Army's later breakthrough against Purple. This project also entailed the first substantial use of early machine technology (such as card sorters) in cryptanalysis. In 1935 Driscoll demonstrated her virtuosity by breaking the M-1 cipher machine, called Orange, used by Japan's naval attachés, and similar to the diplomats' Red machine.

In 1939, Safford set her to crack the Japanese navy's new general purpose code, eventually called JN-25. This system used 30,000 five-figure code groups encrypted with additives from another 300-page book. By 1940, she had stripped away these encrypted values. Safford soon put her in charge of the U.S. Navy's project to break the German navy's Enigma coding system. For more than two years her team made little headway as she had resisted the advice of visiting British experts and persisted in a fruitless search for a solution. Eventually, she was transferred to work new Japanese systems.

After the war Driscoll worked on the Soviet espionage cipher known as Venona, but with no success, at the same time helping to integrate machine technology into naval cryptology. She transferred to the new U.S. cryptologic organizations: the Armed Forces Security Agency in 1949 and the National Security Agency in 1952. She retired in 1958, largely forgotten. She died on 16 September 1971 and was buried in Arlington National Cemetery.

Robert Hanyok

See also Enigma; National Security Agency (NSA); Safford, Laurance F. (1890–1973); Signals Intelligence (SIGINT); Yardley, Herbert O. (1889–1958)

Sources

DeBrose, Jim, and Colin Burke. 2004. *The Secret in Building 26*. New York: Random House.

Hanyok, Robert. 1997. "Still Desperately Seeking 'Miss Agnes': A Pioneer Cryptologist's Life Remains an Enigma." *Cryptolog* (Fall).

Lujan, Susan. 1998. "Agnes Meyer Driscoll." In *Selections from Cryptologia: History, People, and Technology*, edited by Cipher Deavours et al., 269–278. Norwood, MA: Artech House.

National Security Agency Central Security Service. "Hall of Honor: Agnes Meyer Driscoll, 1889–1971." [Online information; retrieved August 2006.] http://www.nsa.gov/honor/honor00024.cfm.

E

Eastern Europe

The several nations of central and eastern Europe experienced varied signaling histories. Many began early military use of telegraphy in the nineteenth century. They became ravaged battlefields in both world wars and later were a part of the Soviet-led Warsaw Pact (from 1955 to 1991) before regaining their independence. A number joined the European Union and the North Atlantic Treaty Organization by the early 2000s.

Czechoslovakia

The first Czechoslovakian signal unit was formed at Fort Josefov in November 1918. It was a telegraph battalion, redesignated as a regiment two years later. During the autumn of 1920, the Central Telegraph School was formed, renamed the Military Telegraph School in 1921. From 1924, telegraph battalions once again became the fundamental signal units and by 1939 there were seven of them. The country was occupied by Germany from 1939 to 1945. After the end of hostilities, special liaison battalions were created. A new

signal corps was established when the socialist republic came into existence.

When the country divided into the Czech and Slovak republics in 1993, each nation formed its own signal corps.

Poland

The first Polish signal units were created in November 1918 at Warsaw Citadel, Krakow, and Lwow. After the outbreak of the Wielkopolskie Uprising on 27 December 1918, signal units were staffed by Polish reserve officers who had seen service in the German army Signal Corps (*Nachrichtentruppe*). The Polish General Staff in Warsaw included a signal section and the inspectorate of the newly formed Polish Signal Corps (*Wojska Lacznosci*). By 1919 the corps included the following units: the general staff sections just noted; two telegraph, one telephone, and one radio battalion at the Warsaw Citadel; a signal regiment in Zegrze; and two wireless companies, a fixed wireless station, and a telegraph battalion in Poznan.

These and additional units fought during the Polish-Russian War in 1920 and served again from 1921 to 1924. New units operated in Zegrze (a signal training center), signal regiments in both Jaroslaw and Grudziadz, and telegraph battalions in both Jaroslaw and Poznan.

Divisional signal companies and brigade signal squadrons (cavalry) had thirty telegraph signal companies by 1930, and ten cavalry signal squadrons were formed by 1935 from cavalry signal troops. Officer signal training schools were formed at Zegrze, and a signal and engineering school was raised in Warsaw.

The Polish army fought against the German invasion in September 1939, and émigrés also fought in France in May and June 1940. These included the Gdanski signal battalion (1 Grenadier Division), the Podhalanska brigade signal company, and the mechanized cavalry brigade signal squadron. After the fall of France (June 1940) a number of Polish signal units were formed in Scotland between 1940 and 1945. Several Polish signals units also served with the 11 Polish Corps in the Italian theater. The Polish General Staff in London had a signal unit and a wireless telegraphy company. After 1945 the Polish army in the West was disbanded and a new army formed with Russian assistance made up of Polish forces that had served in the East.

Romania

Line telegraphy was first introduced into the Romanian army in 1863 when the Post & Telegraph Administration was provided with campaign telegraph sets. A telegraph section in the Miners Company of the Engineers Battalion was established on 14 July 1873 and is considered to be the birth of Romanian army signals. With the experience gained on the battlefield by army signalers and the success of communications (including, according to some reports, the first military use of the telephone) in the battle of Plevna (1877), it was decided to estab-

lish an independent telegraph company. On 19 October 1877 the four telegraph sections from the Engineers Battalion were combined into a telegraph company.

By 1909 the signals operation comprised sections for wireless, motor cars and motorcycles, pigeons, and photography. On the eve of World War I it had added an "aerostation" (flying) company as well as an aircraft training and technical school. A special duties company was responsible for the preparation of wireless operators, signalers, and liaison agents. Only in 1949 did the signal troops of the then socialist republic became an independent corps.

Cliff Lord

See also Baltic Nations; Germany: Army; Polish Code Breaking; Russia/Soviet Union: Army; Warsaw Pact (1955–1991)

Sources
Contribii la Istoria Trupelor de Transmisiuni din Armata Romana. 1973. Rome: Editura Militara.
Rogozinski, Antoni. 1985. *Wojska Lacznosci I Polska Dywizja Pancerna.* Milwaukee, WI: Antoni Rogozinski.

Edelcrantz, Abraham (1754–1821)

Swedish scholar Abraham Niklas Clewberg Edelcrantz invented the first Swedish data communication system, an optical telegraph network. His telegraph acquired great military significance in the wake of the French Revolution and the rise of the Napoleonic Wars. During the first half of the nineteenth century, Sweden operated Europe's second largest telegraph system, exceeded only by that of the French. To reward him for his accomplishments, the Swedish king elevated him to the nobility.

Edelcrantz was born on 28 July 1754 in Åbo, Sweden. He was the son of Carl Abraham Clewberg, a professor of ancient languages at the Royal Academy of Åbo. Edelcrantz attended the University of Turku and in 1772 wrote his first doctoral thesis on optics. In 1773, he wrote a second thesis on literature. He was a member of the Swedish Academy from 1786 until his death in Åbo on 15 March 1821.

After reading an article in the September 1794 issue of *Gentleman's Magazine* about French telegraph inventor Claude Chappe, he immediately began the construction of a Swedish telegraph system. Within two months, he was able to replicate Chappe's design, which utilized articulated arms and flaps. On 1 November 1794, he sent the first Swedish telegraph message to King Gustav IV. By early 1795, Edelcrantz had switched from Chappe's design to a shutter telegraph system, which had also been developed by Chappe (in 1791) but abandoned. Ironically, there is no indication that Edelcrantz knew of Chappe's earlier design nor is there any indication in Edelcrantz's extensive writings why Edelcrantz rejected Chappe's semaphoric arms and utilized shutters. Significantly, both designs were successful. The Swedish system, however, was twice as fast as the French. Unfortunately, bad weather (and thus poor visibility) inhibited the use of both.

The shutter telegraph was a matrix of ten iron shutters positioned on fifty towers that were approximately six miles apart. The position of the shutters formed combinations of numbers that translated into letters and words, which were recorded in codebooks. The shutters could be seen by telescope from the next tower, where operators would immediately replicate the signals. Driven by the fear of a French invasion during the Napoleonic Wars, the shutter system spread rapidly throughout Sweden. When war broke out against Russia in 1808, the system was greatly expanded. Nevertheless,

in 1809, after peace with Russia, the system fell into decline. In the 1830s, however, the tense political system in Europe convinced the Swedish government to reinvigorate the system to protect the Swedish coastline. The Swedish optical telegraph system was only discontinued in 1881 when it was replaced by the electric telegraph.

Michael R. Hall

See also Chappe, Claude (1763–1805); Napoleonic Wars (1795–1815); Semaphore (Mechanical Telegraphs)

Sources
Holzmann, Gerard J., and Björn Pehrson. 1995. *The Early History of Data Networks.* Los Alamitos, CA: IEEE Computer Society Press.
Nickles, David Paul. 2003. *Under the Wire: How the Telegraph Changed Diplomacy.* Cambridge, MA: Harvard University Press.
Wilson, Geoffrey. 1976. *The Old Telegraphs.* Totowa, NJ: Rowman & Littlefield.

Edison, Thomas A. (1847–1931)

Thomas Alva Edison was perhaps the most important American inventor in the nineteenth century. He received more than a thousand patents, more than any other individual, and many had military applications.

Edison was born on 11 February 1847 in Milan, Ohio. He had little formal education but possessed a gifted mind, a visual imagination, and unusual powers of reasoning. While working as a railway newsboy he spent his free time reading scientific books. Edison learned how to operate a telegraph and was a full-time telegrapher for several years. He eventually made his way to Boston in 1868 where, after reading the works of Michael Faraday, he became an inventor.

Edison moved to New York in 1869 and continued to work on inventions related to the telegraph. His first successful invention, an improved stock ticker, earned him $40,000 (a tidy sum in those days), with which he established his first research laboratory in Newark, New Jersey, in 1871. There he developed several devices that improved the speed and efficiency of the telegraph, among them the duplex telegraph, which could send two messages over the same wire at the same time. He soon expanded that idea into the quadruplex and later multiplex, which enabled increased capacity, simultaneous multidirectional capability, and faster transmission of telegraphic messages. All of these became important military communication tools.

In 1876 Edison moved to Menlo Park, New Jersey, and established a larger laboratory designed for a broader program of multidisciplinary research leading to manufacture of any resulting products. At the same time Alexander Graham Bell was working on improvements to his new telephone; and Western Union asked Edison to develop a competitive system. Widely perceived as a scientific soldier of fortune who evaded the patents of others, Edison developed a carbon button transmitter that greatly improved the volume and clarity of voice signals, allowing the telephone to become commercially practical. Edison's carbon transmitter was later used in early microphones for sound motion pictures and radio broadcasting.

Edison then undertook development of a practical incandescent electric light as well as an electrical system that made the new light practical, safe, and economical. In 1887 Edison moved to West Orange, New Jersey, and established his final laboratory complex, which allowed his team to work on ten or twenty projects at once. In the late 1890s, frustrated by competing interests in communications and lighting endeavors, Edison turned to perfecting the phonograph, making it a practical entertainment medium for the early recording industry. Edison also worked to perfect the concept of motion pictures, demonstrating a camera in 1891. He soon began commercial production of "movies" for another new entertainment business. One of his final projects focused on development of a better storage battery for use in electric vehicles, which Edison thought was the best method of powering cars. The alkaline storage battery eventually became his most profitable product, paving the way for the modern alkaline battery.

By the early twentieth century Edison had become a cultural icon, a symbol of American ingenuity. For a lifetime of achievement he was recognized in 1928 with a special Medal of Honor from Congress. Edison died on 18 October 1931 in West Orange, New Jersey, as the most productive inventor in U.S. history—his record of 1,093 individual patents has never been surpassed.

Steven J. Rauch

See also Bell, Alexander Graham (1847–1922); Marconi, Guglielmo (1874–1937); Morse, Samuel F. B. (1791–1872; Tesla, Nikola (1856–1943)

Sources

Israel, Paul. 1998. *Edison: A Life of Invention.* New York: John Wiley.
Millard, Andre. 1990. *Edison and the Business of Innovation.* Baltimore: Johns Hopkins University Press.
Wachhorst, Wyn. 1981. *Thomas Alva Edison: An American Myth.* Cambridge, MA: MIT Press.

Egypt

With a military history tracing back thousands of years, Egypt has nearly always been a power to reckon with in the Middle East. Over the past half-century or so, it has received aid from a variety of nations, depending on its role in the Cold War. In the early 2000s, Egypt was a military and strategic partner of the North Atlantic Treaty Organization, the strongest military power in Africa, and the second largest in the Middle East (after Israel).

From late in the nineteenth century through World War II, Britain maintained a strong influence in the Egyptian military, providing it with equipment, instruction, and technicians. An Egyptian army signal school was established in 1915. Under the terms of a 1936 treaty, British troops remained in the country to defend the Suez Canal. In 1937 the Egyptian Signal Corps became an independent organization, and a training center for signalers and noncommissioned officers was formed a year later. In 1939 the first operational signal unit was formed, followed by many more during World War II. During the war, Egypt became the principal Allied base in the Middle East. An armored signal unit was formed in 1950.

Since the military coup in 1952, career military officers have figured prominently in Egypt's government, and senior officers have played an influential role in Egypt's affairs. The military's involvement in government has diminished since the 1970s, although ranking members of the officer corps have continued to fill the positions of minister of defense (concurrently serving as commander in chief of the armed forces) and minister of the interior.

During each of the several wars with Israel before 1975, the Egyptian army demonstrated weaknesses in command, control, and communications. Under the influence of Soviet military doctrine and advice (dominant after about 1955), higher-level com-

manders had been reluctant to extend operational flexibility to brigade and battalion commanders—a failure poor communications did not help. Even though the Egyptian military became oriented toward the West after the October 1973 war with Israel, it retained large amounts of Soviet equipment (including communications) in its inventory for some years.

After Egypt and Israel signed their peace treaty in 1979, the United States strove to increase deliveries of armaments, advice, and support to Egypt and to provide the country with American military training. With the exception of Israel, Egypt became the largest recipient of U.S. military aid after 1980. Its stock of weaponry and communications equipment from all sources still did not reach the level of Israel's. Equipment from the former Soviet Union has been largely replaced by more modern American, French, and British equipment, a significant portion of which is built under license in Egypt.

The 1990–1991 Gulf War, in which Iraqi equipment, several generations newer than Egypt's Soviet equipment, was badly outclassed by Western types, convinced the Egyptian military that it must devote more effort to replacement than upgrading of old equipment. The Egyptian Air Defense Force (ADF) made progress developing a national air defense network that would integrate all existing radars, missile batteries, air bases, and command centers into an automated command-and-control system. ADF planned to link the system to the Hawkeye early-warning aircraft.

By the late 1990s, many indications pointed to a comprehensive Egyptian effort to create a national information infrastructure that would serve both military and civilian needs. The zeal with which Egypt is approaching its information project reflects a solid understanding of the relationship between information technology and national security. The Internet is perceived as a tool of dual use serving both civilian and military needs.

By the twenty-first century, the Egyptian air arm was completing a long process of transformation to Western systems and technologies. It had procured various modern systems, such as aircraft; attack helicopters; air-to-air and air-to-ground guided munitions; command, control, communications, computer, and information systems; early warning systems; and electronic warfare systems.

Christopher H. Sterling and Cliff Lord

See also Ancient Signals; Gulf War (1990–1991); Israel; Suez Crisis (1956)

Sources

Frisch, Hillel. 2001. "Guns and Butter in the Egyptian Army." [Online article; retrieved April 2006.] http://meria.idc.ac.il/journal/2001/issue2/jv5n2a1.html.

Sobelman, Ariel T. 1998. "An Information Revolution in the Middle East?" [Online article; retrieved April 2006.] http://www.tau.ac.il/jcss/sa/v1n2p4_n.html.

Tartter, Jean R. 1990. "The Military." In *A Country Study: Egypt*, chap. 5. Washington, DC: Library of Congress.

Electric Cipher Machine (ECM Mark II, "SIGABA")

The ECM Mark II (also known as the Navy CSP-888/889 or Army Converter M-134C–SIGABA, a handy code name that masked the equipment's identity) was the chief American cipher machine used during World War II. A high-grade, electromechanical, rotor wheel cipher device, it was apparently never broken by enemy forces. It remained in use in modified form through the 1950s before being replaced with more modern equipment.

The ECM Mark II built on and improved the rotor machine concept developed originally by Edward Hebern early in the twentieth century. That led to the Electric Cipher Machine (ECM) Mark I, a five-rotor system developed by the Navy in the early 1930s. Development of what would become the Mark II or SIGABA device began in the mid-1930s with innovation of the "stepping maze" principle (using some rotors to control the movement of others) by William Friedman and Frank Rowlett, then working for U.S. Army intelligence. Within a year or two Navy researchers (who had more funding) were working to perfect the device with electronic control. The most important difference between previous machines and the ECM was how the enciphering rotors were stepped. The stepping maze used rotors in cascade formation to produce a more random stepping of the ECM's up to ten cipher and five control rotors than existed on previous electromechanical cipher machines such as the German Enigma. The keyboard on the SIGABA had a row of digits like the keyboard on a regular typewriter.

The machine, easily a generation ahead of any other then in use in the world, became operational with both the Army and Navy on 1 August 1941. Within two years, more than 10,000 of the devices were in use. They cost more than $2,000 each. They could send at 45 to 50 words per minute when keyed (operated) by trained personnel. But the SIGABA was a large and heavy device that was mechanically complex and fragile. In that sense it was not as practical a piece of equipment as the Enigma, which was both smaller and lighter. SIGABA was widely used aboard U.S. Navy ships but was rarely used in the field.

Given their centrality to American military communications throughout the war, the

Officially the Electric Cipher Machine (ECM), the complex SIGABA became the mainstay American ciphering device used in World War II. Its signals were never broken by Axis enemy forces. (National Security Agency)

SIGABAs' security was closely guarded. On 26 June 1942 the Army and Navy agreed not to allow the devices to be placed in foreign territory except where armed American personnel were able to properly safeguard the machine. The SIGABA would only be made available to Allies if an American liaison officer prevented allied personnel from direct access to the machine or its operation. Of specific concern were such SIGABA details as its rotors and wiring, or keying or operating instructions. Detailed instructions on how to rapidly destroy threatened machines were issued to all forces.

The SIGABA was adapted for interoperation with a modified British machine, Typex, itself originally based on the Enigma, which had first been used in 1937. The common machine (though neither an ECM nor a Typex) was known as the Combined Cipher Machine (CCM) and was used beginning in November 1943 for messages between American and British forces. The U.S. State Department also made use of the CCM device for many years.

After newer, faster cryptographic systems replaced the SIGABA (and computers made it possible to break their complex codes, which had resisted mechanical methods), the machines were systematically destroyed to protect their design secrets and only a few survive. The National Cryptologic Museum has at least three and the U.S. Naval Security Group has two. Some of the controlling patents were not made public until 2001.

Christopher H. Sterling

See also Arlington Hall; Bletchley Park; Code, Codebook; Code Breaking; Enigma; Friedman, William F. (1891–1969); Magic; Rowlett, Frank B. (1908–1998); Safford, Laurance F. (1890–1973); Signals Intelligence (SIGINT); Ultra

Sources

Andleman, D., and J. Reeds. 1982. "On Cryptanalysis of Rotor Machines and Substitution-Permutation Networks." *IEEE Transactions on Information Theory* IT-28 (4): 578–584.

Deavours, Cipher, and Louis Kruh. 1985. "Billy Friedman and the Electric Super-Code Machine." In *Machine Cryptography and Modern Cryptanalysis*, 35–92. Dedham, MA: Artech House.

Lee, Michael. 2003. "Cryptanalysis of the SIGABA." Master's thesis, University of California, Santa Barbara.

Pekelney, Richard S. 2006. "Electric Cipher Machine (ECM) Mark II." [Online article; retrieved March 2006.] http://www .maritime.org/ecm2.htm.

Savard, John J. G., and Richard S. Pekelney. 1999. "The ECM Mark II: Design, History and Cryptology,. *Cryptologia* 23 (July): 211–228.

Electromagnetic Pulse (EMP)

One of the effects of a high-altitude nuclear explosion is a very short (hundreds of nanoseconds) but intense and widespread blast of electromagnetic radiation. Gamma rays interact with the atmosphere to produce a radio frequency wave that covers every-thing within line of sight of the explosion epicenter. The electric and magnetic fields might couple with electrical and electronic systems producing severely damaging current and voltage surges. In effect, these systems on land, sea, and air may be paralyzed and irreversibly broken. The ionized air might also disrupt radio traffic and radar signals causing serious communication problems. High radio frequencies could be disrupted over large distances for minutes up to an hour depending on the given environment.

Commercial electrical networks could serve as huge EMP antennas, which would cause more severe effects than those of lightning strikes by destroying any equipment connected to electrical cables. When a semiconductive device absorbs EMP energy, it is not able to displace the heat quickly enough. The semiconductor heats up to temperatures near the melting point, which leads to thermal device failure. Modern very-large-scale integrated chips are extremely sensitive to any changes in voltage and would be destroyed by EMP. Particularly vulnerable are computers and radio or radar receivers. Commercial computers are especially susceptible as they are largely built of high-density metal oxide semiconductor devices, which are extremely sensitive to exposure to high-voltage transients. It has been estimated that a single high-altitude nuclear detonation 200 miles above Kansas could produce an EMP encompassing the entire United States.

The design of military equipment is generally supposed to make it resistant to EMP, although any realistic experiments or simulations are very difficult to conduct. Therefore, the effects for military command, control, and communications devices and systems cannot be fully predicted. Radar and electronic equipment, satellites, microwave, ultra-high frequency, very high frequency, high frequency, and low band communication systems as well as television equipment are potentially exposed to EMP damage.

The origins of the idea of using a nuclear burst to paralyze and destroy electrical, electronic, and communication systems of the enemy can be traced back to the U.S. hydrogen bomb test explosion in July 1962, code named Starfish Prime. The bomb was detonated in the Pacific Ocean 800 miles away from Hawaii. The blast generated an EMP that not only caused street lights to go dark and triggered burglar alarms but also blocked radio communication and damaged electrical devices throughout Hawaii. Two years earlier, a Soviet hydrogen bomb detonation over Siberia had a similar unexpected effect of knocking out communication systems.

Nonnuclear means can also produce EMP that would be even greater than that generated by a nuclear explosion. A conventional electromagnetic bomb (E-bomb) is a weapon designed to render inoperative electronics on a wide scale with an EMP. This kind of weapon is highly classified and secret. The United States and Russia are known to possess the technology for designing and producing such a weapon. The military aside, the whole idea inspires popular moviemakers—for example, E-bombs are used in *The Matrix* (1999)—and cyberpunk science fiction, where EMP becomes a "superweapon" destroying the infrastructure core of technologically advanced societies. The EMP could be a devastating means of asymmetric warfare.

Communication and information needs of twenty-first-century military operations require undisrupted flows of information. Modern military platforms developed under the notion of the Information Revolution in Military Affairs are densely packed with electronics, and unless well hardened, their

effectiveness and even functioning could be dramatically reduced by an EMP device. Computer-based communication systems of modern army operations are extremely vulnerable and could be rendered unusable by an EMP attack. Such an occurrence would have a vital effect on war-fighting capabilities.

Łukasz Kamieński

See also Communications Security (COMSEC); Computer; Information Revolution in Military Affairs (IRMA); Jamming; Microwave; Radio; Spectrum Frequencies

Sources

Foster, John S., Jr., et al. 2004. *Report of the Commission to Assess the Threat to the United States from Electromagnetic Pulse (EMP) Attack*. U.S. House of Representatives Armed Services Committee Executive Report, Vol. 1. Washington, DC: Government Printing Office.

Kopp, Carlo. 1996. "The Electromagnetic Bomb—A Weapon of Electrical Mass Destruction." In *Information Warfare—Cyberterrorism: Protecting Your Personal Security in the Electronic Age*, edited by Winn Schwartau, 296–333. New York: Thunder's Mouth Press.

Riddle, Thomas C. 2004. "Nuclear High Altitude Electromagnetic Pulse—Implications for Homeland Security and Homeland Defense." In *A Nation at War in an Era of Strategic Change*, edited by Williamson Murray, 69–93. Carlisle, PA: Strategic Studies Institute.

Spencer, Jack. 2004. "The Electromagnetic Pulse Commission Warns of an Old Threat with a New Face." *Backgrounder, No. 1784*. Washington, DC: The Heritage Foundation.

Electronic Countermeasures/ Electronic Warfare (ECM/EW)

The terms "electronic countermeasures" (ECM) and "electronic warfare" (EW) refer to a large family of technologies that support the interception of enemy signals, jamming of those signals (or antijamming, meaning defense from their jamming efforts), and deception—of any acoustic, optical, radar, or radio communication signals. Put another way, electronic warfare means military action involving the use of electromagnetic energy to determine, exploit, reduce, or prevent hostile use of the electromagnetic spectrum.

Generally speaking, the first use of what would later be termed ECM dates to the early years of the twentieth century and involved the jamming of opponents' radio signals during U.S. naval exercises. Attempts to jam enemy wireless were widespread during World War I naval actions. Between the wars, much attention (in Britain, the United States, and Germany) was paid to the development of radar—and how to protect against electronic or physical attacks on such facilities. The first widespread use of ECM activity began during World War II.

During the mid-1940 Battle of Britain, successful ECM efforts sought to disrupt German Luftwaffe navigational radio beams. Captured aircraft gave away the frequencies being used. The British often jammed German radio traffic—when not monitoring it for signals intelligence purposes. Facing huge losses of aircraft and crews, in November 1943, the British Royal Air Force (RAF) established 100 Group to be responsible for all electronic and radio countermeasures. Some group aircraft carried jamming equipment and flew with the bomber stream; others flew separate missions creating false radar echoes of spoof and decoy raids by nonexistent "ghost" squadrons dropping tinfoil ("window") to deflect enemy radar and other devices. Their radio transmitters also jammed German early warning radar and fighter control communications. A German-speaking RAF crew member would operate the jamming equipment and give false instructions to Luftwaffe fighter pilots. The group's aircraft were thus able to throw out a protective electronic "cloak" to help conceal the attack.

Shortly after the Pearl Harbor attack in December 1941, the U.S. Navy established a radio countermeasures research operation in Cambridge, Massachusetts, under Frederick Terman. Over several years it developed devices used during World War II against the Japanese and Germans. It also marked the beginning of a close working relationship between the military and academic scientists. During the war, Air Force bombers flew "ferret" missions to pick up the electronic signatures of enemy radar installations so they could later be targeted for destruction. ECM aircraft flew on most missions over Japan to confuse their air defense communications and radar.

In the long Cold War, Air Force and Navy bombers (and later U-2 reconnaissance aircraft) flew electronics intelligence (ELINT) missions along the borders of the Soviet Union seeking information on communication networks and radar installations. Such ECM/EW efforts were strongly aided by the solid state electronics revolution after 1960. Growing use of increasingly capable computers, large-scale integration of components to make ever-smaller devices, laser-guided weapons systems, ELINT communication satellites, and effective remote control made ECM/EW possible in all types of vehicles, some of them unmanned drones.

Deception has always been one element of ECM/EW efforts. During the Six Day War in 1967, for example, Israeli radio operators speaking fluent Egyptian Arabic were able to cause havoc with Egyptian fighters and air control. Similar efforts were made by American forces in the Gulf and Iraq wars.

Another kind of ECM/EW is more offensive as it involves using an electromagnetic pulse (EMP) to overpower or burn out electronic devices. This can be used to destroy an enemy's ability to communicate (though nowadays many communication centers, mobile and fixed, are protected—"hardened"—against EMP strikes). EMP can also be a very good psychological weapon as it can render all consumer electronics devices and computers useless.

Countermeasures to defeat enemy ECM/EW efforts are extensive. Sometimes called "counter counter" measures, these include a menu of techniques to overcome the potential damage of enemy efforts. For example, frequency hopping is one often effective way of escaping jamming efforts as it forces the adversary to expend huge sums of money for transmitters covering a wide band of frequencies.

The Association of Old Crows keeps EW veterans in touch and has published a three-volume history of the field. During World War II, operators of ECM equipment were often called ravens, or later, crows.

Christopher H. Sterling

See also Association of Old Crows (AOC); Britain, Battle of (1940); Communications Security (COMSEC); Deception; Intelligence Ships; Jamming; Laser; Meteor Burst Communications (MBC); National Defense Research Committee (NDRC); Naval Research Laboratory (NRL); Radio Silence; Signals Intelligence (SIGINT); Solid State Electronics

Sources
Dickson, Paul. 1976, *The Electronic Battlefield.* Bloomington: Indiana University Press.
Gebhard, Louis A. 1979. "Electronic Countermeasures." In *Evolution of Naval Radio-Electronics and Contributions of the Naval Research Laboratory*, 299–342. Washington, DC: Government Printing Office.
Price, Alfred. 1984, 1989, 2001. *The History of U.S. Electronic Warfare.* 3 vols. Alexandria, VA: Association of Old Crows.
Robb, Stephen C. 1990. "Marine Corps Electronic Warfare—A Combat Power Multiplier." [Online article; retrieved March 2006.] http://www.globalsecurity. org military/library/report/1990/RSC.htm.

E-Mail Systems

Since the 1990s, American military services (and those of most other nations) have developed increasingly sophisticated systems of electronic mail (e-mail) for both tactical and strategic needs as well as individual communication. The Defense Message Service (DMS) was giving way to the improved Military Message Handling System (MMHS) around 2005.

The DMS was created by the Defense Information Systems Agency for defense and related agencies. Begun with testing in 1995, the DMS was designed as a flexible, commercial off-the-shelf (COTS)–based application providing multimedia messaging and directory services using the underlying Defense Information Infrastructure network and security services. The DMS provided electronic message service to all U.S. Department of Defense (DoD) users (including deployed tactical users) and interfaced with other U.S. government agencies, allied forces, and defense contractors. The DMS offered two levels of service: High grade provided organizational messaging/record traffic and replaced incompatible, unsecured e-mail systems. Medium grade was a protected messaging capability for individuals and utilized COTS e-mail products administered as standard network applications across DoD.

Despite its bandwidth and computer equipment requirements, the DMS was installed worldwide. It replaced the earlier Automatic Digital Network and about forty other individual e-mail systems. It is, in turn, being replaced by the MMHS, which is a North Atlantic Treaty Organization standard and offers more sophisticated user identification and security. Both the National Gateway System and the Pentagon Telecommunications System Center provide defense agencies with a continuing capability to satisfy electronic messaging requirements, allied and tactical interoperability, and emergency action message dissemination. Security and delivery assurance mechanisms are approved (or developed) by the National Security Agency for information classified at all levels, including top secret.

By the early 2000s, all branches of the U.S. military offered some sort of e-mail access to individual servicemen and servicewomen. In larger installations, personnel have access to high-speed connections. But in smaller outposts Internet connections are made through satellite linkups and may be limited to a very few computers. American forces in the Middle East found e-mail a vastly improved means of keeping in touch with home than earlier "snail" mail and expensive telephone links. Any use of e-mail, of course, prompts unique security risks. Though military officials believe that the instantaneous interaction e-mail provides to soldiers in remote locations helps to improve morale in the field and at home, many worry that there could be inadvertent leaks of sensitive information from the battlefield. Soldiers in all branches have been instructed not to send certain types of information over the Internet, but policies are generally left up to division and unit commanders.

Christopher H. Sterling

See also Automatic Digital Network (AUTODIN); Defense Information Systems Agency (DISA); Defense Message System (DMS); Global Information Grid (GIG); Internet; National Security Agency (NSA); Voice over Internet Protocol (VoIP)

Source
Defense Information Systems Agency. 2005. "Defense Message System (DMS)." [Online information; retrieved March 2006.] http://www.disa.mil/main/prodsol/dms.html.

Enigma

The Enigma was a multirotor cipher machine widely used by all military forces and most government agencies in Nazi Germany before and during World War II. The breaking of many of its messages by the Allies shortened the war by revealing German plans.

The Enigma device originated with Arthur Scherbius (1878–1929), an electrical engineer who worked for German and Swiss electrical firms before setting up his own company. In the early 1920s, he developed (and named) the Enigma rotor cipher machine, designed for commercial (nonsecret) codes. The key part of the instrument was its four Bakelite (later metal) rotors, which were electrically interconnected to create the coding effect. The first model of the machine was exhibited at a 1923 postal conference in Bern and showed a standard typewriter keyboard. It was both heavy and bulky and was mounted in a wooden case. Though he offered the device to the German navy and the Weimar Republic's foreign office, neither was then interested. In 1923 he sold rights to the machine to another company, which aggressively marketed a series of four improved models, though with only limited results despite favorable publicity and several government purchasers.

In 1926 German naval intelligence began utilizing an Enigma coding machine, modified from one it had purchased from domestic commercial sources. The Italian navy also purchased some Enigma machines. The German army soon followed suit, making fur-

An Enigma cipher machine, used by the German military in World War II to encrypt communications, was the first target of Bletchley Park code breakers. It combined the use of rotors and plugboards to increase the permutations of its signals. (Hulton/Getty Images)

came with their machines. Settings were changed every few months. The number of plugs available increased before and during the war, adding to the machine's security. In 1938, the German army and air force began to require operators to make their own machine settings while the navy retained a standard service approach. During the war, rotor and/or plug settings were changed daily, and sometimes several times in a given day. Two or three people were needed to operate the device in the field.

Some 30,000 Enigma machines of various models were used during the war—more than any other cipher machine by any nation. While this allowed for a standard training practice, it also made it harder to change methods or equipment and made code breaking easier due to the number of messages sent. Perhaps 200 German codes were employed prior to and during World War II, and not all of them were broken. The Germans did not believe that their codes could be compromised, and consequently, the high standards set for their signal staff and security procedures were sometimes relaxed. This contributed to a number of code-breaking breakthroughs for the British and Americans.

The Germans developed several more sophisticated cipher machines for specific uses. Each was given an Allied "fish" code name. The role of all of these machines remained secret for three decades after the war as thousands of Enigmas had survived and were given to other governments—without any notion that the British could read their communications. Examples of most of the Enigma and other cipher machines can today be found in museums.

Christopher H. Sterling

See also Arlington Hall; Bletchley Park; Code, Codebook; Code Breaking; German "Fish" Codes; Germany: Air Force; Germany:

ther modifications to its three-rotor machines. By 1930 the military versions differed substantially from those still on the commercial market, chiefly by the addition of a plugboard (*stecker*) in the front of the device, allowing a huge increase in the number of code permutations that could be transmitted. Indeed, the machine was now considered by its users to be unbreakable. This improved version was first used by the German navy in October 1934 and the reconstituted Luftwaffe in August 1935. By 1938, additional rotors were made available, hugely increasing the difficulty of decoding the machine. By 1939, for example, naval operators could select three operating rotors from among eight that

Army; Germany: Naval Intelligence (*B-Dienst*); Germany: Navy; Nebraska Avenue, Washington DC; Polish Code Breaking; Signals Intelligence (SIGINT); Tiltman, John Hessell (1894–1982); Turing, Alan Mathison (1912–1954); Ultra; Welchman, Gordon (1906–1985); Y Service

Sources

Deavours, Cipher A., and Louis Kruh. 1985. *Machine Cryptography and Modern Cryptanalysis*. Dedham, MA: Artech House.

Mowry, David P. 2003. *German Cipher Machines of World War II*. Fort Meade, MD: National Security Agency.

Winkel, Brian J., Cipher A. Deavours, David Kahn, and Louis Kruh, eds. 2005. *The German Enigma Cipher Machine: Beginnings, Success, and Ultimate Failure*. Dedham, MA: Artech House.

European Late Nineteenth-Century Wars

Changing modes of communication, and especially the electric telegraph, played a growing part in European wars in the last half of the nineteenth century. Military and government use of electric telegraphy was initially dominant as the technology was introduced in mid-century.

The first military test of telegraphy came during the Crimean War (1854–1856), in which Britain and France sought to stop Russian expansion into Ottoman (Turkish) territory. An extensive Russian electric telegraph system, completed by the German firm of Siemens & Halske in 1855, provided a vital link from north of St. Petersburg (then the capital) through Moscow and south to Sevastopol on the Black Sea (site of a long siege) as well as east to Warsaw. On the other side, British Royal Engineers built and operated 21 miles of Wheatstone single- needle telegraph line between British headquarters

at Balaclava and French headquarters in Kamiesch. It was subject to constant battle damage and only marginally useful. In 1855, a private firm under military direction constructed an underwater cable of 340 miles (by far the longest ever constructed to that point) to connect Balaclava across the Black Sea with Varna in present-day Bulgaria (and then connecting with existing continental telegraph lines). It lasted only eight months due to its fragility.

As a result of these new connections, commanders in the field were for the first time interfered with (they felt) by constant questions and suggestions (and sometimes orders) from distant military headquarters in London and Paris. Postwar assessments of telegraphy suggested, however, that it had limited impact on the fighting.

In the war between France and Austria in the early 1860s, both armies made tactical use of telegraphy and often attacked the other side's communication lines. Growing out of its success in rapidly laying field telegraph lines, France established the Telegraph Brigade as well as a school to train telegraphers in 1868. Likewise, Prussia benefited from its effective use of telegraphy in the several wars leading to German unification. The Franco-Prussian War (1870–1871) saw Germany using both military and civil telegraph systems, as well as lines captured from the French. Germany formed special telegraph companies for fighting army units, and her aggressive laying of tactical lines sometimes preceded military actions. French forces surrounded in Paris made notable use of hot air balloons to get messages (and often human and pigeon messengers) above and beyond German siege lines.

The often central role of telegraphy during the American Civil War (1861–1865) prompted European armies and navies to more closely examine use of the technology. The British School of Military Engineering formed a signal wing in 1869 to teach both electric and visual telegraphy methods. In 1886 the School of Signaling focused on visual methods and electric telegraphy remained with the engineers until both methods were again combined on the eve of World War I.

Military forces in all countries were slow to adopt the telephone in the late nineteenth century, however, due to the technology's lack of effective repeaters for long-range use and the widespread preference for paper copies of commands provided by the older telegraph. The full potential of the telephone was only slowly realized. The first military telephone switchboard was not installed by Britain until 1896. Prussian cavalry units experimented with field telephones a year earlier.

On the other hand, wireless telegraphy was pursued vigorously as a method of military communication. The British army and such Royal Navy officers as Henry Jackson were among those who pioneered research on the military potential of wireless telegraphy, applying crude systems to experimental field conditions. The French installed wireless on a gunboat in 1899. German military units were assisted by the work of their countrymen Adolph Slaby and George von Arco in the 1890s. Generally, merchant ships were quicker to adopt wireless than their military counterparts.

Despite the newer systems, old means of communicating remained in use, sometimes because electrical systems were not available.

As with all military communications, however, even the tried and true suffered ill use: the infamous and futile charge of the Light Brigade during the Crimean War was due to a garbled order sent by courier. To the end of the century, most European armies retained extensive military pigeon messaging systems, at least as a backup to other modes of communicating. And European naval forces continued to rely heavily on flag signals by day and Ardois and other light systems by night.

Christopher H. Sterling

See also Airships and Balloons; American Civil War (1861–1865); Ardois Light; France: Army; Germany: Army; Jackson, Henry B. (1855–1929); Spanish-American War (1898); Telegraph; Telephone; Undersea Cables

Sources
Allat, H. T. W. 1886. "The Use of Pigeons as Messengers in War and the Military Pigeon Systems of Europe." *Journal of the Royal United Service Institution* 30: 107–148.

Beauchamp, Ken. 2001. *History of Telegraphy*. London: Institution of Electrical Engineers.

Nalder, R. F. H. 1958. *The Royal Corps of Signals: A History of Its Antecedents and Development*. London: Royal Signals Association.

Scheips, Paul J., ed. 1980. *Military Signal Communications*. New York: Arno Press.

Schowalter, Dennis. 1973. "Soldiers into Postmasters? The Electric Telegraph as an Instrument of Command in the Prussian Army." *Military Affairs* 37 (April): 48–52.

Von Chauvin, Maj. Gen. 1884. "The Organization of the Electric Telegraph in Germany for War Purposes." *Journal of the Royal United Service Institution* 28: 777–808, 1051–1064.

F

Facsimile/Fax

To create an electronic facsimile means to transmit an exact copy of a graphic, photo, or document at a distance. Usually abbreviated as "fax," the process combines some means of scanning the image and its transmission by wire or wireless. It has been in military use since World War II.

Facsimile developed more than a century before it became widespread, the result of work by many inventors in several countries. The first facsimile was the chemical telegraph of Alexander Bain (1811–1877) patented in 1842 and operated a decade later. Shortly thereafter, Frederick Bakewell introduced the notion of scanning a document line by line. Both systems used damp electrolytic paper as a recording medium and a scanning stylus in physical contact with the text. Bain's was a flatbed machine while in Bakewell's model the papers were wound on drums, which long served as a fax standard. For years development of facsimile focused on improving its scanning and reproduction functions. In 1865 the first working trials for a commercially viable facsimile machine

were begun in France by an Italian, Giovanni Caselli. Soon facsimile machines were in service in the French telegraph system, used primarily by the French government to carry stock information. Fax drew usage thanks to elimination of errors in transmission and the availability of a facsimile signature so important in business transactions.

The nineteenth-century contact type of facsimile device limited transmission speed. This was overcome through the 1902 development of the photoelectric cell by Arthur Korn of Germany, and his application of it to phototelegraphy work. By 1910 Korn had established phototelegraphy links from Berlin to Paris and London, and in 1922 he successfully transmitted a picture from Rome to New York by radio. In 1926 a commercial radio link for facsimile was opened between London and New York. Soon pictures for newspaper publication were being transmitted around the world. Developments in the 1930s by Bell Labs and others included transmission of weather maps and wire photo services. The expense of having material photographed for transmission led to a system of transmission based on reflected light. In 1935 the Associated Press installed a countrywide wire photo network, and postal services offered public fax access. Several attempts to introduce facsimile news into the residential market failed to achieve widespread adoption.

During World War II, use of facsimile aided U.S. military forces in several ways. In mid-1942 the Army Communications Service began providing telephotos for domestic newspaper use. In January 1943, the Air Force began transmitting accurate, current weather charts, though each one took twenty minutes to transmit.

Only in the 1960s did cheaper facsimile machines become available for connection by telephone. Growth was prompted in the United States by declining postal services and in Japan by the pictorial nature of its complex alphabet. Solid state digital technology was introduced, and technical standards developed by the International Telecommunication Union (the first in 1968) reduced transmission time for a page to six minutes. Improved standards in 1976 halved transmission time and improved graphic quality. By 1980 fax machines used digital transmission, were smaller and cheaper, and took less than a minute per page with better resolution. Japanese firms began mass production of digital fax machines. Standards have continued to improve, but fax usage is declining in the face of Internet capabilities.

Military use of fax remains important today thanks to secure devices (those that are Joint Interoperability Test Command certified), including TEMPEST (a code name referring to investigations and studies of compromising emanations) models internally shielded to prevent electronic emissions from escaping and allowing detection—though at a sharp premium in equipment cost. Secure fax operation depends on sufficient document memory and ten-keypad dialing as well as the use of digital cryptographic systems.

Christopher H. Sterling

See also Bain, Alexander (1811–1877); Bell Telephone Laboratories (BTL); Internet; Telegraph

Sources

Coopersmith, J. 1994. "The Failure of Fax: When a Vision is Not Enough." *Economic and Business History* 23: 272–282.

Costigan, Daniel M. 1978. "History." In *Electronic Delivery of Documents and Graphics,* 2–21. New York: Van Nostrand Reinhold.

Hatch, Carl H. 1944. "Radiophoto." *Radio News* U.S. Army Signal Corps Issue (February): 218, 316, 318, 320.

HF-Fax Image Communication. "History." [Online information; retrieved September 1995.] http://www.hffax.de/html/hauptteil_faxhistory.htm.

Peterson, M. J. 1995. "The Emergence of a Mass Market for Fax Machines." *Technology and Society* 17: 469–482.

Falklands Conflict (1982)

The 1982 confrontation between Britain and Argentina over the British colony of the Falkland (Malvinas) Islands provided a good example of the central role of communications. When Argentinian forces surrendered to the British on 14 June 1982, their occupation of the Falkland Islands had lasted for seventy-four days. (They held the related but 800-mile-distant South Georgia for only three weeks.) This ten-week interlude had interrupted 142 years of British rule of the Falklands (population less than 2,000) as a Crown colony.

The Argentine forces had landed on 2 April 1982, leading to uproar in Britain and the launching of a naval task force to retake the colony. The task force (which included two carriers) left Portsmouth on 5 April 1982, to be followed by three British liners rapidly converted to troop-carrying status. The first Royal Signals involvement was with SAS (Special Air Service Regiment, or commando) detachments that were inserted onto South Georgia and later East Falkland to obtain information about the enemy. Radio communications over the 8,000 miles back to Britain (the Falklands are just 300 miles offshore from Argentina) were sometimes interrupted by atmospheric conditions in the islands, which suffer a harsh climate. Conditions on the ground also made communication security difficult to achieve, as did constant Argentinian air attacks.

Britain's 30 Signal Regiment established a communications center at the staging post on Ascension Island, the British staging base some 2,000 miles north of the Falklands. Royal Signals detachments provided rear link communications from most fighting units. By 1 June 1982, 5 Infantry Brigade headquarters and a signal squadron had landed at St. Carlos and used the new Clansman-type combat radios. The regiment, with support from other units, formed a unit to support the British land forces headquarters. Members of 50 Signallers ran fifteen radio networks aboard HMS *Fearless*, which was the main headquarters for the British attack.

30 Signal Regiment also provided satellite communications back to Britain and secure telegraph connections for two brigades. Shipborne satellite terminals assisted. This was the first use of satellite communication by the army in a major operation. As one participant noted later, the radio telephone was as clear as if the call had been coming from next door. Approximately 600 Royal Signals men had taken part in the action.

When the short but bitter battle to retake the Falklands was over, the islands' com-munications infrastructure had to be largely replaced. Microwave networks were established to link outlying communities with the capital of Port Stanley. Once again weather (winter in the South Atlantic) made installation of those facilities most difficult.

Christopher H. Sterling

See also United Kingdom: Royal Corps of Signals

Sources

Hastings, Max, and Simon Jenkins. 1984. *The Battle for the Falklands.* New York: Norton.

Warner, Philip. 1989. "'Operation Corporate' The Falklands War." In *The Vital Link: The Story of Royal Signals, 1945–1985*, chap. 8. London: Leo Cooper.

Fateful Day—25 June 1876

Sunday, 25 June 1876, is a little-noted communications landmark in American history. On that one day, separated by several hours but more than 2,000 miles, two events occurred that provide an ironic hint of how changing communications technology would eventually meet military needs.

Philadelphia was the site of the extensive Centennial Exposition in Fairmont Park, which was attracting hordes of visitors that summer. Its several ornate buildings were filled with exhibits of the latest technologies, including a massive Corliss steam engine that dominated Machinery Hall. The exposition's buildings were closed on that hot June day (because it was a Sunday), as judges gathered to award prizes for selected exhibits, a task made easier without the noise from visiting crowds. Brazilian Emperor Dom Pedro, on an extended visit to the United States, was on hand as he paid a return visit to the exposition. He had become interested in deaf education and wanted to see what Alexander Graham Bell was displaying. Bell's exhibit occupied one small table in a back corner of the East Gallery. Dom Pedro led others back to Bell's crude telegraph (as it was called) equipment and soon heard it demonstrated by the inventor. As he listened to the faint words the device transmitted, Dom Pedro exclaimed, "I hear, I hear!" Soon word of mouth spread news of Bell's voice-telegraph display and demonstrations. While few then recognized it, Bell's device was only the beginning of what would become a huge new business that would join and eventually supplant the telegraph.

On that same Sunday, almost 2,500 miles to the west and several hours later, the sun was also hot above the ridge overlooking the Little Bighorn River in southern Montana Territory. Lieutenant Colonel George A. Custer was leading five companies of the U.S. Army's Seventh Cavalry on a punitive expedition against a number of Indian tribes who had left their reservations. Expecting to meet only feeble resistance, Custer instead ran into a huge encampment of thousands of Indians, including about 2,500 fighting men. Before the day was over, he and his less than 200 men would lie dead after a brief but hard-fought battle, overwhelmed by the Indian warriors. Though another seven companies of cavalry were but four miles away, Custer lacked any effective means of rapidly bringing them to the site of the fighting— and he and his men died as a result. While controversy over orders and common sense have swirled around the infamous "last stand" ever since, the fact remains that had Custer an effective means of rapidly signaling his unit's distress, the result might have been different. Then again, it can be argued that the twenty-minute fight did not leave much room for variation.

Putting the two events of 25 June 1876 together with 130 years' retrospective, we can see that what was shown in Philadelphia, crude and tentative though it then was, would grow to become a vital means of communications, military and otherwise. In years to come, improving modes of rapid communication would prove vital to meeting the military needs exemplified by that lonely ridge above the Little Big Horn River.

Christopher H. Sterling

See also Bell, Alexander Graham (1847–1922); Telephone

Sources

Bruce, Robert V. 1973. "Philadelphia, 1876." In *Bell: Alexander Graham Bell and the Conquest of Solitude*, chap. 18. Boston: Little, Brown.

Panzeri, Peter F. 1995. *Little Big Horn 1876: Custer's Last Stand*. Campaign Series No. 39. London: Osprey.

Ferrié, Gustave-Auguste (1868–1932)

A French engineer and scientist as well as an army officer, Ferrié was the World War I head of his country's military communications and accomplished pioneering work in both ground telegraphy and radio.

Born 19 November 1868 in St. Michel in Savoy, France, Ferrié graduated from the prestigious École Polytechnique in Paris in 1891, becoming an engineering officer in the French army. From 1893 to 1898 he worked on improving his country's military telegraph service. When Ferrié was named to a committee exploring the potential for wireless telegraphy, however, he found his real niche. By 1899 he was working with Guglielmo Marconi in Paris on wireless links with England. In 1903 Ferrié invented an electrolytic detector (an early means of receiving wireless signals), which proved more reliable than the Branly coherer then in widespread use.

After he proposed using the Eiffel Tower in 1903 to mount antennas for longer-range radiotelegraphy, under his direction a transmitter was installed in the tower. Over five years of effort, its effective range increased from an initial 250 miles to 3,700 miles by 1908. He then turned to development of mobile transmitters to enable military units to stay in contact with their Paris headquarters.

When World War I began in August 1914, then Colonel Ferrié was appointed to direct French military radio communications. He quickly assembled scientists and technicians who established a network of radio direction finders stretching from the English Channel to the Swiss border. During the war years Ferrié made considerable advances in telegraphy. Using the triode vacuum tube, Ferrié made improvements in the transmitter (signal generator) and the receiver and achieved a usual range of several miles. His simple army transmitter was essentially a buzzer (or, more technically, an electromechanical device that interrupts a circuit at a high rate of speed) powered by a battery. The receiver served as an amplifier. To complete a communications circuit, earth connections were made by driving steel pins into the ground. Additionally, a short length of insulated wire was often laid along the ground surface and anchored at each end by a spike. Thus was born ground telegraphy or earth-currents signaling.

These simple devices began to be used in large numbers in 1916, and by the end of the war the French had produced almost 10,000 of them. In the process of ground telegraphy operations, users discovered that their receivers frequently could pick up other telegraph or telephone signals from lines buried nearby. They could thus tap enemy lines as well as receive their own signals when a line had been severed. These receivers came to play a large role in eavesdropping. Its portability and its freedom from electrical lines made ground telegraphy an important means of communication during the war. Yet even before war's end in 1918, ground telegraphy began to be displaced by radio.

Ferrié created a radio section at the École Supérieur d'Électricité in Gif sur Yvette. He also experimented with radio transmissions from aircraft to direct artillery fire. He became a general in 1919 and continued in service, exempted from retirement in accordance with a special law enacted in 1930. He received many awards and honorary degrees and served as an officer of several scientific groups. Ferrié died on 16 February 1932 in Paris at the age of sixty-five.

Christopher H. Sterling

See also France: Army; Fullerphone; Radio; Vacuum Tube; World War I

Source

Geocities.com. "Gustave-Auguste Ferrié." [Online information; retrieved November 2004.] http://www.geocities.com/neveyaakov/electro_science/ferrie.html.

Fessenden, Reginald A. (1866–1932)

Reginald Fessenden was an important wireless pioneer who developed several important radio devices (using his heterodyne and continuous wave innovations) early in the twentieth century. He was among the first to broadcast voice and music signals, in addition to more traditional telegraphic code.

Born in Quebec on 6 October 1866, Fessenden was introduced to electricity in 1886 when he began working for Thomas Edison's company. By the early 1890s he had worked for Westinghouse and had published several articles and (though he lacked academic credentials) become a professor of electrical engineering, first at Purdue University and then, in 1893, at Western Pennsylvania University (later University of Pittsburgh). In 1900 he began contract wireless development work for the U.S. Weather Bureau. By mid-year he had managed to transmit the human voice to stations a mile apart near Rock Point, Maryland. In 1903 he became the chief researcher of the new National Electric Signal Company (NESCO) with financial support from two Pittsburgh financiers who sought to exploit his newly developed heterodyne principle, which allowed sending and receiving from the same antenna, a notion about a decade ahead of its time.

Fessenden also developed the idea of an alternator device to transmit continuous wave signals (this was further developed and improved by Ernst Alexanderson of General Electric) and a liquid barretter, or electrolytic detector of wireless signals, that was soon widely used by the U.S. Navy—which ignored his patent rights and purchased equipment from other sources. Navy officers also experimented extensively with the Fessenden devices at their research radio station (which became NAA) in Arlington, Virginia. Wartime Navy wireless employed equipment using Fessenden's principles until replaced by vacuum tube devices.

NESCO built a number of coastal transmitters and experimented with transoceanic wireless telegraphy. Fessenden had also successfully transmitted voice and music signals on several occasions, some of them witnessed, by 1905. His difficult personality and lack of marketing ability (or interest), how-

Reginald Fessenden is the Canadian experimenter generally credited with transmitting the first wireless voice and music signals early in the 20th century. He later worked on submarine signaling devices. (Circer, Hayward, ed., Dictionary of American Portraits, 1967)

ever, led to constant bickering with his own backers and many potential clients. Fessenden had largely left the wireless business (his bankrupt firm was sold for the patent rights it held—those rights ended up with Radio Corporation of America) by 1912, ironically just about the time the developing radio industry had begun to agree on the need for the continuous wave transmissions he had pioneered.

Fessenden's final radio work involved the Submarine Signal Company of Boston, which he joined in 1912 to perfect underwater signal transmission and reception, naturally of interest to the Navy. With Navy support, the company tested the Fessenden Oscillator as a means of detecting icebergs, determining water depth, and locating submarines. Again, the Navy used his innovations without paying royalties or even granting him credit until decades later. Fessenden left the firm in 1921 and retired to Bermuda where he died on 23 July 1932.

Christopher H. Sterling

See also de Forest, Lee (1873–1961); Edison, Thomas A. (1847–1931); Naval Radio Stations/Service; U.S. Navy

Sources

Aitken, Hugh G. J. 1985. "Fessenden and the Alternator." In *The Continuous Wave: Technology and American Radio, 1900–1932*. Princeton, NJ: Princeton University Press.

Fessenden, Helen M. 1940. *Fessenden: Builder of Tomorrows*. New York: Coward McCann (reprinted by Arno Press, 1974).

Fessenden, R. A. 1899. "The Possibilities of Wireless Telegraphy." *Transactions of the American Institute of Electrical Engineers* 16: 607–651.

Howeth, L. S. 1963. *History of Communications-Electronics in the United States Navy*. Washington, DC: Government Printing Office.

Seitz, Frederick. 1999. *The Cosmic Inventor: Reginald Aubrey Fessenden*. Philadelphia: American Philosophical Society.

Fiber Optics

A fiber optic telecommunications line or cable combines purified glass and lasers to communicate with broadband capacities at a very high speed. While some of the ideas are anything but new, developing an economically viable fiber optic system for distance communications has occurred only over the past several decades. The chief technical problems in developing such a system included developing a source of power to transmit a message (this became the laser) and improving the purity of the glass used in the cable. Into the early 1960s, most optical fiber was useful only for very short distances—such as in surgery—because of rapid signal attenuation.

After preliminary research at Fort Monmouth, New Jersey, then headquarters of the Army Signal Corps, in 1961 and 1962, the idea of using highly pure glass fiber to transmit light was made public information in a request for proposals issued to all research laboratories. Corning Glass in New York won the contract in 1962. Federal funding for glass fiber optics research at Corning totaled about $1 million by 1970. Signal Corps funding of many research programs on fiber optics continued until 1985, thereby seeding the multibillion dollar industry that all but eliminated copper wire in communications transmission.

The American military adopted fiber optics well before most commercial applications, generally for improved communications and tactical systems. In an early 1970s demonstration, the U.S. Navy installed a fiber optic telephone link aboard the USS *Little Rock*, testing to see how well it eliminated electromagnetic interference from other devices on board. Using fiber optics rather than copper also saves weight—literally tons of it on a vessel of any size. The Air Force followed suit by developing its Airborne Light Optical Fiber Technology program in 1976. Encouraged by the success of these and other applications, military research and development programs sought stronger fibers, tactical cables, more rugged high-performance components, and numerous demonstration systems ranging from aircraft to undersea cable applications. By the mid-1980s, the Pentagon itself began an optical fiber rewiring process, as did many related organizations such as the National Security Agency and the country's atomic laboratories.

Several weapons systems incorporated fiber systems, including the fiber optic guided missile used for short-range tactical missiles. The missile pays out a cable as it flies (at a bit less than 200 miles per hour) and the operator can receive video and data to help guide it more closely to its target. The Navy's Ariadne system, studied in the late 1980s, proposed an antisubmarine listening network on both coasts, linking undersea microphones with fiber optic cables. Fiber links also allow for a central operator to control many and more distant radar or listening posts. The Defense Commercialization Telecommunications Network was a decade-long project through the 1990s to link (with both fiber optic networks and satellites) more than 150 military bases and fifteen major military nodes throughout the United States.

Fiber optics offers a number of military advantages over other modes of communication. These include longer distances between repeaters, immunity from radio frequency and electromagnetic interference, operating without emitting an electronic "signature" that can be picked up by an enemy, and relatively light weight (compared, for example, to copper lines) and space requirements.

Despite widespread assumptions about their relative invulnerability, however, experts say fiber optic networks are susceptible to intrusions and other security threats. Because most intrusion detection systems for fiber optics are not sensitive enough, intruders could read information from a fiber optic network without the knowledge of its administrator or users. The military has encased some fiber links within cement conduits, but that obviously limits access for repair and upgrading.

Christopher H. Sterling

See also Bell Telephone Laboratories (BTL); Communications Security (COMSEC); Fort Monmouth, New Jersey; Laser; Undersea Cables

Sources
Boyle, W. S. 1977. "Light-Wave Communications" *Scientific American* August: 40–48.
Chafee, C. David. 1988. "Refitting the U.S. Military." In *The Rewiring of America: The Fiber Optics Revolution*, 173–190. Orlando, FL: Academic Press.
Hecht, Jeff. 1999. *City of Light: The Story of Fiber Optics.* New York: Oxford University Press.

Field, Cyrus W. (1819–1892)

More than any other person, Cyrus Field was responsible for financing and directing the laying of the first Atlantic telegraph cables that would help revolutionize world communications. While he himself was not involved in military applications of cable telegraphy, he made them possible.

Field was born, one of ten children, on 30 November 1819 in Stockbridge, Massachusetts, and moved to New York City while still in his teens to serve as an apprentice at a large dry goods store. He then joined his older brother's papermaking company. By the end of the 1840s he had retired a wealthy man from his career in the paper business and had built a house facing fashionable Gramercy Park. In 1852, he first heard about the possibilities of submarine telegraphy from Frederick Gisborne, who wanted to build a line to and across Newfoundland, thus saving two days in message transmission from Europe to New York. Field was soon hooked on the new technology, the idea of building a cable from Newfoundland to Ireland, and saving two weeks. He was soon raising funds to build such a transatlantic cable—the laying of a cable under the English Channel had taken place just three years earlier.

After several failed attempts (all of the science and technology was new and mistakes were rife), the first successful cable was laid in August 1858. Sadly, it worked for only about a month—to great fanfare on both sides of the Atlantic—but slowly went dead, probably a victim of faulty insulation or too much power for the lines. Rising political tension that would lead to the American Civil War made seeking investment all but impossible until the mid-1860s when Field tried again. In mid-1865, with improved cable and a huge ship (Brunel's *Great Eastern*, the largest in the world), his consortium nearly completed a cable when the line parted just short of shore. Raising still more funds, Field tried one more time and in 1866 finally achieved lasting success. The 1865 cable was also raised and repaired so there were two strands across the ocean.

With millions earned from the transatlantic cable, Field returned to New York for much of the rest of his life. He seriously explored options for a Pacific telegraph cable, but could not get cooperation of the many governments involved. He invested in the city's elevated railroads as well as railways elsewhere. Ultimately, he was double-crossed by his business partners (one was financier Jay Gould) while his remaining fortune was stolen by his son, leaving Field nearly penniless. Field died at age seventy-two in Stockbridge on 12 July 1892.

Christopher H. Sterling

See also Undersea Cables

Sources

Carter, Samuel. 1968. *Cyrus Field: Man of Two Worlds*. New York: Putnam.

Gordon, John Steele. 2002. *A Thread Across the Ocean: The Heroic Story of the Transatlantic Cable*. New York: Walker.

Hearn, Chester G. 2004. *Circuits in the Sea: The Men, the Ships, and the Atlantic Cable*. Westport, CT: Praeger.

Judson, Isabella Field. 1896. *Cyrus W. Field: His Life and Work*. New York: Harcourt, Brace.

McDonald, Philip B.1937. *A Saga of the Seas*. New York: Wilson-Erickson.

Field Wire and Cable

Wire and cable are used to interconnect activities within command posts and between radio relay terminals and switching centers. Long-haul wire circuits (trunks) are installed to complement radio systems when time, personnel, and equipment are available. Wire or cable is especially useful in military operations where movement is static or limited, as on an established base.

Several types of communications wire and cable exist. A single conductor line is the basic connection for simple telegraphy; it can be bare or insulated. A multiconductor consists of multiple insulated wires. The term "twisted pair" refers to two insulated wires twisted together for strength and ease of laying. The standard means of telephone networking, coaxial cable features an insulated center conductor with a shield (which is also a conductor) and a protective jacket and is used for broadband or video communication. There are many types of wire gauge (smaller gauge wire in World War II worked as well as larger gauge wire in World War I) as well as protective shields.

Among the many advantages of military use of wire and cable communications are that they reduce the need for radio (which can be so easily intercepted) and decrease radio interference; they can lower the electronic "signature" of command posts; and they reduce the enemy's jamming, interference, and direction-finding capabilities. Wire and cable can provide backup and increased traffic capabilities for military radio systems and are not subject to interference or jamming.

Among their disadvantages are that military wire and cable take time to install and maintain, and, as with radio, they are not secure unless encrypted. Wire and cable networks cannot readily react to fast-moving situations and are limited by both terrain and distance considerations. Unlike radio, they are susceptible to damage by friendly action (such as wheeled and tracked vehicle movement across them) as well as being susceptible to damage by direct or indirect artillery fire or bombing. Finally, wire and cable both conduct electromagnetic pulses, which can seriously damage attached telephone and switching equipment.

Wire and cable can be laid in different ways, ranging from an individual pulling lines to specially designed vehicles or, for line burial, cable plows. Special reels can carry wire in such a way as to allow rapid unwinding and laying in battle conditions. These reels were mounted on horseback well into World War I. During World War II, a cable thrower allowed wire to be laid from a rapidly moving truck, the wire projected to the side of the road and into trees. The same unit could recover wire, though more slowly.

Christopher H. Sterling

See also Communications Security (COMSEC); Fiber Optics; Undersea Cables

Sources

Black, R.M. 1983. *The History of Electric Wires and Cables*. London: Peter Peregrinus.

Department of the Army, 1990. "Wire and Cable Operations." In *Communications in a "Come-as-you-are" War*, chap. 5. Field Manual 24–12. Washington, DC: Government Printing Office.

Franzen, Roy O. 1942. "Wire Communication." *Radio News* Special U.S. Army Signal Corps Issue (November): 102–105, 204–208.

Precision Measurement Equipment Laboratories. "Electrical Wire and Cable Glossary." [Online information; retrieved June 2006.] http://www.pmel.org/Wire-Cable-Glossary.htm.

U.S. Army Signal Center. "Wire and Cable Equipment, World War II." [Online information; retrieved June 2006.] http://www.gordon.army.mil/ocos/Museum/AMC/wire.asp.

Fire/Flame/Torch

The use of fire or torches for signaling is surely one of the oldest human means of distant communication. Indeed the use of fire was for thousands of years the only means of sending a nighttime message. Simple fires could be made to flare up (by adding fuel) to make a signal. Or the flames could be hidden (by a blanket or animal skin), allowing very basic "on-off" coded messages.

Both the Greeks and the Romans used bonfires to communicate messages over long distances. A line of bonfires was laid on hilltops from the scene of a battle to the nearest main town. As one fire was lit, the team at the next one in the chain would see it and light theirs, and so on until the last fire was lit. This system lent itself only to simple yes-no, won-lost kinds of messages.

A more complex Roman signaling method, which drew on earlier Greek and Carthaginian "water clocks," combined use of torches and containers (usually wooden barrels) filled with water. Each sending and receiving site would have a numbered list of messages—essentially a code. Each site also had a barrel of water with a scale of numbers running vertically down the inside. The sender would raise his torch to show intent to begin a message. The receiver would raise his torch to indicate readiness to receive. The sender would then remove the bung from the barrel and raise his torch, holding it up while water drained into a container. He would lower his torch when the water level dropped to a level equal with the desired number on the message list and would then replace the bung. His counterpart took the same steps, keeping his torch aloft until the sender lowered his. He would then read the number to determine the intended message. The biggest problem was that the rate of discharge from both barrels might differ due to the size of each (and the bung hole size could vary as well). Therefore, each barrel would need to be individually calibrated. This was cumbersome to operate, let alone carry about on field operations, and the method proved notoriously inaccurate in practice.

To speed up message transmission, the Romans developed a system using multiple torches. To create messages, two men would raise from one to five torches in a predetermined manner. Various combinations could be assigned specific coded meanings. Polybius claimed to have invented such a system, which used five torches on each side and would only have worked at stationary rather than mobile field locations. It required more men to operate than did the water barrel system.

Signal and smoke fires were commonly used by Native Americans (and indigenous people in other areas), both before and after the arrival of European settlers. Several fires might be used at a time to signal specific messages. They were especially useful in rugged terrain or along coastlines to warn of impending enemy landings. Fire arrows (those dipped in burnable material and held together with glue) could be used as warnings when shot into the night sky.

Even in modern times, fire and flames can be used as a standby or emergency means of attracting attention or communicating messages, military or otherwise.

Christopher H. Sterling

See also Ancient Signals; Lights and Beacons; Maori Signaling; Native American Signaling; Night Signals; Smoke

Sources

Acker, Lewis F. 1939. "Communication Systems of the American Indians." *Signal Corps Bulletin* 103: 63–70.

Woolliscroft, D. J. 2001. *Roman Military Signalling.* Stroud, UK: Tempus.

Fiske, Bradley A. (1854–1942)

Bradley Allen Fiske was a career U.S. naval officer and inventor whose inventions greatly improved the efficiency and effectiveness of the U.S. Navy. One of the most successful inventors in the formative years of the modern navy, Fiske is credited with developing an electronic range finder, an electrically powered gun turret, the torpedo plane, various telescopes, and an electromagnetic system for detonating torpedoes under ships. His inventions came at a time when the United States was developing a modern navy and establishing itself as a global power.

Fiske was born on 13 June 1854 in Lyons, New York. He graduated from the Naval Academy in Annapolis, Maryland, in 1874. His first major contribution to the Navy was the installation of electricity on newly commissioned U.S. battleships during the 1880s. During the Spanish-American War (1898), Lieutenant Fiske served as chief navigator on the gunboat *Petrel*. With access to a laboratory in New York City funded by Western Electric, Fiske developed a series of optical devices that he attempted to use as range finders. One of these inventions—the stadimeter range finder, which communicated the ranges of enemy vessels to gunners on U.S. ships—was successfully employed during the Battle of Manila Bay. The stadimeter used a series of mirrors to measure the angular distance between two objects. Fiske was promoted to commander in 1903 and captain in 1907. In 1911, he suggested that torpedoes be launched from aircraft. Although he initially planned to use radio transmissions to guide the torpedoes, he eventually decided to simply drop them from the aircraft so they would travel a straight line toward the target. He obtained a patent for his dropping device in 1912.

In 1913, Fiske was promoted to rear admiral. With World War I on the horizon, Fiske advocated a policy of military preparedness. The start of World War I in August 1914, however, brought Fiske into conflict with Secretary of the Navy Josephus Daniels. Daniels, who was committed to presenting the United States as a neutral power, forbade contingency planning, war games, and the expansion of the Navy's shipbuilding program. Although this conflict with Daniels led to Fiske's resignation in 1916, he headed a team of investigators that unveiled the depth charge and thrower in 1917, which was successfully used against German submarines after the United States entered World War I. Fiske died on 6 April 1942 in New York City.

Michael R. Hall

See also Spanish-American War (1898); U.S. Navy

Sources
Coletta, Paolo E. 1979. *Admiral Bradley A. Fiske and the American Navy.* Lawrence: Regents Press of Kansas.
Fiske, Bradley A. 1919. *From Midshipman to Rear-Admiral.* New York: Century.
Karsten, Peter. 1972. *The Naval Aristocracy.* New York: Free Press.
King, Randolph W., et al., eds. 1989. *Naval Engineering and American Seapower.* Baltimore: Nautical and Aviation Company.

Flaghoist

The most common and longest-used flag signaling system is a series of multiple flags and pennants used among both merchant and naval ships at sea since perhaps 1450. There is thrill and romance to such flaghoist signaling as we sense in the words of a British signalman at the turn of the twentieth century: "Picture a fleet of ironclad in parallel lines . . . only 400 yards apart and rushing though the water at 15 knots . . . Two small flags flutter quickly up to the admiral's yardarm and down again. While they are on their way, the other ships seize their meaning and hang out answering pendants to signify the same. The whole thing is over in 10 seconds and not a scrap of bunting to be seen" (Woods, 1965, 31).

Meanwhile, in response, the entire fleet has turned 90 degrees to starboard, almost as if the multivessel fleet were but a single warship.

Because it required flying multiple flags, flaghoist signaling demanded careful and standardized design. Four shapes of flag design soon became standard: (1) rectangular; (2) rectangular with the triangular cut in the outboard edge (known as a "burgee"); (3) smaller triangular; and (4) slightly longer triangular, coming to a point or rounded end (usually termed a "pennant," or "pendant").

In addition to their shape, flags also varied greatly in their patterns. Among them were squares of one color, vertical and horizontal cross, diagonal cross, one or more diagonal stripes, one or more horizontal stripes, or two or more vertical stripes. Or flag design might be divided into quarters, diagonally, into nine or sixteen small squares, or with a

A flaghoist is shown on the USS Lyman K. Swenson *tied up off the Mare Island Navy Yard, California, in early 1946. The signal flag on the starboard halliards is "H," meaning "I have a pilot aboard." The four signal flags on the port side are the ship's call letters "NTHR." (U.S. Naval Historical Center)*

small square inside, with a larger square inside, with a circle inside, with five crosses inside, seven diagonal stripes, four triangles, a solid burgee, or burgee with vertical stripes. Similar patterns were also used on both burgees and the narrower and longer pennants.

Color was another consideration, although the combination of black and white was most easily seen. Dark colors contrasted to light or noncolored patterns were preferred. Ultimately, colors were restricted to black, blue, red, yellow, and white. Early on, a national or naval ensign was often added

to a square. It soon became clear that a darker versus lighter shaped pattern guaranteed greater visibility, thus dooming any flag designs depending exclusively on color.

P. H. Colomb noted only three objections to the flaghoist: (1) color confusion, which could be eliminated by proper flag deign; (2) the lack of wind while in port or at slow speed, which could harm reading of a flag signal; and (3) complexity as more flags were added. He noted, "With a set of 10 flags, numbered 1 to 0, instead of being able to go steadily on from 1 up to 9999, using no more than 4 flags at a time, all the groups in which the same flag appears *twice*, must be omitted, and this reduces the number of signals by nearly one-half. To obtain the full amount, it is necessary to add at least *three* additional flags, which are called 'repeaters' and which become substitutes for the first, second, or third flags in the series" (Colomb 1863).

Most individual flag signals involved either three or four flags, and a full message might involve no more than twelve.

Essential to the success of flaghoist signaling was use of a codebook by each signal officer. While these books began as guides for one fleet under a single flag officer, they ultimately become useful to the entire navy of a given nation or, internationally, to all merchant ships or allied forces. Hundreds of signals were standardized in these books and could thus be sent quickly by the signalers of one ship and received by all other ships in the group.

Many naval officers, especially those in Britain, France, and the United States, helped develop these systems slowly after about 1700. But the most important progress was initiated by Frederick Marryat, a Royal Navy captain who in 1817 created the Code of Signals for the merchant service. He wisely copyrighted his system, and thus earned considerable royalty income. Eventually, this code became today's International Code of Signals. Marryat offered new flag designs to avoid confusion with the Royal Navy system of the day, beginning with only ten numeral flags, two extras, and four pennants.

For more than 300 years, naval officers have sent tactical maneuvers to their fleets via flaghoist. At Trafalgar (1805), Nelson made but two signals, while during the four-hour Battle of Jutland (1916), 257 were transmitted. As so often happens, even the simplest and most reliable signal system can lead to increased complexity.

David L. Woods

See also Code, Codebook; Color; Flags; Flagship; International Code of Signals; Jutland, Battle of (1916); Trafalgar, Battle of (21 October 1805)

Sources
Colomb, P. H. 1863. "Naval and Military Signals." *Journal of the Royal United Service Institution.* 7 (20): 349–393.
Niblack, A. P. 1892. "Naval Signaling." *Proceedings of the United States Naval Institute* 18 (4): 431–505.
Very, Edward W. 1881. "Marine Signals." *A Naval Encyclopedia*, 751–754: Philadelphia.
Woods, David L. 1965. "Flaghoist & Signal Books." In *A History of Tactical Communication Techniques*, chap. III. Orlando, FL: Martin-Marietta (reprinted by Arno Press, 1974).
Woods, David L., ed. 1980. *Signaling and Communicating at Sea*, Vol. I. 2 vols. New York: Arno Press.

Flags

One of the oldest means of communicating over a distance is the use of colored or patterned pieces of cloth or flags. Flags either displayed in static fashion or waved could extend the visibility of human arms or other physical signaling devices. The use of flags as a primary means of military signaling had largely ended well before World War I. The study of flags is known as vexillogy.

A flag is usually square or rectangular and made up of one or more distinctive colors, often arranged in a pattern. Flags have varied considerably in size. Long used at sea (and still used to some extent), flags as the prime mode of communication for armies lasted only until the mid-nineteenth-century inception of heliograph and then telegraphy systems. Flags provide the benefit of being able to communicate complex ideas but may not be visible in still air (when the flag hangs limp) or in conditions of poor visibility or considerable distance when colors may be difficult to discern.

Using flags for military signaling goes back to ancient times. Roman naval forces used red flags or cloaks to signal. Such systems, often crude and temporary, remained in use, often little changed, but also lacking standardization, for centuries. The late 1660s saw the first English system, the Duke of York (later James II) code, which appears to have named different colored flags for letters of the alphabet. By the middle of the next century about thirty flags and pennants (triangular flags) were used with a set code. In 1792, Admiral Lord Richard Howe's code (actually developed by his secretary, a Mr. McArthur) reduced the total number of signal flags to thirteen and dropped the use of pennants. Four colors were used and flags were identified by number and (in more complex fashion) by letter. Sir Home Popham developed much improved and simplified signal books in the early 1800s. The U.S. Navy adopted the Truxton signal book in 1797, and then the Rogers code in 1846, which used nine square flags and six pennants. It was modified on the eve of the American Civil War to use patterns of twelve flags and nine pennants.

Flag systems are of two basic systems—the one-flag wig-wag and the two-flag, two-hand military signal system generally known as "semaphore flags." The one-flag wig-wag system is characterized by the size of the flags used. They were usually 2, 4, or 6 feet square. The larger the flag, the further it could be seen. The signal pole was 16 feet in length, usually in 4-foot segments that could be joined. It took a strong man to wave a 16-foot pole with a 6-foot square flag on it for an hour or more—especially in any kind of breeze. Flags of such size are seen on college and professional football fields from time to time. But those flags are usually

silk or nylon, and lightweight. Albert Myer's cotton flags were heavy (even more so when wet).

The large square signaling flags were usually white with a red or black square in the center of the flag; some were red with a white square in the center. The Army Signal Corps insignia, worn on the collar of each signal officer, has two crossed wig-wag flags—one red with a smaller white square, the other white with a smaller red square. Many, even in the military service, still confuse these large one-flag wig-wag flags with the smaller, two-flag semaphore flags. Naval flags are often red and white diagonally. Five motions are used for the four-element code, all starting with the flag in front of the signaler in a vertical position: (1) move flag to the left, (2) back to vertical, (3) move flag to the right, (4) back to vertical, and (5) dip the flag—meaning a pause. The code was in numbers—one to the left; two to the right. All letters were turned into numbers to be signaled—"o" was sent as 14 or one left and one right; "d" was 1-1-1 (or three lefts), and so forth. Later a two-element code was used, which eliminated the vertical movement and was deemed simpler and quicker to send and read.

The best system of Army field flag telegraphy was first developed by Albert Myer, founding head of the U.S. Army Signal Corps. While serving as an officer in western military posts in the late 1850s, Myer devised the wig-wag flag communications system, originally made up of four elements (or flag waves representing the numbers one through four), soon simplified to two. The flags were displayed in a prearranged code representing letters and numbers. Flags were red or black, but this soon changed to the standard of white and red with a center block of the opposite color. The chief advantages of the wig-wag system over other modes of communication were its portability and mobility—essential for shifting military forces—that allowed commanders to deliver orders directly to the field.

After extensive testing of flag signals over distances of 5 to 20 miles in New Mexico, Myer's method provided the basis of Army communications (on both sides—many of his assistants joined the Confederacy) during the American Civil War. Myer patented his system (including his code) in 1860. The Myer wig-wag code was widely used during the Civil War by both Union and Confederate armies. The Union Navy also used this system, and it remained the Joint Signal Code between the Army and Navy almost to the end of the nineteenth century.

The system spread to European military forces in the 1860s, though the British were most active in using it, often in various African colonial wars of the late nineteenth century. The British government backed a new International Code, which by 1870 had been adopted by most of the world's navies and merchant fleets. It utilized thirteen square flags, five pennants, and one burgee, or swallow-tailed flag. Combinations of these flown on a flaghoist indicated different letters or numbers. It was steadily revised and improved over the years. To extend the distances covered, telescopes, binoculars, and field glasses were used to read distant flag signals. In comparison to the Myer system, which called only for a response to a completed message, each word transmitted was acknowledged as received. By 1870, the British army established its first regular signals unit, a formal school following in 1886. During the Boer War, flag signaling was central to military operations. After the adoption of the Morse code, the British changed their wig-wag code from ones and twos to dots and dashes.

The French adopted a variation in their flag system, using a single flag for a Morse code dot, and two flags for a dash. The system was simple and quick. Most countries adopted the same Continental Morse code as a basis for operations, allowing parallel use of electric and signal flag telegraphy in the field. The U.S. Army used the Continental Morse code as well, but by that time wig-wag had become outmoded. Development of longer-range rifles brought about the decline in use of wig-wag on the battlefield as signalers could be seen and thus shot too easily. By the early twentieth century, flag signaling was used chiefly for messages sent between Army and Navy units. By World War I, flag signaling had fallen out of favor because battlefield conditions made the effective reading of such messages very difficult (though such methods were employed in the Dardanelles in 1915).

Two-flag semaphore lasted longest among signals controlled by a single person. Starting about the turn of the twentieth century, armies and navies worldwide adopted two-flag semaphore, with the only difference usually being design of flags used.

David L. Woods and Christopher H. Sterling

See also American Civil War (1861–1865); Ancient Signals; Color; Flaghoist; Flagship; Howe, Admiral Lord Richard (1726–1799); Human Signaling; Jutland, Battle of (1916); Myer, Albert James (1828–1880); Napoleonic Wars (1795–1815); Popham, Home Riggs (1762–1820); Signal Book; Truxton, Thomas (1755–1822)

Sources
Myer, Albert J. 1877. *A Manual of Signals for the Use of Signal Officers in the Field.* Washington, DC: Government Printing Office.
Royal Signals Organisation. 2005. "The Royal Signals. Signalling with Flags." 2005. [Online

information; retrieved April 2006.] http://www.royal-signals.org.uk/flagwaving.php.

Wilson, Timothy. 2000. *Flags at Sea: A Guide to the Flags Flown at Sea by Ships of the Major Maritime Nations, from the 16th Century to the Present Day*. Annapolis, MD: Naval Institute Press.

Woods, David L., ed. 1965. "Wig-Wag: The Waving of Flags and Torches." In *A History of Tactical Communication Techniques*, chap V. Orlando, FL: Martin-Marietta (reprinted by Arno Press, 1974).

Woods, David L. 1980. *Signaling and Communicating at Sea*, Vol. I. 2 vols. New York: Arno Press.

Flagship

The term "flagship" (spelled as either one word or two) historically designates the naval vessel carrying the fleet or squadron commander and his identification—his flag of rank. Commands controlling a fleet or squadron were intended to come from this vessel, communicated by a system of flags of different colors and shapes, using a pre-arranged code. In the merchant marine, the flagship is often the largest or newest in a given company's fleet. More generally the word has broadened in meaning to the chief or lead unit of a related group—such as the flagship station in a television firm.

Many famous flagships appear in historical accounts. As a rule, in naval usage, the flagship is either the largest fighting ship or one of that class. Britain's Admiral Horatio Nelson's *Victory* served as his flagship in the seminal Battle of Trafalgar in 1805. The armored cruiser *Olympia* served as U.S. Navy Admiral George Dewey's flagship in the battle with the Spanish fleet in Manila Bay in 1898. The battleship *Iron Duke* was Sir John Jellicoe's flagship at the Battle of Jut-

land in 1916, where signal flag confusion had a strong impact on the outcome of the engagement. Different American battleships served through the twentieth century as flagships for the U.S. Navy's Atlantic and Pacific (or later its numbered) fleets. Between the world wars, HMS *Hood*, a battle cruiser finished at the end of World War I, served as at least the informal flagship of the Royal Navy. By the early twenty-first century, a flagship would more likely be an aircraft carrier, or a nuclear submarine, as these are the most important fighting vessels of a modern navy.

A navy flagship fulfills a specific communications role. Such a ship will carry signals personnel and may feature a flag deck, which combines functions of command and communication of those commands to other ships. While signal flags may be used, more often communications are by radio and other modern technologies.

Christopher H. Sterling

See also Flaghoist; Flags; Jutland, Battle of (1916); Spanish-American War (1898); Trafalgar, Battle of (21 October 1805)

Sources

Coles, Alan, and Ted Briggs. 1985. *Flagship Hood: The Fate of Britain's Mightiest Warship*. London: Robert Hale.

Cooling, B. Franklin. 2000. *USS Olympia: Herald of Empire*. Annapolis, MD: Naval Institute Press.

Goodwin, Peter. 2004. *Nelson's Victory: 101 Questions and Answers About HMS Victory, Nelson's Flagship at Trafalgar 1805*. London: Conway Maritime Press.

Fleming, John Ambrose (1849–1945)

Inventor of the vacuum tube, this long-lived English electrical engineer made possible the early modern era of radio communications by naval and military services. While he played no direct military role himself, he developed the device that, while modified by others, became the basis of all electronic work for a half-century or more.

Born in Lancaster, England, on 29 November 1849, Ambrose (he never used his first name) Fleming earned a bachelor of science degree in 1870 from the University of London. He undertook graduate work at the University of Cambridge and worked for a time at the Cavendish Laboratory under James Clerk Maxwell, the first man to theorize the potential of wireless communications.

Fleming worked for the Edison Electric Light Company of London from 1881 to 1891 and increasingly was also taking on work as a consulting electrical engineer. He became the first professor of electrical engineering at his alma mater in 1885 and would serve in that role for more than four decades. He served concurrently as an adviser to the Marconi Company, beginning in 1899 and continuing for a quarter-century.

The effort that would lead eventually to the first vacuum tube began in 1882. This, clearly Fleming's most important single innovation, was based on the initial electric lights of the late 1870s that had a similar appearance. Thomas Edison and others had noted that when a light remained burning for some time, it often deposited a dark residue on the inside of the glass lamp. The "Edison Effect" was eventually traced to the tiny electric currents moving within vacuum inside the bulb. Fleming built on this and a series of experiments to develop what he (and the British to this day) call a "valve" and the rest of the world refers to as a vacuum tube, the former perhaps better describing the purpose (allowing the passage of electricity), the latter the nature of the device.

The vacuum tube was quickly recognized as a good detector of wireless telegraph or telephone signals and was improved in important ways by Lee de Forest two years later. The "Fleming valve" or tube began the modern era of electronics. He alerted Guglielmo Marconi to his findings in October 1904, noting that his device "opens up a wide field for work," a classic understatement as it turned out. The patent was assigned to Marconi, and Fleming received no direct financial gain for his breakthrough. For years to come, he and de Forest would feud over their respective roles in developing the vacuum tube.

Fleming was widely published during more than a half-century of effort beginning with his first paper in 1883. In addition to many other scientific articles and books, his *The Principles of Electric Wave Telegraphy and Telephony* became a standard text and went through four editions from 1906 to 1919. He retired in 1926, at age seventy-seven. Late in his life, he was honored by many organizations and was knighted in March 1929, the same year he accepted the presidency of the new Television Society. Fleming died at the age of ninety-six on 18 April 1945 in Sidmouth, England.

Christopher H. Sterling

See also de Forest, Lee (1873–1961); Edison, Thomas A. (1847–1931); Marconi, Guglielmo (1874–1937); Vacuum Tube

Sources
Fleming, Ambrose. 1934. *Memories of a Scientific Life*. London: Marshall Morgan & Scott.
Fleming, J. A. 1921. *Fifty Years of Electricity: The Memories of an Electrical Engineer*. London: Wireless Press.
MacGregor-Morris, J. T. 1954. *The Inventor of the Valve: A Biography of Sir Ambrose Fleming*. London: The Television Society.
Shiers, George. 1969. "The First Electron Tube." *Scientific American* 220 (March): 104–112.

Fort Gordon, Georgia

Now the home of the U.S. Army Signal Corps, Fort Gordon dates to the early World War II years. With the threat of war looming in mid-1940, U.S. Army officials began identifying sites suitable for division-level training. By 1941, a decision was made to acquire land near Augusta, Georgia, and the War Department issued a $22 million contract to construct a new installation. At the groundbreaking ceremony on 18 October 1941 the new camp was named for John B. Gordon, a former Georgia governor and lieutenant general in the Confederate Army.

During World War II the 56,000-acre training site was temporary home to three divisions (the 4th and 26th Infantry and the 10th Armored divisions) until they were sent to Europe. From October 1943 to January 1945, Camp Gordon served as a prisoner of war camp. Following the war, Camp Gordon was scheduled to be inactivated, but renewed emphasis on military preparedness during the Cold War affected the Army's plans for Camp Gordon. On 20 September 1948, the Military Police School moved to Camp Gordon and on 1 October the Signal Corps Training Center (SCTC) was activated. Since that time Camp Gordon has served as a crucial communications training installation for the U.S. Army Signal Corps.

In 1950 the demand for signalmen in the Korean War led to a major expansion of the SCTC, making it the largest single source of Army communications specialists. On 21 March 1956 Camp Gordon was redesignated Fort Gordon and made a permanent installation. American involvement in Southeast Asia in the 1960s and 1970s, together with the advances in communications-electronics technology (C-E), placed heavy training demands on Fort Gordon. At the height of

the Vietnam War the renamed Southeastern Signal School (SESS) was the primary source of personnel for tactical C-E units in Vietnam. In September 1965, the SESS activated the Signal Officer Candidate School (OCS). By the time the last class ended in February 1968, more than 2,000 officers graduated from Signal OCS.

The post-Vietnam years found the Army revising training, doctrine, and organization to keep pace with rapid technological advances on the modern battlefield. It was a period of reorganization that resulted in consolidation of all signal training at Fort Gordon on 1 July 1974. The SESS was redesignated the U.S. Army Signal School and on 1 October 1974 was redesignated the U.S. Army Signal Center and Fort Gordon. The 1980s represented a transitional phase for the Army that deeply affected the Signal Center. The Signal Center's efforts included development of mobile subscriber equipment, the Army's communications architecture, and assumption of a lead role for the Army's Information Mission Area, which included the integration of automation, communications, visual information, records management, and publications and printing. In June 1986 the U.S. Army Signal Corp Regiment was established and Fort Gordon designated as the regimental home base.

In 1990–1991, the Signal Center played a vital role in preparing soldiers for deployment during the Gulf War. In the 1990s Fort Gordon became home for training most of the satellite operators and maintenance personnel within the Department of Defense and continued to train signal troops of allied and foreign countries. Today, Fort Gordon serves as a power projection base for several signal units responsible for conducting operations during the war on terrorism and will continue to serve as the home of the

U.S. Army Signal Corps into the twenty-first century.

Steven J. Rauch

See also Army Signal Corps; Fort Monmouth, New Jersey; Gulf War (1990–1991); Vietnam War (1959–1975); War on Terrorism

Source
Command Historian. 1993. *A History of Fort Gordon, Georgia.* Fort Gordon, GA: U.S. Army Signal Center and Fort Gordon.

Fort Huachuca, Arizona

Located near Arizona's border with Mexico, after a long history of border patrol operations, Fort Huachuca has been a center of communications and intelligence operations for a half-century.

On 3 March 1877 two companies of the U.S. Army's 6th Cavalry established a camp located in the heart of the Huachuca Mountains in southern Arizona, and named the post after the mountain range. The camp was intended to protect settlers in the area and to block a traditional Apache Indian escape route to Mexico through the San Pedro and Santa Cruz valleys. It was near clean running water and wood used for fuel, and was located on high ground for greater security.

In 1882 the Army made the camp permanent, and as Fort Huachuca it began to change appearance with construction of durable facilities made out of wood, stone, and adobe. In early 1886 it provided a base for General Nelson A. Miles's campaign against Geronimo, the last Apache leader. With the surrender of Geronimo in August 1886, the Army closed many installations, but Fort Huachuca remained open due to continuous problems along the Mexican border.

In the years that followed the fort was used by the Army in operations against the renegade Indians, Mexican bandits, and American outlaws. From 1913 into the early 1930s, the 10th Cavalry "Buffalo Soldiers" settled at Fort Huachuca to patrol the Mexican border. In 1916 General John J. Pershing joined the 10th Cavalry to command a punitive expedition into Mexico. The general was known for his admiration for the well-disciplined troops, known as the Black Troopers, and acquired the nickname "Black Jack."

During World War II, the 92nd and 93rd black infantry divisions trained at Fort Huachuca and the number of the troops at the fort reached 30,000 men, three times the level of a decade earlier. With the end of the war, the fort was transferred to the state of Arizona, only to be reactivated during the Korean War.

By 1954 the fort was controlled by the chief of Signal Officers as the outpost had been found to offer an ideal climate for electronic and communications equipment testing. In 1967 it became the headquarters of the U.S. Army Strategic Communications Command. The role and importance of Fort Huachuca continued to expand, and in 1971 it became home of the U.S Army Intelligence Center and School.

Today, Fort Huachuca is the major military center in Arizona. It houses and supports missions of the U.S. Army Information System Command and the U.S. Army Intelligence Center and School. The Fort Huachuca museum portrays the history of the U.S. Army in the Southwest.

Arthur M. Holst

See also Mexican Punitive Expedition (1916–1917); Strategic Communications Command (STRATCOM)

Sources
"Fort Huachuca History" website. [Online information: retrieved June 2007.] http://huachuca-www.army.mil/HISTORY/huachuca.htm.

Fort Huachuca Museum website. [Online articles retrieved August 2004.] http:// huachuca-www.army.mil/HISTORY/ museum.html.

"I Sell Arizona!" website. [Online information: retrieved June 2006.] http://www.arizona-broker.com/Fort_Huachuca/page_88775 .html.

Fort Meade, Maryland

Though it became a military installation only upon American entry into World War I, Fort George G. Meade is today one of the largest military installations in the United States and serves as the home of the National Security Agency.

Camp George G. Meade (named after the victor of the Battle of Gettysburg in 1863) first became an Army installation in 1917. As authorized in May 1917, it was one of sixteen cantonments built for troops drafted for the war in Europe. The 8,000-acre Maryland site, located roughly between Washington DC and Baltimore in Anne Arundel County, was then occupied by private farms and orchards. Actual construction began in July and the first contingent of troops arrived in September. Over the next two years, more than 100,000 men passed through Camp Meade, which served as a training site for three infantry divisions, three training battalions, and one depot brigade.

An attempt to rename the post Fort Leonard Wood in 1928 was overturned by Congress a year later when the site became Fort George G. Meade on 5 March 1929. (An earlier Fort Meade existed in Gulf Coast Florida from 1849 to 1900 and has since become a town. There is also a Fort Meade recreation area and cavalry museum in the Black Hills of South Dakota. Neither of these played a role in military communications history.)

Between the wars, Fort Meade served as headquarters of the new tank corps (the last armored units left only in 1967). Fort Meade again became a training center during World War II. Its various ranges and other facilities were used by more than 200 units and approximately 3.5 million soldiers between 1942 and 1946. The wartime peak personnel figure was reached in March 1945 when 70,000 men were on-site. It was also the site of a prisoner of war camp.

Fort Meade reverted to routine peacetime activities after 1946. Second Army headquarters were shifted to Fort Meade from Baltimore in June 1947 (they later merged into and became First Army). A decade later the National Security Agency (NSA) moved its headquarters from Arlington Hall to Fort Meade. From 1954 to 1962, Fort Meade contained several Nike missile batteries designed for the defense of the Washington-Baltimore area. A Fort Meade museum was formed in 1963 and became a permanent part of the base a decade later.

In August 1990 Fort Meade began processing Army Reserve and National Guard units from several states in support of the Gulf War. Some 2,700 personnel from forty-two units deployed from Fort Meade. Fort Meade continues to provide support and services for more than a hundred partner units, which include the Defense Information School, which moved there in 1995; the Defense Courier Service; a number of both Army and Navy intelligence units; and a combat camera unit of the Signal Corps.

NSA occupies a major part of the grounds of Fort Meade. As NSA expanded its operations and more buildings were added to its complex, new roads were constructed connecting the buildings through a huge web of parking lots and access roads. Eventually nine roads were named for deceased American cryptologists. The National Cryptologic Museum occupies a one-time motel building just outside the NSA security area.

Christopher H. Sterling

See also Arlington Hall; Couriers; National Security Agency (NSA)

Sources
Fort Meade. [Home page information; retrieved June 2007.] http://www.ftmeade .army .mil/.
Fort George G. Meade Museum. Home page. [Online information; retrieved April 2007.] http://www.ftmeade.army.mil/Museum/Index.htm.

Fort Monmouth, New Jersey

Fort Monmouth has been the site of some of the most significant communications/electronics advances in American military history. It served as the primary Army Signal Corps base from after World War I to 1976, when it relocated to Fort Gordon, Georgia. From carrier pigeons to frequency-hopping tactical radios, Fort Monmouth has been home to important technological breakthroughs.

The 1,344-acre installation that makes up Fort Monmouth is a far cry from the briar-covered tract that greeted the first thirty-two Signal Corps soldiers in 1917. At the outbreak of World War I, the Army recognized the need for expanded communications facilities. Investigation led them to land that once housed the old Monmouth racetrack, a potato farm at the time. It was ideal as it was close to both river and rail transportation. Originally named Camp Little Silver, the installation was renamed Camp Alfred Vail in September 1917 to honor the New Jersey inventor who helped Samuel Morse develop commercial telegraphy. The installation was granted permanent status and renamed Fort Monmouth in August 1925 to honor the soldiers of the American Revolution who died in the battle of the Monmouth Court House.

The forerunner of the Army Air Corps (eventually the U.S. Air Force) had its roots at Fort Monmouth. Here in 1928 the first radio-equipped meteorological balloon soared into the upper reaches of the atmosphere, an early version of a weather-sounding technique universally used today. The first U.S. aircraft detection radar was developed here in 1938. Space communication was proven feasible when the Diana radar was used in 1946 to bounce electronic signals off the moon. The space age reached maturity thanks in part to key work done here to develop solar-powered batteries, modern teletypewriters for space shuttles, and communications satellites.

Over the last nine decades, the vast majority of communications equipment used by American forces from field radios to transmitters, receivers, walkie-talkies, switchboards, mortar locators, and radar systems had its start here.

The Army Signal Corps rapidly established a presence with a training camp in 1917, a school two years later, the Signal Corps Board in 1924, and its laboratories five years later. With the coming of World War II, a Signal Corps Replacement Center was established in 1941, and a publications office two years later. Finally, in 1949, the Signal Corps Center was established (including engineering labs, the Signal Corps Board, the Signal School, Publications Agency, Intelligence Unit, Pigeon Breeding and Training Center, the Army portion of the Electro Standards Agency, and Signal Corps troop units). The base was redesignated the Signal Corps Center and Fort Monmouth.

From a tiny cluster of Army tents in a clearing not far from the New Jersey seashore, Fort Monmouth became the home of the Communications-Electronics Lifecycle Management Command. The major organizations now located at Fort Monmouth include the U.S. Army Garrison; the Communications-Electronics Command (CECOM); the Program Executive Office for Command, Control and Communications Tactical; and the Program Executive Office for Intelligence, Electronic Warfare and Sensors. Together these organizations are known as Team Command, Control, Communications, Computers, Intelligence, Surveillance, and Reconnaissance.

CECOM and its partners are charged with acquiring, developing, sustaining, and maintaining communications-electronic equipment for the modern multiservice fighting man or woman ("joint warfighter"). This has included work with equipment such as command-and-control systems, situational awareness systems, sophisticated sensors, and electronic jamming systems.

Wendy A. Réjàn

See also Army Signal Corps; Blair, William Richards (1874–1962); Global Command and Control System (GCCS); Greely, Adolphus W. (1844–1935); Identification, Friend or Foe (IFF); Jamming; Joint Tactical Radio System (JTRS); Military Affiliate Radio System (MARS); Miniaturization; Mobile Communications; Myer, Albert James (1828–1880); Signal Book; Signals Intelligence (SIGINT); Squier, George Owen (1865–1934); Voice Relay

Sources

Bingham, Richard. *Famous Fort Monmouth Firsts.* [Online information; retrieved May 2006.] www.monmouth.army.mil/historian/pubupdates/FortMonmouth andTeamC4ISRFamousFirsts_May_2006 .doc.

CECOM and Fort Monmouth historical website. [Online information; retrieved June 2006.] http://www.monmouth.army.mil/historian/history.php.

A Concise History of the Communications-Electronics Command and Fort Monmouth, *New Jersey.* 2003. Fort Monmouth, NJ: Office of the Deputy Chief of Staff for Plans and Operations.

Kozlowski, Melissa. 2004. *Fort Monmouth Landmarks and Place Names.* Fort Monmouth, NJ: Office of the Deputy Chief of Staff for Plans and Operations.

Fort Myer, Virginia

Fort Myer, Virginia, located across the Potomac River from Washington DC, traces its origin as a military post to the Civil War. It served as an important Signal Corps post, an Army cavalry base, the site of the first flight of an aircraft at a military installation, and the home of U.S. Army chiefs of staff for the past century.

The land that would become Fort Myer and Arlington National Cemetery was seized by the Union government when Confederate General Robert E. Lee, owner of the Arlington estate, was unable to pay property taxes in person during the American Civil War (1861–1865). The first occupants of what was initially named Fort Whipple were artillery and infantry units helping to defend Washington. The Signal Corps took over the post by the late 1860s because its high elevation made it ideal for visual communications. In 1881, Fort Whipple was redesignated Fort Myer in honor of Brigadier General Albert J. Myer, the Army's first chief signal officer who served in that post from 1866 to 1880. The Signal Corps continued to staff the post for five more years.

In 1887, the communications units moved out and for two decades, Fort Myer became a cavalry post, playing an important part of the official and social life in Washington. The first military test flight of an aircraft was made from Fort Myer's parade grounds in September 1908. Orville Wright succeeded in keeping the plane aloft for one minute and eleven seconds. The second test flight ended with a tragic crash after four minutes in the air. Wright was severely bruised while his passenger, Lieutenant Thomas Selfridge, became the first powered-aviation fatality. Most of the buildings on the post were built between 1895 and 1908. Many have been designated historic landmarks. Fort Myer served as a military processing station during World War II, and the U.S. Army Band moved to Fort Myer in 1942.

Though only one battalion is active at Fort Myer today, that known as the "Old Guard," it is the Army's official ceremonial and security force in Washington DC. Fort Myer also provides housing, support, and services to thousands of active-duty, reserve, and retired military personnel stationed in the national capital region. Fort Myer's current mission is to operate the Army's showcase community and to support homeland security in the nation's capital.

Danny Johnson

See also Army Signal Corps; Myer, Albert James (1828–1880)

Sources

Belcher, Nancy Hoyt. 2003. "Guarding History, Fort Myer, Next to Arlington Cemetery, is Home to the 3d Infantry Regiment, Formed in 1784." *St. Petersburg Times*, May 25.

Bell, William G. 1981. *Quarters One: The United States Army's Chief of Staff's Residence, Fort Myer, Virginia*. Washington, DC: Government Printing Office.

Fort Myer Military Community Guide. 2005. Gaithersburg, MD: Comprint Military Publications.

France: Air Force (*Armée de l'Air*)

The story of French Air Force communications is a varied one over its first four decades. The nation that pioneered flying in Europe and expanded its air force to substantial size during World War I had little impact on World War II. While some of its early radio equipment was good, technology alone could not overcome decades of politics and pessimism. Two colonial wars (in Indochina and then Algeria from 1946 to 1962) sapped the air arm and only in recent decades has it again become a modern fighting force.

The French War Department began pilot training in December 1909. In March 1910, the Établissement Militaire d'Aviation (EMA) was created to conduct experiments with aircraft. The following month, the Service Aéronautique was formed as a separate air command comprising the EMA and balloon companies. Finally, the army formally established its own air force, the Aéronautique Militaire, on 22 October 1910.

As with many other nations, early French flying during World War I centered on observation activities. The 1915 air battle over Verdun was the first large-scale air battle ever fought. With French observation and reconnaissance aircraft threatened by squadrons of German fighters, French ground commanders were unable to react to German artillery fire and infantry maneuvers. After several weeks of intense air fighting, the French slowly regained air superiority over Verdun. This protracted battle can be seen as the birth of command and control in aerial warfare, for by this time the French air arm had begun using radios to communicate between ground and air. At the armistice (11 November 1918), the Aéronautique Militaire had some 3,225 frontline combat aircraft on the Western Front, making it the world's largest air force.

The French air force took its modern name, Armée de l'Air, in August 1933, though it remained under the jurisdiction of the army for another year. When the country's small aircraft companies proved incapable of producing what the growing air arm needed, the government stepped in. In July 1936 it began nationalizing the sector, creating six giant state-owned firms based on their geographic locations. This included nearly all aeronautical production. But interservice rivalry and political infighting stunted the modernization process. The result was an ill-equipped air force totally unable to face the modern German Luftwaffe.

Effectiveness of the French fighter and bomber force in the face of the German attack of May 1940 was reduced, among many factors, by poor communications that made massing of squadrons impossible and coordination with fighter escorts problematic. Poor liaison relationships between the French army and air force, coupled with slow communications within the air force, led to many squadrons being held too long on forward airfields until they were nearly overrun by German motorized units. Thanks to poor radio communications, coordination between the air force and army barely existed, especially for such a war of movement. The French high command had neglected the preparation of command/control/communications systems and thereby denied the air force the ability to integrate the efforts of its individual units.

With the 22 June 1940 armistice with the Germans, surviving French air units broke into two conflicting camps: those who escaped from France to fighting for De Gaulle's Free French Forces (*Forces Françaises Libres*) and those flying for the French Armistice Air Force on behalf of the Vichy government (*Armée de l'Air de Vichy*). After the Allied landings in North Africa (November 1942), the latter ceased to exist. For the rest of the war, French air units were largely equipped with British or American equipment. French air units were active in the postwar Indochina fighting (1946–1954) and in the battle over Algeria (ending 1962).

French air units operated during the 1990–1991 Gulf War and again during North Atlantic Treaty Organization actions in the Balkans in the 1990s. In the present French air force, the Air Surveillance, Communications and Information Command is charged with means of detection and communication. The 9,000 men and women of the command are spread among 155 units in France, in French overseas territories, and in foreign countries. Since 11 September 2001, the French air force has reorganized and reinforced the air surveillance and early warning network under the responsibility of the Air Defense and Air Operations Command, and it has integrated it into multinational action.

Christopher H. Sterling

See also Airplanes; Airships and Balloons; France: Army; Germany: Air Force; Gulf War (1990–1991); United Kingdom: Royal Air Force; World War I; World War II

Sources

Armée de l'Air. Home page. [Online information (in French); retrieved April 2006.] http://www.defense.gouv.fr/air/.

Cain, A. C. 2002. *The Forgotten Air Force: French Air Doctrine in the 1930s*. Washington, DC: Smithsonian Press.

Van Haute, Andre. 1974. *Pictorial History of the French Air Force: Volume 1 1909–1940; Volume 2 1941–1974*. London: Ian Allen.

France: Army

France pioneered modern military communication with its late eighteenth-century mechanical semaphore systems. During the

Napoleonic Wars, French military communications were the best in the world. Their role over the next two centuries varied, though the French army of the early twenty-first century again uses the most modern systems.

In the early 1790s, the revolutionary French government funded construction of fifteen semaphore telegraph stations from Paris north to Lille, each about 10 to 20 miles apart and equipped with telescopes, covering an overall distance of about 120 miles. The Claude Chappe–designed system was placed into service in mid-1794 and rapidly showed its ability to carry messages far faster than any means of transport. Soon other lines were developed, including east to Strasbourg (1798) and west to Brest and the English Channel. Amsterdam, Milan, and Venice (which could get a signal from Paris in about six hours) were all reached by 1810. Mobile versions of this system were adopted by Napoleon in his military campaigns, and it remained in use until the 1840s.

Conflict with Austria in the early 1860s led to perhaps the first examples of laying electric telegraph cable rapidly ("on the run") from specially equipped wagons. These allowed the French commander to maintain links with his fighting forces on the move. The central role of the telegraph led to the formation of the Telegraph Brigade and the School for Military Telegraphy (1868). During the Franco-Prussian War of 1870–1871, the siege of Paris saw extensive use of balloons to get people and messages across German lines.

In 1872 the Commission for Military Telegraphy was created but not implemented until 1884. The Central Depot was formed at Mount Valerien in 1891 and commanded by Captain Gustave-August Ferrié, who was central in the development of the signal service in the French army. By 1900 one engineers battalion specialized in telegraphy and telephone and was to later become involved in all forms of military signaling. On 30 March 1912 another regiment of engineers was created to provide telegraphists for France and North Africa and included a wireless company. It became the parent regiment for all new signal units. Wireless telegraphy was first used over long distances in 1901 from France to Corsica and Martinique to Guadeloupe in 1902. Further studies in wireless were carried out from fixed stations at the Eiffel Tower, Verdun, Toul, Epinal, and Belfort. The first mobile radio stations were used in Morocco in 1913.

When World War I began in August 1914, now Colonel Ferrié was appointed to direct French military radio communications. French army signals remained under the control of engineer units throughout the war. Field army telegraph services had two divisions—one for communicating to the front, the other to the rear. Radio telegraphy came under the control of the commander in chief.

A signal school was formed in 1923. During the 1930s, the Maginot Line, a defensive series of half-buried border fortifications built to face Germany and Italy, included extensive internal telephone networks as well as telephone and radio telegraph links (featuring 250-watt transmitters), both to other forts and to nearby military commands. Major fortresses such as Hackenberg operated their own telephone exchanges (dubbed "pianos"). Some optical telegraphic systems were also occasionally fitted. In 1942 authorization was given for signals to become independent of the engineers in occupied France and to form a new arm known as *L'Arme des Transmissions*. During the war, Free French forces generally used British and American communications equipment. In the colonial wars that followed in then French Indochina and in Algeria, most modes of communication were based on those from World War II.

The modern French army has long relied on information technology. The innovative ATTILA artillery automation program, launched by the Ministry of Defense in the 1970s, was a precursor of battlefield digitization. Over the next decade the army pioneered a variety of digital systems that entered service in the early 1990s. The next step was networking command information systems with radio communications and distributed sensors. These would deliver real-time situational awareness shared by different levels of command, thereby speeding decision making and execution of orders. The French have embraced the concepts of network-centric warfare emerging in the United States. In its acquisition efforts, the French army is concerned with three priorities: command and information systems in relation to interoperability, intelligence systems, and equipment for crisis reaction forces. Battlefield digitization is coming about with newly implemented systems.

Preceding the introduction of the Information System for Armed Force Command (SICF) was the *Réseau intégré de transmissions automatiques* (RITA), which has been the primary French army tactical network communication system. SICF manages information exchange from an operation center among several other centers. The system supports exchange of tactical information from corps to brigade levels. Combat radio is central to the army combat communication network from platoon up to regiment level. SICF software operates through a network of computer terminals and standard military combat communications systems which are designed to reduce information quantity and

to minimize the transmission capacity required. The army has adopted a three-level horizontal battle management system hierarchy where the top level is SICF; the second level is the Regimental Information System (SIR); and the third level is the Battlefield Management System (SIT). The French approach is similar to British and German systems. Indeed, SIR was the product of a cooperative program with France, Germany, the Netherlands, and Italy. Its design is interoperable with the French air force and navy, and with American, British, and German command-and-control systems.

French army communications are designed to support mission requirements on three levels. The first includes command and support of the top command to ensure interconnectivity with the various military and civil national networks within a national or multinational framework. Second is the planning, preparation, and support of forces in interdepartmental operations with the army, defense forces, or allies. This provides support to metropolitan areas and defense agencies or other ministries with a permanent and reliable service of telecommunications and data processing. Third is the support of communication information systems of army and defense agencies, including design and technical studies to implement and to maintain communication and information systems.

The largest army communications unit is the Brigade of Transmission and Support to Command based at Lunéville with its six regiments and one battalion at Bretteville, Issoire, Thionville, Laval, Agen, and also in Lunéville. The brigade combines mobile communications and information systems and is in charge of deployment and maintenance of tactical means of telecommunications (RITA-radio-satellite) and of associated information systems in external theaters of operation. There are two electronic warfare signals regiments at Mutzig and Haguenau. One regiment is responsible for the communication needs of the Ministry of Defense staff in Paris. There is a satellite communications regiment in Senlis and a signal battalion responsible for army information technology based in Orleans. France has four regional telecommunications and data processing centers as well as those in Paris and overseas locations of the army.

Training for French military communications begins with the École Supérieur of Application of Transmissions at Rennes. The school provides initial officer training as troop commanders in tactical and strategic communications, and in electronic warfare. It also provides initial technical training of senior noncommissioned officers, soldiers, and Ministry of Defense civil servants in communications, electronic warfare, and information technology.

Danny Johnson, Cliff Lord,
and Christopher H. Sterling

See also Chappe, Claude (1763–1805); Ferrié, Gustave-Auguste; (1868–1932); France: Air Force (*Armée de l'Air*); France: Navy (*Marine Nationale*); Maginot Line; Napoleonic Wars (1795–1815); Semaphore (Mechanical Telegraphs); World War I

Sources

Defense Update. 2005. "SIR (Regimental Information System)." [Online article; retrieved June 2006.] http://www.defense-update.com/products/s/sir.htm.

Lattin, Jay D. B. 1930. "The Signal Service of the French Army." *Signal Corps Bulletin 56* (September–October): 1–17.

Mary, Jean-Yves, and Alain Hohnadel. 2001. "Les Transmissions." In *Hommes et Ouvrages de la Ligne Maginot, Tome 1,* 120–126. Paris: Histoire & Collections.

School of Application of Transmissions and School of Information Systems, Communication and the Electronic War. Home page. [Online information (in French); retrieved July 2006.] http://www.esat.terre.defense.gouv.fr/.

Scriven, G. P. 1915. "Notes on the Organization of Telegraph Troops in Foreign Armies." *The Service of Information, United States Army.* Circular No. 8. Washington, DC: Office of the Chief Signal Officer.

Wilson, Geoffrey. 1976. "France." In *The Old Telegraphs,* 120–130. Totowa, NJ: Rowman & Littlefield.

Wodka-Gallien, Philippe. 2004. "The French Army in the 21st Century: Towards Network Centric Warfare." French Army Chapter of Association of Old Crows *Newsletter No. 21* (May).

France: Navy (*Marine Nationale*)

France has enjoyed a long naval history, perhaps second only to Britain's Royal Navy. Indeed, for much of their history, the two navies have been important rivals and often enemies. The French navy's glory years came in the days of sail where it was often at the forefront of naval developments. Yet until the seventeenth century, there was no standard means of signaling among French or other ships at sea.

By the late seventeenth century, however, standard methods of maritime signaling had finally become established in the French, Dutch, and English navies (the three most important fleets of the time). They remained little changed until after the fall of Napoleon in 1815. When the ships were in port, daytime signals were made with guns and by moving sails. At sea, flag signals were best for communicating with the fleet, with guns being used to draw attention to the signal, but only in the eighteenth century was the system of employing small frigates to carry signals developed. In the seventeenth century orders were usually sent through the fleet by boat. At night signals were made by fastening lanterns in the rigging, burning false fires, and firing sky rockets. Fog signaling was very limited in scope and was made with guns, bells, and muskets firing in distinct patterns.

In 1738, a Frenchman, Bertrand-François Mahé de la Bourdonnais, devised the first numerical flag code, on which all later development of flaghoist signaling was based. He assigned a different flag to represent the numbers 0 through 9. With three sets of flags, a ship could make a thousand different combinations of signals. Coupled with a dictionary assigning a meaning to each combination, de la Bourdonnais' system would have permitted a marked advance in the sophistication of naval communications. His idea was not adopted by the French navy, but it was further developed a quarter-century later by another Frenchman, Sebastian Francisco de Bigot (founder of the French Marine Academy at Brest, and also known as Vicomte de Mogogues), who published *Tactique Navale ou Traite des Evolutions et des Signaux* in 1763. In addition to the ten number flags, Bigot prescribed predefined meanings for more than 330 different hoists and added both a preparatory flag to signal that a coded message was to be transmitted and a requirement that the receiving ship acknowledge the signal.

The French continued to develop their tactical communication systems. In 1776 a Captain du Pavillon introduced a signaling system using grid tablature to allow simpler two-flag hoists, flown where most easily seen, to convey hundreds of messages. The American Revolution saw the highest level of competition between French and British fighting and signaling tactics. As late as 1806,

however, the French navy rejected the proposed adoption of a numerical system of signaling (by means of a vote taken at each of the naval bases) and continued using du Pavillon's tabular system until after the end of the Napoleonic Wars.

By the mid-nineteenth century, France had again embarked on fleet expansion as navies experimented with the first metal-hulled ships and the form of large-gunned naval vessels changed more than at any other time. She launched *Gloire* in 1853 as the first major ironclad ship of the line and achieved many other feats though modes of intership communication remained the same flag systems used for decades.

Only in the early twentieth century did France and Britain finally submerge their long naval rivalry to commonly face a resurgent Germany. A 1912 Anglo-French naval agreement gave France leadership of potential naval operations in the Mediterranean. In World War II, however, though having many powerful and well-equipped vessels (the fleet was substantially rebuilt during the interwar period), French naval forces played only a limited role because of the rapid German victory over France in June 1940. The navy was thereafter often divided against itself. Under the Vichy collaborationist regime, elements of the French fleet were moored in several bases in France and North Africa. A few sailed to work with the Allies, but most stayed put—some to be attacked by the British (concerned that French naval units would otherwise fall into German hands) or were scuttled by their crews in late 1942. Those few that survived relied heavily during the war on British and U.S. electronics technology for their communications, radar, and gun control.

French naval development during the Cold War reflected France's changing needs.

At first surviving elements and ships from Britain and the United States supported colonial wars in Indochina and then Algeria. With Charles de Gaulle's government (1958–1968), a strong effort was made to build the fleet into an important power independent of the North Atlantic Treaty Organization (NATO). By the early 2000s, the Marine Nationale was the largest European navy in terms of personnel and operated a wide range of fighting ships.

In February 2004, several firms were awarded a contract for a new naval command-and-control system. The system will be fitted on the nuclear aircraft carrier *Charles de Gaulle* as well as other vessels and shore locations and will allow the vessels to access national or coalition command networks. Likewise, the recent RIFAN secure Internet protocol program represents a radical transformation for the navy, shifting the communications net to one based on Internet protocol. Under the $60 million program, nearly seventy ships will be connected over a secure Internet protocol network designed to provide a common operational picture. The services include voice over Internet protocol, e-mail, videoconference, and cooperative mapping on maneuvers. Both the SIC 21 command-and-control system and RIFAN programs use commercial off-the-shelf technology and international standards, representing a major shift in procurement for the navy but one designed to provide maximum interoperability. The navy also is equipping itself with an upgraded tactical data link network (Prisme), which will evolve to NATO's Link 22 standard.

Early in 2006, the French navy was in the final stages of placing two command ships, the *Mistral* and the *Tonnerre*, into service. They are designed for multiple tasks with the NATO High Readiness Force, which will enter service before 2010. In addition to carrying helicopters and troops, they will also support crisis and humanitarian mission management. The command centers on the two ships include 150 work stations, a fiber optic internal communications network, satellite links, and considerable automation to provide efficient task force command and control.

Christopher H. Sterling

See also Flaghoist; Flags; Napoleonic Wars (1795–1815); Night Signals; North Atlantic Treaty Organization (NATO) Communications & Information Systems Agency; Trafalgar, Battle of (21 October 1805)

Sources

Jenkins, Ernest H. 1973. *A History of the French Navy: From Its Beginnings to the Present Day.* Annapolis, MD: Naval Institute Press.

Palmer, Michael A. 2005. *Command at Sea: Naval Command and Control Since the Sixteenth Century.* Cambridge, MA: Harvard University Press.

Taverna, Michael A. 2006. "Wind and Thunder." *Aviation Week and Space Technology,* April 10.

Tran, Pierre. 2005. "Two Systems to Boost French Navy Interoperability." *C4ISR: The Journal of Net-Centric Warfare* (October 31).

Friedman, William F. (1891–1969)

William Friedman was the most important American code breaker and trainer from the 1930s to 1950s and established much of the scientific basis for wartime and postwar code operations.

Wolfe (later William) Friedman was born 24 September 1891 in Kishinev, Russia, and brought to the United States a year later. He earned a bachelor's degree in genetics at Cornell University in 1914 and married Elizabeth Smith in May 1917. At the time both worked at Riverbank Laboratories, west of Chicago, researching a variety of genetic and then taking on code-breaking assignments from George Fabyan, the operation's eccentric director.

With American entry into World War I, Friedman became a code officer at American Expeditionary Force headquarters in France, serving into 1919, and then returned to Riverbank for another year. He returned to the military a year later, beginning as a cryptographer with the Army Signal Corps in 1921. During the 1930s, Friedman served with the War Department, where he essentially continued (but considerably improved and expanded on) the code-breaking work Herbert Yardley had begun. He trained many of those who would play key roles in the coming war and authored several important training manuals. The operation was based in the War Department building in Washington DC, which moved out to Arlington Hall after the war began and more space was needed.

Often cited as "the man who broke Purple," the Japanese machine code introduced in 1939, Friedman in fact headed the eighteen-month (1939–1940) team effort that accomplished this task, soon dubbed "Magic." The strain was sufficient, however, that it caused a nervous breakdown and his temporary departure from current code-breaking activities. By that time, however, his well-trained and rapidly expanding cadre of code breakers could continue their work without a break. On Friedman's return to work in 1942, he became a civilian employee. He directed communications (meaning code and code breaking) research for the Army's Signal Intelligence Service from 1942 to 1949, and in the early 1950s served as a consultant to the subsequent Army Security Agency and National Security Agency.

He retired from the Army Reserve as a colonel in 1951, and (after a heart attack) from the National Security Agency in 1955, though he continued to consult on secret projects for several more years. Two years later the Friedmans coauthored a book on their lifelong interest—the ciphers said by some authors to have been used by Shakespeare. William Friedman was clearly intellectually brilliant if psychologically insecure, and insisted on many fairly minor formalities—for example, he was always addressed as "Mister" by even his closest colleagues. Friedman died on 2 November 1969 in Washington DC; his wife died 11 years later, on 31 October 1980 in Plainfield, New Jersey.

Christopher H. Sterling

See also Arlington Hall; Bletchley Park; Code Breaking; Electric Cipher Machine (ECM Mark II, "SIGABA"); Enigma; Magic; National Security Agency (NSA); Nebraska Avenue, Washington DC; Rowlett, Frank B. (1908–1998); Signals Intelligence (SIGINT); Yardley, Herbert O. (1889–1958)

Sources
Callimahos, Lambros D. 1974. "The Legendary William F. Friedman." *Cryptologic Spectrum* 4: (1). Reprinted in National Security Agency. 1992. *The Friedman Legacy: A Tribute to William and Elizebeth Friedman*, 241–252. Fort Meade, MD: National Security Agency.
Charles, James R. 1987. "Breaking Codes Was this Couple's Lifetime Career." *Smithsonian* June. Reprinted in National Security Agency. 1992. *The Friedman Legacy: A Tribute to William and Elizebeth Friedman*, 253–264. Fort Meade, MD: National Security Agency.
Clark, Ronald. 1977. *The Man Who Broke Purple: The Life of Colonel William F. Friedman, Who Deciphered the Japanese Code in World War II.* Boston: Little, Brown.
Friedman, William F. 1935. *Advanced Military Cryptography*. Washington, DC: Government Printing Office (reprinted by Aegean Park Press, 1976).

Friedman, William F., and Elizebeth S. Friedman. 1957. *The Shakespearean Ciphers Examined.* Cambridge, UK: Cambridge University Press.

National Security Agency. 1992. *The Friedman Legacy: A Tribute to William and Elizebeth Friedman.* Fort Meade, MD: National Security Agency.

The Fullerphone was, despite its name, a system of portable line telegraphy developed in the British army signals service in 1915. It transmitted over telephone lines without interfering with those signals and was difficult to overhear, making it ideal for the static trench warfare of the Western Front in World War I. (Courtesy Louis Meulstee)

Fullerphone

Despite its name, the Fullerphone was not a telephone but rather a portable telegraph signaling device used in the British army during both world wars. It could be used over either telegraph or telephone lines and was exceedingly difficult for an enemy to overhear.

The Fullerphone was devised in 1915 by then Captain (later Major General) Algernon Clement Fuller of the British Royal Corps of Signals to overcome the common use of earth induction to overhear communications in the closely packed trench warfare of World War I. The commonly used trench buzzer signals could be detected at distances up to 300 yards and speech at 100 yards with only rudimentary equipment from enemy frontline trenches. German listening posts were soon routinely intercepting frontline conversations at ranges of up to 600 yards.

The resulting Fullerphone overcame this problem by using a very small amount of direct current for signaling, making the potential range for overhearing its signals negligible. It first went into use on the Western Front in late 1915 and was ordered in large numbers. Fullerphones eventually replaced earlier equipment to the divisional and corps levels and were widely used (more than 23,000 of them) by 1918. They were also used on some submarine cable links.

Improvements in design continued (the Italians copied the idea in the 1930s), with the Mark IV of 1939 being easier to use and carry. It remained in widespread use during World War II, in part because it could be used over an operating telephone line without disturbing the voice service. An eight-stanza "Ode to the Fullerphone" was published in 1944 in *Jimmy*, the Royal Corps of Signals magazine in the Middle East. The Fullerphone was again used during World War II with submarine cables, achieving a workable range of 200 words per minute upward of 700 miles. The Mark V was combined with a telephone and made for use in tropical regions while the ultimate Mark VI could be fully immersed in water and still used.

The inventor of the device, Algernon Fuller, was born in 1885 and joined the Royal Engineers in 1904. He began experimenting with wireless telegraphy two years later. He built a hobby (ham) wireless station in Bermuda in 1908–1909 and designed a wireless-controlled boat in 1909. He served with the wireless company of the Aldershot command in 1910–1911. Fuller invented a means of electrical recording of speech as well as an automatic alarm signal for making a special call in the absence of a radio operator in 1912. At the time he developed the Fullerphone, he was serving as an experimental officer at the Signals Experimental Establishment in Woolwich (London), where he remained until 1920. He was a member of the Royal Engineers and Signals Board from 1920 to 1933; was chief inspector, Royal Engineers and Signals Equipment, Woolwich, from 1933 to 1937; and served as deputy director of Mechanization at the War Office from 1938 to 1940. His service during World War II included director of Engineering and Signals Equipment for the Ministry of Supply in 1940 and, for a period the next year, deputy director general of the ministry. He retired from the service in 1941 and worked in civil defense for the remainder of the war. Fuller died in 1970.

Christopher H. Sterling

See also Morse Code; Telegraph; Undersea Cables; United Kingdom: Royal Corps of Signals; World War I

Sources

Meulstee, Louis. 1989. "Fullerphone." [Online information; retrieved November 2004.] http://home.hccnet.nl/l.meulstee/fullerphone/fullerphone.html.

Priestly, R. E. 1921. *The Signal Service (France).* Chatham, UK: W. & J. Mackay & Co., Ltd.

War Office, General Staff. 1917. *The Fullerphone, Its Action and Use.* London: Darling and Son, Ltd.

Future Combat Systems (FCS)

The U.S. Army is developing an early twenty-first-century mobile combat capability—the Future Combat Systems (FCS)—that combines various land and air vehicles with a controlling communications network system. The FCS is described as being at the core of Army modernization. The FCS network, interconnecting the eighteen ground and aerial vehicles (some of them unmanned), is the central element in the service's multibillion-dollar program to build its next-generation fighting force. FCS also underscores how vital communications has become to modern military systems.

The FCS network combines and integrates information technology architecture, hardware, software, the Joint Tactical Radio System, and the Warfighter Information Network–Tactical system and intelligence sensors. The Army divides the FCS network into four parts: the System-of-Systems Common Operating Environment (SOSCOE); the communications and computer systems; the battle command software; and the intelligence, surveillance, and reconnaissance system. The communications and computers network provides secure, reliable access to information sources over extended distances and complex terrain. The network will not depend on a large and separate infrastructure because it is to be embedded in the various vehicles, and thus moving with combat units. This enables the command, control, communications, computers, intelligence, surveillance, and reconnaissance network to provide superior battle command on the move to achieve offensive fast-moving operations.

Central to FCS implementation is the SOSCOE—containing some 35 million lines of computer code—which supports multiple mission-critical applications independently and simultaneously. SOSCOE enables straightforward integration of separate software packages, independent of their location, their connectivity mechanism, and the technology used to develop them. SOSCOE uses commercial off-the-shelf hardware and a Joint Tactical–Army compliant operating environment to produce a nonproprietary, standards-based component architecture for real-time, near-real-time, and nonreal-time applications.

Battle command (BC) mission applications include mission planning and preparation, situation understanding, command and mission execution, and the "warfighter-machine interface." These four software packages' combined capabilities enable full interaction among the FCS-equipped battle units. BC capabilities will be common to, and tightly integrated into, the entire FCS network and will share a common framework to achieve the long-desired goal of an integrated and interoperable system with no hardware, software, or information "stovepipes."

The FCS is connected to the command, control, communications, computers, intelligence, surveillance, and reconnaissance network by a multilayered communications and computers (CC) network with unprecedented range, capacity, and dependability. The CC network provides secure, reliable access to information sources over extended distances and complex terrain. The network will support advanced functionalities such as integrated network management, informa-

tion assurance, and information dissemination management to ensure dissemination of critical information among sensors, processors, and fighters both within and outside the FCS-equipped unit.

FCS project development began in 2000 with the Army and the Defense Advanced Research Projects Agency; it was accelerated in 2004, and the first component testing began in 2006, with prototypes expected within two years. Implementation of the first brigade is scheduled for 2014 with a projected total cost of $200 billion for fifteen FCS-equipped brigades.

Christopher H. Sterling

See also Defense Advanced Research Projects Agency (DARPA); Global Information Grid (GIG); Joint Tactical Radio System (JTRS); Mobile Communications; Vehicles and Transport; Warfighter Information Network–Tactical (WIN-T)

Sources

Department of the Army. "Future Combat Systems (FCS)." [Online information; retrieved June 2006.] http://www.army .mil/fcs/.

GlobalSecurity.org. "Future Combat Systems References." [Online information; retrieved June 2006.] http://www.globalsecurity .org/military/systems/ground/fcs-refs .htm.

Tiboni, Frank. 2006. "Visualizing the Army's New Tank: Why the Network is the Main Battle Piece in the Future Combat Systems," *Federal Computer Week*, at www.few.com/ article93979-04-10-86-Print (accessed June 2006).

G

German "Fish" Codes

"Fish" was Bletchley Park's code name for two advanced German teleprinter cipher machines, the Siemens & Halske T 52 series (called "Sturgeon" by Bletchley) and the Lorenz SZ 40/42 ("Tunny"). Tunny was used mainly between the German High Command and army groups and often provided high-level intelligence. "Fish" also referred to a family of codes to which the British assigned fish names (Tunny, Sturgeon) for better coordination of the code-breaking process. The intensive effort to break the Fish codes led to the creation of Colossus, the world's first semi-programmable electronic computer.

Bletchley reconstructed several models of Sturgeon, which was used by the Luftwaffe, and solved some coded messages, or traffic, on them using "depths" (messages transmitted with identical machine settings). However, it decided to concentrate resources on attacking Tunny, as breaking the German army's Enigma was always very difficult, and Bletchley was already deriving a sub-

stantial amount of intelligence from Luftwaffe Enigma ciphers.

Tunny incorporated two sets of five mechanical wheels, with one set stepping irregularly, controlled by two "motor" wheels. The wheels had 501 settable cams, which produced the equivalents of teleprinter "marks" and "spaces" and provided Tunny with a vast number of cipher settings. The two sets of wheels generated streams of key (characters used to encipher plain text), which were added to Baudot-Murray teleprinter code to encipher it.

Contrary to several accounts, Bletchley never saw a Tunny machine until the end of World War II. In an outstanding feat of cryptanalysis, Bill Tutte, a young Cambridge chemistry research student, deduced Tunny's structure from key found by Colonel John Tiltman in August 1941. Bletchley's research section then helped to solve the complete machine by January 1942. Just intercepting the high-speed radio Tunny signals posed immense problems, however, and eventually required more than 800 staff at the Knockholt listening station in Kent.

Depths, near-depths, and poor German operating procedures helped Bletchley to read most Tunny messages from June to October 1942, when a simplistic indicating method was changed. The Germans knew about some of Tunny's weaknesses and constantly improved both the machine and its operating procedures. Being electromechanical, Tunny could produce only a pseudo-random key, which enabled Bletchley to exploit statistical characteristics in its traffic. Tutte invented a statistical method for breaking single Tunny messages in November 1942, but making the calculations manually took far too long. Max Newman, a gifted Cambridge mathematician, therefore, proposed fast machinery for the purpose. Dubbed the "Heath Robinson" after the British cartoon equivalent of Rube Goldberg, it entered service in June 1943. It had few vacuum tubes and was not wholly successful, as it could not fully synchronize two paper tapes being compared. Still, it revealed various problems with the machine breaking of Tunny, and consequently was vital to the subsequent success of Colossus, the special purpose electronic computer developed to solve Tunny messages.

Despite Bletchley's skepticism and disinterest, T. H. (Tommy) Flowers and a Post Office team including S. W. Broadhurst had worked on developing Colossus for almost a year without any official requisition from Bletchley. Due to their foresight and dedication, Colossus I entered service in February 1944. It ran a looped tape containing cipher text at 30 miles per hour, while its 1,500 tubes performed tests and emulated Tunny functions to find Tunny wheel settings. Colossus II, with 2,500 vacuum tubes, entered service just before D-Day to provide crucial intelligence about Hitler's reactions to Allied deception plans. It used parallel processing to analyze data at 25,000 characters per second.

Swedish cryptanalysts also reconstructed Sturgeon from mid-1940 onward, but did not break Tunny until March 1943. They also solved the traffic on both machines using manual methods against depths. They intercepted the traffic on Swedish teleprinter landlines used by the Germans, which generally provided better copy than the sometimes poor radio intercepts that Bletchley had to attack.

Between November 1942 and the end of the war, the Knockholt listening station intercepted almost 168,000 transmissions, from which Bletchley derived 13,500 decrypts containing 63 million characters. Finding Tunny's wheel patterns and settings required the highest cryptanalytical skills, advanced statistical techniques, and the design and construction of the first electronic computer, Colossus. Breaking Tunny traffic was therefore probably the greatest code-breaking feat of World War II.

Ralph Erskine

See also Bletchley Park; Code Breaking; Enigma; Government Code & Cipher School (GC&CS, 1919–1946); Signals Intelligence (SIGINT); Teleprinter/Teletype; Tiltman, John Hessell (1894–1982); Ultra; Y Service

Sources

Copeland, H. Jack, et al. 2006. *Colossus: The Secrets of Bletchley Park's Codebreaking Computers.* London: Oxford University Press.

Erskine, Ralph. 1988. "Tunny Decrypts." *Cryptologia* XII (1): 59–61.

Gannon, Paul. 2006. *Colossus: Bletchley Park's Greatest Secret.* London: Atlantic.

"General Report on Tunny" [1945] Kew: National Archives, Public Record Office, HW 25/4 and 5.

Hinsley, F. H., and Alan Stripp, eds. 1993. "Part Three: Fish." In *Codebreakers: The Inside Story* of *Bletchley Park*, 139–192. New York: Oxford University Press.

Wylie, Shaun. 2001. "Breaking Tunny and the Birth of Colossus." In *Action this Day*, edited by Michael Smith and Ralph Erskine, 317–341. London: Bantam Press.

Germany: Air Force

German air force communications were of superior quality at the start of both world wars, though they declined in capability under the strain of sustained battle conditions and the inability to effectively bring improved designs into service.

Although the German army began experimenting with airships it was slow to see the potential of aircraft. The German Army Air Service was only formed in 1912 because the military authorities became concerned about the growth of the French Aéronautique Militaire as tensions rose in Europe. On the outbreak of World War I in August 1914, German aircraft were unarmed and were mainly concerned with artillery observation and reconnaissance.

German aircraft began air-to-ground experiments with wireless as World War I began. Unique Morse code "sending tables" allowed operation by pilots or other air crew who did not understand Morse code. Improved signal detectors by 1915 greatly increased the efficiency of German aircraft-mounted radios. Power was obtained from a generator driven by the airplane's propeller. After 1916, several Telefunken transmitters were manufactured to allow regular artillery spotting from the air, using more than 300 ground stations and some 500 radio-equipped aircraft. Still later equipment, some of it based on vacuum tube transmitters by 1918, controlled better for interference from other battlefield radio uses. Experimental but not operational use was achieved by wireless telephone (voice) transmitters in the last year of the war, by which time German efforts lagged behind those of the Allies.

Groundwork for a new independent German air force began in secret (because of 1919 treaty requirements) in the mid-1920s. German civil aircraft developed and often shielded military planning and training efforts. German aircraft radio development continued between the wars, chiefly aimed at expanding airline operations and flying clubs and schools. Secret training—including that for developing radio communications—took place in the Soviet Union. The new Luftwaffe was publicly announced in March 1935. The Lufwaffe's "Condor Legion" experience during the 1936–1939 Spanish Civil War made clear the importance of good radio communication between air and ground forces. Although hand signals had sufficed for inter-airplane communications in the past, German pilots learned that air-to-air radio was now essential. Another lesson learned in Spain made the Luftwaffe place greater emphasis on development of navigational aids for both bad weather and night operation.

At the time of the invasion of Poland on 1 September 1939, signal units included nearly 60,000 men (of a total Luftwaffe of 370,000). German aircraft radio equipment was well built and rugged, and generally stayed with prewar designs throughout the conflict. By 1944 the Luftwaffe Signal Service employed 175,000 to 200,000 personnel and came under the director general of Signal Communications, part of Hermann Goering's Air Ministry. The basic operational *truppe* of 10 to 120 men focused on a specific type of signal activity (telephone, cable laying, etc.).

On the other hand Luftwaffe signals security was markedly lax (compared to the German army and navy) and Luftwaffe

Enigma codes were among the first broken (April 1940) by British code breakers at Bletchley Park. By June intercepted messages provided the first information on the *knickebein* air navigation system. The *knickebein* ("crooked leg") navigation technique was first used in the August–September 1940 Battle of Britain, a blind-bombing system that utilized radio direction to assist aerial navigation. Operating on 30 MHz, it was based on the Lorenz blind-landing system that had been pioneered in the 1930s. Pilots flew along one beam, dropping their bombs when they crossed a second beam. The British developed means of locating the two *knickebein* transmitters and either jamming their signals or knocking them out from the air.

One of Hitler's personal aircraft, a four-engine Focke-Wulf Fw 200 Condor transport, was equipped with a high-frequency short-wave transmitter from which messages were sent in Morse code. A long-wave transmitter was also fitted and the aircraft had both fixed and trailing antennas. Later in the war, more sophisticated German aircraft radio designs featured the ability to vary the frequency used as well as either AM or FM modulation.

For more than a decade after World War II, there was, again, no active German air force. From the mid-1950s (when West Germany joined the North Atlantic Treaty Organization) to 1990 two German air forces were in place, one for each half of the country. By the turn of the twenty-first century, however, the Luftwaffe communications network was said to be the most modern in Europe thanks to its new asynchronous transfer mode communications network. The Luftwaffe Communications and Electronics Command reports through the Combat Command based in Münster.

Christopher H. Sterling

See also Airplanes; Airships and Balloons; Bletchley Park; Britain, Battle of (1940); Enigma; Jamming; North Atlantic Treaty Organization (NATO) Communications & Information Systems Agency; Ultra; World War I; World War II.

Sources

AOL Hometown. "Luftwaffe Ground Attack Radio Terminology." [Online information; retrieved November 2004.] http://members.aol.com/dheitm8612/attack.htm.

Air Ministry. 1983. *The Rise and Fall of the German Air Force, 1933–1945.* New York: St. Martin's Press (reprint of 1946 original).

"Battle of the Beams" website: http://www.vectorsite.net/ttwiz7.html (accessed November 2004)

Wood, Tony, and Bill Gunston. 1977. *Hitler's Luftwaffe: A Pictorial History and Technical Encyclopedia of Hitler's Air Power in World War II.* London: Salamander Books.

Germany: Army

German military communications have for nearly two centuries reflected the country's high-quality industrial technology. Germany was an early user of semaphore and then electric telegraphy and telephony. Important experimental work on wireless was undertaken by German pioneers Adolph Slaby and George von Arco in the early 1900s. Blessed with a superior electronics manufacturing capability, as well as the central role of the armed forces within both the Imperial (1870–1918) and later Nazi (1933–1945) governments, Germany eventually developed excellent military communication systems with superior equipment that played a central part in both world wars. Since 1945, German firms have been important providers of analog and later digital military communications equipment.

Line Communications

A military semaphore telegraph system was established by the Prussian government to connect Berlin and Koblenz, becoming fully operational in 1833–1834. About 300 miles long, it included more than sixty semaphore stations, each 7 to 10 miles apart and manned by a crew of two. These stations were constructed on hills or atop tall buildings, including churches. Each was fitted with a wooden mast using three pairs of movable wooden arms, which could send about a thousand prearranged words or symbols. Simple coded messages could be transmitted the length of the system in about fifteen minutes. Personnel were inducted into the uniformed service, the system operated six hours a day, and it came under the control of the Army General Staff. Parts of it remained in service until 1852, when electric telegraphy took over. (Several of the towers survive to this day.)

Field telegraphs were introduced into the Prussian army on 21 August 1856. Two mobile field telegraph detachments, each with three sections of the Pioneer Guard, were created that year. Between 1870 and 1871, seven field telegraph and five lines of communication telegraph detachments were in operation. Prussia (later part of Germany and today mainly incorporated into Poland) and Bohemia (today part of the Czech Republic) first utilized field telegraphy units to coordinate troops during their fighting in 1864. By the time of the larger Franco-Prussian War of 1870–1871, Prussia had three different telegraph units, one operating civilian lines captured from the French. Many of Germany's domestic state telegraph lines were buried rather than strung on poles; this organization provided personnel and equipment to the fighting forces as needed. Field telegraph detachments (a dozen by the end

of the war) were used aggressively, often laying lines under frontline conditions ahead of many fighting troops. More than 7,000 miles of line were laid during the Franco-Prussian War. Telegraph troops proved themselves indispensable and an effective means of military and political command, often on an hourly basis.

The first military signal unit was created in 1887 as part of an engineer battalion, and became an experimental signal company in 1896. On 25 March 1899, the independent German signal corps was born, as on that date the Telegraphentruppe was officially formed. This organization comprised an inspector of telegraphs and three telegraph battalions. A volunteer telegraph section was provided during the Boxer Rebellion in China in 1900–1901. A Bavarian telegraph company was formed in 1901, and a year later a telegraph detachment for the Airship Battalion was created in Berlin. Two field telegraph detachments and two wireless detachments and a signaling section were deployed in German Southwest Africa during the Herero Rebellion of 1904. Signaling in the Airships Group became a Telegraphentruppe responsibility from 1905. All of these units faced a difficult time due to the general military scorn directed at the relatively new and largely volunteer (and nonfighting) signals units. The emphasis of many senior officers was more on how to turn signals personnel into fighting men rather than concern for tactical, let alone strategic, communication links. By 1910, the German army decided the telegraph was obsolete, planning to rely on the telephone for virtually all of its communications.

World Wars

Ten signals battalions were being modernized when World War I began. The Telegraphentruppe had a strength of 550 officers and 5,800 men, which after mobilization rose to 800 officers and 25,000 men. Despite its size, however, the Telegraphentruppe was still insufficient to guarantee telegraphic communications between all forces and headquarters, due in part to the rapid advance of German units over great distances. It was quickly recognized that the Telegraphentruppe was unable to meet the demands of the army and was partly responsible for the failure of the war's opening offensive. Tight secrecy over the overall German plan of attack (the von Schlieffen scheme to move in a massive scythe through Belgium and into northern France) retarded development of any effective role for signals communication. While railway engineers were ready to rapidly replace battlefield infrastructure losses, no similar planning was evident for replacing or constructing signals links.

During the initial August 1914 attack, telegraph and telephone lines were rapidly overwhelmed thanks to this lack of planning and coordination (let alone destruction caused by the fighting). Most units lacked radios given the earlier decision to depend on telephone services. Signals units often lagged far behind the lines, making effective control of the battle extremely difficult and forcing use of traditional courier and other means of signaling. During the early August 1914 siege of Liege, for example, the German High Command was unaware for three days that the city had been occupied by its forces. Many fast-moving frontline elements exceeded the ability of hard-pressed and undermanned signals units to maintain connections to higher command, in part for a lack of redundancy in communication facilities. Where radio was operating and available (typically only at high command levels early in the war), it remained slow due to the need to encode and decode messages. All of

these factors were crucial in the impending Battle of the Marne that halted the German advance before Paris.

The Germans did learn from this experience, reinstating use of the telegraph, adding a motor courier dispatch service, increasing the size of the signals force, and reversing the order of communications responsibility to match that of the Allies—from superior to inferior units. From August 1914 until May 1916, more than 25,000 miles of permanent line and 3,000 miles of cable and underground cable were provided to the 10th Army facing Russia. The army signals corps was reorganized and renamed Nachrichtentruppe in July 1917. By then the German communications network covered nearly 600,000 miles. By the end of World War I, more than 4,000,000 miles of line had been supplied by the signals corps and army command had exchanges with 600 subscribers. The signals corps had a strength of 4,400 officers and 185,000 men. Indeed, German signals forces had grown to 4.3 percent of the total army—a vast expansion from the 1 percent at mobilization. Their huge and complex network enabled General Erich Ludendorff to contact Constantinople and Bucharest from his special train at a railway station on the Western Front. Each German army controlled its own communication links from the front line back to the German border. German subordinate signals units were responsible for communicating up to their superiors (or "front to rear"). But as critiqued after the war, the German system lacked flexibility, in part because officers could be assigned to other units, often bringing untrained personnel into signals operations. Though a third of the quarter-million men in the imperial post and telegraph department were drafted into the military when the country mobilized, markedly few found their way to signals units.

Telefunken was the primary supplier of telegraph/telephone equipment to German forces and had developed a mobile wireless transmitter wagon by 1911. By 1915 Telefunken had perfected a short-range (up to 2,500 feet) spark transmitter for wireless telegraphy signaling in trench warfare. Upward of 200 sets would typically be operating along about 30 miles of the front line. Improved receivers from Siemens & Halske allowed use of several different channels. A Telefunken tube-powered transmitter arrived in 1917, used by both land and air forces. By then, excellent connections were maintained with army command as well as Berlin.

Seventy-one signal detachments were in place by 1939. The ability to communicate and command was largely responsible for the early success of the German army in World War II. German tanks used radio and were thus more flexible than the Allied forces. German radio equipment, having been designed in 1936 to 1940 for use in a mobile army, changed little during the war. Thus, though uniform in design and operation, it did not improve with new knowledge. Equipment was robust but not easily modified. An excellent Telefunken tank radio was developed by 1937, and its effective use in two-way tank communication played an important part in German armored victories at least into 1943, when Allied designs caught up. World War II German radio links utilized the Enigma coding machine (or more advanced "Fish" teleprinter machines), many of whose code systems were increasingly read by the Allies after 1940.

Since 1945

Postwar army communications history dates to 1956 when the German military was reformed. German army (*Bundeswehr*) signal (*fernmelde*) units were soon responsible for voice transmissions, telephone, teleprinters, radio, radio relay links, and later data communications, cable communications, satellite communications, graphics transmission, and fax connections. By the turn of the twenty-first century, the German army Signal Corps was split between the army and the Joint Support Service. The former supports (mobile) tactical or operational command, while the latter provides national strategic command communications and communication links between Germany and military theaters elsewhere. Army tactical and strategic communications units are employed in some multinational North Atlantic Treaty Organization (NATO) units. The Bundeswehr also provided combat and communications support to the Franco-German Brigade of the Euro Corps formed in 1990. During 2000–2002, the corps became a High Response Force for NATO.

These units all employ the German AUTOKO 90 (the Mobile Automated Communication Field Net). It is a digital, mobile, gridlike, automated network with trunk nodes and access nodes. The system consists of communication junction boxes and nodes that are intermeshed by tactical wire/radio relay links, satellite links, and/or terrestrial transmission lines (leased, if required, from commercial providers), and provides digital transmission lines with full-dial service. AUTOKO 90 allows encrypted voice, teletype, facsimile, and data transmission.

Another German system is the Integrated Broadband System for Command Communication Systems. This is a digital system matching the EUROCOM standard and is based on fiber optics. It is the digital local area part of AUTOKO 90 and enables command posts to use both analog and digital terminal equipment. The Terrestrial Trunked Radio system is accommodated in commercial hand-carried containers and is used to network single mobile subscribers within small areas. It integrates these mobile subscribers into the "system of systems" and so enhances the command and control over mobile forces in the area of operations. The Bundeswehr satellite communications system does not yet operate a space segment (satellite) of its own, therefore needed circuits are leased from civilian satellite communication providers (e.g., INTELSAT or EUTELSAT). Finally, the army mobile Command, Control and Information System for digitally supported Command of Operations in Staffs system is deployed by the Bundeswehr operating in Germany and within multinational organizations. It assists the command process from the corps down to brigade level.

Danny Johnson, Cliff Lord,
and Christopher H. Sterling

See also Baltic Nations; Eastern Europe; Enigma; European Late Nineteenth-Century Wars; German "Fish" Codes; Germany: Air Force; Germany: Military Communications School; Germany: Navy; Marne, Battle of (September 1914); North Atlantic Treaty Organization (NATO) Communications & Information Systems Agency; Polish Code Breaking; Tannenberg, Battle of (1914); Ultra; Warsaw Pact (1955–1991); World War I; World War II.

Sources

Arnold, Wilhelm. n. d. "Signal Communications in the Pocket of Stalingrad and Communications with the Outside." [Online information; retrieved November 2004.] http://users.pandora.be/stalingrad/battle_reports/signal_communications.htm.

Beauchamp, Ken. 2001. *History of Telegraphy*. London: Institution of Electrical Engineers.

Bundeswehr. Official home page of the German army. "Locations of Communications Troops in Germany." [Online information (in German); retrieved April 2006.] http://www.deutschesheer.de/portal/a/heer/kcxml/04_Sj9SPykssy0xPLMnMz0vM0Y_QjzKLd483N_AFSYGYZu7m-pEwsa

CUVH1fj_zcVH1v_QD9gtyIckdHRUUARLe1AQ!!/delta/base64xml/L3dJdyEvd0ZNQUFzQUMvNElVRS82X0dfNzBW.

Chauvin, Maj. Gen. 1884. "The Organization of the Electric Telegraph in Germany for War Purposes." *Journal of the Royal United Service Institution* 28: 777–808, 1051–1064.

Evans, Paul W. 1935. "Strategic Signal Communications: A Study of Signal Communication As Applied to Large Field Forces, Based upon the Operations of the German Signal Corps During the March on Paris in 1914." *Signal Corps Bulletin* 82 (January–February): 24–58.

Hofman, Helmut. 2005. "The German Army Signal Corps and Its Equipment." *Military Technology* June/July. In German.

LA6NCA. "LA6NCA's WW2 Radio Page." [Online information; retrieved November 2004.] http://www.laud.no/ww2/.

Porter, Jack J. 2004. "Signaling, Sociology and Structure: Designing German Military Institutions, 1949–1999." Ph.D. diss., University of California, Berkeley.

Radio News. 1944. "Captured Enemy Equipment." 1944. *Radio News* Special Issue: U.S. Amy Signal Corps 31 (2): 163–173.

Showalter, Dennis. 1973. "Soldiers as Postmasters? The Electric Telegraph as an Instrument of Command in the Prussian Army." *Military Affairs* 27: 48–51.

U.S. War Department. 1944. *Signal Communications Equipment Directory. German Radio Communications Equipment*. War Department Manual TM-E 11–227 (June). Washington, DC: U.S. War Department.

U.S. War Department. 1945. "Signal Equipment." In *Handbook on German Military Forces*. War Department Technical Manual TM-E 30–451 (March), 434–477. Washington, DC: U.S. War Department.

Wilson, Geoffrey. 1976. "Germany." In *The Old Telegraphs*, 159–165. London: Phillimore.

Germany: Military Communications School

German military signals training dates back to the Prussian army in the late nineteenth century and has been through many reorganizations, especially during and after the two world wars. For the past half-century, what is now the Communications School and Technical School of the Army for Electro-Technology (FSHElT) has provided telecommunications and information training for the German army.

The *Reichsschule* (Realm School) *Feldafing* was located in a 1912-era country house on Lake Starnberg (once owned by renowned author Thomas Mann). After Hitler's rise to power, it was converted into a private school for Nazi storm trooper leadership. The school was dissolved at the end of World War II, and U.S. occupation forces converted the former Reichsschule into a camp for displaced persons. The camp was closed in 1951 when the revived German army resumed operations in the building (in 1999 it was converted into a Nobel Prize literature museum).

The modern German military communications school was provisionally organized on 24 June 1956 at Sonthofen (in the Bavarian Alps) as the Troop School Communications Troops. That summer it became the *Fernmeldeschule* (Signal School) of the army. Plans were put in motion for the permanent stationing of the school in the Bavarian villages of Feldafing and Poecking, some 20 miles southwest of Munich. The Reichsschule has changed a good deal in the half-century since, as buildings and organization accommodated changes in training. Initially, the school was exclusively responsible for the communications telephone service and, increasingly, various modes of electronic warfare. Curriculum was reorganized in 1972 when the school became the FSHElT. This soon became nationally recognized within Germany for the quality of its technical education. More recently FSHE1T developed into a center of training and advancement in information transfer and data processing.

Students are typically new officers in the technical branches of one of the services or noncommissioned officers who have acquired civilian vocational certification. In 1999, the Luftwaffe technical school was transferred to FSHElT. Training for technical assistants was initiated, as was training of officer candidates for service in army and navy computer science.

Given the continuing transformation of the German armed forces, communications training is constantly being revised and updated as qualified information technology personnel are essential for all military services. German industry has strong demand for those trained in communications support, such as satellite communications.

The location of FSHElT will transfer to Poecking by 2011 and the current school facilities in Feldafing will be sold.

Danny Johnson

See also Germany: Army

Source
Feldafing Fernmeldeschule, Germany. [Online information: retrieved April 2006.] http:// www.gebb-mbh.de/Projekte/ Immobilien/ Portfolio/Bayern/Liegen schaften_in_Feldafing/Fernmeldeschule _Feldafing.html.

Germany: Naval Intelligence (*B-Dienst*)

The German Radio Monitoring Service of World War I continued as a small operation (about twenty people) into the 1920s and 1930s. A number of listening stations (sufficient for effective direction finding as well as listening) were built along the coast of the North Sea and the Baltic Sea, connected by direct telephone cables and telex.

Intelligence formed one of the six German navy war staffs during World War II.

Cryptologic intelligence was the task of the Naval Communications Intelligence Division, generally referred to as the *Beobachtung Dienst* (*B-Dienst*), or Observation Service, which focused on radio intercepts and decoding.

B-Dienst began to study British naval codes in 1936. It achieved an early success in the spring of 1940 when it decoded a British message outlining Royal Navy plans to mine the Norwegian coast. That enabled a radio deception plan that masked true German intentions (to raid the south coast and occupy Oslo), allowing the weaker German naval forces to outwit the stronger Royal Navy, which was focused on the northwest coast as B-Dienst had intended. Capture of some British naval codebooks in mid-1940 opened up the convoy and merchant marine coded communications systems, allowing successful U-boat attacks. The Allies unwittingly contributed to this weakness by not changing codes often enough and sometimes sending the same messages using different codes, a windfall for German code-breaking efforts. Only in June 1943, months after finding out that their convoy code was being read by the Germans, did the British change the code (in June and again in October 1943), thus locking out German code breakers.

Some German U-boats were equipped with two-man teams trained by B-Dienst to intercept voice communications and radio direction finding. On several occasions these teams listened in to low-grade Allied convoy communications, which aided their attack plans.

B-Dienst was divided during World War II into five sections: a main evaluation and intelligence center, a unit focused on decoding British signals, another working on American signals, one dealing with Soviet codes, and a training school. Germany also sought personnel with seagoing experience,

while the British used many civilians. Only late in 1942 did B-Dienst mechanize any of the code-breaking process, using punched-card machines to attack the Allied codes.

Even at its peak, B-Dienst was smaller than Allied code-breaking efforts. In 1944 it operated about fifty intercept stations and had perhaps 5,000 personnel (including about 275 cryptanalytic staff)—about half the staff of Bletchley Park and less than half of that at Arlington Hall. B-Dienst personnel considered traffic analysis as important as cryptanalysis. Radio direction finding, for example, was simply a part of overall intelligence, rather than target acquisition as it was for the Allies. B-Dienst issued the *Radio Intelligence Bulletin* regularly to disseminate its findings.

The German army and the Foreign Office maintained their own code-breaking operations as well, as did the Luftwaffe after its formation in 1935. But the services took a different approach to the code-making process, with the navy observing the best levels of secrecy for its main Enigma ciphers and introducing a four-rotor Enigma machine. While B-Dienst and other units experienced considerable success early in the war, with the introduction by the Allies of the SIGABA, Typex, and combined cipher machines, the Germans were unable to read high-level Allied coded messages. Allied bombing effectively disrupted most B-Dienst activities even before the end of the war in Europe.

Christopher H. Sterling

See also Arlington Hall, Bletchley Park; Code Breaking; Electric Cipher Machine (ECM Mark II, "SIGABA"); Enigma; German "Fish" Codes; Germany: Navy; OP-20-G; Signals Intelligence (SIGINT); Ultra

Sources
Bray, J. K. 1995. *Ultra in the Atlantic, Vol 3. German Naval Communications Intelligence.* Walnut Creek, CA: Aegean Park Press.

Gordon, Don E. 1981. "German Cryptology." In *Electronic Warfare: Elements of Strategy and Multiplier of Combat Power*, 47–52. New York: Pergamon.

Kahn, David. 1978. *Hitler's Spies: German Military Intelligence in World War II*. New York: Macmillan.

Showell, Jak P. Mallmann. 2003. *German Naval Code Breakers*. Annapolis, MD: Naval Institute Press.

Germany: Navy

German naval forces were weak and disorganized and played no important role prior to the early twentieth century. With its huge buildup after 1900, as with the army, the German fleet benefited greatly from the country's excellent radio research and manufacturing capability in both world wars. German radio equipment was among the best produced anywhere and fleet elements constantly practiced in its use.

In the period just before World War I, Germany completed a worldwide network of wireless shore stations to communicate with its naval and merchant fleets. The 200 kilowatt high-frequency station at Nauen (just outside Berlin, then the most powerful in the world) was used in August 1914 to warn German merchant shipping worldwide to seek German or neutral ports. But German stations elsewhere—including several powerful shore transmitters on the East Coast of the United States—were taken over by the U.S. Navy in 1915. In 1914–1915 other German naval shore stations at Kamina (Togoland), Windhoek (southwest Africa), and Zanzibar (African coast) fell to Allied force attacks, as did scattered wireless transmitters on several Pacific islands, mainly to Australian or Japanese forces. Just such a raid in December 1914 by Admiral Maximilian Graf von Spee on the (British) Falkland Islands wireless station led to the loss of his four cruisers when they were ambushed by a stronger British naval force.

Early in World War I, the German light cruiser *Magdeburg* ran aground near the island of Odensholm and could not be refloated. Her loss gave the Allies a huge gift of the German signaling codes. She was carrying three copies of the SKM codebooks, and two of them were taken by the Russians, one shared with the British Admiralty. There, Room 40 code breakers set to work, enabling the Allies to read most German naval messages for the remainder of the war. This ability provided a vital early warning that the German High Seas Fleet was "coming out" at the end of May 1916, enabling the British Grand Fleet to engage the Germans in the Battle of Jutland. German fire control communications improved steadily, especially after Jutland in 1916.

Crude though it then was, airborne radio was vital in communicating with naval Zeppelins. From the inception of the war, Zeppelins carried Telefunken spark transmitters (despite the danger with the hydrogen-filled gas bags) that used low and medium frequencies and often trailed 100-foot or longer aerials. These were heavy modified shipboard transmitters installed in soundproof cabins. Some of the navigation signals could be picked up by the Allies, however, who would then seek and shoot down the huge airships.

After the war, the Naval Communications Research Establishment (it became a command in 1938) was established at Kiel. Sections of it began to investigate what became sonar and radar, as well as general communications technology. The navy itself was reconstituted as the Kriegsmarine in 1935. With the vital exception of its U-boat fleet, however, the German navy played a smaller role in World War II than in World War I.

Other than early sorties of some of its battleships (e.g., *Graf Spee* and *Bismarck*, both of which were lost, the latter thanks to a radio signal breaking what had been effective radio silence, as well as Allied radio direction finding), German surface units had little overall impact.

The submarines were another matter, and their role was either enhanced or badly limited (authorities differ) by the use of radio to vector them in "wolf packs" to Allied convoys. Central command and control of the U-boat fleet was initially hugely successful and relied totally on radio in one of the most successful examples of naval communications. German shortwave radios were less susceptible to direction finding by the Allies than earlier long-wave radio equipment. The importance of radio links to direct the widespread German submarine force is made evident by the use of the most powerful very low frequency transmitter of the period—the German Goliath station located by the Elbe River near Magdeburg. Built in 1941, this antenna was capable of up to two million watts, strong enough to send signals to submarines as far away as the Indian Ocean. This monstrous antenna was composed of some 200 miles of steel wires for the in-ground array (steel was used due to the shortage of more efficient copper), and was built in a swampy area to generate an even stronger signal. It could transmit signals as much as 80 feet below the surface of the water.

The entire system relied, however, on communications security. The Kriegsmarine, and especially the submarine corps, was far more careful about its use of the Enigma cipher equipment than was the Luftwaffe. Still, breaking of the Enigma codes after 1940, and especially those used in U-boat signals by 1943, was a key factor in growing U-boat losses and the eventual Allied win in the Battle of the Atlantic.

At the end of World War II, the detailed May 1945 instructions from General Dwight Eisenhower's headquarters to German naval officials emphasized communications resources to be identified and turned over to the Allies—a final indication of just how important those facilities had been.

Since the 1990 reunification of Germany, the Naval Communications and Electronics Flotilla complements all the capabilities of the German fleet. It is responsible for the coastal radar stations, communications facilities ashore, and three intelligence-collection vessels. A German submarine flotilla is once again active in European and Atlantic waters. And as with other navies, the Germans are integrating Internet links with other modes of communication with their Maritime Command, Control and Information System development.

Christopher H. Sterling

See also Atlantic, Battle of the (1939–1945); Enigma; Jutland, Battle of (1916); North Atlantic Treaty Organization (NATO) Communications &Information Systems Agency; Radio; Ultra; World War I; World War II

Sources

Bauer, Arthur O. 2004. "Aspects of the German Naval Communications Research Establishment." [Online article; retrieved August 2005.] http://www.xs4all.nl/~aobauer/NVK.pdf.

Hezlet, Arthur. 1975. *Electronics and Sea Power.* Briarcliff Manor, NY: Stein & Day.

Global Command and Control System (GCCS)

The Global Command and Control System (GCCS) is the Pentagon's comprehensive automated information network system providing data for strategic command and control. In 1996 the GCCS replaced its existing version—World Wide Military Command and Control System—which had been in use since the 1970s.

The GCCS is one of the significant elements driving the transformation of the American military under the catch phrase of "Information Revolution in Military Affairs." It is thought to be a single, predominant system of global reach for gathering, receiving, sharing, processing, and using military information. The GCCS is the main provider of surveillance and reconnaissance information (data, imagery, intelligence, status of forces, enemy order of battle, air tasking orders, meteorological, oceanographic, etc.). It correlates and merges data from various sensors and intelligence sources. The GCCS is thus the real "system of systems" for military command and control and the cornerstone for American information superiority over its enemies as expressed in the U.S. Department of Defense's *Joint Vision 2020*. Through its workstations it supplies the Joint Staff with a real-time picture of changing battlespace. The GCCS works toward greater interservice "jointness" by enabling commanders to orchestrate actions of air, land, sea, and space forces. At the same time, however, the individual military services have developed particular components for the GCCS that extend its functionality to address specific requirements of the Army (GCCS-A), Navy (GCCS-M), Marine Corps (MAGTF), and Air Force (GCCS-AF). The GCCS's cobweb links numerous information systems for various missions, namely, force projection and employment; situational awareness; force sustainability, readiness, and protection; and intelligence.

The GCCS consists of common hardware, operating systems, and software. It uses classified units of the Defense Information Systems Network for connectivity. The communications backbone of GCCS is the Secure IP Router Network with routers provided by Cisco Company. The GCCS uses a set of integrated software applications operating on common operating environment hardware. There are three basic communication modes: one-way query, one-way data, and two-way data. Commanders can, for example, create their own home pages and communicate through e-mails within the GCCS classified system.

The greatest challenge for the effective functioning of the GCCS and its development is the interoperability and integration of command and control systems into a single broad and interoperable system. Special and demanding standards were introduced to meet this challenge, namely the Joint Interoperability Test Command, which tests and certifies the interoperability of command, control, communications, computer, and intelligence (C4I) systems before their integration with the GCCS.

The GCCS is one of the first steps in the wider Pentagon project called "C4I for the Warrior." Its goal is to merge all major elements of command, control, communications, and intelligence in a single communication network encompassing all the existing military communication systems in the U.S. military. The C4I for the Warrior aims to accelerate the flow of information across the battlefield and between higher and lower command centers. The implementation of the project will allow for unprecedented rapid military communication and for total battlespace information to the warfighter for any mission, at any time, and at any place. The GCCS can be seen as either the midterm solution for C4I for the Warrior or as the first phase for building such a globally connected and fully integrated system.

Łukasz Kamieński

See also Defense Advanced Research Projects Agency (DARPA); Defense Information

Systems Agency (DISA); Global Information Grid (GIG); Information Revolution in Military Affairs (IRMA); "System of Systems"; World Wide Military Command and Control System (WWMCCS)

Sources

Department of Defense. 1996. *Joint Vision 2020.* Washington, DC: Government Printing Office.

Fredericks, Brian. 2002. "Information Warfare: The Organizational Dimension." [Online article; retrieved December 2006.] http://www.ndu.edu/inss/siws/ch4.html.

Joint Interoperability Test Command. 2005. "Global Command and Control System (GCCS) Interoperability (IOP) Home Page." [Online information; retrieved December 2006.] http://jitc.fhu.disa.mil/gccsiop/.

Global Information Grid (GIG)

The Global Information Grid (GIG), initiated in 1999, is designed to integrate all American defense information systems into a network-centric operation that will provide processing, storage, management, and transport of information to support all Department of Defense (DoD), national security, and related intelligence community functions in conditions of war, crisis, or peace. GIG capabilities will be available from all operating locations (fixed or mobile) and will interface with allied nations as well as non-GIG systems. The system will cost at least $21 billion to implement through 2010 and may take another decade and more billions beyond that to fully develop.

The GIG grew out of DoD's search in the 1980s and 1990s for a truly integrated system of communications that would provide information assurance, interoperability of systems, and information sharing across all of its functions. It is much like the Internet in concept, but with less dependence on ground-based and fixed systems and equipment. It will require a new series of transitional military communications satellites that can carry larger volumes of data (the first is to be launched in 2011), the new interoperable Joint Tactical Radio System (which will be fielded in 2007), state-of-the-art optical networking systems, new modes of signal security (being developed by the National Security Agency), and improved network-centric systems across the board.

One element of the larger program, the GIG Bandwidth Extension (GIG-BE), has been designed to provide a secure, robust, optical terrestrial network that delivers very-high-speed classified and unclassified Internet protocol services to key operating locations worldwide (nearly ninety key defense and intelligence sites in the United States as well as in Europe and the Pacific). Each site has 10 gbs of useable dedicated bandwidth. Put another way, GIG-BE was intended to remove bandwidth constraints from military users, limitations that have often proven lethal in the past. After initial procurement purchases in 2003 and a six-site pilot program conducted in 2004, GIG-BE was fully implemented by 20 December 2005.

Development of the GIG has led to DoD defining nine core services to be provided: storage, messaging, enterprise service management, discovery, mediation (between and among systems), information assurance, application hosting, user assistance, and collaboration. Each of these is supported by a community of engineers and architects from all the military services. Defining the information assurance service, for example, the National Security Agency noted on its Web site that "The essential element is that [information assurance] be an embedded feature, designed into every system, holistically, within the family of systems that comprise the GIG. This requires a shift from today's model consisting predominantly of link encryption and boundary protection between multiple discrete networks, to an end-to-end, seamlessly interconnected information environment using 'Defense-in-Depth.'"

Skeptics argue that past experience suggests the huge expenditures called for with such a wide-ranging system (especially one taking decades to innovate and implement) may prove to develop disappointing or short-lived results, especially as the pace of technological change increases. And changing the culture of interservice rivalry to true joint interoperability is another requirement if the GIG is to reach its full potential.

Christopher H. Sterling

See also Communications Security (COMSEC); Defense Communications System (DCS); Defense Information Systems Agency (DISA); Defense Message System (DMS); Internet; Joint Tactical Radio System (JTRS); National Security Agency (NSA); Voice over Internet Protocol (VoIP)

Sources
Department of Defense. 2004. "Chapter 7.2: Global Information Grid (GIG)." *Defense Acquisition Guidebook.* [Online publication; retrieved March 2006.] http://akss.dau .mil/dag/Guidebook/IG_c7.2.asp.
Government Accountability Office. 2004. *Defense Acquisitions: The Global Information Grid and Challenges Facing Its Implementation.* [Online publication; retrieved March 2006.] http://www.gao.gov/new.items/d04858 .pdf.
Miller, Alyson, et al. 2001. "Global Information Grid Architecture." [Online article; retrieved March 2006.] http://www.mitre .org/news/the_edge/july_01/miller.html.
National Security Agency Central Security Service. "Global Information Grid." [Online information; retrieved March 2006.] http:// www.nsa.gov/ia/industry/gig.cfm?MenuID =10.3.2.2.

Weiner, Tim. 2004. "Pentagon Envisioning a Costly Internet for War." [Online article; retrieved March 2006.] http://www .nytimes.com/2004/11/13/technology/ 13warnet.html?ex=1258088400&en=e05f6d9c 70183448&ei=5088&partner=rssnyt.

Global Positioning System (GPS)

The Navigation Satellite Timing and Ranging (NAVSTAR) global positioning system is a U.S. Department of Defense system of twenty-four satellites that provide navigation information to both civilian and military users around the world. It is one of the best current examples of a military development with immediate civilian applications and value.

The GPS program was initiated in 1973 and the first satellites were launched in 1978. The system's initial operational capability was only reached on 8 December 1993 and full operational capability on 27 April 1995. The satellites operate in circular orbits 11,000 miles high, circling the earth every twelve hours. Six orbital planes, usually carrying four satellites each, are equally spaced and inclined at 55 degrees with respect to the equatorial plane. The configuration of the satellites provides the user with anywhere between five and eight satellites that are visible from any point on the earth. The satellites emit continuous signals on two different L-band frequencies (L1 is at 1575.42 MHz; L2 is at 1227.6 MHz).

GPS provides extremely accurate, three-dimensional position data (latitude, longitude, and altitude), velocity, and accurate time; passive all-weather operations; continuous real-time data; support to unlimited users and areas; and a worldwide common grid. The information is available on two levels. The Standard Positioning Service

Global Positioning System (GPS) technology uses multiple communication satellites to allow military forces to determine more precisely their position—and that of their enemies. Here a U.S. Air Force airman uses a handheld GPS device to conduct a data collection survey in Iraq in 2004. (Department of Defense)

(SPS) is a positioning and timing service available to all GPS users (increasingly including automobiles) worldwide on a continuous basis. SPS provides position accuracy of 300 feet horizontally and more than 450 feet vertically with a 340 nanosecond time accuracy. The Precise Positioning Service (PPS) is an extremely accurate military positioning, velocity, and timing service. PPS is available on a continuous, worldwide basis to those users authorized by the United States. Military equipment provides posi-

tion data accurate to at least 70 feet horizontally and 85 feet vertically with a 200 nanosecond Universal Coordinated Time accuracy.

The GPS master control station at Schriever Air Force Base in Colorado monitors and controls the system. In addition, five monitor stations and four ground control antennas are located around the world, which passively track the navigation signals from all the satellites. The data collected by the monitoring stations are analyzed at the master control station and used to update the satellites' navigation messages. The ground antennas also receive telemetry data from the satellites and transmit commands to the various parts of the system.

The designers of the NAVSTAR system originally intended to reduce the number of navigation systems being used by the American military. Since its inception, the number of possible military and civilian uses of the technology have grown dramatically. For the military, receivers have been developed for ships, aircraft, land vehicles, and individual use. The ability to precisely locate a weapons platform and a target has greatly increased the accuracy of precision weapons. In addition, the use of GPS receivers allows the user to know his or her own location more accurately than ever before despite weather conditions, terrain factors, and darkness.

Tommy R. Young II

See also Communication Satellites

Sources
Dana, Peter H. 2000. "Global Positioning System Overview." [Online article; retrieved June 2006.] http://www.colorado.edu/geography/gcraft/notes/gps/gps_f.html.
Kaplan, Elliott D., ed. 1996. *Understanding GPS: Principles and Applications*. Boston: Artech House.

Parkinson, Bradford W., and James J. Spilker, eds. 1996. *Global Positioning System: Theory and Practice. Volumes I and II*. Washington, DC: American Institute of Aeronautics and Astronautics.

Golden Arrow Sections

Golden Arrow sections were self-contained mobile high-speed Morse wireless units with the British Royal Corps of Signals during World War II. Golden Arrow took its name from one of Britain's elite express trains because the name evoked excellence and speed.

The 4th Wireless Group, the parent unit concerned, took the best of operators, wireless (OWL) and line (OKL) and operators from the Royal Signals training centers at Catterick and Huddersfield, and converted them into operators, wireless and keyboard (OWK), by teaching either the wireless or the keyboard skills, as required. After operator training, the group formed mobile Golden Arrow wireless sections.

The purpose of these units was to pass large amounts of traffic efficiently from anywhere in the world. The vehicle-mounted Golden Arrow section and its crew of twenty-three was completely self-contained, carrying its own collapsible mast gear, spare vacuum tubes, power supply, and administrative stores. Most of the sections were sent to the headquarters of army formations around the world and/or to such traditional headquarters as Cairo and Delhi, with the Army Wireless Chain. They sometimes undertook press telegraphy, particularly in the Far East. In northwest Europe, they were also employed to send intercepted enemy signals back to England. The Golden Arrow sections used shortwave band 8 transmitters (with 3.5 kw output), which could trans-mit over long distances. The transmitter was carried in a large semi-articulated vehicle. The receiving vehicle had a similar shape but contained a complex air-conditioned installation as it also formed the traffic office in which the majority of the crew worked. There appear to have been about twenty-five to thirty of these sections.

As the Burma campaign developed, mobile wireless stations were required to move forward as army and corps headquarters advanced. The War Office arranged with Cable and Wireless Ltd. to put into the field civilian detachments to assist in staffing army equipment. They were known as Telcom detachments and retained their international status as civilians. They operated directly with the Cable and Wireless main stations in Ceylon, from whence traffic was transmitted back to London over the existing network.

One example of Golden Arrow work performed in northwest Europe was that done by the 20 M wireless telegraph section. After commencing operations in Normandy in 1944, they were placed with the forward facilities of Allied headquarters (SHAEF) and worked with Royal Air Force personnel who were intercepting German Enigma transmissions and enciphering them into British cipher. The section then sent the encrypted signals to Bletchley Park, where they were sorted out and broken, and sent back for the intelligence staff at SHAEF.

Cliff Lord

See also Bletchley Park; Enigma; High-Speed Morse; Morse Code; Telegraph; Ultra; United Kingdom: Royal Corps of Signals; Vehicles and Transport

Source

Lord, Cliff, and Graham Watson. 2003. *The Royal Corps of Signals: Unit Histories of the Corps*

(1920–2001) and Its Antecedents, 318–320. Solihull, UK: Helion.

Government Code & Cipher School (GC&CS, 1919–1946)

Recognizing the growing importance of radio communications during World War I, in 1919 British government officials created a new signals intelligence agency. Known as the Government Code & Cipher School (GC&CS), the new unit was placed under the British Admiralty. It began with a staff of twenty-five cryptanalysts and thirty support personnel. GC&CS's principal functions were to study foreign powers' methods of encoding radio traffic, with the aim of breaking foreign codes, and advising British government and military agencies on the security methods to be employed in their own communications.

In 1922 GC&CS was moved to the jurisdiction of the British Foreign Office, and the focus of its efforts shifted away from foreign military and toward diplomatic radio traffic. Nonetheless, dedicated sections within GC&CS were created from each branch of the British armed forces. As European and Asian powers drifted toward war in the late 1930s, GC&CS work turned to deciphering the military codes of its potential enemies, particularly Germany. The GC&CS staff working in London increased to about 150 employees.

In 1938 a new property at Bletchley Park (about 50 miles northwest of London) was purchased by Admiral Sir Hugh Sinclair, a former director of Naval Intelligence for the Royal Navy and, at this time, head of the British Secret Intelligence Service (SIS), also known as MI6. SIS had assumed administrative authority over GC&CS, and Sinclair ordered major improvements to the Bletch-

ley Park complex, intending it as emergency accommodation for MI6 and GC&CS personnel in the event of the evacuation of London. GC&CS moved there in 1939.

During World War II the expanded GC&CS headquarters at Bletchley Park included military, commercial, and diplomatic sections. A particular target of its codebreaking efforts was the German military's ciphers produced by the extraordinarily complex Enigma machine, adopted by the German military in the 1920s. Improved versions of Enigma enormously complicated the task of deciphering German military traffic. Such encrypted traffic was provided to GC&CS cryptanalysts by the British army radio monitoring station at Fort Bridgelands, near Chatham; by the Royal Navy's monitoring sites near Scarborough and Winchester; and by the Royal Air Force's signals intercept station at Cheadle.

GC&CS's mathematicians, engineers, linguists, and support staff eventually numbered more than 10,000. Isolated at Bletchley Park, they penetrated enemy diplomatic and military codes and developed the first electronic digital computer. Much (but not all) Enigma traffic was eventually deciphered, and before D-Day, 6 June 1944, decrypted German military communications were being employed in Allied military planning. CG&CS personnel paid less attention to preserving the security of Britain's own communications. British naval codes were regularly compromised by German code breakers in the early years of the war, allowing German U-boats to inflict devastating losses on Allied shipping in the North Atlantic.

After the war the Bletchley Park complex was disassembled. GC&CS was relocated to Eastcote, near London, in 1946, with a smaller staff of 7,000 employees. The name of the organization was changed to Government Communications Headquarters, and in 1952 its headquarters was moved to Cheltenham.

Laura M. Calkins

See also Arlington Hall; Bletchley Park; Code Breaking; Enigma; German "Fish" Codes; Signals Intelligence (SIGINT); Tiltman, John Hessell (1894–1982); Turing, Alan Mathison (1912–1954); Ultra; Welchman, Gordon (1906–1985); World War II; Y Service

Sources
Alvarez, David, ed. 1999. *Allied and Axis Signals Intelligence in World War II.* London: Frank Cass.
Hinsley, F. H., and Alan Stripp, eds. 1993. *Codebreakers: The Inside Story of Bletchley Park.* Oxford, UK: Oxford University Press.
Macksey, Kenneth. 2003. *The Searchers: Radio Intercept in Two World Wars.* London: Cassell.
Smith, Michael. 2004. *Station X: The Codebreakers of Bletchley Park.* Rev. ed. London: Pan Books.

Great Wall of China

The 1,500-mile-long Great Wall of China (actually many different walls built over more than a thousand years) included signaling features from its inception. As early as 400 BCE, beacon fires and drums were used for both warning and general communication along the wall. Flag signals were added later. As early as 200 BCE fairly complex codes were developed for the use of flags and drum signaling.

By the time of the Han dynasty (200 BCE–220 CE), segments of the wall included more signaling towers than had earlier portions. They were built within easy visual sight of one another—often much less than a mile apart, depending on terrain, or in areas of frequent enemy activity. The towers could use any of six different kinds of signaling techniques and predetermined codes (using lights, flag patterns, gunshots), depending on time of day and local conditions. By the Tang dynasty (618–907 CE), messages could be sent up to 700 miles within one day and night.

Beacon fires or torches required a substantial supply of fuel for fires maintained in or near such towers to allow rapid access (some have been recently discovered, carefully covered with mud to preserve them from weather). Once used, the fuel supply was immediately replenished by local garrison troops. Hot coals were kept available as otherwise development of flames for signals or torches would be too time-consuming in times of need. Signal derricks (an early form of semaphore) could raise baskets covered in different colors of cloth or silk. They could also carry baskets of fire or smoke. Flags of different colors could also be used. Drums were often used in wet weather when fires could not be started or in foggy conditions that limited visibility. Different numbers of beats indicated different signals, such as the level of enemy activity, size of an attacking force, or progress of a siege.

The Ming dynasty (1368–1644 CE) added the use of signal artillery. Different numbers of cannon fire could be used to indicate the size of an enemy force. Fire signals made use of color by addition of such fuels as sulphur or saltpeter. Modes of signaling varied by geographic district, and signals could often be sent both ways along the wall.

If one tower failed to relay a signal, a runner would be sent to find out why. Couriers carrying messages in writing were a backup mode to the other methods. Signal tower personnel were required to maintain daily records of signals sent and received and were extensively trained and tested on signal methods and codes. They also had general observation and patrol duties to supplement signaling activity. Punishment for incorrect or false signals or other transgressions could be severe—including imprisonment or even death.

Beacon towers along the wall often served as postal centers. Couriers on foot or horseback were used for short-distance signaling. Very important messages were marked with a feather and had to be carried day and night—the record distance achieved was 250 miles in a day. The hundreds of signal towers remaining in varied states of preservation along the Great Wall attest to their importance in China's long history.

Christopher H. Sterling

See also Ancient Signals; Artillery / Gunfire; China, People's Republic of; Code, Codebook; Couriers; Fire / Flame / Torch; Flags; Horses and Mules; Lights and Beacons; Music Signals; Postal Services; Smoke

Sources

Dalin, Cheng. 1984. "The Wall's Unique Communications System." In *The Great Wall of China*, 198–209. Hong Kong: South China Morning Post.
Lovell, Julia. 2006. *The Great Wall: China Against the World, 1000 BC–AD 2000*. New York: Grove Press.
Waldron, Arthur. 1990. *The Great Wall of China from History to Myth*. Cambridge: Cambridge University Press.

Greece

As with Italy or Egypt in the Mediterranean area, Greek military communications date back to classical history, at least to the time of Alexander the Great. Perhaps the most famous military courier, Philipides brought news of Athens' victory in the battle of Marathon (490 BCE), as he ran 26 miles and then collapsed. His run is the origin of modern marathon races.

The modern Hellenic Army Signal Corps traces its origin to the Army Organization Plan of 1885, which provided for the establishment of one telegraph company within the engineer corps. The company was activated in 1887 and participated a decade later in the war with Turkey. In 1904, two more telegraph companies were formed. Each was organic to three newly established engineering battalions. In 1912 the three telegraph companies were re-formed into two independent telegraph companies and one wireless company. They all saw service in the Balkan Wars of 1912–1913.

During World War I (1914–1918), a telegraph regiment (a depot and training center) was established in 1917. It provided all the communication detachments and support to the Hellenic Army during the war, the subsequent campaign in southern Russia in 1919, and the war in Asia Minor in 1920–1922. By the late 1930s, the Hellenic Army organization provided for one engineer battalion per division. However, only one company of these battalions was an engineer company, the other two being a telephone company and a wireless company, which also included optical signaling equipment. Each army corps was supported by two similar communications companies. The number of wireless sets in a division wireless company was limited to five or six, and these were assigned to the divisional headquarters, the infantry regiments, and the artillery regiments. Most of the Greek signals equipment was of German manufacture.

It was with that organization and equipment that the Hellenic Army communicated during the Italian and later German invasions of 1940–1941. Following the occupation of Greece by the Germans in 1941, the remains of the Hellenic Army escaped to the Middle East, where a small force was organized in the form of a typical British army organization, using British equipment. In November 1942, a Greek brigade participated in the landmark British El Alamein (Egypt) offensive. During that period, the first semi-official separation of signals from the engineers occurred.

An independent signal corps was established only after the liberation of Greece in 1944. It was as a result of the reorganization of the Hellenic Army with the assistance and advice of a British military mission. A royal decree issued on 31 May 1946 established the Signal Corps as the fifth combat arm of the army. A signal training center/school was established at Haidari, on the west side of Athens, in 1946. The buildings had been constructed during the 1938–1940 period, and the Germans had used the area as a concentration camp during the 1941–1944 occupation. The Signal Training Center was opened in 1963, the motto of which is, "He sent forth a dove," from Genesis 8:8.

Cliff Lord

See also Ancient Signals; Couriers

Source

Greek Military Gateway. "Greek Military Photos." [Online information; retrieved December 2006.] http://www.greekmilitary .net/GreekDefenceIndustry.html.

Greely, Adolphus W. (1844–1935)

A man of many accomplishments, Adolphus Greely served the longest tenure of any U.S. Army chief signal officer—from 1887 to 1906—a period of significant development in military communications.

Born in Newburyport, Massachusetts, on 27 March 1844, Greely began his military career during the American Civil War (1861–1865) as a private in the Massachusetts volunteer infantry. Wounded three times, including a bullet to the face, he wore a splendid beard the rest of his life, presumably to hide his scars. Detailed to the Signal Corps in 1867, he served as a signal officer in the field before being assigned to the Signal Office in Washington DC.

When the Signal Corps became responsible for the U.S. Weather Bureau in 1870, Greely became an avid student of meteorology. He made a name for himself by building more than 2,000 miles of telegraph lines in the Southwest and the Northwest over which observers transmitted weather reports. In 1881 Greely volunteered to lead an expedition to Lady Franklin Bay in northern Canada to study Arctic weather and climate as part of the first International Polar Year. Stranded in the far north when relief vessels could not reach them as scheduled, Greely and his men suffered terribly until finally rescued in June 1884. Only six of the original twenty-five members returned home alive. Greely became an internationally known figure, and in 1887 President Grover Cleveland appointed him chief signal officer.

As chief, Greely supervised a rapidly expanding communications network at home and around the world. During the Spanish-American War (1898), the corps laid cable and wire lines in Cuba, Puerto Rico, and the Philippines. With an eye to the future, Greely championed the introduction of new technology to the corps' operations, in particular, aeronautics and radio. In 1892 he authorized the purchase of a captive balloon for reconnaissance, the beginnings of the corps' involvement with aviation. In 1898 Greely urged the Army to support Samuel

P. Langley's aerodrome experiments. He later called his work with Langley the most important peace duty he ever performed. Greely also oversaw the establishment of an experimental laboratory where new signal equipment was constructed and tested. Under his leadership, the Signal Corps built the Washington-Alaska Military Cable and Telegraph System in 1900–1903, and the next year added a wireless portion spanning the 107 miles over Norton Sound.

Greely played an active role in establishing both national and international communications policy. In 1903 he attended both the first international conference on wireless telegraphy in Berlin and the International Telegraph Congress in London. The next year, he was a member of an interdepartmental board, the Wireless Telegraph Board, set up by President Theodore Roosevelt to determine the best means of administration and regulation of wireless telegraphy in the United States. Promoted to major general in 1906, Greely retired two years later at the mandatory age of sixty-four, but remained active throughout the remainder of his long life.

Greely was a founder of the National Geographic Society and the Explorer's Club of New York. He also participated in many social and civic organizations. A prolific writer, he published several books and numerous articles. Shortly before his death, he received a special Congressional Medal of Honor for his lifetime of public service. He died on 20 October 1935 at age ninety-one and is buried in Arlington National Cemetery. Fort Greely, Alaska, is named in his honor.

Rebecca Robbins Raines

See also Airplanes; Alaska Communications System (ACS); Army Signal Corps; Spanish-American War (1898); Wireless Telegraph Board

Sources
Greely, Adolphus W. 1927. *Reminiscences of Adventure and Service: A Record of Sixty-five Years.* New York: Charles Scribner's Sons.
Mitchell, William. 1936. *General Greely: The Story of a Great American.* New York: G. P. Putnam's Sons.
Raines, Rebecca Robbins. 1996. *Getting the Message Through: A Branch History of the US Army Signal Corps.* Washington, DC: Government Printing Office.
Shrader, Charles R. 1984. "Greely, Adolphus Washington." In *Dictionary of American Military Biography,* edited by Roger J. Spiller, 403–409. Westport, CT: Greenwood Press.
Todd, Alden L. 1961. *Abandoned: The Story of the Greely Arctic Expedition, 1881–1884.* New York: McGraw-Hill.

Ground Radio

Widely used during World War I, when constant artillery shelling during trench warfare made it hard to maintain wired links, ground radio (also called earth telegraphy) made use of the earth's ability to conduct an electrical signal for up to several hundred yards.

Hoping to save the cost of stringing expensive wire line, several early telegraph systems took advantage of the ability to send an electrical signal through water and later earth. Experimenters used widely separated ground plates, which proved successful. Indeed, experiments with ground conduction established telegraphic contact through an isthmus of land (by Samuel Morse in 1842), across streams (by Alfred Vail in 1843), across wider rivers (by Lindsay in 1843), across a bay (by Antonio Meucci in 1846), and through the earth (by Nathan Stubblefield from the 1890s on). An accidental discovery proved that one long line system continued operating with great strength of signal, despite the fact that the line had been broken in several places. The realization that signals could actually traverse earth for up to several hundred yards and then reenter a grounded line marked the beginning of conduction systems that relied on ground conduction and energy for their successful operation.

What may have been the first voice "broadcast" was conducted by Nathan Stubblefield at various late nineteenth-century dates (source records differ). He employed what he called "earth cells" and long iron rods to transmit strong voice signals "with great clarity." These traversed a mile or more of ground, a coordinated conduction wireless system providing telephone service for his Kentucky farm community. His experiments offered a technological mystery, for his earth cells never wore out, never produced heat in their telephonic components, and provided power at any time. Being neither activated nor assisted by additional battery power, the system was fully operational around the clock. Unable to obtain financial backing, however, Stubblefield's system was never pursued and he died of starvation in 1928.

Though many others worked on related principles, none were as successful as James Harris Rogers (1850–1929) in the years leading up to World War I. Rogers's wireless telegraphy antennas rested on the ground's subsurface and were relatively easy to construct. Placed into long plowed furrows, the various Rogers antennas performed in a dependable manner, producing strong signals with little static or distortion. His designs attracted the attention of military engineers in their efforts to establish failsafe communications between command centers and distant fleet, ground surface, or submerged forces.

Both sides in World War I made use of ground radio systems once the Western Front stabilized into trench warfare. By 1916 the British Fullerphone, which utilized the earth to complete its telegraph communication circuits, was in service. French army units also used conduction telegraphy devices that used earth circuits. But shortages of this and related equipment well into 1918 (due in part to divided efforts looking into too many different options for trench warfare communication) limited the value of earth conduction telegraphy systems. The U.S. Army Signal Corps had developed and began production of four types of "earth telegraphy" sets by 1918. All of these ground telegraphy systems, however, were really a stopgap until more viable wireless equipment could be developed and distributed.

Christopher H. Sterling

See also Ferrié, Gustave-Auguste (1868–1932); Fullerphone; Radio; Rogers, James Harris (1850–1929); World War I

Sources

Gernsback, Hugo. 1919. "Ground Telegraphy in War." *Electrical Experimenter*.

Lochte, Bob. 2001. *Kentucky Farmer Invents Wireless Telephone! But Was It Radio? Facts and Folklore About Nathan Stubblefield*. Murray, KY: All About Wireless.

"Underground Wireless" (Editorial). 1919. *Electrical Experimenter* VI (11): 833–834.

Vassilatos, Gerry. "An Introduction to the Mysteries of Ground Radio." [Online article; retrieved November 2004.] http://www.borderlands.com/archives/arch/ground-myst.htm.

Gulf War (1990–1991)

The architect of the air power campaign against Iraq in 1990–1991, John Warden III, once described that conflict as the first "hyperwar" because it was based on innovative technology, unprecedented precision, operational and strategic surprise, and the use of advanced modes of military communication. The use of new weapons, including precision laser-guided bombs, unmanned air vehicles (like Predator), the F-117 (invisible to most radar), and the artillery systems of detecting and destroying targets (TAC-FIRE), was made possible by widespread application of command, control, communication, computers, intelligence, surveillance, and reconnaissance (C4ISR) capabilities. Access to information became a primary condition of military success while space, where a lot of crucial military information traveled, gave the war a new dimension. General Merill McPeak, then U.S. Air Force chief of staff, called the conflict the first war of the space age. In the Gulf War, space communications systems played a central role in the effective use of high-tech weaponry. Because (for the first time in military history) precision-guided munitions were used extensively (almost 9 percent of all explosives), the effectiveness of strikes against Iraqi targets depended on the quality and accuracy of information. Precision weapons hinge on precise information—its gathering, processing, interpreting, and transmitting. Thus information and communication became crucial for military victory.

Satellite communication for military purposes was used extensively for the first time during the Vietnam War in the early 1970s. It was continuously developed since then, and the Gulf War saw its widespread application. The allied coalition used about sixty satellites, which fell into two basic systems. The Defense Satellite Communication System consisted of four satellites providing telephone and telegraphic communication,

while the Air Force Satellite Communications System used three satellites securing communication of command over strategic forces. The Defense Support Program early warning satellites, in service since 1970, were used to trace Iraqi Scud missile launchers and launching pads. A crucial function was played by the Joint Surveillance and Target Attack Radar System (JSTARS)—the advanced air radar surveillance system, which at that time was still in its developmental phase. By scanning the earth's surface, it provided information on enemy land forces and detailed images of the terrain. Radar images taken by JSTARS planes were also used to track mobile Iraqi Scud missile launchers. JSTARS provided the allied coalition with the command capability to locate and track moving ground enemy targets. Through extensive communication channels this information was quickly transmitted to air and ground theater commanders.

During the 1980s, the United States orbited a NAVSTAR collection of satellites. By the Gulf War, sixteen of them were providing navigation and positioning data, emitting a steady signal that allowed anyone with a receiver to locate himself or herself in three dimensions. The global positioning system (GPS), which developed from this system, enabled Army elements to determine their position in the vast Iraqi desert. A GPS shortcoming, however, was that it did not work for two hours in the morning and two hours in the evening when the satellites did not cover the Persian Gulf region. Several other systems contributed to the coalition military effort: Defense Meteorological Satellite Program (DMSP) weather satellites, the U.S. LandSAT multispectral imagery satellites, and the Tactical Information Broadcast Service.

The Gulf War developed in two phases: the initial strategic air campaign and subsequent ground warfare backed up with air and naval forces. The war was fought according to the air-land battle doctrine because air (including space) and ground elements were equally important. One of the greatest challenges was to maintain uninterrupted communication that would allow successful conduct of joint air, naval, and army operations. Air space over the Persian Gulf was monitored by Airborne Warning and Control System (AWACS) Boeing 707s filled with computers that by tracking allied and enemy aircraft gave early warning of Iraqi air force movements while supporting coalition strikes. By sending data to ground communication centers, which in turn transferred the information to Air Force planes, AWACS helped direct the air battle. The sky was also scanned by the air defense cruiser USS *Bunker Hill*. The Navy largely relied on E-2C Hawkeye radar surveillance aircraft. Secure communication channels between Air Force AWACS and Navy E-2C aircraft computers was provided by Link 11. It did not, however, work perfectly, experiencing occasional breakdowns resulting in miscues among aircraft and between aircraft and the *Bunker Hill*. Many problems were also experienced with interservice communication. AWACS could communicate information to Air Force F-15s using secure voice but could not communicate with Navy F-14s. Additional surveillance and information systems, such as the Aegis radar system, were located on Navy ships.

To support Operation Desert Storm, U.S. Central Command (CENTCOM) established the largest theater communication system in military history. It connected American sustaining bases, CENTCOM headquarters, coalition forces, and support elements by expanding rapidly. Multichannel satellite systems required detailed frequency man-

agement. There were 115 super high frequency tactical satellite ground terminal relocations during the ground campaign. By the end of the operation, thirty-three multichannel satellite terminals were in Iraq and Kuwait. Due to the distances between units, deploying units also used ultra-high frequency ground terminals.

At the end of the war, the coalition communication system was impressive, consisting of 2,300 personnel, 7,000 radio frequencies, and fifty-nine communication centers. During the war 29 million phone calls were made. Command was heavily dependent on civilian communication satellite networks even for transmitting encoded messages. Much communication traveled over landlines to a commercial satellite terminal in Kuwait City from which it was linked to the United States. After the war this bottleneck appeared to be a potential Achilles heel, for if the Iraqis had realized this heavy dependence on civilian infrastructure, they could have stopped U.S. forces by disrupting their communication with jamming or sabotage.

Military communication (and the war in general) was computer based to such an unprecedented degree that General Norman Schwarzkopf, commander of Operation Desert Storm, admitted that he had problems changing his battle plan because it was so computerized. Among several metasystems that linked computers of C4ISR systems, only one was specially created: Operation Desert Storm Network (ODS NET). Its management center was located at Fort Huachuca in Arizona and linked thousands of computers through satellites and lines. Although ODS NET carried unclassified information, it was essential for providing communication among all the services at bases around the world. Yet the Gulf

War demonstrated limitations in military communication due to poor interservice compatibility. For example, while the Army corps' tactical operation centers used e-mail communication to send messages that were received on cellular phones hooked into a computer, there was no means of confirming that the message had been received.

For allied air operations, Iraqi command, control, and communication sites were a high-priority target. The Iraqi high command's ability to communicate with its forces and control them was destroyed early during the war, giving the allies tactical superiority. This was achieved largely by air power and precision-guided weapons. Targets included microwave relay towers, telephone exchanges, fiber optic nodes, switching rooms, and bridges carrying coaxial communication cables. Because civilian TV and radio facilities could be used for military purposes, they also became crucial targets, as did civilian telecommunication systems. Had the Iraqi command been able to communicate with its forces, its ability to wage war in Kuwait and Iraq would have been far greater.

It was ironic that Iraq's communication infrastructure was being destroyed by sophisticated weapons systems that were completely dependent on communication systems. American information and communication superiority was paralleled by techniques of disinformation against the Iraqi army. For example, the EF-111 Raven aircraft was designed to jam Iraqi radars and thus protect allied aircraft from being detected. The Iraqis failed to create early warning capability when their French-made Tiger radars installed on Soviet-supplied IL-76 transport aircraft did not succeed.

Current information on the war was transmitted to news agencies around the world through the same telecommunication technologies that guided smart bombs and Patriot missiles to their targets. Much media information was carried on the same satellite systems as was military information. Therefore, the Gulf War was a "double hyperwar," for both the military operations and media coverage of them was possible only because of the integrated use of satellites, computers, cellular telephones, microwave relay stations, and related technologies. The increased speed of news transmission resulted in real-time broadcasting, which gave rise to the "CNN effect." This phenomenon created a new dimension of military communication. The reciprocal relationship can be summed up in a series of cycles: war leads to media coverage, which creates public opinion, which places politicians under pressure, who then pressure military commanders, who initiate changes in the conduct of war and/or military censorship. The Gulf War set a new standard for both military communication and media war coverage.

Łukasz Kamieński

See also Airborne Warning and Control System (AWACS); Communication Satellites; Computer; Global Positioning System (GPS); Information Revolution in Military Affairs (IRMA); Iraq War (2003–Present); Microwave; Mobile Communications; Radio; Spectrum Frequencies

Sources

Blackwell, James. 1991. *Thunder in the Desert. The Strategy and Tactics of the Persian Gulf War.* New York: Bantam Books.

Department of Defense. 1992. *Conduct of the Persian Gulf War: Final Report to Congress.* Washington, DC: Department of Defense.

Fialka, John. 1992. *Hotel Warriors: Covering the Gulf War.* Washington, DC: Woodrow Wilson Center Press.

Freedman, Lawrence, and Efraim Karsh. 1993. *The Gulf Conflict 1990–1991: Diplomacy and War in the New World*. Princeton, NJ: Princeton University Press.

Gordon, Michael R., and Bernard E. Trainor. 1995. *The Generals' War. The Inside Story of the Conflict in the Gulf*. Boston: Little, Brown.

Hadrian's Wall

Hadrian's Wall was built in the 120s CE to provide a defensible border at the northern end of Roman-occupied Britain, essentially today's England. It stretched from Wallsend (near Newcastle) on the Tyne River west to Bowness on the Solway River, making good use of terrain to strengthen the barrier. As with other Roman fortifications, the 76-mile-long wall built of stone, wood, and turf (sometimes built to a height of 20 or more feet), was well equipped for military signaling.

The communications system included both the military road that ran along and behind the line of defense and a series of observation and signal towers built directly on the wall, each visible to one of the dozen or so larger residential forts built on or just south of the line. Hadrian's Wall featured dozens of "milecastles," so named because they stood roughly a Roman mile apart from one another. These smaller "fortlets" were carefully sited to remain in signal range (a few hundred yards to a few miles) of the larger forts, or in some cases to intervening towers that could relay a signal, to summon soldiers in case of trouble.

While more complex messages were usually sent by traditional courier, the signal system allowed for more rapid simple emergency communications. The latter made use of a number of visual modes of getting attention and transmitting information—typically fire or prepared beacons of flame. In addition to fire beacons, the Romans operating on Hadrian's Wall may also have used pigeons as well as mirrors or crude heliographs for carrying messages. Using any of these methods, the legions stationed at the larger forts were already alerted and preparing by the time a courier with more complete information arrived on foot or horseback along the military roadways. The obvious nature of using fire for signaling had the additional deterring benefit of letting enemy attackers know they had been sighted and that reinforcing help for the defenders was likely on the way. Presuming sufficient manpower and a careful observation routine, the signaling system made the stone defenses immeasurably stronger.

Roman legions built (in the second century CE), maintained, and manned Hadrian's Wall across the north of England to protect against tribal raids. Signal fires, smoke signals, and couriers were the primary means of communication along the stone and earthen wall. (Corel)

Hadrian's Wall remained active, preventing invasion by the barbarian tribes in the north (present-day Scotland), and was constantly repaired and upgraded, until about 400 CE—in other words, for nearly three centuries. (For a brief period, 143 to about 200 CE, Hadrian's Wall was abandoned for the shorter Antonine Wall, which lay farther north but could not be sustained. That shorter, turf-built wall used similar modes of signaling.) Through those three centuries, signaling methods varied only marginally.

Christopher H. Sterling

See also Ancient Signals; Couriers; Fire/Flame/Torch; Great Wall of China; Heliograph and Mirrors; Lights and Beacons; Military Roads; Pigeons

Sources

Johnson, Anne. 1983. *Roman Forts.* London: Adam & Charles Black.

Johnson, Stephen. 1989. *Hadrian's Wall.* London: Batsford/English Heritage.

Woolliscroft, D. I. 2001. *Roman Military Signalling.* Stroud, UK: Tempus.

Heliograph and Mirrors

The late nineteenth-century heliograph became a sophisticated signaling system combining light and mirrors for tactical communication in the field. It generally used the sun, and occasionally moonlight.

Two sources of light are available for optical signaling: the reflected sun during daylight, and some other form of bright light (a flame or an artificial light source) for use during day or night. Using sun flashes on mirrors, for example, is a very old technique. Many ancient civilizations in Asia and the Middle East as well as Native Americans (notably the Dakota tribes) used small pieces of silica or mica to flash sun signals of recognition and simple messages.

The first technological breakthrough toward a technical system of optical military signaling came in 1821 when German scientist Karl Gauss devised a means to direct a controlled beam of sunlight by mirror to a distant station for use in geodetic surveys in the Hanover region. But Gauss was interested only in surveying, and several decades would pass before the Morse code became the key to communication by heliograph. In 1822 the British Royal Engineers used a flashing instrument with multiple pieces of polished tin in their trigonometric survey of the British Isles. Soon after, the same service devised use of a mirror with a group of telescopes to send flashes directly, calling it a "heliostat." In 1833 in India, Sir George Everest (for whom the mountain is named), devised a "heliotrope," also for use in trigonometrical surveys. A Royal Navy captain at Gibraltar used a mirror from a common looking glass to converse with friends across the strait to Tangier (Morocco) about 1835. And in 1851, Charles Babbage invented a sun-flashing machine he called an "occulting telegraph," which he offered to the Duke of Wellington. By 1860, Monsieur Leseuere, an inspector of French telegraph lines, devised an optical telegraph for use by the French army based on Professor Gauss's earlier device, though his code is unknown.

About 1862, British army Major Francis John Bolton and Royal Navy Lieutenant

Phillip Colomb devised the idea of sending Morse code by signal lamp flashes. Development was pursued with both land and ship-to-ship communication. Colomb lectured on this scheme the next year and later perfected the system. He used burning lime plus a shutter to create signals. Dubbed a "Colomb light," his system used limelight, as had been used in theaters for years, though without any shutter.

While stationed in India in 1869, Henry C. Mance developed the first heliograph by adding a movable mirror. Just a year later, a group of French officers used this system to send flashing signals by day and (with kerosene) by night. The process was used during the Siege of Paris in 1870. Three years later, Captain E. E. Begbie devised an improved mirror signal device using a movable screen that alternately revealed and closed the mirror. The Indian colonial government adopted Begbie's device two years later, and this heliograph subsequently saw considerable use in British colonial wars in Afghanistan, with the Duffla and Jowarki expeditions in India, and during the Zulu War in South Africa.

By this time, two distinct devices had developed. The older heliostat used a fixed mirror to reflect a steady beam of light to a receiving point, and was primarily used in surveying. For signaling, that constant beam was interrupted by a Colomb shutter, generally transmitting the Morse alphabet—with a similar result to the Royal Navy's night Colomb flashing light system. The more advanced heliograph used Mance's oscillating mirror, which, along with a Begbie movable screen, could alternately transmit or stop transmission of a reflected dot or dash to one distant station. Use of a telegraph key to control the Begbie screen permitted short or longer reflection, much as a

The mirror-based heliograph signaling device, shown here with four rather formally-dressed soldiers around 1880, was widely used in the late nineteenth century by both British forces during colonial wars in Africa and Asia, and by the American Army during the Indian wars. (U.S. Army Signal Center Command History Office, Fort Gordon, Georgia)

similar key enabled a short dot or longer dash noise for the electric telegraph. Both heliostat and heliograph had to be set up and calibrated with care, and required a good telescope to read the flashed signals.

While heliograph development took place at Fort Whipple, Virginia, in the later 1870s, little actual field use by the United States came until American forces learned of British success in India. Army use of the heliograph to keep separate forces in constant touch finally turned the tide of the campaign in the Southwest against the tenacious Apaches.

Geronimo and other Native American chiefs were puzzled by the heliograph, and stunned by its speed. While heliograph stations had to be aligned with care and required the use of telescopes to read distant stations, they did not need a wire and were readily portable. The electric telegraph was then rarely used by the Army because of the danger of wire sabotage. Naturally, clear conditions (usually present in the Southwest) were required. Ranges extended from nine to fifty miles, with the Arizona–New Mexico heliograph network covering more than 500 miles. Some 6,000 messages were sent during the extended campaign. The primary challenge with heliograph use was in discerning the difference between the Morse dot and dash. The eventual solution was to make the dash at least three times longer than the dot. Heliographs were adopted by the armies of most developed nations; they were used by both sides during the Spanish-American War (1898) and by the British during the Boer War.

After 1915, the heliograph began to fade into obscurity. Operators were still trained, and systems procured, but trench warfare and poor weather made the systems difficult to use. Improvements in other signal systems (chiefly telegraphy and telephony) pushed the heliograph from its three decades of dominating tactical communication in hot and dry climates. Mesopotamia was the primary theater for heliograph usage during World War I, and the devices were also used on occasion (as weather permitted) on the Western Front.

Heliographs remained part of the signaling equipment of the Australian, British, and Canadian forces well into the twentieth century. Australian forces used the heliograph in Egypt and Libya against Erwin Rommel's Afrika Corps in 1941–1942, and a version was used by Afghan insurgents against the Soviets in the 1980s. An emergency signaling mirror remains a part of survival kits on land and at sea to this day.

David L. Woods

See also Fire/Flame/Torch; Fort Huachuca, Arizona; Lights and Beacons; Spanish-American War (1898)

Sources

Colomb, Philip. 1863, "Naval and Military Signals." *The Journal of the Royal United Service Institution* 7: 349–393.

Goode, Samuel. 1875. "Mance's Heliograph, or Sun-Telegraph." *The Journal of the Royal United Service Institution* 19: 533–548.

Harfield, Alan. 1986. *The Heliograph: A Short History*. 2nd ed. Blandford Camp, UK: Royal Signals Museum.

Woods, David L. 1965. "Optical Telegraphy." In *A History of Tactical Communication Techniques*, 149–166. Orlando, FL: Martin-Marietta.

Wynne, A. S. 1880. "Heliography and Army Signalling Generally." *The Journal of the Royal United Service Institution* 24: 235–258.

Hello Girls

During World War I, the American Expeditionary Force (AEF) in France implemented a program of using technically trained, bilingual female telephone operators, known as "Hello Girls," to help improve American communications as part of the Allied war effort. In October 1917, AEF Commander in Chief General John Pershing asked the War Department for special units of skilled women because he believed they had superior ability as telephone switchboard operators and it would allow male operators to serve in the more dangerous telephone stations at the front. Because the AEF had to communicate with the French armies on its right and left, with French corps in the AEF and the Allied General Headquarters it was vitally important that telephone operators spoke French as well as they spoke English.

In November 1917, the War Department approved Pershing's request and called upon the commercial telephone companies to help identify, recruit, and train physically fit French-speaking American women who would serve in a quasi-military status as uniformed civilian contract employees subject to military discipline. Out of 7,000 applicants, more than 450 women completed

U.S. Army female telephone operators, known as "Hello Girls," operate a switchboard in France during World War I. (U.S. Army Signal Center Command History Office, Fort Gordon, Georgia)

training in signal duties, and 223 were sent overseas in what were officially known as Telephone Operating Units, Signal Corps.

The first unit of thirty-three women departed New York in March 1918 under the supervision of Chief Operator Grace Banker. During American participation in World War I (1917–1918) six operating units were formed and sent to France, where they were assigned to the large headquarters offices such as Paris, Chaumont, and Tours, locations where telephone traffic was especially heavy. In addition, some smaller units of women served at the three Army headquarters. Though technically civilian non-combatants, their military uniforms and

regimen prompted Colonel Parker Hitt, chief signal officer of the First Army, to employ the women at advanced command posts as close to the front as possible.

Shortly after their arrival at Hitt's headquarters, the St. Mihiel offensive began and the Hello Girls received their baptism by fire. They often had to work 48-hour shifts, enduring shell fire, hunger, and fatigue during the later battle for the Meuse-Argonne. They were praised for their skill, particularly Grace Banker, who was awarded the Distinguished Service Medal for her leadership and determination during the Army's offensives. Although the women with First Army were the only ones to experience combat operations, other detachments of Hello Girls worked with the Second Army at Toul and Third Army at Coblenz when it became the army of occupation.

The Hello Girls ensured that efficient command and control were maintained during the most important phase of American operations in France. AEF Chief Signal Officer Brigadier General Edgar Russel proclaimed that the Hello Girls set a standard of excellence responsible for the success of American local and long-distance telephone communication. However, their military status was challenged for more than sixty years until 1977 when the Army granted honorable discharges to the few surviving Hello Girls and recognized them as veterans of World War I.

Steven J. Rauch

See also Banker, Grace (1892–1960); Telephone; World War I

Sources

Gavin, Letty. 1997. *American Women in World War 1*. Niwot: University Press of Colorado.

Schneider, Dorothy, and Carl J. Schneider. 2000. *Into the Breach: American Women Overseas in World War I*. Lincoln, NE: toExcel Press, iUniverse.com, Inc.

Wyman, Thomas Sage. 1998. "A Telephone Switchboard Operator with the A.E.F. in France." *Army History* Fall/Winter: 1–9.

Heraldry/Insignia

As one means of building and maintaining morale and esprit de corps, signaling units from many countries, especially those of the British Commonwealth, made use of various symbols to promote how good they were, or intended to be. Expressed in Latin or in the local language, mottos often appeared on unit badges or uniforms. Special flags and colors were developed, as were, in some cases, coats of arms. These aided with unit identification.

Heraldry is the study and description of coats of arms, and of the rights of individuals and families to bear those arms. The origins lie in the twelfth century, when knights in Europe decorated their shields to identify themselves in battle. Eventually the emblems were reduced in size and became headdress badges and collar badges depicting either country or regiment.

Shakespeare offers a good stage scene built around heraldry, from *King Henry V, Part 2* (Act 5, Scene 1). Warwick, facing battle, places his crest atop his helmet (Shakespeare errs on the origin of the crest: the Kingmaker inherited it from Sir Richard Beauchamp, 13th Earl of Warwick, his father-in-law). And as he is about to ride toward his enemy, he says, "Now, by my father's badge, old Nevil's crest / The rampant bear chain'd to the ragged staff / This day I'll wear aloft my burgonet / As on a mountain top the cedar shows / That keeps his leaves in spite of any storm / Even to affright thee with the view thereof."

With the advent of signal corps in various countries, they too followed suit and introduced their own badges reflecting the nature of their work. These generally fall into four categories: (1) the image of Mercury, the Roman messenger of the gods, worn by British Commonwealth nations; (2) crossed flags, worn by the U.S. Army Signal Corps (see below) and many South American signal units as well as some other nations; (3) lightning flashes, in various forms, worn by many of the world's signal corps; and (4) designs specific to a nation, for example, the heraldic letter T for the French signals (or *transmissions*).

Many modern signal badges, flags, and coats of arms depict Mercury, who was the Roman god of messengers (as well as commerce, games and exercise, story-telling—and even thievery). He is nearly always depicted wearing a winged hat and shoes. Mercury, in turn, was based on the earlier Greek god Hermes, who was depicted in similar fashion. In ancient times, messages from one ruler to another or between armies were often carried by special couriers considered "heralds," who were to be treated with respect and not harmed. They carried a special staff as the sign of their role (this was called a "caduceus," and both Mercury and Hermes were depicted carrying such a staff, which also had wings). The table below provides a brief guide to the variety of some signaling service mottoes.

The Signal Corps device is one of the oldest uniform collar insignia used in the U.S. Army. The torch in the middle comes from the god Mercury. The two square flags with the interval boxes are not semaphore flags;

these are two of the several designs used by Brigadier General Albert Myer, founder of the U.S. Army Signal Corps and inventor of the large, one-flag wig-wag signal flag system widely used in both the Union and Confederate armies during the American Civil War. They continued in use into the twentieth century and were frequently the only signal system that could be used for transmissions between the Army and Navy.

Many signals authorities continue to confuse the two flag designs and systems. The two-hand semaphore flag signal system uses two flags that are marked identically—often divided diagonally red and white. This simple, portable system used two flags about 12 to 14 inches square. In reality, the one-flag wig-wag designs appeared only on large flags usually at least 4 feet square attached to a pole 6 to 8 feet long. It takes a large man with considerable strength to wave any such a flag. Today one of their few uses is at

Signaling Service Mottoes

Country	Slogan	Meaning
Bangladesh	Druto-O-Nishchit	Speed and reliability
Belgium	Ominia Conjungo	All together
Brazil	Sempre Servir	Always serving
Denmark (SjaellandskeTelegrafregiment)	Esse Non Videri	To be, not to seem
India	Tevra Chaukas	Swift and secure
Malaysia	Pantas Dan Pasti	Swift and sure
Netherlands	Nuntius Transmittendus	The message must get through
Nigeria	—	Service and security
Pakistan	Tez O Yaqini	Speed and reliability
Philippines	—	Get that message through
Royal Corps of Signals (U.K., Australia, New Zealand, South Africa, Zambia, Zimbabwe)	Certa Cito	Swift and sure
Sweden	Har Finns Inga Omojligheter	There are no impossibilities
United States	Pro Patria Vigilans	Vigilant for the country
Venezeula	La Vox Del Comando	The voice of command

American football games. The Washington Redskins, for example, send out a dozen men with poles and Redskins flags of this size to be waved in celebrations following the score of a touchdown or field goal. Today's flag is printed on silk and is much lighter than the old denim or cotton signal flags. While the designs of the sports team flag and wig-wag flag differ, the handling of a sports team flag is similar to the way that one-flag wig-wag signals were used in transmitting—with a wave to the left, a wave to the right, and a "pause" centrally in place. As actual wig-wag flags are no longer in use and are confined to a handful of Army museums, it is perhaps not too surprising these designs are confused with semaphore from time to time. Also some may have a hard time mentally seeing a large flag as one of two in the crossed-flag insignia worn on the collar of every U.S. Army Signal Corps officer.

Cliff Lord, David L. Woods,
and Christopher H. Sterling

See also Army Signal Corps; Flags; Myer, Albert James (1828–1880); United Kingdom: Royal Corps of Signals

Sources
Eckholm, Erik. 2006. "A Federal Office Where Heraldry of Yore is Only Yesterday." *New York Times,* June 13, A14.
Lord, Cliff, and Graham Watson. 2003. *The Royal Corps of Signals: Unit Histories of the Corps (1920–2001) and Its Antecedents.* Solihull, UK: Helion.
Mills, T. F. "Heraldry and Vexillogy: A Selected Catalogue of Web Links." [Online information; retrieved September 2005.] http://www.regiments.org/special/ref/flags.htm.
RAF Heraldry Trust. Home page. [Online information; retrieved September 2005.] http://www.griffon.clara.net/rafh/badge_a.htm.
U.S. Army Heraldry. Home page. [Online information; retrieved September 2005.] http://www.qmfound.com/army_heraldry.htm.
Woods, David L. 1965. "Wig-Wag: The Waving of Flags and Torches," In *A History of Tactical Communication Techniques,* chap. V. Orlando, FL: Martin-Marietta (reprinted by Arno Press, 1974).

High-Frequency Direction Finding (HF DF)

High-frequency direction finding (HF DF) was used extensively by both the U.S. Navy and Britain's Royal Navy during World War II, especially against the German U-boats in the Atlantic, a battle that required real-time tactical information by radio from boats in contact with convoys.

German Kriegsmarine radio traffic consisted of standard signals or special short signals, such as convoy sighting reports. Standard signals contained between 40 to 320 letters (lasting from twenty-four seconds to three minutes). "Contact" short signals, giving a convoy's position, course, and speed, lasted only about twenty seconds and were difficult targets for accurate HF DF.

The British used two main types of HF DF set: aural null models, where operators tuned manually to signals using earphones, and instantaneous twin-channel sets using cathode ray tubes. In 1937, the Royal Navy's only HF DF stations were at Flowerdown (England), Gibraltar, Malta, and Hong Kong, but by late 1942 an additional eleven HF DF stations had been established in the United Kingdom. Eventually, the Allied Atlantic HF DF nets consisted of fifteen American, twenty British, and eleven Canadian stations, with plotting rooms in Washington DC, London, and Ottawa.

In addition to aural models, the U.S. Navy used semi-instantaneous cathode ray sets, designed by Henri Busignies. In the Busignies sets, which were designated DAJ (land sets) and DAQ (shipborne sets), spinning goniometers converted an aural signal into images on cathode ray displays. Cooperation on exchanging bearings with the Royal Navy started around October 1940. The U.S. Navy Atlantic DF organization eventually comprised three networks: North American (six stations), with a plotting center at the Naval Communications Annex in Washington; Caribbean (six stations); and South American (three stations).

HF DF stations operated at ranges of 200 to 3,000 miles. Even good bearings could easily deviate by 4 degrees on a signal of a few seconds, resulting in a position difference of approximately 150 miles at 2,000 miles range. A British 1943 report, based on Ultra decrypts, found that fixes in the North Atlantic were between 50 and 170 miles away from the positions reported by the U-boats being targeted. Ionospheric factors limited accuracy, as did physical obstructions near receiving stations.

Installing HF DF in ships presented major difficulties, as ships are a hostile environment with a mass of magnetic fields, re-radiators, and communications equipment emitting radiations. Early shipborne sets left an ambiguity of 180 degrees in a signal's bearing (e.g., the bearing might be 23 degrees or its reciprocal, 203 degrees). In late 1940, W. Struszynski, a brilliant former head of Polish State Telecommunications, joined the British design team and solved the hitherto intractable problem with a superb aerial design.

By December 1942, sixty-four ships in the Western Approaches of the Atlantic were equipped with FH3 aural HF DF. These required skilled operators to determine whether a signal was on the ground wave (generally from a transmitter no farther than about 30 miles distant) or a sky wave (which could be hundreds of miles away). The first U-boat sinking after an HF DF contact occurred on 27 March 1942, when HMS *Leamington* and other escorts sank U-587. Full production of FH4 cathode ray sets did not start until around May 1943: FH3 (not FH4 as sometimes claimed) played a vital role in the Battle of the Atlantic before July 1943.

Shipborne HF DF and radar complemented each other perfectly. Centimetric radar enabled convoy escorts to combat deadly night attacks by surfaced U-boats, forcing the attackers to move 10 to 30 miles from convoys and to send more reports, making them vulnerable to HF DF. The Kriegsmarine was reasonably well informed about British shore HF DF, and later used countermeasures such as "off frequency" transmissions against it. However, U-boat command was unaware of shipborne HF DF until April 1944. "Spurt" transmitters never came into effective service with the Kriegsmarine. An operational research report based on Ultra estimated that without shipborne HF DF, Allied convoy losses in early 1943 would have been 25 to 50 percent higher, with U-boat kills being reduced by one-third. Commanders Kenneth Knowles and Rodger Winn, the heads of the U.S. Navy and British Submarine Tracking Room, respectively (both with full access to Ultra), stated that "accurate U-boat tracking would be impossible without [shore] HF/DF."

Shore HF DF made a major contribution to breaking German naval Enigma signals, especially Shark (used by the Atlantic U-boats), by compelling the Kriegsmarine to use short signals. Shark was broken from mid-December

1942 until July 1943 only because the Atlantic U-boats employed short signals. DF generally, and not just the naval variety, was the code breakers' indispensable aid.

Ralph Erskine

See also Code Breaking; Enigma; German "Fish" Codes; Germany: Navy; Signals Intelligence (SIGINT); Ultra; United Kingdom: Royal Navy; U.S. Navy

Sources
Journal of the Institution of Electrical Engineers. 1947. Vol 94, Part IIIA.
Erskine, Ralph. 1999. "Kriegsmarine Short Signal Systems—And How Bletchley Park Exploited Them." *Cryptologia* 23 (1): 65–92.
Erskine, Ralph. 2004. "Shore High-Frequency Direction-Finding in the Battle of the Atlantic: An Undervalued Intelligence Asset." *The Journal of Intelligence History* 4 (2): 1–32.
Redgment, P. G. 1995. "High-Frequency Direction Finding in the Royal Navy: Development of Anti-U-Boat Equipment." In *The Applications of Radar and other Electronic Systems in the Royal Navy in World War II,* edited by F. A. Kingsley. Basingstoke, UK: Macmillan.
Williams, Kathleen B. 1995. *Secret Weapon: U.S. Navy High-Frequency Direction Finding in the Battle of the Atlantic.* Annapolis, MD: U.S. Naval Institute Press.

High-Speed Morse

During World War II, the British Royal Corps of Signals developed a means of rapidly sending and reading Morse code messages to make signaling more efficient. "Golden Arrow" units were taught the equipment associated with this high-speed operation, which could process 80 to 100 words per minute (wpm) in good conditions.

The Creed high-speed equipment used in these operations required specialist training.

High-speed Morse used a special Creed version of Morse, which was a "two hole" code in paper-tape form and additionally had sprocket holes for use with the auto-head, an instrument used for the transmission of messages previously punched into paper-tape form. During training, the Creed tape was used for "sending" Morse signals in a classroom to students' earphones. A perforator was a typewriter-type machine that, instead of producing hard copy, produced a half-inch-wide paper-punched tape that could then be fed into an auto-head. A reperforator machine was mainly used in static stations and could be coupled to a receiver, which automatically produced a paper-tape version of the message being received so as to facilitate onward transmission on another circuit. The undulator was a machine coupled via a "bridge," which converted the incoming alternating current signal to direct current for a wireless receiver. The standard receiver used in the "M" or Mobile Sections was the Marconi CR100. The incoming signal was "printed" by the undulator as an ink wavy line on an absorbent paper tape, which the operator skillfully wound around his fingers as the message came in. The paper tape then had to be "slip-read." This was the art of reading an undulator tape and typing the message on an ordinary typewriter onto paper. The paper was usually on a continuous roll in order to accommodate long messages. The wavy line on the tape was a readable Morse signal.

For these units, the normal Morse transmission speed by auto-head was 80 wpm, but in good conditions, this could reach 100 wpm. The trade-test speed for Class III operators was 18 wpm for Morse (send and receive); 55 wpm for perforating; and 45 wpm for slip-reading. High-speed operations were expensive in highly trained manpower and after World War II gave way to a variety of newer technologies.

Cliff Lord

See also Golden Arrow Sections; Morse Code; Telegraph; United Kingdom: Royal Corps of Signals; Vehicles and Transport

Source

Lord, Cliff, and Graham Watson. 2003. *The Royal Corps of Signals: Unit Histories of the Corps (1920–2001) and Its Antecedents*, 318–320. Solihull, UK: Helion.

Hooper, Stanford C. (1884–1955)

Stanford Hooper has been dubbed the father of U.S. Navy radio by historian L. S. Howeth, who summarized Hooper's role: "During the period 1915 to 1928, Hooper was the guiding spirit in developing naval radio from little more than a toy to the essential communication medium it became."

Hooper was born in Colton, California, on 16 August 1884. He grew up in San Bernardino and worked as a relief telegraph operator for the Southern Pacific Railway during summer vacations. He graduated from the Naval Academy in 1905, and a year later helped operate the wireless of the USS *Chicago* in San Francisco Harbor, right after the massive earthquake. He taught electricity, physics, and chemistry at the Naval Academy in 1910–1911.

He served for two years (1912–1914) as the Navy's first Atlantic Fleet radio officer (resuming that post again in 1923–1925). With some difficulty and good support, he established coordination and procedures over heretofore independent ships' wireless operators. The tactical and strategic value of U.S. Navy radio was first proven at the April 1914 U.S. occupation of Veracruz in Mexico, where Hooper established a com-plex time-sharing scheme so the vessels of different nations could transmit with their otherwise overlapping spark transmitters. Hooper helped to establish a chain of coastal stations for communication with the fleet. After serving on various ships, he commanded the destroyer *Fairfax* during World War I, winning the Navy Cross.

For a decade after the war (to 1928) Hooper directed the Radio Division of the Navy Department, and then served as director of Naval Communications (1928–1934). He originated the recommendation that led to the formation of the Radio Corporation of America (RCA) in 1919, intended to relieve American dependence on foreign companies, and later published the detailed story of how RCA had come to be formed as a result of combined government and commercial action. Hooper redirected the Naval Research Laboratory from manufacturing to research and tightly defined their priorities, prompting a brief revolt. At the same time he argued for greater naval use of low frequency radio, fearing the ability of enemies to jam the more widely used high-frequency receivers. Later research showed the value of high-frequency long-distance communications. Hooper often represented U.S. interests at international radio conferences. He again directed the Radio Division from 1939 until his 1942 appointment as technical assistant to the vice chief of Naval Operations.

Hooper was a strict disciplinarian and seldom sought or took advice on radio matters, considering himself the final authority. He retired as a rear admiral in June 1945. Over his long career he won awards from the Franklin Institute (Philadelphia), as well as the French Legion of Honor, the Marconi Medal of Merit, and the Institute of Radio Engineers Medal of Honor. Hooper died in Miami Beach on 6 April 1955 at age seventy.

Christopher H. Sterling

See also Jamming; Naval Radio Stations/
   Service; Naval Research Laboratory (NRL);
   Radio; World War I

Sources
Douglas, Susan. 1985. "Technological Innova-
   tion and Organizational Change: The Navy's
   Adoption of Radio, 1899–1919." In *Military
   Enterprise and Technological Change*, edited by
   Merritt Roe Smith, 117–173. Cambridge, MA:
   MIT Press.
Hooper, S. C. 1922. "Keeping the Stars and
   Stripes in the Ether." *Radio Broadcast* June:
   127–132.
Hooper, S. C. 1929. "Naval Communications—
   Radio Washington." *Proceedings of the
   Institute of Radio Engineers* 17 (September):
   1595–1620.
Howeth, L. S. 1963. *History of Communications-
   Electronics in the United States Navy*.
   Washington, DC: Government Printing
   Office.

Horses and Mules

Horses marked the first improvement in the
speed and endurance of the individual military courier. Dispatch riders became a common feature of both diplomacy and war from
prehistoric times. Extensive horse-based
postal and courier systems were in use in the
Far East and India by the twelfth century.
Perhaps ironically, use of the horse in communication was revived by the development
of more modern (but heavier) communications systems—such as the telegraph and telephone, which needed wire, units, and
switching equipment—although now more
horses were carrying the means of communication, rather than messages themselves.
Lighter and faster horses continued to carry
messages between telegraph and telephone
stations, and later between wireless stations.

During the Crimean War (1854–1856),
horses were vital to the construction of
British telegraph lines. Teams of two drew
telegraph office wagons, carts filled with
telegraph cable, and large plough horses
were used to help bury telegraph cable. Similar units operated during and after the
American Civil War (1861–1865). Telegraph
units in the 1870s and 1880s included horses
as "standard equipment" to haul the needed
cable and signaling devices.

During the second Afghan War (1878–
1880), British engineers introduced their first
"telegraph train," which was made up of
mule-drawn carts of telegraph, cable, and
heliograph equipment. The train could carry
as much as 30 miles of telegraph cable for
stringing to and from battlefields as needed.
Smaller amounts of cable, or poles for several miles of service, could be carried in
packs or reels on the backs of individual animals. By the 1890s, cable cart units included
a half-dozen horses and several dozen men,
as well as the telegraph equipment to be
hauled. Fast carts towed by a single horse
carrying a limited amount of cable were
used to deploy lines rapidly. These mobile
units were employed during the Boer Wars.

By World War I, the British army had a
clearly delineated system in place using
horse- or mule-drawn equipment, though
by then these included both wired (telegraph
and telephone) and early wireless services. A
serious problem with using animals in communications, however, was upkeep. All
armies used thousands of horses and mules
during World War I, and just provisioning
them, let alone replacing wounded or dead
animals, became a substantial question of
logistics. While cavalry units averaged a
man per horse, signal companies usually
had far more horses than people. Huge numbers of military personnel were required to
maintain animal stock. Slowly such units
motorized, though horses and mules were
not phased out entirely in the British army
until 1937. Many European armies were still

Pack horses and mules were widely used to carry heavy or cumbersome telegraph and radio equipment. Shown here in 1916, U.S. Army Signal Corps mule carries instruments to be used in wireless telegraphy. (Library of Congress)

using horses widely when World War II began in 1939.

Other animals, including oxen, camels (in the deserts of Somalia and the Sudan in the early 1900s during both world wars) and elephants (in colonial India and Burma) were used by the British military to assist with communications. Extensively detailed orders for the care of these animals became part of British signalers' instructions. Camels were useful in carrying poles and other long items, and later were used to carry radio equipment during and after World War II.

Even in the 1960s, camel-borne radio units included transmitter, receiver, and batteries.

David L. Woods and Christopher H. Sterling

See also Couriers; Dogs; European Late Nineteenth-Century Wars; Heliograph and Mirrors; Pigeons; Telegraph

Sources

Cooper, Jilly. 1983. *Animals at War*. London: Heinemann.

Harfield, Alan. 1989. *Pigeon to Packhorse: The Illustrated Story of Animals in Army Communications*. Chippenham, UK: Picton Publishing.

Woods, David L. 1965. "Messengers: Men, Horses, and Dogs." In *A History of Tactical Communications Techniques*, chap. IV. Orlando, FL: Martin-Marietta (reprinted by Arno Press, 1974).

Hotline/Direct Communications Link (DCL)

On 20 June 1963, the governments of the United States and the Soviet Union signed a memorandum of understanding that established the Direct Communications Link (DCL), better known as the "hotline." This telecommunications system was the first direct channel of contact between the U.S. president in Washington DC and the Soviet leader in Moscow.

The agreement established a full-time telegraph-teleprinter circuit between the capitals routed through Britain, Denmark, Sweden, and Finland and another reserve duplex radio-telegraph circuit through Morocco. Terminals in each country ended in both capitals at "red phones" accessible by the respective national leadership. On the American side, coding equipment at first included the Norwegian-developed Electronic Teleprinter Cryptographic Regenerative Repeater Mixer, four units of which were installed.

The direct impetus for the establishment of the DCL was the Cuban Missile Crisis of October 1962, when the two superpowers had come close to launching a nuclear war. The hotline was designed to prevent any misunderstandings that might lead to the unraveling of the Cold War balance over any point of contention and the consequent purposeful or inadvertent ordering of nuclear missile strikes.

Time and again direct and real-time communications between leaders in Moscow and Washington have proven effective in resolving critical situations. The first situation in which the DCL was key involved a standoff between Soviet and American naval fleets in the Mediterranean during the Arab-Israeli Six Day War in 1967. Five years later, the hotline was essential to avoiding escalation of the Yom Kippur War. In 1979, the hotline was activated by Washington to protest the Soviet invasion of Afghanistan. The last known U.S.-Soviet communication through the DCL was in December 1990, but the hotline continued in use between the United States and a post-Communist Russia. More recently, Russian and American leaders conferred via the "red phones" over stabilization issues during the Iraq War (2003–present).

There were a number of accident-generated interruptions to the physical cable link, exposing the need for reliability. Significant modernization of the DCL occurred beginning in the 1970s to improve the system and make it more secure. One Soviet and one American satellite were stationed in geosynchronous earth orbit to replace the link through Tangier, Morocco. At Fort Detrick, Maryland, the federal government used a fifteen-acre site to construct one of the largest communications facilities in the country, the USA Earth Station, to act as the hub for the satellite system. The Russian terminal of the DCL is run from the space communications center at Valdimir.

By the mid-1980s, the new hotline infrastructure consisted of even more complex satellite telephone channels and graphical imagery transmission capability. The satellites are completely visible between Washington and Moscow for eight hours each day, but alternate acquisition of each satellite by the DCL antennae provides a virtually seamless circuit. Each side receives transmissions in the other's language.

In the United States, the 1110th U.S. Army Signal Battalion operates and maintains the satellite link. A presidentially appointed DCL Operational Oversight Committee oversees the DCL and reviews its procedures; the DCL Configuration Control Board was chartered to ensure systems capability. The DCL continues to be funded by the Department of Defense on behalf of the National Communications System.

Kent G. Sieg

See also Communication Satellites; Cuban Missile Crisis (1962); National Communications System (NCS); Signals Intelligence (SIGINT); Teleprinter/Teletype

Sources

Andrew, Christopher. 1996. *For the President's Eyes Only: Secret Intelligence and the American Presidency from Washington to Bush.* New York: Perennial.

Proc, Jerry. "Electronic Teleprinter Cryptographic Regenerative Repeater Mixer (ETCRRM)." http://www.jproc.ca/crypto/etcrrm.html.

Richelson, Jeffrey T. 1999. *The U.S. Intelligence Community.* Boulder, CO: Westview.

Howe, Admiral Lord Richard (1726–1799)

Richard Howe, who rose to serve twice as Britain's First Lord of the Admiralty, was a prominent Royal Navy flag officer who conducted pioneering work with signal flag systems. Between 1776 and 1793, Howe issued at least eight sets of instructions with dual signal books that sought to standardize Royal Navy flag signal systems.

Howe was born in London on 8 March 1726. Aided by family connections, he entered the Royal Navy at age fourteen in 1740 and served in a variety of locations—rising rapidly to his first command by 1748. He was

elected to Parliament in 1762. Howe served as treasurer of the navy from 1765 to 1770, later was named rear admiral, and rose to vice admiral five years later. He commanded the North American station of the Royal Navy during the early (1776–1778) American Revolution (though—or perhaps because—he was sympathetic to the American cause).

At this time (July 1776) Howe rationalized the chaotic state of naval signaling that often involved use of up to fifty different flag designs. Each fleet, and often each captain, used his own variation of flag signals—there was little standardization. Howe reduced the number of flags needed to twenty-one and developed a standard flag signal book, along with a second explanatory book. The flags were keyed to specific pages in these books. Some flags were of new design, often featuring two or three horizontal stripes. The new system and books were first issued while he commanded HMS *Eagle*, standing off Sandy Hook at the mouth of New York Harbor.

Howe employed a table of squares, sixteen across and sixteen down, numbered from 1 to 256. On the left hand side were shown sixteen signal flags, and the same flags in the same order were shown at the top of the table over squares numbered 1, 17, 33, 49, and so forth. Thus, one flag from the top group and another from the side could indicate together any one of the 256 numbered groups. To signal numbers, Howe had another ten-by-ten table, using different flags. When numbers above 101 were required, a pennant indicating 100 was added. All this section was reserved for the admiral, with a separate private ship section presenting similar signals. Many of these flag designs are still in use.

A revision was issued in 1782, and another, issued about 1790, contained 200 to

300 signal groups. This incorporated a number of flag ideas from French officers (Bertrand-François Mahé de La Bourdonnais and probably Captain Sébastien François de Bigot, Vicomte de Morogues,) by Richard Kempenfelt, who was working on signal systems in this same period. While the Admiralty ruled Kempenfelt's systems were "too complex," he was willing to credit the French and support many of Howe's ideas due to his senior's popularity. Various articles at that time and since have confused the roles of Kempenfelt and Howe. For example, Howe could not have retired and turned his signal system over to Kempenfelt to finish, as the latter died eight years before the former. Thus, the 1790 flag system was Howe's reworking of Kempenfelt's system, rather than the other way around.

Howe was knighted in 1797 (the first Royal Navy officer so honored). Admiral Lord Horatio Nelson credited Howe's flag system for his 1798 victory over the French at the Battle of the Nile. A final development of Howe's system, with 340 signals, appeared in 1799 (the first official Admiralty version). Howe died on 5 August 1799.

Christopher H. Sterling

See also Flaghoist; Flags; Popham, Home Riggs (1762–1820); Trafalgar, Battle of (21 October 1805); United Kingdom: Royal Navy

Source
Syrett, David. 2005. *Admiral Lord Howe: A Biography.* Annapolis, MD: Naval Institute Press.

Human Signaling

Humans are easily overlooked in signal systems, though in one way or another, humans are present as operators in almost every such system. Humans can participate directly as a messenger, voice, or symbol—but in the end are both senders and receivers.

Hand signals are perhaps the oldest signal method as well as being one of the first forms of human communication. In the ninth century, Eastern Roman Emperor Leo VI argued in his *Tactics* that in order to prevent battlefield mistakes, hand signals would be needed. There are many alphabets, usually involving fingers, to allow those who cannot speak, the deaf, those working in high-noise environments, and so forth to exchange messages or directions. Albert J. Myer, who later invented the U.S. Army system of single-flag wig-wag signaling and established the U.S. Army Signal Corps, worked as a telegrapher in early life using a system devised by a Scottish scientist, Alexander Bain. This so interested Myer that on his return to medical study, his doctoral thesis was devoted to a new sign language for deaf mutes. Such efforts led Myer to determine there might be a need for a code that involved tapping on a cheek, hand, or table, thus serving the deaf, blind, and indeed almost everyone. He continued his research, devising a system nearly identical to the dot and dash of the Morse code.

Hand signal systems have also been expanded by using a hat, neckerchief, flag, or some device to render the hand more visible. By the 1800s, such human signal systems were being codified and published. Englishmen including Jack Spratt, Lieutenant Colonel John McDonald, Royal Navy Lieutenant H. Cranmer Philipps, Knight Spencer, and Commander A. P. Eardley-Wilmot; Americans Captain Robert W. Jenks and J. V. Konvalinka; and French Captain Charles de Reynold-Chauvancy all developed varied systems. Even Albert Myer produced various systems for use by a single person. Both

British and American military forces published periodic guidebooks for such signals, including the systems used by landing signal officers aboard aircraft carriers and for replenishing ships at sea.

Other arm and hand signal systems have been devised for use by tugboat crews, aircraft ground crews, police, heavy equipment operators, deep sea divers, astronauts, aircraft and helicopter pilots, Navy frogmen, and military prisoners of war. Many of these same groups, including most military field units, also use arm and hand systems to direct troops and vehicles. Indeed, signalmen often send messages to one another from close-in ships using their arms alone.

David L. Woods

See also Ancient Signals; Bain, Alexander (1811–1877); Couriers; Fire/Flame/Torch; Flags; Maori Signaling; Myer, Albert James (1828–1880); Semaphore (Mechanical Telegraphs); Voice Relay

Sources

Adams, M. R. 1970. *Through to 1970: Royal Signals Golden Jubilee*. London: Royal Corps of Signals Institution.

Myer, Albert. 1872. *A Manual of Signals*. New York: Van Nostrand.

Woods, David L. 1965. *A History of Tactical Communication Techniques*. Orlando, FL: Martin-Marietta (reprinted by Arno Press, 1974).

I

Identification, Friend or Foe (IFF)

Identification, friend or foe (IFF) systems were developed to separate American from enemy aircraft by assigning a unique identifier code to each U.S. aircraft's radio transponder. In 1937 the Naval Research Laboratory developed the first IFF system. Later iterations were developed as follow-ons. The present system is considered a secondary radar system because it operates differently from and independently of the primary radar system that tracks aircraft skin returns only. The same cathode ray tube can be used to display the data from both radar systems.

IFF operates in four modes in military aircraft plus a submode. Mode 1 is a nonsecure method used by ships to track aircraft and other ships. Mode 2 is used by aircraft to make carrier controlled approaches to ships during inclement weather. Mode 3 is the standard system and is also used by commercial aircraft to relay their position to ground controllers throughout the world for air traffic control. Mode 4 is a secure, encrypted identification system and is the only assured method of IFF. Submode C is an altitude encoder.

By 1958, the U.S. Federal Aviation Administration had implemented the Air Traffic Control Radar Beacon System (ATCRBS), which was the civilian equivalent of the military system. The International Civil Aeronautics Organization adopted the ATCRBS, thereby making IFF the basis for the world's air traffic control system.

The IFF system is a query-and-response system. The secondary radar transmits a series of selectable coded pulses. The transponder on the aircraft receives and decodes the interrogation pulses. If the transponder determines that the interrogation code is correct, it transmits a different series of coded pulses in response. A cross-band beacon is employed, the interrogation pulses are transmitted at one frequency, and the reply pulses are at a different frequency.

The IFF concept is in the process of being expanded to cover not just aircraft but also vehicles and even individual personnel on the battlefield. By using the same IFF concepts, it would be possible to reduce the number of "friendly fire" incidents. The advances made in computers and miniaturization have made it possible to reduce the size and cost of the transponders so that it becomes practical to distribute them among vehicles and troops.

Tommy R. Young II

See also Airplanes; Naval Research Laboratory (NRL)

Source

Gebhard, Louis A. 1979. "Radio Identification-IFF." In *Evolution of Naval Radio-Electronics and Contributions of the Naval Research Laboratory,* 251–262. Washington, DC: Government Printing Office.

India

As one of the world's two most populous countries, India ranks as an important center of military communications. After millennia of using couriers or other basic means of signaling, and then an extensive system of semaphores early in the nineteenth century, electrical communications entered India in the mid-nineteenth century and have since expanded to become essential elements of the nation's military forces.

By the time of the horrendous Indian Mutiny of 1857, there were some 4,000 miles of commercial telegraph line in the subcontinent, most constructed within the previous five years. The army controlled some lines and also made extensive use of visual communications, including the heliograph. Aware of the value of the lines, rebels destroyed telegraph links in areas they controlled, though not before warnings were flashed from Delhi to all districts and back to London. On suppression of the mutiny the next year, the British government took over administration of the huge colony from the East India Company, and at the same time overhauled the Indian army with British officers. For the remainder of the nineteenth century, military units were organized under the governments of Bengal, Bombay, and Madras (these were unified only at the end of the century).

Signals detachments operated as part of the sappers and miners (engineers). The earliest record of army telegraphy dates to 1868 when the first internal military telegraph routes were built. By the 1870s, signal units utilizing telegraph and heliograph were a part of army forces in various frontier expeditions. The first school for army signaling (focusing mainly on visual methods) opened in 1881. An improvised sending and receiving set (telephone) was developed during the Jowaki Campaign of 1877–1878 by Captain J. W. Savage of the Royal Engineers. Telephones were also used during the Second Afghan War in 1878—certainly some of the earliest application of the technology to military use. Telephone equipment was being used more extensively by the turn of the twentieth century. Sapper and miner telegraph units served in expeditions throughout the subcontinent as well as in Cyprus, Aden, China, parts of Africa, and the Middle East.

As part of another overall military reorganization, on 15 February 1911, the Indian Signal Service was organized, though still under the auspices of the sappers and miners. By this time, units included some wireless capabilities. Indian units served throughout World War I on the Western Front, in East Africa, and in the Middle East, where service continued into the early 1920s. Indeed, Indian signal troops served in all theaters save Gallipoli and the Balkans.

Increased technical sophistication and enhanced responsibilities of the signaling function saw the 17 April 1920 formation of the Indian Signal Corps as a separate military arm. The corps, still making substantial use of British Royal Corps of Signals officers, formed a signal company for each army division with a nucleus of a wireless company to aid the line of communication. Indian Posts and Telegraphs took over administration and operation of most telegraph and telephone lines in the country. In September 1935, the first Indian officer (from the Indian Military Academy), Second Lieutenant A. C. Iyappa (later director of Signals and signal officer-in-chief) was commissioned into the corps. The corps served on the Northwest Frontier, as well as in Afghanistan, Iraq, and China.

Despite plans for updating, the Indian Signal Corps was still ill equipped and understaffed when the war began in 1939. As Indian units were deployed in the Middle East and elsewhere, they adopted mechanized transport and updated modes of signaling from the Royal Corps of Signals. One signals group was lost in the surrender of Singapore in early 1942. Many Indian units were involved in the fighting in and around Burma from 1942 to the end of World War II. Indian Air Formation Signals units were developed to work with the British Royal Air Force.

As the corps grew to fulfill its expanded deployment, so too did the employment of Indians in more technical fields, and thus their training at multiple sites. The Indian Women's Army Corps helped to provide needed teleprinter, switchboard, and cipher operators. New teleprinter equipment as well as multichannel and long-distance radios were adopted as supplies became available. Signals units assisted in the difficult political transition of 1946–1947 as India was divided into Pakistan and India.

On India's independence on 14 August 1947, the Indian Signals Corps was taken over by Indians. When on 26 January 1950 the country attained full sovereignty, the Indian Signal Corps was renamed the Corps of Signals with the motto *Teevra Chaukas* ("Swift and Secure"). The corps saw duty during the Korean War (1950–1953) as well as in later United Nations peacekeeping efforts in the Congo and Middle East.

The corps, reputed to include 100,000 members in the early twenty-first century, is organized into officers, junior commissioned officers, and other ranks. Officers are employable in all aspects of communication or administration, while the other ranks are organized into specific trades such as Operator Radio and Line, Technician Electronics and Systems, and so forth. The Corps of Signals is the electronic warfare and information technology arm of the Indian army, utilizing an array of computerized/automated state-of-the-art systems. Electronic data processing became a corps responsibility in 1964, and the corps commissioned the army's first computer in 1971. The corps provides networking, an automated message switching system or automated message handling system, and installation of the state-of-the-art exchanges with the latest interactive voice response systems.

Two major factors that have served to keep the Corps of Signals at the top of its form are India's substantial and expanding high technology sector and continued tensions (and occasional clashes) with Pakistan. State-of-the-art communication networks using microwave, ultra-high frequency, optical fiber and satellite systems, and switching systems with security overlays are being implemented. Secure radio and VSAT (very small aperture terminal) equipment have also been introduced to further the reach of the Indian Defense Communication Network to cover communication requirements of all three services (army, air force, and navy) at the strategic level. In addition to applications in and around India, signals personnel go abroad as field detachments for United Nations peacekeeping forces (as in Lebanon and Sierra Leone) and with Indian army training teams in other countries.

Christopher H. Sterling

See also Heliograph and Mirrors; Telegraph; United Kingdom: Royal Corps of Signals

Sources

Corps of Signals Committee. 1975. *History of the Corps of Signals: Volume 1 Early Times to Outbreak of Second World War (1939)*. New Delhi: Corps of Signals Committee, Signals Directorate, Army Headquarters.

GlobalSecurity.org. "Corps of Signals." [Online information; retrieved November 2004.] http://www.globalsecurity.org/military/world/india/signal.htm.

Lord, Cliff, and Graham Watson. 2003. "Indian Corps of Signals." In *The Royal Corps of Signals: Unit Histories of the Corps (1920–2001) and Its Antecedents*, 351–352. Solihull, UK: Helion.

Nalder, R. F. H. 1958. "Signals in India" In *The Royal Corps of Signals: A History of Its Antecedents and Development (circa 1800–1955)*, appendix 2, 493–502. London: Royal Signals Institution.

Subramanyam V. A. 1986. *The Signals: A History of the Corps of Signals*. Delhi: Macmillan India Ltd.

Information Revolution in Military Affairs (IRMA)

The American Information Revolution in Military Affairs (IRMA) began in the 1980s, but a real debate began after the 1990–1991 Gulf War. IRMA combines three components: (1) the information revolution itself, with both military and civilian applications; (2) the use of high-technology conventional weaponry; and (3) how warfare is perceived in American society. This is a revolution that is still under way as it continually develops and reshapes the American way of warfare.

Computer, microchip, and telecommunication innovations all contributed to the information revolution, with "information" understood as both message and medium (system). Contemporary IRMA is information driven, and the changes it is creating in warfare are logical consequences as societies have become inherently information based. IRMA imposes changes in equipment but more importantly reshapes the way operations are conducted and overall strategy as objectives have to be redefined. The information revolution operates on different levels and includes such elements as satellite systems, the global positioning system, warning and control systems (such as Airborne Warning and Control System, Joint STARS, Rivet Joint, Cobra Ball); command, control, communications, computers, intelligence, surveillance, and reconnaissance (C4ISR); and sensors. According to the U.S. Army project Force XXI (1994), every battlefield vehicle will be equipped to allow it to locate itself geographically while maintaining communication among soldiers and between soldiers and command posts.

The information revolution also gave birth to the idea of information warfare (IW), a new type of war, defined by General Colin Powell as "actions taken to achieve information superiority by affecting adversary information, information-based processes, information systems, and computer-based networks while defending one's own information, information-based processes, information systems, and computer-based networks" (Adams 1999, 56). Hence, information becomes both the weapon and the target.

The 1991 Gulf War represented the first application of high technology to war. New types of weapons such as precision laser-guided bombs and unmanned aerial vehicles (e.g., Predator) were used on a battlefield for the first time. Employment of new equipment was backed up by C4ISR capabilities. High-precision, deep-strike, long-range weapons, based on innovations in computer and communication technologies, made it possible to keep soldiers far from the targets. War became somewhat remote controlled.

Given that IRMA is largely an American revolution, it is important to understand the American attitude toward war. This psychosociological factor makes for the third dimension of this revolution. Political leaders are under public opinion pressure that discourages U.S. engagement in a war that may result in many American lives lost. This axiom—the intolerance of casualties—is extremely powerful because it is directly connected with the legitimization of political actions and makes civil-military relations a central factor in designing and implementing IRMA. It is also the part of a wider notion in the West, which is to make war more humane. Standoff (weapons designed to balance or match that of an enemy, not intended for use, but to keep an enemy from employing some other weapon), unmanned vehicles, and nonlethal weapons are used to reduce the risk to human lives and thereby to maintain public support for military involvement.

Łukasz Kamieński

See also Airborne Warning and Control System (AWACS); Army Battle Command System (ABCS); Communication Satellites; Global Positioning System (GPS); Gulf War (1990–1991); Iraq War (2003–Present); Solid State Electronics; "System of Systems"

Sources

Adams, James. 1999. *The Next World War: The Warriors and Weapons of the New Battlefields in Cyberspace*. London: Arrow.

Arquilla, John, and David Ronfeldt, eds. 1997. *In Athena's Camp: Preparing for Conflict in the Information Age*. Santa Monica, CA: RAND Corporation.

Cohen, Eliot A. 1996. "A Revolution in Warfare." *Foreign Affairs* 75 (2): 37–54.

Commonwealth Institute. "The RMA Debate." [Online information; retrieved September 2005.] http://www.comw.org/rma/index.html.

Gray, Colin. 2002. *Strategy for Chaos: Revolutions in Military Affairs and the Evidence of History*. London: Frank Cass.

Krepinevich, Andrew F. 1994. "Cavalry to Computer: The Pattern of Military Revolutions." *The National Interest* 37 (Fall): 30–42.

Schwartzstein, Stuart J. D., ed. 1996. *The Information Revolution and National Security: Dimensions and Directions*. Washington, DC: Center for Strategic and International Studies.

Infrared Signal Systems

Infrared signal systems were used by the U.S. Navy during and after World War II with the original equipment being replaced by more capable devices in the mid-1970s.

The origins of infrared technology date to the mid-nineteenth century, but focused military research began during World War I. With U.S. Army support, Theodore W. Case developed infrared detector devices with which messages could be sent for several miles. British research in the 1930s centered on infrared aircraft detection.

During World War II, infrared research and development programs were under way in both Germany and the United States. During the war, Germany was only able to apply the technology for limited optical telephony. In the United States, such systems became a technological reality during the mid–World War II period, when both means to change visible light to invisible light and a device to reverse the process were discovered. The transmitter lamp used a hood that filtered out the visible spectrum, leaving infrared rays to pass through. The U.S. Navy code name for the system was NANCY HANKS, or just NANCY (after Abraham Lincoln's mother, 1784–1818), though why is no longer clear. A radio message would be sent to the intended recipient that a NANCY HANKS message awaited transmission.

A 1-foot infrared hood was fitted over the standard Navy battery-powered signal searchlight. This provided a very narrow (highly directional) signaling system (probably not more than 2 to 3 degrees of aperture) which had to be continuously trained on the receiving ship, lest it wander off the mark due to relative movement changes and ship roll. International Morse was used as the message medium for all infrared communication. A pair of steady, omnidirectional, point-of-train lights, also with infrared covers, was mounted on ships' masts to provide a transmitting station with a continuous location of multiple ship receiving station(s). During night "darken ship" conditions, it was impossible to determine this optically. Similar equipment was mounted in pairs on each yardarm to transmit to a number of stations simultaneously, using nondirectional procedures. The range of this system was considerably less than with the signal searchlight hood-mounted system, but allowed an officer in tactical command (OTC) to dispatch traffic to all ships in a formation out to a distance of about 3 to 4 miles. During periods of night formation steaming, the OTC issued "NANCY calling periods" on the hour, during which time traffic for all ships could be sent without having to use voice radio call-up procedures.

NANCY was used between ships and shore signal stations when checking in during night port entries, as well as in forward areas.

Though slow and tedious, the system allowed a "no visible light" and near-radio-silence environment while enabling limited tactical/administrative communication within task forces. The method could also be used with shore signal stations. Improved equipment was introduced in the mid-1950s. During the 1970s, infrared systems began to give way to more advanced systems. In the late 1980s, the receiver was replaced by the night vision device or night vision goggles.

David L. Woods

See also Talk Between Ships (TBS)

Sources

Wolfe, W. L. 1965. *Handbook of Military Infrared Technology.* Washington, DC: Office of Naval Research.

Wolfe, W. L., and G. J. Zeiss. 1978. *The Infrared Handbook.* Washington, DC: Office of Naval Research.

Institute of Electrical and Electronic Engineers (IEEE)

The Institute of Electrical and Electronic Engineers (IEEE) was formed in 1963 from two older American professional engineering groups. It is by far the largest world membership organization in and for the field of electrical engineering.

The earlier American Institute of Electrical Engineers (AIEE) was founded in Philadelphia in 1884. Among early members were Alexander Graham Bell and Thomas Edison, who served as vice presidents. While many members were active in the telegraph business, AIEE members included other inventor-entrepreneurs, the relatively few college-trained engineers of the day, teachers, physicists, and even company managers. Publications were planned and even a museum and library were projected. AIEE prospered, but by the early twentieth century, it was focusing more on power and heavy machinery engineering.

Just before World War I, the growth of wireless led to the creation of the Institute of Radio Engineers (IRE) in 1913, formed from two largely local organizations, the Society of Wireless and Telegraph Engineers and the Wireless Institute. From the start of IRE there was some overlapping membership in (and on occasion tension between) the two groups. As an example of just how rapidly the field of radio was expanding and changing, IRE published a massive (more than 1,500 pages) fiftieth anniversary issue of its *Proceedings* that not only reviewed developments of the previous half-century (including four papers on military electronics) but also projected ahead to the world of 2012.

AIEE formed its Military Electronics Group in 1956 as one indicator of the growing symbiosis between the military services and corporate and university electronics research. Rapid changes in both electronics miniaturization and the growing missile programs of each arm of the military spurred growth throughout the 1950s and 1960s.

After several years of negotiation, a merger between the clearly declining AIEE and the rapidly expanding IRE (with about 150,000 members at the time and a thousand new members joining each month) led to the creation of the Institute of Electrical and Electronic Engineers. The new organization adopted the decentralized professional groups of the IRE rather than the hierarchical AIEE structure. Formation of the new Society of Broadcast Engineers was one result of the dissent arising from the larger merger.

In the 1970s opportunities for electrical engineers diminished with the shrinkage of both the aerospace industry, in the aftermath of the Vietnam War, and the National Aeronautics and Space Administration (NASA), with the end of the Apollo moon landing missions. A shrinking employment base paralleled, and may have contributed to, debate in IEEE publications about the role of economic and social (even critical) research to supplement (some said supplant) the purely technical work done by most members. In 1980, IEEE established what has become an extensive history program (on both the organization and the field of electronics). It also began holding a huge annual military communications conference. By 1984, IEEE enjoyed a membership of more than a quarter-million people.

In the twenty-first century, IEEE has become a truly international association with more than 360,000 members in about 175 countries. IEEE produces nearly a third of the world's annual publications on electrical engineering, computers, and control technology; holds more than 300 major conferences annually; and has created nearly 900 consensus-based active technical standards, with another 700 under development.

Christopher H. Sterling

See also Institution of Electrical Engineers (IEE)

Sources
"Fiftieth Anniversary of the AIEE." 1934. *Electrical Engineering* 53 (May): 641–848.
Gannett, Elwood K. 1988. "Proceedings of the IEEE: The First 75 Years." *Proceedings of the IEEE* 76 (October): 1268–1279.
Institute of Electrical and Electronics Engineers. "IEEE History Center." [Online information; retrieved April 2007.] http://www.ieee.org/organizations/history_center/index.html.
Institute of Radio Engineers. 1962. "Fiftieth Anniversary Issue." *Proceedings of the IRE* 50 (May): 1–1450.
McMahon, A. Michael. 1984. *The Making of a Profession: A Century of Electrical Engineering.* New York: Institute of Electrical and Electronic Engineers.

Whittemore, Laurens E. 1957. "The Institute of
    Radio Engineers—Forty-Five Years of
    Service." *Proceedings of the IRE* 45 (May): 597–
    635.

Institution of Electrical Engineers (IEE)

Formed initially by a group of English tele-graph engineers, the Institution of Electrical Engineers (IEE) has since become the premier British membership organization of electrical engineers. Many of its members have worked or been affiliated closely with various branches of British military services. Certainly many people concerned with military communications have been IEE members.

The Society of Telegraph Engineers was founded in May 1871 in London. It had 300 members a year later, from an industry employment base of about 2,500, one-fifth of whom were women. As the field expanded, it changed its name a decade later to the Society of Telegraph Engineers and of Electricians, of which there were nearly a thousand members. The name Institution of Electrical Engineers was adopted in 1889; within two years the organization had more than 2,000 members. An active library was part of the organization from the start.

As just another indicator of expanding opportunities, before World War I, more than twenty other electrical engineering organizations were formed in Britain. IEE members were active in all aspects of World War I—indeed the association gave up its head-quarters building for five years to government needs. IEE had first moved into its Savoy Place headquarters in 1908 (some rooms were leased to the new British Broad-casting Company from 1923 to 1932; the building was substantially reconstructed in 1961). An IEE section devoted to wireless appeared in 1919. A series of annual lectures in honor of inventor Michael Faraday began in 1923.

During World War II, membership rose by 40 percent (it had fallen during World War I), in part due to active training of civilians to assist with the war effort. Members interested in communications, and especially radio, began to outnumber those concerned with power engineering. A full 20 percent of the membership was in one or another of the armed forces.

After the war, IEE membership grew from 20,000 in 1940 to more than 82,000 four decades later—an indicator of the central role of electricity in Britain's postwar expansion. Considerable tension existed between the IEE and the somewhat parallel British Institution of Radio Engineers (formed in 1925, it became the Institution of Electronic and Radio Engineers in 1988) as both sought to speak for radio engineers. Partially because of that competition, IEE reorganized several times after 1945 as the electrical engineering field continued to expand and splinter.

IEE has become the largest professional engineering society in Europe with 120,000 members early in the twenty-first century. It holds conferences and publishes journals, magazines, and a number of online services. On 1 April 2006, IEE merged with the Institution of Incorporated Engineers to become the Institution of Engineers and Technology (IET).

Christopher H. Sterling

See also Institute of Electrical and Electronic Engineers (IEEE)

Sources
Appleyard, Rollo. 1939. *The History of the
    Institution of Electrical Engineers, 1871–1931.*
    London: Institution of Electrical Engineers.

Institution of Engineering and Technology. [Online information; retrieved April 2007.] http://www.theiet.org/.

Reader, W. J. 1987. *A History of the Institution of Electrical Engineers, 1871–1971*. London: Peter Peregrinus for the Institution of Electrical Engineers.

Intelligence Ships

An intelligence-gathering ship is generally an ocean-going vessel carrying electronic means to detect radio signals (and therefore military activity) in its vicinity. Several navies have operated such ships, including those of the United States, Britain, the former Soviet Union, and the People's Republic of China. While most American vessels are operated by the U.S. Navy, many are actually serving the needs of the National Security Agency (NSA) or related entities. The Soviet Union operated a fleet of electronic surveillance vessels, often thinly disguised (given their extensive antenna arrays) as fishing trawlers or other merchant ships. China has at least five such vessels, each operating on a different ocean.

The U.S. Navy has had many radar and radio vessels in commission over the years. Most recently some SWATH (twin hull)

The specialized communications ship USS Pueblo *is shown here in 1967, prior to its seizure off the coast of Wonsan by North Korea in January 1968. (Naval Historical Center)*

vessels have been used in antisubmarine warfare and related tasks. Others have assisted with recording missile launches or space capsule recovery, still others in various kinds of research, both for the Navy and other federal agencies. Some began life as World War II cargo vessels, which years later were rebuilt and loaded with electronic surveillance equipment. One series of ships was dubbed AGER (Auxiliary General Environmental Research) or AGTR (Auxiliary General Telecommunication Research) vessels, denoting joint Navy and NSA operation. They were designed to conduct research in the reception of electromagnetic signals. Equipped with the latest antenna systems and measuring devices, they were highly sophisticated. Three of them became famous—or infamous—in the 1960s.

The USS *Oxford* (AGTR-1) was one of the important surveillance sources used during the Cuban Missile Crisis as she cruised off shore and picked up signals of Russian missile activity on the island in the fall of 1962. She later served in the Far East during the Vietnam War.

On 9 June 1967, the USS *Liberty* (AGTR-5) was sailing off the coast of Egypt, monitoring radio traffic during the Six Day War in the Middle East. She was attacked over a period of two hours, during which time 34 of her crew were killed and 172 were wounded. The attacking aircraft were Israeli—the attack came as Israel was beating Egyptian forces in the Sinai Desert just to the south of the ship's location off shore. A huge controversy arose—and remains—over why the attack took place and over much of what happened—or did not happen—in the immediate aftermath of the attack.

On 23 January 1968, while cruising off the coast of North Korea, the USS *Pueblo* (AGER-2), which was tuning North Korean radio traffic, was attacked and boarded (the first

American ship to be boarded since 1807) by North Korean forces and taken to their port of Wonsan. The crew was held for eleven months before being released—the ship was never released and most of the top-secret equipment on board was lost.

Faced with the loss of two such vessels in six months, making vividly clear how poorly they were or could be defended (and thus how vulnerable their highly secret listening equipment was), the United States withdrew many of its intelligence vessels over the next few years, relying more on aircraft and satellite surveillance sources.

Christopher H. Sterling

See also Cuban Missile Crisis (1962); National Security Agency (NSA); Russia/Soviet Union: Navy; Signals Intelligence (SIGINT); U.S. Navy

Sources

Bamford, James. 2001. *Body of Secrets: Anatomy of the Ultra-Secret National Security Agency from the Cold War Through the Dawn of a New Century*. Garden City, NY: Doubleday.

Gerhard, William. 1981. *Attack on the USS* Liberty. Laguna Hills, CA: Aegean Park Press.

Hounam, Peter. 2003. *Operation Cyanide: Why the Bombing of the USS* Liberty *Nearly Caused World War III*. London: Vision.

Schumacher, F. Carl, Jr., and George C. Wilson. 1971. *Bridge of No Return: The Ordeal of the U.S.S.* Pueblo. New York: Harcourt, Brace, Jovanovich.

U.S. House Armed Services Special Subcommittee. 1969. *Inquiry into the U.S.S.* Pueblo *and EC-121 Plane Incidents: Hearings*. 91st Congress, 1st Session (March–April).

International Code of Signals (ICS)

In 1817, Frederick Marryat (1792–1848), a young British Royal Navy officer, introduced the first edition of his *Code of Signals for the Merchant Service*. While designed for commercial shipping, the flag code was soon utilized by naval vessels as well. Thanks to its versatility, this signal flag code continued being used until at least 1879. Many seafarers continued using Marryat's system beyond 1879, even though it had been officially superseded. His code provided the basis for the present International Code of Signals (ICS), which can be sent by signal flag, blinker light, semaphore, Morse code, or radio. The code was and continues to be intended to ease communication concerning navigation and safety, especially across languages.

Marryat's system was well marketed and was reissued at least eleven times, perhaps due to his father's influence in maritime merchant shipping affairs—but more likely due to the merit of the entire system. Marryat's system used both numeric and alphabetic codes, which allowed ready expansion as needed. Combined with flags indicating 10 or 100 or more, Marryat's approach could be readily expanded while all prior flag codes were limited to stock messages that might number in the hundreds. Further, one could make up new flag messages at will— with more simplicity than in the past. Marryat code revisions did not change existing signals, but added new information that was needed as steamships replaced sail. As a result, versions of his code were used for up to a half-century while other flag codes often saw brief usage.

Marryat's signal code was divided into six parts: (1) the flag codes identifying specific English man-of-war ships; (2) a similar list of flag codes for foreign man-of-war ships; (3) flags for English merchant ships; (4) a flag list of lighthouses, ports, headlands, rocks, shoals, reefs, and so forth; (5) flag codes for a selection of standard and often-used sentences; and (6) flags providing the basic vocabulary. It was this organized approach perhaps more than the actual signal flags that brought Marryat's code such a broad following. Although the growing number of warships and merchant ships made for some problems, Marryat's code was able to expand to handle them. All flag codebooks became enormous (there were hundreds of British and foreign warships, and thousands of merchant vessels—and all the specific locations were noted). The earlier codes were dictionaries, while (comparatively speaking) Marryat's was an encyclopedia. Indeed, for many decades, Marryat had this field to himself.

A British government committee in 1857 not only debated the qualities needed for such a system but also assessed more than a dozen existing official and unofficial signal flag codes. With a brief report, Marryat's code was adopted with some variations. With the Marryat system, eighteen individual signal flags could signal more than 70,000 possible messages. The code was revised three decades later by the British Board of Trade, and again at an 1889 conference in Washington DC. It was widely distributed by the late 1890s. As one example of its naval use, the code was used at the 1905 Battle of Tsushima, when Russian fleet survivors sent the message "XGE" ("I surrender") to the astonished though victorious Japanese.

With the rise of wireless and other technologies, the ICS system began to be applied to other means of communication, and was thus subject to further revision and expansion. The International Radiotelegraph Conference in 1927 considered revision proposals, and three years later a new edition was issued in seven languages: English,

French, Italian, German, Japanese, Spanish, and Norwegian. This new ICS was formally adopted at the Madrid International Radio-telegraph Conference held in 1932. It was published in two volumes—one for visual signaling and the other for radio signals. The Administrative Radio Conference of the International Telecommunication Union suggested in 1947 that the ICS should be controlled by the Intergovernmental Maritime Consultative Organization (IMCO, which later became the International Maritime Organization). In January 1959, this change finally took place. The IMCO Assembly of 1961 approved further revisions and added publications in Russian and Greek, for a total of nine languages. Numerous international organizations contributed to the updating process. The ICS was revised several times in the late 1960s, including dropping the former vocabulary segment, so that each signal has its own complete meaning, thus reducing the size of the code.

David L. Woods

See also Code, Codebook; Flaghoist; Flags; International Telecommunication Union (ITU); Morse Code; Popham, Home Riggs (1762–1820); Tsushima, Battle of (27–28 May 1905)

Sources

National Imagery and Mapping Agency. 2003. *International Code of Signals.* Publication 102. Bethesda, MD: National Imagery and Mapping Agency.
Pocock, Tom. 2001. *Captain Marryat: Seaman, Writer, & Adventurer.* Harrisburg, PA: Stackpole Books.
Report of the Committee Appointed by the Lords of the Committee of Privy Council for Trade to Inquire into & Report upon the subject of a Code of Signals to be Used at Sea. 1857. London: Her Majesty's Stationery Office.
Woods, David L. 1965. "Flaghoists and Signal Books." In *A History of Tactical Communica-tions Techniques*, chap. III. Orlando: Martin-Marietta (reprinted by Arno Press, 1974).

International Telecommunication Union (ITU)

Growing out of the nineteenth-century International Telegraph Union, the modern ITU is a specialized agency of the United Nations and serves as the primary global organization (nearly all nations are members) concerned with international technical standards and development in telecommunication.

From March to May of 1865, the French government hosted a conference of twenty nations in Paris to resolve problems of multiple European telegraph systems of technical standards, codes, and rate structures. The agreement reached, based in part on bilateral treaties dating to 1849, formed the International Telegraph Union, today the world's oldest international organization. It established a priority of messages that is still observed: state (diplomatic), telegraph administration, and private or commercial messages. It also adopted the Morse system as the basis of international operation. Later conferences in Vienna (which established Berne as ITU headquarters), Rome (when Britain joined), and St. Petersburg (the last such plenipotentiary meeting until 1932) revised and strengthened ITU. By the early twentieth century, the organization had fifty-two country members with nationalized telegraph systems, and twenty-five observers who allowed private carriers (including the United States).

One early difficulty for ITU was how to treat coded communications (whether diplomatic, military, or commercial). Only in the 1920s, after considerable debate, did it adopt the Cortina (for the town in Italy where a subcommittee met) report recommending use of no more than five-letter groups.

A series of international conferences concerning wireless telegraphy and telephony (radio) began in Berlin in 1903, outside ITU, with subsequent conferences held in 1906, 1912, and 1927. Only at the ITU administrative meeting in Paris in 1925 did ITU attempt to enforce similar standardization of operations for telephone service. Finally, in 1932 at Madrid, ITU merged with the International Radiotelegraph Conference to become the modern International Telecommunication Union with equal interest in telegraph, telephone, and radio services. After a hiatus forced by World War II, a plenipotentiary conference of seventy-four nations, held in Atlantic City in 1947, reorganized ITU and laid the groundwork for the organization to affiliate with the new United Nations, to shift its base of operation to Geneva, and to establish an International Frequency Registration Board (IFRB). The IFRB seeks to record all uses of radio spectrum by all nations in an attempt to reduce or eliminate interference.

Military services became increasingly interested in (and sometimes involved with) ITU activities as their own use of spectrum-based services became more important in the years after World War II. The 1950s and 1960s saw a constant series of ITU-related conferences, most devoted to specific services. Developments of such new technologies as satellite communication were incorporated into ITU regulations. By the 100th anniversary of ITU in 1965, it had 129 members—forty years later the number was nearly 189. The ITU took on its present structure in 1992 when it reorganized into three sectors: radiocommunication, technical standards, and telecommunication development. The organization adopted its first strategic plan two years later.

Christopher H. Sterling

See also Morse Code; National Telecommunications and Information Administration (NTIA), Spectrum Management

Sources

Channing, Ian. 1995. *International Telecommunication Union: 130 Years, 1965–1995*. London: International Systems and Communications.

Codding, George Arthur, Jr. 1952. *The International Telecommunication Union: An Experiment in International Cooperation*. Leiden: E. J. Brill (reprinted by Arno Press, 1972).

Codding, George A., Jr., and Anthony M. Rutkowski. 1982. *The International Telecommunication Union in a Changing World*. Dedham, MA: Artech House.

Friedman, William F. 1928. *The History of Codes and Code Languages, The International Telegraph Regulations Pertaining Thereto. . .* Washington, DC: Government Printing Office (reprinted by Aegean Park Press).

International Telecommunication Union. Home page. [Online information; retrieved April 2007.] http://www.itu.int/aboutitu/.

Michaelus, Anthony R. 1965. *From Semaphore to Satellite: On the Occasion of the Centenary of the International Telecommunication Union*. Geneva: International Telecommunication Union.

Internet

The Internet's origin can be traced directly to the efforts of the U.S. Defense Advanced Research Projects Agency (ARPA; renamed DARPA in 1972). It became apparent by the 1960s that ARPA researchers at different research centers had to be able to communicate with each other, as well as with various contractors. The most efficient method of communications would be through links between the centers' mainframe computers.

In 1962 ARPA opened a computer research program and appointed John Licklider from the Massachusetts Institute of Technology (MIT) to head the organization. Licklider had just published his first thoughts on what he dubbed the "Galactic Network" in which computers were networked and everyone had access to them. At the same time, Leonard Kleinrock, working at ARPA, was developing the concept of sending information from one point to another in packages or packets. The message would be broken into tiny units that would be transmitted separately, with the packets reassembled on the receiving end. Packets could be sent over more than one transmission line and in any order. Such a system would take advantage of any available means of transmission and make unauthorized interception of the information more difficult.

In 1967 a plan for a computer network called ARPANET was published. When these plans were made public, researchers at MIT, the National Physics Laboratory (NPL) in the United Kingdom, and the RAND Corporation discovered that they had all been working independently for a number of years to develop a wide area network of computers. The switching system took its name from the work done at NPL and became known as packet switching. In December 1968, the firm of Bolt Beranek and Newman (BBN) won the contract to develop the interface message processors (IMPs), commonly called packet switches. The first IMP was installed at the Network Management Center at the University of California Los Angeles (UCLA) by BBN in September 1969. A second host was added at the Stanford Research Institute (SRI) and the first message was sent from UCLA to SRI. Two more nodes were added at the University of California, Santa Barbara and the University of Utah, and by the end of 1969 what we know as the Internet was taking its first steps. In 1970, the first host-to-host protocol, Network Control Protocol (NCP), was completed. In 1972 Ray Tomlinson of BBN wrote the first e-mail program.

Before a truly open-architecture network could be developed, changes would have to be made in the NCP which could only address networks and computers at a destination IMP on the ARPANET. Bob Kahn from DARPA and Vinton Cerf from Stanford began work on a new protocol that would become the Transmission Control Protocol/Internet Protocol (TCP/IP). The first international connections to the ARPANET were made when University College of London and the Royal Radar Establishment of Norway were connected. In a paper presented by Cerf and Kahn on the Transmission Control Protocol, the term Internet was used for the first time in 1974. On 1 January 1983, the ARPANET made the transition from NCP to TCP/IP. In the same year, the University of Wisconsin created the Domain Name System, which allowed packets to be directed to a domain name where they would be translated into IP numbers. The transition to the new protocol allowed the ARPANET to split into the MILNET for operational needs and an ARPANET that still supported research requirements in 1984.

A number of networks, for example, USENET, BITNET ("Because Its Time Network"), CSNET (Computer Science Research Network), Tymnet, TELENET, and JANET in the United Kingdom, had grown up in the late 1970s and early 1980s. TELENET was the first commercial packet-switched network, the civilian equivalent of ARPANET. During the same period the personal computer (PC) made its appearance on the market and a true revolution in the exchange and use of information began.

The introduction of the Intel 4004 chip microprocessor in November 1971 began the computer revolution. The new chip placed all of the parts that made a computer work on one small chip. The Intel chip, and similar chips from other manufacturers, was soon being used to manufacture low-cost computers for office and home. It was natural that owners of the desktop machines would want to connect to networks and exchange information with other users. As the number of users of PCs increased and the capacity and speed of the microprocessors improved dramatically, the number connected to mainframes and networked within organizations increased rapidly. Once the TCP/IP protocol was included in the software loaded on the new machines, their use to access the growing number of networks was assured.

In 1990, Tim (later Sir Tim) Berners-Lee, working at the European Particle Physics Laboratory (CERN) in Geneva, Switzerland, developed three essential parts of the modern Internet: HyperText Markup Language, Uniform Resource Locator, and HyperText Transfer Protocol. The World Wide Web (WWW) was the combination of these developments at CERN, which were adopted and applied to their needs by other users. In 1992, the University of Illinois developed its Web browser "Mosaic." Several years later a commercial version, Netscape, was released. The Internet, as it exists today, is actually a network of computer networks and the WWW is a web of information webs.

In the last twenty years, military organizations around the world have adopted the Internet and the WWW as a means of acquiring and exchanging essential information. Public and secure Web sites are maintained to provide the information necessary to manage and direct military operations. The U.S. Department of Defense has developed a number of security measures to deal with networks. The Secure Internet Protocol Router Network is an interoperable command-and control-network designed to handle classified applications and information. The nonsecure Internet Protocol Router Network handles sensitive information and provides controlled access to the Internet. In addition to the two networks, the FORTEZZA card, which plugs into a computer's PCMCIA (card) reader, contains the capstone cryptographic engines and the user's private key to encrypt and decrypt messages to provide information security.

The PC as a desktop unit became an essential piece of office equipment in the 1980s, and the laptop followed in the 1990s. The ability to utilize commercial communications technology combined with computer security measures has brought personal computers, laptops, wireless networks, personal communications systems, personal digital assistants, satellite telephones, and transmission of streaming video to the battlefield. The Internet has revolutionized the way information is exchanged for both military and civilian users.

Tommy R. Young II

See also Computer; Computer Security (COMPUSEC); DARPANET; Defense Advanced Research Projects Agency (DARPA); Defense Switched Network (DSN); E-Mail Systems; Global Information Grid (GIG); Information Revolution in Military Affairs (IRMA); Solid State Electronics; Voice over Internet Protocol (VoIP)

Sources
Griffiths, Richard T. 2002. "History of the Internet, Internet for Historians (and just about everyone else)." [Online article; retrieved December 2006.] http://www.let.leidenuniv.nl/history/ivh/frame_theorie.html.
Kleinrock, Leonard. 2005. "Internet History" [Online information; retrieved December 2006.] http://www.lk.cs.ucla.edu/internet_history.html.
Leiner, Barry M., et al. 2006. "A Brief History of the Internet." [Online article; retrieved April 2007.] http://www.isoc.org/internet/history/brief.shtml.
Williams, Michael. 1997. *A History of Computing Technology*. 2nd ed. Los Alamitos, CA: IEEE Computer Society Press.
Zakon, Robert H. 2006. "Hobbes' Internet Timeline." [Online information; retrieved December 2006.] http://www.zakon.org/robert/internet/timeline/.

Iraq War (2003–Present)

If the 1990–1991 Gulf War is often called the first Information Age war, then the Iraq War was the first one overwhelmingly dominated by computerized and digital communications. During the twelve-year interlude between these two wars, the American military developed powerful infrastructure for conducting quick wars. Information technology (IT) was the cornerstone of military communication during Operation Iraqi Freedom. Not only did it help to reduce the Clausewitzian "fog" and "friction" of war but it also marked the twenty-first century transformation of the U.S. military toward "network-centric warfare." Based on the Iraq War experience, modern military communication appears to be more about communication among machines (computers, systems, and networks) than among humans. Communication has become real time, automatic, digitized, netlike, multilevel, multiservice, and dependent on commercial IT innovations.

Changing Technology

Communication is now important not merely for transmitting orders but for learning the location of friendly and enemy forces, the changing battlespace map, coordinating joint (multiservice) operations, sustaining interoperability—and for successful use of new high-tech weapons systems (mainly satellite or laser precision-guided munitions [PGMs] and unmanned vehicles). While PGMs amounted to less than 10 percent of explosives used during the 1991 Gulf War, by the Iraq War they accounted for 68 percent. Predator and Global Hawk unmanned aerial vehicles, commonly used for surveillance and reconnaissance missions, provided real-time pictures of remote targets to be destroyed by PGMs. Intelligence analysts working back in the United States reported to the Combined Air Operations Center in Saudi Arabia and to theater commanders in Iraq. This precise and instantaneous communication over great distances was crucial for smart bomb efficiency. Improvement in global positioning system (GPS) theater accuracy by more than 20 percent since the 1990s increased the effectiveness of thousands of GPS-guided munitions used during this war. Pilots could wait for last-minute orders to program a bomb or missile before releasing it. Thanks to GPS, the United States could begin the war with a dramatic air campaign dubbed "Shock and Awe." Full-time GPS coverage was also extensively utilized for location purposes—the Army was supplied with more than 100,000 precision lightweight GPS receivers.

Digital communication networks gave coalition forces unprecedented air-land-naval operations coordination and near-perfect battlespace awareness. This in turn speeded reaction time. Global and tactical communications systems allowed commanders to identify targets and send orders to fire on them within minutes. Never before has the time lag between a target's identification and its destruction ("sensor-to-shooter gap") been shorter. One example is an attempt to take out a probable Saddam Hussein shelter on 7 April 2003—the time between target identification and elimination was less than fifteen minutes. Rapid and massive strikes required streamlined transmission of battle damage assessments as commanders had to make quick decisions of likely re-strikes on undamaged targets. Here communications systems along with intelligence evaluation proved supreme when compared with the earlier Gulf War.

Space-based assets were crucial in Iraq. According to some estimates, 60 percent of all communications at the height of the war were transmitted by satellite. During the opening fighting, almost a hundred different satellites were used for military communication compared to about sixty during the Gulf War. Consequently, fifteen times more satellite bandwidth was available than in 1990–1991. In 1991 American forces numbered 542,000 and could use 99 mbs of bandwidth, while 2003 coalition forces totaled 350,000 but bandwidth grew to 783 mbs. Some 33,500 people at twenty-one American and fifteen foreign sites were involved in space support activities for the Iraq War.

Joint command (at the Central Command level) was conducted via the Global Command and Control System (GCCS), which provided "a God's-eye view" of the battlefield as never before. Eighty aircraft carried out ISR (intelligence, surveillance, and reconnaissance) missions, flying a thousand sorties and collecting 42,000 battlefield images, 3,200 hours of streaming video, and 2,400 hours of signals intelligence coverage. This massive amount of raw data was passed through satellite communication networks and then, after being analyzed, disseminated as processed information across services, command posts, and maneuvering units.

For the U.S. Navy, communication at sea was aided by chat rooms and secure telephones. To enhance speed and effectiveness of command and control (C2), Navy officials used more than 500 chat rooms on Pentagon's SIPRNet (Secret Internet Protocol Router Network). Being functionally a counterpart of the civilian World Wide Web, it became a vital communication channel for all services. SIPRNet and IP connectivity allowed the coalition to rapidly win the initial combat phase in Iraq.

The Iraq coalition was an Information Age force. The key unit responsible for providing communications was the V Corps' 22nd Signal Brigade. The Army Battle Command System (ABCS) enabled commanders to transmit orders, intelligence, logistics information, and other useful data. A new component of ABCS was the Blue Force Tracking (BFT) system for identifying friendly (U.S. or coalition) forces. According to Northrop Grumman, BFT's developer, it is a rugged system of software and hardware that links satellites, sensors, communications devices, vehicles, aircraft, and weapons in a seamless digital network. It provided a real-time "common operational" picture of the battlefield ("battlefield awareness") for commanders and units. It also supported joint operational commands by providing current location of army forces through GCCS. BFT's computer terminals showed blue icons (friendly forces) on digitized maps and provided the latest satellite navigation imagery with regular information updates. Red icons, representing enemy units, could be added to the system, although not automatically updated. BFT was installed on more than 1,200 ground and aviation platforms in Iraq. BFT proved its value as a means for enhanced joint operation among U.S. services and British forces. It significantly reduced incidents of friendly fire ("blue on blue"), as BFT's "common operational picture" allowed everyone to see all fighting units.

Use of "closed loop" operations offered coalition forces a great advantage as feedback between commander and field units allowed information to flow both ways. Soldiers in the field received command, control, communication, computers, intelligence, surveillance, and reconnaissance (C4ISR) information, which provided them with current situation awareness, while the commander, seeing results of operations, could direct further military actions.

The TeleEngineering Kit (TEK) constituted a fairly new pattern of military communication. Units in the field could contact experts at the TeleEngineering Operations Center in Vicksburg, Mississippi, to advise solutions to complex technical problems, such as repairs to damaged bridges, by transmitting information and images. TEK used mobile communication systems of small satellite terminal, laptop, camcorder, and videoconferencing units. Technical advice was usually provided within four hours. TEK is a good example of sharing information and knowledge during combat.

At the beginning of the Iraq War, the coalition managed to destroy most of its priority Iraq communication infrastructure targets. As a result, Iraqi commanders did not have an overall picture of the coalition maneuvers and at times they sent orders to units that had ceased to exist. The coalition's aim was to jam Iraqi reconnaissance and air defense units and to disrupt their communication and radar systems. The Iraqis had at least four systems to jam coalition GPS, but all were damaged in early fighting. Destruction of fiber optic and other networks between southern Iraq and Baghdad cut off enemy forces in the south. In the period following the fall of Saddam Hussein's regime, rising insurgency forces relied on nonradio modes of communication (largely signal flares, light signals, smoke, and couriers). They later worked out a communication system based on portable radios and cell phones.

After the initial (spring 2003) fighting, novel means of sharing experience with and knowledge about fighting insurgencies were created. In April 2004 CavNet was inaugurated at Camp Victory in Iraq as a site (military forum) at SIPRNet. It is a user-driven system for transferring knowledge about the foe, emerging enemy and friendly tactics, techniques, and procedures in various mission categories. CavNet was fashioned to provide commanders the collective best practice to "prepare for the next patrol."

Another new dimension of communication during the war, which also undertook Information Age–like changes, was the pattern of soldiers' communication with home. When in 1948 the Military Affiliate Radio System was established, as a side-effect it enabled soldiers (though on a very limited scale) to call home free of charge. In the Gulf War, e-mail first emerged as a means for deployed soldiers to communicate with families at home. During the Iraq War, with the establishment of forward operating bases where soldiers could rest from the battlefield stress, Internet kiosks were established by Iraqi businessmen. Relying on fiber optic infrastructure, however, they did not survive the war. By mid-2003 a contractor provided satellite broadband Internet access across the Iraq theater. Voice over Internet

Protocol allowed instant messaging from 180 Internet kiosks set up throughout Iraq. Virtually all soldiers used e-mail and instant messaging to stay connected with home.

Lessons

Although the war demonstrated how unprecedented information sharing proved the power of network-centric warfare, there are lessons to be learned from this conflict. Several serious challenges for digitization and modernization of the American military became apparent. While "jointness" acquired with new high-speed communication techniques heavily strengthened coalition forces, there is poor interoperability among service-specific C4ISR capabilities. For example, through unmanned vehicles the U.S. Marines generated data that V Corps badly needed but could not access for the lack of means to connect to the data flow. Interoperability was an even greater challenge for coalition members less advanced in IT technologies. Mobile and wireless C2 must be increased, especially for the Army. Data should be quickly turned into knowledge to remove information overload, which appears to be the twenty-first century version of Clausewitz's fog of war, generating chance and unpredictability.

The Army lagged the Air Force and Navy in use of satellite communications. Although tactical satellite radios for voice communications were used extensively by commanders to communicate, most ABCS information was passed over mobile subscriber equipment (MSE)—an aging line-of-sight voice and data communication system. Its basic shortcoming was the dependence on ground-based nodes. When a subscriber passed outside network coverage, there were no contiguous nodes to carry the signal, so he or she had to turn to FM or military/commercial satellite radios and phones. If the nodes were not within the covered area, field units could not receive updated imagery. Units below the brigade level often lacked even MSE communication. Thus, the Iraq War revealed some shortfalls of the digitized twenty-first century army. One senior official captured this digital divide noting that he could acquire "oven-fresh imagery" but not forward it to the units advancing on Baghdad. The war demonstrated that the greatest IT challenge is to supply an army with systems capable of on-the-move communications backed up with high-bandwidth satellites. Iraq fighting revealed the need for solutions to eliminate this divide, including the Warfighter Information Network–Tactical and the Joint Tactical Radio System.

The Iraq War marked a new phase in the evolution of military communications. It proved the power of information and novel ways of its transmission for achieving decisive and rapid victory in warfare.

Łukasz Kamieński

See also Defense Advanced Research Projects Agency (DARPA); Global Command and Control System (GCCS); Global Positioning System (GPS); Gulf War (1990–1991); Information Revolution in Military Affairs (IRMA); Jamming; Joint Tactical Radio System (JTRS); Military Affiliate Radio System (MARS); Voice over Internet Protocol (VoIP); Warfighter Information Network–Tactical (WIN-T)

Sources

Bradley, Carl M. 2004. "Intelligence, Surveillance and Reconnaissance in Support of *Operation Iraqi Freedom*: Challenges for Rapid Manoeuvres and Joint C4ISR Integration and Interoperability." Newport, RI: Naval War College.

Cordesman, Anthony H. 2003. *The Lessons of the Iraq War: Main Report*, Washington, DC: Center for Strategic and International Studies.

Flynn, Erin. 2006. "Jumping Ahead to WIN-T." *Military Information Technology* 10 (2).

Available online at http://www.military
-information-technology.com/article
.cfm?DocID=1351.

Fontenot, Gregory, et al. 2005. *"On Point"
The United States Army in Operation Iraqi
Freedom*, Annapolis, MD: Naval Institute
Press.

Frontline. 2005. "Innovating & Improvising."
[Online article; retrieved December 2006.]
http://www.pbs.org/wgbh/pages/
frontline/shows/company/lessons.

GlobalSecurity.org. "Warfighter Information
Network–Tactical (WIN-T)." [Online
information; retrieved December 2006.]
http://www.globalsecurity.org/military/
systems/ground/win-t.htm.

Krepinevich, Andrew F. 2003. "Operation Iraqi
Freedom: A First-Brush Assessment."
Washington, DC: Center for Strategic and
Budgetary Assessments.

Moseley, Michael T. 2003. *Operation Iraqi
Freedom*—By the Numbers." United States
Central Command Air Force, Shaw Air
Force Base, SC: Combined Forces Air
Component, Assessment and Analysis
Division (April).

Wong, Leonard, and Stephen Gerras. 2006. *CU
@ The FOB: How the Forward Operating Base Is
Changing the Life of Combat Soldiers*. Carlisle,
PA: Strategic Studies Institute, U.S. Army
War College.

Israel

Founded on 14 May 1948, Israel by the early twenty-first century had put into place the most highly developed (though not the largest) telecommunications system in the Middle East. It is based on a good system of coaxial cable and microwave radio relay and all systems are digital. Israel also has a very proficient high-technology industry.

A signal service was initially developed by the Haganah in the 1930s. By 1937 use of all means of communication from lamps to heliographs to flags to radio were to be found in this underground organization. An underground radio network helped to connect Haganah interests in Baghdad, Damascus, Beirut, and several European and other cities. In May 1948 the Signal Corps was formed from this service, and Jacob Yanovski soon professionalized it. The objectives were to provide communications for the ground portion of the Israel Defense Forces (IDF) and the postal service for ground, sea, and air services. By 1949 the Signal Corps had grown to 3,500 troops. There were approximately fifteen brigade companies, twenty battalion platoons, twenty radio stations abroad, ninety static radio stations, a signal school, and three major electronic equipment laboratories. The corps continued to expand and worked in close contact with the Israeli electronics industry.

IDF has long used technology to make up for what it lacks in size and human resources. Israel has no separate army, navy, or air force. Instead IDF is divided into forces, two of which are the air force (*Heyl Ha'avir*) and navy (*Heyl Ha'yam*, literally, "sea force"). Given its strategic location and situation, IDF requires and has created effective communications to summon and coordinate ground or air forces as needed. Its procurement needs, in turn, feed further technical development. Much of IDF's electronic systems (intelligence, communication, command and control, navigation, etc.) are Israeli developed.

IDF's command, control, communication, and computers directorate is digitizing the military. This effort includes the integration of all ground force assets through fiber optic cables, cellular and broadband communications, and the expansion of military satellite communications. Israel's Ground Forces Command has launched a project called Digital Ground Warfare (*Tsayad*), which is meant to integrate all units of the army and allow the General Staff to obtain a real-time picture of any battlefield.

Many American firms have worked closely with Israel's military. ITT Industries, for example, supplies Israel with communications, electronic, and night-vision equipment. More recently, Motorola established a terrestrial nationwide military cellular network for IDF providing dependable and deployable voice and data services to military commanders. Code-named Mountain Rose (*Vered Harim*), the system became operational in mid-2004, after almost four years of development and installation. It revolutionized IDF communications networks, transforming them from a hierarchical networking model to a spatial connectivity infrastructure. The system replaced outdated means of communications, including terrestrial communications, wireless radiotelephone links, and some combat radio networks. For the first time Israeli commanders can utilize highly secure communications while on the move. The system also supports data transfer. Currently transfer of images and messages is facilitated with planned enhancements including video services. These mobile networks can link to terrestrial networks or satellite communications systems to facilitate direct and seamless connectivity from the lowest echelon up to the national command level.

This military network is maintained by the operator and therefore enables services that had previously been maintained only by commercial providers. These include end-to-end high-level security, assured coverage and capacity based on operational planning (not only by actual demand), and the ability to "kill" a unit that is interfering, lost, or captured by the enemy. Fixed and transportable sites deploy with the military units, positioned at vantage points where they provide optimal coverage and redundancy to maintain effective connectivity and communications capacity for the operating forces. Because the system is not dependent on Israel's commercial infrastructure, communications can be sustained even under critical loads and in emergencies, where other forms of communications fail. When communication links are not available for any reason, each handset is configured to communicate directly with nearby handsets, maintaining a minimum level of local communications.

Israel has used its capability to launch reconnaissance satellites into orbit (a capability shared with but a handful of nations). Both the satellites (*Ofeq*) and the launchers (*Shavit*) were developed by Israeli security industries.

Christopher H. Sterling and Cliff Lord

See also Egypt; Intelligence Ships; Mobile Communications; Suez Crisis (1956)

Sources
Bednarz, Ann. 2005. "There's Battle Tested . . . and Then There's the Israeli Military: The Silicon Valley of the Middle East." *Network World*, May 23.
Israel Defense Forces. Home page. [Online information; retrieved April 2006.] http://www1.idf.il/DOVER/site/homepage.asp?clr=1&sl=EN&id=—8888&force=1.

Jackson, Henry B. (1855–1929)

A British Royal Navy officer who rose to command the service as First Sea Lord, Henry Jackson was a pioneer in experimenting with wireless telegraphy for two years in the late 1890s.

Jackson was born 21 December 1855 in Barnsley, England. As was not uncommon in those days, in late 1868, at the age of thirteen he joined the Royal Navy as a cadet. He rose through the ranks and saw service in Africa, on the torpedo school ship HMS *Vernon* at Portsmouth, and in 1896 was promoted to captain of the HMS *Defiance*, a former sailing ship serving as the navy's torpedo school. Jackson had always been interested in science as it might best serve the navy. He had studied navigation and then the mechanism of the torpedo.

Jackson conceived of the idea of employing wireless waves to signal from one ship to another, specifically to inform a capital ship of the approach of a friendly torpedo boat. He experimented with equipment designed for both sending and receiving messages. While master of the *Defiance*, he succeeded in 1896 in transmitting signals from one end of the ship

to the other. At the same time, although they were unaware of the other's efforts, Guglielmo Marconi had been working along parallel lines. While Marconi was developing long-distance wireless communication over both land and sea, Jackson's main aim was to improve communication service for the fleet. The navy did not seek a patent on Jackson's developments, suggesting they did not see the potential of wireless. Jackson soon achieved intership and ship-to-land transmission distances of up to three miles. Seeing this achievement as well as Marconi's continued efforts, the navy changed its approach and provided more funds for experimentation. But by late 1897, Jackson had become naval attaché at the embassy in Paris. His work from 1895 to 1897 had been central to the Royal Navy's pioneering wireless role. Jackson finally succeeded in persuading the Admiralty to experiment with Marconi's wireless telegraphy devices. Four vessels were equipped in 1899, and Jackson commanded one of them, achieving signals at a distance of 60 to 70 miles. More operational equipment was ordered and installed the next year.

Jackson was elected as a fellow of the Royal Society in 1901 in recognition of his wireless work. He became assistant director of Torpedoes at the Admiralty in 1902, and three years later was appointed Third Sea Lord and controller. In 1908 he returned to the sea as commanding officer of a cruiser squadron in the Mediterranean. In 1911 Jackson became the first director of the newly created Royal Navy War College at Portsmouth. Two years later, on the eve of World War I, he was appointed chief of the War Staff at the Admiralty. When Admiral Lord John Fisher resigned as First Sea Lord over government policy in the Dardanelles, Jackson succeeded him in the uniformed service's highest attainable post in May 1915. Eighteen months later he became president of the Royal Naval College at Greenwich. He was advanced to the ultimate rank of Admiral of the Fleet in 1919.

Jackson continued his interest in wireless and in 1920 was appointed first chairman of the navy's Radio Research Board of the Department of Scientific and Industrial Research. Under his guidance, important experiments were carried out on propagation of wireless waves, the nature of atmospherics, radio direction finding, and precise radio frequency measurements. Jackson received many awards including, in 1926, the Royal Society's Hughes Medal. Admiral Jackson retired in mid-1924 and died on 14 December 1929 at his home on Hayling Island.

Christopher H. Sterling

See also *Defiance* HMS; Marconi, Guglielmo (1874–1937); Radio; United Kingdom: Royal Navy

Sources
Jackson, H. B. 1902. "On Some Phenomena affecting the Transmission of Electric Waves over the Surface of Sea and Earth." *Proceedings of the Royal Society of London* 70: 254–272.

Kent, Barrie. 1993. "Wireless in the Fleet." In *Signal! A History of Signalling in the Royal Navy.* Clanfield, UK: Hyden House.
Pocock, R. F., and G. R. M. Garratt. 1972. *The Origins of Maritime Radio: The Story of the Introduction of Wireless Telegraphy in the Royal Navy Between 1896 and 1900.* London: Science Museum/HMSO.
Rawles, Alan. 1955. "Jackson of the *Defiance.*" *Journal of the Institute of Electrical Engineers* (December).

Jamming

Jamming means to transmit one radio signal in order to block effective reception of another. The jamming signal is most often transmitted to disrupt enemy communication receivers (not transmitters) but may also be intended to throw off radio- or satellite-directed weapons, navigation systems (including global positioning system [GPS]), or radar. A jamming transmitter must operate on the same frequency and with the same type of modulation as the signal it seeks to jam, and it must use at least enough power (often much more than the original signal) to accomplish its job.

The first experiments with intentional radio jamming date to British naval exercises in the Mediterranean in 1902, less than five years after the first shipboard wireless installations. Some jamming efforts took place during the Russo-Japanese War of 1904–1905. Radio jamming was fairly common during World War I though naval jamming often ran up against the greater need to tune in enemy transmissions for intelligence clues. Ground-to-air communication links were also regularly jammed.

One crude but effective means of jamming radar signals during World War II was the dropping of thousands of aluminum tinsel shreds (chaff or "window") from fighter or bomber aircraft. A later effort at selective jamming of radio signals took place in the December 1944 Battle of the Bulge. American B-24 bombers flew over the battle area carrying the high-powered radio jamming transmitter dubbed "Jackal" for the first time. Radio signals transmitted on AM frequencies successfully jammed German radio communications while not interfering with overlapping FM signals from American transmitters. By the end of the war, most participants had developed extensive radio equipment for jamming both communication links and radar systems. Airborne communications jamming equipment was further developed in the postwar years.

The type of jamming probably best known to the public was the long-running Soviet political effort to jam incoming high-frequency shortwave broadcasts (specifically those of Britain, West Germany, Israel, and the United States). By 1956 an estimated 3,000 jamming transmitters were putting up a wall of noise, some jamming ground waves, others sky wave transmissions. With a few respites, jamming continued in Europe for thirty-five years until the beginning of 1988. One Western response was "barrage" transmissions using many transmitters on different frequencies at the same time in the hope that some would get through (the technique parallels one used by the military). The cost of barrage jamming was high—often 100 times that of the signal to be jammed. Such jamming efforts are theoretically illegal in international communications as they often involve unlicensed transmitters that may interfere with services other than their targets.

There are many types of purposeful signal jamming in addition to barrage jamming. Spot jamming, for example, directs concentrated power against a specific channel or frequency. When tuned, a jammed signal most often sounds like random noise, stepped tones (used against voice circuits, these often sound like bagpipes), gull-like sounds (also effective against voice signals), a random pulse tone (useful against teletypewriter and data systems), recorded sounds (such as music, screams, applause or laughter, machinery, or whistles), or what is termed preamble jamming (useful against speech security devices). But jamming transmissions can also be subtle (unmodulated) and obvious in their squelching action only when the desired signal cannot be tuned.

Among methods of overcoming jamming (they vary with the equipment used and signals sought) is increasing transmitter output to overpower the jammer, modifying or relocating antennas, changing frequency, or acquiring another satellite (to overcome jamming of an existing one). Defense Advanced Research Projects Agency–funded research announced in 2001 is developing a software-based radio that can use an antenna to "sniff the frequency" and then convert transmissions to another available frequency for voice or data communications. Operational equipment was said to be five years away.

During the invasion of Iraq in early 2003, American forces destroyed Russian-supplied equipment intended to disrupt reception of GPS signals vital for navigation. Fittingly, the devices were destroyed with a GPS-guided weapon, but they underscored growing concerns about the jamming of satellite-deployed weaponry (especially as the same Russian firm had contracts from the American military). In October 2004, the U.S. Air Force announced that its new Counter Communication System that could jam enemy satellite transmissions was operational. The ground-based jammer (three of which had been delivered to the Air Force Space Command) uses electromagnetic radio frequency energy to knock out transmissions on a temporary basis, without disabling satellite components permanently.

Christopher H. Sterling

See also Communication Satellites; Defense Advanced Research Projects Agency (DARPA); Electronic Countermeasures / Electronic Warfare (ECM / EW); Global Positioning System (GPS); Iraq War (2003–Present); Joint Tactical Information Distribution System (JTIDS); Propaganda and Psychological Warfare; Radio; Spread Spectrum

Sources

Department of the Army. 1990. "Remedial Electronic Counter-Countermeasures Techniques." In *Communications Techniques: Electronic Counter-Countermeasures*, chap. 3, FM 24–33.

Lacrois, R. 1998. "Tactical Radio Jammers." [Online information; retrieved November 2004.] http://www.milspec.ca/jammers/jammers.html.

Poisel, Richard A. 2003. *Modern Communications Jamming Principles and Techniques.* Norwood, MA: Artech House.

Price, Alfred. 1984. *The History of U.S. Electronic Warfare: The Years of Innovation—Beginnings to 1946.* Alexandria, VA: Society of Old Crows.

Wood, James. 1992. "Jamming on the Short Waves." In *History of International Broadcasting.* London: Peter Peregrinus, 162–167.

Japan: Air Force

Japan's air power began to develop early in the twentieth century, and the country was making its own airplanes by World War I. While Japanese army and navy air units dominated Pacific skies early in World War II, they failed to maintain their technical leadership because of the country's limited industrial capacity (never more than 10 percent that of the United States). Japan had counted on winning a short war, and lost a longer one.

The first Japanese military flying took place in 1910, and the country's first aircraft factory, Nakajima, was founded in 1916. The following year Mitsubishi and Kawasaki followed suit. But other than some action in China against weak German colonies, Japan's air units saw little air action during World War I.

Japan did not have an independent air force during World War II, but rather the Imperial Japanese Army Air Force was part of the army while the navy maintained its own air capability (similar to American practice at the time). Each service began the war with about 1,500 fighters and bombers, though the naval air arm was the more important, larger, and better equipped. Banking on a short war, Japan cut back on training new pilots. The Battle of Midway (1942) cost Japan's navy four carriers and hundreds of pilots and aircraft, a loss from which the naval air arm never fully recovered. The Japanese stressed radio silence in its aircraft and thus there was little voice traffic, and what did take place was typically on one channel (unlike the multichannel U.S. aircraft radios), which was easy for a busy pilot to use. Japanese aircraft often relied more on radio telegraphy (code) than on voice, because it had greater range. The risk with the single channel was that it could be and was easily jammed. Radio tubes were generally of American design, manufactured under license before the war began.

Sadly for the Japanese war effort, neither the army nor the naval air units appear to have cooperated with the other on any level. Two examples make this clear. The army used a numerical code for its aircraft communications while naval aviation used Japanese characters—this was never standardized and harmed joint operations. And the two services used different electrical systems so that attempts at identification, friend or foe procedures often failed. The lack of standardization extended to radios. Radio equipment for the air forces of the army and navy alike was compact and generally well made (especially after 1943), though ease of serviceability was often lacking. Radios were small, simple, and light. Transmitters and receivers were often designed for use in specific aircraft rather than along standardized lines. Yet sometimes it appeared as though radio design did not take into account the type of aircraft being used. Aircraft-manufacturer electrical engineers knew little about radio, which did not help matters.

Operationally, aircraft radio left something to be desired, however. Japanese naval aircraft, for example, suffered from high noise levels, making receiving difficult or impossible. Operation of the receivers was difficult because of how the apparatus was placed, and adjustments were difficult. Considerable use was made of earlier American and other designs, though there was little sign of quantity production. Some smaller aircraft lacked any radio equipment, and most Japanese fighters lacked radar even toward the end of the war. Japan's industrial capacity, reeling under increasing American bombing, was unable to produce improved aircraft or radio designs after about 1943, let alone adequately maintain those it had, further hampering air action.

Out of desperation as the Pacific war turned against it, Japan turned to harsh tactics that relied on blind loyalty rather than its declining technology. The first kamikaze (suicide) attack on American warships took place in the late 1944 battle for the Philippines. Suicide pilots had to fly at low altitudes to avoid U.S. radar and were thus vulnerable to anti-aircraft fire. Radios were

usually left off the one-way flights as unnecessary weight.

For a decade after its surrender, Japan had no active air force of any kind. Growing out of rising Cold War tensions, however, Japan began to develop its postwar air force in 1952, and the Japanese Air Self Defense Force was created on 1 July 1954. A year later the Japanese Maritime Self Defense Force received its first naval aircraft. Both made extensive use of American aircraft, radio, and avionics equipment.

Christopher H. Sterling

See also Airplanes; Identification, Friend or Foe (IFF); Japan: Army; Japan: Navy (*Nippon Teikoku Kaigun*); Midway, Battle of (3–6 June 1942); World War II

Sources
Howard, William L. "Collection of Japanese W.W.II Military Radios." [Online information; retrieved April 2006.] http://www.armyradio.com/arsc/customer/pages.php?pageurl=/publish/Articles/William_Howard_Japan/Collection_Of_Japanese_Radios.htm.
Lange, Steve. 1996. "The Imperial Japanese Navy Air Force in the Pacific War." [Online article; retrieved June 2006.] http://www.combinedfleet.com/ijnaf.htm.
Mikesh, Robert C. 2004. "Radio Equipment." In *Japanese Aircraft Equipment 1940–1945*, 72–99. Atglen, PA: Schiffer.
War Department. 1944. "'Airborne' Signal Equipment." In *Handbook on Japanese Military Forces*, Technical Manual TM-E 30-480 (September), 312–322. Washington, DC: Government Printing Office.

Japan: Army

Japan has a longer history of organized fighting forces than most countries. After a long feudal period that ended in the late nineteenth century, the country's military was rapidly modernized. After 1900, Japan made effective use of radio and developed sophisticated ciphers to protect its military communications.

For centuries feudal warriors on Japanese battlefields were identified with symbols, crests, banners, or markings on armor to identify on which side a warrior fought. By the mid-sixteenth century, flags and banners came in a wide variety of styles, sizes, shapes, and colors. Where once only higher-ranking samurai and commanders had standards (flags), lower-ranking warriors also wore flags to communicate their unit or division, along with their clan or lord. Armies were growing larger and the number of clans present had increased as well. This profusion of banners meant that commanders had to have especially large and noticeable standards to identify their location; warriors needed to know where to rally around, whose orders to follow—and what those orders were. The role of standard bearer was one of the most dangerous (and thus one of the most honorable) positions on a battlefield. While all this helped morale, it could also identify key figures for potential enemy attack.

Japanese armies made extensive use of drums, horns, gongs, and bells to announce the call to battle, to set marching pace, and for a number of other basic commands. Conch shells were used as trumpets or horns, and a complex system of calls came into use. Many shell blowers (*yamabushi*) were renowned for their skill and were hired into feudal armies as trumpeters. On the other hand, gongs and bells were rarely brought onto the battlefield. Rather, they would be used at camp to rouse forces to battle or to signal warnings of approaching enemies. For example, one bell could mean to stop eating, the second to put on armor, and the third to move out toward the battlefield.

Communications were necessary between battles as well. As occurred in other countries, one leader set up a system of fire beacons across his province so as to receive notification as soon as his rival made a move. But records suggest the system could be used but once: Wooden towers were filled with flammable material, and as each was lit, the next, some distance away, would see the signal and light its own. The message was sent but the system disappeared (though it could be rebuilt). Couriers were also widely used—with a useful twist for self-preservation of courier and message. A written message might end with "the messenger will provide further details." By not putting the entire message into writing, the messenger enjoyed an element of protection from those who might otherwise kill him to steal the signal.

The late nineteenth-century arrival of huge industrial and political changes in Japan dramatically altered military communications as well. French and German advisers after 1870 helped to create Asia's most modern army. The Imperial Japanese Army (formed in 1873) was directed by a general headquarters with a number of professional bureaus (the third of which included communications responsibilities). A quasi-military signal unit was deployed in 1877, during the Seinan Rebellion; the first fully military signals unit was organized two years later, and in 1880 the army appointed a signal engineer. The signal unit was abolished in 1887 when signal training commenced in the engineers corps. During the Sino-Japanese War (1894–1895), seven field signal units, three signal zone units, and one special signal unit were mobilized. A signal training unit opened in 1902. In the Russo-Japanese War (1904–1905), Japan demonstrated it could apply Western technology, discipline, strategy, and tactics to beat a

European power. Twenty signal companies, seven zone signal companies, and two special signal companies were mobilized. More than 140,000 miles of line were laid, with 883 telegraph terminals and twenty-nine telephone exchanges. A signal battalion was created in 1907. A study committee for wireless communications was established in 1910 and a signal battalion was reorganized with eight telegraph companies.

In World War I, Japan played a limited role in hostilities, but did take over former German colonies in China and the Pacific, thus stretching its communication links. For example, the Japanese Siberia Expedition of 1918 included two field signal companies, a zone signal company, and two wireless companies. A signal school opened in 1924. During the Manchurian Incident of 1931, three signal battalions were involved. More signal units were created during the Sino-Japanese hostilities of 1937. During 1939, a fourth signal regiment was raised. The corps separated from the engineers in 1941, becoming an independent organization. Many additional signal units were formed during World War II.

From 1941 to 1945, Japanese forces operated across a huge area of Asia and the Pacific, making the need for effective communications paramount. Where possible in local battle areas, Japanese military units relied on wired communication (telephone, telegraph), using radio as a secondary mode of transmission for short-term or over long-distance and water links. This lowered the danger of being overheard by the enemy. Equipment designs during the war (usually numbered in accordance with the Japanese year) rarely changed and usually reflected technology of the late 1930s. Radio transmitters, virtually all amplitude modulated, were often small (many could be carried by

one man) except those intended for headquarters use. Most could be operated with batteries and were well made. In addition to wired and wireless electronic means, Japanese forces also used pigeons, dogs, horns and whistles, and pyrotechnic signals for battlefield operations.

Japan did not have much success with wartime signals intelligence. While army cryptographers broke into some low-grade Chinese and American (U.S. Army Air Force) codes, they did not succeed in breaking any high-grade ciphers of any of the Allies. They did, however, carefully monitor Allied radio traffic in the various Pacific theaters of war (learning the frequencies and call signs of B-29 bombers, for example), and from that traffic analysis they were able to make some inferences as to Allied unit locations and plans, and though less often, aims and timing of specific raids. Playing on this, the Allied forces would send false, deceptive transmissions, of which the Japanese often fell afoul. On the other hand, Allied code breakers had considerable success breaking into many Japanese army codes.

On the Manchurian front at the very end of the war (August 1945), the Soviet attack found the Japanese suffering poor communications throughout its Kwangtung Army. Army headquarters possessed no means of military communication. Heavy reliance on public telephone lines proved to be detrimental when the phone lines were disrupted at the beginning of the Soviet invasion. As a result, the Japanese headquarters had little command and control available over its Kwangtung Army, which collapsed under heavy Soviet pressure.

For nearly a decade after World War II, Japan fielded only domestic police forces. The Japan Ground Self Defense Forces were created shortly after the end of U.S. occupation in mid-1954. They are now among the most technologically advanced armed forces, and Japan's military expenditures are the seventh highest in the world. Japan's booming electronics industry has no trouble providing whatever communications equipment is needed. According to the terms of the Treaty of Mutual Cooperation and Security signed in 1960, Japan relies on the United States for defense and hosts a number of American military bases.

Christopher H. Sterling and Cliff Lord

See also Code Breaking; Deception; Flags; Magic; Medieval Military Signaling (500–1500 CE); Music Signals; Signals Intelligence (SIGINT); World War II

Sources

Bennett, J. W., et al. 1986. *Intelligence and Cryptanalytic Activities of the Japanese During World War II.* Laguna Hills, CA: Aegean Park Press (reprint of 1945 classified original report).

Harries, Meirion, and Susie Harries. 1991. *Soldiers of the Sun: The Rise and Fall of the Japanese Imperial Army.* New York: Random House.

Howard, William L. "Collection of Japanese W.W.II Military Radios." [Online information; retrieved April 2006.] http://www.armyradio.com/arsc/customer/pages.php?pageurl=/publish/Articles/William_Howard_Japan/Collection_Of_Japanese_Radios.htm.

War Department. 1944. *Japanese Radio Communications Equipment*, Technical Manual TM-E 11-227A (December). Washington, DC: Government Printing Office.

War Department. 1944. "Signal Equipment." In *Handbook on Japanese Military Forces*, Technical Manual TM-E 30-480 (September), 303–322. Washington, DC: Government Printing Office.

Wikipedia. "Military Communication of Feudal Japan." [Online information; retrieved April 2006.] http://en.wikipedia.org/wiki/Military_Communication_of_Feudal_Japan.

Japan: Navy (*Nippon Teikoku Kaigun*)

As an island nation, Japan's navy and merchant marine trade dominated much of the country's military thinking and technology for the first half of the twentieth century. Generally Japan's naval communications were among the worlds' best, save for the final months of World War II.

The Imperial Japanese Navy was created in 1869 as part of the nation's modernization, though it remained largely a coastal defense force for the next two decades. The 1905 Battle of Tsushima demonstrated to the world Japanese growth and prowess when it demolished a Russian squadron—winning the battle in part by a far more effective use of its use of wireless communications. Japan relied on British and then French ship designs and naval advice but steadily turned to Japanese yards and equipment manufacturers by the start of World War I.

During World War I, Japan focused on the Pacific, first against German colonies and naval units, and then against Germany's commerce raiders through 1917. Japanese naval units helped escort Allied convoys to the Middle East. All of this widespread activity gave naval signals personnel considerable experience. In the 1920s, already ranked as the third largest fleet in the world, the navy began to focus on building a powerful fleet to fight the United States for supremacy in the Pacific. At the same time the country's electronics industry was developing, enabling improved naval communications systems.

Japan entered World War II with what appeared to be huge advantages. It had a large and battle-tested fleet far in excess of any of the Allies. It had more carriers and naval aircraft and well-trained crews. But having to fight to defend its own sea trade routes as well as battling with the United States, Japan was on the road to defeat within less than two years. One key factor was its lack of industrial capacity compared to the United States. In such technologies as radio and radar Japan could not keep up with U.S. developments. By 1943–1944, Japan was producing probably less than 10 percent of U.S. production in electronics and communications gear, and Japan's radio designs were by then increasingly obsolete. Naval forces suffered accordingly.

The Fourth Section of Japan's Naval General Staff focused on fleet communications and code-breaking efforts. (Confusingly, there was also a separate Communications Department in the navy; it was concerned with the training and allocation of radio operators.) Japan's navy made wide use of cipher machines to protect its vital long-distance communication. These were known to the Allies using a color code, such as the "Jade" or "Coral" or, ultimately, "Purple" machines. The machines used a series of rotors and selector switches or plugs to encipher and decipher top secret messages. On the other end of the technology scale, Japan also made effective use of radio silence—as with the naval task force that attacked Pearl Harbor—to confuse Allied efforts.

In the postwar years, the Japanese Maritime Self Defense Force, formed a decade after the war's end, by the early 2000s had grown to once again be the world's third largest naval force. Its communication links are among the best in the world, relying substantially on the country's extensive electronics industry.

Christopher H. Sterling

See also Code Breaking; Deception; Japan: Air Force; Magic; Midway, Battle of (3–6 June 1942); Radio Silence; Signals Intelligence

(SIGINT); Tsushima, Battle of (27–28 May 1905); World War II

Sources

Evans, David C., and Mark R. Peattie. 1997. *Kaigun: Strategy, Tactics, and Technology in the Imperial Japanese Navy, 1887–1941.* Annapolis, MD: Naval Institute Press.

Howard, William L. "Collection of Japanese W.W.II Military Radios." [Online information; retrieved April 2006.] http://www.armyradio.com/arsc/customer/pages.php?pageurl=/publish/Articles/William_Howard_Japan/Collection_Of_Japanese_Radios.htm.

Operational History of Japanese Naval Communications, Dec. 1941–Aug. 1945. Walnut Creek, CA: Aegean Park Press (reprinting a 1946 U.S. Government study).

Whitlock, Duane L. 1995. "The Silent War Against the Japanese Navy." *Naval War College Review* Autumn: 43–52.

Joint Assault Signal Company (JASCO)

In late 1943, the U.S. Joint Chiefs of Staff created a new organization designed to provide improved communications links between land, sea, and air forces during amphibious operations. The Joint Assault Signal Company (JASCO) was formed by adding the naval shore fire control and Army Air Force air liaison parties—which had been too small to be independent units—to special Army signal companies that had handled communications for shore battalions since the summer of 1942. The JASCO was commanded by an Army major because it was much larger than a normal signal company, with an authorization of between 500 and 600 Army, Navy, and Army Air Force personnel. These men were to implement common communications procedures to enable all services to effectively communicate during an amphibious assault.

These procedures included planning for joint radio frequencies, message transmission procedures, coordination for close air support, and control of naval gunfire against shore targets.

The JASCO did not function as an integral unit during operations. When an amphibious landing occurred the various JASCO teams would be attached to the appropriate divisional units needing support. Air liaison teams (each consisting of one officer and three enlisted men, all members of the Air Force) would be attached to battalion and regimental headquarters and to division headquarters. Naval shore fire control teams (two officers, five enlisted men) would be attached to each battalion landing team (the combat battalion and its support units). Communications teams, made up of Army Signal Corps men, would be assigned to each shore battalion to provide radio and wire links between shore battalions and their shore parties, supply dumps, and evacuation stations. Once the situation stabilized and command and control established for the units responsible for sustained ground operations, the JASCO teams would be recalled and evacuated to prepare for the next amphibious operation.

During World War II eleven JASCOs were created that served in the European, Central Pacific, and Southwest Pacific theaters. Three JASCOs were operating on the beaches of Normandy during the landings in June 1944. A platoon of the 294th JASCO provided the only communication system available on Omaha Beach until noon, when other communications units were able to begin operations. At Kwajalein Atoll, a JASCO attached to the 4th Marine Division improved artillery, air, and naval coordination to a great extent. On Iwo Jima, artillery, naval, and air coordination was described as superb due to

JASCO. On hotly contested beaches, such as Saipan, JASCO casualties were often very high, because the men could not provide for their own protection and still carry out their communications missions.

Wherever JASCOs were employed, congestion of radio circuits was reduced and dependable communications were provided for air-ground-sea operations. After World War II, the JASCOs were eliminated and replaced by the air and naval gunfire liaison companies of the Marine Corps. The JASCOs had proven indispensable in linking air, ground, and naval communications during complex joint operations during World War II.

Steven J. Rauch

See also Radio; World War II

Sources

Raines, Rebecca Robbins. 1996. *Getting the Message Through: A Branch History of the US Army Signal Corps*. Washington, DC: Army Center of Military History.

Thompson, George Raynor, and Dixie R. Harris. 1966. *The Signal Corps: The Outcome (Mid-1943 Through 1945)*. Washington, DC: Center for Military History.

Joint Tactical Information Distribution System (JTIDS)

The Joint Tactical Information Distribution System (JTIDS) provides the American military services with theater command-and-control abilities using a secure, high-capacity data link communications system for tactical combat. It uses L-band frequencies (960–1215 MHz) and can handle large amounts of data at high speed. It supplies integrated information distribution, position location, and identification capabilities. Its resistance to jamming and use of data encryption make the JTIDS a remarkably secure network system. The JTIDS provides computer-to-computer connectivity for any military platform—its terminals are found on Navy submarines, Air Force fighters, and Airborne Warning and Control System planes. Its maximum range is between 300 and 500 miles.

The development of the JTIDS began in 1981 with development contracts from the Department of Defense with Singer-Kearfott (later GEC-Marconi Electronic Systems). It is now carried out by Data Link Solutions, a joint company formed in 1996 by BAE Systems Electronics & Integrated Solutions and Rockwell Collins. Multiservice operational testing was completed in 1996 and implementation for the multibillion dollar program took place beginning in 1998.

The JTIDS is a decentralized navigation and communication system as it does not depend on any central location. Instead, each user, as a member of a specific group, independently determines his or her own position. The JTIDS architecture is based on a complex structure of data transmission. It uses a time division multiple access technique, which enables numerous users to exchange information at specific time intervals. However, this exchange is always limited by the length of available time slots and the size of the information package to be transmitted. JTIDS terminals automatically broadcast outgoing messages at predesignated and repeated intervals. Reede-Salomon error-correction mode secures undistorted data transmission against enemy disruption.

The JTIDS is a communication component of a wider North Atlantic Treaty Organization (NATO) data radio network, Link-16, which is also known in the United States as Tactical Digital Information Link type J (TADIL J). Link-16 aims to provide improved communication of information granting U.S. forces situation awareness (dominant battlespace knowledge). Indeed, Link-16 is at times used as a synonym for JTIDS. Sometimes it is referred to as being basically a protocol providing integrated software for data processing. More precisely, it is more than a data link; it is a tactical system providing communication, navigation, and identification. Link-16 was used extensively and proved its effectiveness for the first time during the Gulf War (1990–1991). Being primarily a data network, Link-16 also provides premium voice communication service. For advanced security, both the data and the transmissions are encrypted. One of the crucial features of the security system of Link-16 is frequency hopping—terminals are constantly changing transmitting channels according to a specific pattern. Frequency hopping, along with jitter and pseudo-random noise added to the waveform, prevents jamming and makes the signal exceptionally difficult to detect. Thanks to technical and operational improvements (e.g., jam resistance, improved security, increased amount of information reporting, reduced terminal size), as well as the increased number of participants, Link-16 enables transmission of up to three times more tactical information than its predecessor, Link-11 (also known as TDL A or TADIL A), which was based on 1960s technology.

Link-16 is being employed not only by the U.S. Army but also by some other NATO members and Japan. It is currently the Pentagon's key tactical data exchange system for command, control, and intelligence for each of the military services.

Łukasz Kamieński

See also Airborne Warning and Control System (AWACS); Gulf War (1990–1991); Jamming; Joint Tactical Radio System (JTRS); Mobile

Communications; North Atlantic Treaty Organization (NATO) Communications & Information Systems Agency; Radio; Spread Spectrum

Sources

Federation of American Scientists. "Tactical Digital Information Links (TADIL). [Online information; retrieved December 2006.] http://www.fas.org/irp/program/disseminate/tadil.htm.

Lockheed Martin. "Tactical Data Links—MIDS/JTIDS Link 16, and Variable Message Format—VMF." [Online information; retrieved December 2006.] http://www.stasys.co.uk/defence/datalinks/link_16.htm.

Joint Tactical Radio System (JTRS)

The Joint Tactical Radio System (JTRS, or "Jitters" in Pentagon terminology) is a software-based gateway allowing interoperability of different radio equipment. Focused on tactical battlefield needs and developed as part of the larger Global Information Grid in the early 2000s, JTRS is designed to replace existing separate systems that do not operate well together. Development of civilian software-defined radio equipment made the initiative possible.

JTRS development began in 1997, and the first systems (some 250,000 software-defined radios [SDRs] for the Army's ground vehicles and helicopters) are to be in operation by 2007 at an initial development cost of $14 billion. The new SDRs will number but a third of those being replaced and will require far less maintenance. While the system is being developed centrally for all services, each service is developing its own radios for use within JTRS. The new equipment will integrate voice, data, and video communications links, while providing interoperability with existing radio systems. Spectrum segments used will range from 2 MHz to above 2 GHz.

Procurement of the JTRS system is being phased in clusters to allow incorporation of the latest technologies. The first cluster (initiated in 2002) is for Army and Marine Corps vehicle and helicopter radio; cluster two (initiated in 2003) is for handheld devices; cluster three is for Navy maritime and fixed-site radio systems (initiated in 2003); and cluster four for Air Force and naval airborne radios (initiated in 2003). Cluster 5 (approved in 2003, and led by the Army) focuses on a variety of portable, backpack, and handheld devices. Through each of these clusters—and those yet to be defined—JTRS development includes such goals as effective use of open system architecture, cost-effective utilization of commercial off-the-shelf technology, waveform portability, software reuse, interoperability both with existing legacy communications systems (backward compatibility) and across all JTRS equipment, and the ability to constantly update technology.

Perhaps the best way to understand the aims of the JTRS program is to look at what is being replaced. By the time JTRS is fully in place, one integrated SDR system should replace (or in some cases integrate) three-quarters of a million radios now found in twenty-five to thirty legacy systems (navigation, positioning, location, identification, air-to-ground, air-to-air, ground-to-ground, and satellite communications). These legacy systems date from the 1980s (largely hardware defined, using single channels and requiring regular hardware upgrades) and 1990s (software defined by specific vendors and often not interchangeable, using multiple frequency bands, and updated by software rather than hardware).

All of this comes at a high cost—something approaching $7 billion, or about $40,000 per JTRS radio unit when all the development and managerial costs are included. And the program faces steep technical problems. The desire to use a single antenna for different wavelengths makes it difficult to pull in strong signals across the spectrum. An amplifier working the whole spectrum uses much more electrical power than one tuned for a specific frequency band. And waveforms and transmissions that are speedily handled by analog systems are much tougher to achieve with digital computation. These and related drawbacks have placed the program's future in some doubt.

Christopher H. Sterling

See also Army Battle Command System (ABCS); Future Combat Systems (FCS); Global Information Grid (GIG); Warfigher Information Network–Tactical (WIN-T); World Wide Military Command and Control System (WWMCCS)

Sources

Government Accountability Office. 2004. *Challenges and Risks Associated with the Joint Tactical Radio System Program*. [Online report; retrieved March 2006.] http://www.gao .gov/new.items/d03879r.pdf.
Government Accountability Office. 2004. *Defense Acquisitions: The Global Information Grid and Challenges Facing Its Implementation*. [Online report; retrieved March 2006.] http://www.gao.gov/new.items/d04858 .pdf.
Joint Tactical Radio System. Home page. [Online information; retrieved March 2006.] http://jtrs.army.mil/sections/technical information/fset_technical_sca.html.

Joint Task Force–Global Network Operations (JTF-GNO)

The Joint Task Force–Global Network Operations (JTF-GNO), based in Arlington, Virginia, is the U.S. Department of Defense's operational unit charged with securing the military's information infrastructure and prosecuting offensive information warfare operations.

The JTF-GNO coordinates and controls all aspects of defense information infrastructure protection. To this end, an array of service-specific units interact with and report to the JTF-GNO including the Defense Information Systems Agency, the Computer Emergency Response Team, as well as the 1st Information Operations Command, the Navy Component Task Force–Computer Network Defense, the Air Force Forces–Computer Network Operations, and Marine Forces–Integrated Network Operations, all dedicated to protecting the information infrastructure of their respective services. The JTF-GNO directs these assets to meet threats to defense information networks.

In December 1998, responding to the hacking of U.S. military networks and the lax state of network defense revealed by exercises such as "Eligible Receiver" (1997) and the "Solar Sunrise" event (1998), the Department of Defense set up the Joint Task Force–Computer Network Defense to protect defense information infrastructure. In December 2000, the Department of Defense established the Joint Task Force–Computer Network Attack with the mission to plan and, if necessary, conduct offensive network operations as directed by the government. Both task forces were placed under the direction of the U.S. Space Command.

These task forces were merged in April 2001, renamed Joint Task Force–Computer Network Operations (JTF-CNO), and placed under the army's Strategic Command (now Network Enterprise Technology Command). This was partially prompted by a number of governmental reports about the potential militarization of the Internet by strategic rivals such as China. The unity of command created by this merger would better prepare the United States to face the threats posed by asymmetrical warfare in the post–Cold War era.

In 2004, the JTF-CNO was renamed Joint Task Force–Global Network Operations. The renaming and reassignment of the JTF-GNO from JTF-CNO reflects the awareness of the military that its ongoing overseas operations rely on public infrastructure. The JTF-GNO's mission to protect the Global Information Grid underscores the new reality of extended overseas operations and the reliance of the U.S. military on information networks to create battlefield information dominance.

John Laprise

See also Defense Information Systems Agency (DISA); Global Information Grid (GIG); Information Revolution in Military Affairs (IRMA); National Communications System (NCS); Network Enterprise Technology Command (NETCOM); Strategic Communications Command (STRATCOM)

Sources

Bendrath, Ralf. 2003. "The American Cyber-Angst and the Real World—Any Link?" In *Bombs and Bandwidth: The Emerging Relationship Between Information Technology and Security,* edited by Robert Latham, 49–73. New York: The New Press.
Denning, Dorothy. 2003. "Cyber Security as an Emergent Infrastructure." In *Bombs and Bandwidth: The Emerging Relationship Between Information Technology and Security,* edited by Robert Latham, 25–48. New York: The New Press.
Rattray, Gregory J. 2001. *Strategic Warfare in Cyberspace.* Cambridge, MA: MIT Press.

"Jungle Telegraph"

The widely used term "jungle telegraph" has been applied to many different things during the twentieth century—depending on who is talking and what period is being dealt with. The phrase may have been applied first to the native use of drums in Africa in the late nineteenth and early twentieth centuries. Messages could be sent considerable distances in a fairly short space of time, simply by "talking drum" signals, a kind of signaling system. This was also called the bush telegraph or even (in mid-nineteenth century United States) grapevine telegraph, each of the terms applying the then-new electric telegraph to ancient means of communication. Only on occasion was a specifically military application intended.

Another early use was in Brazil, early in the twentieth century. A jungle telegraph line, formally termed the Strategic Telegraph Line, was built from Mato Grosso north to Amazonas and was one of the first breakthroughs in penetrating the *sertão*, or "backlands." It was constructed between 1907 and 1915 by a government commission headed by an explorer and army engineer, Colonel Candido Mariano da Silva Rondon. Rondon directed the work of the army officers and penal battalions who did the actual work. Telegraph relay stations consisted of a group of straw huts, which were located some 50 or 75 miles from the nearest neighbors on either side. After his 1913–1914 Brazilian expedition, former U.S. President Theodore Roosevelt told a press conference in New York that he had never seen, or knew of, a project equal to the Strategic Telegraph Line. With the introduction of radiotelegraphy, however, the telegraph line soon became obsolete. Its one enduring contribution was access to new settlement regions, for the men who built the line cleared a path about 40 meters wide through the jungle—roughly double the height of the surrounding forest—so that trees would not fall on the telegraph installations. Rudimentary as it was, it was the first overland connection between southern Brazil's population centers and the western Amazon's rich rubber country.

A very different meaning developed in later years. Concern for the "jungle telegraph" was one of the first lessons taught at the military school training to combat tracker teams for guerrilla warfare in Vietnam. Drawing on lessons learned from the British in Malaysia and the French in Vietnam, American forces were trained to move in a stealthy fashion. As one American later described it, one could not touch any small trees as their motion would be a tip-off to enemy troops. In other words, the moving foliage would "telegraph" the troops' location.

Widespread slang usage of the term usually indicates informal modes of communication—a given group of people who know something has happened (or is about to) thanks to word getting around via the so-called jungle telegraph or grapevine. Some have suggested that the Internet is the newest jungle telegraph for organizing action or positions on issues. The term used this way connotes a quiet, informal, or even clandestine mode of communication, whether of military value or not.

Christopher H. Sterling

See also Music Signals; Telegraph; Vietnam War (1959–1975)

Sources

Gall, Norman. 1978. "Letter from Rhondônia: Part II—Strategic Reach." New York: American Universities Field Staff Reports.
Rodgers, Sue. 2001. "Combat Tracker Teams: Dodging an Elusive Enemy." [Online article; retrieved September 2005.] http://www.uswardogs.org/id153.html.

Jutland, Battle of (1916)

The Battle of Jutland (31 May–1 June 1916) was the central naval battle of World War I, as well as the most important engagement involving battleships. The battle was a direct outcome of the early twentieth-century naval rivalry between Germany and Britain, as the former sought to develop a battleship and battle cruiser force to rival that of the latter. Thanks to a furious building program, Britain's Grand Fleet remained larger than Germany's High Seas Fleet when war began in 1914. Both fleets shadowed one another in the first two years of the war as the Royal Navy sought to blockade the German coast and bottle up her naval force.

After months of sparring, raiding, and small engagements (during several of which, British signals experience left much to be desired), elements of the two fleets met off the coast of Jutland (Denmark) in the North Sea on the afternoon of 31 May, and action lasted into the next day. Communications systems and their application played a significant role at Jutland. Indeed, the British fleet, commanded by Admiral John Jellicoe, began the battle with a significant advantage. Thanks to the 1914 capture of codebooks from the German cruiser *Magdeburg*, the British Admiralty's Room 40 had long been able to read German wireless communications. Intercepts of German wireless gave notice that the High Seas fleet had sailed, but due to poor communications between the Admiralty and the fleet, made little effective use of this information.

In the fighting itself, the British ships made heavy use of signals of various kinds—nearly 900 of them, or more than one per minute at the height of fighting. A British seaplane was the first aircraft in history to transmit reports on enemy ship movements, but weather conditions limited further flights. On the other hand, during the action, the Royal Navy relied perhaps too heavily on traditional flag communication among ships, which was often compromised by difficult conditions—increasing gun smoke, the distance between ships, the large number of ships involved, sea conditions, and eventual darkness, all of which contributed to inept signaling or misunderstood signals. Night signaling by color lights was poor and often compromised by enemy interception. As Jellicoe himself later commented, the German system of recognition signals was excellent, while that of the Royal Navy was practically nil.

In too many instances, British messages were either not received at all or were noted late or misconstrued. Wireless telegraphy was not utilized as effectively as it should have been to back up flag signals, especially on Admiral David Beatty's flagship, the *Lion*. Most seriously impacting the outcome of Jutland, captains and other senior officers of participating British vessels failed to keep their fleet commanders sufficiently informed of enemy ship sightings and action. All concerned seemed to presume that others knew more than they in fact did.

In the years of analysis and controversy that followed, signals effectiveness was one focus of discussion. While intership communication within the Royal Navy seemed strong, links with the Admiralty intelligence offices were poor, and individual ship commanders did not keep fleet commanders adequately informed of events. Though more British ships were sunk and they suffered the heaviest casualties, the British tactical defeat somewhat masked their strategic victory as the German High Seas Fleet did not venture out in strength for the rest of World War I.

Marc L. Schwartz and Christopher H. Sterling

See also Code, Codebook; Code Breaking; Flaghoist; Flags; Flagship; Radio; Room 40; Signals Intelligence (SIGINT); United Kingdom: Royal Navy; World War I

Sources

Campbell, John. 1998. *Jutland: An Analysis of the Fighting.* New York: Lyons Press.

Kent, Barrie. 1993. "Jutland." In *Signal! A History of Signalling in the Royal Navy,* 49–66. Clanfield, UK: Hyden House.

Massie, Robert K. 2003. "Jutland." In *Castles of Steel: Britain, Germany, and the Winning of the Great War at Sea,* 553–684. New York: Random House.

Steel, Nigel, and Peter Hart. 2003. *Jutland 1916: Death in the Grey Wastes.* London: Casell.

Yates, Keith. 2000. *Flawed Victory: Jutland, 1916.* Annapolis, MD: Naval Institute Press.

Kilby, Jack St. Clair (1923–2005) and Noyce, Robert Norton (1927–1990)

Jack Kilby and Robert Noyce share the invention of the silicon chip, or integrated circuit, which forms the heart of all modern solid state electronics devices, both military and civilian. Working for different companies located in Texas and California, they independently developed the gist of the idea in 1958–1959. Kilby's patent was granted first by five months, but Noyce's device, the "planar" integrated circuit, would come to dominate the semiconductor market. After years of litigation, the two companies (Texas Instruments and Fairchild Semiconductor) agreed to cross-license their devices.

Jack Kilby was born 8 November 1923 in Jefferson City, Missouri. He earned his bachelor of science degree in electrical engineering from the University of Illinois (1947) and master of science degree in the same field from the University Wisconsin (1950). He joined Texas Instruments (TI) in 1958, and on 12 September demonstrated an early version of what would become the microchip, centerpiece of future integrated circuits.

Kilby went on to pioneer military, industrial, and commercial applications of microchip technology. He headed teams that built both the first military system and the first computer incorporating integrated circuits. He later co-invented both the handheld calculator and the thermal printer that was used in portable data terminals. He retired from TI in 1983, but continued to teach at Texas A&M University. In 2000, Kilby, who held sixty patents, was awarded the Nobel Prize in Physics for his role in innovating the chip. He died 20 June 2005 in Dallas.

Robert Noyce was born in Burlington, Iowa, on 12 December 1927. He graduated with a bachelor of arts degree in physics from Grinnell College (Iowa) in 1949 and a doctor of philosophy degree from Massachusetts Institute of Technology in 1953.

After making transistors for Philco, Noyce began work at Shockley Semiconductor in 1956. He and several others left to form Fairchild Semiconductor in 1957, where he served as research director. In January 1959 Noyce made his first detailed notes about a complete solid state circuit. Six months later Noyce created an integrated circuit made of silicon. He and Gordon Moore left to found

Integrated Electronics (Intel) in 1968, and Noyce served as president until 1975. He eventually held sixteen patents. Often called the "mayor" of Silicon Valley, which he did so much to create, Noyce died in Austin, Texas, on 3 June 1990.

The importance of both men's accomplishments is that they found a common solution to how best to move electronics to the post-transistor stage with the monolithic (formed from a single crystal) integrated circuit. Instead of designing and assembling smaller components as had been the practice to that point, they both found ways to fabricate entire networks of discrete components in a single sequence by laying them into a single crystal (chip) of semiconductor material. Kilby used germanium and Noyce used silicon—and the latter became the most widely accepted material.

Christopher H. Sterling

See also Miniaturization; Solid State Electronics; Transistor

Sources

Berlin, Leslie. 2005. *The Man Behind the Microchip: Robert Noyce and the Invention of Silicon Valley.* New York: Oxford University Press.

Reid, T. R. 1985. *The Chip: How Two Americans Invented the Microchip and Launched a Revolution.* New York: Simon and Schuster.

Riordan, Michael, and Lillian Hoddeson. 1997. *Crystal Fire: The Birth of the Information Age.* New York: Norton.

Wolfe, Tom. 1983. "The Tinkerings of Robert Noyce: How the Sun Rose on the Silicon Valley." *Esquire* December: 346–374.

Korean War (1950–1953)

The North Korean attack on South Korea on 25 June 1950 caught the United States off guard in military communications as in every other aspect of the ensuing war. The U.S. Army had only a few soldiers in South Korea as members of the Korean Military Assistance Group, and they possessed only twelve radio stations. The Republic of Korea (ROK) had a fair communications system, but most of its facilities were centered in Seoul, which the enemy captured in the first days of fighting.

America's Far East Command (FEC), based in Tokyo under General Douglas MacArthur, was little better off. Communications units were under-strength and sometimes ill trained; years of low military budgets and cushy occupation duties in Japan had taken a toll on Army preparedness. MacArthur's principal force in Japan was the Eighth Army. In prewar maneuvers much of its communications equipment got wet and dirty, had not been properly cleaned and stored, and therefore had deteriorated. There were also shortages of basic equipment and spare parts.

Fortunately Korea had a once-magnificent underground telegraph system, the famous Mukden Cable, running from Tokyo to the southern ROK port of Pusan (soon to become the U.S. Army's major supply base) and then north. Built by the Japanese while they controlled Korea (1910–1945), the cable had also deteriorated. As it was immobile it served strategic rather than immediate tactical needs. Nevertheless, it proved vital as Eighth Army communicators entered combat.

Invaluable to Eighth Army survival was the prewar Operation Roll-Up. Much World War II communications equipment had been abandoned all over the Pacific. A good deal had been properly mothballed, and was collected and stockpiled in Japan in 1949–1950. FEC and Eighth Army lived off this equipment during the early, desperate months of the Korean War. The equipment was not enough, however, to save the first of Eighth Army's divisions to enter the conflict; it was badly mauled in July 1950, partly because of inadequate communications. The division's signal company had been split up, with some of its members being detached to perform a strategic theater function (the provision of stopgap communications between Tokyo and Pusan) and thus was not available when the unit entered action. Elsewhere many signalmen were pressed into the fighting as infantry.

As more Eighth Army divisions entered battle in July–August 1950, the Signal Corps discovered just how ramshackle American military communications had become. Radios were increasingly vital because the swift movements of American divisions (actually, retreats during those months) made it difficult for wire layers to keep up. Few in number as they were, these divisions had to stretch their fronts far beyond what they had been trained and equipped to cover, especially in terms of radio ranges. Hastily laid wire, when it could keep up, was vulnerable to artillery fire, tank treads (friendly as well as enemy), and the scavenging of Korean civilian refugees, who cut up wire to serve as harnesses for their packs; indeed American soldiers were guilty of that practice in their precipitous retreat.

Eighth Army also found that its headquarters signal equipment was inadequate to handle its own divisions, let alone ROK units under its command. Like any field army, Eighth Army should have had two or more subordinate field corps headquarters to coordinate its multitude of divisions. However, corps headquarters had been eliminated before the war as an economy measure. Eighth Army signalmen were also expected to provide communications facilities for the news media. As a result, FEC and Eighth

Army signalmen had to make do with a variety of desperate expedients. The range of Eighth Army's very high frequency radios, for example, was extended by banking radio waves off nearby mountains. At one point, lacking in personnel, the acting Eighth Army signal officer helped install communications equipment himself.

Despite these problems, the communications system slowly improved. As American and ROK divisions were forced back into an ever-shrinking perimeter around Pusan, the distances their troops, radios, and wire had to cover also diminished, while reserves were rushed to Korea from FEC and elsewhere. By mid-September, the situation began to stabilize.

With the subsequent Inchon landing and Eighth Army's breakout from the Pusan perimeter, communications resources were stretched again as United Nations (UN) forces moved north. MacArthur then activated three field corps headquarters, two for Eighth Army and one for his Inchon landing force, and they had to be supplied with signal personnel and equipment. The arrival of mobile radio-teletype equipment in September helped a great deal.

The communications situation was never again as poor as it had been in July and August, not even during the sweeping Chinese Communist offensives and UN counteroffensives of November 1950–May 1951. After truce talks began in mid-1951, the front became largely static, and wire and radio operations more routine, as is evident in Signal Corps' situation reports for the remainder of the conflict.

It became possible during this period of a more stable front (lasting to mid-1953) to introduce more rugged, yet lighter, wire and radio equipment, including some radios using transistors instead of vacuum tubes.

Paradoxically, the Signal Corps also experimented with one communications mode revived from the past—carrier pigeons. Unfortunately, the American birds proved vulnerable to an enemy worse than bullets: Korean hawks.

The Korean War demonstrated once again how vital communications are in combat. The North Koreans and Chinese, despite their lack of modern communications equipment (they made extensive use of bugles, whistles, and other crude methods), were dangerous and resourceful. UN commanders had to shuffle their limited resources to cope—and that required the best communications FEC and Eighth Army could provide. Despite the communications inadequacies of the early months of the war, the best turned out to be good enough.

Karl G. Larew

See also Army Signal Corps; China, People's Republic of

Sources

Appleman, Roy E. 1961. *South to the Naktong, North to the Yalu*. Washington, DC: Office of the Chief of Military History.

Raines, Rebecca Robbins. 1996. "The Korean War." In *Getting the Message Through: A Branch History of the US Army Signal Corps*, 321–329. Washington, DC: Center of Military History.

Shiflet, Kenneth E. 1965. " 'Communications Hill' in Korea." In *The Story of the U.S. Army Signal Corps*, edited by Max L. Marshall, 188–191. New York: Franklin Watts.

Westover. J. G. 1955. *Combat Support in Korea*, 86–97. Washington, DC: Combat Forces Press.

Lamarr, Hedy (1913–2000)

Best known as a glamorous film star during Hollywood's golden age, Hedy Lamarr had a first-rate mind and was one of the developers of what later became known as spread spectrum technology. How she got interested in things technical is, however, not entirely clear.

Born in Vienna on 9 November 1913 as Hedwig Eva Maria Kiesler, she attended acting school and appeared in many early Czech and German films starting in 1930. Her fifth film, *Extase* (*Ecstasy*, 1932) became infamous for its nude scenes (she was 19), considered daring at the time.

Hedy Lamarr (she got her last name from film mogul Louis B. Mayer on her arrival in Hollywood in 1937) starred in several feature films before and early in World War II. She married an Austrian armaments manufacturer, Fritz Mandl (the first of her six husbands) shortly thereafter, and it may be from him that her technical interests were first aroused.

Mandl had sought a means of radio-guided weapons that could not be readily jammed. She developed the idea (later dubbed "frequency hopping") that by constantly and quickly changing a signal's frequency, jamming could be prevented. Under her married name (then Hedy Kiesler Markey), she shared patent 2,292,387 (11 August 1942) with her co-inventor, avant-garde music composer George Antheil (who supplied much of the technical knowledge), for what they called their "Secret Communication System."

This seminal invention was the first instance of what would later become known as spread-spectrum communications. Lamarr and Antheil's frequency-hopping techniques, based on available technologies of the time, used player piano rolls to jump among eighty-eight frequencies as a means of making radio-guided torpedoes harder for an enemy to detect or jam. Wartime attempts to interest the Navy in the idea failed (officials figured it could never be made small or robust enough for a torpedo), and the military only took up spread spectrum technology two decades later when digital technology made the idea viable. By the time of the Cuban Missile Crisis the armed forces were routinely using frequency hopping to scramble signals. Many details of the patent, however, remained classified until 1985.

More recently, spread spectrum has been found ideal for interleaving (multiplexing) many messages simultaneously, thus becoming a more efficient transmitting method than ordinary single-frequency techniques and making it the basis of Internet and cell phone traffic. Despite these applications, neither inventor profited because their 1942 patent expired decades before the modern wireless boom. Lamarr's film career began to dwindle after the war, and in the 1950s she retired from making movies. She died 19 January 2000 in Altamont Springs, Florida.

Christopher H. Sterling

See also Jamming; SIGSALY; Spread Spectrum

Sources
Braun, Hans-Joachim. 1997. "Advanced
    Weaponry of the Stars." *American Heritage of
    Invention and Technology* Spring. Available
    online at: http://www.americanheritage
    .com/articles/magazine/it/1997/4/1997
    _4_10.shtml.
Chang, Kenneth. 2004. "Hollywood Star's
    Wartime Secret Becomes a Screenplay. *New
    York Times,* May 4, C2.
Severo, Richard. 2000. "Hedy Lamarr, Sultry
    Star Who Reigned in Hollywood of 30's and
    40's Dies at 86." *New York Times,* January 20,
    A16.

Language Translation

In a world of multiple spoken languages, the ability to understand allied or enemy messages across language lines is a vital part of military communication. The most common historical approach has been to use a human translator who was adept at both languages being used. But translators take time to train, are expensive, and are often overworked. By the early 2000s, computer software was approaching the ability to translate human language in real time.

U.S. involvement in military actions in the Middle East drove the new development. The military needed far more Arabic speakers than it could find. In Afghanistan in 2002 the U.S. Army used a handheld "phraselator" device that could mechanically speak 800 to 1,000 often-used pre-chosen phrases in Arabic that had been recorded by a human speaker. But while the system could be used with many different languages, it offered only one-way communication.

The Army also experimented with the not-for-profit SRI International–developed mobile software system called IraqComm, which provides the beginnings of a more natural two-way language interface in colloquial Iraqi Arabic. IraqComm integrates three advanced software technologies: automatic speech recognition (ASR), machine translation (MT), and text-to-speech synthesis (TTS). To start a dialog, one speaks into a microphone and the system records the voice. The ASR module processes the recording and displays what it heard on a screen. The MT module translates the phrase into Iraqi Arabic. Finally, the TTS module then "speaks" this translation, which is also displayed on the screen. The system began with a vocabulary of nearly 40,000 English and 50,000 Iraqi Arabic words, and runs on commercial off-the-shelf hardware. The Army was experimenting in Iraq with more than thirty of the devices by mid-2006.

The Defense Advanced Research Projects Agency issued a 2001 contract to IBM's Thomas Watson Laboratories. IBM researchers developed the Multilingual Automatic Speech-to-Speech Translator (MASTOR) as a two-way, free-form speech translator that uses natural spoken language for people who do not share a common language. The focus of the MASTOR software program is to convey the meaning of what was said, even if minor errors are made by the speaker(s) or speech recognizer. During normal operation, users speak into a microphone (one at a time) that is interfaced with the MASTOR program. The MASTOR recognizes and translates the speech, then vocalizes the translation in the target language for the foreign-language speaker to hear. The foreign-language speaker can then speak into the microphone in his or her own language, and the MASTOR translates and vocalizes that speech in the original language. Initially developed to work with Mandarin Chinese and English, and later extended to Arabic, the MASTOR can run on a laptop computer or personal digital assistant. It operates with a vocabulary of about 150,000 words.

By 2005, the Army was experimenting with the MASTOR in quiet areas within Iraq. It also employed the Global Autonomous Language Exploitation (GALE) system to read broadcasts and Web sites. GALE experiments took place in both Arabic and Mandarin Chinese, attempting to deal with both the formal languages and regional dialects. By 2009, military officials expect to be using the system in battlefield conditions, and additional languages will be added. While none of these systems are as good as a human translator, they are getting better—faster, more culturally accurate, and more comprehensive.

Christopher H. Sterling

See also Defense Advanced Research Projects Agency (DARPA); Iraq War (2003–Present)

Sources

IBM. "Speech-to-Speech Translation." [Online information; retrieved October 2006.] http://domino.watson.ibm.com/comm/research.nsf/pages/r.uit.innovation.html.

IraqComm. "Speech to Speech Translation System." [Online information; retrieved October 2006.] http://www.iraqcomm.com/.

Willing, Richard. 2006. "Military Tests Portable Translators." *USA Today*, December 20, 8A.

Laser

Though Albert Einstein predicted the phenomenon as early as 1917, the laser (light amplification by stimulated emission of radiation) has developed over the past four decades since the first ones were built in 1960. Military need for improved modes of communication as well as weapons potential has fueled and funded much of the research into laser capability.

More than a thousand different kinds of laser are classified by the type of material used—solid, liquid/chemical, gas, or semiconductor (also called diode types, these were among the first, appearing in 1962). The first two have strong drawbacks for military use—power and cooling requirements with solid lasers, and the substantial chemical plant required for liquid lasers. Once initial problems with heat dissipation were resolved in the 1970s, lasers became widely employed in business (e.g., barcode scanning in retail sales), industry (micromachining, measurement, welding, and cutting), medicine (surgery), and consumer products (printers and compact disc players). Semiconductor lasers form an essential part of commercial and military fiber optic telecommunication systems.

Current applications of lasers on the tactical battlefield include their use as range finders, target designators (e.g., "painting" a target), and various guidance systems. Strategic laser use falls into two categories: near-term research into application as anti-satellite weapons, and longer-term efforts to develop a system for missile defense (also known as the Strategic Defense Initiative). The many military roles of satellites (particularly in surveillance, arms control verifications, and communications) has made them potential military targets. The sensitive optics on such satellites are vulnerable to an overload of light such as would be provided in a laser attack. Military research continues to seek more efficient lasers as well as more rugged ones, able to stand up to battle conditions.

The laser has also proven valuable in communications between submarines and their base because it eliminates the dangers of the traditional but detectable radio signal. A blue-green laser is transmitted to a satellite that, in turn, relays the beam to the submarine. The ray is only relayed for a millionth of a second so there is virtually no chance that it will be detected by anyone else. The submarine's receiver picks up and decodes the signal. Even if someone else did intercept the signal, they would not be able to decode it because the receiver has to be the exact shade of the laser beam.

Most technical experts agree that laser technology is still at relatively early stages of development. Potential laser weapons remain under study, as do other applications.

Christopher H. Sterling

See also Fiber Optics; Satellite Communications; Submarine Communications

Sources

Bertolotti, M. 2004. *The History of the Laser*. Bristol, UK: Institute of Physics Press.
Bromberg, J. L. 1991. *The Laser in America*. Cambridge, MA: MIT Press.
Hecht, Jeff. 2005. *Beam: The Race to Make the Laser*. New York: Oxford University Press.
Holonyak, N., Jr. 1997. "The Semiconductor Laser: A Thirty-Five Year Perspective." *Proceedings of the IEEE* 85 (11): 1678–1693.
Mirra, David R. 1988. "Lasers and Their Potential for Tactical Military Use." [Online article; retrieved June 2006.] http://www.globalsecurity.org/military/library/report/1988/MDR.htm.

Lights and Beacons

Beacons are fires or torches (or, more recently, electronic lights) lit on towers or other high points for a variety of navigational purposes (as in lighthouses) or for military signaling. Beacons are an ancient form of visual signaling and were often used in relays to cover distances beyond line of sight.

Such systems were widely used in ancient times. Greek author Aeschylus's play *Agamemnon* opens with the lines, "And now I am watching for the signal of the beacon, the blaze of fire that brings a voice from Troy, and tidings of its capture." In Scandinavia, many hill forts were part of networks of beacons to warn about pillaging expeditions from other Scandinavians ("Vikings"). The "Brecon Beacons" in Wales take their name from beacons used to warn of approaching English raiders in the Middle Ages. The best-known British example is the beacons used in 1588 to warn of the approaching Spanish Armada. This chain of beacons gave the name to many "Beacon Hills" in the south of England.

During the American Revolution, beacons were often used to warn one side or the other of troop movements. In central New Jersey, beacons were placed atop the Blue Hills as part of a network of twenty-three beacons located on strategic heights around the central part of the colony where they were visible to most members of the New Jersey militia. Lord Stirling directed construction of the network in March 1779 under the orders of George Washington.

Beacons have often been used to mislead, especially by enemy forces or pirates. A fire could direct a ship against cliffs or beaches, so the cargo could be looted after the ship sank or ran aground. Likewise, military forces could be misdirected.

Large light beacons were installed at many American coast defense installations. Kept inside buildings or bunkers much of the time, these lights could be rolled out and used to illuminate enemy ships not far off shore, thus aiding coast artillery in targeting those vessels. This was clearly more of a tactical rather than signaling use of a light beacon.

All light and beacon systems suffered from high cost (because many people were required to build and then maintain them), concerns about visibility in poor weather conditions, and time (unless they were staffed at all times). Over the past several decades, the term "beacon" has also been used to apply to radio and audio signaling devices.

Christopher H. Sterling

See also Ancient Signals; Ardois Light; Coast Defense; Coston Signals; Fire/Flame/Torch; Native American Signaling; Night Signals; Searchlights/Signal Blinkers

Sources
Holzmann, Gerard J., and Björn Pehrson. 1995. "Fire Beacons." In *The Early History of Data Networks*, 15–20. Los Alamitos, CA: IEEE Computer Society.
Raleigh, James. 1983. "Beacons: Means of Communication and Celebration." [Online article; retrieved March 2006.] http://www.greenbrooknj.com/main6_04.htm.
Sheil, T., and A. Sheil. "Light Signals." [Online information; retrieved March 2006.] http://www.thortrains.net/RRLIGHT1.HTM.
Woods, David L. 1965. *A History of Tactical Communications Techniques*. Orlando, FL: Martin-Marietta (Reprinted by Arno Press, 1974).

Lincoln in the Telegraph Office

While serving as president during the American Civil War (1861–1865), Abraham Lincoln was able to play a far more direct and real-time role in planning and directing military actions than had any prior national leader. What made this possible was the telegraph, and specifically a telegraph sending and receiving office within the War Department, housed next door to the White House.

Lincoln was first exposed to the telegraph's potential while still practicing law in Illinois in 1857. By the time he reached the White House four years later, he readily understood the technology's potential and value. In April 1861, Secretary of War Simon Cameron created the U.S. Military Telegraph Corps, and it was that organization that also served Lincoln. The telegraph office was soon relocated next to Edwin Stanton's office (he had replaced Cameron on 15 January 1862) and both the president and Stanton could often be found there, either reading telegraph reports or sending messages.

Lincoln would come to the office, often on a daily basis, especially when major battles were under way. He would generally read the telegraphic traffic received since his last visit and might send up to a dozen messages a day to specific leaders in the field. The ability to send and receive messages far faster than in the past underscored the growing disagreements between Lincoln and General George McClellan, the commander of the Union armies in 1862–1863. Likewise the messages of 1864–1865 between Lincoln and General Ulysses Grant ranged over strategy as well as tactics and logistics. The amount of traffic always increased during major engagements.

Lincoln's messages to and from the War Department telegraph office were usually

President Abraham Lincoln drafts the Emancipation Proclamation in the Military Telegraph Office, located in the War Department next to the White House. (Library of Congress)

transmitted in hours, despite the time-consuming need for encipherment or decoding. On occasion, however, as much as a week could pass due to cut lines, mobile troops, or the need to utilize couriers in some places where lines were down or did not exist. Such lapses were more likely for distant engagements—such as the Battle of Mobile Bay in mid-1864—rather than battles in the main theater of war in northern Virginia.

Lincoln came to the telegraph office as one means of gaining respite from the pressures and office seekers in the White House and would sometimes spend hours, even staying overnight, in the telegraph office. Indeed, he drafted the first (June 1862) version of his landmark Emancipation Proclamation while there. Lincoln made active and virtually daily use of the telegraph to the end of the war, just shortly before his assassination.

Christopher H. Sterling

See also American Civil War (1861–1865); Stager, Anson (1825–1885); Telegraph; U.S. Military Telegraph Service (USMTS)

Sources

Bates, David Homer. 1907. *Lincoln in the Telegraph Office: Recollections of the United States Military Telegraph Corps During the Civil War.* New York: Century.

Markle, Donald E., ed. 2003. *The Telegraph Goes to War: The Personal Diary of David Homer Bates, Lincoln's Telegraph Operator.* Hamilton, NY: Edmonston Publishing.

Wheeler, Tom. 2006. *Mr. Lincoln's T-Mails: The Untold Story of How Abraham Lincoln Used the Telegraph to Win the Civil War.* New York: Collins.

Lowe, Thaddeus S. C. (1832–1913)

Nineteenth-century innovator Thaddeus Lowe provided balloon observation and artillery spotting for Union Army forces during the first two years of the American Civil War (1861–1865), presaging later aeronautical intelligence and aerial military communications.

Lowe was born in New Hampshire in August 1832, and left school after the fourth grade. He first learned of balloons while working his way toward Portland, Maine. For a time he sold patent medicines and adopted the "professor" title he used throughout his life. He apprenticed to a shoemaking firm in Boston and on his own time experimented with lifting cats with kites. By 1856, a year after his marriage (he would father ten children), he was experimenting with tethered balloons inflated with hydrogen gas.

Learning more about balloons and their operation, Lowe sought to make a transatlantic aerial voyage. An experiment working in that direction involved a 650-mile, nine-hour trip in April 1861 by his balloon *Enterprise* from Cincinnati to the Chesapeake Bay area to prove his theory of easterly winds at altitude, but winds carried him instead toward the Carolina coast and then back to Unionville, South Carolina, where he was briefly interned as a Union spy just as tensions gave way to war.

Lowe was but one of several who attempted the use of balloons in the Civil War. With the backing of Smithsonian secretary Joseph Henry, Lowe demonstrated what he might accomplish. On 17 June 1861 his *Enterprise* rose in a tethered experiment near the White House for President Abraham Lincoln and other officials. Lowe and two telegraphers ascended to 500 feet and sent

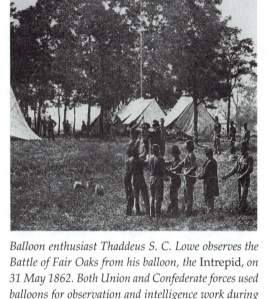

Balloon enthusiast Thaddeus S. C. Lowe observes the Battle of Fair Oaks from his balloon, the Intrepid, *on 31 May 1862. Both Union and Confederate forces used balloons for observation and intelligence work during the early part of the Civil War. (National Archives)*

telegraph messages to the ground using a battery-powered telegraph key and a line along the tether to the ground—essentially the first aerial telecommunications. Lowe was soon appointed by the president as the chief of the new Balloon Corps, a civilian agency under the Bureau of Topographical Engineers of the Army. His balloon was providing Army aerial reconnaissance in the northern Virginia area within days.

On 24 September 1861, from his *Union* balloon tethered about 1,000 feet up, Lowe helped to direct artillery fire from Union gun batteries at Fort Corcoran (west of Washington DC) on to Confederate lines near Falls Church, Virginia. As the gunners on the ground could not see their targets, this was the first such aerial artillery spotting. Lowe used a white flag in prearranged fashion to signal where Union cannon fire was landing.

Lowe developed portable gas generating equipment to ease the use of balloons in the field. The Balloon Service of the Army of the Potomac was widely utilized. In his two years in his post as chief of the Balloon Corps, Lowe and others made some 3,000 flights over Confederate territory. With the relief of George McClellan as Union commander, however, he lost an important supporter. Faced with growing opposition from traditionalists, he left in April 1863, and the Balloon Corps was eliminated in August.

Lowe staged extensive balloon exhibitions for large crowds in Philadelphia and New York, but soon moved on to other interests. He eventually held about forty patents and worked on mechanical refrigeration, among other fields. He moved to southern California in 1887 and focused on astronomy; he also operated a hotel, bank, and local railroad. He died in January 1913 in Pasadena.

Christopher H. Sterling

See also Airships and Balloons; American Civil War (1861–1865)

Sources

Block, Eugene. 1966. *Above the Civil War: The Story of Thaddeus Lowe*. Berkeley, CA: Howell-North Books.

Evans, Charles M. 2002. *War of the Aeronauts: A History of Ballooning in the Civil War*. Mechanicsburg, PA: Stackpole Books.

Haydon, F. Stansbury. 1941. *Military Ballooning During the Early Civil War*. Baltimore: Johns Hopkins University Press.

Lowe, Thaddeus S. C. 2004. *My Balloons in Peace and War: Memoirs of Thaddeus S. C. Lowe, Chief of the Aeronautic Corps of the Army of the United States During the Civil War*. Lewiston, NY: Edward Mellen Press.

Magic

The American breaking of Japanese army and naval coded communications during World War II is often given the overall term "Magic," though in fact that term applied only to the Japanese machine-generated Purple code. Code breaking against Japan generally was referred to as "Ultra" by mid-1943 in accordance with the code-breaking treaty between the United States and Britain. Unlike many other wartime coding operations, the successful efforts against Japanese codes were revealed right after the war ended, in large part because of congressional hearings into the Pearl Harbor attack.

Several Americans, working in the State, War, and Navy departments, notably Herbert Yardley and later William Friedman, had begun working with various decoding and decrypting methodologies during and after World War I. Yardley's team enjoyed some success in breaking Japanese codes from the time of the Washington Naval Conference of 1921 and thereafter during the 1920s. But the State Department's code-breaking activities were temporarily scuttled after 1929, when

U.S. Secretary of State Henry Stimson laid down the famous dictum that "Gentlemen do not read each other's mail." A small Army code-breaking operation under Friedman continued through the 1930s, creating a cadre of experienced personnel. Growing American concern about Axis intentions in the late 1930s slowly increased the support given to code-breaking activities.

The Japanese employed a number of increasingly intricate pen-and-paper codes, which were designated by various color names by American intelligence, beginning with Orange in the 1920s, and then Red. Purple was a coding machine first utilized by the Japanese in February 1939 and known to them as the Type 97 Alphabetic Typewriter. It used telephone stepping switches, but has been described as a substantial modification of an Enigma machine given to the Japanese by the Germans under terms of the Axis treaty. The Japanese also employed a variety of diplomatic codes, which were sometimes easier to break. Not all of the fifty-plus codes used by the Japanese before and during World War II were broken, but most information intercepted and interpreted by the

Americans was shared with the British from the time of the Pearl Harbor attack.

In 1940, a team led by Friedman and Frank Rowlett reverse-engineered the Japanese Purple machine, constructing an analog device, from which others were eventually fabricated. All consisted of two typewriters connected by a plug box and telephone stepping switches. Messages typed in clear language on one typewriter emerged enciphered from the other. Friedman's version enabled the Americans to read some of the Japanese codes nearly in real time (as their intended recipients were seeing the same messages). The Japanese diplomatic ultimatum, sent in the Purple code for transmission to the American government, was received by Japan's embassy in Washington DC on 6–7 December 1941. It was to be handed to Secretary of State Cordell Hull at a specific time—but was already in his hands earlier, thanks to this intelligence effort. The message did not make clear, however, the intended target, and Pearl Harbor commanders (who were in any case unaware that Japanese codes were being read) were surprised by the Japanese attack.

Until early 1942, understaffed American civilian and military intelligence made uncoordinated efforts to break further Japanese diplomatic and naval codes, but Army and Navy rivalry, and the resulting reluctance to share information, greatly hindered code and cipher work. Not until just after Pearl Harbor did both services finally allocate sufficient personnel to this activity. Ordinarily, the Japanese changed details of their codes monthly to forestall decryption, but for a variety of reasons (chiefly the difficulty of distributing new code instructions to their expanding empire) did not always follow this policy.

Two examples demonstrate the military impact of the breaking of Japanese codes.

Unable to get new sets of codebooks to all naval commands in advance of their planned invasion of the island of Midway in mid-1942, the Japanese delayed making scheduled changes in their administrative code (JN-25 to the Americans) for several months. This gave American intelligence officers sufficient time to determine enemy intentions for the projected operation, and the Navy was able to inflict a landmark defeat on the Japanese. In a later success due to Magic intelligence, the Americans in April 1943 deployed fighter planes that intercepted and shot down an aircraft carrying Japanese Admiral Isoroku Yamamoto, commander of the Imperial Japanese Navy. By mid-1945, most essential Japanese military codes had been broken. No complete Japanese-made code machines were captured, however, all having been destroyed prior to the Japanese surrender. Highly secret during the war, the Magic operation became generally known during the congressional investigations into the Pearl Harbor attack held in 1946.

Keir B. Sterling

See also Arlington Hall; Bletchley Park; Code, Codebook; Code Breaking; Friedman, William F. (1891–1969); Midway, Battle of (3–6 June 1942); Nebraska Avenue, Washington DC; OP-20-G; Rowlett, Frank B. (1908–1998); Safford, Laurance F. (1890–1973); Signals Intelligence (SIGINT); Ultra; Yardley, Herbert O. (1889–1958)

Sources

Department of Defense. 1978. *The "Magic" Background of Pearl Harbor.* 7 vols. Washington, DC: Government Printing Office.
Lewin, Ronald. 1982. *The American Magic: Codes, Ciphers and the Defeat of Japan.* New York: Farrar, Straus & Giroux.
Rowlett, Frank B. 1998. *The Story of Magic: Memoirs of an American Cryptological Pioneer.* Laguna Hills, CA: Aegean Park Press.
Spector, Ronald H., ed. 1988. *Listening to the Enemy: Key Documents on the Role of Communications Intelligence in the War*

with Japan. Wilmington, DE: Scholarly Resources Inc.

Maginot Line

From 1929 to the late 1930s, France constructed an extensive series of largely underground defense lines facing Germany in the north and Italy in the south. This system of fortresses featured advanced telephone, radio, and acoustic communications links.

Having been invaded by Germany twice in the previous sixty years, France undertook, at huge effort and expense, to develop an invincible armored wall of defense to prevent further incursions. The fortifications were especially necessary, it was argued, as French manpower fell behind that of Germany due to losses in World War I. Andre Maginot (1877–1932), like most of his contemporaries, had served and been wounded on the Western Front in World War I. By the late 1920s he had become minister of war in France and, reading the national mood, spearheaded the planning, funding, and initial construction of the defense line that would bear his name after his death. The

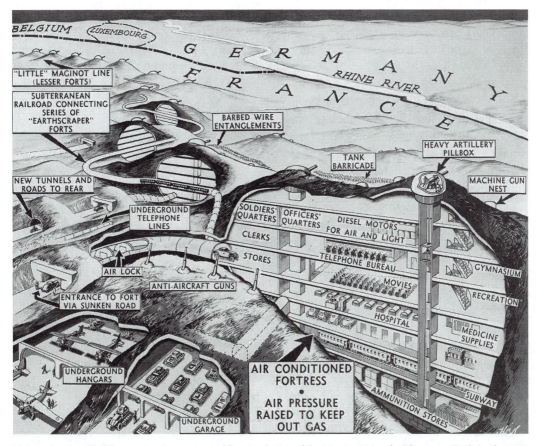

This rather fanciful illustration demonstrates the complexity of the Maginot Line fortifications. Built in the 1930s by France along its borders with Germany and Italy, communication within and among the many underground fortresses used telegraph, telephone, and radio links. (Library of Congress)

Maginot Line consisted of a series of fortresses (*ouvrage*), some built around artillery and others around infantry, with smaller defensive bunkers in between—it was not a line, per se, but defense in depth along the French border. Individual garrisons ranged from a few dozen to as many as 1,200 men.

Each Maginot unit was tied to all the others as well as central command by wired telephone, the cable facilities for which were duplicated and also buried to protect against artillery or air attack. Some of the artillery *ouvrage* had numerous separate artillery blocs, or positions, covering an extensive area, and all were tied to a central command post by telephone. Each command post featured telephone switchboards that were operated with electricity generated within each fort.

For internal communications, individual observation sites communicated with the command center using voice tubes or telephone. In turn, the command center sent orders by use of bells and lights as indicators, and the movement of indicator needles on circular dials. These were essentially electrical order transmitters, allowing visual confirmation of commands despite the din of gunfire, which might impede telephone messages. Optical telegraphy (mirrors, lights, and the like) could also be employed from one external observation point to another. Study had begun as to whether these should be supplemented or replaced by infrared systems when the Germans attacked in May 1940.

Radio telegraphy served only as an alternate mode of communication as French wireless technology lagged that of other countries and radio generally was in the nascent stages of its development. Further, radio messages would have to be enciphered, which would delay communication, and radio antennas had to be stretched hor-izontally along the external face of the *ouvrage* entrance, and were thus vulnerable to attack. Finally, the Maginot Line's radio system transmitters, which ranged from 50 to 250 watts, only serviced a range of about 15 miles.

In May and June 1940, Maginot fortresses successfully resisted frontal (and some air) attacks from both the Germans and Italians, but were eventually encircled from the rear as France fell. But at no time did the internal communication links within individual fortresses fail, and most interline communications remained intact as well.

Christopher H. Sterling

See also Atlantic Wall; France: Army; Underground Communication Centers

Sources

Kaufmann, J. E., and H. W. Kaufmann. 1997. *The Maginot Line: None Shall Pass*. Westport, CT: Praeger.

Kemp, Anthony. 1982. *The Maginot Line: Myth & Reality*. Briarcliff Manor, NY: Stein & Day.

Mary, Jean-Yves. 1980. "Les Transmissions." In *La Ligne Maginot*, 150–155. Cuneo, Italy: SERCAP.

Mary, Jean-Yves, and Alain Hohnadel. 2001. "Les Transmissions." In *Hommes et Ouvrages de la Ligne Maginot, Tome 2*, 120–129. Paris: L'encyclopédie de l'Armée Française—Editions Histoire et Collections.

Rowe, Vivian. 1959. *The Great Wall of France: The Triumph of the Maginot Line*. London: Putnam.

Truttmann, Philippe. 1987. "Transmissions." In *La Muraille de France*, 409–414. Thionville, France: Gerard Klopp.

Maori Signaling

The Maori (indigenous people) of what is now New Zealand developed a very sophisticated system of different types of wartime signaling.

Large battle groups of warriors were controlled by the chief in the field by use of a unique signaling device. The Maori sling (*he kotaha*) had a dual role of being both a weapon and a communicator. A number of darts were provided, which had either fire bundles or feathers mounted at the top. When shot into the air they signaled for warriors to advance to left or right or to withdraw. Some darts used fire to indicate a change of direction. In effect each was a prearranged command. It took many years to learn to use the sling and prepare the darts, and only a few had that honor.

Other forms of signaling in the field were provided by the use of the *tewha tewha*, a battleaxe-like weapon, that could also indicate a change of direction by the chief. The quarter-staff (*taiaha*) was used for signaling over a distance. Movement of the staff indicated to which tribe the warrior belonged.

Fixed communication was practiced in a number of ways. The Maori developed long-distance communication by using the resources available. These included the *pahu*, a large wooden gong, that was located on what is now the One Tree Hill area of Auckland. The *pahu* was reputed to be audible over most of the Auckland isthmus. The *pu kaea* was a form of Alpine horn. Fire and smoke were also used, and with the arrival of European settlers, cow horns came into use as well. Another method of communicating was to simply shout between fortifications or from cliff top to cliff top. This was known as *pari karangaranga*.

The native trumpet shell was the *pu tara*, or war trumpet. This prized shell was used by *iwi* (tribes) to issue a challenge to a potential enemy. If the challenge was answered then battle would ensue. Explorer Abel Tasman unwittingly accepted such a call to battle when he first heard the challenge, and ordered his sailors to trumpet a reply. This misunderstanding of communications highlights the need for all communicators to understand their medium and exploit it to its fullest potential.

Cliff Lord

See also Ancient Signals; Music Signals; Native American Signaling

Marconi, Guglielmo (1874–1937)

Innovator of the world's first successful wireless telegraph system, Marconi is often considered the father of the radio industry. His wireless firms in Britain (founded 1897) and the United States (1899) played central roles in introducing naval and military radio early in the twentieth century.

Born in Bologna, Italy, on 25 April 1874, Marconi began experimenting with wireless on his father's estate two decades later. Eliciting little interest from Italian naval authorities, he traveled to England in 1896 to experiment further and develop a wireless business. The British Post Office, Admiralty, and army were all soon interested and involved in perfecting the system, transmitting wireless telegraph signals over ever-greater distances over both land and water. Marconi received a Morse code signal of the letter "S" sent across the Atlantic in late 1901.

Marconi wireless sets were used by the British army (briefly) and Royal Navy (more successfully) as early as the Boer War. Some were used by the Japanese navy in the Russo-Japanese War of 1904–1905, a contributing factor in its eventual victory. The number of British naval ships equipped with wireless expanded to 42 by late 1900, to 80 by 1905, and to 435 by the eve of World War I. By 1913, Marconi had also established an extensive system of navy shore wireless transmitters and direction-finding stations.

Italian inventor Guglielmo Marconi poses with some of the equipment that formed an early version of his wireless system. Marconi equipment was furnished to the Royal Navy and other forces in both world wars. (Library of Congress)

The Admiralty took control of the Marconi factory on the outbreak of World War I in August 1914. Marconi himself was commissioned in the Italian army during the war, and helped develop low-frequency radio facilities that aided the Italian navy's operations. His firm operated extensive training schools for the Admiralty and army, while the Royal Flying Corps took over Marconi's Brooklands experimental site. The British Expeditionary Force landed in France with only one mobile transmitter, but had ten units within a month. Marconi's Chelmsford works developed radio links for British headquarters to use on the stabilized Western Front by 1915. Vacuum tube–powered

sets were replacing crystal-driven equipment. Development of lighter aircraft radios (down to 20 pounds by late 1915) from Marconi greatly aided artillery spotting from the air. During 1916 Marconi-built vacuum tube radios began to equip the Royal Navy and were soon fitted in British airships.

After the war, Marconi conducted extensive experiments with shortwave and helped establish international radio links using the technology. Many were done on his yacht *Elettra*, purchased in 1919. Long enamored of Mussolini, he joined the Fascist Party in 1923, and in 1930 he became a part of the Fascist Grand Council. Two years later he returned permanently to Italy. From his yacht he conducted microwave experiments and some work with the principles of radar. In declining health for several years, he died on 20 July 1937 in Rome.

Even then increasing orders for the coming war were flowing to the Marconi Company, which developed communication and navigation equipment for all three British service arms. Unlike in World War I, however, Marconi was not alone in the British market. Considerable emergency work was accomplished in 1939–1940 for the British Expeditionary Force in France. By 1943, a quarter of company manufacturing capacity was devoted to radio needs of the Royal Air Force and another 30 percent served Royal Navy requirements. That year alone, nearly 11,000 transmitters and 15,000 receivers were manufactured.

Christopher H. Sterling

See also Airplanes; Airships and Balloons; Jackson, Henry B. (1885–1929); Radio; Tsushima, Battle of (27–28 May 1905); United Kingdom: Royal Navy

Sources

Baker, W. J. 1971. *A History of the Marconi Company*. New York: St. Martin's Press.

Dunlap, Orrin E. 1937. *Marconi: The Man and His Wireless*. New York: Macmillan (reprinted by Arno Press, 1971).

Godwin, George. 1946. *Marconi: A War Record*. London: Chatto & Windus.

Jolly, W. P. 1972. *Marconi*. New York: Stein & Day.

Vyvyan, R. N. 1933. *Wireless Over Thirty Years*. London: Routledge (reprinted by EP Publishing, 1974, as *Marconi and Wireless*).

Marne, Battle of (September 1914)

The first Battle of the Marne was a series of engagements fought along the Marne River between Paris and Verdun during the German invasion of France in September 1914. While the Germans guarded their left flank with two weak armies, five larger German armies on the right flank swept through Belgium and northern France. They quickly shattered the French armies and the British Expeditionary Force (BEF), and by 1 September the Germans were within 30 miles of Paris. Fortunately for the Allies, extended logistics, inadequate command and control, and human exhaustion affected German operations greatly.

A significant element in the eventual failure of the German offensive was inadequate communications systems that failed to provide German Chief of Staff Helmut von Moltke with timely or accurate information from the front. During the operations, Moltke remained at his headquarters in Luxembourg more than 200 miles away. He thus lost touch with his commanders, leading to German failure to exploit operational opportunities at decisive points on the battlefield. In contrast French commander General Joseph Joffre maintained good communications with his commanders, primarily through direct personal visits and constant movement to critical areas of the battle as he sought an opportunity for a counterattack along the Somme-Verdun line.

Many of the problems with German communications began with inadequate planning because the chief of the field telegraph service was not included in preparations for the advance. Extensive secrecy regarding the pending violation of Belgian neutrality made it impossible to preplan communications through the country. The Germans had also resolved to rely on telephone lines and radio instead of the telegraph, though forward units were not told and thus destroyed much of the wire communication infrastructure of Belgium and France.

As the German right wing advanced across Belgium, a gap opened between the First and Second armies because the aggressive First Army commander ordered a move east of Paris to destroy the flank of the retreating French army. This moved the First Army far ahead of other German armies, exposing their right flank to the French. Because of the lag in communications, Moltke ordered the First Army to guard the flank of the Second. First Army shifted south of the Marne River on 4 September.

The Allies identified the exposed German flank using air reconnaissance and radio intercepts. The military governor of Paris ordered a French army to attack the exposed enemy flank on 5 September with more than 150,000 men. First Army then moved away from Second Army as it turned to deal with this threat, which opened a gap of almost 30 miles between the two German forces. The remaining French armies held the line to the east, and the battle along the Marne raged for three days. Because of his firsthand knowledge of the situation, Joffre identified and exploited the gap between the German armies. On 9 September the BEF crossed the Marne and moved unopposed into the gap.

Frustrated by poor communications, Moltke sent a general staff officer forward on 8 September to coordinate the actions of his army commanders. He arrived at Second Army headquarters just as that unit's flank was being turned by the French while the BEF threatened First Army's rear. In Moltke's name, he ordered First Army to withdraw or risk envelopment. From 10–12 September the Germans conducted a 40-mile fighting withdrawal to the Aisne River, where they halted. Soon both exhausted armies dug trenches and extended their front from Switzerland to the English Channel.

The Battle of the Marne proved to be one of the most decisive in military history. It was a strategic victory for the Allies and was the closest the Germans ever came to victory. It also ended all the belligerents' hopes for the short war their prewar plans had projected.

Steven J. Rauch

See also France: Army; Germany: Army; World War I

Sources

Blond, Georges. 1966. *The Marne*. Harrisburg, PA: Stackpole Books.

David, Daniel. 1987. *The 1914 Campaign*. New York: Military Press.

Evans, Paul W. 1935. "Strategic Signal Communications—A Study Based upon the Operations of the German Signal Corps During the March on Paris in 1914." *Signal Corps Bulletin* 82 (January–February): 24–58.

Schniewindt, Lt. Gen. 1933. "Signal Communication Between the Headquarters Staffs During the Warfare of Movement in 1914." *Signal Corps Bulletin* 74 (September–October): 1–26.

Mauborgne, Joseph Oswald (1881–1971)

Joseph Mauborgne served as chief signal officer and was a key figure in the early development of the U.S. Army's signals intelligence capabilities.

Mauborgne was born on 26 February 1881 in New York City. A graduate of the College of St. Francis Xavier in New York (1901), he entered the Army as an infantry officer in 1903. A student at the Army Signal School (1909–1910), he was among the first to experiment with radio to and from airplanes in 1912–1914. In 1914, he was the first to solve the Playfair complex field cipher system then used by the British.

Detailed to the Army Signal Corps in 1916, Mauborgne worked on eliminating radio static during World War I. He also developed the first theoretically unbreakable cipher and promoted use of an automatic cipher machine. Named chief of the Signal Corps' Research and Engineering Division during World War I, he transferred to the Signal Corps (1920) and directed a signal laboratory at the National Bureau of Standards from 1923 to 1927. He served as a technical adviser at several international communications conferences. He was a graduate of the Army War College in 1932, and in 1934 was assigned to San Francisco as a signal officer. Mauborgne did pioneering work in his quarters during off-duty hours, seeking foreign radio transmissions on his radio, attempting to determine where they came from and with whom the senders were communicating. Promoted to colonel in 1934, Mauborgne directed the Aircraft Radio Laboratory in 1936–1937.

Promoted to major general and appointed chief signal officer in October 1937, Mauborgne urged expansion of the Signal Corps telegraph system. He contended that military "double tracking" with commercial firms would be essential in meeting increased wartime service demands. He opposed the single national telegraph company, which Congress mandated in 1943. Mauborgne began converting Signal Corps administrative offices from telegraph to teletype. By 1939, he was receptive to the idea that Army communications systems should eventually switch from AM to the newly developed FM, especially for communication with aircraft. Unfortunately, early military tests of FM transmission proved inconclusive, and the civilian radio industry seemed uninterested in its use. As General Electric had not supplied the necessary equipment before Pearl Harbor, the Army relied on AM systems early in World War II.

Mauborgne was a highly capable cryptologist who organized the Signal Intelligence Service (SIS), gave it a substantial budget,

expanded its operations and staff, started correspondence courses, and added more intercept facilities. He continued to provide strong encouragement to those working in this field. When, in September 1940, Frank A. Rowlett and other SIS operatives broke the Japanese Purple code after eighteen months of effort, Mauborgne dubbed Rowlett and his associates "magicians" and the product of their decryptions as "Magic."

Long before Mauborgne took office as chief, however, the Army Air Corps contended that the Signal Corps was not moving fast enough to meet its various requirements, including improved communications and detection capabilities such as radar. In addition, ground troops needed long-range radios, particularly for vehicles. Some felt the Signal Corps was not doing enough to ensure communications preparedness in the event of American involvement in the war in Europe. These concerns may have contributed to his termination as chief signal officer in mid-August 1941, six weeks ahead of schedule, when Mauborgne was retired at the direction of Army Chief of Staff George Marshall. He died in Little Silver, New Jersey, on 5 June 1971.

Keir B. Sterling

See also Army Signal Corps; Magic; Rowlett, Frank B. (1908–1998); Signals Intelligence (SIGINT)

Sources

Alvarez, David. 2000. *Secret Messages: Codebreaking and American Diplomacy, 1930–1945.* Lawrence: University Press of Kansas.

Kahn, David. 1967. *The Codebreakers: The History of Secret Writing.* New York: Macmillan.

Raines, Rebecca R. 1996. *Getting the Message Through: A Branch History of the US Army Signal Corps.* Washington, DC: Center of Military History.

Terrett, Dulany. 1956. *The United States Army in World War II: The Technical Services. The Signal Corps: The Emergency (to December, 1941).*

Washington, DC: Office of the Chief of Military History.

Medal of Honor Winners, Signal Corps

During U.S. Army Signal Corps history, five individuals have been recognized for acts of personal bravery or sacrifice above and beyond the call of duty through award of the Medal of Honor. This is the highest American military award and, since its inception in 1862, has been awarded to approximately 3,400 recipients out of the millions who have served in the U.S. armed forces.

Morgan D. Lane (1866)

Morgan Lane enlisted in August 1862 in a Michigan cavalry regiment and transferred to the newly authorized Signal Corps in April 1864. He served at the 5th Corps headquarters as an orderly to Lieutenant P. H. Niles, one of the corps signal officers. Lane achieved recognition in April 1865 at Jetersville, Virginia, midway between Petersburg and Appomattox, during the Union pursuit of General Robert E. Lee's Confederate Army. Confederate naval forces on the Appomattox River also attempted to escape and burned the CSS *Nansemond*, an 80-ton wooden steamer on 4 April. Lane, Niles, and an engineer captain were manning a small signal station atop a house in Jetersville when they observed and captured the escaping Confederate sailors. Lane seized the colors of the *Nanesmond* from the escaping captain. During the Civil War, capturing an enemy organization's colors was deemed a valiant act, because they were defended to the death and reflected the nature of personal close combat. The War Department awarded the Medal of Honor to Lane on 16 March 1866. He was a common soldier who performed his duty faithfully and effectively and was the first Signal Corps soldier to receive the Medal of Honor.

Will Croft Barnes (1882)

Will Barnes enlisted in the Signal Corps in 1879 for five years, and attended signal training at Fort Whipple, Virginia, where he studied flag, torch, and telegraph signaling. In December 1879, Barnes was assigned to Fort Apache, Arizona, as the post telegrapher and weather observer. During 1881 Barnes sent more than 4,000 messages and four daily meteorology reports to the Office of the Chief Signal Officer in Washington DC. Trouble with Apache Indians near the fort in late August 1881 set the stage for Barnes to demonstrate his courage. When an Apache medicine man began predicting the defeat of the white men and the return of Indians to power, conflict erupted. Fort Apache's commander set out with 117 men to arrest the Indian leader, and Barnes remained behind at the fort with less than 70 other soldiers and civilians, who had been cut off from wire communication by the Indians. Uncertain about the status of the expedition, Barnes volunteered to climb a 2,000-foot mesa and use his signal flags to alert the post to any threatening Indian activity. During further operations in September, Barnes went out with an armed escort to repair the telegraph line. Barnes's abilities as a soldier and signalman impressed his superiors for being "prompt and unhesitating in the discharge of all duties assigned to him, more than once being exposed to great danger." On 8 November 1882, General William T. Sherman, commanding general of the Army, approved award of the Medal of Honor, which then-Sergeant Barnes received the following spring at Fort Apache.

Charles E. Kilbourne, Jr. (1905)

Charles Kilbourne, Jr., was the only signal officer to win the Medal of Honor while performing a combat communications mission. A Signal Corps officer's son, Kilbourne became an observer with the U.S. Weather Bureau until the war with Spain in 1898, when he joined the Volunteer Signal Corps, an expansion of the regular corps assigned to provide tactical communications to the rapidly expanding Army. He shipped out to the Philippines, where he participated in the campaign against Spanish forces resulting in the seizure of Manila. When the Philippine Insurrection began in February 1899, Kilbourne earned a place in history and the Medal of Honor for his actions, where "Within . . . 250 yards of the enemy and in the face of rapid fire, he climbed a telegraph pole at the east end of Paco Bridge and, in full view of the enemy, coolly and carefully repaired a broken telegraph wire, thereby re-establishing telegraphic communication to the front." Kilbourne later applied for and was accepted in the Regular Army as an infantry officer, eventually transferring to the artillery. During World War I he served as the chief of staff of the 89th Infantry Division, and, though wounded by a mortar shell, his performance earned him the Distinguished Service Cross. In October 1918, he earned the Distinguished Service Medal, making him the only soldier at that time to hold the nation's three highest military awards.

Gordon Johnston (1910)

Gordon Johnston, the son of a Confederate general, began his military service as an enlisted man during the Spanish-American War, first in Cuba and eventually in the Philippines, where he won a Distinguished Service Cross while fighting insurgents in 1902. During a second tour of duty in the Philippines, on 7 March 1906 he distinguished himself at Mount Bud-Dajo, where, "while gallantly raising himself up to gain a foothold to climb up in advance of the others, he was severely wounded. This especially brave action . . . distinguished his conduct above that of his comrades." Johnston received the Medal of Honor four years later. Camp Gordon Johnston, a 155,000-acre World War II training installation (1942–1946) in coastal Franklin County, Florida, was named for him and served as an amphibious-warfare training center.

Adolphus W. Greely (1935)

Adolphus Greely, who served most of his long Army career in the Signal Corps, was unique in that his Medal of Honor was awarded by special act of Congress for service, joining the elite ranks of Richard Byrd, Floyd Bennett, and Charles Lindbergh as the only people to receive a Medal of Honor as a "special legislation" award. After Civil War service, in 1867 he was detailed to the Signal Corps and served during the campaign against the Cheyenne Indians. In 1870 he was assigned to Washington DC to help Colonel Albert Myer organize the meteorological service. In March 1887, President Grover Cleveland jumped Greely from captain to brigadier general and appointed him chief signal officer, a post he held for nineteen years. He fought numerous battles to save the Signal Corps' existence. Under Greely's tenure the Signal Corps was a leader in technological innovation, including use of wireless telegraphy, the airplane, the automobile, and other modern devices. Greely was retired for age in 1908, and on his ninety-first birthday (27 March 1935), he was presented with a special Medal of Honor "for his life of splendid public service."

Steven J. Rauch

See also Army Signal Corps; Greely, Adolphus
W. (1844–1935); Spanish-American War
(1898)

Sources

Brown, J. Willard. 1896. *The Signal Corps, USA in
the War of the Rebellion*. Boston: U.S. Veteran
Signal Corps Association (reprinted by Arno
Press, 1974).

Command Historian Office. 1990. *Signal Corps
Recipients of the Medal of Honor*. Fort Gordon,
GA: U.S. Army Signal Center.

Lang, George, et. al. 1995. *Medal of Honor Recipients: 1863–1994*. New York: Facts on File.

Raines, Rebecca Robbins. 1996. *Getting the
Message Through: A Branch History of the US
Army Signal Corps*. Washington, DC: US
Army Center of Military History.

Medieval Military Signaling (500–1500 CE)

Military communication during the medieval period was accomplished by foot courier,
mounted courier, pigeon, identifying banner, and music signals. Ships communicated
using flags, light, or their sails. Use of military communication was vital in order to
facilitate and coordinate appropriate movement of armed forces, including infantry,
cavalry, and naval forces.

It was easier to get a messenger into a
besieged town or castle than for the besieged
to dispatch a messenger out, as those under
attack were also under constant surveillance
by their enemies. Vital military messages
were often written using encryption or using
a substance visible only when moistened
and held to a fire. Messages were also hidden in the messenger's food, written in the
scabbard of a sword, concealed in the collar
of the messenger's dog, or hidden on the
messenger's person.

On the battlefield, music became an
important ally. Battle signals were commu-

nicated using a curved animal horn, and the
drum communicated marching pace.

Flags were also an important part of military communication. The banner, gonfanon,
pennon, and standard are just a few examples, and each type had its own particular
use. The banner identified an individual,
while the standard was used as the rallying
point for troops in battle. The gonfanon, like
the pennon, was carried at the head of a lance
and served to identify the knight. During the
twelfth century, crusaders bearing the flag
with the cross of St. George communicated
country of origin as well as religion.

Information concerning the enemy's position could come from an unexpected source.
A civilian, townsperson, or distraught
enemy soldier was often willing to betray his
army. Therefore a messenger was never to be
ignored. Messengers bringing good news
were often well rewarded. In twelfth-
century England, Henry II's messenger
brought news that the invading king of Scotland had been captured. Henry promptly
awarded the messenger with an estate in
Norfolk. Those bearing bad news sometimes
did not fare well.

The need for rapid communication between armies or kingdoms gave rise to use of
mounted couriers. The Battle of Poitiers in
732 was among the first in Europe to be
fought by cavalry, with the subsequent tra-
jectory in the use of mounted couriers.

In the late twelfth century, Genghis Khan
used homing pigeons as couriers, establishing pigeon messenger posts and relay sites
from his Mongol capital, extending to
Europe and Asia. A pigeon carried messages
up to a speed of 50 miles per hour and flew
over mountains, rivers, and enemy territory,
while a mounted courier could only travel a
few miles per hour. Using pigeons as messengers, Genghis Khan was able to send

expedited commands to his various armies and distant sovereignties.

Medieval ships, like the carrack and smaller caravel, used flag and lantern communication. A ship flew its nation's flag to convey identity, and pennants were flown from the mastheads and yardarms. Lantern signals were also transmitted, received, and understood. In the sixteenth century, codes based on the position and number of lights, flags, and cannon shots were developed.

Kathleen Hitt

See also Ancient Signals; Artillery/Gunfire; Couriers; Flags; Horses and Mules; Lights and Beacons; Music Signals; Pigeons

Sources

de Joinville, Jean and Geffroy de Villehardouin. 1963. *Chronicles of the Crusades.* Baltimore: Penguin Books.
Machiavelli, Niccolo. 2001. *The Art of War.* 2nd ed. Cambridge, MA: Da Capo.
Oman, C. W. C., and John H. Beeler, eds. 1953. *The Art of War in the Middle Ages.* Ithaca, NY: Cornell University Press.
Poole, Austin Lane. 1951. *Doomsday Book to Magna Carta.* Oxford: Clarendon Press.

Mercury, **HMS**

A land-based series of buildings rather than a ship, HMS *Mercury* has served from 1941 as the center of British Royal Navy signals and communications training. The name derived from the twelfth ship of the name, a cruiser launched in 1878, which in 1903 became the floating school to teach navigation. The school moved ashore (though maintaining the ship's name) to a navigation school at the old Naval College in Portsmouth, which opened in 1906.

After years of operation at the Portsmouth Navy Yard, wartime space pressure and the increasing intensity of enemy bombing raids in the fall of 1940 made imperative the relocation of navy signals training and several related functions (the navigators, for example, moved to Southwick House). A brief survey of options led to the privately owned Leydene House (completed in 1924, with its lush gardens finished in 1926), near East Meon, in Hampshire, northwest of Portsmouth. The stately home was requisitioned by the government and on 16 August 1941 was formally commissioned as HMS *Mercury.*

Some 300 ratings (enlisted personnel) assigned for training in modes of communications were soon accommodated in rows of tents until a row of Nissen hut barracks could be constructed. A host of other temporary buildings soon cluttered the grounds. More than a thousand men—and sometimes twice that—were being trained at any one time.

After the war, Leydene House and about 160 surrounding acres were purchased by the government so that signals training could continue. Remaining parts of the large estate were sold to tenant farmers, among others. Construction of training and activities buildings continued in the postwar years, considerably extending the facility's capabilities.

In 1948 the training establishment was renamed the Admiralty Signal and Radar Establishment (ASRE), by which time the first buildings on the new site at Portsdown had been completed. Moves to Portsdown took place progressively over the next ten years. ASRE was again renamed, becoming the Admiralty Surface Weapons Establishment, and eventually it became the Admiralty Research Establishment, part of the Defence Research Agency.

Christopher H. Sterling

See also United Kingdom: Royal Navy

Sources

Kent, Barrie. 1993. *Signal! A History of Signalling in the Royal Navy*, 122–125, 317–330. Clanfield, UK: Hyden House.

Royal Naval Communications Association. Home page. [Online information; retrieved May 2004.] http://www.rnca.org.uk/frameindex.htm.

Meteor Burst Communications (MBC)

Meteor burst communications (MBC)—also known as meteor scatter—systems use the ionized trails of the small particles entering the earth's atmosphere to reflect radio waves between stations. Various studies in the 1940s and 1950s examined different methods that might be used to establish an effective telecommunications system.

The MBC system works by transmitting packets of digitized information when a meteor trail is available. The time available for transmission of a signal is dependent on the size and type of meteor trail, which may last from a few milliseconds to a few seconds. Early experiments were not entirely successful, but the development of high-speed data transmission and data compression technologies allows the transmission of bursts of information at high data rates. A complete message might require the transmission of a number of packets spread over a period of time. After the complete message is transmitted, it is reassembled by equipment at the receiving station. Signals propagated by an MBC system have a low probability of interception and detection and are difficult to jam because of the burst mode of transmission, the random nature of the communication, and the small signal footprint.

The Canadians implemented their version of an MBC system, JANET, in 1952. JANET operated through the decade, but because of complicated storage and signaling equipment, it failed to gain widespread acceptance. JANET consisted of a full duplex circuit and a communication path of more than 1,000 km with a data rate of thirty-four words per minute.

The first operational military MBC was Communications by Meteor Trails (COMET), implemented by the North Atlantic Treaty Organization's Supreme Headquarters Allied Powers Europe in 1965. COMET operated between stations in the Netherlands, France, United Kingdom, Italy, West Germany, and Norway. The system was capable of maintaining from two to eight sixty-words-per-minute teletype circuits, depending on the amount of meteor activity.

The introduction of satellite communications in the late 1960s reduced interest in MBC. However, when the many vulnerabilities of satellite communications were recognized and the number of satellites was found insufficient to meet requirements, interest in MBC returned.

Two large civilian systems, the Snow Pack Telemetry System (SNOTEL) and the Alaskan Meteor Burst Communications System (AMBCS) became operational in 1978 and 1977, respectively. The SNOTEL system consists of two master stations and more than 500 remote stations located in nearly inaccessible sites in ten Western states. The remote sites are solar powered and transmit reports on snow pack, precipitation, and temperature every twenty-four hours. The AMBCS is used by five federal agencies to gather information from remote areas of Alaska. Both the SNOTEL and the AMBCS demonstrate that large MBC systems are not only feasible but also practical.

The U.S. Air Force's Alaskan Air Command MBC became operational in the mid-1980s. The Air Force system was used as a backup communications system between the

Regional Operations Center and thirteen long-range radar sites throughout Alaska. The system was able to send data in sufficient quantity to maintain a real-time radar display.

Tommy R. Young II

See also Communication Satellites; North Atlantic Treaty Organization (NATO) Communications & Information Systems Agency

Sources

Jernovics, John P. 1990. "Meteor Burst Communications: An Additional Means of Long-Haul Communications." [Online article; retrieved January 2007.] http://www.globalsecurity.org/space/library/report/1990/JJP.htm.
Schilling, Donald L. 1993. *Meteor Burst Communications: Theory and Practice.* New York: Wiley.

Mexican Punitive Expedition (1916–1917)

In March 1916 a Mexican guerrilla force led by Pancho Villa raided the border town of Columbus, New Mexico, and inflicted two dozen American casualties and thousands of dollars of property damage. In response to this terrorist act, President Woodrow Wilson ordered mobilization of forces along the border and directed Brigadier General John J. Pershing to lead a punitive expedition into northern Mexico to capture Villa. This invasion of Mexico was not welcomed, and Pershing's force of 12,000 men was soon fighting both the Mexican army and Villa's guerrilla forces. During the expedition, the Americans called on the latest technological advancements, including radios, motor vehicles, and airplanes, all employed in combat for the first time by the U.S. Army.

Columbus became the center for command, control, and communications for the operation. Signal units included three field signal companies and the First Aero Squadron, with a total of eighteen officers and 284 men. They employed wire and wireless wagons, wireless sets, telegraphs, telephones, switchboards, cameras, and pigeons. Early in the campaign, two wireless (radio) wagon sets were in service—one at Columbus and the other at Colonia Dublan, about 125 miles from Columbus. The wireless equipment was so large and heavy, however, that it could not keep pace with the quickly advancing cavalry columns, and the uncertainty of radio contact failed to satisfy commanders in the field. As a result almost all messages were sent via wire.

Pershing's expedition was notable for its long lines of communication wire. As troops moved deeper into Mexico, wire was laid from the tailboards of wagons, and Pershing was never out of communication with his base at Columbus, an eventual distance of almost 400 miles. At first only a single bare wire was laid, as the signal units lacked insulated wire. The ground was dry sand, and when it rained the wire shorted out. Even morning dew shorted the circuit until sunrise, when heat burned away the moisture. After insulated wire was obtained, connection was still an issue due to breakage by animals and sabotage by enemy guerrillas. To resolve that problem, maintenance stations were established at 25-mile intervals along the line. Signalmen traveled on horseback and light motor trucks to repair any breaks. A test message was sent every ten minutes, and trucks were ready to make needed repairs should the test fail.

The unique contribution of this expedition was the first American use of airplanes to support military operations. The mission of the First Aero Squadron was to carry messages and conduct reconnaissance and observation flights. It also carried mail for the troops from Columbus to Pershing's head-quarters in the field. Flying was dangerous due to the mountains and wind currents, which caused several accidents and damaged aircraft. Pershing often employed the aircraft to carry messages directly back to his headquarters or to other commanders in the months of frustrating effort to capture the elusive Villa. However, by April 1916 most of the First Aero Squadron was used up and only two aircraft were left in service. Unable to capture Villa and hoping to avoid a general war with Mexico, Pershing's punitive expedition returned to the United States in February 1917—just months before the country entered World War I.

Steven J. Rauch

See also Airplanes; Army Signal Corps; Field
   Wire and Cable; Radio; Telegraph

Sources

Mason, Herbert M. 1970. *The Great Pursuit.* New
   York: Random House.
Raines, Rebecca Robbins. 1996. *Getting the
   Message Through: A Branch History of the US
   Signal Corps.* Washington, DC: Center of
   Military History.

Microwave

Microwaves are high-frequency radio waves used for point-to-point and omnidirectional communication of audio, data, and video signals, both on land and to and from satellites. Microwave frequencies (generally 1–30 GHz) require direct line of sight to operate; obstructions can distort or block the signal.

Microwave links offer several advantages, and countervailing drawbacks. Though traditionally such radio links were less expensive than buried or aerial cable lines, the growth of high-capacity fiber optic networks has tended to curtail both the growth and use of microwave relays. While microwaves make reliable and fast mobile communications possible (sometimes transmitted and received via satellite), this capability has led directly to microwave espionage, where signals are intercepted and decoded.

Usefulness of shortwaves for radio communication made researchers curious about what awaited them at wavelengths shorter than 10 meters (30 feet) and higher in frequency than 30 MHz. Throughout the 1930s, scientists and engineers began experiments with what they called "ultra-short waves" or "microwaves." Because there were then no obvious commercial applications for such waves, experiments were generally restricted to laboratories. The U.S. Navy installed its first experimental microwave communication system in 1937 on the destroyer USS *Leary*.

During World War II extensive research on search radar moved the technology forward substantially. As the war ground to a close, Philco, RCA, Raytheon, and Westinghouse all began to exploit the technology further for both civilian and military needs. Military microwave applications focused on radar, both mobile and fixed. Other important applications included electronic countermeasures and (by the 1990s) the global positioning system (GPS).

Over the final two decades of the twentieth century, military needs substantially drove microwave and millimeter-wave technology in the United States. The highly successful $90-million-a-year Microwave and Millimeter-Wave Integrated Circuit (MIMIC) program was a major source of research funds, but other significant research and development programs included funding for microwave tubes. The three-service MIMIC program pushed the frontiers of microwave integrated-circuit technology, focusing on a comprehensive capability for design, manufacture, and testing. The program successfully transformed many military systems from tubes to solid state and from hybrids to monolithic microwave integrated circuits. Budget constraints after 2000 began to impinge on this work, forcing more adaption of commercial systems.

High-powered microwave (HPM) bombs were an option under consideration early in the twenty-first century for ruining enemy electronic components and communication without harming military personnel. By sending out a microwave pulse, HPM bombs fry the electrical innards of electrical equipment and communication links, including command-and-control systems. Such devices can be guided by central controllers (only 10 percent of bombs in the 1990–1991 Gulf War were so controlled—by the 2003 Iraq War, some 80 percent were).

Christopher H. Sterling

See also Communication Satellites; Electromagnetic Pulse (EMP); Electronic Countermeasures/Electronic Warfare (ECM/EW); Fiber Optics; Global Positioning System (GPS); Gulf War (1990–1991); Iraq War (2003–Present); Solid State Electronics

Sources
Cantelon, Philip L. 1993. "The Promise of Microwaves." In *The History of MCI: The Early Years, 1968–1988*, appendix A, 508–524. Dallas: Heritage Press.
Glasser, Lance A. n.d. "Breakthroughs in Affordability of Military Microwave Systems." Washington, DC: Defense Advanced Research Projects Agency. http://www .darpa.mil/mto/Articles/Article8.html.
IEEE Virtual Museum. 2006. "Post–World War II Military Applications of Microwaves." [Online information; retrieved June 2006.] http://www.ieee-virtual-museum.org/ exhibit/exhibit.php?id=159265&lid=1& seq=7.

O'Neill, E. F., ed. 1985. "Ultrahigh Frequencies, Microwaves, and Radio Relays." In *A History of Engineering and Science in the Bell System: Transmission Technology (1925–1975)*, 141–192. New York: AT&T Bell Laboratories.

Midway, Battle of (3–6 June 1942)

The three-day Battle of Midway was a decisive turning point in the Pacific conflict with Japan and was World War II's most important naval battle. Midway's result was determined largely by signals intelligence, which revealed Japanese plans to the U.S. Navy.

After devastating the U.S. Pacific Fleet in its December 1941 Pearl Harbor attack, Japan embarked on a lightning campaign to conquer the western Pacific and its many islands. The primary threat to that campaign was the American aircraft carriers, none of which had been at Pearl Harbor. When its confidence was shaken by a carrier-borne U.S. bombing attack (the Doolittle Raid) against Tokyo on 18 April 1942, Japan initiated plans to lure the American carriers into a decisive engagement that would destroy them. The Battle of the Coral Sea in early May bloodied both the Japanese and American fleets (each lost a carrier), and Japanese invasion forces heading for Port Moresby, New Guinea, were turned back. Against that American strategic victory, the Japanese Imperial Navy next resolved to seize the American-held Midway Island, the westernmost part of the Hawaiian chain and site of an important airfield. Holding such a base was deemed vital to defending the newly conquered reaches of the Pacific.

Thanks to the American breaking of Japan's diplomatic Purple and naval JN-25 codes used in radio communication, however, and especially the efforts of a team led by Commander Joseph J. Rochefort, U.S. Navy OP-20-G's intelligence "Station Hypo" in Honolulu was able to identify Japan's focus on Midway. This was accomplished by a neat piece of deception. To determine that Japan's coded target (dubbed "AF" in radio messages) was, in fact, Midway, Honolulu contacted Midway by means of submarine cable connections (that could not be read by enemy forces) and told island forces to send a clear (uncoded) radio signal that the garrison was short of fresh water. Subsequently decoded Japanese messages affirmed that their intended target lacked sufficient water supplies—and thus American naval leaders knew both when and where the next Japanese attack would fall. Signals intelligence also revealed a good deal about the order of battle of Japanese forces and some of their intentions.

This vital knowledge allowed the badly stretched American fleet to concentrate its fighting forces, including its (only) three carriers in the Pacific, in the right place and time, ignoring Japanese attempts to deflect attention with attacks on the Aleutian Islands far to the north. The Japanese force of approximately 200 vessels included eight carriers. The outclassed American side included the carrier *Yorktown*, which had been rushed to repair (from damage received in the Coral Sea fight) in just forty-eight hours at Pearl Harbor. The ensuing battle for Midway was a fierce air engagement between carrier-based fighter and bomber groups. Adding to their vital signals intelligence–derived knowledge, however, American forces were also lucky. After several failed attempts, their key air strike against the Japanese carriers came as the Japanese were reloading aircraft and were thus at their most vulnerable.

The battle resulted in Japan's loss of four fleet aircraft carriers (and related aircraft and trained crews), among other vessels. The U.S. lost *Yorktown* and a few other ships. Failing to gain Midway, the Imperial Navy also lost its carrier-based initiative and was forced into defensive operations for the rest of World War II.

Marc L. Schwartz and Christopher H. Sterling

See also Code Breaking; Magic; OP-20-G; Signals Intelligence (SIGINT)

Sources
Fuchida, Mitsuo, and Okumiya Masatake. 1955. *Midway: The Battle That Doomed Japan.* Annapolis, MD: Naval Institute Press.
Lord, Walter. 1967. *Incredible Victory.* New York: Harper & Row.
Parker, Frederick D. 1993. *A Priceless Advantage: U.S. Navy Communications Intelligence and the Battles of Coral Sea, Midway, and the Aleutians.* Cryptologic History Series IV, World War II, Volume 5. Fort Meade, MD: National Security Agency.
Prados, John. 1995. *Combined Fleet Decoded: The Secret History of American Intelligence and the Japanese Navy in World War II.* New York: Random House.
Prange, Gordon W., et al. 1982. *Miracle at Midway.* New York: McGraw-Hill.

Military Affiliate Radio System (MARS)

The Military Affiliate Radio System (MARS) was organized in 1948 as the Military Amateur Radio System, a network of volunteer licensed civilian "ham," or amateur, radio operators who provided auxiliary communications services for America's military. The MARS system traces its origins back even further, however, to the formation in 1925 of the Army Amateur Radio System (AARS), a small civilian volunteer network sponsored by the U.S. Army Signal Corps. Its purpose was to enlist enthusiasts in the new field of radio operations and communications in the Signal Corps' programs of radio-wave research and radio equipment development. During World War II, the AARS system became moribund because national security regulations prohibited civilians from using broadcast equipment.

After the war, however, the U.S. Army reactivated AARS and shortly thereafter replaced it with the MARS system. The objective of the change was to cultivate a new pool of experienced personnel capable of assisting with the American military's communications needs in the event of national or local emergencies. Each branch of the armed services eventually developed its own MARS system, the last being the formation of the Navy–Marine Corps MARS in 1963.

During the early Cold War period, expansion of the MARS systems was driven by the government's emphasis on civil defense preparedness, especially for a nuclear attack on the United States by the Soviet Union. By the 1960s, however, the emphasis in MARS development began to shift to more global coverage, and a worldwide network of civilian radio operators was recruited to help provide communications links to support potential deployments of American troops overseas.

MARS expansion in East and Southeast Asia was especially rapid during the period of American military involvement in Vietnam. The MARS system in South Vietnam was launched in 1965 with only six small stations. By late 1969, when the United States had a half-million troops in South Vietnam, the Army system alone had forty-seven sta-

tions in the country, while the Navy–Marine Corps MARS had nearly thirty. All of the MARS stations in South Vietnam used civilian-produced, commercially available single-sideband radios. These stations provided "phone patch" services for American military personnel serving in Southeast Asia. Once contacted via radio by a station in South Vietnam, a U.S. civilian MARS network operator would place a collect telephone call to a serviceman's home in the United States. By 1970 MARS connections were reportedly accessible to every American unit in Vietnam. Radio use imposed a different vernacular, however, and many Vietnam-era veterans fondly remember punctuating their brief conversations with the word "over."

During the1980s MARS networks provided communications conduits for American military personnel overseas, as well as disaster response functions at home. In the United States, MARS operators work with the Federal Emergency Management Agency and with the National Disaster Medical System, which coordinates the work of federal, state, and local agencies providing medical and public health services during peacetime disasters.

Although use of the Internet narrowed demand for MARS services, in the early 2000s MARS operators transmitted simplified text messages, known as "morale messages," to American soldiers in Afghanistan and Iraq and placed long-distance telephone calls to the United States for active duty personnel.

Laura M. Calkins

See also Army Signal Corps; Iraq War (2003–Present); Radio; Vietnam War (1959–1975)

Sources

Marine Corps Institute. 1992. *The MARS Operator.* Washington, DC: Marine Corps Institute, Marine Barracks.

Rienzi, Thomas M. 1972. *Communications-Electronics 1962–1970.* Washington, DC: Department of the Army.

Thompson, Paul. 1968. "MARS Calling." *Leatherneck* 51 (January): 84–85.

Military Communications-Electronics Board (MCEB)

After years of competition and disagreement, cooperation in military communications across the American military services was forced by the exigencies of World War II, and despite many organizational and name changes, it continues today. For nearly a half-century, the Military Communications-Electronics Board has fulfilled the coordinating role.

The word "joint," to designate cooperating or combining of often competitive military arms, was a relatively new term in Washington DC when, in July 1942, the Joint Chiefs of Staff (JCS, itself newly formed) commissioned the Joint Communications Board. To be staffed with four members, two each from the Army and the Navy, the board was to have oversight regarding communications and electronics issues, operating under the JCS umbrella. In 1948 the board was reorganized as the Joint Communications-Electronics Committee (JC-EC) and in 1949 expanded its responsibility for communications electronic matters as well as added membership from the recently formed U.S. Air Force. The JC-EC mission continued oversight of all military communications and electronics, an expanding sector in all of the services. The director of Communications Electronics for the JCS Joint Staff was added a few months later. Due to another reorganization of JCS in 1958, JC-EC functions and structure were shifted to a new Joint Communications Electronics Group, still as part of JCS, in midyear.

The Military Communications-Electronics Board (MCEB) was established in October 1958 with the creation of the JCS Joint Staff. The board's oversight function was supported with communications and electronics expertise from the several military departments. The chairmanship of MCEB was assigned to the director for Communications-Electronics (J6) until, four years later, the director of the Defense Communications Agency became chairman. The National Security Agency also became part of MCEB and at the same time the level of the board was raised to that of an advisory body serving the secretary of defense. In 1966 the manager of the National Communications System became chairman of MCEB. In June 1976, the director, Tri-Service Tactical Communications System became another participant on MCEB. Late in 1993, the Joint Commanders Group for Communications-Electronics began to participate in the deliberations of MCEB.

The deputy secretary of defense revised MCEB's mission, organization, functions, responsibilities, and relationships in 1998. The board became the decision-making instrument of both JCS and the secretary of defense for determining the military needs for and components of command, control, communications, and computers (C4) strategy to support American forces in peace or war conditions. As such, the board resolves issues related to the interoperability, compatibility, and integration of C4 and intelligence and coordinates these efforts with other federal agencies. MCEB also coordinates with other nations, usually via the Combined Communications-Electronics Board (CCEB). This is a five-nation joint military communications-electronics (C-E) organization that coordinates any military C-E matter that is referred to it by a member nation. CCEB member nations are Australia, Canada, New Zealand, the United Kingdom, and the United States. CCEB consists of a senior C4 representative from each member nation.

MCEB continues to be chaired by the director for Command, Control, Communications, and Computer Systems (J6) of the Joint Staff and is composed of flag officer— or senior executive service—level representatives of more than twenty-two organizations from the services and defense agencies.

Danny Johnson

See also Defense Communications Agency (DCA, 1960–1991); National Communications System (NCS); National Security Agency (NSA)

Sources

Department of Defense. 1998. *Military Communications-Electronics Board (MCEB): Department of Defense Directive, Number 5100.35.* 1998. Washington, DC: Department of Defense.

Department of Defense. 2002. *Military Communications-Electronics Board, Organization, Mission and Functions Manual.* Washington, DC: Government Printing Office.

Joint Chiefs of Staff. 1995. *Doctrine for Command, Control, Communications and Computer (C4) Systems Support to Joint Operations.* Joint Publication 6-0 (May 30). Washington, DC: Joint Chiefs of Staff.

Military Roads

Roads built by the military are an excellent though not unique example of the melding of manmade transport and communications links (waterways could obviously serve the same purpose, as, after about 1830, could railways). Especially prior to the late-eighteenth-century appearance of optical or mechanical semaphore systems, sending a courier on a direct road was nearly always the fastest way to transmit military messages (think of Paul Revere's famous ride in 1775).

Carl von Clausewitz, in *On War* (1832), underscored the value of military roads in chapter XVI on lines of communication: "Only those roads on which magazines, hospitals, stations, posts for dispatches and letters are organized under commandants with police and garrisons, can be looked upon as real lines of communication."

As in so many activities in which they excelled, the Romans promoted empire expansion with the building and maintenance of a superior road system. The legions and others built perhaps as many as 50,000 miles of hard-surfaced roadway, of which the 160-mile Appian Way heading south from Rome is probably the most famous. Roman roads (such as that behind Hadrian's Wall) provided the right of way for many later highways in Britain and elsewhere.

Under orders from British monarch George I to suppress a rebellion in Scotland, Major General George Wade (1673–1748) spent sixteen years (1724–1740) directing the construction of a widening web of some 250 miles of military roadways across the country to link old and new fortresses and barracks. His designated successor, Major William Caulfield, continued the process for another quarter-century (1740–1767) after the second Jacobite invasion (1745–1746). Stone bridges (more than forty of them in Scotland) were usually the most expensive part of these building campaigns—and many survive today.

In western Europe and the American colonies, late eighteenth-century post roads (e.g., the Boston Post Road) connected cities to encourage more and faster mail service. Congress helped to fund construction of post roads as the country expanded, and military roads to help extend communication (and control) to the frontier. The latter appeared first in the old Northwest (now the upper Midwest) and then in the trans-Mississippian region from at least the 1820s to the post–Civil War period. The short-lived Pony Express (1860–1861) from St. Joseph, Missouri, to California was an expensive private example of the same idea.

In the American Civil War (1861–1865), both sides sought to build and control military roads (and railroads) while denying their use to the enemy. But the major change in the role of military roads was already apparent: given the availability of telegraphy, the roads now rarely served communications needs. World War I, being largely static save for its opening and closing months, did not lend itself to much road building. World War II military road-building projects such as the Alaska Highway and Burma Road were built largely for supply needs rather than communication. Even the interstate highway system approved by the U.S. Congress in 1956 was constructed with military needs very much in mind, though those needs no longer focused on supporting communication.

Christopher H. Sterling

See also Couriers; Hadrian's Wall; Horses and Mules; Mobile Communications; Vehicles and Transport

Sources

Clausewitz, Carl von. 1832 (1976). *On War*. Princeton, NJ: Princeton University Press.
Hulbert, Archer Butler. 1904. *Military Roads of the Mississippi Basin: The Conquest of the Old Northwest*. Cleveland, OH: Arthur H. Clark.
Overland Trail Links. "Military Roads of the Old West." [Online information; retrieved April 2007.] http://www.overland.com/militaryroad.html.
Taylor, William. 1996. *The Military Roads of Scotland*. Colonsay, Argyll, Scotland: House of Lochar.
War Office. 1935. *Military Engineering, Vol V: Roads*. London: His Majesty's Stationery Office.

Miniaturization

Efficient use of electronic circuits and the military equipment based on them has greatly improved over the past half-century thanks to increasingly small, portable, and capable equipment with lower power demands and less heat production. With mechanical devices, miniaturization was a slow and serial process accomplished by a few experts. While the trend to miniaturize electronics was especially driven by Cold War military needs, it began before World War II with the drive to shrink vacuum tubes to reduce their power needs and heat output.

Three parallel and overlapping paths of technology development have pushed miniaturization in electronics. First came the Bell Laboratory's development of the transistor (1948), followed by the Kilby-Noyce invention of the integrated circuit (1959), which revolutionized electronics beginning in the 1960s. Yet the notion of printed circuit boards dates back to 1943. Components that had relied for a half-century on cumbersome and fragile vacuum tube technology could now be made far smaller and less power hungry. The public saw this breakthrough in terms of shrinking hearing aids (and other medical devices) and ever-smaller portable radios, while all military services gained greater communication capabilities, though the devices used took up less space and power.

The second was development of both military and civil missile systems, from the German V-2 of World War II to liquid-fueled intermediate-range and then intercontinental ballistic missiles, and finally to solid-fuel rockets. The cost of developing sufficient power to launch missile payloads—and later to place them in orbit for space exploration purposes—strongly supported development of miniature components. The case is made when one compares early Soviet and American missiles. The former were huge largely because Russian electronics lagged behind those of the West, and brute power was needed to launch the archaic electronic systems into orbit. American missiles and spacecraft had smaller engines, which drove the need for them to be far more capable per pound launched.

The third (and most obvious to the public) has been the development of the digital computer, and the solid state electronics–driven shrinking of computer components from room-size mainframe devices to stand-alone units, to desktop devices, and now laptop computers. The first computer to use integrated circuits was the PDP-8 of 1965. The first integrated circuit microprocessor came six years later with the Intel 4004. The constant press for faster operation and greater memory capacity puts more power in the hands (literally) of a user in the early 2000s than a whole room-size computer could generate a half-century earlier. And while capacity rises, size shrinks, as does the price per unit of computing power—not a bad combination.

But there are clear limits to the process of electronics miniaturization—the laws of physics for one, and the specific problem of heat dissipation of components jammed ever closer to one another. Such limits—at least as they are understood at the beginning of the twenty-first century—suggest

that the process of miniaturization may have run its course.

Christopher H. Sterling

See also Bell Telephone Laboratories (BTL); Communication Satellites; Computer; Kilby, Jack St. Clair (1923–2005) and Noyce, Robert Norton (1927–1990); Mobile Communications; Solid State Electronics; Transistor; Vacuum Tube

Sources

Electronics, Editors of. 1980. *An Age of Innovation: The World of Electronics, 1930–1980.* New York: McGraw-Hill.

Keyes, R. W. 1988. "Miniaturization of Electronics and Its Limits." *IBM Journal of Research and Development* 32: 1.

Kovacs, G. T. A. 2000. "The Past, Present and Potential Future of Miniaturization Technologies." Washington, DC: Defense Advance Research Projects Agency.

Stevenson, William R. 1966. *Miniaturization and Micro-miniaturization of Army Communications-Electronics 1946–1964.* Historical Monograph 1, Project Number AMC 21M. Fort Monmouth, NJ: Headquarters and U.S. Army Electronics Command.

Missile Range Communications

During and after the 1960s, the U.S. Air Force Eastern Test Range supported both military missile test launches and the civilian space program. The range extended from Cape Canaveral, Florida, 5,000 miles south to Ascension Island in the South Atlantic Ocean. Missiles were launched from the cape and were tracked over the range by facilities on a number of Caribbean islands that included Grand Bahama, Antigua, and Ascension. In addition, several ships were stationed in the Atlantic to serve as floating tracking sites.

During a missile launch, all of those tracking sites had to intercommunicate on a real-time basis, both with each other and with the cape. Each location needed voice, data, and video communications for routine, ongoing, daily work. The Air Force's 2862 Ground Electronics Engineering Installation Agency (GEEIA) Squadron was responsible for the installation and depot-level maintenance of that communications equipment.

On the cape, those communications traveled through a total of approximately 1,000 miles of lead-covered, buried cables that contained hundreds and sometimes several thousand pairs of copper wires. GEEIA personnel interconnected these cables by splicing them together, one wire at a time. Since the cape is at sea level, water put those buried cables at risk. Therefore, they were pressurized with an inert gas to keep water from entering. Cape Canaveral and the various tracking locations all had their own electromechanical telephone systems that required frequent depot-level maintenance from GEEIA personnel. Expansion of the telephone systems was ongoing to support the ever-expanding needs of the Eastern Test Range. High-frequency radio equipment was used to provide communications between the cape and the downrange tracking sites. At all of those locations, GEEIA personnel installed and maintained that equipment, including the antenna systems.

Each launch complex had an extensive complement of missile intercommunication equipment. It provided a multichannel voice communications capability on the launch pad to the nearby control blockhouse and to downrange sites. Often, the heat from a missile launch would damage the missile intercommunication equipment on a launch pad, and GEEIA personnel would perform maintenance work and install new equipment as needed. Public address systems were widely used on the launch complexes and in the assembly hangars and buildings on the cape. That equipment served a critical function in advising personnel about launch and normal work activities. Because of the size of the buildings, making those systems work effectively was a challenging task. On each launch complex, closed circuit television cameras provided a view of the missile to personnel in the blockhouse and mission control.

By the early twenty-first century, many of the Cape Canaveral launch facilities from the 1960s had been abandoned in place—no longer needed and too expensive to remove. GEEIA organization activities were transferred to other Air Force organizations.

Ronald R. Thomas

See also Communication Satellites

Source

National Aeronautics & Space Administration. "Kennedy Space Center History." [Online information; retrieved January 2007.] http://www.nasa.gov/centers/kennedy/about/history/index.html.

Mobile Communications

Effective mobile communications are central to the operation of any fighting force. With the exception of ancient and traditional methods of message sending, technology has made truly mobile communications possible only in the past few decades. Mobile communications have evolved from supporting military action to becoming an integral military force. With the mid-nineteenth-century invention of the telegraph, land-based military signaling has served less to carry messages than to coordinate widespread use of various wheeled, and eventually motorized, vehicles. By the 1930s, mobile radio began to vastly increase the coordinated use of all military transport and fighting vehicles.

For thousands of years, mobile military communications meant carrying a message by courier, pigeon, animal, or vehicle. Using vehicles to carry military communication dates at least to Roman times when military roads were maintained for use by, among others, military couriers, some of whom traveled by chariot or coach. For centuries, however, land vehicular speeds were no faster than a horse. This continued into the early days of military telegraph (1850s) and telephone (1870s), save for rapid cable laying by special teams using cable carts.

Mobile military communications in the modern sense begins with the coming of radio at the turn of the twentieth century. For only with wireless technology were military forces able to move and still communicate without being tied by wire to higher headquarters. In 1906, the U.S. Army developed a portable wireless pack set that could be carried by three mules. It was powered by batteries and used a 60-foot telescoping antenna, and could soon be mounted on a single wagon. The original induction coil was replaced by a quenched spark-gap set by 1911. The motorcycle became another useful means of dispatching military messages. Harley-Davidson motorcycles, for example, were used by the U.S. Army during the Mexican Punitive Expedition of 1916.

World War I saw a push to develop smaller and lighter radios, primarily for use in airplanes, airships, and submarines rather than trench-bound land warfare where mobility was rare for much of the fighting. Several factors limited radio's portability in the early twentieth century, chief among them the use of fragile spark-gap, and later,

bulky and heat-producing vacuum tube equipment. Battery-powered "trench" radios were bulky but at least allowed some use on the move, usually carried by trucks or horses and by 1918 sometimes in the new tanks. Though some 10,000 wireless sets were made in the United States, American participation in World War I was too brief to see most of them put to use. Further, tactical radio was rarely more than a backup for line telecommunications, though British forces in the Middle East (with little line telegraphy or telephony) made good use of animal- or wagon-borne pack radio sets from 1915 to 1918.

Radio technology developed further during the interwar period. Both the British and American army signal arms actively pursued vehicle radio development. Development of FM radio techniques greatly aided development of U.S. Army vehicular and man-pack radio systems. As early as 1938 Germany had manufactured a complete line of portable and mobile radio equipment for its army, links that would prove vital in the forthcoming blitzkrieg warfare. Germany's integrated use of ground armor and air power in 1939–1940 was tied together with effective tactical radio communications. Rapid movement by German motorized divisions as well as their close air support were made more effective by their use of shortwave radio communications.

World War II's wide-ranging battles required tactical radio communications, perhaps best exemplified in the war of movement across North Africa from 1940 to 1943. More than 90,000 Harley-Davidson motorcycles were produced in the United States during World War II, many of them used in dispatch duty. Lighter motor scooters were also used. The ubiquitous "jeep" began to replace both by the mid-1940s. Specialized radio trucks were vital to fast-moving Axis and Allied armies, especially in the European and African theaters of World War II. With transmitters and receivers built and tested to stand rugged treatment over difficult terrain, wide temperature and humidity variation, and constant use, these vehicles were essential means of keeping active commanders in touch with fast-changing battle fronts. Multiple spare parts (especially fragile vacuum tubes) were supplied, waterproofing was standard, and antennas were mounted on springs.

Often, sufficient equipment was not the problem—sufficient trained personnel was. The public perception of portability became the U.S. Army's "walkie-talkies" that looked something like the earliest cell phones of four decades later. Bricklike in size, shape, and weight, they allowed some portability as well as links to frontline fighting forces. High-powered land mobile radio sets became common at division and regimental levels. Tank radios initially suffered from battery shortages and recharging, and often from varied equipment. With improved radios, telegraph (code) communication could be conducted by 1944 at distances of more than 100 miles from vehicles in motion. Fleets of tanks and personnel carriers were connected to central command by radio communication. U.S. Army vehicles made early use of FM multichannel radio for static-free high-frequency communications, despite the many sources of interference in the vehicle itself. Throat and then lip microphones were developed to improve communication in high-noise situations. Virtually all armored vehicles, Allied or Axis, contained at least one form of radio to meld them into an effective mobile force.

Postwar radio development centered on FM's capabilities, on which the U.S. Army

Signal Corps focused. In general, goals in developing a new generation of combat radios included lower power consumption, smaller size, lighter weight, ability to use more frequencies with closer channel spacing for efficient operation, and higher reliability. By the 1970s and 1980s, additional requirements included more attention to internal communications security (which had become a serious problem in the Vietnam War) and the ability to send and receive data along with voice.

Engineers sought to make vehicular and portable radios more compatible. Antennas were improved in an attempt to make them less obvious to enemy forces by means of telescoping or use of ground trailing types. Batteries (primary type were longer lasting but could not be recharged; secondary type could be recharged and used again) were made more heat and water resistant and longer lasting. Vietnam saw the introduction by 1965 of squad-level combat FM radios, some of them belt mounted, others with receivers built into helmets, though they saw limited use in the jungle combat conditions.

Over the last few decades, a fundamental revolution in mobile military communication has integrated digitization, solid state circuits, and miniaturization with ever more capable military communication satellites. Radio types by the last quarter of the twentieth century varied by their intended use and range. Tactical types included the squad radio (a small, handheld FM unit) for very local communication within ground forces, a main ground force communication device that was also FM and was carried in a backpack for longer-distance communication, a forward air controller AM radio in a backpack for communicating with ground support aircraft, and a special forces high-frequency radio using single-sideband technology over longer distances. Nontactical types included search and rescue AM radios on various frequencies, used for downed air personnel or other rescue duties, and a guard duty/fire rescue/other use type of radio, which could be low or high band, using FM. The U.S. Army has generally taken the lead in developing most of these, with the Marine Corps using similar equipment.

The Gulf War of 1990–1991 made clear the role of mobile communications. Integrated air and ground unit communications kept up with a fast-changing battlefield area. The expansive desert terrain called for flexible use of multiple spectrum channels and constant command-and-control links made possible by increasingly digital equipment. The importance of data over voice communications became immediately evident, supported by use of more than sixty military satellites. At the same time, Iraqi communications were steadily interdicted, with immediate impact on the battlefield.

Now being developed are the first fully integrated combat systems, developed from the ground up and incorporating various communications capabilities and links as central features. In October 1999, for example, the Army announced development of the first two technology-enhanced, rapidly deployable Stryker brigades (named for two Medal of Honor winners) using off-the-shelf technology from the private sector. Heavy tracked vehicles (armored personnel carriers and tanks) are being replaced by a family of eight lighter, faster, more fuel-efficient wheeled vehicles. The Army is developing the capability to put brigade combat teams anywhere in the world within 96 hours, a division on the ground in 120 hours, and five divisions within thirty days. The brigades build on the strike force concept, which focuses on the ability to rapidly

deploy a lethal modular and network-centric force. Six brigades are planned (most oriented toward the Pacific) by 2008. The first were employed in Iraq in 2003.

The developing Future Combat Systems and the Warfighter Information Network–Tactical are further examples of this multiservice trend toward full integration of communications with fighting units on the ground and in the air.

Christopher H. Sterling

See also Airmobile Communications; Combat Information Transport System (CITS); Communication Satellites; Couriers; Fiber Optics; Field Wire and Cable; Fire/Flame/Torch; Future Combat Systems (FCS); Global Information Grid (GIG); Global Positioning System (GPS); Gulf War (1990–1991); Heliograph and Mirrors; Internet; Iraq War (2003–Present); Joint Tactical Radio System (JTRS); Mexican Punitive Expedition (1916–1917); Pigeons; Radio; Single Channel Ground and Airborne Radio System (SINCGARS); Single Sideband (SSB); Smoke; Vacuum Tube; Vehicles and Transport; Vietnam War (1959–1975); Walkie-Talkie; Warfighter Information Network–Tactical (WIN-T); World War I; World War II

Sources
Beauchamp, K. G. 2001. "Telegraphy at War" In *History of Telegraphy*, 266–307. London: Institution of Electrical Engineers.
Bergen, John D. 1985. *Military Communications: A Test for Technology*. Washington, DC: U.S. Army Center for Military History.
Campen, Alan D., ed. 1992. *The First Information War: The Story of Communications, Computers and Intelligence Systems in the Persian Gulf War*. Fairfax, VA: AFCEA International Press.
Gonzalez, Dan. 2005. *Network Centric Operations Case Study: The Stryker Brigade Combat Team*. Santa Monica, CA: Rand Corp.
O'Connell, J. D. 1942. "Development of Vehicular Equipment." *Radio News* Special Signal Corps Issue (November): 106–109, 198–202.

Rice, M. A. 1994. *Command & Control Support Systems in the Gulf War: Land Warfare.* London: Brassey's Battlefield Weapons Systems & Technology.

Tasker, Alan D. "U.S. Military Portable Radios." With rebuttal by Dennis Starks. [Online article; retrieved June 2006.] http://hereford.ampr.org/history/portable.html.

Woods, David L. 1965. "Tactical Wireless, Radio, and Radiotelephone." In *A History of Tactical Communication Techniques,* 209–239. Orlando, FL: Martin-Marietta (reprinted by Arno Press in "Telecommunications," 1974).

Modulation

Modulation is the process by which voice or other intelligence is added to radio waves produced by a transmitter (an unmodulated radio signal is called a carrier). Each modulation mode has strengths and weaknesses, some technical and some economic. Amplitude modulation (AM) was the only mode in general use until frequency modulation (FM) became available in the late 1930s. AM and FM transmissions are subject to an inherent and relatively poor signal-to-noise ratio, though FM is much better than AM. Both are analog systems and dominated radio into the 1980s and 1990s, when digital services began to appear. The newest modulation approach is software-defined radio, developed by the military.

AM was the only mode of military radio available up to the beginning of World War II. "AM" simply indicates that the signal's strength is being modulated (several thousand times per second) in accordance with the amplitude or strength of the carrier wave. But AM is prone to natural and most manmade electrical interference, which cannot be electronically separated from the desired signal. Constant research to finds ways to overcome static (by use of narrower channels or more transmitter power, for example) failed. AM is subject to varied coverage depending on time of day—skyway propagation at night can send semipredictable signals a long distance. Most fiber optic transmissions use AM, as do single-sideband transmissions, which are a more efficient mode of AM.

FM radio was developed in 1928–1933 by prolific radio inventor Edwin Howard Armstrong. He was awarded the key patents in late 1933, and commercial FM radio began in 1941. Armstrong gave free use of his patent rights to the military during World War II. FM radio was an important mode of military communications during (and since) World War II, especially for mobile communications, as with tanks. In Armstrong's FM system, signals are varied by frequency rather than power output. He found that using a channel twenty times wider than an AM channel (200 kHz) would create an analog signal with vastly improved frequency response (up to 15,000 cycles per second, three times that of AM) that could avoid both artificial (manmade) and atmospheric interference (e.g., static from electrical storms). An FM signal need be only twice as strong as a more distant competing transmitter to suppress the interfering signal. Generally using a very high frequency (VHF) spectrum (often called VHF radio outside the United States), FM signals are propagated by direct line-of-sight means day or night, limiting transmitter coverage to a radius of no more than 60 to 70 miles depending on local terrain.

Phase modulation (PM) is a variation of FM and modulates the polarity of the wave. The two methods are very similar in the sense that any attempt to shift either the frequency or phase is accomplished by a change in the other. PM is not very widely used because it tends to require more complex receiving equipment.

Pulse code modulation (PCM) was developed in 1939 by English inventor Alec H. Reeves. PCM is the most important of several forms of pulse modulation because it can be used to transmit information over long distances with hardly any interference or distortion; for this reason it has become increasingly important in the transmission of data in the space program and between computers.

Software-defined radio (SDR) involves computer software defining the modulation method to be used. One of the first SDR units was an early 1990s U.S. Army project dubbed SpeakEasy. Its primary goal was to use programmable processing to emulate nearly a dozen existing military radios, operating in frequency bands between 2 and 200 MHz. Another design goal was to be able to easily incorporate new coding and modulation standards in the future, so that military communications can keep pace with advances in coding and modulation techniques. The project was also defined to operate with existing ground force radios (such as "frequency agile" VHF, FM, and Single Channel Ground and Airborne Radio System), Air Force radios (VHF AM), Navy radios (VHF AM and high-frequency single-sideband teleprinters), and communication satellites. The SpeakEasy project produced a demonstration radio only fifteen months into a three-year research project, and it proved so successful that further development was halted and the radio went into production with a 4 to 400 MHz range. As a military project, the radio strongly distinguished "red" (unsecured secret data) from "black" (cipher-secured data).

Christopher H. Sterling

See also Armstrong, Edwin Howard (1890–1954); Communication Satellites; Fiber Optics; Joint Tactical Radio System (JTRS); Mobile Communications; Radio; Single Channel Ground and Airborne Radio System (SINCGARS); Single Sideband; Spectrum Frequencies; Spread Spectrum

Sources

Defense Science Board Task Force. 2003. *Wideband Radio Frequency Modulation: Dynamic Access to Mobile Information Networks.* Washington, DC: Department of Defense.

Department of the Army. 1990. "AM Radio Operations." In *Communications in a "Come-as-you-are" War,* Field Manual 24–12. Washington, DC: Government Printing Office.

Department of the Army. 1990. "FM Radio Operations." In *Communications in a "Come-as-you-are" War,* Field Manual 24–12. Washington, DC: Government Printing Office.

Marks, William S. 1944. "FM in World War II." *Radio News* Special U.S. Army Signal Corps Issue (February): 243, 426–428.

McNicol, Dennis. 1946. *Radio's Conquest of Space.* New York: Murray Hill Books (reprinted by Arno Press, 1974).

National Association of Broadcasters. 1999. *NAB Engineering Handbook.* Washington, DC: NAB.

Morse Code

The Morse telegraphic code was largely developed by telegraph inventor Samuel F. B. Morse and his long-neglected assistant, Alfred B. Vail, in 1843.

In the eight years of telegraph experimentation to that point, Morse's system communicated by leaving a series of long, wavy lines on a strip of paper—a long, wavy ink line was termed a dash, while a shorter line was considered a dot. A year later, Vail invented a telegraphic sounder, which promptly replaced most ink recording devices and converted the electric telegraph from a written to a sound-based system. As do some modern electronic voting machines, the telegraph also left a written record. Telegraph messages were later again written as typed messages, only to change back to electrical sound, and ultimately to digital signals.

Most signal "codes," including the Morse code, did not intend to be secret. Codes simply made the telegraph more efficient and thus less expensive to use. If the message must be kept secret, then it must be encrypted into a true code or cipher. Like modern signal flag codes, the Morse code is simply a means to send messages by relating short and longer sounds to numbers and the letters of the alphabet. Numbers and letters are "coded" in plain text—via the electric telegraph, sound radio, flashing light, or single flag wig-wag. Because it could readily be applied to many different signal/communication methods, the Morse code became the most useful.

After the Pearl Harbor attack (7 December 1941), a U.S. Navy signalman proved vital to a dramatic rescue that saved 300 sailors trapped in the hull of the overturned battleship *Oklahoma*. For nearly four hours he "read" (by listening to) Morse messages tapped by sailors within the ship, and with his pocket knife tapped back messages promising help was on the way. After a hole was cut in the hull, the trapped sailors were guided to safety. Almost every signalman or radioman in the U.S. Navy learned how to send and receive Morse by sound over a telegraph line or radio, a tap on a ship's hull, or by flashing light visible day or night.

A little help was needed for Albert Myer's wig-wag flag code to use the Morse code. Myer had initially declared that a wave of

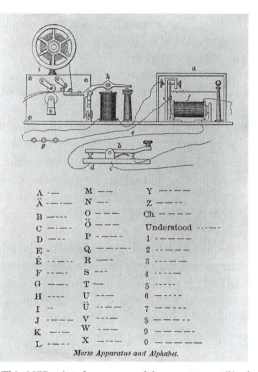

This 1877 print shows some of the apparatus utilized for sending and receiving coded telegraph messages using the alphabet and numbers that made up the "Morse code." (Library of Congress)

the large flag to the right meant the number one while a wave left meant a two. Dropping the flag in front the of the signaler meant a "pause" or number three and served as the end of the letter in the message being sent. Myer also evolved a second code in which sending a two equaled the letter "T," while twenty-two equaled the letter "A," and 222 equaled "D," just as one equaled "L," eleven equaled "N," and 111 equaled "Y," and so on.

During the 1840s, British army signalmen began to use the dot/dash of the Morse sound telegraph code instead of Myer's ones and twos. The Royal Navy also began to use Morse in their flashing light signals. The modern International Morse Code was invented by Friedrich Clemens Gerke in 1848 and used for telegraphy between Hamburg and Cuxhaven in Germany. After some minor changes in 1865 it was standardized at the telegraphy congress in Paris.

By 1896 the U.S. Army (after twenty-six years of using Myer's system) converted to the Continental Code for electric telegraphy, but retained Myer code for heliograph flashes and wig-wag flags. Three years later, all American railroads and commercial firms dropped the Continental Code in favor of American Morse. Ultimately, military services of both Britain and the United States adopted American Morse, finally providing a single code for electric telegraphy, one flag wig-wag, and flashing light signals via either blinker or heliograph. Though painfully slow, pyrotechnic signals can also employ Morse code. As it can take as long as five seconds to fire and view each burst (using, say, red flares as dashes and white flares as dots), such messages are not of much value in most tactical military or naval signaling. Since Morse code relies on an on-off keyed signal, it uses simpler equipment than voice radio communication, requires less spectrum space, and can be "read" in such high-noise/low-signal environments as military actions.

Morse is used today by amateur radio (ham) operators, even though in late 2006 the Federal Communications Commission announced it would no longer require that capability. Old-fashioned stock tickers using a long strip of paper to record stock prices using Morse code (the mechanism often covered with a transparent glass dome) are evident in photos and motion pictures of the turn of the last century. Morse code is also used as an assistive technology, which can help people with a variety of disabilities to communicate.

David L. Woods

See also Code, Codebook; Flaghoist; Flags; Heliograph and Mirrors; High-Speed Morse; International Code of Signals (ICS); Morse, Samuel F. B. (1791–1872); Myer, Albert James (1828–1880); Night Signals; Signal Book; Telegraph

Sources

Helft, Miguel. 2006. "A Fading Signal." *New York Times,* December 27, C1, C4.
Perera, Tom. n.d. "The 'Morse' Code and the Continental Code." [Online article; retrieved December 2006.] http://chss.montclair.edu/~pererat/percode.htm.

Morse, Samuel F. B. (1791–1872)

Inventor of the world's most widely used system of electric telegraphy, Samuel Morse was a key figure in introducing the telecommunications era. Arrival of the telegraph would open unforeseen opportunities for military communications, first made clear in mid-nineteenth-century wars in both Europe and the United States.

Morse was born on 27 April 1791 in Charlestown, Massachusetts, outside Boston. He graduated from Yale University in 1810 and then studied art in Britain. Until the 1830s, he trained to be a painter and practiced fine painting of both individuals and scenes, though he also produced a few mechanical inventions. He also worked in early photography, training, among others, Matthew Brady. Morse unsuccessfully ran for political office on an anti-immigration ticket, and published anti-Catholic pamphlets. He studied and painted in Europe from 1829 to 1832.

On the voyage home from Europe in 1832, Morse, always interested in science though lacking training, first developed the gist of a telegraph system in conversations with a fellow passenger. He demonstrated a working model late in 1835 and focused full time on developing his new invention by 1837. He had great trouble getting a telegraph signal to travel very far through a wire until a colleague suggested a stronger battery. By 1838 Morse and Alfred Vail had worked out the basics of what became known as Morse code to simplify and thus speed up the sending of messages. Granted a patent in 1840, he also sought patent protection in several European nations.

After several failed attempts, in 1843 Congress voted to allocate $30,000 (more than a half-million dollars in 2007 terms) for a test line along the 40 miles between Baltimore and Washington DC. Initially constructed underground, overhead lines on poles were found to be cheaper and more reliable. On 24 May 1844, the first message, "What Had God Wrought," was sent by Morse from the capital north to Baltimore.

Over the next two years, the telegraph was extended to New York, Boston, and Buffalo; other firms entered the business (often starting patent fights); and Morse again traveled to Europe to secure patent protection. Several years later a number of European governments awarded him a financial prize for his telegraph work. His American patent rights were upheld by the Supreme Court in 1854, and he began to collect royalty payments. He worked closely with Cyrus Field on several initial—and failed—attempts in the late 1850s to lay an Atlantic telegraph cable.

The remainder of Morse's life was often difficult, as he responded to attacks by other would-be telegraph inventors, dealt with the problems of his seven children, and became active in national conservative political debates over slavery and states' rights. While he played no direct part, his telegraph invention was increasingly applied to military needs in such conflicts as the Crimean (1854–1856) and American Civil (1861–1865) wars. A number of the original backers of the telegraph fell out with Morse and one another, adding to the bitterness of his final years. Morse died on 2 April 1872 at his home in New York City.

Christopher H. Sterling

See also American Civil War (1861–1865); European Late Nineteenth-Century Wars; Morse Code; Telegraph

Sources
Library of Congress. "Samuel F. B. Morse Papers at the Library of Congress, 1793–1919." [Online information; retrieved April 2007.] http://memory.loc.gov/ammem/sfbmhtml/sfbmhome.html.
Mabee, Carleton. 1943. *The American Leonardo: The Life of Samuel F. B. Morse*. New York: Knopf.
Morse, Edward Lind, ed. 1914. *Samuel F. B. Morse, His Letters and Journals*, 2 vols. Boston: Houghton Mifflin (reprinted in one by Da Capo, 1973).
Prime, Samuel Irenaeus. 1875. *The Life of Samuel F. B. Morse, LL.D, Inventor of the Electro-Magnetic Recording Telegraph*. New York: Appleton (reprinted by Arno Press, 1974).
Silverman, Kenneth. 2003. *Lightning Man: The Accursed Life of Samuel F. B. Morse*. New York: Knopf.
Thompson, Robert Luther. 1947. *Wiring a Continent: The History of the Telegraph Industry in the United States, 1832–1866*. Princeton, NJ: Princeton University Press.

Music Signals

While sounds, ranging from gunfire to vocal shouts, have undoubtedly been the most common means of signaling since warfare began, sounds can be easily misunderstood or overlooked. Among the many forms of viable signals cited by General Albert J. Myer in his comprehensive 1872 manual, perhaps the most unusual were those provided by musical tones and instruments. Indeed, some were also used to promote morale, such as bagpipes in some Scottish regiments.

The oldest musical signaling instrument is the drum. Signal drums are still used in parts of Africa, although more as a kind of newspaper than military device. In the Congo and other parts of Africa, a two-tone, wooden-slit drum is commonly used to broadcast news within a single village, and then pass it from village to village. The African drum does not communicate by rhythm or beat, but rather by tone. The *Lokele* drum, for example, is made from the red heartwood of a wlee tree. A log is allowed to lie on the forest floor until the yellow sap wood has rotted, and is removed. The drum maker chisels a narrow slit down the length of the log, and about halfway into it. The inside of the drum is hollowed on both sides of the slit. The two sides of the drum are made into different tones; one is more hollow, thus providing a lower tone. The low voice is the *limiki lia otomali*, or voice of the female; the high voice is *limiki lia otolone*, or the voice of the male. The drum is beaten with two short branches from the bokofe tree, bound on the tips with rubber. Females understand the drum language, but the men do all the beating. The drum is never sold; it is a village institution.

Military drum activities were more prosaic. As early as 500 BCE, the Persians used kettle drums both to control cavalry formation and frighten their enemies. The snare drum was the standard battlefield infantry communication device from the 1700s until well into the 1860s. A list of drum calls for the British army in about 1800 included the following: "caution"—a short roll; "do something specific" (by prearrangement)—a slam; "form a line or battalion"—to arms;

"advance"—the march; "advance quickly"— the quick march; "march and charge"—the point of war; "retreat"—the retreat; "halt"— drum ceases; "per-form flank firing"—two short rolls; "open the battalion"—dragoon march; "form the column"—grenadier march; "double division"—the troop; "form the square"—the long roll; "make ready and fire"—the preparative; "cease firing"—the general; and "bring the colors"—two long rolls. The traditional use of the drum has been for keeping time for marching troops. The most recently reported use of the tactical drum in war was by guerrillas in the Philippine Islands during World War II.

Trumpets, horns, and drums were used in ancient Greek and Roman armies and navies although seldom for a more specific signal purpose than to order an attack. Early Greek trumpets were made of goat horn or wood, and joined with brass wings. The *cornu* was a common Roman trumpet, a large curved instrument with a fairly high tone used to pass along the signals of the *tuba*—a long straight instrument with a fluttering end. Deep notes signaled advances or retreats. The *bucini* sounded reveille divisions of the day and other orders common to army foot solders.

By the reign of Alexander the Great (336–323 BCE), trumpets and fifes (as well as standards and raised weapons) were used to control the phalanx of his army. Perhaps the earliest recorded use of specific signals via musical tones were the three-toned whistling arrows used by Genghis Khan's Mongol cavalry in the late twelfth and early thirteenth centuries.

Trumpets (most often modified into a more compact bugle) are undoubtedly the longest-used military musical signal instrument. By 1800, a bugler was a key member of most military units and was also found aboard most ships. Bugle calls for meals (soupee) and sleep (taps) are well known even outside military services. During the first Boer War, British infantry were closing on an enemy force when a Boer bugler sounded the call "Retire." The well-trained British units began to stumble smartly in confusion, until a bright British bugler realized what was happening—and sounded "Advance"—loudly and continuously. This restored order, and the British eventually triumphed. The British infantry bugle was tuned to E flat and had five open notes: C, G, C, E, and G. There were no keys nor slides, for a bugle was shorter and smaller than the larger trumpet used with the cavalry. The small American bugle was deemed too small to play songs during long marches, so the American army normally had a trumpeter play songs during long infantry marches, as a trumpet (with three valves) offered a full range of several octaves.

The British army has also used gongs for many years, generally at regimental barracks, but at times in field camps. The gong may indicate time of day, certain formations, and duties. The corporal of the guard usually handles this duty, which seems to be a holdover from the periodic voice reports given by a town crier: "12 o'clock and all's well."

Navies have their own special device for dividing a sailor's day into segments. Properly played, the boatswain's pipe can be a musical instrument. Modern devices have gradually replaced this ancient instrument, however. Recorded pipe calls are often used in the Navy now, combining ease with tradition.

David L. Woods

See also Ancient Signals; Native American Signaling

Sources

Downey, Fairfax. 1971. *Fife, Drum & Bugle.* Fort Collins, CO: Old Army Press.

Ferguson, Allan J. 1984. "Trumpets, Bugles and Horns in North America, 1750–1815." *Military Collector & Historian* 36 (Spring): 2–7.

Myer, Albert J. 1872. *A Manual of Signals for the Use of Signal Officers in the Field, and for Military and Naval Students, Military Schools, etc.* Washington, DC: Government Printing Office.

"Piping the Boatswain's Call." 1961. *All Hands* 531 (April): 30–31, 34.

Woods, David L. 1965. "Signaling by Sound." In *A History of Tactical Communication Techniques.* Orlando, FL: Martin-Marietta (reprinted by Arno Press, 1974).

Myer, Albert James (1828–1880)

An Army doctor and founder of the U.S. Army Signal Corps, Myer invented the wig-wag system of signaling, using flags and torches to convey messages.

Born in Newburgh, New York, on 20 September 1828, Myer's interest in communications began while he was a medical student and working in the Buffalo office of the New York State Telegraph Company. For his medical dissertation, he developed a sign language for deaf mutes that used taps on the cheek or hand to spell out words.

After joining the Army in 1854 as an assistant surgeon, Myer spent a number of years at Western outposts. During this period, he converted his sign language into a visual signaling system that used flags by day and torches at night to communicate over long distances. Under ideal conditions, messages could be sent and received for up to 15 miles. He developed a signal code by assigning numerical values to the movements of the flag or torch to the left or right of center. By representing each letter of the alphabet with a combination of numerals, messages were transmitted by moving the flag or torch accordingly. A consummate lobbyist, Myer won War Department approval to conduct a series of tests to prove the system's value. Among his assistants was Edward Porter Alexander, who would eventually head the Confederate Signal Corps for a time.

In June 1860, Congress approved Myer's system, making the U.S. Army among the first in the world to have a branch dedicated solely to communications. Myer became the Army's first signal officer with the rank of major.

During the Civil War, he established a wartime organization with signal officers assigned to Army and corps headquarters. In addition to flags and torches, Myer introduced the use of electric telegraphy and adapted the Beardslee magneto-electric telegraph for field use. Because it used a dial rather than a key, the Beardslee did not require an operator trained in Morse code. Soldiers carried instruments and equipment onto the battlefield in wagons, known as telegraph trains. Technical difficulties, however, eventually forced Myer to adapt the Beardslee to use Morse equipment. In doing so, however, Myer came into direct competition with Secretary of War Edwin M. Stanton and his U.S. Military Telegraph, composed of civilian operators. Stanton ultimately relieved Myer of command of the Signal Corps in 1863, and Myer spent the remainder of the war largely on the sidelines. He used the time, however, to complete his text, *A Manual of Signals: for the Use of Signal Officers in the Field*, which codified signal doctrine for the first time.

After Stanton's removal as secretary of War in 1867, Myer won reinstatement to his position as chief signal officer. He spent the postwar years fighting for the Signal Corps' continued existence in the face of skeptics who saw no value in a permanent communications branch. In 1870 he found a peacetime mission for the branch in the form of the national weather service. Signal soldiers forwarded weather reports to Washington via telegraph three times daily. In the signal office, "computers" compiled the data into weather forecasts, then called probabilities, that were published in newspapers across the nation. Thus, Myer, as head of the weather service, became widely known as "Old Probabilities."

While most of the Signal Corps' efforts in the 1870s were devoted to weather reporting, some new advances in communications were made, such as the adoption of a standard heliograph and improvements to the field telegraph train. The corps also began its first experiments with the telephone. Myer established a signal school to which students from foreign armies were admitted and built up an official library of technical publications. Having married into a wealthy family (the Waldens of Buffalo, New York), Myer moved in elegant social circles. As head of the Signal Corps he also became an international figure and attended the International Meteorological Congress in Vienna in 1873.

Myer became a brigadier general in 1880, but he would not live long to enjoy his elevation in rank. He had suffered from serious health problems as a young man, but had apparently been healthy ever since. He became ill while traveling in Europe in 1879 and grew gradually worse after his return. Myer died in Buffalo on 24 August 1880 from nephritis. He was just fifty-one years of age.

The following year, Fort Whipple, Virginia, just across the Potomac River from Washington DC, was renamed Fort Myer in his honor. As Myer's legacy, the U.S. Army Signal Corps has grown to become one of the Army's largest and most vital branches.

Rebecca Robbins Raines

See also Alexander, Edward Porter (1835–1910); Army Signal Corps; Beardslee Telegraph; Fort Myer, Virginia; U.S. Military Telegraph Service (USMTS)

Sources

Raines, Rebecca Robbins. 1996. *Getting the Message Through: A Branch History of the US Army Signal Corps*. Washington, DC: Government Printing Office.

Scheips, Paul. J. 1963. "Union Signal Communications: Innovation and Conflict." *Civil War History* 9: 399–421.

Scheips, Paul J. 1965. "Albert James Myer, Founder of the Army Signal Corps: A Biographical Study." Ph.D. diss., American University, Washington, DC.

N

Napoleonic Wars (1795–1815)

For two decades bridging the late eighteenth and early nineteenth centuries, Napoleonic France pursued wars of conquest across Europe and the Middle East, both on land and at sea. During these various wars and countless battles, both traditional and improved means of military communications played a key part in Napoleon's highly centralized military and diplomatic operations.

European armies all made extensive use of traditional means of signaling, from couriers (both runners and on horseback) and signal flags for tactical messages to the mails (especially the French military postal service) and postal coaches for strategic and diplomatic notes. Napoleon's forces also utilized the newer semaphore communications networks to rapidly transmit military messages. They had to, as armies were growing larger (and were made up increasingly of conscripts, sometimes poorly trained), making them harder to control. Artillery and other guns were rapidly improving—though adding more noise to the battlefield. And as more countries became allied in larger wars,

language differences often slowed message communication.

As early as 1793, a French force besieged in Valenciennes tried to use a hot air balloon to send out reports of their status (unfortunately, it floated over enemy lines)—the first known use of communication by air other than birds. In 1794, the newly constructed Chappe semaphore (or mechanical telegraph) system informed Parisians of the capture of Condé-sur-l'Escaut from the Austrians less than an hour after it occurred. Numerous additional semaphore lines were soon built, including one from Paris south to the naval port of Toulon on the Mediterranean coast. The Chappe system lent itself far more to diplomatic and strategic military messages rather than tactical battle communications. As French forces extended their control into new areas, additional semaphore lines were constructed for communication back to Paris.

Napoleon's Military Telegraph Service operated the Chappe semaphore system and could achieve message transmission speeds as high as 120 miles per hour in ideal conditions. Attempts to develop a wagon-mounted mobile semaphore system foundered for lack of sufficient funds. A constant risk was the potential enemy theft of signal books from semaphore stations, which would compromise military secrecy.

Where the semaphore did not reach, Napoleon's forces utilized a system of signal flag relays. Flags or couriers were used for such tactical tasks as artillery spotting. But as with the semaphore network, these optical means all required clear weather, and fog or snow (let alone hours of darkness) too often intervened and effectively shut the systems down. In attempting to use the flag system in 1809 to communicate between Napoleon's headquarters at Vienna and Strasbourg, for example, poorly placed signalers doomed the system to failure. In several other instances, courier messages meant to follow on and extend a semaphore or flag signal (which was presumed to be faster and thus to arrive first) arrived though the original semaphore or flag-transmitted message did not, adding further confusion to battlefield conditions.

During the bitter 1808–1814 Peninsular Campaign in French-occupied Portugal and Spain, the British constructed a string of more than a hundred strong points or forts along the Torres Vedras defensive lines in Portugal (1809–1811), connecting them with a semaphore network. Royal Navy personnel operated the semaphore system, which had signal stations located about eight miles apart and allowed for flexible army support when a fort was attacked. Signals combined standard naval usage with specialized army terms as needed. A military road, hidden from sight of French forces, also connected the strong points and eased courier and postal connections. Napoleon's infamous retreat from Moscow in 1812 was hampered by, among many other things, poor visibility and thus limited semaphore communication links.

The Chappe semaphore (sometimes confusingly called a telegraph) system was quickly and widely copied by other European states. Norway, allied to France, installed a heavily used military semaphore system with three connected coastal networks in 1809, though it was closed down after Napoleon's fall at Waterloo. The extensive Edelcrantz system in Sweden (1794) was another Scandinavian semaphore service. The British Admiralty adopted a semaphore system linking Deal on the east coast with London to warn of potential invasion danger. It also developed a semaphore system somewhat similar to Chappe's in the years to follow, and soon linked London with major port cities and naval bases on the south coast. Offered an early electrical telegraph system by Francis Ronalds in 1816, the Admiralty turned it down as unnecessary. In 1797, the British army had introduced its Radiated Telegraph (semaphore) System, which proved to be more mobile than the already antiquated Murray Telegraph semaphore system.

The semaphore networks that had so aided Napoleon's armies were also used to report his final defeat at Waterloo in 1815.

Christopher H. Sterling

See also Airships and Balloons; Chappe, Claude (1763–1805); Edelcrantz, Abraham (1754–1821); Flags; France: Army; Military Roads; Popham, Home Riggs (1762–1820); Postal Services; Semaphore (Mechanical Telegraphs); Trafalgar, Battle of (21 October 1805); Waterloo, Battle of (18 June 1815)

Sources
Belloc, Alexis. 1888. *La Télégraphie Historique: Depuis les Temps les Plus Recules Jusqu'a nos Jours.* Paris: Fermin Didot.
Chandler, David G. 1966. *The Campaigns of Napoleon.* New York: Scribners.
Esdaille, Charles. 2001. *The French Wars, 1792–1815.* London: Routledge.
Fletcher, Ian. 2003. *The Lines of Torres Vedras 1809–11.* Wellingborough, UK: Osprey (Fortress 7).

Koenig, Duane. 1944. "Telegraphs and Telegrams in Revolutionary France." *The Scientific Monthly* LIX (December): 431–437.

Norsk Telemuseum. Home page. [Online information; retrieved January 2005.] http://www.norsktele.museum.no/mambo/content/view/255/155/.

National Bureau of Standards (NBS), National Institute of Standards and Technology (NIST)

The National Institute of Standards and Technology (NIST) was founded as the National Bureau of Standards (NBS) in 1901 in order to maintain a system of weights and measures for the United States. Like many a new government agency, the bureau was formed by expanding a division of an established office, the Coast and Geodetic Survey, which had strong ties to the American military and a clear interest in communication. Survey scientists had helped develop the electrical telegraph as a communications tool and an instrument for determining longitudinal differences.

During the first decade of the twentieth century, NBS personnel began working on electrical standards: the standard volt, the standard ohm, and the standard ampere. In 1911, this work led to an investigation of wireless telegraphy. The most pressing problems of the day involved signal interference, transmitting and detecting signals in a fixed frequency band, and radio direction finders. NBS expanded its radio research during World War I and worked closely with both the Army Signal Corps and the Naval Radio Laboratory. It created a detailed standard for radio broadcasting, the "National Bureau of Standards Circular on Radio Instruments and Measurements," often referenced as "Circular 74." NBS also published an influ-

ential text, *The Principles Underlying Radio Communication*, which helped train a generation of radio engineers and operators.

After the 1918 armistice, the government reduced the overall NBS budget but expanded its radio research. During the 1920s, bureau scientists created a refined quartz oscillator to keep stations on frequency, explored long-distance shortwave transmission, began broadcasting standard time signals, and developed radio guidance systems for both the Navy and Army Air Corps. Staff members also served as advisers to the newly formed Federal Radio Commission and designed a circuit that allowed home radios to use current from the power grid rather than a battery.

Between 1940 and 1946, NBS worked with both the Army and Navy to develop the LORAN (long range) radio navigation system, the radio proximity fuse, and the radio tracking of weather fronts. In the years following World War II, the bureau was a major center of research on digital computers and digital communication. NBS provided funds for the construction of the first UNIVAC and produced a series of memos that outlined a system of long-distance digital communication between computers.

Following a 1954 review of operations, the bureau relinquished its military research units and directed its focus to civilian problems. Most communications research continued untouched at a new radio propagation laboratory in Boulder, Colorado. In 1965, the bulk of this laboratory was removed from NBS and placed under the control of the Environmental Science Services Administration, and still later (1978) the National Telecommunications and Information Administration. Renamed in 1988 as the National Institute for Standards and Technology, NIST continued to conduct some research on measuring and detecting communications signals at Boulder and at a central facility, constructed in 1964, in Gaithersburg, Maryland.

David Alan Grier

See also Computer; National Telecommunications and Information Administration (NTIA); Navy Radio Laboratory; Quartz Crystal for Radio Control

Sources

Aspray, William, and Michael Gunderloy. 1989. "Early Computing and Numerical Analysis at the National Bureau of Standards." *IEEE Annals of the History of Computing* 11(1): 3–12.

Cochrane, Rexmond. 1974. *Measure for Progress: A History of the National Bureau of Standards.* Washington, DC: Government Printing Office.

National Bureau of Standards. 1922. *The Principles Underlying Radio Communication.* Washington, DC: U.S. Army Signal Corps.

National Institute of Standards and Technology. 2000. *A Century of Excellence in Measurements, Standards, and Technology: A Chronicle of Selected NBS/NIST Publications, 1901–2000.* NIST Special Publication 958. Washington, DC: Government Printing Office.

Perry, John. 1955. *The Story of Standards.* New York: Funk and Wagnalls.

Pursell, Caroll. 1968. "A Preface to Government Support of Research and Development." *Technology and Culture* 9: 145–164.

Schooley, James. 2000. *Responding to National Needs: The National Bureau of Standards Becomes the National Institute of Standards and Technology (1969–1993).* NIST Special Publication 955. Washington, DC: Government Printing Office.

National Communications System (NCS)

The National Communications System (NCS) supports the American president and senior military and civilian officials with effective telecommunications links and coordinates planning for and provision of national security and emergency preparedness communications for the federal government under all circumstances, including crisis or emergency, attack, and system recovery.

NCS can be traced back to the October 1962 Cuban Missile Crisis, when communications problems threatened to further complicate events. After the showdown between the United States and the Soviet Union, the National Security Council formed an interdepartmental committee to examine existing networks and needed changes. The result was the formation of NCS on 21 August 1963 to coordinate a unified communications system to serve the president, Department of Defense, diplomatic and intelligence activities, and other federal leaders. NCS was assigned to direct communications for the federal government under all conditions ranging from normal to national emergencies and international crises, including nuclear attack. The agency was to focus especially on system interconnectivity and survivability. The Defense Communications Agency served as the executive agent. On 3 April 1984, President Ronald Reagan expanded NCS into an interagency group of twenty-three federal departments and agencies. NCS began coordinating and planning national security and emergency preparedness (NS/EP) telecommunications during crises, natural disasters, and humanitarian aid efforts. NCS is also involved in training military and civilian personnel for NS/EP communications needs. On 1 March 2003 NCS was made a part of the new Department of Homeland Security.

NCS and its industry partners (including, for example, amateur radio operators) triggered a series of emergency response actions immediately after the terrorist attacks of 11

September 2001, and again after the disastrous hurricanes of mid-2005. The Government Emergency Telecommunications System and Telecommunications Service Priority programs of NCS were vital in helping to restore emergency telecommunications in these situations. NCS has also evaluated ways to deploy wireless priority access service in selected metropolitan areas and eventually across the country. This allows NS/EP users in emergencies to gain access to the next available wireless channel without preempting calls already in progress.

Danny Johnson

See also Cuban Missile Crisis (1962); Defense
Communications System (DCS);
Hotline/Direct Communications Link
(DCL); National Security Agency (NSA);
White House Communications Agency
(WHCA)

Sources

Barrett, Steve. 2003. "National Communications System Joins Homeland Security Department." *American Forces Press Service,* March 10.
Lake, Timothy L. 2004. *Reliable and Relevant National Communications System.* Strategy Research Project. Carlisle Barracks, PA: U.S. Army War College.
National Communications System. [Online information; retrieved November 2005.] http://www.ncs.gov/index.html.

National Defense Research Committee (NDRC)

The National Defense Research Committee (NDRC) was a U.S. government agency that oversaw scientific research for the military during World War II. It was created in June 1940 at the instigation of Vannevar Bush, a Massachusetts Institute of Technology (MIT)

electrical engineer. The committee consisted of a dozen senior academic scientists, representatives of the military, and a few officers of major industries. It evaluated the research needs of the country's war effort, recruited scientists or companies qualified to do the scientific work, and offered them contracts to do the work. These contracts, which had rarely been used before the war to fund science, would state the goals for the research and the resources that the government would provide. They left the scientists free to determine how the research would be conducted. In its six years of operation, NDRC negotiated 2,300 contracts worth a half-billion dollars with 321 private companies and 142 academic institutions.

Initially, NDRC was organized in five divisions: A for armor and ordnance; B for bombs, fuels, and chemicals; C for communications; D for detectors and controls; and E for external relations and patents. Division C was overseen by Frank Jewett, president of Bell Telephone Laboratories and the National Academy of Sciences. This division worked with the largest research contractors of the war (outside of the Manhattan Project), including the Radiation Laboratory of MIT, AT&T's Western Electric, RCA, and the California Institute of Technology. It helped develop microwave radar, secure voice communication systems, radio jamming systems, the Combat Information Center, the LORAN navigation system, electromechanical computing devices, and aircraft communications systems.

The bulk of NDRC research was conducted in the northeastern segment of the United States, the area that contained most of its major universities and corporate headquarters. The research was often given to graduate students or young professors, who used the opportunities to become leaders in scientific communication. Most of the research for aircraft communications systems was done at the Harvard University Psycho-Acoustic Laboratory by a new engineer named Leo Beranek. After the war, Beranek used his NDRC contacts to found a research company named BBN. BBN quickly became a leading consulting firm on acoustics issues. It eventually developed substantial expertise in computer communication and created much of the early technology for what became DARPANET.

In May 1941, NDRC became part of the Office of Scientific Research and Development (OSRD), a coordinating body that reported to the government's Office of Emergency Management. Bush, who became head of OSRD, appointed Harvard University President James Conant as the new director of the NDRC. In November 1943, Conant reorganized NDRC into nineteen divisions. Division 13 dealt with electronic communication, Division 14 with radar, and Division 15 with radio coordination. By 1944 NDRC reached its largest extent with 1,400 staff members and 450 scientists as technical volunteers, headquartered at the Carnegie Institution in Washington DC.

The key figure in both NDRC and OSRD, Vannevar Bush, was by nature a conservative man who distrusted government intrusion in the scientific process. He intended that the OSRD would be a temporary agency. In September 1944, he notified all divisions that OSRD would go out of business after defeat of Germany, which he assumed might happen as early as November 15. The Battle of the Bulge, in which the German army temporarily repulsed Allied troops in December 1944, delayed Bush's plans. However, by April 1945, he had begun demobilization in earnest. He transferred certain crucial OSRD contracts to the Army and Navy before terminating the remainder.

During the last days of the organization, scientists attempted to establish a similar organization, the Research Board for National Security, to guide postwar science. This organization lasted barely a year before collapsing. In 1950, five years after the closure of OSRD, the government founded the National Science Foundation as the country's peacetime scientific agency.

David Alan Grier

See also Airplanes; Bell Telephone Laboratories (BTL); Bush, Vannevar (1890–1974); Combat Information Center (CIC); DARPANET; Jamming

Sources

Baxter, James Phinney III. 1946. *Scientists Against Time.* Boston: Little, Brown.

Genuth, Joel. 1988. "Microwave Radar, the Atomic Bomb, and the Background to U.S. Research Priorities in World War II." *Science, Technology and Human Values* 13 (3–4): 276–289.

Gruber, Carol. 1995. "The Overhead System in Government-Sponsored Academic Science: Origins and Early Development." *Historical Studies in the Physical and Biological Sciences,* 25 (2): 241–268.

Owens, Larry. 1994. "The Counterproductive Management of Science in the Second World War: Vannevar Bush and the Office of Scientific Research and Development." *Business History Review* 68: 515–576.

Stewart, Irvin. 1948. *Organizing Scientific Research for War.* Boston: Little, Brown.

National Reconnaissance Office (NRO)

The National Reconnaissance Office (NRO) is a combined activity of the U.S. Department of Defense (DoD) and the Central Intelligence Agency (CIA). As part of the fifteen-member U.S. Intelligence Community, it is staffed by DoD and CIA personnel and is responsible for the research, development, acquisition, and operation of innovative space reconnaissance systems to support global information gathering. National and military leaders use data obtained from NRO satellites to plan and prosecute military actions, as well as to monitor weapons of mass destruction programs, track terrorists, enforce arms control and environmental treaties, and assess the impact of natural and manmade disasters. NRO is funded through the National Reconnaissance Program, which, in turn, is part of the National Foreign Intelligence Program.

NRO was created following months of intense controversy between the White House, CIA, DoD, and U.S. Air Force over the allocation of responsibilities for satellite reconnaissance. In the aftermath of the May 1960 downing of an American U-2 spy plane over the Soviet Union, President Dwight Eisenhower directed the intelligence community to develop recommendations on the future of space-based intelligence collection. The subsequent report to the National Security Council on 25 August 1960 marked the formation of NRO.

The principal decision to form a "national" agency was to ensure that the interests of all parties, including the military and civilian intelligence communities, would be represented in the utilization of space systems. For the next thirty-one years NRO's very existence was classified secret, and, except for the DoD directive that served as a charter, its name or initials could not be used in any government document that did not carry a special security classification. Throughout the Cold War of the 1960s, the détente of the 1970s, and the renewed arms race of the 1980s, NRO remained a classified organiza-

tion as it continued to develop, build, and operate advanced space-based intelligence systems.

However, in recent years, NRO took a series of actions declassifying some of its operations. Its existence was finally acknowledged in September 1992, followed by the location of its headquarters in Chantilly, Virginia, in 1994. In February 1995, CORONA, a photo reconnaissance satellite program in operation from 1960 to 1972, was declassified and 800,000 CORONA images were transferred to the National Archives and Records Administration. In December 1996, NRO announced for the first time, in advance, the launch of a reconnaissance satellite.

NRO is organized into five operational directorates: Signals Intelligence, Imagery Intelligence, Advanced Systems and Technology, Communications Systems Acquisition, and the Office of Space Launch. The director of NRO reports to the secretary of defense who, in concert with the director of central intelligence, has ultimate management and operational responsibility for the agency. NRO's programs and activities are overseen by six congressional committees: House Permanent and Senate Select Committees on Intelligence, House and Senate Appropriations Committees, House National Security Committee, and Senate Armed Services Committee.

Brett F. Woods

See also Communication Satellites; Signals Intelligence (SIGINT)

Sources

Handberg, Roger. 2000. *Seeking New World Vistas: The Militarization of Space*. Westport, CT: Praeger.
Richelson, Jeffery T. 1999. *The U.S. Intelligence Community*. Boulder, CO: Westview Press.
Worden, Simon P., and John E. Shaw. 2002. "Whither Space Power? Forging a Strategy

for the New Century." Maxwell Air Force Base, AL: Air University Press.

National Research Council (NRC)

The National Research Council (NRC) is the operational arm of the National Academy of Sciences. The academy was founded in 1863 as an independent organization that would bring the best American scientists into a single institution where they might share the results of their work. As part of its charter, the academy was charged, "whenever called upon by any department of the Government, [to] investigate, examine, experiment, and report upon any subject of science or art." However, during the nineteenth century, the academy was consumed with internal issues and offered little advice to the government.

The academy formed NRC in 1916, in anticipation of American involvement in World War I. The two scientists most instrumental in forming the council, physicist Robert A. Millikan and astronomer George Ellery Hale, had also helped the academy develop ties to academies of science in Europe and recognized that these organizations took a more active role than the American academy in directing scientific research. NRC included academic scientists, representatives of the industrial giants engaged in research (notably American Telephone & Telegraph, General Electric, and Dupont Nemours), and key military officers.

The purpose of the council was not to conduct research. During World War I, most scientific research was undertaken by university scientists who held reserve military commissions and worked at government facilities. Millikan, the chair of the council, for example, studied radio propagation as a reserve officer in the Army Signal Corps. During the war, the council surveyed the stock of the nation's laboratories and scientists and advised the American military on possible research opportunities.

After the war, the council was reorganized "to stimulate research in the mathematical, physical, and biological sciences." It raised funds for postdoctoral fellowships and, in the process, built strong ties with the Carnegie and Rockefeller foundations. It also organized small committees to survey the literature of specific scientific disciplines and recommend research strategies. The members of these committees were usually not members of the academy but university scientists who volunteered their services for this work. Among the reports prepared by these committees were papers on radio communications, radar, and nuclear fission.

During the 1930s, NRC tried to develop a research facility but failed to gain congressional support. At the start of World War II, NRC created two new organizations to direct research: the National Defense Research Committee and the Office of Scientific Research and Development. In 1950 the government chose to fund scientific research through the National Science Foundation and directed NRC to survey scientific endeavors and recommend strategies for research. Increasingly, the council took up problems from the fields of medicine and engineering. The National Academy of Science was joined by the National Academy of Engineering in 1964 and the Institute of Medicine in 1970. By the start of the twenty-first century, NRC was producing about 350 reports a year, based on requests from Congress, the military, the National Science Foundation, and other offices of the American government.

David Alan Grier

See also American Telephone & Telegraph Co. (AT&T); Bell Telephone Laboratories (BTL); National Defense Research Committee (NDRC)

Sources

Bugos, Glenn. 1980. "Managing Cooperative Research and Borderland Science in the National Research Council." *Historical Studies in the Physical and Biological Sciences* 20: 1–32.

Christman, Albert B. 1971. *Sailors, Scientists and Rockets*. Washington, DC: Naval History Center.

Cochrane, Rexmond. 1963. *The National Academy of Sciences: The First Hundred Years, 1863– 1963*. Washington, DC: National Academy of Sciences.

Dupree, Hunter. 1957. "The Founding of the National Academy of Sciences, A Reinterpretation." *Proceedings of the American Philosophical Society* 101: 434–440.

Kevles, Daniel. 1968. "George Ellery Hale, the First World War and the Advancement of Science in America." *Isis* 59 (4): 427–437.

Kevles, Daniel. 1971. "Federal Legislation for Engineering Experiment Station: The Episode of World War I." *Technology and Culture* 12 (2): 182–189.

Reingold, Nathan. 1977. "The Case of the Disappearing Laboratory." *American Quarterly* 29: 79–101.

National Security Agency (NSA)

The National Security Agency (NSA) has for a half-century been the chief American cryptologic organization. The largest such organization in the world with nearly 40,000 employees (15,000 of whom are civilian), its director, a flag-rank military officer, reports to an assistant secretary of defense. NSA has more budget and personnel than the better-known Central Intelligence Agency.

The mid-1952 Brownell Committee report to President Harry Truman called for unification of all U.S. communications intelligence activities. Formation of the committee grew out of dissatisfaction with the Korean War activities of the existing Armed Forces Security Agency, which had been set up just three years earlier to combine the work of the military services. As a result of the committee's recommendations, NSA was established late in 1952 at Arlington Hall, just outside Washington DC. It moved to new headquarters at Fort Meade, Maryland (between Washington and Baltimore), in 1957 and has been expanding and upgrading them ever since. In 1972, the Central Security Service (CSS) was formed to promote a closer partnership between NSA and the cryptologic elements of the armed services (the director of NSA is also chief of CSS). To record and preserve its history and that of its predecessors, NSA established the National Cryptologic Museum and research facility at Fort Meade, which opened to the public in 1993.

NSA has three primary missions: to develop means to better protect information infrastructures critical to U.S. security; to exploit, collect, and process intercepted foreign communication signals or signals intelligence (SIGINT); and to train personnel for operations security. NSA produces SIGINT as specified by the director of central intelligence and the National Foreign Intelligence Board. NSA "customers" include the White House, the Joint Chiefs of Staff, component military commands, multinational forces, and U.S. allies.

NSA seeks ways to better protect information and communications thought critical to the country's security. NSA develops technologies that allow policy makers and military commanders to communicate free of concern over being heard by foreign intelligence agencies. Military command-and-control systems are designed and produced by NSA. To do this NSA employs many of the country's top cryptologists, mathematicians, computer scientists, physicists, linguists, researchers, engineers, and related positions.

A decade after its formation, NSA faced its most serious crisis during the October 1962 Cuban missile confrontation with the Soviet Union. Signals intelligence crucially contributed to the human and photographic intelligence findings that have been long known. Pressure to rapidly decode Cuban and Soviet information led to the first twenty-four-hour command center. Interception came from ground stations, aircraft circling the island, and the USS *Oxford* SIGINT collection vessel. SIGINT provided the first indications that Soviet ships were turning back before reaching a U.S. Navy blockade, and that possible war had been averted. Later SIGINT results showed the "other side" standing down as well.

Another American SIGINT surveillance vessel, the *Liberty*, was tuning in Egyptian and Israeli military signals during their 1967 war when the vessel was attacked and nearly sunk by Israeli aircraft (34 were killed, 171 injured). A potential international incident was largely hushed up. A similar vessel, the *Pueblo*, was tuning military information off shore from North Korea in December of the same year when she was boarded and taken, though in international waters. A good deal of secret NSA material was captured before it could be destroyed, and the American crew was held for months.

NSA code breakers played a central part in later conflicts as well. Airborne and ground SIGINT played a substantial role during the long Vietnam War (the first American casualty of that war was working for NSA). NSA-generated SIGINT was central to military operations in central Europe in the mid-1990s and in Afghanistan and Iraq in the early 2000s.

In order to effectively intercept and decode foreign signals, NSA established numerous monitoring stations around the world and also in satellite orbit. This global eavesdropping network is interconnected with those of selected foreign intelligence agencies such as those of Britain, Canada, Australia, and New Zealand. This "UKUSA" network assigns each participating agency a separate section of the globe. NSA monitors Russia and related states east of the Ural Mountains and most of the Americas; Britain monitors Europe, Africa, and Russia west of the Urals, and Australia monitors the South Pacific and Southeast Asia. The largest NSA overseas monitoring station is at Menwith Hill, in Yorkshire, England. With access to Britain's communication networks, it has twenty-two satellite terminals and about five acres of buildings. The network is interconnected with the Echelon computer software system. Every monitoring center in the UKUSA network is equipped with its own supercomputer capable of processing all the information intercepted there and filtering out communications that match certain search parameters.

Given continuing and ever-faster advances in technology, NSA's job has become steadily more complex. High-end encryption technologies previously available only to governments can often be obtained today at relatively low cost—indeed, encryption software can be found on the Internet at no cost. The huge increase in the number of cell phones, e-mails, fax machines, and other means of electronic communication and their increasing speed of transmission adds greatly to the challenge of monitoring the ever-increasing volume of information exchange. This volume caused NSA supercomputers to overload and stop processing for three-and-a-half days in early 2000. Technological advances are reducing the advantage that NSA once held. Fiber optic cables, for example, carry huge amounts of information yet are extremely difficult to intercept without physical access to the cables. For several years, NSA has been working to substantially expand its research and development efforts into development of new code-breaking technologies.

Once totally secretive (NSA was jokingly said to stand for "no such agency") and sometimes dubbed "Crypto City," NSA has become better known as it seeks to recruit the best and brightest to its code-breaking and protection missions.

Arthur M. Holst and Christopher H. Sterling

See also Arlington Hall; Code Breaking; Communications Security (COMSEC); Computer; Cuban Missile Crisis (1962); Fort Meade, Maryland; Intelligence Ships; Signal Security Agency (SSA, 1943–1949), Signals Intelligence (SIGINT)

Sources

Bamford, James. 1982. *The Puzzle Palace: A Report on America's Most Secret Agency.* Boston: Houghton Mifflin.

Bamford, James. 2001. *Body of Secrets: Anatomy of the Ultra-Secret National Security Agency.* New York: Random House.

Brownell, George A. n.d. *The Origin and Development of the National Security Agency.* Laguna Hills, CA: Aegean Park Press.

Center for Cryptologic History. 1998. *NSA and the Cuban Missile Crisis.* Fort Meade, MD: Center for Cryptologic History.

National Security Agency. 2002. *Cryptologic Excellence: Yesterday, Today, and Tomorrow.* Fort Meade, MD: National Security Agency.

National Security Agency. Home page. [Online information; retrieved April 2007.] www.nsa.gov.

National Telecommunications and Information Administration (NTIA)

The National Telecommunications and Information Administration (NTIA) is the U.S. president's chief adviser on telecommunication and information policies. It also controls electromagnetic spectrum allocations for the federal government, including the Department of Defense and the individual military services.

NTIA was created as an agency within the Department of Commerce in 1978 in a reorganization of telecommunications functions within the executive branch of the federal government. NTIA combined functions of the White House's former Office of Telecommunications Policy (OTP) and the Commerce Department's Office of Telecommunications (OT). Formed in 1970, OTP had been responsible for telecommunications policy making and radio spectrum management on behalf of the president. OT provided staff support for OTP's spectrum management, including frequency allocation and assignment, as well as technical research and analysis. All of this transferred to NTIA.

NTIA activities are directed by an assistant secretary of commerce. The agency has nearly 300 employees (quite small by federal standards) and operates a laboratory facility, the National Institute for Telecommunication Sciences, in Boulder, Colorado. It is concerned with both domestic and international policy issues.

NTIA houses the Interdepartment Radio Advisory Committee (IRAC), which advises the agency on telecommunications policy, technical, and other matters affecting federal agencies using spectrum. Operating since 1922, it now comprises representatives from some twenty federal agencies (including the military services) and has observers from several more, including the Federal Communications Commission, which represents all private and state government spectrum users. IRAC reviews major radio systems planned by federal agencies to ensure that they comply with applicable technical standards and can be supported in the frequency bands their proponents plan to use. IRAC also coordinates federal space satellite systems with other domestic and foreign satellites.

Of most immediate concern to the military is NTIA's Office of Spectrum Management (OSM), which oversees and coordinates federal agency spectrum use. Understandably a good deal of what it does is classified. But overall, OSM issues policy regarding allocations and regulations governing federal spectrum use; develops plans for both peacetime and wartime use of spectrum; participates in international radio conferences; assigns frequencies for federal agency users; and participates in all aspects of the federal government's communications-related emergency readiness activities. It also publishes and frequently revises the official U.S. frequency allocation chart.

Christopher H. Sterling

See also Spectrum Management

Sources

National Telecommunications and Information Administration, Office of Spectrum Management. Home page. [Online information; retrieved April 2007.] http://www.ntia.doc.gov/osmhome/osmhome.html.

National Telecommunications and Information Administration. "Welcome to NTIA." [Online information; retrieved April 2007.] http://www.ntia.doc.gov/.

Native American Signaling

Native Americans made effective use of traditional modes of communication, including fire, smoke, and couriers. Two specific seventeenth-century examples demonstrate especially effective signaling methods to coordinate multiple attacks on encroaching European colonies.

The first took place in Virginia in 1622, and was apparently years in the planning. Tribes in the tidewater region were all accessible by water—both Indian and European settlements in the tidewater were usually built near rivers—as well as by traditional couriers carrying memorized messages. However, a much more sophisticated signal triggered the 1622 attack. Early planning took place at funeral ceremonies for a chief in which all of the tribes participated. This supplied perfect cover for tribal war planning that would eventually lead to the 1622 attack and another uprising in 1644.

The tactical problem was how to surprise the English colonists with simultaneous strikes in several locations. The Native American leader apparently synchronized his colonywide ambush by using Native American sensitivity to the moon's changing appearance as an ingenious low-tech signaling system. The first visible crescent moon in a month's lunar cycle appeared twenty-one days before both the 1622 and the 1644 attacks. Attuned to the lunar cycle, Native Americans could simply count the number of days between one moon phase and the next, even if bad weather obscured the sky. The means to synchronize the multitarget strike was thus a reliable natural phenomenon of which native people were already aware. On the night of 1 March 1622, the new moon rose over the Virginia colony.

Exactly twenty-one days later, the attack came as a stunning surprise as Indians swarmed over the unsuspecting English with weapons they had hidden ahead of time in haystacks, barns, kitchens, and stables. It was the worst attack the English in the colony had ever suffered. Although the Indians successfully interrupted settlement for a short time, the attack did nothing to shake growing English domination of the region.

In a final, desperate effort to halt the obliteration of his people and their way of life, two decades later the same leader tried the same trick again. And again it was tactically successful. On 18 April 1644, again twenty-one days after the appearance of the first visible crescent moon, the ambush was repeated. This time close to 500 white settlers died, but that was a much smaller proportion of the growing British population, and the overall impact on the burgeoning colony was almost negligible.

Decades later and more than 2,000 miles to the west, Pueblo Indians rose up against Spanish occupiers of what is now New Mexico. One of the revered Pueblo medicine men, Popé, survived capture by Spanish authorities in 1675 and began to plot ways to overthrow the colonizers. Within five years, his plans matured. To ensure that many Pueblos would act at the same time, Popé dispatched runners to the various pueblos, each courier carrying a knotted cord, with the number of knots signifying the number of days remaining until the chosen day of attack. Each day the Pueblo leaders were to untie one knot from the cord, and when the last knot was untied, that would be the signal for them to rise in unison against the Spaniards. The day for the attack had been fixed for 11 August 1680, but the Spaniards

learned of the revolt after capturing two Tesuque Pueblo youths entrusted with carrying the message to the pueblos. Popé then ordered the execution of the plot on 10 August, before the uprising could be put down.

Such signaling methods, though in the end fruitless, demonstrated considerable ingenuity as well as social cohesion.

Kerric S. Harvey

See also Ancient Signals; Couriers;
  Fire/Flame/Torch; Maori Signaling; Smoke

Sources

Acker, Lewis F. 1939. "Communication Systems of the American Indian." *Signal Corps Bulletin 103* January–March: 63–70.

Aveni, Anthony. 2005. "How Was 'The Tyme Appointed'?" *Colonial Williamsburg Journal* 27 (4): 27–32.

Fauze, J. Frederick. 2006. "The First Act of Terrorism in English America." [Online article; retrieved September 2006.] http://www.hnn.us/articles/19085.html.

Ponce, Pedro, 2002. "Trouble for the Spanish: The Pueblo Revolt of 1680." *Humanities* 23 (November–December): 6.

Naval Radio Stations/Service

Growing out of recommendations in 1904, in the years before and during World War I the U.S. Navy constructed an extensive chain of fifty medium- and high-powered radio shore stations along the Atlantic and Pacific coasts and in Alaska, Panama, Hawaii, and the Philippines. They were not built to a common plan but rather as needs dictated. Some operated only for a short time, and as signal ranges increased they were shut down in favor of others. Intended primarily for communications with the fleet, they often shared similar designs and facilities (though power varied from 2 to 100 kw). As technology was in constant flux, their transmitters were regularly upgraded or replaced. Other than the several stations located at Navy yards, the transmitters handled commercial wireless work if a private transmitter was not available. Most broadcast time signals in Morse code coordinated from the Naval Observatory in Washington DC as well as weather reports.

From 1913 until 1941, the Navy operated radio station NAA from "Radio" (Arlington), Virginia. It was the first and chief facility among the chain. Construction began in 1912 on a low hill acquired from neighboring Fort Myer, Virginia (the same year the Navy dropped use of the term "wireless" in favor of "radio"). As completed, the facility consisted of one 600-foot, four-leg, self-supporting steel antenna tower and two others of 450 feet (soon dubbed "the three sisters"; budget limitations had prevented building all three to the 600-foot height) arranged to form a triangle about 350 feet on a side. Two substantial two-story buildings, one housing the transmitter and the other for reception and operation spaces plus living quarters, completed the station.

December saw installation of a Fessenden 100 kw synchronous rotary spark transmitter, which was to be compared with a 30 kw Poulson arc transmitter. Initial results showed the latter to be a more effective transmitter. On 13 February 1913 the station was commissioned and was soon testing signals (on 12 kHz) with a transmitter on the Eiffel Tower in Paris as well as Marconi stations in Britain and Ireland. During October 1915, AT&T experimenters at the Arlington facility established voice communication with Panama, Honolulu, and—a first for transatlantic service—Paris. Used for these signals was a 3,000-watt transmitter made by Western Electric, using about 500 small vac-

This early-twentieth-century postcard shows the three tall wireless towers at the Naval Radio Station at "Radio" (Arlington), Virginia. This facility formed the headquarters of an expansive network of similar stations at American naval bases around the world by 1920. (Courtesy Christopher H. Sterling)

uum tubes on a frequency of 50 kHz. Yet the same year, NAA ceased its role as a reception facility with establishment of "Radio Central" in the State, War, and Navy building next to the White House. From then on NAA was operated remotely as a transmitting operation only.

As with several of the other stations, NAA transmitted calibrated time signals twice a day, and weather forecasts even more often. These were intended chiefly for vessels at sea and by 1927 were going out on shortwave bands as well as the original low frequency. In 1922, two 200-foot antenna towers were added, for a total of eight towers. A vacuum tube transmitter was placed into use in mid-1925, replacing the older spark equipment. Beginning in early 1923, NAA transmitted music and other programs (from the Navy Yard in downtown Washington) at select times in the broadcast band (690 kHz). By the late 1920s, station NAA (as well as NAL at the Navy Yard and NSS in Annapolis) was being operated from Radio Central, which had been relocated to the Navy Building in downtown Washington.

By the late 1930s, however, the facility had become outmoded by rapid changes in radio technology and may have been used for burial of obsolete ammunition and chemicals. The antenna towers were dismantled in 1940 as they endangered approaches to the new National Airport, less than two miles away on the Potomac River. (Some sources suggest at least one was reassembled at the Naval Academy at Annapolis, and only replaced in the late 1990s.) The rest of the station was decommissioned in mid-1956, though the two buildings (and more recent shorter antennas) remain and are used by the Defense Communications Agency. The call letters NAA were later applied to a very low frequency (VLF) Navy station in Maine.

Twenty-one U.S. Navy stations were located along the Atlantic Coast from Portland, Maine, south to Key West, and in Pensacola, New Orleans, and the Texas coast along the Gulf, several of them built at Navy yards. Along the Pacific coast, nine stations were built from San Diego in the south all the way up to the Bremerton Navy Yard in Washington. Seven other stations were constructed in the Territory of Alaska, in the Pribilof and Aleutian island chains.

The transmitter near the Naval Academy at Annapolis, for example, went on the air on 6 August 1918 as station NSS using two antenna towers. The Annapolis transmitters operated in conjunction with a large antenna receiver facility at Cheltenham, Maryland. Two additional towers were added in 1922. In August 1938, the erection of three "Eiffel Towers" was completed. In 1941, a 50-kw transmitter was installed and high-frequency operations established; the station was used for all communications with the Atlantic Fleet during World War II. Extensive modification of the antenna system was begun in 1969. The four 600-foot radio towers were demolished to make way for a new communications link with vessels of the Atlantic Fleet. A new 1,200-foot guyed center tower was erected and surrounded with nine 600-foot towers (three of which were identical to those erected in 1917). The modified towers covered about 200 acres. As need for the facility declined, the station was closed down. At the end of 1999, sixteen of the nineteen radio towers were demolished with the remaining three turned over to Maryland authorities for telecommunications or training purposes.

Naval stations were also constructed in San Juan, Puerto Rico, and at Guantanamo Bay in Cuba; at Honolulu; on the islands of Guam and Samoa; and two in the Philippines (at Cavite and Olongapo). Stations in Panama were built on both the Atlantic and Pacific ends of the canal that had opened for shipping in 1913. The station at Colon, Panama, began operating in 1904 and was rebuilt in 1915; the one at Darien, Panama, opened in 1912. A Balboa, Panama, transmitter was added a year later. Three freestanding antenna towers at Darien were 600 feet high; those at Balboa half as tall.

As modes of telecommunication steadily improved, many of these Navy coastal stations, designed in an era of spark-gap wireless telegraphy transmission, were upgraded to vacuum tube technology while others were closed down. As the effective range of radio increased, many of the stations became redundant. The need for shore stations had largely diminished before World War II, though some remained active in that period. Virtually all are gone today, or converted to very different uses.

Christopher H. Sterling

See also Defense Communications Agency (DCA, 1960–1991); Fessenden, Reginald A. (1866–1932); Fort Myer, Virginia; Hooper, Stanford C. (1884–1995); Morse Code; Radio; U.S. Navy; Vacuum Tube; World War I

Sources

Bullard, W. H. G. 1915. "The Naval Radio Service: Its Development, Public Service, and Commercial Work." *Proceedings of the Institute of Radio Engineers* 3 (March): 7–28.

Bullard, W. H. G. 1916. "Arlington Radio Station and Its Activities in the General Scheme of Naval Radio Communication." *Proceedings of the Institute of Radio Engineers* 4 (October): 421–447.

Crenshaw, R. S. 1916. "The Naval Radio Stations of the Panama Canal Zone." *U.S. Naval Institute Proceedings* 42 (July–August): 1210–1218.

Hooper, S. C. 1929. "Naval Communications— Radio Washington." *Proceedings of the Institute of Radio Engineers* 17 (September): 1595–1620.

Howeth, L. S. 1963. *History of Communications- Electronics in the United States Navy.* Washington, DC: Government Printing Office.

Todd, David W. 1911. "The Navy's Coast Signal Service." *Journal of the American Society of Naval Engineers* 23 (November): 1092–1116.

Todd, David W. 1913. "The Arlington Radio Station." *Journal of the American Society of Naval Engineers,* 25 (February): 60–80.

Naval Research Laboratory (NRL)

The Naval Research Laboratory (NRL) was established in 1923 and has been the pri-mary home of U.S. Navy research efforts since.

NRL was created at the suggestion of the Naval Consulting Board, chaired in the early 1920s by American inventor Thomas Edison. The board included specialists from eleven major American technical societies who reviewed new inventions for their potential military applications. The board recommended that the U.S. Navy maintain its own industrial-style research laboratory, which was organized in 1923 at Washington DC as the Naval Experimental and Research Laboratory.

Originally consisting of three sections, Sound, Metallurgy, and Radio, the laboratory incorporated into its Radio Division both the Naval Aircraft Radio Laboratory and the Radio Test Shop, which dated from World War I. The Naval Experimental and Research Laboratory pioneered the development of high-frequency radio equipment during the mid-1920s, and in 1929 it demonstrated the long-distance capabilities of such devices in transcontinental transmissions, including broadcasts from Antarctica. The laboratory supported and evaluated both basic and applied research, including among its projects research utilizing data developed during the late 1930s on atomic fission. The laboratory, by then given its present title (NRL), began experiments to assess nuclear fission as a potential power source for submarines. Just before the United States entered World War II, NRL, which had been administered by the Office of the Secretary of the Navy, was transferred to the Navy's Bureau of Ships.

NRL's World War II programs, implemented by a staff of 4,400 working on 900 projects, focused on immediately applicable innovations for America's naval fleets. Under Secretary of the Navy James Forrestal, in 1945 NRL interests again expanded to encompass basic research. A broad program of research and development was initiated to study the Navy's operational environments. Work performed in NRL facilities was supplemented by research performed under contracts at American universities. High-priority programs included development of radar-absorbing materials; stress testing; and new formulations for metals, paints, and polymers, as well as research on radiation safety monitoring and nuclear fission–based propulsion systems for submarines.

Bureaucratic changes in 1946 strengthened the NRL program. The laboratory, while reduced to just 1,100 professional staff, was placed within the Navy's Office of Naval Research (ONR), which was given the same status within the Department of the Navy as its powerful bureaus. ONR included overseas offices, an international scientific and technical monitoring service, and several laboratories in addition to NRL. However, post–Korean War federal funding cuts and changing defense priorities that highlighted the U.S. Air Force's strategic bombers, missiles, and satellites put the Navy and NRL at a disadvantage. The Navy's own satellite project, known as Vanguard, developed at NRL, proved a technical failure and left the Navy far behind the Air Force. NRL veterans of the Vanguard program formed the core staff of the National Aeronautics and Space Administration when it was established in 1958.

NRL research opened a new era in 1959 as it began work on a radio telescope for space research. Research for this system, based near Sugar Grove, West Virginia, was terminated in 1962, but NRL activities already occupied a key location within the National Radio Quiet Zone. Established by the Federal Communications Commission in 1958,

the zone covers more than 13,000 square miles in Virginia and West Virginia and is relatively free of electromagnetic interference. In 1965 NRL's share of the zone was converted to support monitoring of foreign and ship-to-shore communications traffic. Construction of two enormous arrays for capturing high-frequency signals was completed in 1969. The Sugar Grove installation became known as NAVRADSTA (Naval Radio Station) Sugar Grove.

NRL scientists made several crucial breakthroughs in communications, location, and navigation technologies. Innovations included voice processing algorithms for secure voice communication, high-frequency radar, missile launch and nuclear explosion detection systems, satellite-based terrain and weather imaging equipment, and, in 1977, in cooperation with the Air Force, the first satellite-based global positioning system (GPS), known as Navigation Satellite Timing and Ranging, or NAVSTAR.

Utilization of high-frequency communications systems by America's Cold War rivals declined during the 1980s, and the Sugar Grove arrays became less critical to signals intelligence gathering. They were finally deactivated in the late 1990s. The Navy, however, maintained the Sugar Grove site as a monitoring facility for satellite communications and renamed it the Navy Information Operations Command (NIOC)–Sugar Grove. The complex now hosts sophisticated equipment for satellite communications monitoring, as well as intelligence specialists from the U.S. Air Force, the National Security Agency, and the U.S. Department of Defense. Published analyses agree that NIOC–Sugar Grove continues to be a key installation in the Anglo-American Echelon signals intelligence system.

Laura M. Calkins

See also Communication Satellites; Global Positioning System (GPS); National Security Agency (NSA); Navy Radio Laboratory; Signals Intelligence (SIGINT)

Sources

Gebhard, Louis A. 1979. *Evolution of Naval Radio-Electronics and Contributions of the Naval Research Laboratory.* NRL Report 8300. Washington, DC: Government Printing Office.

Keefe, Patrick Radden. 2005. *Chatter: Dispatches from the Secret World of Global Eavesdropping.* New York: Random House.

Naval Research News. 1996. "Office of Naval Research 50th Anniversary." *Naval Research News* Special issue, XLVIII: 1.

Rath, Bhatka, and Don J. De Young. 1998. "The Naval Research Laboratory: 75 Years of Materials Innovation." *Journal of Materials 50:* 7, 14–17.

Richelson, Jeffrey. 2000. "Desperately Seeking Signals." *Bulletin of the Atomic Scientists 56:* 2, 47–51.

Sapolsky, Harvey M. 1990. *Science and the Navy: The History of the Office of Naval Research.* Princeton NJ: Princeton University Press.

Naval Security Group (NSG)

The Naval Security Group (NSG), with some variance in title, had charge of U.S. Navy communications intelligence activities for more than a half–century. It followed and built on the important signals intelligence activities of the OP-20-G organization before and during World War II.

Early in 1943, OP-20-G moved from the Army-Navy Building on Constitution Avenue in Washington DC to the new Communication Supplementary Annex on Nebraska Avenue in Washington. This later became the Naval Communication Station Washington DC, and in September 1950 it became the Naval Security Station. It would remain the center of naval communications intelligence until 1995.

A closer alliance with Army and Air Force cryptologists was formalized in 1949 with the establishment of the Armed Forces Security Agency. On 28 January 1950 the following functional organizations were designated as the Naval Security Group: Communications Supplementary Activities, Communications Security Activities, and Special Electronics Search Projects. The Navy signals intelligence unit did yeoman work during the Korean War (1950–1953). In 1953 the organization, now designated as the Naval Security Group, included naval communication units, security group departments of Naval Communication Stations, naval security detachments, and registered (classified) publication issuing offices.

In 1956, the U.S. Naval Security Group Headquarters activity was established. The Naval Security Group Command, reporting directly to the chief of Naval Operations, was activated on 1 July 1968. The Naval Security Group moved from the Naval Security Station north to Fort Meade, Maryland, in November 1995.

In 2003 the former Nebraska Avenue communications complex became the new home of the Department of Homeland Security. Two years later, the separate Naval Security Group Command was disbanded (30 September 2005) and aligned with the Naval Network Warfare Command based in Norfolk, Virginia.

Christopher H. Sterling

See also Korean War (1950–1953); National Security Agency (NSA); Nebraska Avenue, Washington DC; OP-20-G; Signals Intelligence (SIGINT)

Sources

Grobmeier, Al. 2006 "Naval Security Group History." [Online article; retrieved April 2006.] http://coldwar-c4i.net/NSG/NAVSECGRU-history.html.

Safford, Laurance, and J. N. Wenger. 1994. *U.S. Naval Communications Intelligence Activities.* Laguna Hills, CA: Aegean Park Press.

Naval Tactical Data System (NTDS)

The Naval Tactical Data System (NTDS) was a computerized information processing system developed by the U.S. Navy in the 1950s, approved for implementation in 1956, and first deployed in the mid-1960s for use in combat ships. In service into the 1990s, the NTDS was the first digital system installed on any American naval vessel, as well as in a number of foreign fleets. It paved the way for the full integration of digital systems throughout American combat vessels.

UNIVAC developed the transistorized hardware and Seymour Cray (later famous for developing a line of supercomputers) was a critical figure in designing the original NTDS system architecture. Before installing anything on a combat ship, the Bureau of Ships' Naval Electronics Laboratory worked out system mockups and then began to lay out components in a shore facility. Early in 1961 computer training classes began for officers who would be assigned to operate the NTDS. Two ships, the newly built guided missile frigates *King* and *Mahon*, were designated for the first shipboard installations, along with the carrier *Oriskany* and the guided missile cruiser *Long Beach*.

Until the advent of computers compact and robust enough to be used aboard ships at sea, collection (and display) of information about the position of nearby aircraft, ships, and submarines was done manually. The NTDS was the Navy's first step to automate this information flow for use in either attack or defense, to reduce the chance of error and to allow ship commanders to cope with a more complex and faster-moving threat environment. The NTDS and wireless data links allowed ships to readily share information with other elements of a task force.

Installation of the first test system aboard three vessels began in late 1961, followed by a six-month operational evaluation. Equipment and program reliability varied greatly—sometimes the programs failed several times in the course of a single day. But testing continued and bugs were worked out. Early in 1963, the improved NTDS system was ordered installed on other fighting ships. Five NTDS-equipped ships were at sea within a year, ten by the end of 1965, with twenty-two more systems being installed. Partially due to the space requirements for radar and combat information center installations, implementation focused first on larger vessels—carriers and cruisers.

Over the next several years, as the Navy became increasingly involved in operations off Vietnam, the system was modified to fit other uses (for example, the Marines developed the Marine Tactical Data System, and antisubmarine patrol aircraft utilized the Airborne Tactical Data System, both NTDS-compatible systems). And other navies, most particularly Britain's Royal Navy and the smaller fleets of Canada, Belgium, and the Netherlands, were developing their own similar systems at the same time. The allied services worked together in sharing equipment and operational ideas, and variations of the NTDS were often installed, as happened later with German, French, Italian, and Japanese naval units. In all, by the late 1980s, forty-two foreign ships were carrying the NTDS along with 175 American vessels.

Naturally the system evolved as computers and related equipment were improved.

Consoles and display units became more capable, as did other components. Successful operation of the NTDS in combat conditions off Vietnam helped to reduce the last of naval resistance to the needed changes that the technology represented. By the late 1980s, follow-on systems, under the rubric of Advanced Combat Direction System, were progressively replacing NTDS installations.

Christopher H. Sterling

See also Combat Information Center (CIC); Computer; Transistor; U.S. Navy

Source

Boslaugh, David L. 1999. *When Computers Went to Sea: The Digitization of the United States Navy.* Los Alamitos, CA: The IEEE Computer Society.

Navy Commands and Systems

Changing U.S. Navy communications organizations and systems over the years have often been confusing, made more so by ever more complex names (and their sometimes odd abbreviations). Unlike the Army Signal Corps or the U.S. Air Force, the U.S. Navy has usually lacked a single command structure overseeing all of its communication systems and needs.

Regular organizational and related nomenclature changes afflict all military services, and while some modifications may sometimes seem inconsistent or even whimsical, they also reflect broadened responsibilities. Regardless of name, the mission of naval communications has always been to provide and maintain reliable, secure, and rapid communications, based on war requirements, to meet the needs of naval operating forces. The term "telecommunications" is now taken to include all types of information

systems in which electric or electromagnetic signals are used to transmit information between or among points.

As with other military services, the Navy realized that commercial off-the-shelf information technology (IT) was mature enough that the Navy could depend on it, rather than building and operating its own separate system. The Navy also realized that IT infrastructure could be treated like a utility that someone else capitalized, operated, and maintained. Today's Naval Telecommunications System (NTS) comprises all the end-terminal processing equipment, transmission, switching, cryptographic, and control devices used to transmit operational information in the Navy. It provides electrical and optical communications to all naval forces under its command. The NTS is used primarily to exercise command and control over naval operating forces at sea (not the shore establishment, which is served through the Defense Communications System). The Naval Communications Processing and Routing System is an automated system that serves as the interface between shore networks and operational units of the Navy.

In 1986, the Naval Telecommunication Command became the chief communications unit within the service. In 1993 it was renamed the Naval Computer and Telecommunications Command, and in 2001 changed again, becoming the Naval Network and Space Operations Command (NNSOC). NNSOC was also the result of a merger of the Naval Space Command and the Naval Network Operations Command, the latter formed only one year earlier.

On 1 May 2002, the Navy formed the Naval Network Warfare Command (NETWARCOM) as the headquarters for operational decisions and directions, with a global staff of 7,000. The establishment of NET-WARCOM reflected the Navy's recognition that networks are warfare enablers, and are thus becoming increasingly important. NET-WARCOM is responsible for coordinating all information technology, information operations, and space requirements and operations within the Navy. It controls twenty-three subordinate selected naval information technology/information operations or organizations. These include the Naval Network and Space Operations Command based in Dahlgren, Virginia; the Fleet Information Warfare Command in Norfolk, Virginia; and the Navy Component Task Force Computer Network Defense in Washington DC.

The U.S. Navy divides the world into four operational communications areas: Western Pacific headquartered on the island of Guam; Eastern Pacific in Honolulu; Atlantic in Norfolk, Virginia; and the Mediterranean in Naples, Italy. All communications activities within each area are under the operational control of a Naval Computer and Telecommunications Area Master Station (NCTAMS). These master stations (the one in Oahu dates to a Pearl Harbor predecessor that first aired in 1906) are the primary keying stations for their region, are the entry points for Navy tactical satellite systems, and operate and maintain one or more Defense Satellite Communications System terminals. The NCTAMSs include fleet telecommunications operations serving as the focal point for fleet communications support. While all NCTAMSs have similar operational capabilities, no two have identical facilities. They also control the use of assigned naval tactical radio frequencies and disseminate interference information.

Global Command and Control System–Maritime (formerly the Navy Tactical Command System–Afloat) is the system by which all Navy seagoing forces maintain a common operational picture. This system enables the warfare commander to exercise effective command. The Navy/Marine Corps Intranet (NMCI) is an unclassified wide-area network that is (or is being) installed at all U.S. Navy shore commands. The system is intended to improve efficiency and security by having all Navy e-mail accounts maintained centrally. EDS won the contract for NMCI in the 1990s, but the system has cost billions of dollars and been plagued by problems. NETWARCOM serves as program administrator.

Implementation of "Copernicus" architecture has contributed to this major restructuring of U.S. Navy command, control, communications, computers, and intelligence systems to place the operator at the center of the command-and-control process. Rather than "push" data to the battle group/battle commander, data are collected, correlated, and melded to efficiently disseminate them when required. Copernicus uses existing communications systems and equipment and a communication support system (CSS) to integrate naval communications assets. The CSS is the communications subarchitecture that provides multimedia access and media sharing, permitting users to share total network capacity on a priority demand basis in accordance with a tactical commander's communications plan. Communications pathways are automatically selected as needed rather than dedicated, making the transmission medium invisible to the user.

Christopher H. Sterling

See also Defense Communications System (DCS); National Communications System (NCS); Naval Radio Stations/Service; Satellite Communications; U.S. Navy

Sources

GlobalSecurity.org. 2005. "NCTAMS PAC, Wahiawa, Hawaii." [Online information; retrieved January 2007.] http://www.globalsecurity.org/military/facility/wahiawa.htm.

Naval Network Warfare Command. Home page. [Online iinformation; retrieved January 2007.] http://www.netwarcom.navy.mil/.

Navy Radio Laboratory

The U.S. Navy's earliest activities with radio date from 1899. Naval research into uses of radio waves was assigned to the Navy's Bureau of Equipment in 1903. As experimentation with radio increased, private entrepreneurs, foreign governments, and the U.S. military all saw multiple applications for the new technology. Efforts by the federal government and by international organizations to create control structures for frequency usage, wireless telegraphy, and radio communications in the early 1900s added urgency to the Navy's research and management activities. Hoping to use radio-based communications in both on-shore installations and ships of the fleet, the Navy developed research initiatives to improve the reliability, distance, security, and speed of radio message traffic. In 1908 the U.S. Naval Wireless Telegraphic Laboratory, later known as the U.S. Navy Radio Laboratory, was organized. Its equipment, quarters, and personnel were obtained from the research wing of the U.S. Bureau of Standards.

The new laboratory conducted precision experimental work with receivers, circuit efficiency, and wavelength measurements in its facilities, while development of antennas and measurements of atmospheric factors was performed in the field and aboard ships. Laboratory personnel kept abreast of technical innovations in the fast-changing radio field, as private companies moved quickly to introduce radio equipment of all types into the American and European markets. The Navy also had security concerns about Britain's development of a worldwide cable-based communications system, so one key area of research at the Radio Laboratory involved producing and measuring radio signal strength over long distances and point-to-point transmission and reception.

A Congressionally mandated reorganization of the Navy Department in 1910 produced a decision to divide oversight of naval radio-related activities: Naval radio communications, including operations, land-based stations, and fleet requirements became the province of the Division of Operations, while radio equipment, maintenance, and research were housed in the Bureau of Steam Engineering. The Navy Radio Laboratory was placed within the latter, which also had a Radio Telegraphy Division; this became the Radio Division in 1917, when the Naval Aircraft Radio Laboratory was also created to research shortwave radio for use in naval aviation. With the leadership of the Navy Radio Laboratory, the Steam Engineering Division introduced the Navy's first organized plan for radio frequency allocation and usage. Specific frequencies were designated for "calling" purposes in the short-, medium-, and long-wave bandwidths, and increasingly reliable transmission and reception of messages between naval vessels was achieved.

By 1912 sufficient long-distance signal strength and reception accuracy had been measured by laboratory personnel to permit a major initiative in radio traffic development by the Navy. The Navy requested congressional funding of $1 million to construct a high-powered network of wireless communications stations in the Pacific that would use arc transmitters, which utilized "continuous wave" transmissions. This technology made long-range signal transmission practicable, and the Navy proposed to build ground-based transmission and reception stations in Virginia, California, Hawaii, Samoa, Guam, and the Philippines. The first station to become operational was at La Playa Naval Coaling Station, a facility formerly owned by the U.S. Army, which was also the Navy's first installation in San Diego.

In 1920 the Bureau of Steam Engineering was renamed the Bureau of Engineering, and in yet another reorganization in 1930, its Radio Division became the Radio and Sound Division and a part of the Navy's new Bureau of Ships. The Navy Radio Laboratory was also renamed the Navy Radio and Sound Laboratory. During the 1930s and World War II, the laboratory focused much of its research effort on evaluating underwater radio and sound waves, eventually testing and modifying submarine-based communications and countermeasure technologies as well as radio wave-based harbor and surface ship defense systems. In 1947 the laboratory was merged with elements of the University of California's Division of War Research to become part of the Navy Electronics Laboratory.

Laura M. Calkins

See also National Bureau of Standards (NBS), National Institute of Standards and Technology (NIST); Naval Radio Stations/Service; Naval Research Laboratory (NRL); Radio; U.S. Navy; Wireless Telegraph Board

Sources

Douglas, Susan J. 1985. "Technological Innovation and Organizational Change: The Navy's Adoption of Radio, 1899–1919." In *Military Enterprise and Technology Change:* *Perspectives on the American Experience,* edited by Merritt Roe Smith. Cambridge MA: MIT Press.

Douglas, Susan J. 1987. *Inventing American Broadcasting, 1899–1922.* Baltimore: Johns Hopkins University Press.

Hammond, P. H. 1944. "The U.S. Navy Radio and Sound Laboratory." *Journal of Applied Physics* 15 (3): 240–242.

Howeth, Linwood S. 1963. *History of Communications-Electronics in the United States Navy.* Washington, DC: Government Printing Office.

Yeang, Chen-Pang. 2004. "Scientific Fact of Engineering Specification? The US Navy's Experiments on Wireless Telegraphy circa 1910." *Technology and Culture* 45: 1–29.

Nebraska Avenue, Washington DC

The building complex at 3801 Nebraska Ave. NW has played a large part in signals intelligence and even the development of the computer. For over a half-century it housed the U.S. Navy's communications and signals intelligence operations.

The Mount Vernon Seminary, a private finishing school and later a college for women, opened in Washington DC in 1875 and moved to new buildings on Nebraska Avenue in 1917. The college campus doubled from 15 to 31 acres in 1928 as more buildings went up. With the onset of World War II, however, many sites in the Washington area (this one is 5 miles from downtown, located across from American University) were taken over for military needs. In 1942, the seminary property, including all of its dormitories and classrooms, became one of these, taken over by the Navy. (The school was reimbursed two years later, and in 1945 purchased land on Foxhall Road for a new campus with the same name. It remains there today, since 1999 a part of George

Washington University.) At the same time, the Army was taking over another women's school, Arlington Hall, for its own signals intelligence operation.

The number of employees increased steadily during the war, growing at least fivefold. As the amount of code-breaking activity increased (including all theaters of war, not just the Pacific), so did the need for mechanical assistance if messages were going to be broken on any schedule to be worthwhile to military and naval planners. That led to the "Bombe" project—the building of dozens and then hundreds of electro-mechanical machines used to solve each day's Enigma cipher settings. Without the bombes, Allied code breakers would have been overwhelmed.

Originally developed in Poland and perfected in Britain, many bombes were made in the United States, with its greater manufacturing capacity and freedom from enemy attack. The American version was designed in great secrecy at Dayton, Ohio, in the facilities of National Cash Register, with the resulting machines being installed in the newly constructed Building 4 on Nebraska Avenue. By 1945, 121 of the clanking 5,000-pound machines (which had cost about $6 million to manufacture) were operating on two floors, all of them operated by some 600 members of the naval women's auxiliary—thus bringing women back to the site of the seminary. Running twenty-four hours a day, the bombes helped greatly to speed the reading of Enigma-coded U-boat messages as well as Bletchley Park's "Hut 6" coded traffic. Improved models had been steadily introduced. Most were destroyed after the war to preserve their secrets; today a few are on exhibit in museums.

The Nebraska Avenue location was named the Navy's Communications Supplementary Annex in February 1943 (it was renamed NAVCOMMSTA—for Naval Communication Station—Washington on 7 July 1948, and the Naval Security Station on 21 September 1950). The site remained a naval facility for six decades (though the communications intelligence units moved to Fort Meade, Maryland, in 1995), transferring to the then Office of Homeland Security in 2003, and becoming headquarters for the cabinet-level Department of Homeland Security a year later. In 1994, what had been the Naval Security Station District was identified as a historic property, and it is listed in the National Register of Historic Places, administered by the National Park Service.

Christopher H. Sterling

See also Arlington Hall; Bletchley Park; Enigma; Magic; Naval Security Group (NSG); OP-20-G; Polish Code Breaking; Signals Intelligence (SIGINT); Ultra

Sources

MSN Groups. 2003. "3801 Nebraska Avenue." [Online information; retrieved April 2006.] http://groups.msn.com/ctoseadogs/3801.msnw.

Wilcox, Jennifer. 2001. *Solving the Enigma: History of the Cryptanalytic Bombe.* Fort Meade, MD: National Security Agency, Center for Cryptologic History.

Network Enterprise Technology Command (NETCOM)

Headquartered at Fort Huachuca, Arizona, the Network Enterprise Technology Command (NETCOM) is the central executive institution responsible for the full spectrum of U.S. Army "infostructure" and integrates ground forces' command, control, communication, and computers. It was established in October 2002, when the 9th Army Signal Command was renamed as Network Enterprise Technology Command and the 9th Army Signal Command (NETCOM/9th ASC). Its creation was part of the Army Knowledge Management Strategy with the aim of transforming itself into a network-centric and knowledge-based service. The origins of NETCOM/9th ASC, however, can be traced back to 1918 and the setting up of the 9th Service Company in Hawaii, which over time was subject to a number of reorganizations.

NETCOM was established as the single authority assigned to operate and manage the Army's information network infrastructure at the enterprise level. It provides central technical control over all functions associated with Army networks. Its mission also includes management and protection of the Army frequency spectrum. It provides critical communication means also for nonmilitary governmental agencies in support of emergency operations, for example, during hurricanes and subsequent relief actions. NETCOM is a global organization comprising approximately 14,000 soldiers and civilians at 104 sites around the world. It possesses strategic tactical entry point sites in South America and along the Pacific Rim so that the "sun never sets on NETCOM operations."

Cooperating with other services, NETCOM provides timely distribution of critical information. It acts in response to instant demands to set up communication services in distant places. For command, control, and combat purposes it is capable of quickly extending such services as e-mail, the Secret Internet Protocol Router Network, the Unclassified but Sensitive Internet Protocol Router Network, video teleconferencing capabilities, and voice telephone.

NETCOM/9th ASC is an important agent of a secure all-embracing information network that is being built by the Pentagon, known as the Global Information Grid (GIG), which interconnects communications at strategic, operational, and tactical levels. NETCOM's task is to ensure that the Army's segment of the GIG is protected (from hackers, viruses, worms, etc.) and on hand whenever and wherever necessary. NETCOM operates, engineers, integrates, sustains, and protects the LandWarNet, the Army's portion (in terms of networks) of the GIG.

The 11th Signal Brigade is crucial for NETCOM's operations. It consists of three tactical and one strategic battalion. The latter is the brigade's interface with the GIG. The brigade possesses the only tri-band terminals in the Army, which allow it to use both military and commercial satellite terminals. The brigade's soldiers were deployed in eight different countries in 2006. Its great advantage is data package capability, where combinations of multiplexers, firewalls, servers, and hardware are packaged and ready for prompt transportation.

Although when the Iraq War began in March 2003 NETCOM had been functional for only six months, it proved to be successful in securing safe and on-time communication for the Army.

As an element of overall Pentagon transformation toward network-centric warfare, NETCOM faces some challenges generally associated with the evolution of the American way of war. The two greatest ones are the constant improvement of network defense and securing appropriate technology upgrades.

Łukasz Kamieński

See also Army Battle Command System (ABCS); Army Signal Corps; Fort Huachuca, Arizona; Global Information Grid (GIG); Information Revolution in Military Affairs (IRMA); Iraq War (2003–Present); "System of Systems"

Sources

Clarke, Patrick E. 2003. "Sun Never Sets on NETCOM Operations." *Military Information Technology* 7 (8). Available at http://www.military-information-technology.com/article.cfm?DocID=231.

GlobalSecurity.org. 2005. "Network Command History." [Online information; retrieved December 2006.] http://www.globalsecurity.org/military/agency/army/netcom-history.htm.

GlobalSecurity.org. "Network Enterprise Technology Command." [Online information; retrieved December 2006.] http://www.globalsecurity.org/military/agency/army/asc.htm.

"Network Operator: Interview with Brigadier General Carroll F. Pollett, Commander Army Network Enterprise Technology Command 9th Army Signal Command." 2005. *Military Information Technology* 9 (8). Available at http://www.military-information-technology.com/article.cfm?DocID=1184.

U.S. Army Network Enterprise Technology Command/9th Army Signal Command. [Online information; retrieved December 2006.] http://www.netcom.army.mil/.

New Zealand: Royal New Zealand Corps of Signals

New Zealand military communications began with Maori systems in ancient times. Modern signaling systems date to the 1860s and expanded through both world wars as New Zealand signalers worked around the world.

Corporal Alexander Brodie of the Royal Engineers is considered to be the father of New Zealand army signaling. Fully conversant with the latest military techniques in telegraphy, he arrived in New Zealand in 1863, during the Second New Zealand War between British and Maori forces. On 11 March 1863, Brodie and others commenced construction of a military telegraph line from the Albert barracks in Auckland to Queens Redoubt, about 35 miles to the south. They utilized local resources and the assistance of selected infantry personnel to lay more than 100 miles of line from Auckland to Te Awamutu, including a spur to Cambridge, in little more than a year. Telegraph stations at the various armed posts into the Waikato were manned by army telegraphists. Brodie's telegraph line was in constant use, providing a vital link from the campaign directly back to Auckland through hostile territory. When military operations in the area concluded, the troops turned over the telegraph line to civilian authorities on 30 September 1866.

Military signaling continued to the end of the nineteenth century within the armed constabulary and volunteer engineers. It was not until 1905, however, that signaling detachments were added to volunteer infantry and cycle units. The Cycle and Signaling Corps was established in 1909 as the first dedicated signal unit in New Zealand. It was one of several similar units that, by 1 July 1913, became the New Zealand Divisional Signal Company. Two years earlier, the New Zealand Post and Telegraph Corps had been formed and it soon provided very highly trained civilian telegraphists. This became a part of the New Zealand Engineers Signal Service on 1 July 1913.

New Zealand engineer signals troops participated in the capture of German Samoa in August 1914. The Divisional Signal Company saw service in Gallipoli and in Egypt before moving on to France in 1916. New Zealand has the only signal corps that can boast a Victoria Cross (V.C.) winner. Corporal Cyril Royston Guyton Bassett won his V.C. for conspicuous bravery during the Gallipoli campaign. The Mounted Signal Troop served at Gallipoli, and later operated in Palestine. A New Zealand wireless troop served in Mesopotamia and Persia with the

Australians in a combined wireless signal squadron. On 1 June 1921, the New Zealand Corps of Signals was formed from the New Zealand Post and Telegraph Corps.

During World War II, New Zealand signal regiments served in North Africa, Syria, Greece, Crete, Italy, and the Pacific. Coast watchers were also established at many Pacific islands. A signals intercept section was located at the Army Signal Company at Wellington and intercepted Japanese Morse signals, which were sent to Brisbane to be decoded. In 1945, a signal company was sent to Japan as part of the British Commonwealth Occupation Force.

King George VI granted the New Zealand Corps of Signals the prefix "Royal" on 12 July 1947. The Royal New Zealand Corps of Signals provided two signal troop units for the Korean War (1950–1953). During the latter half of the twentieth century the corps sent personnel to Malaya, Borneo, and Singapore, and on many peacekeeping duties around the world including Rhodesia, Sinai, Bosnia, and Cambodia, Iraq, and Afghanistan. A number of signal detachments were also sent to the Southwest Pacific, in particular, East Timor.

Cliff Lord

See also Australia: Royal Australian Corps of Signals; Maori Signaling; Signals Intelligence (SIGINT); United Kingdom: Royal Corps of Signals

Sources
Barber, Laurie, and Cliff Lord. 1996. *Swift and Sure: A History of the Royal New Zealand Corps of Signals and Army Signalling in New Zealand*. Auckland: New Zealand Signals Incorporated.
Borman, C.A. 1954. *Divisional Signals*. Wellington, New Zealand: War History Branch Department of Internal Affairs.
Ellis, Roy F. 1968. *By Wires to Victory*. Auckland: 1st NZEF Divisional Signal Company, War History Committee.
History of the New Zealand Engineers. 1927. Wanganui, New Zealand: Evans, Cobb and Sharpe Ltd.

Night Signals

How to send visible signals at night was a complex problem in the period before electrical communication developed in the mid-nineteenth century. The usual means of visual signaling (flags, smoke) or even pigeons to carry messages, were of little use during hours of darkness. For centuries, military signalers working at night were limited to traditional resources such as couriers (on foot or horseback) or some means of generating sound signals.

In ancient times, means of generating sound included horns and drums, while light modes included torches (later, lanterns). But neither was good for signaling over more than a few miles—and that only under good conditions (fog could do them all in). By the late Middle Ages, gunfire could also be used for sound signaling. Some handheld visual signals could be used to communicate at night by adding lanterns—but again, only for relatively short distances. Distress rockets, first developed in the early eighteenth century, could also be applied to military nighttime signaling needs. Trumpet or bugle calls were utilized also. Well into the nineteenth century, such traditional methods were about all commanders could call on, and reliance on human couriers (and occasionally animals, especially dogs—but usually not birds, which were more suitable to daytime use) remained essential.

As technology created new options in the mid-nineteenth century, however, new visual methods appeared, including signal flares (Coston signals) and other pyrotechnics; blinking colored lights (Ardois lights), which were soon electrified; and even large electrical searchlights for signaling to and from ships at sea, or from coastlines out to sea. Night signals using balls of red and green fire shot from a pistol appeared in 1877, their arrangement in groups denoting numbers that had a prearranged code significance. Star shells of different colors, as well as rockets to carry tactical messages, were widely used in World War I, especially in the final year, as were lights dropped from aircraft. Naval vessels made widespread use of shutter light signaling in both world wars.

The arrival in the mid-nineteenth century of the practical electric telegraph—followed later in the century by the telephone and finally wireless/radio—largely eliminated most day-night signaling differences.

Christopher H. Sterling

See also Ardois Light; Artillery/Gunfire; Color; Coston Signals; Couriers; Fire/Flame/Torch; Lights and Beacons; Music Signals; Searchlights/Signal Blinkers; Signal Rockets; Telegraph

Sources

Niblack, A. P. 1892. "Naval Signaling." *U.S. Naval Institute Proceedings* 18: 431–505.

Woods, David L. 1965. *A History of Tactical Communication Techniques*. Orlando, FL: Martin-Marietta (reprinted by Arno Press, 1974).

North Atlantic Treaty Organization (NATO) Communications & Information Systems Agency

The North Atlantic Treaty Organization (NATO) Communications & Information Systems Agency (NCSA) was formed only in 2004 but has an involved history going back to the 1970s. When NATO was founded, it relied initially on signals services provided by the United States and Britain.

Over the past three decades, there have been numerous restructurings of the various NATO communications organizations. The first specialized communications and information entity was the NATO Integrated Communications Systems Central Operating Authority, established to control, operate, and maintain NATO communications. These included the Initial Voice Switched Network, Telegraph Automated Relay Equipment, Status Control Alerting and Reporting System, satellite communications systems, and the ACE High Tropospheric Scatter trunk communication network. With changing technologies by the early 1990s, it became necessary to reorganize. This coincided with a major restructuring of NATO to take advantage of the "peace dividend" with the end of the Cold War. In 1993 the NATO Communication and Information Systems Operating and Support Agency (NACOSA) was formed by adding some elements of the Communications and Information Systems Division of the Supreme Headquarters Allied Powers Europe (SHAPE). Soon it became apparent that further streamlining to improve management and control and to trim staffing was needed. NACOSA took command of four subordinate elements including the Integrated System Support Centre; Allied Command Europe Communications Security; NATO Communication and Information Systems School at Latina, Italy; and Regional Signal Group SHAPE. In the following years, NACOSA developed into an organization with responsibilities for the operation and support of communication and information systems on both sides of the Atlantic and all NATO operations.

By 1997 multiple factors (including the arrival of new systems and technology, lessons learned in operations in the Balkans, the introduction of "Partners for Peace," and NATO's study of its long-term needs) led again to NACOSA reorganization. Its charter was redefined and remained in force until 2003, when, after yet another study, the North Atlantic Council endorsed further change. All of NATO's fragmented communication and information service elements were integrated into a centralized organization designed to separate customers from suppliers. All deployable communication and information service capabilities were combined in two NATO signal battalions and became part of the new NCSA. Created were the NATO Signal Battalion North (Army) in Brunssum, Netherlands, and the NATO Signal Battalion South (Navy) in Naples, Italy. Each has four deployable communication modules, comparable in size and mandate to signals companies.

NCSA's 3,000 military and civilian personnel provide service to NATO and national customers. The central staff is co-located with SHAPE in Mons, Belgium. The NCSA director is accountable to NATO's Consultation, Command and Control Board for executing general policy decisions associated with provision of communication and information services throughout NATO. NCSA personnel provide technical advice; install equipment; conduct hardware and software maintenance; configure and control networks; and train personnel on NATO communications and information systems. They also provide secure computer network, telephone, and videoconference services to the International Assistance Force in Afghanistan, the NATO Training Mission in Iraq, units in the Balkans, and disaster relief operations such as for a 2005 earthquake in Pakistan. They also provide secure and non-secure computer, telephone, and videoconference services to NATO's headquarters in Europe, North America, and Asia.

Danny Johnson

See also Canada; Eastern Europe; France: Air Force; France: Army; France: Navy; Germany: Air Force; Germany: Army; Germany: Navy; Greece; United Kingdom: Royal Air Force; United Kingdom: Royal Corps of Signals; United Kingdom: Royal Navy; Warsaw Pact

Source

NATO Communication and Information Systems Services Agency. Home page. [Online information; retrieved August 2006.] http://www.ncsa.nato.int/index_sm.htm.

O

Office of Strategic Services (OSS)

The Office of Strategic Services (OSS) was developed in mid-1942 from the Coordinator of Information (COI), established a year earlier. This legendary and highly controversial intelligence agency, ancestor of today's Central Intelligence Agency (CIA), operated until September 1945 under the direction of Colonel (later Major General) William "Wild Bill" Donovan, a charismatic New York attorney who had been a highly decorated infantry officer during World War I.

Most COI/OSS personnel were civilians. Under COI, the Radio News and Features Division of the Foreign Information Service (FIS) provided (beginning in August 1941) background information concerning events in Europe to eleven U.S. shortwave stations—all but one in the northeastern United States—for use as they saw fit. At first, FIS had no broadcasting capability of its own. By November 1941, the Radio Production Division was broadcasting abroad in seventeen languages, and FIS had begun to analyze German radio transmissions. The first Voice of America broadcast (in German) was made from New York in February 1942, and within three months, FIS was broadcasting in twenty-seven languages around the clock. Soon, FIS had begun utilizing news items from Axis countries in a very effective propaganda/intelligence initiative. When COI became the Office of Strategic Services in June 1942, FIS transferred to the Office of War Information.

In September 1942, Donovan established the OSS Communications Branch, which was eventually responsible for communications training of agents. Divisions took charge of a wide range of technical support issues, to include sound and light modes of signaling as well as radio. The branch provided equipment for code transmission, reception, and interception. One important example was its "Joan/Eleanor" ground-to-air FM transmission system first used in late 1944 behind the lines in the Netherlands. It used a tiny and highly focused vertically directional transmitter signal (Eleanor) to reach a receiver (Joan) and wire recorder in a circling airplane. It was almost impossible to detect on the ground. The names for the small devices came from the OSS practice of assigning random female names for projects.

An OSS message center had responsibility for all incoming and outgoing cable traffic. At first, commercial facilities were utilized, but Army and Navy networks later transmitted OSS messages abroad. The center's operations began with a staff of three clerks in December 1941, but by the end of the war, 530 persons (400 in the field) handled the activities of a code room, paraphrasing and distribution, teletype, typing room, maintenance, and cryptographic security. The Communications Branch also had responsibilities for technical support of direction-finding apparatus, while OSS's Secret Intelligence Division dealt with all intelligence issues. By 1944, OSS was utilizing new high-speed enciphering and deciphering methods on a cable channel provided by Western Union. Though radio listening stations in New York and California had been established earlier, the shortwave intelligence they collected did not come within the purview of the Communications Branch, though the branch did maintain the stations after 1943.

Donovan, who had originally persuaded President Franklin Roosevelt that the nation needed a centralized intelligence organization, faced a continuing challenge to maintain the cohesiveness of his brainchild. While COI had operated under the Office of the President, OSS was placed under the Joint Chiefs of Staff. More traditionally oriented intelligence personnel in the uniformed services and Federal Bureau of Investigation Director J. Edgar Hoover resented this new entity. They made every effort to persuade Roosevelt to either limit the scope of OSS operations (by ruling out OSS activities in the Western Hemisphere and the Pacific Theater) or by transferring its work to the uniformed services. Their ultimate objective was to close OSS down.

They appeared to succeed when President Harry S. Truman abruptly terminated Donovan's operations in September 1945 (the Research and Analysis Division survived as an agency of the State Department). Within a year after the war ended, however, the beginnings of what is now CIA were in place when the Joint Chiefs realized that they were not receiving as good communications and other forms of intelligence as had been the case during World War II.

Keir B. Sterling

See also Code, Codebook; Modulation; Signals Intelligence (SIGINT); World War II

Sources

Chalou, George C., ed. 1992. *The Secrets War: The Office of Strategic Services in World War II*. Washington, DC: National Archives and Records Administration.

Katz, Barry M. 1989. *Foreign Intelligence: Research and Intelligence in the Office of Strategic Services, 1942–1945*. Cambridge, MA: Harvard University Press.

Roosevelt, Kermit, ed. 1976. *War Report of the OSS (Office of Strategic Services)*, vol. I. New York: Walker.

Troy, Thomas. 1981. *Donovan and the CIA: A History of the Central Intelligence Agency*. Lanham, MD: University Press of America.

Ohio, USS

In the early 1920s, the U.S. Navy converted an obsolete battleship, the USS *Ohio*, to use as an experimental vessel for the installation and development of radio communications.

Construction of the *Ohio* began 22 April 1899 and was completed 18 May 1901 as BB-12, part of a class of three vessels. The Navy commissioned her on 4 October 1904, at which time she was designated flagship of the Asiatic Fleet. After a fifteen-year career, in August 1919, the *Ohio* was turned over to the Bureau of Engineering to become an experimental radio ship. The purpose of designating the *Ohio* for such a task was to free up more modern battleships to save resources but still allow for needed experimentation and development of radio communications.

In Portsmouth, Virginia, the Navy removed the battleship's guns and refitted her with a series of new radio transmitter and receiver systems. This work took nine months. The refit included converting two rooms below decks into large radio facilities, designed to handle the new systems. One of the new rooms was fitted with transmitting equipment; the other was fitted with new receiving equipment. The Navy left the vessel's original radio room unchanged in order to process routine traffic. As part of the refitting process, the Navy added two antenna trunks to the ship, positioned between the new radio rooms and the deck. One was made of steel, the other of copper. An arrangement of topmasts, which could be varied in five-foot increments of height, was attached to the *Ohio*'s main cage masts in order to improve communication distances.

After her refit, the Navy placed the *Ohio* under the Naval Experimental Station. The *Ohio* also was assigned a small crew in which every member played a vital role in carrying out the experiments.

The greatest benefit of the *Ohio*'s radio experiments came in the form of information about future radio installations. The Navy learned a lot about antenna performance, closed-circuit systems, and arc transmission techniques.

In addition, the *Ohio* assisted in a series of experiments involving the USS *Iowa*. The Navy installed equipment designed by inventor John H. Hammond to make the *Ohio* a control platform that could remotely control *Iowa*. On 21 June 1921, more than a hundred transmissions were sent to the *Iowa* at the range of about 8,000 yards, all of which functioned to control the unmanned battleship. Although the following day's tests failed because of problems aboard the *Iowa*, the Navy had proven that a ship could be controlled by radio. After these tests the *Ohio* continued with her duties until she was sold for scrap in early 1922 as a condition of the Washington naval treaties.

Charles A. Swann

See also Hooper, Stanford C. (1884–1955); Navy Radio Laboratory; U.S. Navy

Sources
Bauer, K. Jack, and Stephen S. Roberts. 1991. *Register of Ships of the U.S. Navy 1775–1990: Major Combatants.* Westport, CT: Greenwood Press.
Howeth, Linwood S. 1963. *History of Communications-Electronics in the United States Navy.* Washington, DC: Government Printing Office.

OP-20-G

OP-20-G was the primary U.S. Navy signals intelligence organization from 1922 until after World War II. Navy interest in signals intelligence began 28 July 1916 when a code and signal section was established in the Office of the Chief of Naval Operations. It worked at breaking German naval codes. Two years later, during World War I, the first modern American codes were issued, copied after British codes used by the United States during the war. After the armistice was signed (11 November 1918), an intelligence clerk from the cable censor's office was transferred to the code and signals section for research in the development of codes and ciphers. It soon became apparent that to learn the weakness of existing codes and ciphers (as well as how to construct secure ones), the first essential was to learn the basics of cryptanalysis. After the war, naval code activities were merged for several years with the Army's cipher bureau.

In July 1922, what had been the code and signals section was assigned the soon-to-be-familiar organizational title OP-20-G. The odd acronym came from the fact that the new office was the 20th Division of the Office of the Chief of Naval Operations, while the "G" indicated the communications security section. A year later Laurance F. Safford first became involved in communications intelligence. In 1923 the Office of Naval Intelligence requested that all ships of the Asiatic Fleet forward intercepted Japanese and commercial code messages. In 1924 (and possibly before), the naval radio station (dubbed simply "Station A") at the Navy Purchasing Office within the U.S. Consulate in Shanghai was intercepting and forwarding Japanese traffic. The naval radio station San Francisco was also forwarding all official Japanese traffic to OP-20-G's code and signals section.

Operations were limited by budget constraints in the late 1920s. A handful of officers and a small cadre of enlisted personnel trained themselves in the specific skills and knowledge of naval signals security. The enlisted intercept specialists who trained on the roof of the old Navy Department building in Washington DC became known as the "On-the-Roof Gang" and were the core of the vastly expanded effort during World War II. More listening and monitoring stations were opened—Station B in Guam and another in Beijing, China. Station C was soon established at Subic Bay (it shifted location three times before the Japanese occupation in 1942) in the Philippines. Additional stations (including H, or Hypo, at Pearl Harbor) slowly followed as funds allowed. In early 1935, in accordance with joint action of the Army and Navy, radio intelligence was determined to be a function of communications and the

Navy portion of radio intelligence was assigned to the Office of Naval Communications. On 11 March 1935, OP-20-G became a part of the Communication Security Group.

OP-20-G personnel were intimately involved with breaking the continuing series of Japanese naval and other codes in the period leading up to World War II. They also played a central part in the development of the SIGABA electric cipher machine that provided unbreakable Allied communication links. In 1942, OP-20-G expanded into seventeen subsections and its chief became the assistant director for communication intelligence in the Office of Naval Communications. Navy cryptologists were successful in breaking the latest Japanese naval code (dubbed JN-25 by the Allies) in time for the Battle of Midway in mid-1942, and were instrumental in providing information for the American fleet commander to defeat the Japanese fleet. They also broke the Japanese merchant shipping code, giving American submarines locations of Japanese ships. By war's end, five-sixths of the Japanese merchant fleet was sunk. At the height of the war, nearly 10,000 naval specialists participated in the worldwide activities of OP-20-G.

Only after the war, in yet another reorganization, did OP-20-G give way to what became the Naval Security Group.

Christopher H. Sterling

See also Electric Cipher Machine (ECM Mark II, "SIGABA"); Magic; Midway, Battle of (3–6 June 1942); Naval Radio Stations/Service; Naval Security Group (NSG); Nebraska Avenue, Washington DC; Pearl Harbor, Hawaii; Safford, Laurance F. (1890–1973); Signals Intelligence (SIGINT)

Sources
Benson, Robert Lewis. 1997. *A History of U.S. Communications Intelligence During World War II: Policy and Administration.* United States

Cryptologic History, Series IV, Vol. 8. Fort Meade, MD: National Security Agency.

Grobmeier, Al. 2006. "Naval Security Group History." [Online article; retrieved April 2006.] http://coldwar-c4i.net/NSG/NAVSECGRU-history.html.

Lewin, Ronald. 1982. *The American Magic: Codes, Ciphers and the Defeat of Japan.* New York: Farrar, Straus & Giroux.

Parker, Frederick D. 1994. *Pearl Harbor Revisited: United States Navy Communications Intelligence, 1924–1941.* United States Cryptologic History, Series IV, Vol. 6. Fort Meade, MD: National Security Agency.

Safford, Laurance, and J. N. Wenger. 1994. *U.S. Naval Communications Intelligence Activities.* Laguna Hills, CA: Aegean Park Press.

Pearl Harbor, Hawaii

When the Japanese Imperial Navy attacked the American naval base at Pearl Harbor on 7 December 1941, American forces were taken by surprise, and losses of personnel (more than 2,200), ships, and aircraft were heavy. Numerous wartime and postwar investigations of the disaster focused in considerable part on the poor state of communications between army and naval forces on the island—and communication failures between Washington and Hawaii. There was plenty of blame to go around in what some termed the worst failure of military communications in the nation's history.

The Army and Navy had divided up the task of protecting Hawaii. The Navy's ships and aircraft were assigned to locate and intercept any enemy naval force that might be heading for Hawaii, out to a distance of 500 miles from Oahu. The Army's air arm was assigned to patrol up to 20 miles off the coast, while the Army's Coast Artillery was responsible for defending the islands (and especially the Navy's ships in Pearl Harbor) to the maximum range of their fixed artillery

batteries (the largest 16-inch guns could fire about 25 miles). This division of labor seemed a logical approach in 1940–1941.

The Army's coastal defenses in Hawaii were extensive, designed to repel an attempted enemy landing. Batteries had been built beginning early in the twentieth century, largely to defend Honolulu and the growing naval anchorage at Pearl Harbor just west of the city. The Army Signal Corps' fire control command and communications system employed on Oahu in late 1941 relied on a series of subterranean telephone cables that ringed the island to provide a means of communicating with the numerous airfields, observation posts, and coastal gun batteries. Few of the coast defense fire control or outlying base end stations were equipped with radio, however, and only a few of the larger coastal gun batteries included radio capability. With its cable system, the Army's Hawaii command could communicate with its coast defenses located around the perimeter of the island and could telephone sightings of enemy vessels, including elevation and range data, to the plotting rooms of the coastal gun batteries. Telephone links included

Army airfields and support facilities as well as an experimental radar installation on the north side of Oahu, which detected and reported the incoming Japanese aircraft on the morning of 7 December, but was ignored. The Navy's communication (telephone and radio) facilities were totally separate and centered on the Pearl Harbor base, as were links to Marine Corp facilities elsewhere on Oahu.

Limited coordination between the services existed only at the jointly staffed Harbor Entrance Control Post (HECP), which controlled ships' entry into Pearl Harbor. HECP provided communication between the island's defense facilities and ships offshore, either by signal flag, lights, or radio, depending on conditions. Fatally compromising all these efforts, as events would prove, however, was the lack of cooperation between the competitive Army and Navy commands. They often refused to share information or intelligence and even lacked a common radio frequency with which to communicate with each other at the time of the Japanese attack, and often had to rely on couriers. Combined with the Japanese fleet's effective use of radio silence, surprise was complete. The senior Army and naval officers, General Walter C. Short and Admiral Husband E. Kimmel, respectively, were relieved of command in the immediate aftermath of the attack.

The extensive postwar congressional joint investigation (which ran to forty published volumes) provided considerable detail of what Washington DC knew from "Magic" decrypts of Japanese diplomatic messages, the poor communication between the nation's military leadership and the commanders on Oahu (the final warning that an attack might be imminent was sent from Washington by commercial telegram— which arrived after the attack was underway), and the almost nonexistent cooperation, let alone communication, among the Army and naval commands on the island.

Lessons learned the hard way, however, were quickly applied once the war began, as cooperation increased, resulting, among other victories, in the landmark Battle of Midway just six months later.

Christopher H. Sterling

See also Coast Defense; Magic; Midway, Battle of (3–6 June 1942); OP-20-G; Radio Silence; Signals Intelligence (SIGINT)

Sources
Prange, Gordon W., et al. 1981. *At Dawn We Slept: The Untold Story of Pearl Harbor.* New York: McGraw-Hill.

U.S. Congress. 1946. *Investigation of the Pearl Harbor Attack: Report.* 79th Cong, 2d Sess, Senate Document 244. Washington, DC: Government Printing Office.

U.S. Congress. 1946. *Pearl Harbor Attack: Hearings, Part 39: Reports, Findings, and Conclusions of Roberts Commission, Army Pearl Harbor Board, Navy Court of Inquiry, and Hewitt Inquiry.* 79th Cong., 1st Sess. Washington, DC: Government Printing Office.

Wohlstetter, Roberta. 1962. *Pearl Harbor: Warning and Decision.* Palo Alto, CA: Stanford University Press.

Philippines

Other than native means of communicating, military signals in the Philippines were long those of Spain, the colonizer of the islands. After the Spanish-American War (1898) and uprising against American forces (1898–1903), signaling developed along lines used in the American Army.

Origins of the Philippine Signal Corps lie within the Philippine Constabulary, formed by the Americans in 1901. Under Filipino officers by the 1920s, the unit provided communications with homemade radio sets during the intensified campaign in 1935 against bandit groups operating in Tayabas (now Quezon) Province. When the Philippines were granted commonwealth status by the U.S. Congress in 1936, this communication success led to the creation of the Signal Corps in the newly formed Armed Forces of the Philippines. The first Commonwealth law made this corps one of the first technical service units of the srmy to provide communications for the country's ten military districts.

After the Japanese invasion of December 1941, the Signal Corps played a vital role providing communications for joint Philippine and U.S. Army units defending Bataan and Corregidor. After the May 1942 surrender, a Signal Corps officer helped organize the first guerrilla unit in the Visayas. This was also the first resistance unit to establish radio contact with the American forces. Vital information was passed to the Americans regarding Japanese strength and disposition. This aided the reconquest of the country by American forces in early 1945. The Philippines achieved independence the next year.

The new nation focused its army communications on a signal operations company, a signal light construction battalion, and a base depot company. An extensive communications network linking army headquarters with subordinate units was gradually established. At the same time the Military Police Command Signal Corps installed and operated a broadcasting station, KAIMP ("Voice of Peace and Order"), to support the corps' psychological warfare activities. Military forces played a strong political role in the nation.

With reorganization of the armed forces on 15 April 1950, the Signal Corps underwent major changes. All of its functions, including the signal school, were transferred to the Service Command. Later that year all units were transferred to general headquarters. The Office of the Chief Signal Officer maintained technical supervision and control of operational activities.

A Signal Service Group was activated on 27 September 1954, whose units included the Office of the Chief Signal Officer, Signal Service Battalion, Signal School, and Signal Intelligence Service. The Signal Group was redesignated in 1965 as Communications-Electronics Group.

By the early 1980s, the largest single user of Philippine telecommunications was the U.S. military, which then had massive installations at Clark Air Base and Subic Naval Base. The Philippines also provided strategic regional communication functions for the United States, hosting the U.S. San Miguel Communications Center, the Southeast Asian headquarters of the Central Intelligence Agency, and the China transmitters of the Voice of America.

In the early twenty-first century, American Special Forces trainers worked with elements of the Philippine army to bring them up to date after nearly three decades of anti-insurgency warfare. The biggest expense is buying modern communications systems to replace some of the Philippine military's Vietnam War–era equipment. New radios will help Philippine forces communicate within a combat area and back to headquarters.

Cliff Lord and Christopher H. Sterling

See also Spanish-American War (1898)

Sources

Library of Congress. 1991. "Philippines Military Profile." Washington, DC: Library of Congress.

Sussman, Gerald. 1983. "Philippine Information System Geared Toward Multinationals and

Security." [Online article; retrieved December 2006.] http://multinational monitor.org/hyper/issues/1983/06/sussman.html.

Phonetic Alphabet

For radio and telephone communication, making messages absolutely clear sometimes involves spelling out key words, almost all numbers, or even whole messages. This has to be done in such a fashion that no letter is in doubt—a requirement that led to the need for a standardized phonetic alphabet. Attempts to develop such a standard began in the late nineteenth century. While military forces became important creators and users of such systems by World War I, civilian needs (as in air transport) played a role as well.

Even during World War I, it became increasingly clear that a growing proportion of military and naval communication would rely on the voice of operators using telephones, sound-powered phones, wireless, and radio telephones. Yet given the many languages and dialects in the world, operators often had trouble communicating with others using different languages. Unless one is very familiar with the speech patterns of other languages, one may be forced to spell out the more challenging technical terms letter by letter or go over numbers carefully one by one.

Perhaps the first standardized phonetic alphabet evolved informally in the British Royal Corps of Signals to teach Morse code. Each Morse symbol had a vocal equivalent, such as a short and long syllable to equal a dot followed by a dash. This alphabet, however, was merely used in training to master

the coded alphabet. Phonetic alphabets were used daily as one soldier in a trench might communicate on the phone to another at forward headquarters. Over the years, several such alphabets developed, as summarized in the table below. The first column shows that used by the British Royal Navy during World War I; the second shows the U.S. Army phonetic call signs used during the same period; and the third column shows the joint U.S. Army–U.S. Navy phonetic alphabet in use during World War II.

Of course by then others were using radio and telephone communication professionally, including several important international bodies. Among these were the International Civil Aviation Organization (ICAO), the International Telecommunication Union (ITU), the International Maritime Organization (IMO), the U.S. Federal Aviation Administration, and the American National Standards Institute, each of which had evolved differing "standard" alphabets of their own. The fourth alphabet shown in the table is that first adopted by ITU in 1927, as revised slightly in 1932, and then adopted by the International Commission for Air Navigation (predecessor of ICAO) and used by airlines before World War II. This alphabet was continued by IMO until 1965. Note the logical use of common travel names and the considerable variation in number names.

The final column shows the present-day North Atlantic Treaty Organization (NATO) phonetic alphabet. The first NATO alphabet was a subset of the much older International Code of Signals, which originally included visual signals by flags or flashing light; sound signals by whistle, siren, foghorn, or bell; and one-, two-, or three-letter codes for many phrases. Issued soon after World War II, the Allied Tactical Publication (ATP-1)

Phonetic Alphabets

	(1) WWI Royal Navy	(2) WWI U.S. Army	(3) WWII U.S. Army/Navy	(4) ITU/IMO 1927–1965	(5) NATO 1956
A	apples	able	able	amsterdam	alfa
B	butter	boy	baker	baltimore	bravo
C	charlie	cast	charlie	casablanca	charlie
D	duff	dock	dog	denmark	delta
E	edward	easy	easy	edison	echo
F	freddy	fox	fox	florida	foxtrot
G	george	george	george	gallipoli	golf
H	harry	have	how	havana	hotel
I	ink	item	item	italia	india
J	johnnie	jig	jig	jerusalem	juliett
K	king	king	king	kilogramme	kilo
L	london	love	love	liverpool	lima
M	monkey	mike	mike	madagascar	mike
N	nuts	nan	nan	new york	november
O	orange	opal	oboe	oslo	oscar
P	pudding	pup	peter	paris	papa
Q	queenie	quack	queen	quebec	quebec
R	robert	rush	roger	roma	romeo
S	sugar	sail	sugar	santiago	sierra
T	tommy tare	tare		tripoli	tango
U	uncle	unit	uncle	upsala	uniform
V	vinegar	vice	victor	valencia	victor
W	william	watch	william	washington	whiskey
X	xerxes	x-ray	x-ray	xanthippe	x-ray
Y	yellow	yoke	yoke	yokahama	yankee
Z	zebra	zed	zebra	zurich	zulu
1				unaone	one
2				bissotwo	two
3				terrathree	three
4				kartefour	four
5				pantafive	five
6				soxisix	six
7				setteseven	seven
8				oktoeight	eight
9				novanine	niner
0				nadazero	zero

included this alphabet in its second volume, *Allied Maritime Signal and Maneuvering Book,* used by all allied NATO navies. Technically, however, ATP-1 is classified and not publicly available. Yet the name NATO Phonetic Alphabet became widespread as these signals and this alphabet became a true global standard. In the original version of late 1951, the alphabet included the words coca, extra, metro, nectar, and union. By early 1956 they were replaced as this version was implemented by ICAO and became the established phonetic alphabet for ITU's 1959 *Radio Regulations*.

David L. Woods

See also Airplanes; Code, Codebook; International Code of Signals (ICS); Morse Code; Radio; Telephone; Walkie-Talkie

Sources

Albright, Robert William. 1958. "The International Phonetic Alphabet: Its Backgrounds and Development." *International Journal of American Linguistics* 24 (1, Part 3): 78 pp.

International Phonetic Association. 1999. *Handbook of the International Phonetic Association: A Guide to the Use of the International Phonetic Alphabet*. Cambridge: Cambridge University Press.

Logan, Robert K. 1986. *The Alphabet Effect: The Impact of the Phonetic Alphabet on the Development of Western Civilization*. New York: William Morrow.

Rose, L. J. 1956. "Aviation's ABC: The Development of the ICAO Spelling Alphabet." *ICAO Bulletin* 11 (2): 12–14.

Woods, David L. 1965. *A History of Tactical Communication Techniques*, plate XI-6. Orlando, FL: Martin-Marietta (reprinted by Arno Press, 1974).

Photography

Combat photography brings to mind famous scenes of Pearl Harbor, the Normandy invasion, raising the flag on Iwo Jima, the Tet Offensive in Vietnam, or scenes from the Gulf War, Somalia, Panama, or the recent military actions in Iraq and Afghanistan. This entry concerns photography taken by and for military forces, as opposed to the better known journalistic variety.

Military combat photography dates back to the Crimean War in 1855 when Englishman Roger Fenton photographed carefully posed images of British army camp life. The British set up the first military photography school a year later. During the American Civil War (1861–1865), photographers such as Matthew Brady were able to show the aftermath of battles. Bulky and technologically crude glass plate equipment, however, generally prevented war photographers from producing images of ongoing battles.

In 1898, American military photographers were the first to use celluloid film rather than glass plates. During the Philippine Insurrection in 1899, J. D. Salisbury became the first U.S. Army photographer to be captured by the enemy. In 1900, Frances Johnson became the first female photographer assigned to a combat zone. When World War I broke out in Europe in 1914, photographers followed troops into battle. Cameras were smaller and film was faster as shutter speeds increased, allowing photographers to be more mobile and closer to combat action. During World War II, cameras were totally manual in operation, yet combat photographers worked in the midst of savage destruction to capture vital events on film. World War II combat camera crews were trained by the Army's First Motion Picture Unit near Hollywood, California. Each crew was composed of seven officers and twenty to thirty enlisted men.

American military photography is provided today by a small group of professionals. These combat camera (COMCAM) soldiers, sailors, air personnel, and marines provide commanders and decision makers with essential battlefield information in support of strategic, operational, and tactical mission objectives. COMCAM forces come from the Army's 55th Signal Company, the Air Force 1st Combat Camera Squadron, three Marine Corps COMCAM units, and the Navy's Fleet Combat Camera Groups.

A U.S. Army combat photographer is shown with his digital video camera before conducting a sensitive site exploration outside Kabul, Afghanistan, in July 2002. Combat photography has long provided important information in the planning and evaluation of military operations. (Department of Defense)

There are also COMCAM units in the reserve forces and National Guard. These units play an important role in every contingency operation, training exercise, and humanitarian relief mission. COMCAM units are capable of worldwide deployment on short notice and are skilled in digital and conventional still photography, film processing, digital image transmission, digital and conventional video photography, and video editing.

The Department of Defense established the Joint Combat Camera Center (JCCC) at the Pentagon. It serves as the hub for COMCAM imagery of significant defense operations and exercises worldwide, and is the central reception center for all COMCAM still and video imagery. The JCCC is a division of the American Forces Information Service, and its mission is to provide commanders with imagery support of operational and planning requirements during worldwide crises, contingencies, exercises, and wartime operations. COMCAM imagery may also be used as a secondary intelligence resource. Military COMCAM units have served in virtually every American military action in recent years.

The World War II truism is as valid today as it was then: "The brave ones were shooting the enemy. The crazy ones were shooting film."

Danny Johnson

See also Television

Sources
Department of Defense. 1996. *Joint Combat Camera (COMCAM) Program.* Directive

Number 5040.4 (30 September). Washington, DC: Department of Defense.

"Images of War: Combat Photography, 1918–1971." 2000. Eyewitness to History. [Online information; retrieved December 2005.] http://www.eyewitnesstohistory.com/cbpintro.htm.

Military Intelligence Division, War Department. 1945. *Choosing the Right Photograph: Part IV: Military and Technical Photography.* Washington, DC: Government Printing Office.

Moyes, Norman B. 1996. *Battle Eye: A History of American Combat Photography.* New York: Metro Books.

Phu Lam, Vietnam (1961–1972)

The American military established its first communications system in Vietnam in 1951, relying on a single high-frequency radio link from Saigon to Clark Air Force Base in the Philippines. In 1961 President John F. Kennedy ordered an increase in the number of American military personnel in the Republic of Vietnam (South Vietnam), necessitating improvements in these communications capabilities. Phu Lam, a suburb of Saigon, was selected as the site for America's new military communications hub in South Vietnam. The U.S. Army managed Phu Lam, placing high-frequency radio transmitters there in 1961.

Meanwhile the National Security Agency (NSA) was laying an undersea cable from the Philippines to Nha Trang, on the central coast of South Vietnam, as part of NSA's new secure communications system in the Western Pacific and Southeast Asia, code-named WETWASH. Completed in 1962, the WETWASH system allowed Phu Lam to send messages to Nha Trang by tropospheric scatter radio. From there the messages were transmitted by cable to the Philippines, then on to Hawaii and Washington DC. By mid-1962 the Phu Lam station was in operation twenty-four hours daily, operating high-frequency radio circuits to Thailand, Okinawa, and the Philippines. Less than a year later, Phu Lam was included on forty-four teletype and nine voice communications circuits.

In late 1963 U.S. Army engineers installed the Saigon Overseas (telephone) Switchboard and a paper tape message relay system at Phu Lam, marking the shift of virtually all U.S. military communications conduits from Saigon to Phu Lam. In early 1964 Phu Lam handled some 185,000 messages per month. After the Gulf of Tonkin crisis in 1964, an experimental satellite messaging terminal was installed, and Phu Lam was placed under the Pacific headquarters of the Army Strategic Communications Command.

In 1965 American ground forces were deployed to South Vietnam. Phu Lam's facilities were expanded with the introduction of the Integrated Wideband Communications System, which provided reliable radio links between American military units and South Vietnam's provincial capitals. An IBM punch card–based data relay replaced the tape message system, allowing greater speed and accuracy in message production and transmission. In March 1968 the new Automatic Digital Network (AUTODIN) switching center became operational, and use of the IBM card system declined. AUTODIN permitted accelerated ordering of equipment and supplies, as well as intelligence reporting from the field. By late 1969 AUTODIN processed almost all U.S. military message traffic in and out of Saigon.

The phased withdrawal of U.S. forces from Vietnam in the early 1970s reduced demand for Phu Lam's services. Beginning in 1972, when the post was reorganized as a signal battalion, some of its equipment was turned over to the South Vietnamese army under President Richard Nixon's "Vietnamization" program. However, most of Phu Lam's sophisticated communications technology was removed and transferred to American forces stationed in South Korea. Phu Lam's buildings were transferred to South Vietnam in November 1972, and were eventually seized by Communist Vietnamese forces in April 1975.

Laura M. Calkins

See also Automatic Digital Network
(AUTODIN); Communication Satellites; National Security Agency (NSA); Teleprinter/Teletype; Tropospheric Scatter; Undersea Cables; Vietnam War (1959–1975)

Sources

Rienzi, Thomas M. 1972. *Communications-Electronics 1962–1970*. Washington, DC: Department of the Army.
Rokus, Josef W. n.d. "The Phu Lam, Vietnam U.S. Army Communications Base." [Online information; retrieved December 2004.] http://phulam.com/history.htm.

Pigeons

The use of homing, or carrier, pigeons in military signaling over thousands of years suggests several contradictions. Despite the lack of attention to their role, pigeons are among the oldest means of military communications. Though Britain and the United States led in the introduction of most modes of military signaling, both lagged in pigeon use in signaling (though they captured more coverage than the true pioneering pigeon-using nations). And while few signal systems are equally suitable for short-, mid-, or long-range communication, pigeons could handle all of these and, until the advent of electrical communications, were for centuries the only message system that could do so.

Pigeons have from ancient times formed a key portion of much long-range communi-

cation. Genghis Khan (1162–1227) established a pigeon relay system across Asia and much of Europe. Even earlier, Syrians and Mesopotamians had active pigeon programs. Raising and racing pigeons became a hobby for many, and pigeon fanciers were often helpful to national interests during periods of war. Pigeons were used to transmit vital news in the nineteenth century by the new Reuters service just as the Rothchild financial empire was informed by frequent signals via pigeon. Perhaps the first wide attention came to pigeons as messengers during the German siege of Paris in 1870–1871. Some reports indicate homing pigeons were carried out on balloons to permit them to carry messages back into the city. Messages were reduced in size by photography—40,000 messages were reportedly received on just one day (3 February 1871). During the six-month siege, only 57 of 302 birds actually reached Paris, but these were untrained birds working in unfavorable winter weather.

Nations' use of pigeons soon flourished. Germany established pigeon lofts or bases in sixteen major cities, France built seventeen military lofts along the German frontier with a central loft in Paris, and both Italy and Portugal built more than a dozen. Austria, Russia, Switzerland, Denmark, Canada, and Sweden all had active pigeon programs. Belgian pigeon expert Lieutenant Felix Gigot underscored the importance of using experienced birds for longer missions. For distances up to 60 to 90 miles, for example, he recommended dispatch of two pigeons at least six months old. For up to 120 miles, he called for three birds each at least a year old; and so on—up to sending six three year-old birds for distances up to 240 miles. By late in the nineteenth century, U.S. Army General Nelson Miles had attempted to work with

Pigeons were used for centuries to send military signals, often over enemy lines. Here one of the birds is shown fitted with a film-message capsule during World War II. (U.S. Army Signal Center Command History Office, Fort Gordon, Georgia)

pigeons in the Dakota Territory as early as 1880, though local hawks ate most of his pigeons. By 1890, Naval Academy professor Francis Marion and Lieutenant E. B. Eberle had begun experiments and were advocating pigeons for use in the U.S. Navy, and by 1897 the Royal Navy began pigeon experiments under Commander Lionel Tufnell.

By World War I, both the British army and Royal Navy operated major pigeon programs, both begun by former pigeon fancier A. H. Osman, who later accepted an army commission and brought his son into the program. Osman later advised the U.S. Army pigeon program. Pigeons turned out to be conveniently immune to tear gas, then so common in trench warfare. An Italian program used 50,000 pigeons, reporting that

one pigeon message had helped save 1,800 Italians and led to the capture of 3,500 Austrians. R. F. H. Nalder wrote that by the end of the war, the British army used 20,000 birds and some 350 handlers as part of its Signal Service, although he attributed this use largely to the difficult conditions on the Western Front and lack of more satisfactory alternatives. During both world wars, pigeons were dropped into occupied territory in the hope that partisans would find them, write descriptions of events and fortifications, and then release the pigeons to come home with this needed data.

The U.S. Army pigeon program almost disappeared just prior to World War I, but was revived to enjoy considerable success, particularly in North Africa. Most naval pigeons carried messages from ship to shore, although some British pigeons flew messages to nearby warships. A highly trained pigeon could fly both ways—if food and family were maintained ashore.

David L. Woods

See also Ancient Signals; Cher Ami and the "Lost Battalion"; Medieval Military Signaling (500–1500 CE)

Sources

Allatt, H. T. W. 1886. "The Use of Pigeons as Messengers in War and the Military Pigeon Systems of Europe." *Journal of the Royal United Service Institution* 30 (188): 107–148.

Harfield, Alan. 1989. "The Pigeon Service." In *Pigeon to Packhorse: The Illustrated Story of Animals in Army Communications*. Chippenham, UK: Picton.

Marion, H. 1892. "Pigeons for Sea Service." *U.S. Naval Institute Proceedings* 18 (4): 589–596.

Nalder, R. F. H. 1958. *The Royal Corps of Signals: A History of its Antecedents and Development*. London: Royal Signals Institution.

Osman, A. H. 1928. *Pigeons in the Great War: A Complete History of the Carrier-Pigeon Service During the Great War, 1914–1918*. London: The "Racing Pigeon" Publishing Co.

Osman, W. H. 1950. *Pigeons in World War II.* Norwich, UK: The "Racing Pigeon" Publishing Co.

Wilson, James. 1899. "The Naval Pigeon Post." *The Navy & Army Illustrated,* May 27, 222–223.

Polish Code Breaking

Code breakers in Poland were the first to solve the German military Enigma machine and the messages sent on it in 1932 in a project known as GALE. Their pioneering work contributed enormously to the Allied success in reading secret German military communications during World War II.

Project GALE

Project GALE (*Wicher*) was conducted from 1933 to 1939 by the Cipher Bureau (CB) of the Second Department of the Polish General Staff. The first attempts to break the military Enigma machine were made by Lieutenant Antoni Palluth and Major Maksymilian Ciężki, of CB, starting in 1928. They established that the first six characters of each Enigma message were important. To solve the problem of a machine cipher, Major Franciszek Pokorny, then head of Polish Radio Intelligence, organized a cryptological course for mathematics students at Poznań University from 1928 to 1929. Its purpose was to train those who understood higher mathematics to become cryptanalysts. Two participants, Jerzy Różycki and Henryk Zygalski, were chosen to work in the CB German Section. In 1930 Marian Rejewski joined the team part time (he shifted to full time in fall 1932), and became the best of them all. Jointly this team broke a book code of the German Reichsmarine in September 1932.

Transferred to the Cipher Bureau in Warsaw in mid-1932, Rejewski soon obtained a commercial version of the Enigma coding machine and several dozen intercepted military messages, which proved useful in helping to break the more complex military version of the machine. He also received a German description of the machine and tables, with its rotor and plugboard settings, in the fall of 1932, discovering only years later that these had come from Captain Gustave Bertrand of French radio intelligence. It took Rejewski ten weeks to solve the Enigma's complex internal wiring, and thus be able to develop methods for solving its traffic. While his mathematical work and an inspired guess had played a crucial role, he acknowledged that the French material had saved at least two years. Intercepted 1932 German Christmas messages enabled him to verify his mathematical reconstruction of Enigma. Beginning in January 1933, the Polish CB was able to regularly decipher Enigma messages as it tracked the steady German improvements of the device.

CB soon produced copies of Enigma with the aid of the AVA radio factory in Warsaw. By January 1938, the cryptologists were able to decipher about 75 percent of intercepted signals. Information gained from GALE was so incredible that Polish intelligence officers in Germany were ordered to check it out on several occasions. CB was able to monitor the German military and naval exercises as well as German units entering Austria and occupying Czechoslovakia in 1938, and German cruisers operating near Spain. To keep GALE secret, for seven years the Polish intelligence authorities did not tell their own analysts (or their French collaborator, now Major Gustave Bertrand) about the real source of their data.

The team created a catalog of Enigma positions, observed and listed the mistakes of careless German operators, and developed mechanical aids such as the "cyclometer." When the Germans improved their coding system in September 1938, the three cryptanalysts invented the Polish "Bomba," a mechanical device that synchronized the rotors of six Enigmas, to speed discovery of daily coding keys. As an additional aid, Zygalski invented his "Zygalski sheets." Additional Enigma rotors (IV and V) introduced by the Germans at the end of 1938 were reconstructed mathematically by Rejewski, thanks to the carelessness of one network (of the *Sicheheitsdienst*, or SD), whose messages were fully read until the end of June 1939. German army and air force messages from February 1939 to the end of the year were only partially broken (about 10 percent of the traffic during that time) because of the new rotors and additional plugs. CB lacked resources to build more Bombas and to cut additional sets of sheets: To continue daily reading as quickly as before would have required fifty-four more Bombas (each with six sets of rotors) and fifty-eight additional sets of Zygalski's sheets (each set comprising twenty-six items).

Seeking another solution, Colonel Gwido Langer, chief of Polish radio intelligence, and his deputy, Major Maksymilian Ciężki, attended the first Allied conference of cryptanalysts in Paris on 10 January 1939. At that time the French had minimal knowledge of Enigma, and the British had been balked by one of the machine's interior connections. The Poles were forbidden to disclose their success. Eventually, General Wacław Stachiewicz, chief of the Polish General Staff, gave permission to share the Polish Enigma success in mid-1939. On 25–26 July, a second conference took place, at the CB center in Pyry, south of Warsaw. Polish cryptanalysts not only shared their knowledge of Enigma and methods of breaking its keys with the French

and British but they also gave the Allies two Polish replicas of the Enigma device. In mid-August (just two weeks prior to the German invasion), Langer gave London an incomplete set of Zygalski's sheets. The Polish GALE operation ended with its last decipherment of Enigma on 25 August.

After the German and Soviet invasions of Poland, the Polish code breakers escaped to Romania on 16–17 September 1939. They soon reached Paris with help from Bertrand's people. There was no Allied cryptographic success until January 1940 when Zygalski's perforated sheets were supplied from Bletchley Park to the French army radio intelligence center, and with them, the Poles were again able to decipher German codes. From 17 January 1940, they broke nearly a fifth of daily German codes, and during the spring German invasions of Norway and France they deciphered 1,151 and 5,084 messages, respectively.

After the June 1940 collapse of France, the Polish team was transferred to North Africa and then back to Vichy France. There the team worked at the secret French cryptological center set up near Nimes in Provence until the German occupation of Vichy France in November 1942. Rejewski and Zygalski escaped to Spain and transferred through Portugal to London. As suspect aliens, however, they were not allowed into Bletchley Park and could not even regain the Polish copy of the Enigma given to the British in mid-1939. Polish-British cooperation unfortunately ceased after the June 1944 D-Day landings, as the Polish General Staff transferred Rejewski to the Russian section, the results of which remain unknown. The Polish code-breaking role was largely forgotten until publication of Bertrand's memoirs in 1973. The British eventually honored the Poles with a special monument at Bletchley Park in 2002.

Key Polish Personnel

Gwido Langer (1894–1948) was an Austrian officer who fought on the Eastern Front during World War I, escaped from Russia in 1920, and graduated from the Military Staff College in Warsaw in 1925. In the 1930s, he headed and reorganized CB and intercept stations. Cooperating closely with Major Bertrand, he organized and supervised Project GALE, though he was not a code breaker himself. Together with Major Maksymilian Ciężki, Colonel Langer created the Polish cipher machine Lacida, which because of its limitations did not see use during the September 1939 invasion. However, copies that survived evacuation to France helped him maintain secret communication with his superiors in London. He supervised the Polish sections of CB in France from 1939 to 1942. In March 1943 Langer was arrested by the Germans and sent to Schloss Eisenberg, a prisoner of war camp in Czechoslovakia. Despite interrogation, he managed to withhold the breaking of Enigma. He was liberated by the American Army, but soon died in London.

Maksymilian Ciężki (1898–1951) was a radio operator with the German army in World War I (what is now western Poland was then part of Germany), participated in the Polish-Bolshevik War of 1920, and by 1923 was a signals intelligence officer in CB. Deputy to Langer, he supervised the work of Polish cryptologists in Project GALE, the production of Enigma analog devices, and Lacida coding machines. In 1941–1942, he was responsible for the radio work of a Polish outpost in Algiers. Arrested by the Germans, he spent the rest of World War II with his superior in Schloss Eisenberg. Interrogated by the Germans in spring 1944, he convinced them that Enigma had defeated Polish code breakers after the 1938 changes. Liberated, he died in England.

Marian A. Rejewski (1905–1980) studied math and physics at Poznań University, attending a course in cryptology run by the army's general staff in 1928. From 1930 to 1932 he worked at the cryptological outpost of the Cipher Bureau in Poznań, breaking hand ciphers of the German army (*Reichswehr*). In late 1932, Rejewski made the key breakthroughs in understanding how the Enigma machine worked—and thus how it could be broken. By mid-1944 he was working on Soviet codes. He spent 1945–1946 in Scotland taking part in the Military Administration's Officers Training Course (in fact an intelligence school of the Polish Army in Exile), returning to his family in Bydgoszcz in November 1946. He never worked with codes again, being employed in various local industry cooperatives until retiring in 1967.

Jerzy Różycki (1909–1942) entered CB as a student after taking a cryptological course in Poznań. During Project GALE, he invented the "clock" method for solving the order in which the rotors were inserted into Enigma (e.g., III, I, IV, etc.). He participated in the invention of the Polish Bomba. By mid-1940, he was sent to the Algiers outpost to assist Ciężki. He was drowned in the loss of the SS *Lamoricière*, off the Balearic Islands in January 1942.

Henryk Zygalski (1908–1978) was another brilliant student at the Poznań cryptological course, entered CB and closely cooperated with Rejewski on breaking Enigma in the 1930s. He helped the latter to create the Bomba device and also invented the special Zygalski sheets to break Enigma anew in autumn 1938. The method was used at Bletchley Park from mid-January on (except for a net used in the invasion of Norway). Zygalski reached London in August 1943 and, together with Rejewski, achieved mastery in solving German police ciphers. In doing so he may have helped the British in breaking Enigma daily codes even though he was not allowed into Bletchley Park. After World War II he remained in England and became a lecturer in mathematics at the Battersea Institute of Technology.

Zdzislaw J. Kapera

See also Bletchley Park; Britain, Battle of (1940); Code Breaking; Enigma; Signals Intelligence (SIGINT); Ultra

Sources

Bloch, Gilbert. 1990. "The French Contribution to the Breaking of 'Enigma.'" *The Enigma Bulletin [The Enigma Press]* 1 (December): 3–13.

Ciechanowski, J. S., et al., eds. 2005. *Marian Rejewski 1905–1980. Living with the Enigma Secret.* Bydgoszcz, Poland: City Council.

Kahn, David. 1991. *Seizing the Enigma: The Race to Break the German U-Boat Codes, 1939–1943.* Boston: Houghton Mifflin.

Kapera, Zdzisław J. 2002. *Before ULTRA There Was GALE.* Kraków: The Enigma Press.

Kapera, Zdzisław J. 2005. *Marian Rejewski Pogromca Enigmy [Marian Rejewski. The Man Who Defeated ENIGMA].* Kraków: The Enigma Press.

Kozaczuk, Wladyslaw. 1984. *Enigma: How the German Cipher Machine Was Broken and How It Was Read by the Allies During World War II.* Washington, DC: University Publications of America.

Medrala, J. 2005. *Les reseaux de renseignements franco-polonais 1940–1944.* Paris: Harmattan.

Stirling, T., W. Maresch, and J. Tebinka, eds. 2005. *Intelligence Co-operation Between Poland and Great Britain During World War II, Vol. 1: The Report of the Anglo-Polish Historical Committee.* Portland, OR: Vallentine Mitchell.

Popham, Home Riggs (1762–1820)

Sir Home Riggs Popham was a British admiral who saw service during the French Revolutionary and Napoleonic wars. He is remembered for his scientific accomplishments, particularly the development of a signal code that was adopted by the Royal Navy in 1803.

Popham entered the Royal Navy in 1778 at age sixteen and served during the American Revolution. In 1783 he was promoted to lieutenant and was for a time engaged in survey service on the coast of Africa. Between 1787 and 1793 he was engaged in a series of commercial adventures in the Eastern Sea, sailing first for the Imperial Ostem Company and then in a vessel he purchased and in part loaded himself. He undertook several surveys for the East India Company, but in the 1790s became involved in litigation with the firm and soon resumed his naval career. He achieved higher ranks and was engaged for years in naval cooperation with the troops of Britain and its allies in various military expeditions. He ran into further difficulties as several senior admiralty officials did not like him. Popham was not a man to be quashed without an effort. He brought his case before Parliament and was able to prove that there had been, if not deliberate dishonesty, at least the very grossest carelessness on the part of his assailants.

Popham was one of the most scientific seamen of his time. While commanding the Royal Navy ship HMS *Romney* off Copenhagen, he drew on his ideas and those of others to develop a new numeric code using traditional signal flags. First published privately in 1800, an expanded version was adopted by the Admiralty in 1803 and used for many years. Ships would initially fly a single "telegraph" flag to indicate they were using Popham's system. Popham's signal flag system allowed more detailed communication—initially a thousand and soon more than two thousand words as well as some sentences. Admiral Lord Horatio Nelson liked the system and used it at the Battle of Trafalgar to send one of naval history's most famous signals, "England expects that every man will do his duty." Seeking to expand his system he added flags indicating letters and soon had some 11,000 three-flag signals (more if four flags were used), a system that was issued to the Royal Navy in 1813. A final version was published in 1816 as an official "Vocabulary Signal Book." With this, naval officers could carry on simple two-way conversations. Later versions appeared after Popham's death, and similar signal systems were adopted by the Merchant Navy as well.

Despite numerous later conflicts, Popham was appointed to other commands. In 1812–1813 he worked with Spanish guerrillas to successfully harry occupying French forces and facilities while the Duke of Wellington was advancing through Spain. He was promoted to rear admiral in 1814, and made a knight in 1815. He died at Cheltenham on 20 September 1820. Popham's son and namesake also entered the navy and helped perfect British semaphore systems.

Christopher H. Sterling

See also Flags; Signal Book; Trafalgar, Battle of (21 October 1805)

Sources

Mallinson, Howard. 2005. "Popham's Naval Vocabulary Code." In *Send It by Semaphore: The Old Telegraphs During the Wars with France*, 91–94. Ramsbury, UK: Crowood Press.

Popham, Hugh. 1991. *A Damned Cunning Fellow: The Eventful Life of Rear-Admiral Sir Home Popham*. Tywardreath, UK: Old Ferry Press.

Postal Services

Most nations with fighting forces have developed some means of distributing mail to those forces. This is partially a matter of communication, of course, but also con-

tributes hugely to military morale, as attested in countless cases. Organized systems to deliver mail to military forces date back to early Egyptian armies around 2000 BCE. In modern times, virtually all such systems interface with government/civilian mail services. Only a few more recent examples are noted here.

A need for a postal service for British troops posted abroad was evident in the late eighteenth century. Only in 1808, during the Peninsular War in Spain, however, was the first army post office placed into operation. In 1840 another army post office was established during operations in Hong Kong. The Indian Army Postal Service dates to British colonial field post office systems established in 1856.

During the American Civil War (1861–1865), mail service to soldiers and sailors was erratic, especially if forces were on the move. The post office acknowledged that few soldiers carried stamps and permitted them to send letters without them. A soldier's envelope had to bear his name, rank, and unit. Such mail was marked "postage due," and the amount indicated was collected from the addressee. The post office at the headquarters of the Union Army saw thousands of letters pass every week. Each regiment had a post boy, who carried the letters of his command to brigade headquarters. There the mails of the different regiments were placed in one pouch and sent up to division headquarters, and thence to corps headquarters, where mail agents received and delivered them at the principal depot of the army. The work required a large number of men, nearly all private soldiers detailed for such duty. Confederate and Union prisoners were allowed to exchange mail through flag-of-truce ships and other designated points. Little mail was censored.

In Britain on 22 July 1882 the Post Office Corps was formed using volunteers for service in Britain's colonial campaigns in Egypt and the Sudan. The Post Office Corps was followed by a second army postal corps called the Royal Engineers Telegraph Reserve. In 1889 both reserve corps were reorganized to create an efficient postal and telegraph service during the 1899–1902 South African (Boer) War. In 1908 a further reorganization amalgamated the two reserve companies into the Royal Engineers (Postal Section), or RE (PS).

Major fighting powers in World War I developed extensive military mail services (*Feldpost* in German-speaking countries; *Bureau Postal Interarmees* in France). The British RE (PS) served in France, Belgium, the Dardanelles, Egypt, Palestine, East Africa, Greece, Italy, and North Russia. In addition to conventional means, mail was transported by mule, sleigh, trawler, minesweeper—in fact, any form of transport available at the time. At the outbreak of World War I, army postal personnel totaled 300 men, and they were presumed sufficient to service mails for the British Expeditionary Force. By 1918 this task required some 2,500 people, nearly half of them women. Experiments were carried out that year using modified aircraft for transporting mail by air, and the first regular airmail service (from Folkestone to Cologne) was set up in March 1919 to provide British troops in Germany with a fast mail service.

Levels of mail censorship varied by country. Allied enlisted men's mail was closely censored (officers were to censor their own mail) to prevent communication of important military information. Army or air force post office or fleet post office mail services controlled U.S. service mails during and after World War II. The British RE Postal Section (PS) served on all fronts worldwide and was detached with forward troops. RE (PS)

personnel landed by parachute and glider on D-Day in 1944, and field post offices were established on the beachhead within hours of their arrival. Likewise, Australian and New Zealand forces serving in World War II were supported by military postal units from those nations.

RE (PS) served with British troops in the Korean War. The Home Postal Depot took over responsibility for Royal Naval Mails and HM Ships mail from the Civil Post Office in 1962. Thus the RE Postal and Courier Communication (PCC) became a British forces tri-service organization (having previously accepted responsibility for Royal Air Force mails), as well as an international military service with British units in the North Atlantic Treaty Organization. A further reorganization took place in 1979 to form the Royal Engineers Post and Courier Services, RE (PCS).

Each American military service managed its own mail program until 1980, when the Department of Defense (DoD) designated the secretary of the army as the single military mail manager. The Military Postal Service Agency (MPSA) was created to be the DoD point of contact with the U.S. Postal Service. MPSA is headquartered in Alexandria, Virginia, manages the Military Postal Service, and handles both official and personal military mail. Security concerns since 2001 have slowed traditional ("snail") mail transport—for example, it was taking two weeks to get a letter to soldiers in Iraq in 2003. MPSA utilizes civilian and military air and sea transport to serve approximately 2,000 military post offices in eighty-five countries as of early 2006.

The Military Postal History Society (founded in 1937) is but one example of a number of collector groups around the world interested in military mail over history.

Christopher H. Sterling

See also Couriers; E-Mail Systems; V-Mail

Sources

AOL Hometown. "Centenary of the Forces Postal Service." [Online information; retrieved March 2006.] http://members .aol.com/reubique/aps.htm.

Boyden, Peter B., and Alan J. Guy. 1990. *Tommy Atkin's Letters: The History of the British Army Postal Service from 1795.* London: National Army Museum.

Postal and Courier Services (UK). Home page. [Online information; retrieved March 2006.] http://www.regiments.org/regiments/ uk/corps/postal.htm#biblio.

PostalCensorship.com. "Censored and Military Postal History." [Online information; retrieved March 2006.] http://www .postalcensorship.com/.

Samachar, Sainik. 2005. "Army Postal Service: A Soldier's Messenger." [Online article; retrieved March 2006.] http://www .bharat-rakshak.com/LAND-FORCES/ Army/Articles/Article45.html.

Wells, Edward. 1987. *Mailshot: A History of the Forces Postal Service.* London: Defence Postal & Courier Services, Royal Engineers.

Propaganda and Psychological Warfare

Propaganda is a type of military communication designed to weaken an enemy before and during operations. Put another way, propaganda seeks military gains without, or more usually in support of, military force. While utilized well before nineteenth-century warfare (there are many references to propaganda efforts; both sides used it during the American Civil War), propaganda and psychological warfare really came into their own during the two world wars. While many efforts were made to propagandize civilians, this entry focuses on military applications.

"Military propaganda" (an old term based on "propagating" ideas) is the process of applying planned, manipulative communi-cation to achieve a desired tactical or strategic response. It involves organized and often emotional campaigns that may employ graphic, print, film, or radio (including loud-speakers) media.

"Psychological warfare" first appeared as a term around 1920 and involves a broad and continuing campaign of propaganda intended to confuse an enemy, weaken their resolve, and make them surrender. It is employed in both traditional warfare and terrorism and antiterrorism activities. "Psychological operations" (PSYOPS), first used in 1945 and now the term of choice (as it does not reference "warfare"), is the military use of propagandistic communication content to discredit, demoralize, and intimidate enemy forces. All three terms are often (and confusingly) used interchangeably, and can be offensive (the most common) or defensive in nature.

Propaganda in support of military operations is rarely political in emphasis, but rather serves a variety of more specific aims. It can be used to encourage enemy surrender by emphasizing the futility of the enemy's situation; build up enemy fear of the effects of your weapons; counter enemy propaganda directed at your own forces; encourage friendly partisan or guerrilla activities; control enemy and friendly citizens in combat areas; and disseminate useful military information and proclamations.

The impact of all such efforts was poorly understood for most of military history. Practitioners hoped or believed that their efforts had a direct or "hypodermic needle" effect, such as using surrender leaflets to encourage enemy soldiers to stop fighting. Only with careful research in the mid-twentieth century was it learned, for example, that ridicule seldom works, and that clearly defined messages designed for reception by specific audiences usually had greater impact.

World War I

As a modern psychological weapon of war, propaganda was first systematically applied by all major combatants in World War I. French (until 1916) and German efforts were largely controlled by the military, while most British and American efforts were under civilian control.

In sharp contrast to its World War II experience, Germany was not as clearly organized as the British or Americans. The American military propaganda effort, primarily one of morale and surrender leaflets aimed at German soldiers, was headed by the Propaganda Section of the Allied Expeditionary Force General Headquarters. Leaflet content often focused on how food would be supplied for the ill-fed German soldiers if they surrendered. Americans built their propaganda approach and messages on extensive British and French experience.

Some military propaganda was "black" in that it purported to originate on the enemy side of the line. This might take the form, for example, of a German-language newspaper that provided detailed reports of hunger and other trouble behind the lines. Other efforts sought to divide the frontline fighter from his officers (or higher leadership at home), showing the former suffering so that the latter could safely live the good life.

Allied efforts to divide German forces from their Austro-Hungarian allies were often successful as they built on existing differences and cultural thinking. Allied propaganda (some dropped from airplanes or unmanned balloons) was very effective in promoting defeatist thinking among (and surrender from) multinational Austro-Hungarian forces facing the Italians in April 1918. Likewise as the war turned against Germany in the summer of 1918 on the Western Front, heretofore pointless Allied surrender leaflet campaigns began to have some effect, as did millions of leaflets urging replacement of the Kaiser and military government.

World War II

All sides applied lessons from the first world war to the second. Of all the fighting powers, German propaganda was clearly the best synchronized with their military effort. Film and radio (broadcasting was new to this war) helped promote the mighty power of German arms, as did bright poster art and printed media. Edmund Taylor's 1940 book, *The Strategy of Terror*, labeled the German approach as a strategy of terror. Later in the war, much German military propaganda was defensive in nature—seeking to hold up the morale of the German fighting man.

Both sides again used black propaganda against enemy forces, only this time messages were greatly enhanced by the use of shortwave radio. The Germans set up a station in 1939–1940 that seemed to be coming from inside France, seeking to get French soldiers to save themselves while they could. Likewise a later Allied shortwave station was made to appear as though it was really operated by renegade German soldiers, ranting about the inequities of the German system in the tone of a griping frontline fighter.

The American military effort, directed by the War Department's Propaganda Branch, provided research and coordination with civilian efforts, but operational efforts were left to theater commanders under the assumption that psychological warfare was a function of command. Indeed, psychological operations on the tactical level were first used on a large scale in World War II. By late in the war, psychological warfare units often operated at the small-unit level. One effective American effort closely coordinated the use of artillery leaflet shells and radio broadcasts to surrounded German forces in the French port city of Lorient in 1944. Among many other broadcasts, captured family letters to the defending German soldiers were read on the air. In China, picture leaflets urged local people to assist downed Allied fliers.

The most successful Allied military efforts were carefully designed leaflets intended to lower enemy soldier morale and/or induce his desertion or surrender. They emphasized the decent treatment a prisoner would receive as well as bad conditions back home, and that officers were getting better food and shelter than frontline soldiers. These were particularly effective in Europe, less so in the Pacific because of cultural differences. Many millions were dropped by aircraft (belly fuel tanks or bomb bays were converted to leaflet distribution uses). All types of artillery shells (especially mortars) were used for leaflets as were many small arms such as rifle grenades or even leaflet bundles tossed like grenades.

Given the distances covered by Japan's conquests at their height (from the borders of India to the mid-Pacific in 1942), the Japanese military relied on extensive use of shortwave radio. This included the use of "Tokyo Rose" and others broadcasting to American troops to weaken their morale. Allied counterefforts by late in the war included messages transmitted by loudspeakers mounted on tanks that were timed to give enemy soldiers time to surrender before an attack. More complex language problems made this a limited option in parts of the Pacific Theater.

Korea and Vietnam

Coming almost on the heels of World War II, the Korean War saw almost immediate use of propaganda leaflets (more than two billion by the end of the war) and broadcasts by Allied forces against those of North Korea

(and later China as well). The Psychological Warfare Section of the Far East Command (headquartered in Tokyo) became the focus of such efforts, including widespread use of loudspeakers on the ground and from the air. Media and methods were essentially those of World War II, with extensive use of printed material of all types (nearly always printed in Japan) and the use of broadcast female voices to elicit male responses.

Efforts aimed roughly equally to hit the morale of North Korean fighters and beef up that of the defenders of South Korea. Estimates suggest upward of 100,000 enemy soldiers may have surrendered due to these efforts, especially picture leaflets aimed at those who could not read. The North, in turn, made often very effective use of prisoner-of-war broadcasts back to frontline Korean and American troops.

A dozen years later, expanding U.S. psychological warfare operations in Vietnam were controlled by the 4th PSYOP Group, based in Saigon from 1967 to the end of American involvement in 1973. Unlike earlier wars, however, tactical military and larger political concerns were very closely intertwined, often confusing messages and effects. Once again broadcasts, loudspeakers, and leaflets were the primary means of transmitting messages against the Viet Cong and North Vietnamese throughout the fighting areas. But both enemy forces were more complex targets (they were far more committed to their fighting role than earlier opponents) in what many considered a civil war.

The dismal end of the war in Vietnam had a debilitating impact on military psychological operations and their importance sharply declined in the American military services for several years. But based on all of this experience and considerable research effort, PSYOPS are once again an integral part of

This propaganda leaflet was dropped over North Korea by American military forces in November 1950, as part of a psychological warfare operation. It shows the United Nations flag and the text: "The U.N. is working for the establishment of a united, independent and democratic Korea. Only the Communists oppose this, and insist on continuing the war." (Bettmann/Corbis)

American military efforts, as seen in post–Cold War fighting in the Persian Gulf and Iraq.

Christopher H. Sterling

See also Airplanes; Gulf War (1990–1991); Iraq War (2003–Present); Jamming; Korean War (1950–1953); Radio; Vietnam War (1959–1975); World War I; World War II

Sources

Daugherty, William, and Morris Janowitz, eds. 1958. *A Psychological Warfare Casebook.* Baltimore: Johns Hopkins Press for the Army Operations Research Office.

Lerner, Daniel. 1949. *Sykewar: Psychological Warfare Against Germany: D-Day to VE-Day.* New York: George W. Stewart (reprinted by MIT Press, 1971).

Linebarger, Paul M. A. 1954. *Psychological Warfare.* New York: Duell, Sloan & Pearce (2nd ed. reprinted by Arno Press 1972).

Margolin, Leo J. 1946. *Paper Bullets: A Brief Study of Psychological Warfare in World War II.* New York: Froben Press.

McLaurin, Ron D., ed. 1982. *Military Propaganda: Psychological Warfare and Operations.* New York: Praeger.

McLaurin, Ronald, et al., eds. 1976. *The Art and Science of Psychological Operations: Case Studies of Military Application.* Pamphlet No. 525–7 (2 vols.). Washington, DC: Department of the Army.

Pease, Stephen E. 1992. *Psywar: Psychological Warfare in Korea, 1950–1953.* Harrisburg, PA: Stackpole Books.

Roetter, Charles. 1974. *The Art of Psychological Warfare.* Briarcliff Manor, NY: Stein & Day.

Taylor, Edmund L. 1940. *The Strategy of Terror.* Boston: Houghton Mifflin

Quartz Crystal for Radio Control

Of all the components of a radio transmitter and receiver, the most important is that which controls its operating frequency. Though different methods of controlling radio frequencies exist, by far the most dependable is the quartz crystal oscillator. Methods of using quartz oscillators for radio frequency control were developed in the early 1920s. Making use of the piezoelectric property of quartz (i.e., the relationship between physical vibrations and electrical conductance), a unit consisting of a small, accurately ground wafer of quartz is inserted into the tuning circuit of the radio. The natural oscillating frequency of the quartz wafer then becomes the operating frequency of the radio.

The initial market for quartz oscillators in the late 1920s and the 1930s was made up almost entirely of ham (amateur) radio enthusiasts and two-way radio manufacturers (such as the Galvin Corporation, later Motorola). This relatively limited market was served by a small number of manufacturers producing their oscillators by hand, one at a time. With no real need for mass pro-

duction, no techniques or equipment were developed for carrying out the required orientation, cutting, and grinding of quartz in mass.

The Army Signal Corps took the better part of two decades to make the switch to quartz crystal control for its own equipment. Not until the development of its highly mobile air and armored branches did the Army pay any real attention to the need for dependable and mobile radio communications. Though radios utilizing methods other than crystal control were dependable while sitting still, they became almost impossible to use while in motion. As a result of tests carried out during field maneuvers throughout 1940, the Signal Corps committed to full-scale utilization of quartz oscillators.

The wisdom of this decision was questioned when, after the December 1941 attack by the Japanese on Pearl Harbor, the military found itself requiring millions of crystal oscillators for its communications equipment and lacking any real industrial capacity to produce them (prior to the war, the largest numbers of oscillators produced annually was on the order of 100,000). A mass production industry would need to be built, that industry would need to be supplied with raw quartz, and manufacturing-related defects in the oscillators would need to be overcome.

Through the Office of the Chief Signal Officer, calls went out to current oscillator manufacturers, radio and electronics companies, and anyone else interested to join this new enterprise. Along the way, physicists, radio engineers, and geologists were recruited by the Signal Corps to serve as instructors and troubleshooters for the nascent industry. Government funding through such agencies as the Defense Supplies Corporation and the Reconstruction Finance Corporation was secured for manufacturers to ramp up their manufacturing capacity. Through the efforts of private manufacturers as well as Signal Corps research laboratories, equipment for orienting, cutting, and grinding large numbers of blanks were developed. These efforts led to the creation of an industry that produced more than five million oscillator units during 1942 and more than twenty million during 1943.

In order to supply this new industry with needed raw materials, the War Production Board devoted many resources (both human and financial) to securing the entire production of the Brazilian quartz mining industry and transporting it to the United States. This program required tremendous cooperation between the Signal Corps, the Army Air Transport Service, the War Production Board and its attendant agencies, and the U.S. State Department.

All of these concerted efforts resulted in the adequate supply of dependable communications technology for the U.S. armed forces. Push-button tuning while on the move allowed units to maintain contact while maneuvering. The extreme stability of the crystal oscillators allowed for the operation of great numbers of radios within limited ranges of the spectrum and the quick establishment of radio monitoring networks. These benefits gave the Allies a distinct edge over the Axis and contributed greatly to the winning of the war.

Richard J. Thompson, Jr.

See also Army Signal Corps; Fort Monmouth, New Jersey; Mobile Communications; Radio

Sources
Bottom, Virgil. 1981. "A History of the Quartz Crystal Industry in the USA." *Proceedings of the 35th Annual Frequency Control Symposium*, 3.

Thompson, Richard J. 2005. "The Development of the Quartz Crystal Oscillator Industry of World War II." *IEEE Transactions* 52: 694.

Thompson, Richard J. 2006. *Crystal Clear: the Struggle for Reliable Communications Technology in World War II.* New York: IEEE Press/Wiley.

Radio

For more than a century, radio in various forms has been a central means of military communication. Wireless (as the British long termed it) or radio communications have played an expanding part in fighting, diplomacy, and propaganda from the turn of the twentieth century. Major military powers developed significant land and sea wireless capability before World War I, though radio's use in aircraft was still experimental. Radio came fully into its own during World War II and was dramatically transformed in the decades to follow.

Origins

Practical use of radio began with the work of Guglielmo Marconi and others in the late 1890s in the form of wireless telegraphy or code, sent with the use of spark-gap transmitters. It slowly progressed after about 1920 to radio telephony or voice signaling, made possible by vacuum tube continuous wave transmitters. Depending on the need of the moment, in many cases the two operated side by side.

Many early wireless demonstrations in Britain, the United States, and Germany were well attended (and sometimes funded) by military and naval personnel. Some attempts to use wireless during the Boer War (1899–1902), however, were not successful. Wireless first proved a valuable factor in the Japanese victory over a Russian fleet at the 1905 Battle of Tsushima, and Marconi equipment was used by both the Romanians and the Turks in the little-remembered Balkan War of 1912.

Both the British Royal Navy and the U.S. Navy experimented with and then adopted wireless early in the twentieth century. Within the first decade, both services were installing improved wireless transmitters and receivers on combat vessels and developing extensive networks of shore stations. Airborne radio was first demonstrated in British and German airships. The first successful two-way wireless between an airplane and the ground came in 1910 in a test with a Curtiss aircraft. At this stage radio sets were heavy, bulky, and hard to tune—all drawbacks to their aerial use.

Key innovators after Marconi included Americans Edwin Armstrong, Lee de Forest, and Reginald Fessenden, among many others. Though hotly competitive, in the years leading up to 1920 they spearheaded vital developments (the regenerative and super-heterodyne circuits, three-element vacuum tube, and radio telephony, respectively) that would reshape and dramatically expand what radio could do. Other early radio innovators were active in Britain, France, Germany, and Russia as well, most working closely with military authorities.

World War I (1914–1918)

The outbreak of war in August 1914 led to severe limitations being placed on private or commercial use of radio in the countries involved, as most commercial and amateur stations were closed down or taken over by the government. The British Royal Navy supplemented its own facilities by taking over in August 1914 the extensive Marconi-developed "All-Red" or British Empire chain of wireless stations, which provided especially useful Southern Hemisphere links where little other communication modes existed. Likewise, American authorities took over all foreign-owned radio facilities when the United States entered the war in April 1917. Those who tried to elude these limitations and operate transmitters without a license were prosecuted out of fear of radio's use by enemy agents. The U.S. Navy closed down private (ham) radio upon American entry into the war in 1917 and retained supervision of all radio transmitters in the United States until early 1920. Extensive training programs were established in many countries to develop the thousands of radio operators needed to supplement the few available.

Early in the war, enemy radio transmitters were often targeted, one indication of their growing importance. At the same time, Ger-man undersea telegraph cables were cut by the British in the early days of the war, forcing Germany to use radio transmissions, which the British could intercept—and eventually understand as their code-breaking expertise expanded.

Radio direction-finding techniques, developed before but vastly improved during the war, made wireless signaling at sea dangerous, as use of triangulation could readily locate a ship's transmitter, thus placing the vessel at risk from submarine attack. Knowing this danger, Allied convoys of merchantmen usually maintained radio silence (relying on visual signals), as did most military vessels while on patrol. The German cruiser *Emden*, for example, was successful for a long period in late 1914 largely by keeping radio silence. Electronic jamming of enemy radio signals was often attempted, though usually with little effect.

On the other hand, the use of radio was generally effective in both the British and German fleets and became an essential element in such large naval battles as Jutland (31 May 1916). Distance, darkness, or smoke all made visual signals questionable. As spark-gap equipment was replaced (1916–1917) by better arc, and then vacuum tube–powered equipment (1918), naval radio's value increased further. Wartime needs and growing equipment procurement greatly accelerated the pace of radio's technical development. Tube-based equipment, rare in 1914 (when obsolete spark-gap wireless telegraphy was still widespread), was becoming standard by 1918, vastly increasing radio's capabilities by adding voice to code communication.

On the American home front, the U.S. Navy supervised a mandatory pooling of private patents "for the duration" to encourage manufacture of the best possible equipment. The U.S. Army established a large Army Signal Corps research center that became Fort Monmouth, New Jersey, which developed improved transmitters for use on land and in the air. Large government stations (such as Nauen in the Berlin suburbs, and the U.S. Navy's NAA near Washington) were often used to transmit news reports (for use by newspapers), to stay in touch with distant bases or colonies, or to communicate important diplomatic messages such as President Woodrow Wilson's "Fourteen Points" in late 1918.

Army radio in 1914 was crude on both sides of the conflict. Antennas were obvious targets, and equipment was fragile, cumber-

some, and vulnerable to weather or enemy action. There were few trained operators, nor were enough radios available (a U.S. Army division of 20,000 men rarely had more than six radios, even in 1918). But military radio's biggest drawback was the lack of senior commanders willing to use or trust it in battlefield conditions. Poorly organized at first, Army radio users also suffered from security breaches such as sending vital messages in the clear rather than in code. Wireless systems on the Western Front after 1916 made use of conduction with the Fuller-phone and French systems.

Several key battles—those of the Marne and Tannenberg (both 1914) among them—

Wireless or radio first became a central part of military operations during World War I. Equipment became more efficient and lighter in the course of the fighting. This is a German army radio station before Tarnopol in August 1917. (National Archives)

were decided in part by which side made the most effective use of communications, including wireless. Radio was more useful away from the Western Front (in the Middle East, for example), where alternative modes of communication were rare, as was the likelihood of signal interference or enemy code breaking. Radio developments during World War I included creation of trench transmitters and receivers so that radio could keep commanders in better touch with frontline troops, and the use of wireless to connect observation forces watching for enemy air attacks.

An early exception to radio's limitations was the use of airplane radios to report artillery target spotting. Demand for such service led to rapid development of lighter equipment with sufficient transmission range and various means of avoiding interference. Voice (radio telephony) communication to and from airplanes became possible by 1917. By the end of the war some 600 British fighter and bomber aircraft were radio equipped. American forces experimented at the end of the war with radio-controlled fleets of bombers.

The two decades between the wars saw further, if rather slow, radio progress. Vacuum tube ("valve" in British terminology)–powered continuous wave equipment became standard and more rugged. Transmitter efficiency and stability greatly improved. British tanks (by 1935) and some French armor (in 1939) began to fit radios to allow better control of larger forces, sometimes by a commander in the air. Shortwave equipment was being installed at some bases and naval vessels by the late 1920s. Edwin Howard Armstrong developed FM radio in the early 1930s, which would prove invaluable in the coming war. Military services in many major nations became increasingly involved in radio research and equipment design. Air-

plane radio improved dramatically in all ways—equipment was lighter, range was greater, and operation was easier. Led by amateur operators, users of radio explored use of higher frequencies—into the very high-frequency (VHF) spectrum range. This allowed for more compact equipment that used less power while often offering greater range. Radio technology also provided the basis for development of radio direction finding (radar) in the late 1930s. Vehicular FM radios were just coming online in 1939–1940 in the United States.

World War II (1939–1945)

Radio proved central to the command and control of virtually all military forces by the start of World War II in September 1939. This was partially a matter of geography—the huge areas of the Pacific Front, or the Eastern Front in Europe, for example—but it was also a matter of the huge military forces that were spread out over that geography, making radio the only effective means of control.

And this was generally a war of movement, unlike the previous war, in which the Western Front was essentially static. The primacy of air power required radio for vital communication to and among fighter and bomber forces. The narrow margin of victory in the 1940 Battle of Britain was, in part, due to the Royal Air Force's effective integrated use of both radio and radar. Indeed, radio had become irreplaceable.

Radios had become both smaller (and thus lighter, but also more robust) and more efficient since the war two decades earlier. Established radio industries in all the major fighting nations were able to supply needed equipment—and (in the case of the United States and Britain) able to provide it to allies as well. While Allied force radios improved throughout the war, Germany and Japan were forced to rely on 1939–1940 designs, which were standardized but could not be improved because of heavy Allied bombing damage. That said, Axis nation equipment was generally well designed and well made. The British exploited VHF radio more than the Germans (who used the band for radar). German fighter aircraft used voice radio, while German bombers generally used radio telegraphy—meaning the two arms of the Luftwaffe could not intercommunicate well.

Portable radios, from "manpacks" such as the "walkie-talkie" to "handie-talkie" devices (about the size of an early analog cell phone and at least as heavy), greatly expanded the value of radio in frontline operations. As in World War I, training was ramped up considerably and large numbers of radio operators and technicians were provided for all the fighting services.

To a degree unprecedented in warfare, radio also provided one key to ultimate Allied victory when code breakers were eventually able to read many, if not most, German, Italian, and Japanese coded radio communications, while the reverse was generally not the case (there are important exceptions). While news of the breaking of Japanese codes was known right after the war, British and American success against German codes was held secret for three decades. Not all codes were broken, nor were many read in sufficient time to have an impact on operations. But the Allied code-breaking operations—which employed thousands of personnel by the end of the war at Bletchley Park north of London, Arlington Hall in northern Virginia, and Nebraska Avenue in Washington DC, among other places—helped immensely and also contributed to early computer technology (e.g., the analog "bombe" devices and especially the British digital Colossus).

Since 1945

The fundamental changes in military radio in the last six decades have included (1) an increasing variety of delivery modes, such as microwave and especially communication satellites; (2) the transistor after 1948 and the solid state revolution after 1959; and (3) by the 1980s, increasing digitization. Signal quality was improved, communication was faster, power requirements declined, and capacity was increased thanks to signal compression, among other factors. Combined, these trends have made radio more effective and secure, even in an Internet data-driven age. Changing weapons systems—including jet aircraft, missiles, and the nuclear submarine—have all added important radio communications requirements as well.

Major proving grounds for military radio included the Korean War (1950–1953) and the longer Vietnam conflict (1959–1975). Korea represented essentially a replay of World War II radio techniques, albeit in a much smaller space. The fighting in Vietnam occurred during the transition to solid state electronics and satellite communications, making strategic use of radio from distant Washington headquarters more viable. Tropospheric scatter radio and microwave radio links helped to tie Vietnamese bases to a single command-and-control system. The first generation of digital communications, the Automatic Digital Network, was introduced in 1968 at the height of fighting. Miniaturization of components made radio more portable.

The Falklands conflict (1982) between Britain and Argentina was possible thanks to modern satellite and other radio links between London and the South Atlantic battlefront. The Gulf (1990–1991) and Iraq (2003–present) wars introduced more digital radio links for both strategic and tactical use.

Between the two, most remaining analog radio systems were phased out. At their heart, however, even the new systems preserved the basic concept of "wireless," or radio.

Christopher H. Sterling

See also Airplanes; Airships and Balloons; Arlington Hall; Armstrong, Edwin Howard (1890–1954); Army Signal Corps; Automatic Digital Network (AUTODIN); Bletchley Park; Boer War Wireless (1899–1902); Britain, Battle of (1940); Code Breaking; Communication Satellites; de Forest, Lee (1873–1961); Enigma; Falklands Conflict (1982); Ferrié, Gustav-Auguste (1868–1932); Fessenden, Reginald A. (1866–1932); Fort Monmouth, New Jersey; Fullerphone; Ground Radio; Hooper, Stanford C. (1884–1955); Jamming; Jutland, Battle of (1916); Korean War (1950–1953); Magic; Marconi, Guglielmo (1874–1937); Marne, Battle of (September 1914); Modulation; Naval Radio Stations/Service; Nebraska Avenue, Washington DC; Propaganda and Psychological Warfare; Radio Silence; Spectrum Frequencies; Submarine Communications; Tannenburg, Battle of (1914); Tropospheric Scatter; Tsushima, Battle of (27–28 May 1905); Ultra; United Kingdom: Royal Corps of Signals; Vacuum Tube; Vietnam War (1959–1975); Walkie-Talkie; Y Service

Sources
Beauchamp, Ken. 2001. *History of Telegraphy*, 268–388. London: IEE.
Devereux, Tony. 1991. *Messenger Gods of Battle: Radio, Radar, Sonar: The Story of Electronics in War*. London: Brassey's.
Hezlet, Arthur. 1975. *Electronics and Sea Power*. New York: Stein & Day.
Howeth, L. S. 1963. *History of Communications-Electronics in the United States Navy*. Washington, DC: Government Printing Office.
Nalder, R. F. H. 1958. *The Royal Corps of Signals: A History of Its Antecedents and Development*. London: Royal Signals Institution.
Schubert, Paul. 1928. "Era of Military Use." In *The Electric Word: The Rise of Radio*, 85–187. New York: Macmillan.
Wedlake, G. E. C. 1973. *SOS: The Story of Radio Communication*, 88–129, 188–198. North Pomfret, VT: David & Charles.

Radio Silence

Radio silence generally means avoiding military use of radio communications to avoid detection by an enemy force. Typically it indicates the ability or willingness to receive but not transmit radio messages.

When transmitting a signal, any radio's location can usually be pinpointed by use of triangulation or other methods. Thus observing radio silence is intended to deny an enemy the ability to locate a force (including ships and aircraft) by honing in on its radio transmissions. Radio silence can also be a valuable type of communications deception designed to confuse an enemy.

The concept of radio silence dates from early in the wireless/radio era when it was realized that active electronic signaling carried the danger of giving away the location of the transmitter, and thus the location of forces using or relying on the transmitter. One can observe radio silence and still receive messages, as reception does not create electronic pulses that can be traced. A more specific concern is to preserve coded communication—use of line telegraph or telephone links (or even older means of communicating) can sometimes substitute for more easily intercepted radio signals, though they are subject to wiretapping. But a coded message not sent by radio is virtually impossible to detect by Y (listening) services.

There are countless historical examples of successful military application of radio silence. The radio silence observed by the German High Seas Fleet prior to the Battle of Jutland (1916) worked well enough to hide from the British Admiralty that Germany's ships had put to sea. Another familiar example is the radio silence maintained by the Japanese fleet sent to attack Pearl Harbor (1941). By maintaining total radio silence after departing the Japanese naval base at Kure (in other words, by receiving but not transmitting radio messages), the location of the fleet was successfully hidden from American patrolling ships and aircraft, as well as listening code breakers. A decade later, infiltrated Chinese "volunteers" sent in to assist North Korea (1951) went largely undetected by U.N. forces until they attacked, thanks to their careful observation of radio silence. More recently, terrorists often avoid using radio (including cell phones) as their signals can too readily be traced—sometimes quickly enough to call in an air strike.

One often effective means of avoiding detection of radio signals when radio silence is not an option is to use burst communications, which are signals sent too quickly to be successfully located. Observing radio silence could also be useful when trying to tune distant or weak radio signals.

Christopher H. Sterling

See also Code Breaking; Deception; Electromagnetic Pulse (EMP); Jutland, Battle of (1916); Korean War (1950–1953); Meteor Burst Communications (MBC); Signals Intelligence (SIGINT); Y Service

Reber, Samuel (1864–1933)

A prominent U.S. Army Signal Corps officer of the late nineteenth and early twentieth centuries and closely associated with the corps' aviation program, Reber played a significant role in the growth and expansion of military communications as the United States became a global power.

Born in St. Louis, Missouri, on 16 October 1864, Reber graduated from West Point in 1886 and received a commission in the cavalry. After studying electrical engineering at Johns Hopkins University, Reber transferred to the Signal Corps in 1894. He caught the eye of Chief Signal Officer Adolphus W. Greely as a man of talent and began his rise through the ranks. Lieutenant Reber authored the Signal Corps' first *Manual of Photography* in 1896 and taught courses in the subject. During the Spanish-American War (1898), Reber initially commanded the telegraph train and balloon company in Tampa, Florida. He subsequently served in Puerto Rico, where he was in charge of land communication and repaired equipment destroyed by the Spaniards.

After the war, Reber served in Cuba as superintendent of military telegraph lines and acting chief signal officer. From 1899 to 1901, he was chief signal officer of the Department of the East, headquartered at Governor's Island, New York. As such, he conducted some of the corps' early wireless experiments between stations in New York Harbor. He became a captain in 1900 and a major in 1903. That year, he was among the first officers detailed to the Army's newly created General Staff. In 1904 he was a delegate to the International Electrical Congress held in St. Louis. Based on his experimental and practical work during this period, Reber prepared the Signal Corps' *Handbook of Telephones* (1903) and contributed a chapter to the *Handbook of Submarine Cables* (1905). From 1907 to 1909 he served as chief signal officer in the Philippines, where he oversaw the ongoing transfer of the Signal Corps' communications system to civilian control. His next assignment was a second tour as chief signal officer of the Department of the East.

Promoted to lieutenant colonel in 1913, Reber became head of the Signal Corps

Aeronautical Division, which became a section the next year. His tenure in that position proved to be controversial, however, and Secretary of War Newton D. Baker removed him in May 1916. Although Reber remained in uniform and served overseas with the American Expeditionary Force during World War I, his military career was effectively over. He retired from the Army as a colonel at his own request in 1919.

Reber became an executive with the new Radio Corporation of America (RCA) in 1923, where he continued work similar to that he had performed in the Army. As RCA's general foreign representative, Reber participated in a number of international communications conferences. He was in Tokyo in 1923 to conduct radio negotiations with the Japanese when a devastating earthquake struck the city. Escaping uninjured, Reber took charge of restoring the city's cable and wireless communications with the outside world, for which feat the Japanese government decorated him. Reber died in Washington DC on 16 April 1933 at age 68, and is buried in Arlington National Cemetery.

Rebecca Robbins Raines

See also Army Signal Corps; Greely, Adolphus W. (1844–1935); Spanish-American War (1898)

Sources

Cullum, George P., et al., comps. 1891–1950. *Biographical Register of the Officers and Graduates of the U.S. Military Academy at West Point, N.Y.* 9 vols. Cambridge, MA: Riverside Press and others.

Harbord, James G. 1934. "Samuel Reber." *Sixty-fifth Annual Report of the Association of Graduates of the United States Military Academy at West Point, New York*, 150–153. New York: The Association.

Raines, Rebecca Robbins. 1996. *Getting the Message Through: A Branch History of the US Army Signal Corps*. Washington, DC: Government Printing Office.

Renaissance and Early Modern Military Signals (1450–1800)

Modes of military signaling during the European Renaissance and early modern era were largely bypassed in the revolution in military technology, which included a rediscovery of classical Greek and Roman military thinking and methods. Yet the need for effective communication grew with the size of armies committed to battle. From the late sixteenth to the late eighteenth century, fighting forces became both better trained and more professional—and expanded by a factor of ten, making coordination and signaling that much more important and, at the same time, difficult. Bastioned artillery fortresses made siege warfare both significant and complex, yet even modes of stationary communications failed to keep up.

Indeed, the technology and methods of military communication changed very little through this period of nearly four centuries. Land transport remained crude and slow, as did the movement of messages and men. Naval forces made the transition from oared fighting galleys to more efficient sailing ships of war, but maritime signaling methods remained crude at best. Battlefield communication remained largely as it had for hundreds of years, heavily reliant on—and subject to the problems of—couriers. Old systems, long used, dominated.

At the time of the Spanish Armada (1588), for example, large beacon signal fires set on English hilltops could communicate messages from the south coast to London (and then the rest of England) within hours. This allowed relatively rapid mobilization of thousands of men to repel expected invaders. When the Armada ships were first sighted off the Hampshire coast, prepared fire beacons were lit and men flowed into Portsmouth to protect the naval base against a possible attack. To prevent misuse or confusion, the beacons were often placed under the control of local justices of the peace.

In the on-and-off fighting of the Thirty-Years War (1618–1648) and other seventeenth-century wars between Catholic and Protestant forces, communications methods resembled those of previous centuries. Likewise, in the often convoluted English Civil Wars (1642–1651), slow communications contributed to the confusion that plagued both Parliamentarian and Royalist forces. Two Scottish uprisings against England in 1705 and again in 1745–1746 relied on use of a "fiery cross" (a wooden cross singed on the ends) carried by runners to call up Scots aged sixteen to sixty to an agreed place of rendezvous. Bagpipes led the Scots to battle at Culloden (1746) and elsewhere. The conquering English built an extensive series of military roads to better control occupied areas of Scotland and increase the pace of their communications. The Seven Years War (the French and Indian War in North America, 1756–1763) saw usage of traditional modes of Native American signaling often not much different from those of the European powers, which had changed little over time.

There were some innovations. Many systems of mechanical semaphore were developed. The invention of the telescope in 1608 helped to revive the use of visual signaling methods and prompted several early semaphore systems. In 1684, Robert Hook offered a semaphore system that utilized various suspended shapes in the daytime and the use of torches at night. Irishman Richard Lovell Edgeworth, in the late 1760s, proposed his "tellograph," a series of windmill sails of specific shapes and colors for which he recommended a system of towers and trained operators—one of the first proposals for a complete signaling system.

Other modes of communication appeared during this period, and some were used by military authorities during wartime emergencies. The modern newspaper was born in the form of business newsletters and then weekly papers. Postal services developed and expanded to distribute mail—and were often used for military messages aside from wartime situations. Town criers came into widespread use as well.

Christopher H. Sterling

See also American Wars to 1860; Fire / Flame / Torch; Flags; Horses and Mules; Lights and Beacons; Medieval Military Signaling (500–1500 CE); Military Roads; Music Signals; Pigeons; Postal Services; Semaphore (Mechanical Telegraphs)

Sources

Hale, John Rigby. 1986. *War and Society in Renaissance Europe, 1450–1620.* Baltimore: Johns Hopkins University Press.

Hall, Bert S. 2001. *Weapons and Warfare in Renaissance Europe: Gunpowder, Technology, and Tactics.* Baltimore: Johns Hopkins University Press.

Kitchen, Frank. 1988. *Fire over England: The Armada Beacons.* Brighton, UK: Tower Publications.

Parker, Geoffrey. 1996. *The Military Revolution: Military Innovation and the Rise of the West, 1500–1800.* Cambridge: Cambridge University Press.

Somerset (UK) County Council. "Beacons and Coastal Defences." [Online information; retrieved September 2005.] http://www.somerset.gov.uk/archives/ASH/Beacons.htm.

Woods, David L. (1965). *A History of Tactical Communications Techniques*. Orlando, FL: Martin-Marietta (reprinted by Arno Press, 1974).

Robison, Samuel Shelburne (1867–1952)

One of the brightest and most innovative officers of his generation, Samuel Robison was a pioneer in the U.S. Navy's adoption, development, and use of radio communications.

Born in Juniata County, Pennsylvania, on 10 May 1867, Robison attended the Naval Academy from 1884 to 1888. He was commissioned an ensign in the summer of 1890 and spent most of his early career on the Asiatic Station. During the Spanish-American War, he saw action at Manila Bay on USS *Boston*, fighting alongside George Dewey's flagship *Olympia*. After the war, Robison served on a battleship (*Alabama*) and a destroyer (*Hull*) before being placed in charge of the Radio Division at the Bureau of Equipment. Robison had a small staff and spent much of his time personally supervising tests of wireless apparatus. Pursuing a policy initiated by his predecessor, Robison strove to procure as many American-made radios as possible. When his tour ended in July 1906, the Navy was using radio equipment manufactured by at least five different American companies.

While serving as head of the Radio Division, Robison, in cooperation with several others, wrote an instruction manual on wireless telegraphy for use by naval electricians. First published in July 1906, it covered both the theoretical underpinnings and the practical applications of wireless. Robison's manual went through eight revised editions and served as the U.S. Navy's standard textbook on radio communications for the better part of two decades.

Between 1911 and 1917 Robison had three seagoing command tours (*Cincinnati, Jupiter, South Carolina*), and during World War I he commanded the Atlantic Fleet Submarine Force. After a series of brief assignments—including Boston Navy Yard commandant, military governor of Santo Domingo, and General Board member—Robison hoisted his flag as commander-in-chief of the United States Battle Fleet on 30 June 1923.

Robison's expertise in radio communications surpassed that of any previous fleet commander in the U.S. Navy, and he used his expertise as a basis for reform. He pushed vigorously for modern equipment, oversaw the establishment of communications departments on combatant ships, and encouraged the building of a new radio school on the West Coast. Robison also took aggressive steps to improve the communications efficiency of his subordinates. Toward this end he achieved remarkable success. The month before Robison assumed command of the Battle Fleet, the average time to deliver a radio dispatch within the fleet was slightly more than half an hour. Two years later, the average was down to just four minutes. By the time Robison relinquished command in August 1926, ship-to-ship radio had become the fleet's most important system of tactical communication.

Robison served as commandant of the Thirteenth Naval District from 1926 to 1928 and as superintendent of the Naval Academy from 1928 until his retirement in 1931. He later coauthored a comprehensive history of naval tactics with his wife, Mary. Robison died in Glendale, California, on 20 November 1952.

Timothy Wolters

See also Fiske, Bradley A. (1854–1942); Hooper, Stanford C. (1884–1955); Radio; Spanish-American War (1898); U.S. Navy

Sources

Howeth, L. S. 1963. *History of Communications-Electronics in the United States Navy.* Washington, DC: Government Printing Office.

Robison, S. S., et al. 1906. *Manual of Wireless Telegraphy for the Use of Naval Electricians.* Washington, DC: Government Printing Office.

Robison, Samuel S. 1911. *Manual of Wireless Telegraphy for the Use of Naval Electricians.* Revised 2nd ed. Annapolis, MD: Naval Institute Press (and later editions, as revised by others).

Robison, Samuel S., and Mary L. Robison. 1942. *A History of Naval Tactics from 1530 to 1930: The Evolution of Tactical Maxims.* Annapolis, MD: Naval Institute Press.

Rogers, James Harris (1850–1929)

James Rogers was an early twentieth-century radio pioneer who developed important underground and underwater radio reception systems used by the U.S. Navy during World War I. His work helped to lay the groundwork for Cold War very low frequency submarine communications.

Rogers was born on 13 July 1850 in Franklin, Tennessee, and was educated by private tutors and then at St. Charles College in London. His initial experience in electrical communications concerned telegraphy, and in 1872 he shared a patent with his brother for a system of embossed telegraphy—the first of nearly fifty patents he would receive. He served as chief electrician at the U.S. Capitol from 1877 to 1883.

Rogers settled in the Hyattsville, Maryland, area in 1895. He was one of the inventors of printing telegraph devices, and his full-size working models saw commercial service on a circuit between Baltimore and Washington DC, as well as in New York, in the 1890s. Improved elements of this were patented in 1893.

About 1908, Rogers began to experiment with underground and underwater wireless reception, trying out different types of wire and cable antennas with varied designs to receive distant wireless signals. To improve reception, he utilized an extensive underground (or underwater) array of antenna wire, with multiple "legs" often extending out many yards from the central reception point. He experimented with many designs and types of antenna material. After working in other areas (including airplane stability and means of generating wireless signals), he resumed his experimental wireless reception work in 1916.

The Rogers system, the first successful low-frequency approach, allowed reception in North America of European radio signals. His system was first tested in front of naval officials late in 1916 and again early in 1917. Rogers's work was the subject of nine patents granted to him from 1916 to 1919.

Rogers's health began to decline in 1917 after he was overcome by monoxide gas in a Maryland cave while working to improve his reception system. With public announcement of the system and its use after World War I, he received two honorary doctorates and other awards. Rogers died at his Hyattsville home on 12 December 1929.

Christopher H. Sterling

See also Radio; Submarine Communications; Telegraph

Sources

Bearden, Tom. "The Tom Bearden Website." [Online information; retrieved April 2007.] http://www.cheniere.org/books/part1/toc.htm.

Rogers, John H. "Underground & Underwater Radio." [Online information; retrieved

April 2006.] http://www.rexresearch.com/rogers/1rogers.htm.

Secor, H. Winfield. 1919. "America's Greatest War Invention." *Electrical Experimenter* March: 787–789, 834–835.

Taylor, A. Hoyt. 1948. "1917–1918: World War I, Great Lakes and Belmar." In *Radio Reminiscences: A Half Century.* Washington, DC: U.S. Naval Research Laboratory.

Room 40

Room 40 was the designation (and originally the actual location within the Old Admiralty building in London) of the British Naval Intelligence Division during World War I. It was created in October 1914 by Rear Admiral H. F. Oliver, chief of the War Staff, and operated throughout the war. In 1917 it became more formally known as the Intelligence Division of the Naval Staff.

In order to obtain vital intelligence, Britain cut Germany's undersea telegraph cables on the first full day of World War I, thus forcing Germany to use radio—which could be heard and intercepted. But the British could not read the German codes. In a stroke of luck, Britain obtained a naval codebook from the wreck of the German cruiser *Magdeburg* (off the coast of what was then Russian Estonia), thanks to fast work by its Russian ally. Within months, the code breakers of Room 40 had copies of all three German naval codes and were thus able to read most German wireless traffic for much of the war.

Captain (later Admiral Sir) Reginald "Blinker" Hall directed much of this effort, under the overall leadership of Sir Alfred Ewing. Hall gathered a group of naval personnel (and soon some civilians) who could be counted on to keep quiet about what they knew. Some were fluent in German, others interested in puzzles or math. Few knew anything about ciphers and codes when the war began. Starting with one wireless listening post (in Stockton), Room 40 soon set up many others, the origin of the "Y Service" that operated in both world wars. These posts, often staffed in part with volunteers as well as advisers from Marconi, focused on intercepting as many German signals as possible—by the end of the war, Room 40 had dealt with some 15,000 messages. But having information was no help if it was not effectively communicated. The British fleet suffered at Jutland (May–June 1916) because of poor or late communication from the Admiralty of what Room 40 had learned about German naval plans and actions.

On 17 January 1917, Room 40 intercepted a secret communication from German Foreign Minister Arthur Zimmermann to the German ambassador in Washington DC. The message took cryptographers nearly a month to fully decode, but its importance was quickly realized. The Zimmermann Telegram, as it would soon become known, revealed German plans to begin unrestricted submarine warfare in the Atlantic. Knowing that this could bring the United States into the war, Germany offered an alliance to Mexico if it would keep the United States occupied, plus a commitment to return former Mexican territory in Texas, New Mexico, and Arizona. British intelligence shared the contents of the memo (but not how they had intercepted and decoded it) with the American ambassador in London, who immediately informed Washington, thus airing and thwarting the German plan. Zimmermann, perhaps more honest than diplomatically astute, admitted the telegram's content. The United States declared war on Germany in April 1917.

In 1919, the separate naval signals intelligence operation was combined with the parallel army entity to form the Government

Code & Cipher School, which would operate in London until World War II, moving in 1939 to Bletchley Park. Unlike the situation after World War II, knowledge of Room 40 and its role was released to the public by the mid-1920s, just a few years after the end of World War I.

Christopher H. Sterling

See also Bletchley Park; Code, Codebook; Government Code & Cipher School (GC&CS, 1919–1946); Jutland, Battle of (1916); Signals Intelligence (SIGINT); United Kingdom: Royal Navy; World War I; Y Service

Sources

Beesly, Patrick. 1982. *Room 40: British Naval Intelligence 1914–1918.* New York: Harcourt Brace Jovanovich.

Grant, Robert M. 2004. *U-Boat Hunters: Code Breakers, Divers and the Defeat of the U-Boats, 1914–1918.* Annapolis, MD: Naval Institute Press.

Hoy, Hugh Cleland. 1934. *40 O.B., or How the War Was Won.* London: Hutchinson.

James, William. 1956. *The Code Breakers of Room 40.* New York: St. Martin's Press.

Tuchman, Barbara. 1966. *The Zimmermann Telegram.* Rev. ed. New York: Macmillan.

Rowlett, Frank B. (1908–1998)

An important American cryptographer for six decades, Frank Rowlett helped to develop the American SIGABA code machine, break the Japanese Purple code, and served with the Central Intelligence Agency (CIA) in the 1950s and then the National Security Agency (NSA) in the 1960s.

Rowlett was born in Rose Hill, Virginia, on 2 May 1908 and graduated with an honors degree in chemistry and mathematics in 1929 from Emory and Henry College. On 1 April 1930 he was hired by William F. Friedman, who was building a small staff of army cryptologists for the new Army Signal Intelligence Service.

During the 1930s, Rowlett and his handful of colleagues, after a lengthy period of training under Friedman, worked as both cryptologists and cryptanalysts. They compiled codes and ciphers for use by the U.S. Army and began solving a number of foreign systems, notably Japanese. In the mid-1930s, Rowlett and his colleagues solved the first Japanese machine system for encipherment of diplomatic communications, known to the Americans as Red. He played a crucial role in protecting American communications when he originated the "stepped maze" concept for a coding machine, which became the electric cipher machine, or SIGABA, the device that was never solved by the Axis during the war. (In 1964, Congress awarded Rowlett $100,000 as partial compensation for his classified cryptologic inventions.) From 1939 to 1940, Rowlett played a major role in solving a much more sophisticated Japanese diplomatic cipher machine, nicknamed Purple by the United States When asked what his greatest contribution to this effort was, Rowlett once said that he was the one who believed it could be done. He was credited with leading the team that did the mind-numbing work over a period of eighteen months. At American entry into World War II, Rowlett became an Army officer and rose to the rank of colonel.

In addition to having highly developed cryptanalytic skills, Rowlett was a good manager, and he rose quickly within the Army's signals intelligence organization. From 1943 to 1945 he was chief of the General Cryptanalytic Branch, and from 1945 to 1947 he served as chief of the Intelligence Division. From 1949 to 1952, he was technical director in the Office of Operations of the Armed Forces Security Agency, the predecessor to NSA. Rowlett differed with General Ralph Canine, the first director of NSA, over personnel movements, including his own. Acting on his differences, he transferred to CIA from 1952 until 1958. He then returned to NSA as a special assistant to the agency's next four directors. In 1965, Rowlett founded and became commandant of the National Cryptologic School. He retired from federal service in 1966.

In 1990, NSA's highest achievement award was named for Rowlett. He died at the age of ninety on 29 June 1998 in Gaithersburg, Maryland, last of the original trio of Army code breakers hired by Friedman.

Christopher H. Sterling

See also Arlington Hall; Bletchley Park; Electric Cipher Machine (ECM Mark II, "SIGABA"); Friedman, William F. (1891–1969); Magic; National Security Agency (NSA); Signals Intelligence (SIGINT); Ultra

Source
Rowlett, Frank B. 1998. *The Story of Magic: Memoirs of an American Cryptologic Pioneer.* Laguna Hills, CA: Aegeon Park Press.

Russia/Soviet Union: Air Force

The Soviet (later Russian) air force has gone through a varied history, developing from a backward service with obsolete aircraft in the 1930s to one of the world's pre-eminent services at the height of the Cold War, to the decline of recent years. Its communication facilities have followed a similar arc.

While Russian flying preceded the start of World War I, the Soviet air force was founded as the "Workers' and Peasants' Air Fleet" in 1918. After being placed under control of the Red Army in 1930, its influence on aircraft design became greater. Germany helped advise the buildup of Soviet air power in the 1920s and 1930s. The first big test of the Soviet air force came in 1936 with the Spanish Civil War, when Russian pilots helped to support the Republic. The purge of

many senior leaders in 1939 weakened the force, however, and it fared poorly against the Finns in 1939–1940 and the German invasion a year later. A huge number of fighter aircraft and large amounts of related equipment were provided by the United States under lend-lease.

During the Cold War the Soviet air force was divided into three segments: Strategic Aviation was focused on long-range bombers; Frontal Aviation was concerned with battlefield air defense, close air support, and interdiction; and Military Transport Aviation served both. The Air Defense Forces focused on air defense and interceptor aircraft as a separate and distinct service. Some 500 air bases were operational, about a fifth of them in the Arctic regions of the country. Coordination over this huge territory required effective communications.

Following the collapse of the Soviet Union in December 1991, the aircraft and personnel of the Soviet air force were divided among the many newly independent states. Russia received the majority of these forces—approximately 40 percent of the aircraft and 65 percent of the manpower—to form the new but smaller Russian Federation air force. By the late 1990s, limited funding severely restricted what had become a defensive and declining service. Declines in Russia's electronics industry, no longer as cutting-edge as it had been under Soviet rule, contributed to the deterioration. Further, the country's air surveillance and command system changed dramatically after 1991, as Russia lost the opportunity to maintain forward-positioned, ground-based air surveillance networks.

Christopher H. Sterling

See also Russia/Soviet Union: Army

Sources
Lee, Asher. 1959. *The Soviet Air and Rocket Forces.* New York: Praeger.

Murphy, Paul J. 1984. *The Soviet Air Forces.* Jefferson, NC: McFarland.

Nikunen, Heikki. 2005. "The Current State of the Russian Air Force." [Online information; retrieved November 2006.] http://www .sci.fi/~fta/ruaf.htm.

Steinman, Victor A. 1995. "Soviet Air Power In Perspective: Development and Impact, 1925–1942." [Online article; retrieved April 2006.] http://www.globalsecurity .org/military/library/report/1995/SVA .htm.

Russia/Soviet Union: Army

Russia (to 1917), the Soviet Union (1917–1991), and then Russia again (since 1991) share a fascinating and complex military communications history. Through the early nineteenth century and Napoleon's march on Moscow (1812), Tsarist Russia was backward and well behind European military practice. Modes of communication were traditional ones, used for hundreds of years, including flags, couriers, and pigeons. Message transmission was slow.

Mechanical semaphore networks were established during the reign of Nicholas I as the first line opened in 1824 between the capital of St. Petersburg and Lake Ladoga. By 1834 it had been extended to the naval base of Kronstadt and by 1839 reached southeast to Warsaw (then part of Russia). The system and signaling method used was based on that of Claude Chappe by Pierre-Jacques Chatau. Some 2,000 men were employed, with four to six at each signaling tower. The St. Petersburg terminal station (on the roof of the Winter Palace) survives to this day. Elements of this system may also have been employed as late as the Crimean War, used primarily for government and military messages.

The German firm of Siemens & Halske started construction of the Russian long-distance electric telegraph network in 1853 and completed the project two years later. The network was approximately 6,000 miles in length and extended from Finland down to the Crimea (where it was useful in the 1854–1856 Crimean War against Britain and France) via St. Petersburg, Moscow, Kiev, and Odessa. Further lines led to the Baltic provinces and to Warsaw. Military mobile telegraph parks were formed in September 1870. They were independent units under the control of the General Engineers Department. These were disbanded in 1894, but one telegraph company was introduced into each engineer battalion. The telephone was more slowly adopted and was long limited to a few large cities, connecting St. Petersburg and Moscow only in the 1890s.

Russian telegraph signalmen were organized as part of the army engineers, as in many other European forces. In actual battle, they would be attached to a corps headquarters. Thirteen telegraph sections were based in specific Russian fortifications. By the early twentieth century, after the disastrous Russo-Japanese War (1904–1905), these forces operated both wire and wireless telegraphy equipment (as well as heliographs for daytime and lanterns for nighttime signaling). The wireless companies were based in fortresses with mobile Marconi systems. By 1912, specialized training had been established. The same forces also provided horse and bicycle courier services.

The Russian army was an early user of radio communication in a military operation, but Russian signaling forces crumbled under the pressure of World War I, as demonstrated at the Battle of Tannenberg, 23–29 August 1914. During the fighting, Russian forces used wireless to transmit orders to their army forces. But this was also the first time that radio intercept was employed in warfare, as the Germans were monitoring the airwaves and received the Russian orders (which were sent in clear language, and not code) almost as soon as the intended Russian recipients did. By the time Russia pulled out of the war (1917), most army signaling had reverted to couriers and pigeons with occasional use of wired and wireless telegraphy.

Russian leader Vladimir Lenin ordered the manufacture of wireless equipment, which began in 1918. Operators were in such short supply that they had to be trained in the field. The Chief Signal Department of the Red Army was created in October 1919, and the posts of chiefs of the signal troops of the fronts, armies, divisions, and smaller units were instituted. The Civil War (1918–1922) destroyed much of the country's communications infrastructure, and thus heavy use was made of couriers and mounted dispatch riders. Combat exploits of the signalers were highly regarded by the Revolutionary Military Council of the new regime.

The new Soviet Union sought communications technology from abroad. Ericsson, for example, provided designs for telephone networks and equipment that were by 1927 built under license in what had become Leningrad. Russian forces lost a huge amount of their communications equipment and thus capability during the German mid-1941 invasion. It took about a year before Soviet factories, relocated to the Ural Mountains, could begin to replace radios and other tactical and strategic communications gear. In the interim, Soviet forces made extensive use of traditional couriers for military messaging. Production of wireless equipment was stepped up, and during the Battle of Stalingrad, 9,000 wireless sets were in use, while in the Belorussian operations of 1944, as many as 27,000 wireless sets were used. Considerable American radio equipment

was shipped to the Soviet Union as part of the Lend-Lease Program during World War II. Other U.S. radio and electronic equipment was taken from downed American aircraft, and some was reverse-engineered for Soviet manufacture.

Through the Cold War decades, Soviet signal troops operated tactical radio and wire communications networks and intercepted enemy signals for combat intelligence purposes. They also operated strategic underground cable, microwave, and satellite communications systems. The Soviets began launching their military Cosmos and other communication satellite series in 1962. There were signal corps academies and schools in many areas, including Kiev, Cherepovetz, Ryazan, Gorky, Kemerovo, and Ulyanovsk.

By the early 1970s, Soviet planners used the term "radio-electronic combat" (REC) to refer to their integrated program to disrupt enemy military command, control, and communications (C3) at all levels. Embodied in the Soviet doctrine for REC is an integrated effort centered on reconnaissance, electronic countermeasures (jamming), physical attack (destruction), and deception operations. Each of these elements contributes to the disruption of effective command and control at a critical decision point in battle at strategic, operational, and tactical levels. At the strategic level, the Soviet REC effort may involve simultaneous operations to deceive Western intelligence collection programs and to jam strategic C3. The Soviets continued to enhance their strategic REC mission capability right to the end of the Cold War.

Soviet attempts to counter enemy strategic command and control in wartime would involve disrupting the entire range of communication media available for strategic C3. Using their concept of *radiablokada* (radio blockade), the Soviets would attempt to isolate entire geographic regions and prevent deployed forces from communicating with their headquarters.

In the mid-1980s, the Soviets stopped their routine jamming of foreign radio broadcasts directed at Soviet audiences, though high-frequency (HF) jamming antennas remained in all major Soviet urban areas, available for wartime or crisis use as a strategic counter-measure asset. The transmitter power and range capability of these systems made them suitable for employment against North Atlantic Treaty Organization (NATO) HF communications. The large number of high-power transmitters and long-range directional antennas under the Soviet Ministry of Communications constituted an additional pool of strategic jamming assets. Used for the worldwide broadcast of such programs as Radio Moscow, these facilities could be employed effectively against U.S. and NATO high-frequency communications.

In the bitter 1990s war with Chechen nationalists, the Russian army's most significant technical problem was establishing and maintaining communications. The breakdown occurred at platoon, company, and battalion levels. Some of the problems were clearly the fault of Russian planners, such as the decision during the battle for Grozny to transmit all messages in the clear. This misstep obviously allowed the Chechen force not only to monitor all transmissions and thus prepare for what was coming next, but also to insert false messages in Russian communications traffic. The Russians soon turned to message scramblers.

The chief factor in the communications breakdown, however, was simply urban structures. High-rise buildings and towers impeded transmissions, especially those in the high to ultra-high frequencies. Communication officers had to consider the nature of radio wave propagation and carefully select operating and alternate frequencies, and they had to consider the interference caused by power transmission lines, communications lines, and electric transportation contact systems. Many radio transmitter operators were killed in the initial battles, as Chechens focused on soldiers carrying radios or antennas. To solve this problem, Russian radio operators began concealing their antennas. However, this led them to hide their whip antennas in a pocket or under a shirt, and in their haste to reassemble the radio while under fire, forgetting to reconnect the antenna. The Russians noted that the Chechen forces used Motorola and Nokia cellular radios and leased satellite channels on foreign relays. This enabled them to establish communications between base stations and to maintain quality mobile radio communications.

Multiple after-action recommendations by Russian communication specialists included the need to develop more convenient and lighter-weight gear for radio operators, including wire-type antennas; outfitting units with cellular and trunk-line adaptable radios; putting an indicator lamp on the radio sets to highlight problems; developing a common radio storage battery; and providing alternate antennas capable of automatic connections in case primary antennas become disabled. Other recommendations included using radios with automatic frequency tuning together with devices for guaranteeing scrambling and masking speech; using HF radios of armored vehicles with a supplementary receiver; developing an ability to bounce signals off buildings or retransmitting them at intersections or via airborne platforms; locating very high frequency/ultra-high frequency radios at a distance of three to five times the height of reinforced concrete upper stories or iron roof structures; putting antennas near windows or doors of upper stories when a radio is in a building; using coaxial cable (or existing television cable) to remotely operate radios from basements; and using beam antennas to maintain communications with a distant site.

Christopher H. Sterling and Cliff Lord

See also Chappe, Claude (1763–1805); European Late Nineteenth-Century Wars; Russia/Soviet Union: Air Force; Russia: Navy; Tannenberg, Battle of (1914); Warsaw Pact (1955–1991); World War I; World War II

Sources

Department of Defense. 1989. "Radio-Electronic Combat." In *Soviet Military Power 1989: Prospects for Change.* Washington, DC: Department of Defense.

Howard, William L. 2002. "Russian Military Radios." [Online information; retrieved April 2007.] http://www.armyradio.com/publish/Articles/William_Howard_Russian/Russian_Mil_Radio.htm.

International Collectors Group. "USSR Military Tube Transistor Radio Gallery." [Online information; retrieved April 2006.] http://users.iptelecom.net.ua/~ussradio/.

RussiaSpaceWeb.com. 2005. "Spacecraft: Military." 2005. [Online information; retrieved April 2006.] http://www.russianspaceweb.com/spacecraft_military.html.

Thomas, Timothy L. 1999. "The Battle of Grozny: Deadly Classroom for Urban Combat." *Parameters* (Summer): 87–102.

Wilson, Geoffrey. 1976. "Russia." *The Old Telegraphs*, 180–182. Totowa, NJ: Rowman & Littlefield.

Russia/Soviet Union: Navy

The Soviet navy of the twentieth century was often called the Red Navy, and was one of increasing power into the final decades (1970–1990) of the Cold War.

The Soviet navy traces its history back to at least Peter the Great in the 1700s. Because of its huge landmass and location, the Soviet Union's naval forces were not a primary part of the Tsarist regime in Russia. This was never more evident than with the fleet's stunning loss to Japan in the 1905 Battle of Tsushima. With the 1917 revolution, vessels of the former imperial fleet made up the new Red Fleet, though well into the 1930s it was a dilapidated coastal defense force of little power. U.S. destroyers obtained by the navy under the Lend-Lease Program made up part of the growing Soviet fleet during World War II, their main role being to protect Allied convoys to Murmansk. The postwar Soviet submarine fleet, initially based on German U-boat designs, grew substantially in the Cold War years. The emphasis on submarines (between 300 and 400 ships after 1955, with perhaps half using nuclear propulsion by the 1980s) meant that communication links with those submarines were among the top electronics concerns for the fleet.

The first helicopter carrier aircraft appeared only in 1968–1969. The Soviet navy never embraced the American fascination with carrier-based aviation, but fearing American aircraft carriers it invested considerable resources in antishipping cruise missiles launched from submarines, surface ships, and shore-based aircraft. By the mid-1980s the Soviet navy, by then with some carriers of its own, was the largest in the world in terms of number of ships, and second in tonnage only to the United States.

During the Cold War, the Soviet navy was divided into several major fleets including the Northern, Pacific Ocean, Black Sea, and Baltic fleets. The Caspian Flotilla came under the Black Sea Fleet command, while the Indian Ocean Squadron drew its units from and was under the jurisdiction of the Pacific Ocean Fleet. Other components included the Naval Aviation, Naval Infantry (their equivalent of the U.S. Marine Corps) and coastal artillery. Naval doctrine recognized the importance of electronic warfare at least by the 1960s and within two decades had developed a strong ability to jam, deceive, or intercept enemy communications, while at the same time developing redundant systems for Soviet vessels to ensure their survival. The need to strike at and destroy Western naval communication facilities was a central part of naval planning and war games.

As Norman Polmar reported in his guide to the Cold War Soviet navy, "Soviet combat aircraft, surface ships, and submarines have electronic warfare equipment to (1) detect threats, (2) collect Electronic Intelligence (ELINT), (3) identify friendly forces (IFF), and (4) counter threats (ECM)." The Soviet navy operated a fleet of intelligence collection vessels, many looking like the merchant fishing trawlers or factory ships from which they were converted. Various classes of these included satellite and other communication links as well as extensive electronics eavesdropping capability. These and a number of communications ships were launched in different classes from the 1950s into the 1980s. The navy also operated nearly a dozen cable ships by the 1980s to lay and repair undersea communication cables as well as seafloor hydrophone (listening) devices.

Access to ports and airfields in Vietnam, Syria, Libya, Ethiopia, South Yemen, and Seychelles in the 1980s enabled Soviet naval forces to repair their ships, fly ocean reconnaissance flights, establish communications (fleet radio as well as listening or intercept) posts, and maintain forward deployments. The Soviet fleet was designed primarily to intercept convoys across the Atlantic intended to support North Atlantic Treaty Organization forces.

With the demise of the Soviet Union and end of the Cold War in 1991, the maritime force was re-formed into the Russian navy. The navy quickly declined to a mere shadow of its once powerful profile, however, as many ships were laid (or broken) up, quality and morale suffered, and accidents rose.

Christopher H. Sterling

See also Electronic Countermeasures/
Electronic Warfare (ECM/EW); Identification, Friend or Foe (IFF); Tsushima, Battle of (27–28 May 1905)

Sources
Polmar, Norman. 1991. *The Naval Institute Guide to the Soviet Navy.* 4th ed. Annapolis, MD: Naval Institute Press.
"Signal Flags: Soviet Navy." 2005. http://www.fotw.net/flags/xf~ru.html (accessed April 2006).

Safford, Laurance F. (1890–1973)

Often called the "father" of U.S. Navy cryptography, Safford was a key figure in the development of American military cryptology between the world wars.

Laurance (some sources spell it Laurence) Safford was born in 1890 in Massachusetts and graduated fifteenth in the Naval Academy class of 1916. His early career on board several different naval vessels gave no indication of his future role in cryptologic history, and his constantly rumpled look hid an affinity for mathematics and machines. He was also attracted to chess and other intellectual pursuits. In January 1924 he was shifted from command of a minesweeper off the China coast to head the "research desk" (the code and signal section) within the Office of Naval Communications (OP-20), located in the Navy Building in Washington DC. In the beginning his prime task was to exploit a Japanese naval codebook (from the Japanese consulate in New York) that had been secretly photographed. To do this he had four civilian clerical employees. This was the beginning of the OP-20-G naval signals intelligence unit.

Safford turned out to be perfect for the task at hand. He promoted the effort throughout the Navy, attracting brilliant minds like his own, including Agnes Meyer Driscoll, Joseph Rochefort, Joseph Wenger, and others who were to lead the Navy's cryptographic effort through World War II and into the postwar period. He began organizing a worldwide naval collection and direction-finding effort, so that when the United States entered World War II it already had a system of established radio intercept and listening stations (the first was in Shanghai). Due to naval officer rotation policies, Safford was reassigned in 1926, returning three years later. He remained with the code work except for one final sea tour of duty (1932–1936). Meanwhile, the effort that he headed broke Japanese naval codes and began mechanizing its code operations with the addition of IBM equipment. Safford was directly involved with building cryptographic machines and collaborated with the Army's Frank Rowlett in the invention of the SIGABA device, one of the few cipher machines never broken by any country during World War II.

Safford promoted collaboration with the Army on several fronts and was largely responsible for the Navy entry into a joint effort with the Army on the Japanese diplomatic systems. He recognized the signs of war that appeared in the diplomatic traffic (on which OP-20-G had been told to concentrate) and tried to get a warning message to Pearl Harbor several days before the attack, but was rebuffed by the director of Naval Communication.

Organizationally, he promoted a decentralized system with naval communications intelligence sections near Seattle, in Honolulu, and in Manila (with the Japanese invasion in 1941, it shifted first to Corregidor and then Australia). He assigned the chief Japanese naval code problem to the Hawaii station and named Joseph Rochefort to head the effort, using the very best Navy cryptanalysts. Rochefort's team broke JN-25 (the American designation for the Japanese naval operational code) in time to help a U.S. Navy task force to win the landmark battle of Midway in mid-1942.

Disputes over organization (and his being one of those blamed for U.S. forces being surprised by the Pearl Harbor attack) eventually froze his career path, and he was shunted aside for the remainder of the war. Safford retired from active duty as a captain in early 1953 and died two decades later, on 2 March 1973.

Christopher H. Sterling

See also Electric Cipher Machine (ECM Mark II, "SIGABA"); Magic; Midway, Battle of (3–6 June 1942); Nebraska Avenue, Washington DC; OP-20-G; Rowlett, Frank B. (1908–1998); Signals Intelligence (SIGINT)

Sources

Parker, Frederick D. 1994. *Pearl Harbor Revisited: United States Navy Communications Intelligence 1924–1941.* Fort Meade, MD: National Security Agency.
Safford, Laurance, and Joseph N. Wenger. 1994. *U.S. Naval Communications Intelligence Activities.* Laguna Hills, CA: Aegean Park Press.

Satellite Communications

Military satellites are usually strategic or tactical. Strategic satellites are typically networked through fixed ground stations. They allow communications between stations served by the same satellite using any number of routes. Tactical satellite systems, on the other hand, utilize mobile earth stations. Military users have traditionally avoided commercial satellites because of security concerns, though increased use of encryption eases that worry.

A communications satellite must have a receiver and a transmitter, antennas for both functions, a method to convert the received message at the transmitter, and a source of electrical power. The ground portion of a satellite system consists of a transmitter, a receiver, antennas, and a means of connecting the station to end users. The most obvious difference between a satellite ground station and a point-to-point microwave station is that the satellite high-gain antenna is able to track the satellite.

The U.S. Army and Navy first experimented with reflecting radio signals off the moon in the 1940s and 1950s. On 11 January 1946 the Army reflected radio signals off the moon. On 24 July 1954, as a part of the Navy's Communication Moon Relay Project (CMR), James H. Trexler, an engineer at the

Naval Research Laboratory, became the first person to transmit his voice into space and have it returned to earth. The CMR was first tested and publicly revealed in January 1960 and operated between Hawaii and Maryland with sixteen teleprinter channels at the rate of sixty words per minute. Within two years, the system had been expanded to include ship-to-shore communications. The CMR was the only operational satellite communications relay system in the world until the Defense Satellite Communications System began operation on 16 June 1966.

All of these experiments were intended to utilize the theoretical advantages that satellite communications offer over the traditional methods of long-haul communications, such as underwater cables, landlines, microwave transmission, and television signals. Submarine cables are expensive to lay and lack the large capacity necessary to meet the continual demand for more circuits. Because microwave transmissions travel in a straight line, relay stations have to be constructed about every thirty-five miles. The relay stations must receive, amplify, and retransmit the signal. Normal radio transmissions are subject to atmospheric disturbances, such as sun spots. The optimum altitude for a communications satellite is 22,300 miles above the equator, where the satellite appears to be stationary because it is in a geosynchronous orbit. A constellation of three such satellites, positioned at 120 degrees from each other, with the capability of relaying communications between the satellites, provides communications to virtually every part of the earth except the North and South poles.

On 4 October 1957, military and civilian communications changed with the launch of the Soviet Union's Sputnik 1. On 18 December 1958, the U.S. Signal Communi-cations by Orbiting Relay Equipment (SCORE) was launched, and a taped Christmas message from President Dwight Eisenhower was broadcast from orbit. SCORE was also used to transmit messages between Arizona, Texas, and Georgia. SCORE was a store-and-forward satellite, receiving a message from earth, storing it on a tape, and then retransmitting it on command from an earth station. On 12 August 1960, the ECHO 1 satellite, a passive aluminized Mylar balloon, was launched, and experiments with radio and television transmission began in earnest. The first geosynchronous satellite, Syncom III, launched in August 1964. The Syncom series was a joint project of the Department of Defense and the National Aeronautics and Space Administration to demonstrate the economic viability of satellite communications.

The Soviet Union followed its initial Sputnik by launching more satellites than any other nation. The Soviet space program ranked second only to the United States in the resources devoted to its efforts. Most Soviet military satellites, regardless of type, were named Cosmos. In addition, "civilian" satellites, the use of which the Soviets did not want to explain, also received the Cosmos designation. In the three decades to 1990, most, if not all, satellites launched by the Soviets had some military functions. In the post-Soviet era, Russian military satellites are identified as such, but still receive the Cosmos identifier.

Development of military satellite communications drew heavily on advancements in the construction of commercial satellites. The fact that the Intelsat IV satellite had more than 4,000 two-way voice channels was a powerful incentive for developers of high-capacity military communications systems.

The number of nations providing domestic satellite service has increased dramatically since Canada started the service in 1972 and the United States launched its first in 1974.

Planners at the U.S. Department of Defense increasingly realized that a specialized architecture for military satellite communications (MILSATCOM) was necessary. The first MILSATCOM architecture was published in 1976 and has been refined numerous times to meet changing requirements and advances in technology. The architecture has three parts: mobile and tactical, wideband, and protected systems. Users are grouped together according to their requirements that can be met by a common satellite system.

Development of more sophisticated electronics has increased the capability of satellite communication. Its importance to military operations during the Gulf War (1990–1991) was summarized by Lieutenant General James Cassity, Joint Staff Directorate for C3 (command, control, and communications) Systems, who said, "From day one, satellite communications have been our bread and butter. From first deployment through today, military and commercial satellite communications systems have been vital in providing essential command and control. . . . In 90 days, we established more military communications connectivity to the Persian Gulf than we have in Europe after 40 years." The essential role played by satellites in that conflict was noted by military planners around the world.

Present U.S. MILSATCOM architecture has three basic systems: the Fleet Satellite Communications system (FLTSATCOM); the Defense Satellite Communications System (DSCS); and Milstar. The satellites of each system operate in the geosynchronous orbit (22,300 miles high), and each system uses specific frequency ranges. FLTSATCOM satellites operate in the ultra-high frequencies at 225 to 400 MHz; DSCS satellites operate in the super-high frequencies at 7,250 to 8,400 MHz; and Milstar satellites operate in the extremely high frequencies at 22 to 44 GHz. A fourth system, the Air Force Satellite Communications System (AFSATCOM), is supported by the three basic systems. AFSATCOM has no dedicated satellites but uses channels or transponders on the satellites of the MILSATCOM system. The AFSATCOM is used to transmit Emergency Action Messages and Single Integrated Operation Plan messages.

The FLTSATCOM system provided near worldwide coverage through its constellation of geosynchronous satellites. The FLTSATCOM system was the first operational system fielded by the Department of Defense to support tactical operations. The first FLTSATCOM satellite was launched in 1978 and the last in 1989. The system was utilized by naval aircraft, ships, submarines, and ground stations. In addition, it supported communications between the National Command Authority and high-priority users, such as the White House Communications Agency.

In an effort to increase the use of leased commercial satellites, Congress directed that the follow-on system for FLTSATCOM be leased. The LEASAT program primarily served the Navy, Air Force, and mobile ground forces, using FLTSATCOM terminals and communications channels very similar to FLTSATCOM. The first LEASAT was launched in 1984 and the last in 1990. By 1999, all of the FLTSATCOM satellites had been removed from service.

FLTSATCOM and LEASAT satellite systems were both replaced by UHF Follow-On (UHF F/O) satellites. The Navy's requirements for additional UHF capacity had increased dramatically after the FLT-

SATCOM system was initiated. The UHF F/O constellation of satellites was implemented to meet the increased demand for more capacity. The first successful launch was in 1993 and the last in 1999. Two UHF F/O satellites are located at each of the FLTSAT-COM locations. The new satellites more than double the capacity of the system. All of the UHF F/O satellites are electromagnetic pulse protected. The satellites carry transponders for use by the Milstar ground terminals and the Global Broadcast Service (GBS). The enhanced capability of the satellites has allowed a reduction in the size of terminals; for example, the Army's Enhanced Manpack UHF terminal can be carried, set up, and used by individual soldiers to communicate using the UHF F/O satellites.

The GBS utilizes technology from commercial television to broadcast large streams of data to numerous small antennas. The system broadcasts only one way and resembles the system used for home satellite television reception. The need for the GBS system grew out of the Gulf War when service-operated and commercial leased communication channels were overloaded and essential information had to be moved to fighting units by airlift assets. Since the GBS can transmit to small, phased array antennas on mobile platforms, data can be transmitted to forces while they are in motion. Commercial off-the-shelf and government off-the-shelf technology was used to quickly acquire and field the GBS capability.

The Defense Satellite Communications System (DSCS) provides secure voice, teletype, television, facsimile, and digital data services. The primary users of the DSCS are the Global Command and Control System, White House Communications Agency, Defense Information Systems Network, Defense Switched Network, Defense Mes-

sage System, Ground Mobile Forces, the Diplomatic Telecommunications Service, and several allied nations. THE DSCS evolved through three phases: DSCSI, or the Initial Defense Satellite Communications System (IDSCS), began in 1967; DSCSII began in 1971 with the launch of two satellites; and DSCSIII began in 1982 when its first satellite was launched. The five DSCSIII satellites allow most earth terminals to access two satellites. The Ground Mobile Forces (GMF) operate on a subnetwork using the DSCS satellites. The GMF subnetwork requires use of a gateway terminal, as it is not compatible with the DSCS network's strategic terminal.

The Milstar Satellite Communications System is the most advanced satellite communications system. It provides secure, jam-resistant, worldwide communications to meet joint service requirements. The Milstar system consists of five satellites in geosynchronous orbits, the first of which was launched 7 February 1994. Milstar terminals allow a user to transmit encrypted voice, data, teletype, or facsimile communications. The satellite functions as a switchboard by routing traffic from terminal to terminal anywhere on earth. The system has reduced requirements for ground-controlled switching because the satellite processes the communications signal and can link with other satellites in the constellation through crosslinks. One of the driving aims behind the Milstar program is to provide interoperable communications between Army, Navy, and Air Force Milstar users.

The capability of the Milstar system to operate under adverse conditions, such as jamming and nuclear attack, are achieved by frequency hopping, extensive on-board processing, and crosslinks. The flexibility of the Milstar system is improved by multiple uplink and downlink channels operating at different rates; multiple uplink and downlink beams; and routing of individual signals between uplinks, downlinks, and crosslinks.

Tommy R. Young II

See also Defense Message System (DMS); Electromagnetic Pulse (EMP); Global Command and Control System (GCCS); Gulf War (1990–1991); Spectrum Frequencies; White House Communications Agency (WHCA)

Sources
Butricia, Andrew J., ed. 1997. *Beyond the Ionosphere: Fifty Years of Satellite Communication.* NASA History Series SP-4217. Washington, DC: Government Printing Office.
Cassity, James. 1991. "Operation Desert Storm—The J-6 Perspective." *AFCEA News* February: 2.
Chun, Clayton K. S. 2006. *Defending Space: U.S. Anti-Satellite Warfare and Space Weaponry.* Oxford: Osprey Publishing.
Elfers, Glen, and Stephen B. Miller. 2001. "Future U.S. Military Satellite Communication Systems." [Online article; retrieved December 2006.] www.aero.org/publications/crosslink/winter2002/08.html.
Federici, Gary. "From the Sea to the Stars: A History of U.S. Navy Space and Space-Related Activities." [Online information; retrieved December 2006.] http://www.history.navy.mil/books/space/index.htm.
Martin, Donald H. 2001. "A History of U.S. Military Satellite Communication Systems." [Online article; retrieved December 2006.] www.aero.org/publications/crosslink/winter2002/01.html.
National Aeronautics and Space Administration. "DSCS (Defense Satellite Communications System)." [Online information; retrieved December 2006.] http://msl.jpl.nasa.gov/Programs/dscs.html.
RussianSpaceWeb.com. 2006. "Spacecraft: Military." [Online information; retrieved December 2006.] http://www.russianspaceweb.com/spacecraft_military.html.

Scott Air Force Base, Illinois

For many decades the headquarters of U.S. Air Force communications activities (under varied titles), Scott Air Force Base traces its background to World War I.

Some 624 acres of land in Belleville, Illinois, about 20 miles east of St. Louis, were leased to the U.S. government in mid-June 1917, two months after the country's entry into World War I. Two thousand workers and a $10-million appropriation converted the former farmland into an Army airfield with sixty buildings and a railway connection to existing lines. A month later the field was named after Corporal Frank Scott, the first enlisted man killed in an air crash (in College Park, Maryland, five years earlier).

The training of pilots began at Scott Field in September 1917, much of it in the familiar Curtiss JN-3D "Jennies." By 1918, two modified Jennies had been constructed to serve as air ambulances for pilots hurt in accidents. Scott's first public air show was held in mid-August 1918. After some postwar confusion and worry about the future, the War Department in 1919 purchased the land on which the airfield operated.

In 1920 Scott became the Army's only inland airship facility for experiments with military uses of blimps and balloons. This role lasted until 1937, when Scott again became an airplane base. Just a year later, Scott became home for the General Headquarters of the Air Force, leading to demolition of most existing buildings (some of them two decades old) and construction of more permanent administration, housing, and hangar buildings, more than seventy in all. The field was considerably expanded during World War II (it served as a major induction center for draftees) and again in the 1950s when several housing areas were added.

In 1941, Scott Field was designated as the communications training center for the Army Air Force, beginning nearly five decades of Scott's identification with Air Force communications operations. In January 1958, Scott Air Force Base became for twelve years the headquarters of the Air Force Communications System, later Command. Though the headquarters shifted for seven years to Richards-Gebair Air Force Base, Missouri, the function returned to Scott in November 1977 and has remained since.

In the early twenty-first century, Scott Air Force Base was also the headquarters of the U.S. Transportation Command, the Air Mobility Command, and the Defense Information Technology Contracting Organization, as well as nearly thirty other tenant organizations.

Christopher H. Sterling

See also Air Force Communications Agency (AFCA, 1991–2006); Air Force Communications Service (AFCS,) Air Force Communications Command (AFCC) (1961–1991)

Sources

Miller, Linda G., and Cora J. Holt. 1989. *Air Force Communications Command Chronology, 1938–1988*. Scott Air Force Base, IL: Air Force Communications Command.

Snyder, Thomas S., gen. ed. 1991. *Air Force Communications Command: 1938–1991—An Illustrated History*. 3rd ed. Scott Air Force Base, IL: Air Force Communications Command Office of History.

Searchlights/Signal Blinkers

The first known naval searchlight was employed aboard a Union warship blockading a Southern port during the American Civil War (1861–1865). In the very dark night the Confederate ship tried to break through the blockade. One Union ship managed to fire up a feeble, poorly reflected, and unfocused beam of light, which, following the noise of the escaping ship, managed to illuminate it enough to permit discovery and engagement.

Searchlight technology was simple. The searchlight was similar to lights used to illuminate the outside of theaters with what was, logically enough, called "limelight." It was produced by playing an oxy-hydrogen flame on a candle of calcium oxide in front of a crude, spherical, polished metal mirror, which reflected only about half the light generated. Soon, a more efficient and brighter arc light was developed for use in lighthouses.

During the siege of Paris (1870–1871), an improved arc light was developed as a searchlight. By 1876, some lights featured a silvered glass reflector, which was the forerunner of modern searchlight mirrors. In the winter of 1881–1882, the Imperial Austrian Navy won a naval battle in the Bay of Cattaro by combining use of searchlights with machine guns. An English fleet used searchlights in 1882 to prevent Egyptians from erecting artillery batteries at Alexandria. Later, French and British forces landed troops under searchlights. By 1886 British naval maneuvers at Milford Haven demonstrated that squadron searchlights could blind and confuse gunners on shore and reduce their firing effectiveness.

In fall 1903, the U.S. Atlantic Fleet conducted joint maneuvers with the Army at the eastern entrance of Long Island Sound. As the fleet neared Fort Michie, all its searchlights were concentrated suddenly on the fort upon a signal from the flagship. The fort was lit so plainly that movement of individual soldiers could be readily seen, and the fleet reached the sound without a shot fired from the fort's main batteries. Officers in the

Searchlights became important means of signaling and operations in the late nineteenth century as improved electric technology allowed the use of bright, focused beams. Here, the cruiser USS Philadelphia is playing her searchlights on USS Alarm (left) and USS Vesuvius in this 1892 watercolor by Fred S. Cozzens. (U.S. Naval Historical Center)

fort reported they were so blinded by the concentrated light that they could see nothing.

By 1907, the value of searchlights was widely recognized. One new use was to illuminate attacks by fast torpedo boats by blinding firing crews on targeted ships. Other uses were to detect enemy ships at greater distances, as a signaling device over considerable distance, and to illuminate where landing parties were to go ashore. Searchlights also were most helpful in locating and signaling the presence of the enemy during the Battle of Jutland (1916), where German searchlights appeared to be technically superior to those used by the British.

During the early days of World War II, searchlights again played a valuable role. The Royal Navy had remarkable success using searchlights in the Battle of Matapan (1941). During the Battle of Guadalcanal (1942), a U.S. destroyer lit up a Japanese cruiser just as the cruiser lit the destroyer, which fired five torpedoes, one scoring a hit. The Navy later achieved some success in blinding kamikaze pilots attempting night attacks.

The advent of radar soon confined searchlight use at sea largely to use as signal blinkers. There were 24-inch and 12-inch searchlights, as well as a smaller, handheld Aldis signal light, which was very effective in sending messages to airplanes. While limited largely to operator speed, blinkers provided an invaluable, reliable, and often secure means for close-range message traffic within fleets and convoys during both day and night. While technological advances continue, the blinker light, like its daytime partners, the flaghoist and the two-flag hand semaphore, still keeps sailors and commanders well informed.

David L. Woods

See also Aldis Lamp; Jutland, Battle of (1916); Lights and Beacons; Night Signals

Sources

Boghosian, Ernest. 1956. "History of Naval Searchlights." *Journal of the American Society of Naval Engineers* 69 (August): 3.

Bureau of Steam Engineering. 1918. "Signaling Apparatus." In *Searchlights and Signal Lights*. Washington, DC: U.S. Navy Bureau of Steam Engineering.

Semaphore (Mechanical Telegraphs)

Two common words in much early signaling—"telegraph" and "semaphore"—have often been misused. The Greek words *teele*, meaning "at a distance," and *grapho*, meaning "to write," combine logically to form the term "telegraph." Likewise, the Greek *seema*, "a sign," and *phero*, "to bear, or to carry," form the highly popular signal term "semaphore." The term "telegraph" has described many ancient signal systems, and several all but forgotten large networks of mechanical telegraphs, as well as various means of electric telegraphy. While all these systems had the same purpose (rapid communication over a distance), each was physically different. Likewise, while "semaphore" was often used as a synonym for the mechanical telegraph, it gained lasting popularity as a descriptor for one-man, two-flag signal systems, as well as a large number of multishaped, fixed, and partially mobile signal systems employed from sea to shore, aboard ship, or on land for military use—and which still exist in railroad applications. "Tele-

graph" is also used as a verb, while "semaphore" is normally a noun.

This entry focuses on the use of mechanical systems for signaling over distances on land. Wooden shutters or arms (which could be moved to arrange different prearranged patterns to designate letters, numbers, or even words or phrases) were mounted on one or more wooden or metal poles or structures. These mountings, in turn, were usually found on the tops of buildings, church steeples, old fortifications, or specially built towers of either wood or stone. Prior to the development in the mid-1800s of the electric telegraph, they were the most sophisticated and rapid means of communicating information over considerable distance. But they were also expensive to build (signaling towers or stations had to be within the line of sight of two other such stations, typically not more than 20 miles or less apart) and to operate (one or more trained operators at each site who knew the code and how to operate the sometimes complex devices), and were largely limited to daytime operation in clear weather conditions (when operators in one tower could see others). The high cost of their construction and operation limited semaphore telegraph application to government and military entities. Frenchman Claude Chappe was first to devise a workable optical semaphore or telegraph that gained widespread practical application. With four brothers, he transmitted successfully from Paris to Bulon in March 1791. He used a 30-foot post, with a movable, 14-foot regulator at the top. There were also two shorter, movable indicators. This system did not spell, but in various positions indicated a word, phrase, or number of a word or phrase. Initial success of the line from Paris to Lille led to rapid expansion after 1795, and especially after Napoleon took power, as Strasbourg, Brussels, Boulogne, Amsterdam, Milan, and Mantua were added. Telegraph lines reached hundreds of miles north, south, east, and west from Paris by 1815. By 1844, and the arrival of the electric telegraph, 534 mechanical telegraph stations connected twenty-nine of Europe's largest cities. Meanwhile, Irishman Richard Edgeworth was working on a military "tellograph," as was a Swede, Abraham Edelcrantz, who erected ten large tabletop devices that could be moved either to follow military forces or in case it was necessary to hide them. As reduced by Lord George Murray to only six tabletops, the British Admiralty established shutter telegraph lines (with stations from 3 to 10 miles apart) from London to Portsmouth

between 1796 and 1816. Plymouth was added in 1806 and Yarmouth in 1808. Others in Britain who tried to adapt similar systems for mobile land use were Reverend John Gamble (whose very effective system was rebuffed by the Admiralty) and Lieutenant Colonel John Macdonald.

A semaphore line following a different track of closer stations and using a semaphoric system devised by Sir Home Riggs Popham and Sir Charles Pasley, was developed from the Admiralty in London to the Royal Navy base at Portsmouth from 1822 to 1847, along with an uncompleted branch to Plymouth from 1825 to 1831. Later, Popham simplified his land telegraph to something akin to modern railroad semaphores. His

This semaphore signaling device, aboard the battleship USS Utah around 1915, could send ship-to-ship signals across limited distances to supplement flag or radio signals. The horizontal arms could move to represent different letters. (Library of Congress)

three movable pieces could send numbers and letters. A portable land system much like Popham's remained in use within the U.S. Army through 1916, at which time a more portable one-man, two-flag semaphore system took over.

Geoffrey Wilson's *The Old Telegraphs* summarizes the near worldwide glut of similar semaphore, mechanical, and optical telegraphic systems during these decades. In addition to the three best-known systems and the several pioneers already mentioned, he comments on more than a half-dozen others in the British Isles; a coastal semaphore in France in addition to the Chappe system, which was extended to Italy, Switzerland, and the Netherlands; two each in Germany and Sweden; one each in Denmark, Norway, Spain, Portugal, and South Africa; and several systems in Russia.

Simple semaphore systems found several decades of use aboard ship, known as masthead semaphores. U.S. Navy Admiral Bradley Fiske devised such a system as a junior officer. Various systems of cones, forms, shapes, and drums were devised by many for use aboard merchant ships and in the navies of at least Britain, the United States, Prussia, and Austria. By 1920, these somewhat complex concepts of optical signaling by shape had been largely superseded by other methods, including a signalman with two small, portable semaphore flags—which on occasion continues even today.

David L. Woods

See also Chappe, Claude (1763–1805); Edelcrantz, Abraham (1754–1821); Fiske, Bradley A. (1854–1942); Flags; Human Signaling; Popham, Home Riggs (1762–1820); United Kingdom: Royal Navy

Sources

Burns, Russell W. 2004. "Semaphore Signalling." In *Communications: An International History of the Formative Years*, 29–55.
Stevenage, UK: Institution of Electrical Engineers.
Chappe, Ignace V. J. 1840. *Histoire de la Telegraphie*. AuMans, France: Ch. Richelet.
Holmes, T. W. 1983. *The Semaphore: The Story of the Admiralty-to-Portsmouth Shutter Telegraph and Semaphore Lines, 1796 to 1847*. Ilfracombe, UK: Arthur H. Stockwell.
Mallinson, Howard. 2005. *Send It by Semaphore: The Old Telegraphs During the Wars with France*. Ramsbury, UK: Crowood Press.
Wilson, Geoffrey. 1976. *The Old Telegraphs*. Totowa, NJ: Rowman & Littlefield.
Woods, David L. 1965. "Mechanical Telegraphs and Semaphores." In *A History of Tactical Communication Techniques*, 13–29. Orlando, FL: Martin-Marietta (reprinted by Arno Press, 1974).
Woods, David L., ed. 1980. *Signaling and Communicating at Sea*. 2 vols. New York: Arno Press.

Semi-Automatic Ground Environment (SAGE)

By 1948 the Soviets were developing nuclear weapons and the aircraft to drop them on American cities. Effectively countering an airborne attack when the attackers could approach from a wide variety of directions over an area covering thousands of miles was seen as a critical problem. The solution was the Semi-Automatic Ground Environment (SAGE), a network of twenty-three computerized command-and-control centers located in the United States and Canada that operated from 1959 until 1983. Telephonically connected computers at these centers allowed the North American Air Defense Command (NORAD) to detect approaching Soviet aircraft. Controllers could then direct and coordinate response by interceptor aircraft or air-to-ground missiles. Until its replacement, SAGE formed a large part of the total NORAD air defense effort in the 1960s and 1970s.

Work on SAGE began in the late 1940s. The first part of the problem, the short range of radar stations, was mitigated by installing many of them to cover potential paths of approach. Second, the amount of data from these stations could not be processed manually. By this time, though, a computer existed, the Whirlwind, developed at the Massachusetts Institute of Technology. Whirlwind, it was hoped, could process this data in time for decisions to be made. A prototype system connecting the Whirlwind to radar stations was developed that proved the concept well enough to encourage developers. Through the early to mid-1950s, SAGE was developed. In 1959, the first SAGE Center was installed, and four years later, the entire system was operating.

Each site contained two computers, designated as Whirlwind II and later as AN/FSQ-7, one as primary and the other on a "hot standby" basis. As was typical of the time, these computers were huge: each weighed about 275 tons with approximately 50,000 vacuum tubes. Data were presented to the users on a cathode ray tube in real time so that decisions were being made based on the nearly instantaneous transfer of data over phone lines using modems.

Had the Soviets attacked, SAGE would have picked up their aircraft on a radar. Information indicating the aircraft's location, height, and flight path would have been conveyed to a SAGE Center, which would convey information to both NORAD command and to air defense units. Through the ensuing battle, all information would pass through the centers at the same time that further radar reports, if there were subsequent attacks, would be tracked and processed as well.

SAGE was a huge design, manufacturing, implementation, and operations effort. It successfully combined existing technologies as well as new ones. It operated with a high degree of reliability and provided large amounts of information processed quickly and in such a way as to allow intelligent decisions to be made about air defense. It also provided technologies that would form the basis for civilian air traffic control. On the most immediate basis, SAGE apparently succeeded as a deterrent by its very presence. There were no attempts to attack the United States by Soviet bombers, and some of the credit must be given to the system. It has, however, been questioned as to whether it would have worked in a real attack: At least once an Air Force exercise penetrated the defenses.

Robert Stacy

See also Airplanes; Bell Telephone Laboratories (BTL); Computer; Telephone

Sources

Everett, R. R., et al. 1958. *SAGE, A Data Processing System for Air Defense.* Bedford, MA: MITRE.

Everett, Robert R., ed. 1983. "Special Issue: SAGE (Semi-Automatic Ground Environment)." *Annals of the History of Computing* 5: 4.

Gray, Colin S. 1972. *Canada and NORAD: A Study in Strategy.* Toronto: Canadian Institute of National Affairs.

Radomes, Inc. "SAGE Documents." [Online information; retrieved December 2006.] http://www.radomes.org/museum/sagedocs.html.

Redmond, Kent C. 2000. *From Whirlwind to MITRE: The R&D Story of the SAGE Air Defense Computer.* Cambridge, MA: MIT Press.

Signal Book

A signal book is typically issued by an agency—usually, though not always, a Navy—to include all the means of signaling and their meanings. It differs from a code-book in that the signals are not intended to be secret, merely efficient. There have been many kinds of signal books. In the earliest days of flaghoist usage, most flag signal codes were issued by flag (commanding) officers to a squadron or larger body of ships under his command, and each admiral had his own. The term "signal book" commonly applies to this usage. At the same time, how-ever, an entire fleet or navy might also issue a signal book that contained more signals and hundreds of written meanings for vari-ous combinations of flags. The term "signal book" was common, but "book of signals" was also used. As the merchant class began to use extensive signaling (at first by sema-phore, later by telegraphy), it too developed signal books, usually referred to and pub-lished as *International Code of Signals* vol-umes. These were typically issued by each nation. As ciphering came into use to pre-vent enemy reception of signals, books of code (codebooks) began to appear. Unlike signal books, these had little to do with signals and nothing to do with signal flags. They continued in use through World War II, and designated officers got out the code-book to decode messages usually sent by wireless in the Navy or by line on land. Codebooks could be made up of numbers, of letters, or might feature both. Each number or lettered group meant a given word—which the codebook revealed. Ulti-mately, there were codes on top of these codes to take every fifth word for true mean-ing, or various patterns of word substitu-tion that were preplanned by various correspondents.

David L. Woods and Christopher H. Sterling

See also Code, Codebook; Code Breaking; Flag-hoist; International Code of Signals (ICS)

Sources

Department of the Army. 1916. *U.S. Army Signal Book.* Washington, DC: Government Printing Office.

U.K. Royal Navy. n.d. *HMS Manual of Instruc-tion of Army Signalling.* London: His Majesty's Stationery Office.

U.K. Royal Navy. 1918. *Handbook of Signalling.* London: His Majesty's Stationery Office.

U.S. Navy Hydrographic Office. 1931. *Interna-tional Code of Signals, American Edition— Visual.* Washington, DC: Government Printing Office.

Signal Rockets

Rockets carrying colored explosive signals (much like modern fireworks) allow simple messages to be sent for considerable distances as the rocket's achieved altitude can often be seen for miles, depending on terrain.

Signal rockets may have been used in China in ancient times, a spin-off of their development of both gunpowder and crude rockets. Sir William Congreve (1670–1729) developed a rocket light ball that shot into the air and slowly descended on a small parachute, allowing a light to be seen for several minutes. Marine rockets were devel-oped by the early eighteenth century. Per-haps the best example of marine signal rocket use occurred in April 1912 when the foundering *Titanic* shot off numerous emer-gency rockets to try to attract the attention of a nearby vessel—to no avail.

Signal rockets were one mode of commu-nication included in an 1840 U.S. Army ord-nance board manual. A signal rocket announced the start of the American Civil War (1861) in Charleston Harbor. Signal corps on both sides used chronosemic, or timed, rocket signals. Use of color signals sent at predetermined intervals could signal fairly complex messages. The modern Very pistol is a descendent of such rocket signals.

World War I saw extensive use of signal rocket communications. The Germans and French both utilized searchlight shells early in the war. Tracer shells were also used early on, their (usually) red path communicating to the ground artillery how close their firing was getting to the target. After 1917 signal rockets came into more general use. Some made use of colors to communicate Morse code, with red indicating a dot and white or green a dash. Smoke rockets were often used during the day when colors could not be easily discerned. Schermuly line-throwing rockets were used in World War I to shoot telephone lines along or across trench lines rather than risking men to do the same job.

Rocket signals featured many drawbacks. Experience in World War II suggested that simple signals were usually the most successful, whether communicated by color or the pattern of rocket explosion—or both. The meanings of various signals could vary as they were often peculiar to individual commands. As noted in many conflicts, visibility of rocket signals was apt to be overrated by inexperienced personnel. They could not be successfully used in wooded country. Sometimes when clouds are low, rockets throw out their signals above the clouds, making them invisible to the ground. In mountainous areas rockets may well not attract the attention of the observing party unless the observers have a comparatively unobstructed view.

Christopher H. Sterling

See also Artillery/Gunfire; Lights and Beacons; Night Signals

Sources

Cyberheritage. "Schermuly and His Rockets." [Online information; retrieved March 2006.] http://www.cyber-heritage.co.uk/schermuly/.

Woods, David L. 1965. "Pyrotechnic Signals." In *A History of Tactical Communication Techniques*, chap. 6. Orlando, FL: Martin-Marietta (reprinted by Arno Press, 1974).

Signal Security Agency (SSA, 1943–1949)

The Signal Security Agency (SSA) was a new name introduced in 1943 for the U.S. Army Signal Corps' Signal Intelligence Service (SIS), which had been organized in 1930. SIS remained a minor bureau until the late 1930s. The opening of World War II brought a rapid increase in staff, and in 1942 its operations were moved to Arlington Hall, a former women's college near Washington DC. The following year SIS, already renamed the Signal Intelligence Division, was again renamed the Signal Security Division, the Signal Security Service, and finally the Signal Security Agency.

The old SIS working arrangements involved State Department–style country desks (staff arranged by country). SSA adopted a new workflow pattern based on the type of task being executed, whether statistical analysis, deciphering, or code reconstruction. In 1943, using this new system, Arlington Hall was intercepting more than 380,000 messages per month, about half of them Japanese military traffic.

Cooperation with Britain's Government Code & Cipher School (GC&CS) was a key element in SSA's operations. In March 1944, arrangements were made for more comprehensive distribution of intelligence information among the Allies. This agreement followed a 1942 SIS-Canadian arrangement under which Ottawa passed intercepts of

Vichy French diplomatic traffic to Washington. Another agreement, reached in May 1943, ratified United States–United Kingdom working-level arrangements in place since April 1942 that allocated general responsibility for global monitoring of enemy military communications. Under these agreements, SIS/SSA focused on Japan's traffic while GC&CS worked chiefly on German codes. The 1944 agreement, known as the "BRUSA" (or sometimes "UKUSA") agreement, extended the cooperation to involve other Allied powers and covered the exchange of raw radio intercepts, cryptanalysis techniques, deciphering solutions, and other technical data. Direction of these cooperative efforts rested with SSA. Soon both Australian intercepts of Japan's military traffic, monitored in Brisbane and Darwin, and British monitoring material based on German transmissions were being exchanged through SSA communications facilities.

Beginning in early 1943, SIS/SSA code breakers prioritized work on Japan's military, diplomatic, and administrative traffic in the Far East. The Purple cipher machine, used by Japan's diplomats, had been largely penetrated in 1940, but Japan's military traffic remained a major problem. By the end of 1943, breakthroughs were achieved in decoding Imperial Japanese Army messages, and in 1944 SSA Purple experts were transferred to work on military codes.

SSA led America's efforts to accelerate the decryption of intercepted traffic and the search for decryption solutions. While Britain's GC&CS developed the Colossus computer to sort German military messages encrypted by the "fish" codes, SSA employed a sophisticated microfilm-based machine, the 5202. By comparing strips of microfilmed message traffic, 5202 reported coincident appearances of coded message elements, and operators were able to attack multiple encryption permutations using the machine.

By summer 1945 SSA had eleven intercept stations, located at Vint Hill Farms, Virginia; Two Rock Ranch, California; Indian Creek Station, Florida; Asmara, Eritrea; Fort Shafter, Oahu, Hawaii; Amchitka in the Aleutian Islands; Fairbanks, Alaska; New Delhi, India; the island of Guam; Tarzana, California; and Bellmore, New York. The stations operated twenty-four hours daily, monitoring some 300 foreign transmitters. Using these and intercepts and material shared by the Allies, SSA code breakers routinely worked on about 350 different cryptosystems deployed in the traffic of at least sixty different governments or political entities.

The Allies' wartime signals intelligence (SIGINT)–sharing agreements continued into the postwar era, and eventually covered open radio broadcasts as well as encrypted transmissions. SSA remained the principal U.S. agency involved in monitoring efforts, although the Navy, the newly organized U.S. Air Force, and the Office of Strategic Services each fielded smaller monitoring and cryptanalysis operations.

The reorganization of American intelligence operations in the late 1940s soon engulfed SSA. In 1949 it was amalgamated into the Armed Forces Security Agency (AFSA), along with Navy and Air Force SIGINT entities, and placed under the U.S. Joint Chiefs of Staff. In 1952, AFSA was placed under civilian control of the U.S. secretary of defense, renamed the National Security Agency, and moved to Fort Meade, Maryland.

Laura M. Calkins

See also Arlington Hall; Bletchley Park; Enigma; Fort Meade, Maryland; Government Code &

Cipher School (GC&CS, 1919–1946); Magic; National Security Agency (NSA); Office of Strategic Services (OSS); Rowlett, Frank B. (1908–1998); Signals Intelligence (SIGINT); Turing, Alan Mathison (1912–1954); Ultra; World War II

Sources

Aldrich, Richard J. 2000. *Intelligence and the War Against Japan: Britain, America, and the Politics of Secret Service*. Cambridge: Cambridge University Press.

Alvarez, David, ed. 1999. *Allied and Axis Signals Intelligence in World War II*. London: Frank Cass.

Alvarez, David. 2000. *Secret Messages: Codebreaking and American Diplomacy, 1930–1945*. Lawrence: University of Kansas Press.

Haufler, Hauvie. 2003. *Codebreakers' Victory: How the Allied Cryptographers Won World War II*. New York: New American Library.

Smith, Michael. 2000. *The Emperor's Codes: The Breaking of Japan's Secret Ciphers*. Harmondsworth, UK: Penguin Books.

Signals Intelligence (SIGINT)

Signals intelligence (SIGINT) is one of four important sources of intelligence information. The oldest and most traditional of the four is human intelligence (now dubbed HUMINT), and the others include imaging intelligence (IMINT) and measurement and signatures intelligence (MASINT). SIGINT is composed of two different categories of intelligence collection: communications intelligence (COMINT), or the practice of collection and analysis of communications (of whatever type and source) from foreign countries, and—since about World War II—electronic intelligence (ELINT), the collection of information from electromagnetic signals other than communications signals. This includes foreign instrumentation sig-

nals intelligence (FISINT) and its subset, telemetry intelligence (TELINT). Information collected from nonimaging radars (RADINT) is a subset of MASINT.

In the United States, each of these intelligence streams of information is the responsibility of different federal agencies: SIGINT is the province of the National Security Agency (NSA); HUMINT is a shared responsibility of the Central Intelligence Agency and the Defense Intelligence Agency (DIA); IMINT is the responsibility of the National Geospatial-Intelligence Agency; and MASINT is conducted by DIA.

No matter what source is used, SIGINT poses a basic problem for military planners: By its very nature, the information is perishable (it is valuable for a short time), yet too direct a response to SIGINT information can inadvertently give away the fact that enemy codes are being read.

Origins

The collection of COMINT has been a common practice as long as people have communicated with each other. One of the most famous efforts was the Geheim Kabinets-Kanzlei in Vienna, Austria. This "Viennese Black Chamber" of the 1700s intercepted mail and then supplied intelligence to the emperor and also sold information to other governments. Similar organizations were established by other governments to gather information that would further their national objectives.

Once communications moved from the written word to the telegraph and subsequently the telephone and radio, the problems associated with collecting intelligence increased. Telegraph and telephone lines could be intercepted, but only if they crossed the territory of the nation intercepting the transmissions, where wires could be tapped.

Introduction of radio communications meant that listening stations located elsewhere could monitor the signals being sent to and from military forces, government offices, and foreign embassies.

During World War I (1914–1918), all of the combatant nations established organizations to gather intelligence from the signals transmitted by their enemies. Listening, analyzing, and sometimes jamming enemy radio signals became a basic part of military operations. Lack of proper signals procedures cost the Russians the Battle of Tannenberg (1914) when Germany read Russia's military orders. Closely contested trench warfare led to SIGINT results by simple induction. Large organizations were necessary to effectively collect, decipher, analyze, and distribute the information collected. Beginning in June 1917, the U.S. War Department's Military Intelligence Division (MI-8), directed by Herbert O. Yardley, conducted cryptographic operations.

Following the war, MI-8 became the Cipher Bureau and was jointly funded by the War Department and the State Department. In 1929, the organization lost much of its funding when Secretary of State Henry L. Stimson famously pronounced that "Gentlemen do not read each other's mail." Yardley's organization was closed, and on 24 April 1930, the Army established its Signals Intelligence Service (SIS). The U.S. Navy's World War I cryptologic bureau had closed in 1918, and beginning in 1924, Navy COMINT activities were carried out by OP-20-G, which soon turned its attention to breaking Japanese naval codes.

World War II

The years leading up to World War II (1939–1945) marked the inception of electromechanical machine-generated codes and ciphers, making the job of code breaking much more complex. The major achievement of the Army's SIS in the immediate pre–World War II period was the breaking of the Japanese diplomatic (Purple) codes. Polish, British, and eventually American SIGINT was an important factor in the Allied victory in 1945.

In England, the primary task of the Government Code and Cipher School (GC&CS), located by late 1939 at Bletchley Park, was to break German machine-generated ciphers. The two major, and most famous, successes were the breaking of the Enigma and more complex Lorenz ciphers. Messages sent in both ciphers were encrypted using extremely sophisticated machines. The Germans believed that the Enigma messages were unbreakable, and more than 200 variants were identified, not all of which were broken. This process of interception, decryption, and analysis was dubbed Ultra.

Two electromechanical inventions aided the breaking of numerous German codes. Alan Turing further developed a Polish machine called the Bomba, which could simulate the actions of Enigma machines and provided a high-speed check of all potential settings. Once the settings were determined, a message could be decrypted. The Lorenz codes were broken by early 1942, but it took weeks to work out the proper settings to decrypt each message. In March 1943, design work began on a machine that would reduce the time required to break "fish" messages. The Colossus, a pioneering computer, was operational at Bletchley Park by January 1944 and allowed decryption of Lorenz messages in hours rather than weeks. In May 1943 a formal agreement to share Ultra information with the United States was signed. The British observed one essential element of any successful SIGINT program by maintaining the secret that they had broken the German codes. Indeed, the breaking of the German ciphers remained a secret until 1974, and details of the effort were still being revealed in the 1990s.

One successful factor involved in safeguarding communications was the use of Navajo "code talkers" by the U.S. Marines during World War II. Because Navajo is an extremely complex unwritten language and was spoken only on the Navajo lands of the U.S. Southwest, no Japanese knew the language (the Japanese chief of intelligence reported after the war that Japan was unable to break the Marine "code"). Another factor was that Allied electric cipher machines were not broken by the Axis powers. American reading of Japan's army, navy, and diplomatic codes was dubbed Magic. Army and Navy code breakers worked (and sometimes even cooperated) in the effort, and results were shared with the British under the agreement between the two nations.

Cold War

The United States formed the Armed Forces Security Agency (AFSA) in 1949. The new organization was responsible for conducting communications intelligence and communications security activities within the military. Because it lacked a central agency for cryptologic activities, however, AFSA was unable to perform its mission effectively. Consequently, the military as well as nonmilitary cryptologic activities became a part of NSA, established in November 1952. The British continued their GC&CS and later renamed it the Government Communications Headquarters (GCHQ).

The beginning of the Cold War shifted the focus of the SIGINT activities of the Western nations. Large listening posts were established around the border of the Soviet Union

and its allies, but the vast distances meant that the coverage was less than adequate. Attempts were made to overfly the territory, but such flights were dangerous, increased international tension, and were thus rare.

The development of satellites offered the opportunity to monitor communications without the dangers associated with overflights. NSA is responsible for the collection and analysis of information collected by a system of satellites. The first constellation of American SIGINT satellites, known as Rhyolite, consisted of three or four satellites in geostationary orbit, launched in the early 1970s. The second group, launched in the late 1970s, was designated Chalet or Vortex. The third generation, known as Magnum, was launched in the late 1980s.

Each series of satellites incorporated the most recent advances in technology to collect more and more information. One of the most notable improvements was in the size of the antennas, which increased with each generation. The larger the antenna, the more low-powered transmission can be intercepted and the transmitter more accurately located.

Development of computers with increased speed, capacity, and capabilities added to the ability to analyze SIGINT interceptions. At the same time, the computers also increased the ability of those charged with developing codes to protect information. NSA operated one of the first Cray supercomputers to manage and analyze the vast amount of information collected from a wide variety of SIGINT sources. Likewise, the British GCHQ uses similar computer resources consisting of the latest Cray machines and high-end Sun workstations.

One part of the SIGINT process that has not changed is the role of the human analyst. Interpretation of the information captured by SIGINT efforts remains labor intensive. Perhaps 10,000 people worked at Bletchley Park during World War II. In 1997, it was reported that just one NSA monitoring station (at Menwith Hill in Yorkshire) employed more than 1,200 civilian and military personnel. It has been rumored that NSA employs more mathematicians than any other employer in the world. Analysis of SIGINT is usually done in a secure location in order to protect the expertise and knowledge of the analysts from falling into enemy hands.

In addition to breaking and analyzing SIGINT, both NSA and GCHQ develop the ciphers and other items necessary to protect the communications of their respective governments. Codes and ciphers must be changed or upgraded regularly—any country has to operate under the assumption that other nations are using computers to break into its communications.

Tommy R. Young II

See also Arlington Hall; Bletchley Park; Chicksands; Code Breaking; Code Talkers; Driscoll, Agnes Meyer (1889–1971); Electric Cipher Machine (ECM Mark II, "SIGABA"); Enigma; Friedman, William F. (1891–1969); German "Fish" Codes; Germany: Naval Intelligence (*B-Dienst*); Government Code & Cipher School (GC&CS, 1919–1946); High-Frequency Direction Finding (HF DF); Magic; Mauborgne, Joseph Oswald (1881–1971); National Reconnaissance Office (NRO); National Security Agency (NSA); Nebraska Avenue, Washington DC; Op-20-G; Polish Code Breaking; Room 40; Rowlett, Frank B. (1908–1998); Safford, Laurance F. (1890–1973); Signal Security Agency (SSA, 1943–1949); SIGSALY; Tannenberg, Battle of (1914); Turing, Alan Mathison (1912–1954); Ultra; Welchman, Gordon (1906–1985); Y Service; Yardley, Herbert O. (1889–1958)

Sources
Alvarez, David J., ed. 1999. *Allied and Axis Signals Intelligence in World War II*. London: Frank Cass.

Bamford, James. 2002. *Body of Secrets: Anatomy of the Ultra-Secret National Security Agency*. London: Government Communications Headquarters.
Kahn, David. 1996. *The Codebreakers: The Comprehensive History of Secret Communication from Ancient Times to the Internet*. 2nd ed. New York: Scribner's.
Pincock, Stephen. 2006. *Codebreakers: The History of Codes & Ciphers*. New York: Walker & Co.
Richelson, J. 1985. *The U.S. Intelligence Community*. Cambridge, MA: Ballinger.
Singh, Simon. 1999. *The Code Book: The Science of Secrecy from Ancient Egypt to Quantum Cryptography*. New York: Doubleday.

Signals Research and Development Establishment (SRDE)

The British Signals Research and Development Establishment (SRDE) was for many decades the primary research center for the Royal Corps of Signals.

SRDE antecedents date to 1903, when the army chose two men to develop telegraphy and posted them to the School of Military Engineering at Chatham, in Kent. Later that year, the work and equipment were transferred to a telegraph battalion at Aldershot. A reorganization of the Royal Engineers Telegraphs followed in June 1905, when wireless telegraph companies were formed. In 1911, the unit was renamed the Experimental Wireless Telegraphy Section Royal Engineers.

In August 1914, many of the officers of the Royal Engineers Signal Service, who had been seconded from a variety of other regiments, were recalled to their parent units, which meant that the Experimental Wireless Telegraphy Section lost most of its military personnel. Those civilians and remaining military staff were transferred to Woolwich Dockyard and became involved with the bulk manufacture of line and telephone equipment. Toward the end of 1915 emphasis turned again to wireless. In September 1916, the unit, now with a staff of some 150, was transferred to a new site at Woolwich Common and was renamed the Signals Experimental Establishment (SEE). SEE worked with communications, both wireless and line, for the army, which included the Royal Flying Corps. This work included design, manufacture, and experimentation. Later additions included the Searchlight Experimental Establishment (an early ancestor of the Royal Signals and Radar Establishment Malvern) and the Experimental Bridging Establishment (a forerunner of the Military Engineering Experimental Establishment). Some of the subjects studied included vacuum tube circuitry, test and specification, line and radio telephony, microphones, direction-finding radio compass, standards, jamming, tank communication, aircraft communication, switchboards and generators, batteries and accumulators, and enemy equipment. Following the formation of the Royal Air Force and the Air Ministry in April 1918, some personnel transferred to Biggin Hill (south of London) to form the Wireless Experimental Establishment, Air Ministry. In 1922 this unit moved to the Royal Aircraft Establishment at Farnborough, Hampshire, where it was redesignated the Radio Department.

By the early 1920s, SEE had become a mainly civilian establishment, controlled by Royal Signals officers. Between the wars SEE suffered from shortage of staff and funding. This placed severe limitations on what it could do. One of the tasks that SEE advanced was the use of vacuum tube transmitters and receivers in mobile radio stations. SEE also pioneered radio telephony for tanks and vehicles generally and assisted in the specification and test of improved valves and components. It also devised a "transceiver" and was involved in telephony, telegraphy, power supplies, and aerial systems.

Partial evacuation of SEE to Warnham Court in Sussex took place early in 1941, because of the bombing of Woolwich. SEE was renamed the Signals Research and Development Establishment (SRDE) in 1942, and the next year, the entire operation was concentrated at Christchurch, Hampshire, at a site vacated by the Air Defence Research and Development Establishment. An outstation was opened in the nearby New Forest at Broomy Lodge because of a new requirement to keep highly classified work more than 10 miles from the coast.

SRDE absorbed the radio laboratory of the Polish Research Institute, which was staffed by the Polish army. This brought particular expertise on mine detection to supplement that already existing at SRDE. Work on improved components and reliability came to prominence, with particular application to jungle and tropical warfare. A tropical testing outstation was established in Nigeria in 1944. Development of the multichannel microwave link set was one of the major SRDE successes during the war. By mid-1945, total strength of SRDE was about 1,500.

In the 1950s, SRDE undertook development of "active" infrared viewing systems for the army. This helped to foster a new and effective industry in Britain for the design and production of image intensifiers, with associated electronics and fast optical systems rugged enough to withstand battlefield conditions. SRDE was to become involved in organizing groups of equipment into viable operating systems. It dealt both with highly specialized radios (such as Larkspur and Clansman) for combat, and with very large systems (such as Project Ptarmigan) for rear tactical areas. Worldwide strategic systems using cable, high-frequency radio, and satellites (Project Skynet) were also studied. This led SRDE into the computer and digital information technology age. Among the postwar achievements of SRDE was the development of a mobile tactical satellite communications earth station. SRDE established considerable expertise in computer software and in the use of computers offline to simulate the operation of complex systems.

In 1976, the Royal Signals and Radar Establishment was formed by the amalgamation of three defense establishments: the Royal Radar Establishment at Malvern, SRDE at Christchurch, and the Services Electronics Research Laboratory at Baldock. By the end of 1980, the unified establishment was concentrated at Malvern, with outstations at former airfields at Defford and Pershore.

Cliff Lord

See also United Kingdom: Royal Corps of Signals

Source

Lord, Cliff. 2003. *The Royal Corps of Signals: Unit Histories of the Corps (1920–2001) and Its Antecedents.* Solihull, UK: Helion.

SIGSALY

A secure means of voice communication between London and Washington DC, SIGSALY (the odd name did not stand for anything) was a secret telephony system designed by Bell Telephone Laboratories. It was used from 1943 to 1946 and remained secret for another three decades.

When fighting began in Europe in 1939, a voice-scrambling radio coding system called A-3 (also developed by Bell Labs) was employed for voice communications between

military and political leaders in Washington and London. But it was not robust enough to resist concerted code breaking. Indeed, it was suspected of being read by the Germans (as was the case, in nearly real-time terms, from a listening post in the occupied Netherlands). Thus users were told they could probably be overheard and to speak in guarded terms. A better solution was needed, and as quickly as possible.

In 1936 Bell Labs had begun to develop a voice code (vocoder) system that could break up speech into digital bits on the sending end to be reconstructed at the receiving end. While many patented systems existed by 1939, none offered truly secure messaging. Bell Labs personnel continued research into a workable secure voice system that would allow encoded telephonic communications over great distances. By 1942 the basic work on a system that dissected and then reassembled twelve different audio channels had been perfected and was demonstrated for the U.S. Army.

The new system utilized an entirely random means of generating key signals that used no repeats, thus making it unbreakable. The key signals generated electrical noise, which could be recorded on hard vinyl 16-inch phonograph records that ran for twelve minutes. These were carried by courier to the sending and receiving locations and were destroyed after a single use—in other words, a key was only used once. Thus many of the special recordings were made, each one destroyed after its specified use. Both the sending and receiving ends, however, had to be absolutely synchronized for up to an hour for effective communication. This was accomplished by a mechanical timing device on each terminal. The process was complex and expensive, but it did work and was never broken. (Due to the buzzing sound some of the equipment could make, SIGSALY was often called "The Green Hornet," after a popular radio drama of the time.)

An Army contract was placed with Bell Labs for two systems in 1942, and they were placed into service in mid-1943. The new system allowed for protected communications via actual conversations and the first military conference among top Army officers took place between London and Washington on July 15, 1943. The London terminal was built into a basement of the Selfridge department store while the telephone terminal was in the Cabinet War Rooms located underground about a mile away. The Washington terminal was in the Pentagon. Eventually twelve SIGSALY terminals were developed and located in Paris, Algiers, Honolulu, Guam, Australia, one on a ship following General Douglas MacArthur's shifting headquarters and, toward the end of the war, in reoccupied Manila in the Philippines. Together, they supported some 3,000 voice conferences between military and political leaders, including President Franklin Roosevelt and Prime Minister Winston Churchill. After the war, units were also located (somewhat ironically) in the former Luftwaffe headquarters in Berlin, the I. G. Farben headquarters building in Frankfurt that served as the center of the occupation, and in Tokyo.

The 350 personnel of the special 805th Signal Company operated the terminals in teams of fifteen at each location, which required twice the maintenance time (16 hours) compared to actual usage (eight hours a day). The large and cumbersome SIGSALY equipment filled a room with vacuum tube equipment and required extensive power supplies and cooling. The forty racks of relevant equipment weighed some 55 tons. A half-century later the same capa-

bilities could be contained in a briefcase, with space left over.

Christopher H. Sterling

See also Bell Telephone Laboratories (BTL); Code, Codebook; Code Breaking; Modulation; Signals Intelligence (SIGINT); Spread Spectrum

Sources

Bennett, William R. 1983. "Secret Telephony as a Historical Example of Spread-Spectrum Communications." *IEEE Transactions on Communications* Com–31 (1): 98–104.

Boone, J. V., and R. R. Peterson. 2000. *The Start of the Digital Revolution: SIGSALY Secure Digital Voice Communications in World War II.* Fort Meade, MD: National Security Agency.

Fagan, M. D., ed. 1978. "Secure Speech Transmission." In *A History of Engineering and Science in the Bell System: National Service in War and Peace (1925–1975)*, 291–317. New York: Bell Telephone Laboratories.

Mehl, Donald E. 1997. *SIGSALY: The Green Hornet—The World War II Unbreakable Code for Secret High-Level Telephone Conferences, The Beginning of the Digital Age.* Kansas City, MO: Donald E. Mehl.

Silicon Valley, California

Located primarily in Santa Clara and San Mateo counties, among the many communities north and west of San Jose south of San Francisco, the former fruit orchards of the central California coast became known as "Silicon Valley" at least by the early 1970s, named after the main element used in integrated circuits. The region has for decades been a major center of electronics research, design, and manufacturing, much of it funded by military communications equipment contracts.

At least four waves of technology entrepreneurs created what would become Silicon

Valley. Firms such as Federal Telegraph had manufactured radio equipment before World War I—Federal was a major radio supplier to the U.S. Navy. But most radio and electronics patents were controlled by General Electric and the Radio Corporation of America, both in New York. Thus, the first wave of change, stretching from the 1920s into early World War II, centered on those interested in radio (both broadcasting and shortwave) who helped to expand an existing small vacuum tube–manufacturing base, building on an active amateur radio community. Companies such as Eitel-McCullough (founded in 1934 to make radio tubes), Hewlett-Packard (begun in a garage in 1937), and Litton Industries (1932) were formed and soon grew. Stanford University faculty, especially engineer Frederick Terman, played a substantial role in the university's formation of one of the first university-centered research "parks" in the country. Engineers and others were drawn to the region by their ties to the university or the wonderful weather and then-inexpensive lifestyle of the area.

After substantial electronics growth and technical developments during World War II, the microwave tube business found a base in the region, supported largely by growing Cold War defense contracts for radar and other complex equipment. Varian Associates (formed in 1948) became a major player, manufacturing complex specialized microwave and klystron vacuum tubes. The Korean War (1950–1953) accelerated the defense focus for most research and manufacturing in the region.

From the mid-1950s on, the region centered increasingly on silicon-based electronics components, beginning with Shockley Semiconductor (formed in 1955) and Fairchild Semiconductor (1957), .which in turn spun off many other firms, among them Intel, based on solid state electronics. Military procurement—for communications, radar, and the growing military missile and civilian space programs—helped to speed development of more reliable and miniaturized components. Defense contracts remained dominant until the early 1960s, when changes in defense procurement policies led to dramatic change. Sharply reduced defense orders and tighter contract accounting led to company retrenchment, layoffs, and mergers, and surviving firms in the region increasingly diversified to commercial markets. Another downturn in the early 1970s was caused by cuts in defense spending for electronics systems and resulting manufacturing overcapacity. Once again, many firms retrenched or got out of the business.

Consumer electronics demand for Silicon Valley solid state products expanded strongly in the early 1970s. Later in the decade, Silicon Valley experienced a fourth wave as the region focused on computer hardware and (later) software, driven first by the almost overnight success of Apple (started in another garage, in 1976), and then Oracle and many other firms based on the soon-thriving personal computer business. Standardization and mass production led to sharp drops in component prices at the same time speed and capability increased (Moore's Law). Defense contracts remained an important, but no longer dominant, feature of Silicon Valley economic life.

Silicon Valley today is a center of electronics innovation, sparking the creation of many other "valleys" elsewhere in the United States and the world.

Christopher H. Sterling

See also Computer; Kilby, Jack St. Clair (1923–2005) and Noyce, Robert Norton (1927–1990); Miniaturization; Solid State Electronics; Transistor; Vacuum Tube

Sources

Enochs, Hugh. 1962. *Electronics Research in the Space Age: The Story of Electronics Research and Development in the Palo Alto-Stanford Area.* Palo Alto, CA: Chamber of Commerce.

Lécuyer, Christophe. 2006. *Making Silicon Valley: Innovation and the Growth of High Tech, 1930–1970.* Cambridge, MA: MIT Press.

Leslie, Stuart. 1993. "How the West Was Won: The Military and the Making of Silicon Valley." In *Technological Competitiveness: Contemporary and Historical Perspectives on the Electrical, Electronics, and Computer Industries,* edited by William Aspray. New York: Institute of Electrical and Electronic Engineers.

Morgan, Jane. 1967. *Electronics in the West: The First Fifty Years.* Palo Alto, CA: National Press Books.

Rogers, Everett, and Judith K. Larsen. 1984. *Silicon Valley Fever: Growth of High-Technology Culture.* New York: Basic Books.

"Silicon Valley: How It Really Works," 1997. *Business Week,* August 18, 64–110.

Single Channel Ground and Airborne Radio System (SINCGARS)

The Single Channel Ground and Airborne Radio System (SINCGARS) is a family of FM combat radios that operate on the VHF spectrum band. They were designed as the primary means of tactical command and control for infantry, armor, and artillery units, and, more recently, airborne units as well. They replaced a variety of radios used by U.S. forces in Vietnam in the late 1960s and early 1970s.

Design began in 1974 to create a modular voice system with maximum equipment commonality, and production began in 1983. Prototype SINCGARS ground radios passed initial tests in January 1988, and production deliveries began at that time. An airborne version of the SINCGARS radio followed in the mid-1990s. The SINCGARS radio system operates on any of the 2,320 channels between 30 and 88 MHz. When in the jam-resisting frequency-hopping mode, the unit can send or receive, but not both at once. More than a quarter-million receivers (at an average unit value of about $6,500) have been produced.

SINCGARS uses a transceiver designed for easy transport in a backpack or vehicle. Designed initially for voice traffic, improved SINCGARS radios can transmit and receive voice, tactical data, and record traffic messages and are consistent with North Atlantic Treaty Organization interoperability requirements. SINCGARS radios provide improved data capability and forward error correction for low-speed data, as well as a global positioning system interface and Internet controller, which allows SINCGARS to interface with a variety of military computers.

The SINCGARS System Improvement Program of the 1990s made the radios more compatible with the Internet. SINCGARS equipment (there are easily a dozen different types) has been sold to a number of American allies. By the early 2000s, the SINCGARS system was beginning to give way to digital replacement systems within the Global Information Grid system, especially the Joint Tactical Radio System.

Christopher H. Sterling

See also Global Information Grid (GIG); Global Positioning System (GPS); Internet; Jamming; Joint Tactical Radio System (JTRS); Mobile Communications; North Atlantic Treaty Organization (NATO) Communications & Information Systems Agency; Radio

Sources

Department of the Army. 1996. *Talk II-SINCGARS Multiservice Communications Procedures for the Single-Channel Ground and Airborne Radio System.* Army Field Manual

11–1. Washington, DC: Government Printing Office.

Olive-Drab.com. "Military Radios: SINCGARS." [Online information; retrieved April 2006.] http://www.olive-drab .com/od_electronics_sincgars.php.

Single Sideband (SSB)

Single sideband (SSB) is a type of AM radio transmission first experimentally developed in 1915 by what later became Bell Telephone Laboratories. It was perfected and used by AT&T for transatlantic radio-telephone calls starting in 1927, and over the next decade to increase domestic network capacity.

By eliminating the duplicated sideband and carrier from a radio transmission, required bandwidth is reduced by half. This allows far more radio communication within a given segment of spectrum. Because the carrier radio frequency is also filtered out, there is no transmission unless information is being sent, a factor especially useful for covert operations protected by radio silence. Efficiency is also notably improved. But there is a cost for these gains—the improved performance adds complexity to the design of the equipment. Therefore SSB is normally employed in already expensive radio devices or cases where the gains are vital—such as in military situations.

At first, however, the necessary equipment for SSB was both bulky and expensive—and potential benefits of the technology were often ignored in an era before spectrum conservation became important. SSB was taken up by a few amateur radio operators in the mid-1930s and by more of them after World War II to help reduce crowding. Collins Radio introduced a mechanical filter in 1952, and soon SSB was coming came into widespread amateur use as transmitters became more stable.

Military SSB applications developed more slowly. Western Electric developed a four voice-channel SSB transmitter by 1938. It was purchased by both the U.S. Army and U.S. Navy for military high-frequency fixed-station communications. The Naval Research Laboratory developed key elements of a workable and economically viable system in the mid-1950s. By the early 1960s the U.S. Navy, United Kingdom Royal Navy, and others had almost completely converted to SSB radio operation both at sea and on shore. By international agreement, ships completed after 1973 had to be equipped with SSB equipment.

Christopher H. Sterling

See also Modulation; Naval Research Laboratory (NRL); Radio Silence; Spectrum Frequencies; Spectrum Management

Sources

Benton, Mildred. 1956. *Single-Sidebands in Communication Systems: A Bibliography.* Washington, DC: Naval Research Laboratory.

Single Sideband for the Radio Amateur. 1954. West Hartford, CT: American Radio Relay League.

Site R

Site R is the shorthand name for the Alternate Joint Communications Center (AJCC), a facility north of Washington DC that houses the Alternate National Military Command Center.

As Cold War tensions increased after World War II, U.S. military authorities sought a location to which they could be evacuated in the event of a Soviet nuclear attack on the Washington DC area. In 1950, Raven Rock Mountain, near the border dividing Maryland and Pennsylvania, was chosen as an optimal site. It was located near Camp (later Fort) Albert C. Ritchie, which had housed intelligence activities during World War II. The "alternate Pentagon" project took more than $35 million to construct. A significant technical achievement was the excavation of a half-million cubic yards of rock in less than a year. More than three miles of tunnels are associated with the complex. Equipped with emergency power and advanced filtration, the center is three stories high and can withstand immense blast effects. Connecting transmitter stations were built at Greencastle, Pennsylvania, and Sharpsburg, Maryland. By 1953 the secret AJCC was established.

Between 1953 and 1971, the Army's communications element at Site R (for Raven Rock), a part of the Army Joint Support Command, provided support for the facility. This unit eventually became the Directorate of Telecommunications, remaining under the Fort Ritchie commander. After 1976, it underwent a series of reorganizations and changes in name and reporting structure. Most base operations activities were removed from its mission, leaving its focus on communications. With the increased importance of AJCC throughout the 1960s, Fort Ritchie's primary mission evolved into installation support for Site R—indeed, after the early 1970s, Fort Ritchie became a premier provider of military information services in general. In 1971 the Army Strategic Communications Command relocated to the post, followed within three years by the Army Information Systems Engineering Command–Continental United States and related units.

For a few years in the late 1970s, a considerable improvement program was implemented at Site R, and a Department of Defense special projects office extended the tunnels and began construction of a survivable command-and-control center. By the 1990s, more than 2,000 personnel worked at Fort Ritchie, primarily in support of Site R. In spite of this activity, the 1995 base closure commission listed Fort Ritchie for deactivation, and it closed as an active base on 1 October 1998. Its federal employees were relocated to an Army depot in Letterkenny, Pennsylvania, or to Fort Detrick, Maryland, about 30 miles away. Site R (which continued to function) came under the command of Fort Detrick in late 1998.

Currently located at Site R are computer services that support the Joint Staff and the Office of the Secretary of Defense, as well as other defense elements. Technical support at the facility includes switching, transmission, distribution, and power operations. Atop Mount Quirauk, overlooking the Fort Ritchie site, are other related and active military communications facilities. The military services maintain an emergency operations center at Site R that is active twenty-four hours a day.

In early 2002, the Bush administration acknowledged publicly that Vice President Dick Cheney had been secreted away at Site R during the weeks following the 11 September 2001 attacks. As with the military at Site R, the legislative branch had its continuity of government facility underneath a wing of the posh Greenbrier Resort in West Virginia, though it closed soon after the *Washington Post* exposed its existence in 1992. Another secure operating facility is maintained by the Federal Emergency Management Agency at Mt. Weather, located near Bluemont, Virginia.

Kent G. Sieg

See also Underground Communication Centers

Source
Bamford, James. 2004. *A Pretext for War: 9/11, Iraq, and the Abuse of America's Intelligence Agencies.* New York: Doubleday.

Smoke

Signaling by the use of puffs of smoke from a fire is a form of long-distance visual communication developed by both Native Americans and personnel manning signal towers along China's Great Wall—and probably used by others.

By covering an open fire with a blanket and quickly removing it, a puff of smoke can be generated. Adding green or wet material to an existing fire can create more smoke. With some training, the sizes, shapes, and timing of smoke puffs can be controlled, though this often requires two to four men to control the blanket. Depending on weather conditions and time of day, of course, such puffs may be observed by anyone within its visual range.

With this in mind, signaling was often done from heights—natural or manmade—to maximize the viewable distance. The towers along the Great Wall of China are one example of artificial signaling stations that used, among other methods, smoke signals. In the Tang dynasty (618–907 CE) wolf droppings were used in signal fires in the belief that such smoke would rise straight up without dispersing in air currents.

There was no generally understood or standardized code for smoke signals. Signals were more often of some predetermined pattern developed and shared by a given tribe or even a specific sender and receiver. Smoke signals tend to convey only very simple messages and are thus a very limited form of communication, and one useful only in hours of daylight.

Colored smoke was an additional option, though some of the problems involved are evident in a nonmilitary application—as in the practice of announcing the election of a new pope for the Catholic Church—and the occasional confusion caused thereby. Smoke was a logical choice for communicating papal election results, because church tradition called for cardinals to burn their ballots after each vote to maintain conclave secrecy. But there have been occasional troubles in discerning whether the smoke was black (no pope choice made) or white (a new pope has been elected).

Smoke can also be used to obscure enemy communications or to send deceptive signals. Smoke bombs can be sent by means of artillery or dropped from airplanes.

Smoke signals are still used today in fire and rescue work as well as some military missions. Use of smoke signals is one feature of survival training in the military. Indeed, one can purchase colored smoke signal devices and smoke grenades on the open market. The term "smoke signals" has also entered the lexicon to indicate a message that may not be very clear.

Christopher H. Sterling

See also Ancient Signals; Color; Fire/Flame/ Torch; Great Wall of China; Hadrian's Wall; Native American Signaling

Sources
Acker, Lewis F. 1939. "Communication Systems of the American Indians." *Signal Corps Bulletin* 103 (January–March): 63–70.
Conway, Emmet A. "Smoke Signal Bowls—The First WWW." [Online article; retrieved September 2005.] http://www.oldeforester .com/sigbo.html.

Department of the Army. 1984. *Deliberate Smoke Operations*. Field Manual 3–50. Washington, DC: Government Printing Office.

Department of the Army. 1992. "Mortar Smoke Operations." In *Tactical Employment of Mortars*, Appendix C. Field Manual 7–90. Washington, DC: Government Printing Office.

Woods, David L. 1965. *A History of Tactical Communication Techniques*. Orlando, FL: Martin- Marietta (reprinted by Arno Press, 1974).

Solid State Electronics

The solid state electronics revolution began with the late 1940s' development of the transistor and became possible with the innovation of integrated circuits a decade later. Modern solid state technology was driven by defense needs and has had an immense impact on all military electronics.

The notion of solid state electronics had been suggested in principle in the early 1950s and was of central interest to the armed services. If workable, such systems promised huge benefits of special value to military applications—robustness, lower weight and power requirements, and far greater capacity. The U.S. Air Force contracted with Westinghouse in 1959 to experiment with "molecular electronics." The Army Signal Corps was already developing a "micro-module" project to shrink component size across a variety of military needs. Research and development work was underway at many companies, usually funded by Air Force or Navy contracts.

Over the space of a few months in 1958–1959, Jack Kilby (1923–2005) of Texas Instruments and Robert Noyce (1927–1990) of Fairchild Semiconductor independently developed similar notions of an "integrated" circuit (IC), for which Kilby belatedly shared the Nobel Prize in 2000. They both determined that squeezing all elements of an electrical circuit—transistors, connections, and other electronic devices—onto a tiny silicon chip could be accomplished and would save considerable space while speeding up signal processing speed. Eliminating the need for individually handwired connections between transistors and other elements would also greatly increase circuit reliability, reduce manufacturing cost, and save time. The potential for further IC improvement was huge.

These substantial benefits became a vital part of the Cold War era of miniaturization being driven by developing missile technology. Thus the Air Force was immediately interested in the IC innovation and provided research funding vital to further research. The Navy was not interested at first, and the Army was uncertain how the IC breakthrough might fit into its existing projects. U.S. electronics manufacturers, many of them focused on the thriving market for military equipment (inadvertently leaving the consumer electronics field open to foreign firms), were initially more skeptical, but were soon won over by the obvious IC benefits. The first products using ICs (which then cost between $50 and $100 each) were in mass production by 1962.

Today's solid state electronics rely on use of the microscopic, sandwichlike IC "chip," which is a careful microscopic arrangement of transistors, other devices, and all of their connections. Development of the steadily improving IC chip virtually created the modern computer industry, transforming once room-size vacuum tube–powered machines into today's more capable and flexible array of solid state mainframes, minicomputers, and personal computers. Gordon Moore of Intel expressed his famous "law" more than four decades ago—that every eighteen months the capacity of the chip will double while its price drops. Moore's Law has been most publicly evident in the improving capacity and declining price of personal computers—from the Intel 8086 chip of 1978 (featuring 29,000 transistors), to early twenty-first-century chips with more than 50 million transistors.

Paced by steady improvements in solid state technology, the worldwide electronics market has grown from $29 billion in 1961 to nearly $1.2 trillion by the early twenty-first century—it may well become the world's single largest industry.

Christopher H. Sterling

See also Kilby, Jack St. Clair (1923–2005) and Noyce, Robert Norton (1927–1990); Miniaturization; Transistor

Sources

Braun, Ernest, and Stuart Macdonald. 1982. *Revolution in Miniature: The History and Impact of Semiconductor Electronics.* New York: Cambridge University Press.

Malone, Michael S. 1995. *The Microprocessor: A Biography.* Santa Clara, CA: TELOS/Springer-Verlag.

Morris, P. R. 1990. *A History of the World Semiconductor Industry.* London: Peter Peregrinus.

Queisser, Hans. 1988. *The Conquest of the Microchip.* Cambridge, MA: Harvard University Press.

Reid, T. R. 1984. *The Chip: How Two Americans Invented the Microchip and Launched a Revolution.* New York: Simon and Schuster.

South Africa

The Boer republics were quick to embrace modern communications technology at the end of the nineteenth century, establishing proficiency in telegraphy, telephony, and semaphore. They also understood the interception of phone and telegraph lines and were able to put this skill to good use in their war against the British. Wireless technology was well understood, but sets that they had ordered were impounded by British authorities when the equipment arrived.

The South African Republic's State Artillery had a field telegraph section from 1890 to 1896 and members were also trained in use of the heliograph. The section was re-formed again in 1898, and was finally disbanded in 1902 after the Boer War. The Orange Free State also had a telegraph section from 1898 to 1902.

Signaling detachments in Natal were amalgamated with the Natal Telegraph Corps in 1903. This comprised two units of fifty men each. During the Zulu Rebellion of 1905–1906, the unit was reinforced by post and telegraph staff. Correspondingly, the Transvaal Signalling and Field Telegraph Section was formed in 1903 and administered as part of the Transvaal Light Infantry until 1907, when it became independent and was renamed Transvaal Signalling and Field Telegraph Corps. In 1908, it amalgamated with the Volunteer Company of Military Signallers, which had been established on 14 September 1904. By 1910 it had a strength of fifty, largely composed of government telegraphists.

In 1912, the South African Field Telegraph and Postal Corps was formed. On 1 July 1913, both the Natal and Transvaal signaling units were absorbed into the Active Citizen Force while retaining their original titles. With establishment of the Permanent Force in 1913, arrangements were made for a signalling branch at the South African Military School at Tempe. The Permanent Force Engineer Signal Service was formed in 1914 and lasted until 1922. South Africa sent 900 signalers to

Europe and 1,500 to East Africa. In 1914, the Natal Telegraph Corps amalgamated with the Transvaal Signalling Corps, and a year later the units were incorporated into the South African Field Telegraph and Postal Corps. The corps was disbanded on 30 September 1915. British signaling equipment was used by all of these South African units.

The Cape Fortress Engineers included a signal section from 1914 to 1920, when the unit was absorbed by the South African Engineer Corps. Fortress Engineers provided communications at fortified static defense installations such as those at Cape Town. This included defense, telephone, and electrical duties. In 1922, it became the Fortress Engineers and Signal Section and after 1931 the 4 Company, Cape Garrison Artillery. The unit was disbanded in 1933.

On 1 November 1923, the South African Corps of Signals (Active Citizen Force) was established. An alliance with the Royal Corps of Signals lasted from 1926 until 1961. This close tie ensured that the latest doctrine and technology was available to the South African Corps. During World War I, the corps served in the advance through East Africa, and also in North Africa, Italy, and Madagascar. Tactics and equipment were similar to other dominions of the time and were based on British-manufactured wireless and associated equipment. A number of signal units were raised for service abroad, and a brigade signal company saw service in Madagascar.

Of a more diverse nature was the Special Signal Services (SSS), formed at Johannesburg in 1939, to deal with radio direction finding, as radar had become a signals responsibility. The first radar set was successfully designed and built in South Africa and tested at the University of the Witwatersrand in 1939. SSS operated radar sites in Kenya, in the Sinai Desert, and along the South African coast. After the end of the war, SSS was demobilized.

On 18 October 1946, the South African Corps of Signals (Permanent Force) was formed. Citizen Force Signals remained to provide communications in conjunction with the Permanent Force in times of emergency. A small signal corps was built up to provide communications for the various commands within the country and support for the infantry and armored divisions. During the 1970s and 1980s, the corps expanded to meet the perceived external military threat to South Africa. The corps was on operational duty along the Angolan border. With the political changes of the 1990s, the army was reorganized and the corps downsized. In 1999, the Command and Management Information Division was established to meet the changing demands of the twenty-first century.

Cliff Lord

See also Boer War Wireless (1899–1902); United Kingdom: Royal Corps of Signals

Sources

Buchan, John. 1920. *The History of the South African Forces in France*, 279–316. London: SA Signal Company (reprinted by Imperial War Museum and Battery Press, 1992).

Jacobs, F. J., et al., eds. 1975. *Suid-Afrikaanse Seinkorps/South African Corps of Signals*. Publikasie No. 4. Pretoria: Dokumentasiedi-ens S.A.W.

Lord, Cliff, and Graham Watson, 2003. *The Royal Corps of Signals: Unit Histories of the Corps (1920–2001) and Its Antecedents*. Solihull, UK: Helion.

Spanish-American War (1898)

This short but "splendid little war" of a few months proved more important to subsequent world politics than to warfare. It pushed the United States into the league of world powers while dropping Spain from the rank it had held for more than three centuries. From the standpoint of signal systems, the entire war might well be summed up by the early observation of the commanding U.S. Army general in Cuba—the portly General William R. Shafter—who said he did not want men carrying signal flags, but rather men with guns. The good general, as many leaders before and since, failed to realize the vital importance of accurate two-way communication, as well as apparently being unaware of the brawn required to wave for hours the 4 × 4-foot wig-wag flags used most commonly in Army signals. There were also several historic firsts in many Army signal modes from the use of field telephones, field telegraphy, and observation signal balloons. It took less than a month for the Navy to organize a coast signal system of 230 coast observation stations equipped with binoculars and telescopes connected by telegraph and telephone to central headquarters. Couriers and messenger animals and pigeons were also widely used in Cuba. The irony of this war's mixed signal success seems best illustrated by the continuing frustration of Navy Secretary John D. Long, who attempted to exercise personal command and control over naval units in Cuban waters—most unsuccessfully concerning the "Flying Squadron" led by Commodore Winfield Scott Schley. Secretary Long sent telegrams that were quickly transmitted to the naval base at Key West, Florida. There, however, his messages had to be typed out on paper, placed in a sealed envelope, and handed to the commanding officer of the next available small naval patrol craft, which then had to seek out Commodore Schley's flagship, the USS *Brooklyn*, somewhere in the waters surrounding Cuba.

There was no radio, radar, or scouting aircraft to locate Schley's squadron—merely a week-old (or older) report on where that squadron had been and where it might be heading. It was natural for Long to expect that his telegrams would elicit a response in a short time. Instead he soon concluded Schley was a dilettante, simply unreliable, disliked orders—or all three. A growing lack of trust plagued the careers of both men.

Off Santiago, Cuba, naval fighting began with a simple flaghoist signal to disregard movements of the commander in chief, Admiral William T. Sampson (who was aboard the flagship USS *New York*, moving to Siboney for a prearranged meeting with Shafter). The USS *Brooklyn*'s morning signal record logs sixteen key signals (three via wig-wag and thirteen flaghoist) reporting "enemy ship's escaping," "clear for action," "close up," "the enemy has surrendered," "report your casualties," and "this is a great day for our country."

Communications on Cuba included an Army Signal Corps company with fifteen red and fifteen white signal flags, each four feet square; another ten red and ten white signal flags of half that size; fifteen three-piece poles 12 feet long (for flag waving); eight heliographs; six aluminum signal lanterns; ten telescopes; ten pairs of field glasses; six compasses; four sets of telegraph instruments; and ten dry-cell batteries. After the war, the unit commander concluded that there had never been a campaign in which electric communication was more imperative. Visual signals were used in the Santiago, Cuba, campaign only between ships and between ships and shore. The communications situation was different in the Philippines. Admiral George Dewey used both Army and Navy wig-wag flags for signaling during the Battle of Manila Bay. Flags also provided communication under fire during the fight for Manila while telephone lines were being laid.

Yet despite Long's frustrated efforts at control from Washington DC, this remained a war where field commanders relied—as before—largely on their own judgment. The Army knew intelligence reports on the location of the Spanish fleet came from a spy in the Havana telegraph office, and so they believed them. But naval commanders Sampson and Schley, knowing only that these reports came from the Army, remained skeptical. Dewey, on his own and much farther away in the Philippines, had more success than anyone with the possible exception of Rough Rider Colonel Theodore Roosevelt, whose men took San Juan Hill without any major Signal Corps contribution.

David L. Woods

See also Couriers; Horses and Mules; Human Signaling; Pigeons; Semaphore (Mechanical Telegraphs); Telegraph; Telephone

Sources

Freidel, Frank. 1958. *The Splendid Little War.* Boston: Little, Brown.
Giddings, Howard A. 1900. *Exploits of Signal Corps in the War with Spain.* Kansas City, MO: Hudson-Kimberly Publishing.
Schley, W. S. 1910. *Forty-five Years Under the Flag.* New York: Appleton.
Woods, David L. 1965. *A History of Tactical Communication Techniques.* Orlando, FL: Martin-Marietta (reprinted by Arno Press, 1974).

Spectrum Frequencies

The use of radio spectrum frequencies is vital to modern military communications and to most aspects of electronic warfare, whether analog as in the past, or digital as now and increasingly in the future. Military needs often conflict with civilian demand and must be resolved through spectrum management policies. Several frequency bands are especially important for national security needs.

Electromagnetic radiation is the propagation of energy (including radio signals of all kinds) that travel through space in the form of waves. Radio spectrum is that relatively small portion of the overall electromagnetic spectrum that carries these radio waves. And only part of that radio spectrum is technically and economically viable for communications use, though the proportion of usable spectrum is increasing all the time—as is demand for it.

Many spectrum terms have passed into general usage, including very high frequency (VHF) and ultra-high frequency (UHF), where, among many other services, one finds broadcast television channels (a "channel" is a set of frequencies used to transmit a single outlet of any given service) and FM radio. But so have terms defined by their wavelength, such as shortwave and microwave. Converting these to the actual frequencies they occupy, we find shortwave services use the HF, or high frequency, band, and microwave is found in the UHF and higher bands.

Historically, spectrum use for telecommunication purposes began with the first wireless experiments in the late 1890s in the lower ranges of what are now called the medium frequencies (MF), or about 300 kHz to as high as 3 MHz. As technical knowledge of spectrum capabilities and how to use them improved, driven especially by technological developments during the two world wars, ever higher bands of spectrum became viable for military and later civilian communications use.

Major recent changes include far more efficient use of spectrum by many users (such as

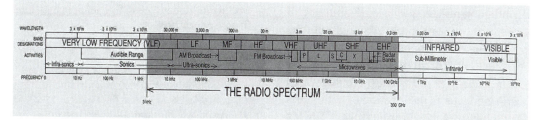

This chart shows the radio spectrum frequencies that are used by both military and civilian applications. The shaded portion is useful in telecommunications and most frequencies are shared, though some are reserved for military use. Spectrum never "wears out" but can be overused, leading to interference and other problems. (U.S. Department of Commerce)

digital compression of signals to use less spectrum) and far greater use of optical fiber cable links (replacing spectrum-using microwave and satellite links for point-to-point communications), which allow massive capacity while freeing up spectrum for other uses. Furthermore, a greater degree of spectrum sharing among commercial and military users is likely, as is commercial provision of many military links.

Frequencies are measured in terms of thousands of cycles per second, or Hertz (named after the German physicist who first transmitted wireless signals in the late nineteenth century). These are expressed in thousands (kilohertz, or kHz), millions (megahertz, or MHz), or billions (gigahertz, or GHz) of cycles per second. For convenient reference, over time we have come to divide spectrum into specific "bands" that share propagation characteristics (how they carry a wave or signal). The different bands vary in their mode of propagating signals. Lower frequencies (the LF through HF bands) utilize groundwaves, where radio waves move along the surface of water or earth, or indeed through surface layers. These would include AM or shortwave radio services. Medium frequencies (MF band) use both groundwaves and sky waves (where radio waves

are reflected back to earth from upper levels of the atmosphere, much as a flashlight will reflect off a mirror), as in AM radio broadcasting. As the radio waves travel very different paths, this can lead to interference, especially at night. Higher frequencies (those at VHF and above) use direct (line of sight) waves. These different characteristics are important to understand when considering specific applications. The following is a description of frequencies, listed from lowest to highest.

ELF (extremely low frequencies) range below 30 kHz and are of special value to the Navy. Making use of ground conductivity, these frequencies are used for submarine communication from large transmission facilities that require huge buried antenna arrays.

HF (high frequencies) range from 3 to 30 MHz and are widely used for international shortwave radio broadcasting, such as the Voice of America. Some third-generation mobile digital telephones have apparently caused interference with military satellites in the 1,755–1,850 MHz band—just one example of growing problems of too many services attempting to use limited frequencies.

VHF (very high frequencies) range from 30 to 300 MHz and are among the most hotly contested frequencies, as they can serve a variety of conflicting needs equally well—but not all of them at any one time. Among military applications in this band are both fixed and mobile services for all three services.

UHF (ultra-high frequencies) are known to most Americans as the location of many television channels; these range from 300 MHz to 3 GHz. Put another way, all radio waves at this range and higher fall into the microwave category.

SHF (super high frequencies) range from 3 to 30 GHz and include many military radar applications such as radar systems of various kinds. Included are the "C" band satellite uplink and downlink channels, and (though higher up) Air Force and Navy "K" band (20–21 GHz) satellite links (that band is restricted by the North Atlantic Treaty Organization to military use). Use above 60 GHz is more difficult due to higher power needs and other costs.

EHF (extremely high frequencies) range from 30 to 300 GHz, are the latest frequencies now being used, and about which more is learned all the time. Radar installations operate in this band. Anything higher verges into infrared spectrum bands.

Even applying spectrum-use labels becomes a security issue because in so doing, users reveal basic mission information (needed to identify any potential or actual radio frequency interference)—and thus can expose system vulnerabilities that should not be communicated outside classified channels. Recognizing this in a post-9/11 world, the spectrum-management process is moving toward greater confidentiality.

Christopher H. Sterling

See also Communication Satellites; Electromagnetic Pulse (EMP); Fiber Optics; Jamming; Meteor Burst Communications (MBC); Microwave; Modulation; National Telecommunications and Information Administration (NTIA); Single Sideband (SSB); Spectrum Management; Spread Spectrum; Tropospheric Scatter

Sources
Defense Science Board Task Force. 2003. *Wideband Radio Frequency Modulation: Dynamic Access to Mobile Information Networks*. Washington, DC: Department of Defense.
Devereux, Tony. 1991. "Frequency Bands of Electromagnetic Radiation, Military History and Importance." In *Messenger Gods of Battle: Radio, Radar, Sonar: The Story of Electronics in Battle*, 80–81. London: Brassey's.
General Accounting Office. 2001. *Defense Spectrum Management: More Analysis Needed to Support Use Decisions for 1755–1850 MHz Band*. Washington, DC: Government Printing Office.
Hurt, Gerald, et al. 1995. *Spectrum Reallocation Final Report*. Special Publication 95–32. Washington, DC: National Telecommunications and Information Administration.
Joint Spectrum Center. Home page. [Online information; retrieved November 2004.] http://www.jsc.mil/.
Kobb, Bennet Z. 1995. *Spectrum Guide: Radio Frequency Allocations in the United States, 30 MHz—300 GHz*. Falls Church, VA: New Signals Press.
Merrill, Albert, and Marsha Weiskopf. 2001. "Critical Issues in Spectrum Management for Defense Space Systems." [Online article; retrieved November 2004.] http://www.aero.org/publications/crosslink/winter2002/02.html.
National Telecommunications and Information Administration. 2003. "United States Spectrum Allocations Chart." [Online information; retrieved August 2005.] http://www.ntia.doc.gov/osmhome/allochrt.pdf.

Spectrum Management

Spectrum management is a process intended to allow the most effective use of the natural resource of electromagnetic (or radio) frequencies by the greatest number and variety of services and users consonant with the need to limit mutual interference. Such management combines technical, economic, and political elements and is nearly always administered by governments, within a regional and global context of spectrum allocations and relevant technical standards. The military services have always been the primary federal government users of spectrum in the United States.

Technically and economically useful radio frequencies, while slowly increasing all the time, make up but a fraction (about 20 percent) of the total electromagnetic spectrum. Most military applications are found in the VHF (very high frequency, or 30–300 MHz), UHF (ultra-high frequency, or 300 MHz to 3 GHz) and SHF (super high frequency, or 3–30 GHz) spectrum bands. Very little spectrum is designated for the exclusive use of the military; rather it is shared with other users, with transmitters separated by distance, time, or frequency to reduce interference. Spectrum management involves three related processes: allocation, allotment, and assignment. "Allocation" means the setting aside of frequency blocks or bands for a specific service and user (private, commercial, government). "Allotment" is the location of specific channels within an allocation to specified locations, while "assignment" is the actual licensing of a transmitter to use an allotment.

American spectrum regulation began with the Wireless Telegraphy Board, convened by President Theodore Roosevelt in 1904. A panel made up of one Army and three Navy officers and a representative of the Department of Agriculture outlined recommendations primarily concerning maritime wireless use. The first global maritime wireless conference had taken place a year earlier in Berlin. At a 1906 Berlin conference, the United States and twenty-seven other powers discussed maritime communication and agreed to establish an international bureau to gather and distribute information on wireless stations around the world. Despite support from the Army and Navy, commercial opposition prevented American ratification of the resulting treaty until 1912.

Initial American wireless legislation came in 1910 with a brief act establishing minimal requirements for the use of radio at sea. In light of the *Titanic* disaster it was strengthened two years later. Later in 1912 a separate Radio Act was the first to deal with allocation of frequencies. By that time government, amateur, and commercial wireless stations were suffering mutual interference. The 1912 law provided the country's first allocations (including 187.5 to 500 kHz for federal, including military, use) and established the Department of Commerce as licensing authority, but granted it no discretion to deny any application. The Navy briefly took control of all wireless transmitters during American participation in World War I, but lost an attempt to continue that role afterward.

Though it remained in force for fifteen years, the 1912 law began to break down in the early 1920s under pressure from newly established broadcasters demanding more spectrum space. It was replaced by the Radio Act of 1927, which divided authority for spectrum allocation between the Federal Radio Commission for commercial users and the Department of Commerce for federal needs. Finally, this was superseded by the Communications Act of 1934, which, though amended, still forms the basis for American spectrum management.

As government use of wireless and thus need for spectrum allocations expanded to more agencies, the Interdepartmental Radio Advisory Committee (IRAC) was established in 1922 to coordinate spectrum use by federal and private users, including burgeoning broadcasting. Housed within the National Telecommunications and Information Administration (NTIA, part of the Department of Commerce) since 1978, IRAC continues to function today, providing essential coordination across nearly two dozen federal agencies (including the armed services) and with the Federal Communications Commission representing all other spectrum users. NTIA has overall responsibility for and management of all federal spectrum allocations, including those for the military.

As telecommunications/electronics assumed an ever more central role in the Army, Navy, and (since 1947) Air Force, so too did the spectrum needs of those services. Even in the 1930s, IRAC focused on growing Army and Navy demands for more spectrum space for tactical purposes. The Army alone was operating some 1,500 transmitters by 1932. These needs expanded exponentially during World War II, and by 1943 some requests were being denied for lack of available spectrum. At the same time war-driven research made technically and economically viable the use of more frequencies in the UHF and higher ranges.

Spectrum-using modes of communication expanded further during both the Korean and Vietnam wars. As the latter wound down in the early 1970s, the Army was operating more than a half-million transmitters (a typical field army using more than 75,000). The Navy and Marine Corps operated about 300,000 transmitters and more receivers on ships, aircraft, and land. The Air Force added about 130,000 transmitters, for a Department of Defense total of nearly a million transmitters and far more receivers. Spectrum frequency needs to support all of this were considerable, and the pace of technological change was increasing demand.

Political pressure on the Department of Defense to give up some of its allocated spectrum space increased after 1970 with the growth of various commercial mobile communication services. Arguments were made that the military was "warehousing" spectrum for possible future use. The conflicts increased as military and civilian spectrum usage needs increasingly focused on much of the same spectrum space. The income-generating potential of spectrum auctions to commercial users during the 1990s added congressional pressure on the military to transfer underused spectrum allotments for use by the commercial sector. This process continued into the early twenty-first century, often stretching over many years to allow time for military users to relocate elsewhere.

The three military services present their spectrum needs through IRAC, through a layered process of supervision by several specialized agencies, beginning with the individual service and coordinated at the Department of Defense level. The deputy undersecretary for command control communications and intelligence has overall responsibility for U.S. military spectrum management policy. The individual services center their spectrum management concerns in either the Naval Electromagnetic Spectrum Center, the Army Communications-Electronics Services Organization, or the Air Force Frequency Management Agency. The U.S. Military Communications-Electronics Board (MCEB) is the main coordinating agency working with these three service entities. MCEB reports to the secretary of defense and the Joint Chiefs of Staff. It guides defense preparation and coordination of technical directives in allocating spectrum allotments received from NTIA.

The Joint Frequency Panel (JFP) is the principal defense coordinating agency for spectrum management and works closely with other federal agencies represented on IRAC. JFP also reviews, develops, coordinates, and implements Department of Defense directives, studies, reports, and recommendation for MCEB. Any service application for frequency allocation must be approved by JFP before funds are authorized for the development of new equipment that will radiate electromagnetic energy. An application is also required for equipment receiving signals, if interference protection is desired. In addition, an assignment in the appropriate frequency band must be obtained from the Frequency Assignment Subcommittee of IRAC prior to the operation of any transmitting equipment for testing, training, or operational use.

Given the complexity of spectrum management, considerable ongoing training takes place. NTIA runs regular spectrum management courses for U.S. and overseas officials. The Army operates the Interservice Radio Frequency Management School at Keesler Air Force Base in Biloxi, Mississippi. The intensive curriculum provides exposure to techniques common to all defense spectrum personnel. Emphasis is placed on national and international regulations and standards with particular impact on the global mission of the American military.

Christopher H. Sterling

See also Electromagnetic Pulse (EMP); International Telecommunication Union (ITU); Jamming; Microwave; National Telecommunications and Information Administration (NTIA); Single Sideband (SSB); Spectrum Frequencies; Spread Spectrum; Wireless Telegraph Board

Sources

Defense Science Board Task Force. 2003. *Wideband Radio Frequency Modulation: Dynamic Access to Mobile Information Networks*. Washington, DC: Department of Defense.

Levin, Harvey J. 1971. *The Invisible Resource: Use and Regulation of the Radio Spectrum*. Baltimore: Johns Hopkins University Press.

National Telecommunications and Information Administration. "Office of Spectrum Management (OSM)." [Online information; retrieved November 2004.] http://www.ntia.doc.gov/osmhome/osmhome.html.

Office of Telecommunications Policy. 1975. *The Radio Frequency Spectrum: United States Use and Management*. Washington, DC: Government Printing Office.

Robinson, John H. 1985. *Spectrum Management Policy in the United States: An Historical Account*. OPP Working Paper Series No. 15. Washington, DC: Federal Communications Commission, Office of Plans and Policy.

Roosa, Paul C., Jr. 1992. *Federal Spectrum Management: A Guide to the NTIA Process*. Special Publication 91–25. Washington, DC: National Telecommunications and Information Administration.

Spies

A vital if clandestine seeker of military information, dating from ancient times, has been the spy. A spy's methods of communicating the information gained are the focus here, for lacking such means, no spy can fulfill his or her function. Many long-used methods, such as secret writing (disappearing ink, hidden messages), concealed messages (in everyday objects such as cigarettes, buttons, batteries, or cosmetics), and the use of dead drops (using a prearranged location for the dropping off and picking up information) are not described here—nor are the many methods used over the years for encipherment of written materials (including one-time pads).

Photographic methods have been one prime method of communicating secret information. Making photos as small as possible (yet readable with sufficient magnification) has been a goal at least since the American Civil War (1861–1865). Microdots are photographs (of messages or copied documents) reduced to be no larger than a period on this page—and often smaller yet. Such microscopic photos are more easily hidden in a variety of ways. The cameras that take such pictures can also be very small and easily hidden—and some have even been carried by birds (or more recently drone aircraft). Application of digital technology in recent years has made the process of making and communicating such tiny pictures even easier.

Since World War I, radio has been an important mode of rapid spy communication. During the interwar years, both German and French intelligence services developed radios that fit within suitcases (not easy in the days of bulky and fragile vacuum tube technology). A prime concern with such radios was ensuring sufficient transmission range—usually a few hundred miles. Many allowed either code or voice messages. Code could be dangerous, as the hand one uses to transmit code varies by individual, making "radio fingerprinting" possible. And radio signals of any kind could always be monitored for content—and often transmitter location. With that concern in mind, easily portable and hidden radios were central to Allied communication with resistance groups (as well as spies) behind German lines in occupied Europe. Many of these were made in separate sections (receiver, power supply, transmitter, plus smaller parts including the antenna, headphones, Morse key, and microphone) to allow greater portability and ease of hiding. Postwar radios could fit into attaché cases.

The post—World War II arrival of transistors and later solid state electronics along with extreme miniaturization allowed the manufacture of very tiny spy radios for the Central Intelligence Agency and other agencies. But their transmissions could still be picked up and traced, leading to the application of burst communication methods (also developed after World War II) so individual transmissions would be of microsecond length, making effective tracing nearly impossible. Another option, especially useful in urban areas, was infrared transmission, which made radio signaling difficult to intercept.

As most modes of electronic communication have steadily evolved from analog to digital, so have options for spy communication. Hacking into (or tapping) computer systems is now a prime means of both national and industrial espionage, as is encoded use of the Internet or digital cell telephones. The National Security Agency is the leading American entity focused on this problem today. On a far less sophisticated level, many so-called spy shops sell various electronic devices usable in low-grade (usually interpersonal) spying efforts.

Christopher H. Sterling

See also Code Breaking; Communications Security (COMSEC); Computer Security (COMPUSEC); Deception; National Security Agency (NSA); Radio Silence; Signals Intelligence (SIGINT); Solid State Electronics; Transistor; Ultra; War on Terrorism

Sources
Bamford, James. 2001. *Body of Secrets: Anatomy of the Ultra-Secret National Security Agency from the Cold War Through the Dawn of a New Century.* New York: Doubleday.
Kahn, David. 1967. *The Codebreakers: The Story of Secret Writing.* New York: Macmillan.
Melton, H. Keith. 1996. "Clandestine Communications." In *The Ultimate Spy Book*, 110–133. New York: DK Publishing.

Polmar, Norman, and Thomas B. Allen. 1997. *Spy Book: The Encyclopedia of Espionage.* New York: Random House.

Pujol, Juan, with Nigel West. 1985. *Garbo: The Personal Story of the Most Successful Agent of World War II.* New York: Random House.

Spread Spectrum

Dating to a World War II innovation, spread spectrum was a military communications application for decades before the technology became commercially available. Military research at the Massachusetts Institute of Technology's Lincoln Laboratory, Magnavox, and Sylvania lead to the first spread spectrum equipment in the early 1950s. Sylvania-developed equipment, for example, was used by the U.S. Navy during the Cuban Missile Crisis of 1962, about the time the term "spread spectrum" (if not the classified technology) began to come into general use. Parallel research on radar systems and a technologically similar concept called "phase coding" also had an impact on spread spectrum development.

Spread spectrum works by transmitting signals that sound like electrical noise, spread over (by rapid switching or hopping) a wide band of frequencies. Indeed, signals are intentionally spread over a much wider band than the information they are carrying to make them more noiselike. Combined, these two features make signals hard to detect, jam, or intercept and thus are invaluable for military signaling. This technique decreases the potential interference to other receivers while achieving privacy. While commercial spread spectrum systems use bandwidths of 10 to 100 times the information rates, military systems have used spectrum widths from 10 to 1,000 times wider.

If the sequence of channel changes is not known to potential adversaries, spread spectrum signals are highly resistant to deliberate jamming. Military radios use cryptographic techniques to generate the channel sequence under the control of a secret transmission security key that only the sender and receiver share. By itself, frequency hopping provides only limited protection against eavesdropping, so military frequency-hopping radios often employ separate encryption devices. U.S. military radios that use frequency hopping include the Single Channel Ground and Airborne Radio System.

The basic elements of spread spectrum were declassified only in the 1980s, allowing the development of commercial applications. Spread spectrum has been recently combined with digital technology for spy-proof and noise-resistant battlefield communications. In civilian life, it is seen most often in cordless phones and wireless local area networks.

Christopher H. Sterling

See also Communications Security (COMSEC); Cuban Missile Crisis (1962); Global Positioning System (GPS); Jamming; Lamarr, Hedy (1913–2000); Mobile Communications; Satellite Communications; SIGSALY; Single Channel Ground and Airborne Radio System (SINCGARS)

Sources

Dixon, Robert C. 1994. *Spread Spectrum Systems with Commercial Applications.* 3rd ed. New York: Wiley-Interscience.

Institute of Electrical and Electronic Engineers. 1982. *Milcom '82: IEEE Military Communications Conference—Progress in Spread Spectrum Communications.* New York: Institute of Electrical and Electronic Engineers.

Malik, R. 2001. "Spread Spectrum—Secret Military Technology to 3G." IEEE History Center. [Online article; retrieved June 2006.]

http://www.ieee.org/organizations/history
_center/cht_papers/SpreadSpectrum .pdf.

Squier, George Owen (1865–1934)

George Squier served as the U.S. Army's Chief Signal Officer from 1917 to 1923 and was an active innovator of communications technology as well as military aviation.

Squier was born in Dryden, Michigan, on 21 March 1865. Though he completed only the eighth grade, after working for two years, Squier entered West Point, graduating seventh in his class in 1887. He then attended Johns Hopkins University and earned a doctorate in electrical engineering in 1893. He entered the Army as an artillery officer and served in the Volunteer Signal Corps during the Spanish-American War. In 1896, the city of Philadelphia, upon the recommendation of the Franklin Institute, awarded Squier the John Scott Legacy Medal for his polarizing photochronograph. In February 1899 he transferred to the Army Signal Corps and rose to major by 1903. With help from Lieutenant Colonel James Allen (chief signal officer from 1906 to 1913), Squier developed a wireless system initially used in April 1899. From 1900 to 1902, Squier commanded the cable ship USS *Burnside* during the laying of the Philippine telegraph cable, which formed the basis for the communication net in the Philippine Islands. He also served as the superintendent of telegraph lines.

In 1905, Squier became assistant commandant of the new Signal School at Fort Leavenworth, Kansas. The inclusion of aeronautics in the curriculum evidenced Squier's own interest in aviation. He was key to the Army Signal Corps' early developments of an aeronautical program. In 1907 Squier transferred to Washington DC as assistant chief signal officer. It was not long after his arrival that Chief Signal Officer Allen created an aeronautical division under the control of his office. Major Squier directed the board, which supervised the Army's trials of Wright brothers' airplanes at Fort Myer, near Washington, in 1908–1909. Squier drafted the Army's original airplane specifications.

During a tour of duty from 1909 to 1911 at the National Bureau of Standards, Squier experimented with the transmission of radio waves along wires, a technique he termed "wired wireless." According to this method, signals could be multiplexed (many verbal messages could be sent simultaneously along the same wire) without the interruption of telephone traffic, part of the basis for modern communications systems. Squier also discovered that voice signals could be transmitted by radio along telephone lines. He demonstrated his multiplex system for Allen in September 1910.

After his 1912–1916 tour of duty as military attaché to London, Lieutenant Colonel Squier headed the Signal Corps' Aviation Section. With Chief Signal Officer George Scriven's retirement in February 1917, Squier became the new chief and was promoted to major general on 6 October 1917. With America's entry into World War I, Squier managed an expanding Signal Corps and its aeronautical and radio programs. The corps made several advancements including airborne radiotelephony, which made it easier for a pilot to communicate with the ground. Squier worked with private industry to perfect radio tubes. These wartime efforts were one basis for the development of radio broadcasting in the 1920s.

Squier remained the Chief Signal Officer until 31 December 1923. He was the inventor of the monophone for broadcasting over telephone wires. In addition to his other inventions, he is credited with developing piped-in music, or what was soon dubbed

"Muzak." In 1919 he was named to the National Academy of Sciences. For his contributions to science, he received the Elliott Cresson Gold Medal and the Franklin Medal from the Franklin Institute. General Squier died at the age of sixty-nine in Washington DC on 24 March 1934.

Kathryn Roe Coker

See also Airplanes; Army Signal Corps; National Bureau of Standards (NBS), National Institute of Standards and Technology (NIST); World War I

Sources

Bache, Rene, 1911. "Many Talk on One Wire." *Technical World Magazine,* March: 32–35.

Clark, Paul Wilson. 1974. "Major General George O. Squier: Military Scientist." Ph.D. diss., Case Western Reserve University, Cleveland.

GeorgeSquier.com. "Who Was Major General George O. Squier?" [Online article; retrieved April 2006.] http://georgesquier .com/george/.

"Multiplex Telephony and Telegraphy by Means of Electric Waves Guided by Wires." 1911. *Proceedings of the American Institute of Electrical Engineers* May: 857–862.

Raines, Rebecca Robbins. 1996. *Getting the Message Through: A Branch History of the US Army Signal Corps.* Washington, DC: Government Printing Office.

Squier, George O. 1933. *Telling the World.* Baltimore: Williams & Wilkins.

Stager, Anson (1825–1885)

Anson Stager directed military telegraphs for the Union during the American Civil War and played important management roles in Western Union and other firms. He also developed the first system of cryptography formally adopted by the American military.

Stager was born in Ontario County, New York, on 20 April 1825. At the age of sixteen, he began to work for Henry O'Reilly, a printer and pioneer in the building and operating of telegraphs. He was placed in charge of O'Reilly's telegraph office at Lancaster, Pennsylvania, in 1846. He later moved to Pittsburgh, and then Cincinnati, Ohio, where he made several improvements in the construction of batteries and the arrangement of wires. In 1852 he was made general superintendent of the principal lines in the American West at that time. After the initial consolidation of the Western Union company in 1856, Stager became general superintendent of operations.

With the inception of the American Civil War early in 1861, Stager was appointed to manage the U.S. Military Telegraph in the Department of Ohio (which included Indiana and Illinois), reporting to General George McClellan. He soon organized military and civilian telegraph lines into an efficient system. He also developed a field telegraph system to follow the Army, sometimes moving upward of ten miles per day. Though he lacked any background in cryptography, Stager soon prepared a cipher by which he could safely communicate with others who had the key (and such people were very few, one reason for the system's success). Consisting of ten numbered cipher systems, it was never broken during the war.

When McClellan took over the Union Army in Virginia after the Battle of Bull Run, he appointed Stager to run his telegraph operations. In November 1861, Stager became general superintendent of the U.S. Military Telegraph (which assumed emergency operation of commercial lines for the duration of the war), reporting by January 1862 directly to Secretary of War Edwin Stanton. Stager remained at this post until September 1868, continuing all the while to also serve as general manager of Western Electric (in what today would be a clear conflict of interest). During the war, the system carried some 3,000 telegrams per day and constructed 15,000 miles of telegraph line, all of which was transferred to Western Union after the fighting ceased. Stager's unit operated in some competition with the separate Army Signal Corps.

In 1869 General Stager returned to Chicago, and, in addition to his duties as general superintendent of the central region of the United States, he promoted related enterprises, among them the Western Electric Company, the largest manufacturer of telegraph equipment in the United States, of which he became president in 1872. He secured a consolidation of the two telephone companies in Chicago and became their president as well as heading the Western Edison electric light company in the same city. Stager died in Chicago on 26 March 1885.

Christopher H. Sterling

See also American Civil War (1861–1865); Army Signal Corps; Code Breaking; Telegraph; U.S. Military Telegraph Service (USMTS)

Sources

Plum, William R. 1882. *The Military Telegraph During the Civil War in the United States.* Chicago: Jansen, McClurg (reprinted by Arno Press, 1974).

Romano, Kevin. "The Stager Ciphers and the U.S. Military's First Cryptographic System." [Online article; retrieved October 2004.] http://www.gordon.army.mil/AC/Wntr02/stager.htm.

Thompson, Robert Luther. 1947. *Wiring a Continent: The History of the Telegraph Industry in the United States 1832–1866.* Princeton, NJ: Princeton University Press.

Strategic Communications Command (STRATCOM)

Operational from 1962 to the late 1970s, the U.S. Army's Strategic Communications Command's (STRATCOM) origins date to early 1945, when the Pentagon established the 9423rd Technical Services Unit, War Department Signal Center (Traffic Operations Branch). It became the U.S. Army Command and Administrative Communications Agency in 1947, and the U.S. Army Communications Agency (ACA) a decade later. On 1 April 1962, ACA merged with the Army's Signal Engineering Agency to form the U.S. Army Strategic Communications Command, which would later become known as STRATCOM. The new agency took charge of all Army communications engineering, installation, operation, and maintenance.

The Cuban Missile Crisis (October 1962) revealed serious flaws in communications between the State Department, American embassies, and the Soviet Union. Post-crisis analysis of communication delays confirmed a need for an upgrade of both interdepartmental and international communication capabilities. As a result, President John Kennedy ordered creation of the National Communications System, and STRATCOM became its Army element. STRATCOM's roles soon included (1) management of strategic mobile communications, fixed signal communications, the Military Affiliate Radio System, frequency interference resolution, and communications equipment research and development; (2) worldwide test and evaluation, maintenance planning, and development of engineering for plant and equipment; (3) acquisition management of automatic data processing equipment for Army use; and (4) supervision of transportation and traffic management of the signal field command.

On 1 March 1964, the Army established the Office of the Chief of Communications-Electronics and discontinued the century-old post of chief signal officer. At the same time, STRATCOM achieved major Army command status with full control of worldwide strategic communications. It expanded with creation of STRATCOM-Europe in July 1964 and STRATCOM-Pacific in September 1964 (adding facilities in Hawaii, Vietnam, Okinawa, Taiwan, and Thailand in November). STRATCOM's growing role in Vietnam led to formation of the 1st Signal Brigade in 1966, which controlled all Army communications-electronics resources in Southeast Asia. Scattered across 200 sites in Vietnam and Thailand, it became the largest combat signal unit ever formed.

STRATCOM headquarters moved from Washington DC to Fort Huachuca, Arizona, in 1967. In 1973, STRATCOM took responsibility for all communications systems at Army installations, including telephone, telecommunications centers, nontactical radio operations, television distribution, and public address systems. As the war increasingly blurred the distinction between strategic and tactical communications, STRATCOM became the U.S. Army Communications Command in 1973 and later the U.S. Army Network Enterprise Technology Command.

Christopher H. Sterling

See also Army Signal Corps; Cuban Missile Crisis (1962); Defense Communications Agency (DCA, 1960–1991); Military Affiliate Radio System (MARS); National Communications System (NCS); Network Enterprise Technology Command (NETCOM); Spectrum Management; Vietnam War (1959–1975)

Source
GlobalSecurity.org. 2005. "Network Command History." [Online information; retrieved December 2006.] http://www.global security.org/military/agency/army/netcom-history.htm.

Submarine Communications

Communicating with submarines at sea has always presented special problems. As sub-marine capabilities improved after the mid-1950s thanks to nuclear power, the vessels could stay deeply submerged for extended periods, making detection of their location nearly impossible. But if they had to rise to the surface for communication, much of that capability disappeared.

During World Wars I and II, the only way a submarine could communicate with its home base was to surface in order to use shortwave or other radio signaling. This made the vessels vulnerable, and after the British broke the German Enigma codes, many submarines were located (and some sunk) through their regular signaling process. After the war, though submarines improved, means of signaling from a land base through deep water remained impossible.

In the late 1950s, to resolve the submarine problem, the Navy proposed an extremely low frequency (ELF) antenna system, which would face strong opposition throughout its proposal and development and into its operational stages. The Navy first became interested in ELF signals in 1958 when it was discovered that low-frequency radio waves could penetrate seawater deep enough to send one-way signals to submerged submarines. Tests in the early 1960s proved the idea to be practical. The original project would have required a grid of cables over 22,500 square miles of northern Wisconsin and the Upper Peninsula of Michigan (an area larger than Belgium and Holland combined), as well as 240 transmitters and 800 megawatts of power, and would have cost billions of dollars to build. In 1969, a more modest replacement, "Project Seafarer," was proposed, relying on newer technology to eliminate the need for such a huge grid. But with both projects, concern over potential harmful effects on fish, birds, and animals, as well as delayed effects on humans, was at the heart of concerted public opposition.

In the end, the further downsized $400-million "Project ELF" became operational in October 1989, consisting of just two transmitters in Wisconsin and Michigan, connected by a 165-mile underground cable. Operated for twenty-four hours a day, each transmitter consisted of a 14-mile-long antenna strung on hundreds of 40-foot poles across dozens of miles of forest. Annual operating costs for both ELF transmitters was $13 million. Consideration was given to a mobile ELF system (using trucks on land or balloons in the air to avoid enemy attack), but cost precluded implementation. The Soviet Navy developed a similar system, called the ZEVS, located on the Kola Peninsula near Murmansk. It was first detected in the 1990s and, unlike the American system, is also used for geophysical research. The British Royal Navy also considered building such a system in Scotland, but decided against it given the high cost.

As is evident from the huge size of the ground antennas used, the ELF communication link was obviously one way. Further, on such low frequency, information can only be transmitted very slowly, on the order of a few characters per minute. Although the actual codes used were secret, the transmissions could be received all over the world. Naturally, when a submarine is on the surface, it can use ordinary radio communications. Today, this usually means use of dedicated military communication satellites (the U.S. Navy calls its system Submarine Satellite Information Exchange Sub-System).

The Navy's ELF system was closed in September 2004, the official explanation being that technological progress in very low frequencies had made use of the huge ELF antenna no longer necessary.

Christopher H. Sterling

See also Communication Satellites; Spectrum Frequencies

Sources
Aldridge, Bob. 2001. "ELF History: Extreme Low Frequency Communication." Santa Clara, CA: Pacific Life Research Center.
Jacobsen, Trond. "ZEVS, the Russian 82 Hz ELF Transmitter: A[n] Extrem[e] Low Frequency Transmission System." [Online article; retrieved April 2006.] http://www.vlf.it/zevs/zevs.htm.
Merrill, John. 2003. *A History of Extremely Low Frequency (ELF) Submarine Radio Communications*. Southington, CT: Publishing Directions.
Navy Extremely Low Frequency Communications System Facilities Closure. 2004. [Online information; retrieved April 2006.] http://www.navyspace.navy.mil/home/elf/overview/pdf.
"The Wireless Equipped Submarine." 1916. *Wireless Age* III (9): 605–616.

Suez Crisis (1956)

The Suez Crisis was generated by Egyptian nationalization of the Suez Canal on 26 July 1956. The Egyptian takeover of this Anglo-French–owned canal brought both Britain and France into a conflict with President Gamal Abdel Nasser's Egyptian Republic. With the failure of diplomacy, Britain and France undertook a combined military operation, in concert with an Israeli invasion, to reassert control over the canal. Communication problems were a central part of the resulting campaign.

In 1952, Nasser and others overthrew Egypt's King Farouk and quickly moved to establish an Arab republic. Their new policy normalized relations with Communist China and sought military equipment from Soviet-bloc nations. These actions led Britain and France to withdraw support from Nasser's

Aswan Dam construction project on the Nile River, jeopardizing its completion. At the same time, Egypt and Israel were fighting an undeclared border war. In July 1956, Nasser ordered nationalization of the Suez Canal in an effort to use its revenues to fund the Aswan Dam project. Britain and France decided to use military force to retake the canal. To ensure success, they agreed to act in concert with Israel, which would invade the Egyptian-controlled Sinai Peninsula. An Anglo-French force would use that attack as an excuse to invade the Port Said Canal Zone by sea and air in what became known as Operation Musketeer Revised.

Command and control of the operation initially was to be aboard the HMS *Tyne*, which was to handle communications of both air and sea elements of the invasion force. The French decided to equip another ship to provide an additional communication platform for the invasion force and chose the *Gustave-Zede*, a French naval stores vessel. That vessel was fitted with additional aerials and carried radio trucks to increase communications capacity from ship to shore.

The Royal Navy was in the process of converting from TYPEX to KL7 for coding messages, and the Suez operation was the first campaign in which its wireless operators were using this new system. Despite success in working with United Nations allies in Korea, the British had difficulty in coordinating their communications with the French warships participating in the Suez operation. The French armed forces were a late entry into the North American Treaty Organization armed forces, and their communications were at odds with the Royal Navy. In addition, the adding of ships to the invasion fleet overwhelmed the transmission of messages to the *Tyne*, and the Royal Navy switched

back to its tested capability with Morse code. Unfortunately, use of code extended the time for message translation.

On 29 October 1956, Israeli forces launched their attacks into Egypt and the Gaza Strip, driving toward the Canal Zone. On 5 November, Allied airborne battalions made landings within Port Said and quickly secured the canal zone. French airborne troops used a circling aircraft as a communications center to direct naval support and reinforcements to deal with Egyptian attacks. By the next day, British land forces had reinforced the paratroopers within the zone. Within several days, however, U.S. and U.N. diplomats established a ceasefire and by March 1957 Allied and Israeli forces had evacuated the canal zone and the Sinai Peninsula.

William H. Brown

See also Combat Information Center (CIC); Egypt; Flagship; France: Navy (*Marine Nationale*); Israel; Korean War (1950–1953); Signals Intelligence (SIGINT); United Kingdom: Royal Navy

Sources

Beaufre, Andre. 1969. *The Suez Expedition 1956*. New York: Frederick A. Praeger.

Bowie, Robert R. 1974. *Suez 1956*. London: Oxford University Press.

Dayan, Moshe. 1965. *Diary of the Sinai Campaign*. New York: Harper & Row.

Haykal, Muhammad Hasanayn. 1987. *Cutting the Lion's Tail: Suez Through Egyptian Eyes*. New York: Arbor House.

Lucas, W. Scott. 1996. *Britain and Suez: The Lion's Last Roar*. Manchester, UK: Manchester University Press.

"System of Systems"

The "system of systems" is one of the most popular concepts associated with the American Information Revolution in Military

Affairs (IRMA). It was proposed in the mid-1990s by Admiral William A. Owens, then vice chairman of the Joint Chiefs of Staff. The system of systems concept integrates three elements: (1) sensors, satellites, radars, and remote acoustic devices; (2) computer and communication systems; and (3) modern precision-guided weapons. It merges such capabilities as command and control, surveillance, reconnaissance, intelligence, and targeting.

In such a military architecture, individual units are incorporated into a powerful joint war-fighting structure. New technologies allow one to gather, process, store, and transmit an enormous amount of information. The Army, with its superiority in information revolution technology, knows more (and more rapidly) about its enemy and the potential battlefield. Dramatic improvements in military communication systems made possible a real-time knowledge, which produces a situation awareness or a "dominant battle knowledge." One can know almost everything about the movements of an enemy, and thus have the ability to predict and counteract that enemy's actions. Such a system of systems allows the modern army not only to locate, fix, and destroy military targets but to do so from a distance.

Building a system of systems, understood to include the integration of sensors, high-tech weapons systems, and command, became the goal of the American military, explicitly expressed in *Joint Vision 2010* (1996) and *Quadrennial Defense Review* (1997). Additionally, the system of systems concept requires integration of all military services and their full cooperation. Traditional service-oriented structures are slowly being replaced by interservice cooperation. This need for "jointness" is one of the most demanding aspects of the IRMA. Decisions based on a near real-time situation awareness have to be made quickly and thus often by lower levels of command. Operations under the system of systems cannot be strictly preplanned, as they must adapt to changing battlefield conditions with a much greater flexibility than before.

The system of systems concept exploits John Boyd's "OODA [observe, orient, decide, and act] loop," which offers a universal logic of conflict. The one who is able to carry out the whole cycle quicker and more effectively wins. Admiral Owens' system of systems promises the U.S. military to gain unchallenged superiority in the OODA loop and thus to win both battles and wars. Like many addicted proponents of IRMA, Owens announced the end of one of Karl von Clausewitz's dictums: The U.S. system of systems would lift the "fog of war" by making it predictable and fully plannable due to American information and communication supremacy. The idea that new information and communication technologies could eliminate the effect of friction and fog (chance and uncertainty) in war is naturally debatable.

Reliance on the system of systems architecture of computers, communications, and precision-guided weapons, however, could create its own source of vulnerability and friction. Information noise (the problem of identifying valuable information within the vast flow of superfluous data), information overload, and the ever-present threat of temperamental electronic systems might serve as a source of friction and confusion in the twenty-first-century battlefield.

Łukasz Kamieński

See also Communication Satellites; Computer; Global Command and Control System

(GCCS); Information Revolution in Military Affairs (IRMA); Internet; Signals Intelligence (SIGINT)

Sources

Nye, J. S., and William A. Owens. 1996. "America's Information Edge." *Foreign Affairs* 75 (2): 20–35.

Owens, William A. 1996. "The Emerging U.S. System-of-Systems." [Online article; retrieved September 2005.] http://www .ndu.edu/inss/strforum/SF_63/forum63 .html.

Owens, William A. 2001. *Lifting the Fog of War*. Baltimore: Johns Hopkins University Press.

Talk Between Ships (TBS)

The talk between ships (TBS) transceiver was a line-of-sight voice radio employed by the U.S. Navy for ship-to-ship communications during World War II.

The Navy's interest in radio dated to 1899, when Secretary of the Navy John Long made arrangements for officers to observe Guglielmo Marconi's wireless reporting of the America's Cup yacht races. They reported favorably on Marconi's apparatus, but the Navy waited until 1902 to purchase its first spark sets for sending code. Voice communication was not possible with these early sets because they produced damped waves.

The service purchased its first voice radios in late 1907. Inventor Lee de Forest had developed a working radio-telephone system earlier that year by utilizing arc transmission to generate continuous (undamped) waves. Though the Navy bought more than two dozen sets from de Forest, production problems and an overly aggressive installation schedule led to poor performance during the world cruise of the Great White Fleet

(1907–1909). With that the Navy abandoned serious efforts to adopt voice radio until World War I.

By then, radio experts in the Navy's Bureau of Steam Engineering had concluded that the vacuum tube offered a superior alternative to the arc. In March 1917, the bureau ordered several vacuum tube radio-telephone transceivers from Western Electric. Testing confirmed their suitability for shipboard use, and during the war the Navy ordered more than a thousand sets. This equipment provided the service with its first reliable system of ship-to-ship voice communications and served as standard equipment for more than a decade. As a high frequency system, however, messages often could be intercepted hundreds of miles away. One solution to this problem was radio equipment that could operate at a higher frequency, as very high frequencies propagate along a line of sight and the earth's curvature limits the maximum range between transmitter and receiver. The Naval Research Laboratory (NRL) began experimenting with very high frequency equipment in 1929, but due to technical difficulties and limited funding, most of the fleet did not receive operational sets until 1936.

These first-generation line-of-sight voice radios had a maximum operating frequency of 60 MHz, but fleet personnel asked for equipment that could transmit and receive at still higher frequencies. In 1939, the Navy's shore establishment met this request by introducing the TBS radio transceiver. Developed by NRL and manufactured by the Radio Corporation of America, the new transceivers had a frequency range of 60 to 80 MHz and provided American naval officers with an extremely reliable means of short-range tactical communication. By 1941 the Navy had installed TBS on most warships, and it served as the fleet's primary system of tactical ship-to-ship communications throughout World War II. The system proved especially valuable during amphibious landing and convoy operations.

Although TBS was simply the alphabetic designation for the new equipment (other contemporary naval radios included models such as the TBM and TCZ), sailors soon began referring to it as "Talk Between Ships." The moniker quickly stuck. TBS remained in service with the U.S. Navy until the mid-1950s, when it was replaced by more advanced higher frequency systems.

Timothy Wolters

See also de Forest (1873–1961), Lee; Naval Research Laboratory (NRL); Radio; Spectrum Frequencies; U.S. Navy; World War I; World War II

Sources

Aitken, Hugh G. J. 1985. *The Continuous Wave: Technology and American Radio, 1900–1932.* Princeton, NJ: Princeton University Press.

Douglas, Susan. 1987. *Inventing American Broadcasting, 1899–1922.* Baltimore: Johns Hopkins University Press.

Gebhard, Louis A. 1979. *Evolution of Naval Radio-Electronics and Contributions of the Naval Research Laboratory.* Washington, DC: Government Printing Office.

Howeth, Linwood S. 1963. *History of Communications-Electronics in the United States Navy.* Washington, DC: Government Printing Office.

Tannenberg, Battle of (1914)

Perhaps no other battle of the early twentieth century illustrates the importance of communications planning, supply, and operations in modern warfare better than the Battle of Tannenberg. A key opening battle of World War I, it was fought on the Eastern front 26–30 August 1914.

In accordance with prewar mobilization plans, the Russian First and Second armies advanced toward East Prussia to defeat the German Eighth Army. The Russian advance had to consider an enormous swamp known as the Masurian Lakes, which divided Russia's armies as they sought to outflank the Germans. The lakes effectively cut off lateral communication between the Russian armies. In addition, their Northwest Front commander failed to assign either army to maintain communications and ordered each to advance separately, resulting in a 60-mile gap between them.

The Russians had failed to plan for communications at any level. Signal communication was primarily a function of Russian engineers. Telegraph companies were trained and equipped to install and maintain telegraph lines and also had some telephone equipment. Independent telegraph companies assigned to army corps had a limited supply of wire. Field radio stations were also at corps and army headquarters but had only limited mobility for equipment that had a maximum range of about 100 miles.

Shortly after First Army began the advance, it outran its wire communication and resorted to sending orders by radio. The messages were sent without encryption, due to Russian fear of using codes that could not be deciphered by the intended recipient, a fear greater than the risk of the Germans intercepting the signal. This calculated risk failed as the Germans easily intercepted the transmissions and used the information to win a minor engagement. After the Russians inflicted a local defeat on the Germans at Gumbinnen and the Russian Second Army crossed into Prussia, however, the German commander was replaced by Paul von Hindenburg. His chief of staff, Erich Ludendorff, quickly developed a plan to counterattack the Second Army. At the same time, one Russian general moved his army to the left while another issued orders for it to move toward the First Army on the right. Second Army's wire supply had also run out, and it resorted to sending uncoded radio transmissions.

The Battle of Tannenberg began on 26 August with a coordinated German attack on the Russian Second Army that had devolved into separate corps (due to difficult terrain) that could not communicate with each other or headquarters. This total absence of lateral signal communication between Russian corps commanders made them ignorant of what was happening on their flanks. By the evening of 27 August, the German attack had broken both the right and left flanks of the Second Army, and the Russian commander did not know where his corps command posts were located. The breakdown of the brittle Russian signal system deprived him of vital information.

On 28 August, von Hindenburg ordered an attack on the Russian center while his other units moved to outflank the Russian Second Army. On 29 August the Russians tried to withdraw from the encirclement, but their retreat soon became a rout. By 30 August the Russian army had disintegrated into small groups of men escaping to the rear, having suffered more than 50,000 casualties with another 90,000 captured by the Germans. The Russian commander, who had become lost in the woods, committed suicide. The First Russian Army would meet a similar fate at the Battle of the Masurian Lakes in early September.

Tannenberg illustrates the importance of proper signal planning for large operations. Russian command and control suffered from poor leadership, lack of secrecy, inadequate prewar planning, and inadequate supplies of signal equipment, such as wire. Frequent moves of unit headquarters disrupted the wired systems, which forced the use of radio signaling using open channels. The open signaling permitted the Germans to fully understand Russian plans, with fatal results for the latter.

Steven J. Rauch

See also Germany: Army; Russia/Soviet Union: Army; World War I

Sources

Ingles, Harry C. 1929. "Tannenberg—A Study in Faulty Signal Communication." *The Signal Corps Bulletin* 49 (July–August): 1–14.
Showalter, Dennis. 1991. *Tannenberg: Clash of Empires*. Hamden, CT: Archon Books.

TELCOM Mobile Wireless Units

Cable and Wireless Limited, a British worldwide telecommunications company, sent a mobile wireless assembly (MWA) to Algiers in 1942, which was composed of five vans and a trailer manned by nine operators and three engineers. Known as the "Blue Train," the MWA operated during the remainder of the British campaign in North Africa in World War II and was then attached to the public relations office of the British army for the invasion of southern Italy in late 1943.

During the fighting in North Africa and the early stages of the Italian campaigns, Cable and Wireless staff suffered the shared risks, discomforts, and frustrations of servicemen in the field but without any formal claim to the support of the armed services with whom they worked in close association. While the acquisition of food and accommodation presented the MWA staff with particular problems, as civilians in plain clothes, they faced the greater and very real risk of being treated as irregular soldiers if taken prisoner by the enemy.

To rectify this situation, Cable and Wireless proposed to the army that those of their staff who were working in forward areas be enrolled in a uniformed organization supported by the services. The status of the TELCOM personnel was the same as for war correspondents. No provision was made in the TELCOM charter concerning rank, and the personnel did not wear rank insignia, although it was generally accepted that senior operators were equivalent to lieutenants, managers to captains, and divisional managers to lieutenant-colonels.

TELCOM, as a new noncombatant force, wearing its own uniform but unarmed, joined the British Empire's forces in overseas theaters of war for the assault on Europe and the Far East. They saw service in Ceylon, Burma, Malaya, Dutch East Indies, and Hong Kong. They assisted the services by providing operational and administrative communications duties and carrying to and from the forward areas messages for government departments and the press. Expeditionary force messages were also handled by TELCOM. These were sent between the troops and their families at home.

Cliff Lord

See also Golden Arrow Sections; Mobile Communications; United Kingdom: Royal Corps of Signals; Vehicles and Transport

Sources

Bairstow, J. P. 1994. *East of Colombo 1945–1949: A Record of the Cable and Wireless Ltd Australasian Telegraph Operator Classes of '44 and the TELCOM Teams in Which They Served.* Padbury, Australia: J. P. Bairstow.
Graves, Charles. 1946. *The Thin Red Lines.* London: Standard Art Book.
Lord, Cliff, and Graham Watson. 2003. *The Royal Corps of Signals: Unit Histories of the Corps (1920–2001) and Its Antecedents.* Solihull, UK: Helion.

Telegraph

Electric or line telegraphy was quickly recognized as a breakthrough technology for military communicators. Its application, beginning in the 1850s, transformed command-and-control functions for land warfare, and its tactical and strategic use carried through more than a half-century before being replaced by newer technologies.

While the first workable telegraph was developed by Francis Ronalds in 1816, the first practical system that saw active use was the needle telegraph developed by William F. Cooke and Charles Wheatstone, which was adopted by the expanding British railway systems. Many others also experimented with telegraph ideas. Samuel F. B.

Morse first began to develop his telegraph system in the early 1830s. He demonstrated a working model late in 1835 and focused full time on developing his new invention by 1837. By 1838 Morse and Alfred Vail had worked out the basics of what became known as Morse code to simplify and thus speed up the sending of messages. Granted a patent in 1840, Morse also sought patent protection in several European nations. After Congress underwrote the costs of his initial line between Washington DC and Baltimore, commercial operators dominated the service's subsequent development.

Europe took a different path in that governments generally built and operated most telegraph systems. The French, building on their use of the Chappe mechanical semaphore system, were building their first electric telegraph line by 1845 and restricting it to government (and military) use. Military use also dominated the first Prussian state telegraph in 1847. Many other European nations followed suit. British telegraph services were originally shared between commercial (the new railways) and government/military needs. The first British colonial telegraph lines were being constructed in India by 1848. By the time of the Sepoy Indian Mutiny a decade later, those telegraph lines were vital to warn British outposts (from headquarters in Delhi) that the uprising had begun. In addition to a spreading network of stationary lines, special telegraph circuits were built to support the armies on the move. During the siege of Lucknow, a telegraph line was built to more rapidly communicate with headquarters.

The first military test of telegraphy, however, came during the Crimean War (1854–1856), in which Britain and France sought to stop Russian expansion into Ottoman (Turk-ish) territory. An extensive Russian electric telegraph system, completed by the German firm of Siemens & Halske in 1855, provided a vital link from north of St. Petersburg (then the capital) through Moscow and south to Sevastopol on the Black Sea (site of a long siege) as well as east to Warsaw. On the other side, British Royal Engineers built and operated 21 miles of Wheatstone single needle telegraph line between British headquarters at Balaclava and French headquarters in Kamiesch. It was subject to constant battle damage and only marginally useful. In 1855, a private firm under military direction constructed an underwater cable of 340 miles (by far the longest ever constructed to that point) to connect Balaclava across the Black Sea with Varna in present-day Bulgaria (and then connecting with existing continental telegraph lines). It lasted only eight months due to its fragility. Commanders in the field were for the first time interfered with (they felt) by constant questions and suggestions (and sometimes orders) from distant military headquarters in London and Paris.

During the American Civil War (1861–1865), telegraphy proved vital given the need to manage large armies spread over a wide geographic area. As the war began, civilian telegraph networks were widespread (primarily in the north), but military experience with the service was limited. The Confederacy established its own telegraph arm in 1862. The Union took over the commercial operators early in 1862 and also established the U.S. Military Telegraph, which was staffed by civilians and soon developed mobile field units using specially designed wagons ("telegraph trains") to keep up with shifting armies. The Beardslee telegraph system was widely used, though with varying results, as was telegraphy from

This American Civil War engraving shows signals personnel laying a "flying telegraph" line during combat. Such telegraph services could be moved with armies, keeping commanders in touch with frontline conditions. (U.S. Army Signal Center Command History Office, Fort Gordon, Georgia)

tethered observation balloons. President Abraham Lincoln maintained close touch with his commanders through the War Department telegraph office next to the White House. To protect their communications, both sides resorted to coding messages—and trying to read the enemy's messages. More than 300 telegraph operators died from disease or battle injuries.

In a war between France and Austria in the early 1860s, both armies made tactical use of telegraphy and often attacked the other side's communication lines. Growing out of its success in rapidly laying field telegraph lines, France established the Telegraph

Brigade as well as a school to train telegraphers in 1868. Likewise, Prussia benefited from its effective use of telegraphy in the several wars leading to German unification. The Franco-Prussian War (1870–1871) saw Germany utilizing both military and civil telegraph systems, as well as lines captured from the French. Germany formed special telegraph companies for fighting army units, and its aggressive laying of tactical lines sometimes preceded military actions. The first separate British telegraph troop was established in the Royal Corps of Engineers in 1870. British and colonial forces slowly perfected pack animal transport to carry needed telegraph equipment. Telegraph units also served to link British forces during operations in China (1900) and Tibet (1904).

Telegraphs were widely used in British colonial areas in Africa, where logistical problems arising from both limited experience and the hot and wet climate complicated military campaigns. Royal Engineer telegraph units supported many of these actions from the 1860s to the turn of the twentieth century. For the Egyptian campaign, victory was telegraphed directly from the battlefield to London for the first time.

British forces also made extensive use of the telegraph during the Boer War (1899–1902), although this introduced a new drawback when the Boers tapped British lines to intercept messages. The British commander responded by trying to deceive his enemy with false troop movement messages sent in the clear. Cable carts traveled with the troops, enabling rapid connection with headquarters. Railways were protected by a series of blockhouses and armored trains connected by telegraph. Several thousand miles of telegraph line were installed during the conflict, much of it along railway rights of way.

During World War I, military telegraph services were active within all the fighting powers and civilian/commercial networks were widely applied to military needs. Telegraphers (not yet part of the British signal arm, they operated as a part of the Royal Engineers until 1920) began to take precedence. Wire lines for telegraphy (and telephony) had to be either strung or buried. That was best done along roadways, but as opposing forces often shelled roads to interdict communications, handcarts were used to string wire cross-country. Wire strung from poles could all too easily be cut by rifle or shell fire. Along front lines, wire had to be laid, buried if conditions permitted, or run along special communication trenches. High-speed Morse operations were introduced during the war, speeding up message transmission.

Telegraphy as a military service finally gave way to other technologies during and after World War II. Having reached its peak application about 1930 (in terms of telegrams sent and Western Union employment), the commercial business had gone into a steady decline. Growing use of wireless telegraphy and expansion of telephone, telex, and teleprinter networks in the 1920s and 1930s removed much of the need for line telegraph services dedicated to military use. Later fax technology, let alone the Internet and e-mail, marked the final demise of a once-dominant service.

Christopher H. Sterling

See also Army Signal Corps; Beardslee Telegraph; Confederate Army Signal Corps; Facsimile/Fax; Field Wire and Cable; High-Speed Morse; Morse Code; Morse, Samuel F. B. (1791–1872); Semaphore (Mechanical Telegraphs); Stager, Anson (1825–1885); Teleprinter/Teletype; Undersea Cables; United Kingdom: Royal Corps of Signals; U.S. Military Telegraph Service (USMTS)

Sources

Bauchamp, Ken. 2001. "Military Telegraphy." In *History of Telegraphy*, chap. 4. London: Institution of Electrical Engineers.

Marland, E. A. 1964. *Early Electrical Communication*. London: Abelard-Schuman.

Nalder, R. F. H. 1958. *The Royal Corps of Signals: A History of Its Antecedents and Development*, chaps. 2, 3. London: Royal Signals Association.

Raines, Rebecca Robbins. 1996. *Getting the Message Through: A Branch History of the US Army Signal Corps*, chaps, 1–3, 5. Washington, DC: Government Printing Office.

Scheips, Paul J., ed. 1980. *Military Signal Communications*. 2 vols. New York: Arno Press.

Telephone

The telephone was adopted for military use more slowly than the telegraph. There were several reasons for this—for example, the telephone left no physical record of a message as the telegraph provided, and until World War I, telephone signals could be sent only a limited distance, far less than the telegraph. On the other hand, the telephone could be easily used by any personnel (no need for a crew of trained specialists), allowed for faster transmission of longer messages without the use of code, and encouraged two-way communication. The telephone was used first in military headquarters, as application in the field called for lighter and portable equipment, which took some time to develop.

As early as 1877, just a year after Alexander Graham Bell's telephone invention, English telegraph engineer W. H. Preece, in a talk to British engineer officers, predicted military use of the instrument. But he also noted its drawbacks for military use—fragility and susceptibility to interference, for example. At the same time, he suggested that a telephone could transmit the actual words of command as well as the tones of voice. He concluded that such an apparatus would be valuable for military purposes. The telephone saw occasional use over short distances in Britain's African colonial campaigns and siege operations, as well as in India, in the late 1870s and into the 1880s.

The U.S. Army Signal Corps installed its first experimental telephone line in 1878. Soon thereafter the telephone was adopted as the prime means of communication for messages that did not require a physical copy between Fort Whipple (now Fort Myer) in Virginia and the Office of the Chief Signal Officer in Washington DC. Some experimental telephone links were also established at sea coast defense facilities for fire control. Questions of equipment weight and portability dominated early Army concerns with telephone use—as did the often poor voice quality provided.

The first experimental U.S. Army field telephone appeared in 1889 but proved too expensive to manufacture in large numbers. In the meantime, Siemens & Halske of Germany were making a field telephone with a drum of cable that could be rapidly deployed. Telephone wire was soon converted from iron to copper and several weights were tried. Following telegraph procedure and precedents, both man-carried and horse-borne means of laying wire in the field were developed. Hand generator and battery systems were both used, the former in combat conditions, the latter on individual posts.

British headquarters were making active use of telephones during the Boer War (1899–1902). Some were using commandeered civilian equipment, but the first purpose-designed military telephones were also being used. Telephones were found in major British and American fortifications, among those of other nations. During the Spanish-American War, the Army Signal Corps established telephone networks within bases and headquarters, and between President William McKinley and his secretaries of war and navy in Washington DC and Tampa, Florida, the main port used to support American forces. After fighting ceased, the Signal Corps built Cuba's first telephone network.

When the British War Office moved to Whitehall in 1906, the building included a

400-line telephone switchboard. Switchboards were constantly improved to add capacity and flexibility. In the American West, telegraph lines that had once connected military posts began to give way to telephone networks. Telephone lines were also built to connect General John J. Pershing's Mexican Punitive Expedition headquarters back to his American base in New Mexico.

By World War I, the telephone had come into widespread military use. French civilian telephone networks were initially pressed into use, but demand quickly surpassed their capacity. Telephone repeaters allowed for service over longer distances and for thinner (and lighter) lines. Static trench warfare on the Western Front favored use of telephones if their connecting lines could be buried deep enough, and often they were not. Massive artillery barrages by both sides repeatedly tore up enemy line communications. The other important problem was security, and listening by induction to enemy telephone signals was widespread by 1915. For subsequent field operations, British (and later American) forces used a combined buzzer and telephone set, of which the British Fullerphone was perhaps best known (the U.S. equivalent was the EE-1).

The British Post Office manufactured more than 40,000 "trench" telephones that were used on all fronts, linked by manual switchboards. The U.S. Army standardized the use of a field telephone housed in a wooden case and an improved version based largely on commercial equipment and thus available for rapid and relatively inexpensive mass production. Dedicated telephone links were soon established between Allied headquarters and both London and Paris, and a cadre of some 200 "Hello Girls" operated the American switchboards at Chau-

An American army officer makes a telephone call on the Western Front in 1918. The telephone proved a significant, if unreliable, mode of communication during World War I, but was vastly improved in the two decades before World War II. (National Archives)

mont after 1917. A huge dedicated network of 20,000 miles of wire served both telegraph and telephone networks in France.

Telephones also proved invaluable for onboard communication in both British and German airships (where crew members were often widely separated from one another), though equipment had to be airtight (to reduce the danger of fire), as light as possible, and resistant to vibration. Telephones were also used to connect artillery spotters in tethered balloons with their ground controllers.

European fortifications constructed before and during World War II made extensive use of internal telephone communications. German fortifications along the border and later the Atlantic Wall were connected by telephone by deeply buried telephone cables, as well as telephone links between the outside and the inside of a given structure (speaking tubes were installed in many of the works in case of failure of the telephone system). The French Maginot Line was similarly equipped.

During World War II, telephones carried two-thirds of communications within the United States and some overseas sites (telegraphy remained the more secure long-distance communication mode). In combat theaters, alternative routing helped to ensure communications continuity. Switchboards, however, had changed little since World War I. Britain's Fighter Command connected its more than forty key airfields and radar installations during the Battle of Britain with an extensive dedicated telephone network, making use of duplicate facilities where possible to allow continued connectivity even with battle damage. German and Japanese forces made extensive use of telephone services, though the latter's extensive water-separated holdings made radio more valuable. Security was of concern, as with any voice-based system, leading to many ingenious means of coding messages, of which the SIGSALY system was perhaps the most advanced.

The standard American field equipment during the war was the EE-8 portable field telephone, which (with battery) weighed about 10 pounds and could send a signal from 11 to 17 miles, depending on conditions. It came in a leather (later canvas and, by 1967, nylon) bag and remained in use through the Vietnam War. The rugged, lighter-weight, and smaller telephone set TA-312/PT, which entered service in the 1950s, was the main successor to the EE-8, though both were used interchangeably for decades. The newer unit could also be hand cranked. Later equipment featured small push-button number pads.

By the late twentieth century, telephone links were so common as to have become part of the military background—presumed to be always available and ready. The fundamental technical change has been a steady progression from analog to digital technology in switching and transmission.

Christopher H. Sterling

See also American Telephone & Telegraph Co. (AT&T); Atlantic Wall; Automatic Secure Voice Communication (AUTOSEVOCOM); Bell, Alexander Graham (1847–1922); Bell Telephone Laboratories (BTL); Britain, Battle of (1940); Coast Defense; Fullerphone; Hello Girls; Maginot Line; Mexican Punitive Expedition (1916–1917); Mobile Communications; SIGSALY; Spanish-American War (1898); Telegraph; Underground Communication Centers; Undersea Cables; World War I; World War II

Sources
Beck, George I. 1928. "The Telephone: Commercial v. Military History and Development." *Signal Corps Bulletin* 42 (March): 1–17.
Beresford. C. F. C. 1892. "The Telephone at Home and in the Field." *Journal of the Royal United Service Institution* 36 (170): 347–368.
Fagan, M. D., ed. 1978. *A History of Engineering and Science in the Bell System: National Service in War and Peace (1925–1975)*. New York: Bell Telephone Laboratories, Inc.
Fay, Frank H. 1927. "A.E.F. Telephone and Telegraph System." *Military Signal Communications* I (May): 10–21.
Insulator Collectors on the Net. "Military Phones." [Online information; retrieved April 2006.] http://www.myinsulators.com/commokid/telephones/militaryphones.htm.
Lavine, A. Lincoln. 1921. *Circuits of Victory*. Garden City, NY: Country Life Press.
Olive-Drab.com. "Military Telephones: EE-8 Field Phone." [Online information; retrieved April 2006.] http://www.olive-drab.com/od_electronics_ee8.php.
Povey, P. J., and R. A. J. Earl. 1988. "First World War and Post-War Telephones." In *Vintage Telephones of the World*, 140–152. London: Peter Peregrinus and the Science Museum.
Preece, W. H. 1878. "The Telephone and Its Application to Military and Naval

Purposes." *Journal of the Royal United Service Institution* 22 (January): 209–216.

Scheips, Paul J., ed. 1980. *Military Signal Communication,* vol. II. New York: Arno Press.

Teleprinter/Teletype

For much of the twentieth century, teleprinters (the European term; in the United States they were called teletypes), which used radio or line telegraphy, were employed extensively throughout the world by civilian carriers as well as military services. They began to fade from use when newer facilities, including facsimile, and later the Internet, better filled military needs.

A teletype, or teleprinter/teletypewriter, is a now-obsolete electromechanical typewriter that communicates messages/signals from one point to another through a simple electrical communications channel, line, or wireless. The most modern form of these devices was fully electronic and used a visual display unit with a hard copy printer.

The mechanical typewriter was developed in 1867 and was in large-scale U.S. production within a decade, directed primarily at

The teleprinter or teletype allowed rapid communication of printed military orders and information. Most ground forces in World War II made good use of these devices which could send coded signals. (Library of Congress)

government and business office use. In telegraph offices, operators would listen to the Morse sounder and directly type plain language messages (transcription) onto telegram forms for hand delivery to recipients. Mechanizing that transfer helped to speed up communication. A company was formed in 1906 to make machines (it became Teletype Corporation in 1925) into which an operator would type alphanumeric characters (not Morse code). New York and Boston were linked in 1910, and the Associated Press began to transmit war news to American newspapers four years later. The first general purpose teletype appeared in 1922. The Teletype Corp. became part of AT&T in 1930, but its name was synonymous in America with teleprinters.

The "torn tape" system was initially developed by Donald Murray of New Zealand just after the turn of the twentieth century. His machine involved code-punched or "chadless" tape using teleprinters and "reperforators." A teletypewriter was designed that could print and read these paper tapes as well as print out the characters. If the message had to be forwarded, the paper tape was torn off one machine (thus the name) and sent on another connected to the next point-to-point link in the network. Large communication centers that were filled with teleprinters, reperforators, and autoheads had tape factories or racks holding messages—the first store-and-forward facilities. The basic techniques used still form the basis of all asynchronous message systems such as e-mail. This system not only acted as a buffer if there were more inputs than output facilities but also permitted a system of manual prioritization as shown on the preamble of the message. The preamble consisted of motor startup characters, circuit sequence number, priority, routing

indicators, date-time group and originator, classification, and short break. The classification denoted the level of security required. Before the advent of online cipher, offline encryption was performed on sensitive signals.

Concurrent with the teleprinter networks was telex. Starting in the 1930s, large telegraph carriers began to develop systems that used telephone-like rotary dialing to connect teleprinters. These new devices were called "telex," (combining *tele*printer and *ex*change) and sent five-unit Baudot code in a system of automated message routing. The first wide-coverage automatic public telex network was implemented in Berlin and Hamburg by the German Post Office in 1932 and was quickly followed by other technically capable nations before World War II. Teleprinter operations gradually declined with the introduction of fax and visual display units (cathode ray tubes) from the late 1970s. Today, any personal computer with its associated printer equipped with a serial port can emulate the functionality of a teleprinter.

Military forces in Britain and its empire, the United States, Germany, and some other countries began to use teleprinters in their networks during the 1930s. Experimentation by various organizations took place, including Britain's Royal Navy. After a successful 1937 test aboard a battleship, the Royal Navy made extensive use of teleprinters during World War II. Royal Air Force Bomber Command relied on nearly a thousand dedicated teleprinter circuits by 1945. Wireless/radio links were used extensively to link teleprinter networks.

Wartime demand forced American Teletype Corp. machine production up fifteenfold from 1939 to 1944, and similar demand no doubt impacted Creed, the famous British teleprinter firm. Communication between

Winston Churchill in London and Franklin Roosevelt in Washington often used teletype machines with encrypted communication. After Western Union and AT&T's installation in the new Pentagon building of the Army Communications Service, direct circuits connected British and American military and diplomatic offices and War Department offices to posts in the United States and overseas. They could carry 50 million words a day, up from less than a million when the war began.

After World War II, British forces gradually shifted from dependency on wireless and telegraph circuits (and some high-speed Morse networks) to teleprinter links, which were largely strategic in application. The use of five-unit tape became extensive by the 1950s, applying the torn-tape concept. An operator at a tributary, or small site, typed signals, which caused a tape to be produced by a reperforator unit at the receiving end of the circuit. The tape was then manually torn off and placed in an autohead tape transmitter on another circuit and dispatched to the next destination. An operator could read the routing from the routing indicator in the preamble of the tape either by reading the chadless tape holes (visualization) or in some cases by reading the print on the reperforator tape.

Message switching automation, which in Britain was heralded by the Signal Transmit Receive and Distribution system and Telegraph Automatic Routing Equipment (TARE) came into use in the early 1960s. Signals received from tributaries or relay stations were automatically routed by TARE to the next message switching equipment from whence it was dispatched to its destination.

The Telegraph Automatic Switching System was the British military telex system linking permanent military installations and communication centers. Introduced in 1955, the system lasted well into the 1980s.

Cliff Lord and Christopher H. Sterling

See also Automatic Digital Network (AUTODIN); Bell Telephone Laboratories (BTL); Commonwealth Communications Army Network (COMCAN); Facsimile/Fax; High-Speed Morse; Internet; Telegraph

Sources

Beauchamp, Ken. 2001. *History of Telegraphy.* History of Technology Series No. 26, 391–401. Stevenage, UK: Institution of Electrical Engineers.

Calvert, J. B. 2002. "Teletypewriter." [Online article; retrieved June 2006.] http://www.du.edu/~jacvert/tel/teletype.htm.

Department of the Army. 1954. *Fundamentals of Telegraphy (Teletypewriter).* Technical Manual TM11–665. Washington, DC: Government Printing Office.

Huurdeman, Anton A. 2003. "Teleprinters." In *The Worldwide History of Telecommunications,* 300–307. New York: Wiley-Interscience.

Nalder, R. F. H. 1958. *The Royal Corps of Signals: A History of Its Antecedents and Development (circa 1800–1955),* 479–481. London: Royal Signals Institution.

Nelsen, R. A. 1963. *History of Teletypewriter Development.* Skokie, IL: Teletype Corp.

Oslin, George P. 1992. "Early to Modern Operating Progress." In *The Story of Telecommunications,* 297–317. Macon, GA: Mercer University Press.

Teletype Corporation. 1957. "The Teletype Story." Skokie, IL: Teletype Corp. [Online information; retrieved September 2005.] http://www.kekatos.com/teletype/The_Teletype_Story_50th_Anniversary.htm.

Television

The military potential of television was studied early on during the medium's development. From use in guided weapons to all types of training, television or video appeared to have distinct uses for the military, though few focused at first on communication.

Articles in Britain and the United States suggested military applications of the technology even as television began regular broadcast service (1936 in Britain, 1941 in the United States). During the war numerous experiments were conducted using television to navigate aircraft and bombs by remote control. In 1944, RCA developed the image orthicon (IO) tube, which was more light sensitive than existing iconoscope equipment. About 4,000 of a smaller IO version were produced for various military requirements. Further experiments developed television gun cameras for aircraft and film equipment to record video images. Television allowed for remote monitoring of some of the manufacturing facilities supporting the atomic bomb project. Initial experimental work on color television was accomplished by British inventor John Logie Baird in 1942, and by CBS engineer Peter Goldmark in 1944.

After World War II, television technology was used to make flight simulator training more realistic. The first example of a simulator with an outside view appeared in the 1950s, when suitable video equipment became available. With this equipment, a videocamera could be "flown" over a scale model of terrain around an airport, and the resulting image was sent to a television monitor placed in front of the pilot in the simulator. His movement of the control stick and throttle produced corresponding movement of the camera over the terrain board. Now the pilot could receive visual feedback both inside and outside the cockpit.

During the 1960s, the U.S. Navy experimented with airborne television in what became known as "Project Jenny." Early in the decade, Northwestern University built and tested the first airborne TV broadcast test platform using very high broadcast frequencies. In 1962 the Navy temporarily installed RCA radio/TV broadcast equipment in two propeller air transports with the intent of using their capabilities during the Cuban Missile Crisis. Completed too late, the aircraft were placed in storage for later use. The Department of Defense began to develop plans for airborne radio/TV broadcast capabilities to be used in the Southeast Asia conflict in psychological warfare. RCA provided equipment and technical expertise to support project completion.

Early in 1965 construction of the first "Blue Eagle" aircraft was begun, configured as a platform to test the design of various TV broadcast antennas. Technical training began in May. The first applications were in September, flying psychological operation missions in support of the revolution going on in the Dominican Republic, when the country's radio stations were taken over by rebels. The mission continued for about two weeks. A month later, one of the three (later six) Blue Eagle aircraft was ordered to Saigon to fly its first broadcast mission (broadcasting the baseball World Series) out of Tan Son Nhut Air Force Base and in support of South Vietnamese operations. Two more aircraft joined by the end of the year and all continued a combination of broadcast and psychological warfare missions. Operations ceased in 1970, though some equipment was left for South Vietnamese forces.

The Defense Advanced Research Projects Agency supported experiments with high-definition television technology in the 1990s, looking into digital compression and equipment design. Television monitoring was widely used as a part of security systems protecting military bases.

Christopher H. Sterling

See also Defense Advanced Research Projects
Agency (DARPA)

Sources
Abramson, Albert. 2003. "Television and World
War II." In *The History of Television, 1942 to
2000*, chap. 1. Jefferson, NC: McFarland.
American Forces Vietnam Network. "History of
Project Jenny." [Online information; retrieved
March 2006.] www.afvn.tv/ProjectJenny/
history.html.
Schechter, Maurice. 2004. "Military Television
Equipment Built by RCA, 1942–1945."
[Online article; retrieved March 2006.]
http://www.qsl.net/w2vtm/mil
_television_history.html.
Slee, J. A. 1935. "Potentialities of Television for
Warlike Purposes." *Journal of the Royal United
Services Institute* 80 (August): 522–528.
Van Deusen, G. L. 1939. "Television and Its
Possible Military Applications." *Signal Corps
Bulletin* July–September: 17–20.

Tesla, Nikola (1856–1943)

A Serbian-American electrical inventor
active in the United States from the late nineteenth into the early twentieth century, Tesla
innovated communications and automation
ideas of potential interest to the military,
though he achieved few contracts. He has
become a semimythical cult figure to many
people today, and sorting out reality from
fiction is not easy.

Tesla was born on 10 July 1856 in what is
now Croatia, then part of the Austro-Hungarian Empire. He studied mechanical and
electrical engineering at the Austrian Poly-
technic School in the 1870s, and later worked
as an electrical engineer in Budapest and
Paris. Tesla moved to the United States in
1884 and worked briefly for Thomas Edison
before moving on to Westinghouse. He
turned to independent research and invention by 1887.

His initial electrical efforts focused on
alternating current (AC) power sources and
X-ray technology. By the end of the 1880s he
had demonstrated his polyphase AC power
system, which is much like that used worldwide today. It was introduced at Niagara
Falls in 1896, though he had already sold
his AC patents to George Westinghouse.
He developed his Tesla Coil, or transformer,
in 1891. Tesla experimented in Colorado
Springs with high-voltage electricity and the
possibility of transmitting and distributing
large amounts of electrical energy over long
distances without using wires. Some have
argued he invented radio, based on his work
beginning in 1893 and two U.S. patents of
1900. His later proposed world wireless system failed in development for lack of the
substantial funds needed to construct it.

Tesla patented a wireless means to
remotely control a boat in 1898. He demonstrated a small version just months later in
New York. He believed the Navy would be
interested in such a device as well as in radio-
guided torpedoes, yet they did not take up
either idea at the time. Officials argued his
remote-control system was too fragile for use
in combat and could be easily jammed by an
enemy force. He also proposed the essentials
of radar and remote-control missiles decades
before they actually appeared. Indeed, radio
remote control of weapons remained largely
a novelty until well after his own relevant
patents had expired.

In the mid-1930s, Tesla proposed a "death
beam" device that, using high power, was
said to be able to destroy aircraft hundreds of
miles away. He suggested the use of such
beams could defend nations like an "invisible Chinese Wall," only they would be more
impenetrable. He briefly negotiated with the
British government to help develop such a
system, though no agreement resulted.

Tesla received a total of 112 patents between 1886 and 1928. After he died at the age of eighty-six on 7 January 1943 in New York City, agents of the Federal Bureau of Investigation took away many of his surviving papers, leading to years of conspiracy supposition about what the bureau held (and why) and what information was in them. Six months after his death, the U.S. Supreme Court held that his wireless patents preceded those of Marconi.

Christopher H. Sterling

See also Edison, Thomas A. (1847–1931); Marconi, Guglielmo (1874–1937)

Sources

Cheney, Margaret. 1981. *Tesla: Man Out of Time.* Englewood Cliffs, NJ: Prentice-Hall.

Martin, Thomas C., ed. 1894. *The Inventions, Researches, and Writings of Nikola Tesla.* New York: Electrical Engineer.

Secor, H. Winfield. 1917 "Tesla's Views on Electricity and the War." *Electrical Experimenter* V (August): 229.

Seifer, Marc J. 1996. *Wizard: The Life and Times of Nikola Tesla—Biography of a Genius.* Secaucus, NJ: Birch Lane Press.

Tesla, Nikola. 1982. *My Inventions: The Autobiography of Nikola Tesla.* New York: Barnes & Noble.

Tiltman, John Hessell (1894–1982)

John Tiltman's remarkable career as a cryptologist spanned almost sixty years, from 1921 to 1980: with the British until 1964, and then with the U.S. National Security Agency (NSA).

Tiltman was born in London on 25 May 1894. He worked as a teacher from 1911 to 1914, when he joined the army. He was wounded in France in 1917 and won the Military Cross. He was assigned to the Government Code and Cipher School (GC&CS) to translate Russian diplomatic messages in 1920, while taking a Russian language course. He showed such a flair for code breaking that he never returned to his regiment.

Tiltman was posted to India in late 1921, still mainly working on Russian diplomatic traffic, but also designing some cipher systems. He became a civil servant in 1925 and returned to England 1929 as head of the new military section at GC&CS, to work on Russian and Japanese codes. Starting at least by 1933, he made significant success against the constantly evolving Japanese systems. This work undoubtedly helped him subsequently to break into JN-25, the principal Japanese naval code when it was introduced in June 1939. Tiltman solved its indicator system within a few months—a year ahead of the U.S. Navy's OP-20-G. He also helped Dillwyn Knox to break the coded traffic of the Communist International with Communist parties in the United Kingdom and Europe throughout the 1930s.

Tiltman was recalled to the army in September 1939 as a lieutenant-colonel, but remained at GC&CS. He quickly solved two German army field ciphers, including the difficult double Playfair (*Doppelkastenschlüssel*). By April 1940, he had also solved a commercial Enigma machine (without a plugboard) used by the Swiss, together with a German meteorological cipher used for artillery purposes, and the Russian meteorological cipher. In mid-1940, he read messages on a commercial Enigma used by the German railways, which enabled others at Bletchley Park to determine the machine's rotor wiring. In mid-1941, he solved a Kryha machine cipher used in traffic between Spain and Germany.

One of Tiltman's biggest contributions to the war effort came in mid-1941 when he read two messages enciphered on the Lorenz SZ 40/42 teleprinter cipher system (code-named "Tunny" by GC&CS). These became the basis for GC&CS's solution of the Tunny machine in early 1942.

By March 1942 Tiltman and his unit had partially recovered the indicating system of the Japanese military attaché system. To cope with the shortage of Japanese linguists, he organized intensive six-month courses in Japanese for talented linguists. These were very successful, although language experts had disparaged them, presuming that learning Japanese would take several years. He invented the important stencil subtractor frame, which from 1943 onward replaced the vulnerable conventional subtractor tables previously used for enciphering British military and civil codes.

Tiltman was a member of important liaison visits to the United States in 1942, and always pressed for the fullest cooperation with American Army and naval code breakers, even when some senior GC&CS figures were less enthusiastic. He was promoted to brigadier in June 1944 and was later always known as "the Brig." He became the first head of the cryptanalytic group when it was established at GC&CS in 1945, returned to civilian status in April 1946, and was named assistant director at what became Government Communications Headquarters (GCHQ) in 1947. By 1954, when he formally retired from GCHQ, he had spent upward of thirty years breaking into previously unexploited ciphers from scratch. He was immediately re-employed by GCHQ for another decade, after which time NSA recruited him as a researcher and consultant troubleshooter.

Recipient of numerous awards and honors, in 1980 he was honored by the directors of both NSA and GCHQ for his "uncountable contributions and successes in cryptol-

ogy." Tiltman was admitted to NSA's Hall of Honor in 2004, the only Briton ever to be so honored. He died in Hawaii on 10 August 1982.

Ralph Erskine and Peter Freeman

See also Bletchley Park; Code Breaking, Enigma; German "Fish" Codes; Germany: Naval Intelligence (*B-Dienst*); Government Code & Cipher School (GC&CS, 1919–1946); Magic; National Security Agency (NSA); OP-20-G; Signals Intelligence (SIGINT); Ultra

Sources

Erskine, Ralph, and Peter Freeman. 2003. "Brigadier John Tiltman: One of Britain's Finest Cryptologists." *Cryptologia* 27: 289–318.

Nicoll, D. R. 2004. "Tiltman, John Hessell (1894–1982)." in *Oxford Dictionary of National Biography*, edited by H. C. G. Matthew and Brian Harrison. Oxford: Oxford University Press.

Tiltman, John H. n.d. "Some Reminiscences from Bg. Tiltman." National Archives and Records Administration, College Park, MD, RG 457, Historic Cryptographic Collection, Pre–World War I Through World War II, Box 1417, Nr. 4632.

Trafalgar, Battle of (21 October 1805)

The Battle of Trafalgar was the most significant naval engagement of the Napoleonic Wars and the pivotal naval battle of the nineteenth century. The British victory ended the threat of an invasion of England by Napoleon and guaranteed British domination of the seas for more than a century. Central to the victory was effective use of naval signaling.

Fought 20 miles off Cape Trafalgar, west of Gibraltar on the Atlantic coast of Spain, the battle saw a Royal Navy fleet under the command of Admiral Lord Horatio Nelson (1758–1805) destroy a large combined French and Spanish fleet of thirty-three ships under the command of Vice Admiral Pierre de Villeneuve. Nelson's daring plan was to divide his smaller fleet of twenty-seven vessels into two groups. One would attack portions of the opposing enemy line and destroy them before other ships could come to their aid. Simultaneously, the other group would attack the enemy at right angles, break through their lines, and then cut off their retreat. The strategy would prove decisive, as it caught the French and Spanish ships by surprise. Nelson's sailors achieved a total defeat of the enemy fleet, which lost twenty ships (and 14,000 men, half of them prisoners) while the British lost no vessels. Nelson was mortally wounded and died toward the end of the five-hour battle, though not before he knew of his fleet's victory.

Trafalgar was also significant because Nelson effectively utilized a recently developed system of alphabetical flag signaling that had been devised by Sir Home Riggs Popham. Nelson's ability to pursue and retain control of his daring battle plan depended completely on his use of Popham's range of signal flags, which offered great flexibility in passing information from his flagship *Victory* to other ships in his fleet on a moment-by-moment basis.

Using these flag signals, Nelson encouraged his British sailors with the now famous message "England expects every man to do his duty." Lieutenant John Pasco (later a rear admiral, 1774–1853) who was serving as signal officer for Nelson, obtained the admiral's agreement to substitute the verb "expect" (which was included in Popham's code) for Nelson's original word "confide" (which was not included, and would thus have to be spelled out using more flags),

speeding up the signal process. As it was, Pasco still had to spell out "d-u-t-y," which was also not in the flag code. The famous signal was posted shortly before noon (sources differ) and took but four minutes to transmit. Nelson's equally famous order to "Engage the Enemy More Closely" (number 16 in the Popham flag code) followed at 12:20 p.m. It stayed up until shot away in the heat of the battle.

Use of these battle flags showed both the strength and weakness of such signaling methods. While the standard system allowed ready understanding by multiple vessels, the process was still cumbersome, requiring the flying of a total of thirty-one flags (seven of which spelled out "duty") plus the initial red-and-white telegraph flag, which announced a signal was forthcoming. Each word or (in the case of "duty") letter had to be separately hoisted. Only highly trained personnel could have accomplished this in just four minutes. Further, in the heat, smoke, and confusion of battle, clearly reading flag signals was anything but easy to do.

Jaime Olivares and
Christopher H. Sterling

See also Flaghoist; Flags; Napoleonic Wars (1795–1815); Popham, Home Riggs (1762–1820)

Sources

Bennett, Geoffrey Martin. 1977. *The Battle of Trafalgar.* Annapolis, MD: Naval Institute Press.

Kent, Barrie. 1993. "John Pasco and the Trafalgar Signal." in *Signal! A History of Signalling in the Royal Navy,* 7 and plate I. Clanfield, UK: Hyden House.

Lavery, Brian. 2004. *Nelson's Fleet at Trafalgar.* Annapolis, MD: Naval Institute Press.

Morriss, Roger, ed. 1997. *The Campaign of Trafalgar, 1803–1805.* London: Chatham, in association with the National Maritime Museum.

Transistor

Created by a team of Bell Telephone Laboratories scientists in the late 1940s, the transistor initiated the solid state revolution, which transformed electronic equipment of all kinds. Developed as a vacuum tube replacement for telephone applications, the Nobel Prize–winning invention spawned a new industry and revolutionized military electronics. It is widely considered the most revolutionary electronic development of the twentieth century.

At its most basic form, a transistor is a tiny (today it is microscopic) solid state device, made with a chip of a specially processed crystal substance, with three tiny terminals. A single transistor can amplify, rectify, detect, and switch signals as only a bulky and fragile vacuum tube could do before. A transistor is a semiconductor triode in engineering terms. As means of manufacturing the tiny devices became more efficient, the benefits of the transistor became rapidly apparent: compared to vacuum tubes they offered longer life and greater reliability, used less power and thus created less heat and took less space, and were far cheaper to make in bulk lots. They provided dramatic improvements in the circuit capacity of wired and radio telecommunications as well as early computers.

In December 1947 three scientists at Bell Labs, John Bardeen (1908–1991), William Shockley (1910–1989), and Walter Brattain (1902–1987) succeeded in sending an electrical signal through a specially prepared crystal of germanium—what was called a point-contact transistor. John Pierce of Bell Labs suggested the name of the device, drawing on its functions. Improved by Shockley as the more practical junction transistor, the invention was announced six months later, and its first practical application was in a Bell System telephone switching office. Bell Labs' Morgan Sparks determined how to make transistors more capable of handling complex signals—such as the human voice. Bell Labs held a conference about all aspects of the transistor in September 1951 and a detailed technical symposium in April 1952. These began the rapid development of the technology by a host of American and a few overseas companies.

The first mass-produced transistors appeared in 1953; they were soon followed by transistorized hearing aids and (in September 1954) initial pocket-size AM radios. By 1955 the first silicon-based transistors were being made. Shockley had left Bell Labs to form Shockley Semiconductor Laboratory, the pioneering San Francisco Bay company that soon initiated development of what became Silicon Valley. Bardeen (who would later win a second Nobel Prize) and Brattain moved on to other research. In 1956 the three scientists shared the Nobel Prize for their invention.

Aside from the more widely publicized consumer applications, transistors were first utilized in the developing U.S. missile and space program, and then were applied to other equipment where robustness was vital. Transistors made that equipment far lighter and somewhat less complex to manufacture. Both the Air Force and Army Signal Corps began extensive research projects into how best to develop and utilize the transistor.

Modern transistors included in integrated circuits are usually field-effect devices—and a single silicon chip today can contain more than 50 million transistors. Some estimates are that by 2010, transistors may be only half the microscopic size they already are now.

Christopher H. Sterling

See also Bell Telephone Laboratories (BTL);
Miniaturization; Silicon Valley, California;
Solid State Electronics; Vacuum Tube

Sources

Bell Telephone Laboratories. 1958. "The Transistor 1948–1958: Ten Years of Progress at Bell Telephone Laboratories." *Bell Laboratories Record* 36 (June): 190–236.

Institute of Electrical and Electronic Engineers. 1976. "Special Issue: Historical Notes on Important Tubes and Semiconductor Devices." *IEEE Transactions on Electron Devices* ED-23 (July): 595–790.

Institute of Electrical and Electronic Engineers. 1998. "Special Issue: 50th Anniversary of the Transistor!" *Proceedings of the IEEE* 86 (1): 1–217.

Ridenour, Louis N. 1951. "A Revolution in Electronics." *Scientific American* 185 (2): 13–17.

Tri-Service Tactical Communications Program (TRI-TAC)

The Tri-Service Tactical Communications Program (TRI-TAC) is a digital, large volume, circuit-switched communication system with analog-to-digital converting capability. Development began in 1971, and continually updated versions of the system have been used in military actions since the 1980s.

Army Signal Corps equipment into the 1960s provided separate voice, record, and data communications circuits. Multichannel communications used radio spectrum by combining several channels for transmission over one radio. Multichannel equipment using digital transmission was introduced in the field in the late 1960s, and approximately 25 percent of the Army's requirement had been fielded through fiscal year 1970. For the most part, equipment was solid state and represented state of the art. It was smaller, lighter,

easier to maintain, and more reliable than older equipment; it provided greater channel capacity; and it was more mobile and responsive. "Project Mallard" was established in 1968 at Fort Monmouth to develop cellular phone technologies for the battlefield. This was a development and procurement program intended to provide a secure tactical communications system for American, British, Canadian, and Australian forces in the 1980s. In 1971, however, Congress killed Mallard in favor of the TRI-TAC program.

TRI-TAC began as a concept in 1971 as military operations in South Vietnam were drawing to a close. It served as the principal voice communications system employed in a joint tactical circuit-switched network to support joint task force exercises, deployments, and contingency operations. TRI-TAC communications systems were originally fielded as means of voice command and control during the 1980s. The Army and Air Force began fielding new equipment that significantly enhanced tactical voice communications, providing the capability to install a robust hybrid (analog and digital) backbone network. This afforded the flexibility to interface with the myriad switchboards in the military inventory.

During the 1990–1991 Gulf War, Army, Air Force, Joint Communications Support Element, and Marine Corps equipment was employed to establish the theater circuit switch network. In a theater devoid of communications capabilities, these switches successfully supported both strategic and tactical users. TRI-TAC systems were also used during 1990s' operations in Somalia, Bosnia, and Kosovo, and 2002–2003 operations in Afghanistan and Iraq.

TRI-TAC communications networks consist of components that ensure users have the capability to transmit and receive voice, data, and video, regardless of location. Transmission systems are based on common TRI-TAC standards, and all interoperate. Similar to mobile subscriber equipment, the TRI-TAC network forms a communications grid of area nodes, which covers a given area of operations. The area nodes normally interconnect by line-of-sight links up to 25 miles apart. Tactical satellite and tropospheric links can further extend that range. The system also provides packet-switched data communications service for local area networks and individual host computers. TRI-TAC can operate at top secret and compartmented levels.

As users embraced commercial off-the-shelf data and video teleconferencing applications, however, TRI-TAC data capacities were quickly overwhelmed. Thus both the Army and Air Force are replacing older switches and terminals with state-of-the-art digital equipment, procuring commercial telephone switches and lightweight, multiband satellite terminals. The switches are capable of entering the Defense Integrated Switched Network or public switched telephone network.

TRI-TAC and mobile subscriber equipment (MSE) systems are now nearing the end of their planned life cycle. Their replacement will be the Warfighter Information Network–Tactical (WIN-T) in the Army's version. WIN-T will provide an advanced seamless multimedia transport system that will connect and serve all Army echelons. It will be a mobile, high-capacity, secure, and survivable network.

Danny Johnson

See also Gulf War (1990–1991); Iraq War (2003–Present); Mobile Communications; Telephone; Television; Tropospheric Scatter; Warfighter Information Network–Tactical (WIN-T)

Sources

Department of the Army. 1995. *The Signal Leaders Guide.* Field Manual 11–43 (June). Washington, DC: Government Printing Office.

Department of the Army. 2005. *The Signal Leader's Guide.* Field Manual Interim 6-02.43 2-9 (30 November). Fort Gordon, GA: U.S. Army Signal Center.

Hamilton, Brian, and Walton Brown. 2000. "Tactical High-Speed Data Network: The Army's Interim Answer to Battlefield Data Transport." *Army Communicator* 25 (Spring): 1.

Williams, Charles F., Jr. 1974. "What is TRI-TAC?" *Air University Review* 25 (May–June): 4.

Tropospheric Scatter

Also known as troposcatter, or simply tropo communications, such systems bounce signals off particles in the troposphere (the atmospheric layer closest to earth). Troposcatter systems were developed before communication satellite systems became available to provide long-distance links. The quality of early troposcatter communications often varied from hour to hour. As troposcatter signal strengths were normally low, they required high-power, high-gain antennas and sensitive receivers. However, their advantages—a cost-effective communications system for data and voice over medium and long distances—long outweighed its disadvantages.

In the 1950s and early 1960s, troposcatter systems were used for communications systems operating over longer distances. The Pinetree Line, which became operational in 1952, was the first of three communication lines supporting air defense radar sites constructed across Canada. Tropo links connected the forty-four Canadian and six U.S.

Air Force manned radar sites. The WHITE ALICE Communications System was built to connect the various aircraft control and warning radars located in Alaska. WHITE ALICE attained full operational capability on 26 March 1958. The system would eventually be expanded to connect the Distant Early Warning Line and Ballistic Missile Early Warning System line of Canadian radar stations. The systems provided communications with a reliability of more than 99 percent in the harsh Arctic conditions.

The North Atlantic Treaty Organization used troposcatter for its ACE High system as early as 1956. The ACE High system consisted of forty-nine troposcatter links and forty line-of-sight microwave links extending from Norway to Turkey. In the mid-1980s, troposcatter systems were used to extend the long-haul capability of the Joint Tri-Service Tactical Communications Program network. While advances in satellite communications in the 1980s and 1990s seemed to portend the end of troposcatter systems, ever-increasing demand for more communications capacity exceeded the capabilities of the satellite systems. Consequently, tropospheric scatter systems continued to be used for tactical communications systems.

During Operation Desert Storm in 1991, troposcatter systems provided the long-haul communications backbone for one of the longest tactical communications networks ever established. During the 1990s, new troposcatter systems were fielded by the U.S. Army, Air Force, and Marine Corps. During the Iraq War (begun in 2003 and continuing at the time of publication), troposcatter systems again provided the essential long-haul communications.

Troposcatter systems offer reliable, cost-effective, and high-capacity (up to 4 mps) long-haul communications without relying on availability of satellite channels. The systems are utilized not only by a number of the world's armed forces, including China and India, but also by commercial entities that require reliable long-haul communications.

Tommy R. Young II

See also Gulf War (1990–1991); Iraq War (2003–Present); North Atlantic Treaty Organization (NATO) Communications & Information Systems Agency; Tri-Service Tactical Communications Program (TRI-TAC)

Sources
Chaukas, Treevra. "Corps of Signals." [Online information; retrieved April 2007.] http://indianarmy.nic.in/arsig1.htm.
Emmerson, Andy. "ACE HIGH." [Online article; retrieved December 2006.] http://www.subbrit.org.uk/rsg/features/ace_high/index.html.
Pinetree Line. 2006. Home page. [Online information; retrieved December 2006.] http://www.pinetreeline.org.
Rhodes, Brad E. 2005. "What is the Future of Troposcatter in the Army? History, Successes, Usage and Upgrades Supporting the Integrated Theater Signal Battalion." [Online article; retrieved December 2006.] http://www.radio-electronics.com/info/propagation/troposcatter/troposcatter.php.
Snyder, Thomas S., et al. 1986. *The Air Force Communications Command: 1938–1986 An Illustrated History.* Scott Air Force Base, IL: Air Force Communications Command Office of History.

Truxton, Thomas (1755–1822)

Thomas Truxton (sometimes spelled Truxtun) was an American naval officer who in 1797 wrote the first naval signal book to organize the flag signal codes of the nascent American Navy.

Truxton was born on 17 February 1755 near Hempstead, New York, on Long Island. With the minimal level of education common in those days, at the age of twelve he joined the crew of the British merchant ship *Pitt*. Over the next eight years, he impressed many of his superiors with his leadership abilities. In 1775, the Royal Navy offered the twenty-year-old Truxton command of his own merchant vessel, the *Andrew Caldwell*, as a reward for his exploits. The outbreak of hostilities in the American Revolution would transform Truxton's career. He operated as an American privateer commanding at different times four ships: the *Congress, Independence, Mars,* and *St. James*. He became a national hero as he successfully captured numerous English ships while never suffering defeat.

Truxton returned to the merchant marine for another dozen years. In 1786, he commanded one of the first American ships to engage in trade with China, the *Canton*, operating from Philadelphia. When it became evident that the United States was being pulled into the continuing French Revolution in 1794, Truxton was appointed a captain in the new American Navy.

In 1797, Truxton published the first naval signal book for use by the recently organized Navy. His system utilized ten numeral pennants, made of combinations of red, white, blue, and yellow bunting, with flags for repeaters. The codes contained approximately 290 signals. During darkness or fog, signals were indicated by gun and musket fire or lights. The Navy would utilize Truxton's book to modernize its signaling technology and strategy, though the book itself was soon withdrawn when discrepancies were discovered between Truxton's manuscript and the printed version. Over the next several years, elements of his system would become the part of the basis of improved flag signaling codebooks in both the American and British navies.

Truxton died on 5 May 1822 in Philadelphia.

Jaime Olivares

See also Artillery/Gunfire; Flags; Night Signals; Popham, Home Riggs (1762–1820); Signal Book; United Kingdom Royal Navy; U.S. Navy

Sources
Ferguson, Eugene S. 1956. *Truxtun of the Constellation; the life of Commodore Thomas Truxtun, U. S. Navy, 1755–1822*. Baltimore: Johns Hopkins University Press.
Truxton, Thomas. 1797. *Instructions, Signals, and Explanations, Ordered for the United States Fleet*. Baltimore: Printed by John Hayes, in Public-Alley.

Tsushima, Battle of (27–28 May 1905)

The naval battle of Tsushima, the ultimate contest of the 1904–1905 Russo-Japanese War, was one of the most decisive sea battles in history. Superior communications capability and application played a large part in Japan's victory over a hapless Russian fleet.

Admiral Z. P. Rojdestvensky, commander of Russia's Baltic Fleet, recast as the Second Pacific Squadron, sailed to replace losses sustained in the earlier defeat of the Russian Pacific Fleet at the Battle of Shantung in August 1904. His fleet's voyage took a tedious nine months to travel 18,000 miles from the Baltic, around Africa and out to East Asian waters, an ordeal for which his coal-fired warships were ill equipped. Though the Russian objective was to break Japan's blockade of Port Arthur, by the time the exhausted fleet finally arrived, the city had already fallen. The only remaining Russian Pacific port of refuge was Vladivostok. Of the three possible passages to that port, the narrow strait of Tsushima, between Korea and Japan, was the simplest, and was chosen by Admiral Rojdestvensky—and, for the same reason, was guessed by the Japanese.

The Russian ships utilized German Slaby-Arco wireless signaling equipment with a range of not more than 65 miles, and were thus often out of touch with the Russian Admiralty. Equipment constantly broke down on the long voyage, and wireless operators were neither well trained nor well supervised. As the fleet approached the Philippines, the admiral complained that wireless traffic among his vessels was hopeless, and restricted his fleet to sail within visual signaling distance. As he approached Tsushima, he imposed radio silence, resisting a suggestion to jam Japanese wireless messages.

Japanese vessels employed an improved version of Marconi wireless equipment, and all ships could, and did, readily intercommunicate. Admiral Heihachiro Togo relied on wireless reports from outlying patrolling vessels to tell him when the Russian ships approached. Elements of his fleet spotted two Russian hospital ships on 26 May and reported immediately. At 2 p.m. on 27 May, Japanese and Russian battleships began to exchange gunfire. The Japanese ships succeeded in "crossing the T" in front of the Russian fleet twice. In the heat of battle, both fleets resorted to visual flag signals rather than wireless. Early in the morning of 28 May (after ships on both sides had scattered during darkness), the Japanese used wireless to pull their fleet together to finish off the Russian remnants.

The Japanese enjoyed several advantages in addition to their superior tactical use of wireless. Their ships were newer and faster and featured more effective artillery crewed by highly trained men who hit their targets more often. Thus the battle became a massacre of the Russians, and only four of their ships escaped. The Japanese lost only three torpedo boats, and their total casualties were tiny: 117 dead and nearly 600 injured, compared to nearly 4,400 Russian dead and 6,000 injured. This final crushing action of the Russo-Japanese War forced the Russians into U.S.-brokered peace negotiations. Tsushima established Japan as a major naval power and demonstrated the importance of effective maritime wireless communications in battle.

Arthur M. Holst and Christopher H. Sterling

See also Japan: Navy (Nippon Teikoku Kaigun); Russia/Soviet Union: Navy

Sources

Busch, Noel F. 1969. *The Emperor's Sword: Japan vs. Russia in the Battle of Tsushima.* New York: Funk & Wagnalls.

Hazlet, Arthur. 1975. *Electronics and Sea Power,* 44–49. New York: Stein & Day.

Hough, Richard. 1958. *The Fleet that Had to Die.* New York: Viking Press.

Pleshakov, Constantine. 2002. *The Tsar's Last Armada: The Epic Voyage to the Battle of Tsushima.* New York: Basic Books.

Russo-Japanese War Research Society. 2002. *Admiral Togo's Report on the Battle of Tsushima.* [Online report; retrieved September 2004.] http://www.russojapanesewar .com/ togo-aar3.html.

Turing, Alan Mathison (1912–1954)

Alan Turing was a British mathematician who pioneered development of electronic computers for the decoding of enemy electronic signals.

Turing was born 23 June 1912 in London, the son of a British official in the government of India. He graduated in mathematics in 1935 from Cambridge University's King's College. His 1935 article "On Gaussian Error Function" (concerning probability theory) won a Smith's Prize in 1936. That same year Turing began graduate work on mathematical logic at Princeton University with Alonzo Church. In 1937 Turing published his most important paper, "On Computable Numbers with Application to the Entscheidungs Problem." This addressed the question posed by David Hilbert whether all mathematical problems could be solved. Turing's answer was a definitive "no." Turing received his doctor of philosophy degree from Princeton in 1939.

To prove his mathematical conclusion Turing developed the concept of what became known later as the "Turing Machine." Turing imagined a mechanism that could read and write to a tape according to its design. The design was set forth in a table of features. While the table defining the machine was finite, the machine could do an infinite amount of work.

On 4 September 1939, the day after Britain's declaration of war on Germany, Turing joined the Government Code and Cipher School at Bletchley Park, the center of Britain's project to decode German Enigma signals. Nazi signal traffic was encoded by a typewriter-like machine called the Enigma. Turing played a central role in helping to develop an electromechanical device—dubbed a "bombe"—that could assist in the reading of German signals by reducing the number of permutations to be decoded. Over time, this and related innovations helped the Allies to ultimately defeat the U-boats in the Battle of the Atlantic.

After the war Turing joined the National Physical Laboratory in Teddington, England. He helped to design an early computer called the Automatic Computing Engine. He next accepted a position at Manchester University as a reader (member of the faculty) and assisted in the development of Britain's first large computer, the Mark I. While at Manchester, Turing worked on the Manchester Digital Machine, which was soon to become one of the most advanced computers of its day.

In 1950 Turing published "Computing Machinery and Intelligence," arguing that machines could be built to mimic human thinking. To illustrate he created the "Turing Test," in which an operator, remotely connected to another human over one line and a machine over another line, would pose a series of questions. When the examiner could no longer tell the difference between the two, artificial intelligence would have been achieved. He was one of five authorities presenting a series of five lectures on computers broadcast by the BBC in 1951.

Brilliant but sometimes odd and absent-minded in his behavior, Turing could be difficult to work with. Under increasing police surveillance because of his homosexuality, Turing took his own life on 7 June 1954 at his home in Cheshire.

Andrew J. Waskey, Jr.

See also Atlantic, Battle of the (1939–1945); Bletchley Park; Code, Codebook; Code Breaking; Computer; Enigma; Government Code & Cipher School (GC&CS, 1919–1946); Nebraska Avenue, Washington DC; Signals Intelligence (SIGINT); Ultra

Sources

Gottfried, Ted. 1996. *Alan Turing: The Architect of the Computer Age.* New York: Franklin Watts.

Hodges, Andrew. 1983. *Alan Turing: The Enigma.* New York: Simon and Schuster.

Lavington, Simon. 1980. *Early British Computers.* Manchester, UK: Manchester University Press.

Millican, P. J. R. 1996. *The Legacy of Alan Turing.* New York: Oxford University Press.

Strathern, Paul. 1999. *Turing and the Computer.* New York: Anchor Books.

U

Ultra

"Ultra" and "Top Secret Ultra" were the code terms applied by the British to their secret World War II code-breaking efforts, focused primarily on attacking the German Enigma machine-generated coded communication. The successful effort had an important impact on military and naval actions in the European and Atlantic theaters from 1940 through 1945.

Polish cryptographers first learned of the Enigma device in 1928, and through mathematical analysis began devising solutions to German message traffic. In 1930, French intelligence began working cooperatively with the Poles. In 1931, a French intelligence officer received parts of an Enigma instruction manual from a dissident German official. Several Polish mathematicians spent the next half-dozen years developing several functioning analog machines, and in July 1939, fearing that their country would soon be attacked, gave them to the French and British.

The British Government Code and Cipher School at Bletchley Park (BP) collectively designated the German machine systems as Ultra in 1940 to describe decrypted enemy radio intelligence communications—principally German, some Italian, and a few Japanese army and naval ciphers. The coded material was intercepted by Y Service radio listening posts all over Britain and around the Mediterranean for final analysis at BP.

The British first broke the codes used by the Luftwaffe in the spring of 1940. The Luftwaffe code could be used to develop some information about German army activities, but in general, German army decrypts, many of them having to do with the army's order of battle—the disposition of their land units—could not be fully interpreted until the summer of 1942. Not until mid-1943 did the British finally break the code used by the German submarine service, with the result that losses of Allied Atlantic convoys dropped off sharply.

For some months following American entry into the war in late 1941, the British were reluctant to share what they had with their new allies, but Prime Minister Winston Churchill briefed General Dwight Eisenhower on Ultra in late June 1942. Eisenhower fully grasped the value of the program, but some of his subordinates, notably Generals Mark Clark and George S. Patton, Jr., were dubious about its utility. British General Bernard Montgomery was another officer who often disregarded Ultra intelligence. The two countries eventually signed secret agreements on sharing the effort and results of their code breaking—a relationship that continues to this day.

Although the British did share some intelligence information with the French, they did not share the Ultra secret or code-breaking technology with the Russians. Occasionally, selected intelligence information such as advance warning of the German invasion of the Soviet Union in June 1941, was passed on to Josef Stalin, though to no avail.

The British, and later the Americans, utilized Special Liaison Units (SLUs) to transmit sensitive top secret Ultra material to commanders in the field on a need-to-know basis. British SLUs merely handed intelligence intercepts to their commanders, whereas American SLUs synthesized, summarized, and interpreted intercepts for their recipients. The Allies used German Ultra intercepts with care, partly owing to uncertainty about their authenticity. But the principal limitation on the use of Ultra intelligence was that the British, and later the Americans, had to identify and utilize some other pertinent piece(s) of information apart from broken codes before acting on Ultra, lest the Germans draw the conclusion that their communications had been compromised. Most details concerning the operation of Ultra remained secret until the publication of F. W. Winterbotham's *The Ultra Secret* (1974) opened the floodgates.

Keir B. Sterling

See also Arlington Hall; Bletchley Park; Code Breaking; Enigma; German "Fish" Codes; Government Code & Cipher School (GC&CS, 1919–1946); Magic; Polish Code Breaking; Signals Intelligence (SIGINT); Turing, Alan (1912–1954); Welchman, Gordon (1906–1985); Y Service

Sources
Bennett, Ralph. 1989. *Ultra and Mediterranean Strategy.* New York: Pantheon.
Calvocoressi, Peter. 1980. *Top Secret Ultra.* New York: Pantheon.
Kahn, David. 1991. *Seizing the Enigma: The Race to Break the German U-Boat Codes, 1939–1943.* Boston: Houghton Mifflin.
Kozaczuk, Wladyslaw, and Jerzy Straszak. 2004. *Enigma: How the Poles Broke the Nazi Code.* New York: Hippocrene Books.
Lewin, Ronald. 1978. *Ultra Goes to War: The First Account of World War II's Greatest Secret, Based on Official Documents.* New York: McGraw-Hill.
Sebag-Montefiore, Hugh. 2000. *Enigma: The Battle for the Code.* London: Weidenfeld & Nicolson.

Underground Communication Centers

The growing strength of artillery and bombing aircraft forced a proportion of command and communications facilities into underground bunker structures as early as World War I. The rising cost and complexity of such facilities during World War II and especially in the Cold War decades that followed underscored the growing centrality of communications in modern military conflict as well as continuity of government amid nuclear war. Numerous once-secret but now obsolete facilities have become museums in recent years—but many more remain in active use.

Perhaps the best known of the World War II sites is the Cabinet War Rooms in central

London, not far from the Houses of Parliament. Now operated by the Imperial War Museum, they were originally built in the late 1930s as tensions between Britain and Germany grew, in an attempt to protect vital communications links in a city subject to aerial bombing. They were built into a subbasement of a government office building, with specially reinforced ceilings to resist bomb impact. There were several related sites in or near London, but this set of rooms was occupied for the entire war. On occasion during the 1940 blitz and again during the 1944–1945 V-weapon attacks, Winston Churchill stayed

there. Communications facilities included a transatlantic telephone room where Churchill and Franklin Roosevelt, among others, communicated; BBC equipment for wartime broadcasts; a telephone exchange; and a large map room with numerous secure telephone links. To the west of London, at Royal Air Force Uxbridge, Fighter Command maintained its primary underground communications control during the Battle of Britain—also now a museum.

From the 1950s well into the 1970s, numerous Cold War command-and-control bunkers for both governments and military

Underground headquarters and communications centers became important in the twentieth century. This is a portion of the Cabinet War Rooms in London, located 50 feet under a government building as part of a maze of work spaces with accommodation for up to 270 people. It is now part of the Imperial War Museum. (Hulton-Deutsch Collection/Corbis)

services were constructed in (among other nations) Britain, Canada, and the United States. Several have since become museums. Less than 20 miles west of Ottawa is Carp, site of what is now derisively called the "Diefenbunker" (after the prime minister who ordered it built), designed to continue Canada's government and military capabilities in the event of nuclear war. Built between 1959 and 1961, it became a museum in the 1990s. Several similar continuity-of-government sites operated in England and Scotland, and some are now museums.

One of the better known (and still active) American sites is Cheyenne Mountain, near Colorado Springs, Colorado. Begun in 1961 as the center of North American air defense, and fully operational before the end of the decade, this massive underground site with multiple roles has constantly updated its communication facilities. Some 1,250 people from all the service branches and the Canadian armed forces staff the North American Aerospace Defense Command, U.S. Space Command, and Air Force Space Command. There are also civil defense personnel. The site can survive at least a month on its own resources, independent of any outside supplies. In 2006 plans were announced to shift many of its functions to a nearby air base.

Another (though lesser known) example is the former U.S. Strategic Air Command (SAC) center, constructed at Offutt Air Force Base outside Omaha, Nebraska, beginning in 1955. A special three-story structure below ground served SAC as its command post throughout most of the Cold War period. Made of hardened reinforced concrete, the underground command post had 24-inch thick walls and a 24- to 42-inch-thick roof and blast- and gas-proof doors. An extended tunnel led up to an above-ground office

building. The facility was always called the "molehole" due to its ramped tunnels and self-contained condition. The structure featured lavish and modern connections to the world outside. Its "big board" featured a series of huge maps and screens showing military conditions worldwide. The first Air Force computers were installed there in 1957. A "red phone" system, with dedicated connections to 200 operating locations internationally, further supported communications with the SAC underground post. An expanded center built from 1986 to 1989 included protection against electromagnetic pulse as well as state-of-the-art communications links and information displays. Through satellites and radio networks on a variety of spectrum bands, the center (now the Strategic Command Center) can communicate with aircraft in flight over any part of the world.

Both sides in the Vietnam War made extensive use of underground communications bunkers. Those in Saigon were located under the Presidential Palace and served as headquarters for the South Vietnamese government. The Viet Cong and North Vietnamese became expert builders of low-technology (but still quite effective) communication centers underground. During the decades of fighting in Afghanistan, underground facilities were extensively used by both sides. During the Gulf and Iraq wars, destruction of extensive Iraqi underground bunkers became a priority for Allied aircraft.

Indeed, going underground has become so pervasive worldwide that in 1997, the Central Intelligence Agency formed the Underground Facility Analysis Center (UFAC) as a military service and intelligence agency consortium effort to detect, characterize, coordinate, and assess potential adversarial underground facilities (or hardened and deeply buried targets—HDBT). More specifically, UFAC's mission is to provide intelligence data that would support enemy HDBT defeat. As part of this effort, the Defense Advanced Research Projects Agency formed the Counter Underground Facilities Program to focus research efforts on detection and defeat of potential enemy underground facilities.

Christopher H. Sterling

See also Britain, Battle of (1940); Defense Advanced Research Projects Agency (DARPA); Site R; Vietnam War (1959–1975); Zossen, Germany

Sources

Blair, Bruce, and Henry Kendall. 1990. "Accidental Nuclear War." *Scientific American* 263 (6): 19–24.

Esterbrook, Mark. 2005. "Underground Facility Analysis Center." [Online article; retrieved September 2005.] http://www.military-geospatial-technology.com/article.cfm?DocID=1042.

Federation of American Scientists. "C3I: Communications, Command, Control and Intelligence, United States Nuclear Forces." [Online information; retrieved September 2005.] http://www.fas.org/nuke/guide/usa/c3i/index.html.

Federation of American Scientists. "U.S. Strategic Command Command Center." [Online information; retrieved September 2005.] http://www.fas.org/nuke/guide/usa/c3i/cmdctr.htm.

Free Republic. "A List of All Known 'Cold War' Nuclear Bunkers and Subterranean Complexes in the U.K." [Online information; retrieved September 2005.] http://209.157.64.200/focus/f-news/873564/posts.

Hough, Henry W. 1970. *NORAD Command Post: The City Inside of Cheyenne Mountain.* Denver, CO: Green Mountain Press.

McCamley, N. J. 1998. *Secret Underground Cities: An Account of Some of Britain's Subterranean Defence, Factory and Storage Sites in the Second World War.* Barnsley, UK: Leo Cooper.

McCamley, N. J. 2002. *Cold War Secret Nuclear Bunkers: The Passive Defence of the Western World During the Cold War.* Barnsley, UK: Leo Cooper.

Patton, Phil. 1999. "Going Ballistic!" *Wired* November: 7–11.

Ozorak, Paul. 1998. *Bunkers Bunkers Everywhere.* Ottawa: Paul Ozorak.

Simpkins, Peter. 1983. *The Cabinet War Rooms.* London: Imperial War Museum.

Undersea Cables

Undersea communication cables have long had considerable strategic military and political value. Countries controlling access to cable networks—such as the British to at least 1930—enjoyed a substantial military benefit with this first means of global communication.

Submarine cable communication dates to about 1850, when the first short-range cables allowed telegraph signals to be sent under bodies of water, such as the English Channel, in 1851. After several failures, the first successful transatlantic cable was laid in 1866 and soon others followed in other major bodies of water, culminating with the transpacific cable of 1903. The first successful transatlantic telephone (TAT-1) cable was laid in 1956. By 1988, the TAT-8 cable employed fiber optic construction that provided far greater capacity. Military use of such cables dates from their very beginning.

The first specifically military undersea telegraph cable was laid during the Crimean War in the mid-1850s and traversed the Black Sea from Romania to the Crimean Peninsula. Though it operated for only a few months due to the crude technology of the time, it enabled connection with European land telegraph networks, and thus put London and Paris in direct touch with their troops in the field. Shortly thereafter, the Indian Mutiny of 1857 convinced the British of the need to develop rapid imperial communications. They soon developed an "all-Red" submarine telegraph network to tie their empire together. The first important link in 1870 connected London to India by way of Gibraltar, Malta, Suez, and Aden—all British colonies—and then across the Indian Ocean to Bombay. By the turn of the century, submarine telegraph cables reached virtually around the world, and Britain had funded about 75 percent of their length. Government (including military) messages received priority transmission and often cut rates. Further, the government was empowered to take over submarine cables in time of emergency.

British colonial (as opposed to British) troop concentrations could now be controlled from London, stationed where needed, and sent where required rapidly—as they often were. And orders could be more easily changed when shifting troop concentrations could maintain at least occasional contact with home commanders. Submarine telegraphy allowed for a smaller but far more mobile number of troops to be stationed abroad, and at considerable savings. Royal Navy conversion to steam—and thus the need for maintaining coaling stations at various points around the world—led to another geographic convenience when telegraph cable stations were often colocated with the coaling stations. This was a good example in which imperial administrative needs, commercial trade possibilities, and both military and naval communication all conveniently coalesced in a single system. Other countries, including the United States, had to rely on British cable networks for much of their international communication.

From 1899 to 1902, the U.S. Army developed inter-island submarine cable communications in the Philippines. Several vessels were converted to lay cable, and hundreds of miles were put in place. Eventually 1,300 miles of undersea cable (and forty-one cable stations) connected with hundreds of miles of land telegraph to tie American military forces together. Only in 1902 with the cessation of most fighting were the lines opened for limited commercial use. Both the Army and Navy developed their own small fleets of dedicated cable vessels

The British and Americans each opened transpacific cables in 1903, the delay after the Atlantic cables being due to the great distances and lack of multiple intermediate landing points. By 1904, an undersea cable and 107-mile wireless telegraph link completed an all-American communications route (previous lines included a run through part of Canada) from Alaska to Washington DC and elsewhere in the continental United States. By 1906 the Washington-Alaska Military Cable and Telegraph System was handling more than 300,000 messages per year—about 20 percent of them military in nature. The lines, constructed at a cost of around $2 million (or about $40 million in 2006 dollars), were maintained by the Army Signal Corps.

As early as the Spanish-American War (if not earlier yet), cables were recognized as important means of military communications and were regularly cut during hostilities. Military use of cables required coded messages given the number of people involved in handling the traffic. By the turn of the twentieth century the U.S. Navy claimed to have a superior coding system in place—and used it to keep in touch with naval attachés during the Russo-Japanese War of 1904–1905.

While the inception of wireless radio after 1900 began to siphon off some of the cable traffic, ironically the newer mode of transmission underscored a special value of the old—communication security. At the inception of World War I, the British cut five German telegraph cables in the English Channel, thus forcing the enemy to use radio—which could be intercepted and decoded. (At the time there was no capacity for tapping cables to learn what was being communicated.) Among the intercepted radio signals was the infamous German "Zimmermann" telegram, which was the proximate cause of American entry into World War I early in 1917.

Even as cable technology improved, however, liabilities remained. Chief among them were the landing sites for cables where the system became highly vulnerable to natural or manmade service cut-offs. Cable landing sites were often noted on ships' maps (to avoid fouling the cable), which reduced their security that much more.

Maps of the world's submarine cables reveal another important political and economic, if not military, factor—there are few lines to or around Africa or South America. Most Southern Hemisphere nations (Australia and New Zealand are exceptions) must communicate with the rest of the world by cables connecting Northern Hemisphere nations.

With the inception of communication satellites by the 1970s, undersea cables began to lose their hegemony over long-distance communications. Satellites had greater capacity and could be designed and launched more rapidly than a cable could be constructed. With the later development of fiber optic cable in the 1980s, however, the tables slowly turned again, as the new cables now offered greater capacity, as well as the option of repairing problems, rarely possible with satellites. Increasingly both modes are used to back up the other.

During the 1970s, American submarines began placing taps on undersea cables along the Soviet Pacific coast. Submarines had to return every few months to pick up tapes that recorded the communications. Soon similar "listening pods" were implanted on other Soviet cables, able to pick up magnetic emanations from the cable without penetrating it. The mission was ultimately betrayed by a spy, and the recording device is now at the KGB Museum of Security Service in the Lubyanka in Moscow. But additional taps continued for several years. The "Ivy Bells" tapping project, for example, allegedly involved hooking up a nuclear radioisotope-powered pod (which could be 20 feet long) containing tape recorders, which was left in place for almost a year between submarine visits to recover the tapes.

This would be harder to do with the gigabytes per second flowing through a modern fiber cable, as there is no unclassified recording device with anything like the storage capacity to record everything, or even a significant fraction of everything, for that long a period in a form that would fit in a pod on the sea floor. According to published accounts, in the early Reagan years the intelligence community considered running its own fiber cable to tap sites on the Soviet analog cables to recover the data in real time, but the end of the Cold War terminated the need.

The USS *Jimmy Carter*, a Seawolf-class nuclear submarine, entered the U.S. fleet early in 2005 with enhanced signals communications intelligence abilities, reportedly including the ability to tap into fiber optic cables. Her hull is 100 feet longer than that of her sisters, thus allowing stowage of undersea intelligence devices and vehicles. The submarine's ability to tap fiber optic cables, however, may be unique in the fleet.

Christopher H. Sterling

See also Communication Satellites; European Late Nineteenth-Century Wars; Field, Cyrus W. (1819–1892); Signals Intelligence (SIGINT); Submarine Communications

Sources

Finn, Bernard S., and Vary T. Coates. 1979. "War and National Security." In *A Retrospective Technology Assessment: The Transatlantic Cable of 1866*, 97–116. San Francisco: San Francisco Press.

Haigh, K. R. 1968. "United States Army, United States Navy." In *Cableships and Submarine Cables*, 285–299. London: Adlard Coles.

Hecht, Jeff. 1999. "Submarine Cables: Covering the Ocean Floor with Glass (1970–1995)." In *City of Light: The Story of Fiber Optics*, 201–215. New York: Oxford University Press.

Lumpkin, John J. 2005. "USS *Carter* Will Be Able to Eavesdrop." Associated Press, February 18.

Russel, Edgar. 1902. "The Military Cable System of the Philippines." *Transactions of the American Institute of Electrical Engineers* May 28: 629–641.

Schenck, Herbert H., and Leo Waldick. 1991. *1990 World's Submarine Telephone Cable Systems*. Washington, DC: National Telecommunications and Information Administration.

Sontag, Sherry, and Christopher Drew. 1998. *Blind Man's Bluff: The Untold Story of American Submarine Espionage*. New York: Public Affairs Press.

Williams, Charles E., Jr. 1978. "Communications and Crisis Actions." [Online article; retrieved June 2006.] http://www.airpower.maxwell.af.mil/airchronicles/aureview/1978/mar-apr/williams.html.

United Kingdom: Royal Air Force

Britain's Royal Air Force (RAF) has pioneered many modes of communication, both tactical and strategic, during its long history. The Royal Flying Corps (RFC) was created on 13 May 1912, superseding an air battalion of the Royal Engineers formed just the year before as part of the British army. RFC pioneering began with an experiment that year using spark-gap radio equipment at an airfield at Hendon (near London) transmitting to an aircraft circling overhead.

On 15 September 1914 the RFC made its first use of wireless telegraphy during observation flights over enemy artillery positions. During the Battle of the Aisne, the RFC made its first operational use of aerial photography. The corps was responsible for observation balloons as well as artillery spotting over the Western Front. Reports were originally dropped to the ground tied to rocks. Early RFC aircraft radios were heavy and cumbersome and difficult to operate, and only received signals from the ground. As radios improved, however, low-flying RFC aircraft equipped with two-way wireless cooperated with ground forces and attacked enemy forces, facilities, and airfields.

The RFC also researched how wireless telegraphy could be used to help defend against German airplane or Zeppelin bombing raids. By 1916 the corps had developed a lightweight aircraft receiver and a Marconi half-kilowatt ground transmitter, which could be located on aerodromes in raid-threatened areas. The aircraft receiver was tuned in advance, and the pilot had to unreel a 150-foot aerial from its drum and switch it on. Initial trials in May 1916 demonstrated that signals were clearly heard up to ten miles. Further development by November provided clear signals over twenty miles. Pilots could be informed about enemy aircraft and attack them before they could bomb Britain.

After 1917, much RFC wireless training took place in Canada (at Camp Borden,

Ontario). After considerable debate, the RFC and the Royal Navy Flying Service were merged to form the Royal Air Force on coequal status with the army on 1 April 1918.

Between the wars, the RAF was dramatically scaled down in equipment and personnel, only beginning to rebuild in the late 1930s. Technical development was also slowed, save for the innovation of radar on the eve of World War II. On Britain's entry into the war on 3 September 1939, only one of 135 RAF squadrons was devoted to communications. It became the RAF Signals Organization, and much of its emphasis was on the vital radar technology.

On 1 January 1940 the RAF introduced identification, friend or foe (IFF) signals to help identify bomber, coastal, and fighter aircraft on radar screens. Radio likewise played a central role in the Battle of Britain. On 7 October 1940, No. 80 (Signals) Wing became the RAF's first electronic warfare unit. As an example of what could be accomplished, on 13–14 November 1940, two aircraft of the Wireless Intelligence and Development Unit made the first direct attack on enemy navigational radar installations on the Cherbourg Peninsula by homing in on their transmission signals.

The RAF developed an extensive teleprinter network linking its ground control and airfield facilities. Communications hubs for these and voice communications were located in several underground centers around the country, interconnected by coaxial cable and high-frequency radio links. Links to aircraft included both voice (for fighters) and telegraphy (more for transports and bombers), both using code systems for security. On 18 July 1944 VHF radios fitted in tanks were first used to call for close air support during the ongoing breakout from the D-Day landing areas. By 1945, the term "sig-

nals" in the RAF spanned different disciplines. It comprised radio communications (air and ground); radio aids to navigation; radio as an airborne bombing or interception aid; airborne and ground radars (both those used for fighter control and for air traffic management); electronic intelligence and electronic warfare; and teleprinter, telegraph, and telephone services. The worldwide intercommand telecommunications system was supplemented by an air traffic control organization with its associated communications systems and approach aids, and maintenance organizations to address the needs of both ground and airborne systems. But there was little centralized control over all of these functions.

Post Design Services (PDS) was formed at the Telecommunications Research Establishment at Malvern during the war to provide a direct link between the designers of electronic equipment in the laboratories and the service users in the field. The organization was manned by civilian scientists and serving officers and worked predominantly in the fields of airborne radar and ground control interception. In 1946, PDS was disbanded and a successor organization, the Radio Introduction Branch (RIB), was formed at RAF Medmenham. In 1952, RIB became the Radio Introduction Unit responsible for the introduction of all airborne and ground radio systems. The unit had a complement of ten officers dealing with airfield approach aids, airborne tail warning, Doppler navigation, weapon aiming, and airborne interception for various RAF aircraft

In the 1950s, No. 90 (Signals) Group provided a single focus for all signals matters, including the design, manufacture, installation, operation, and maintenance of RAF signals systems. Its principal units included the Central Signals Establishment and the Radio Engineering Unit. No. 90 Group became the

Signals Command on 3 November 1958. But British military forces were drawing down around the world, and on 1 April 1964 a unified Ministry of Defence (MOD) was created, and the Air Ministry became MOD's Air Force Department. A common signals staff serving all three services was one outcome. The RAF signals staff was reduced to just one branch, and Signals Command reverted to group status once again, within Strike Command, on 1 January 1969. Further interservice rationalization led to the RAF assuming responsibility for all strategic defense networks. Continued reductions in British commitments overseas meant the return of overseas garrisons and headquarters, and a consequent reduction in needed telecommunications. 90 Group became Support Command's Signals Headquarters.

By the early twenty-first century, RAF signals communications (still a part of the RAF Strike Command) could be divided into three categories. First, there is a large complex of high-frequency transmitter and receiver facilities in Britain, including communications centers with automatic message routing equipment. Operations include those on behalf of Strike Command, the Military Air Traffic Organisation, the North Atlantic Treaty Organization (NATO), and the meteorological office.

Second, the RAF Signals Staff operate both automatic and manual message relay centers, and also manage the RAF's general purpose telephone network. For the use of all British armed forces, MOD has procured a fixed telecommunications network called Boxer under an outside contract, which will save the increasing expense of renting lines from the private sector. RAF Henlow has been a ground-training base specializing in electronics since the end of World War II and was for many years the base for the RAF

Signals Engineering Establishment. The station is now home to the Directorate of Engineering Interoperability, which is part of the Defence Communications Services Agency.

Third, the main operation of the Skynet Satellite Communications System, which offers overseas formations telegraph, data, and speech communications, is controlled by the RAF Command. RAF Oakhanger is the focal point of military satellite communications in the United Kingdom. During 1998, three Skynet 4 Stage 2 satellites entered service. The RAF also manages the NATO 4 series of satellites. Skynet 5 is expected to enter service in 2008 and provide the next generation of flexible and survivable satellite communications services for military use. Robust military satellite communications services are essential to support inter- and intratheater information exchange and to ensure that deployed and mobile forces are not constrained by the need to remain within the range of terrestrial communications. RAF command operating procedures are monitored on all networks to ensure high standards are maintained.

The RAF Tactical Communications Wing (TCW, formed in 1965 and taking its present name in 1969) installs, operates, and maintains transportable tactical communications and information systems in support of RAF squadrons and units deployed worldwide for what can include support of United Nations operations or acting as part of the NATO Reaction Forces. Its capability can be divided into three main areas: bare base operation, tactical satellite communications (with equipment delivered by small vehicles), and trunk communications. The last is achieved by using the new RAF Transportable Telecommunications System, which enables the switching of voice and data services around a mesh network, effectively creating a wide area network extension of what is available in Britain. TCW has about 450 personnel.

To reduce risk of compromise, all RAF communications facilities are designed to carry classified information and are regularly checked for communications electrical security. Their signals operation has a large engineering design staff of engineers, technicians, and draftsmen. Manufacturing resources include a general mechanical engineering and calibration capacity at RAF Henlow, plus a facility for the system design, development, and installation of certain airborne signals role equipment.

An RAF signals museum at RAF Henlow is open on occasion.

Christopher H. Sterling

See also Airplanes; Airships and Balloons; Britain, Battle of (1940); Defence Communications Service Agency (DCSA); Falklands Conflict (1982); Identification, Friend or Foe (IFF); North Atlantic Treaty Organization (NATO) Communications & Information Systems Agency; Teleprinter/Teletype; United Kingdom: Royal Corps of Signals; World War I; World War II; Y Service

Sources
McLaughlan, S. 2003 "TCW: The Tactical Communications Wing." [Online information retrieved April 2006.] http://www.raf.mod.uk/history/.
Nutting, C. W. 1942. "Signals and Radio." *Flying: Special Royal Air Force Issue* September: 138–140.
Reader, Dennis. The Sound of Trumpets: History of the RAF Signals Service, 1945–1975 (in preparation). [Online information; retrieved March 2006.] http://members.aol.com/ DenReader/RAF_History.html.
Royal Air Force, Air Historical Branch. Various dates. *Royal Air Force Signals in the Second World War*. 7 vols. London: Air Ministry.
Royal Air Force History. Home page. [Online information; retrieved March 2006.] http://www.raf.mod.uk/history/.
Royal Air Force. "RAF Communications." [Online information; retrieved March 2006.] http://www.armedforces.co.uk/raf/listings/l0051.html.

United Kingdom: Royal Corps of Signals

As the chief information and communications provider for the British army, the Royal Corps of Signals deploys everywhere the army goes. The corps provides communications links throughout the army's command-and-control system. While individual units are responsible for their own internal communications, most communications from brigade level and above are the responsibility of the corps. In modern terms, Royal Signals acts as a significant "force multiplier."

Origins

The Royal Corps of Signals was established on 28 June 1920, but its ancestry is as a direct descendant of the Royal Engineers. The Royal Engineers' interest in military communications began during the Crimean War (1854–1856), when they were first assigned the task to build and operate electric telegraph links. Telegraphers and signalers gained further active field experience during the Abyssinian War of 1867.

Partly because of the experience gained during these two campaigns, authority was given in 1869 to form a separate signal wing at the Royal Engineer Depot at Chatham. During 1870, "C" Telegraph Troop was formed and was responsible for providing telegraph communications for the field army. This troop saw active service in the Zulu War of 1879, where the heliograph first gained recognition. Many heliographs were made in India, and the device would be used in combat from the northwest frontier of

India through World War I and into the desert campaign of World War II.

The Royal Engineer Telegraph Battalion was formed in 1884 and took part in the Nile Campaign and later played an important role in the Ashanti Campaign of 1895–1896. During this campaign the Telegraph Battalion hacked a path for an overhead line from the Cape coast to Prahsu, covering 72 miles through jungle. As members of the Telegraph Battalion staggered out of the jungle, they confronted King Prempeh, who was so surprised by their unexpected appearance that he surrendered his forces (his throne is now displayed in the Royal Signals Museum at Blandford).

The corps' first wireless telegraph companies were formed in 1907, followed a year later with establishment of the Royal Engineer Signal Service, which became responsible for all forms of army communication.

World War I

At the outbreak of war in August 1914, the British army had few wireless sets. These spark transmitters operated on long wave and were cumbersome, heavy, and unreliable. The Royal Flying Corps had begun to use wireless to direct artillery fire. A Marconi transmitter was fit into an aircraft that allowed sending of a Morse signal to be picked up on the ground. By 1915 trench sets were used on the Western Front but suffered as the enemy could easily overhear the messages.

Thousands of miles of cable and line were used during the four years of war, constantly being repaired or replaced due to damage by shell fire and movement of troops. French civilian telephones were pressed into frontline service, but were not designed to operate in damp, muddy conditions. Equipment slowly improved. One field switchboard was self-contained with its own instrument, calling generator, night bell, and speaking set. Having provided excellent service, it went on to serve during the next war two decades later. The standard army field telephone incorporated a buzzer unit and a Morse key so it could be used to send and receive Morse if the circuit was too noisy for voice transmissions.

Visual signaling methods included flags, lamps and lights, and the heliograph. Signal flags were normally blue and white, and lightweight silk flags could, with a competent operator, reach about twelve words per minute. Although visual signaling was generally unsuitable for trench warfare (because the operator had to show himself), in 1915 a system of signaling discs and shutters was introduced that could be operated from within a trench and read using a periscope. The heliograph, flags, and lamps were especially valuable when the army was moving too quickly to establish a telephone network. The trench signaling lamp featured a bull's-eye lens to concentrate the light and a Morse key to switch it on and off. Useful in signaling from trench to trench, operators could see its signal using a periscope or telescope. It was always dangerous to transmit toward the battlefield, as this attracted enemy fire. Finally, many traditional methods were in continual use. Dogs carried messages between trenches, and horses, mules, and dogs were all used to lay wire and cables. At various periods during the war, more than 20,000 pigeons and 370 pigeoneers were in the war zone. Very often pigeons were the sole means of communication.

The idea to establish a separate signal corps was considered in 1918, but various institutional and policy obstacles delayed action until 28 June 1920, when a royal warrant gave the king's approval to its formation. George V conferred on the new corps the honor of using the title "Royal" on 5

August 1920. During the 1920s and 1930s, the corps increased its strength and had personnel serving in a variety of overseas stations of the empire. The largest portion of corps personnel were overseas, nearly a third in India.

World War II

Once again, the British army was ill equipped when war broke out in September 1939. Royal Signals units traveled to France with the British Expeditionary Force, though some of the signalers were not fully trained and much of the equipment was obsolescent. As happened two decades earlier, the civilian telephone system was used in France and Belgium as messages were less likely to be intercepted this way.

The long North African campaign (1940–1943) was fast moving, and Royal Signal units had to lay and retrieve telephone cables and establish wireless links at great speed. Lessons learned in the desert proved invaluable in the mobile warfare that followed the Normandy D-Day landing in June 1944. The corps developed an armored command vehicle equipped with signaling capabilities that was used throughout campaigns in North Africa and Europe. The Wireless Station No. 10 was the technological wonder of its time and something of a forerunner of modern radio relay equipment. The station was contained in a 2-ton trailer and provided telephone circuits over a duplex radio path. If the route was longer, up to seven relay stations could be inserted in the chain.

As the Allies moved through northwest Europe, Royal Signals laid hundreds of miles of telephone and telegraph cables and made use of civilian networks wherever possible. Communications to the United Kingdom were made via a cable laid under the English Channel connected to signal stations at Bayeaux and Cherbourg. All fighting forces used machines to encrypt messages, the British version being the Typex. Members of the corps served in every theater, and by 1945 the corps had a serving strength of 8,500 officers and 142,500 soldiers. Nearly 4,400 members of Royal Signals were killed.

Since 1945

The corps played a full and active part in numerous postwar campaigns including operation of the British Mandate in Palestine (1945–1948); the long antiguerrilla campaign in Malaya (1949–1960); the Korean War (1950–1953); the Suez Crisis (1956); and various operations in Cyprus, Borneo, Aden, the Arabian Peninsula, Kenya, and Belize. Until the end of the Cold War in 1990, the main body of the corps was deployed with the British Army of the Rhine confronting the Communist bloc forces, and providing much of the North Atlantic Treaty Organization's (NATO) communications infrastructure. Corps personnel also spearheaded individual operations, including the Falkland Islands campaign (1982); peacekeeping force in Lebanon; supervising the peaceful transition of Namibia to independence; and the 1990–1991 Persian Gulf campaign. Since then, members of the corps have been deployed to East Timor; Kurdistan; the states of Bosnia, Croatia, and Kosovo; the western Sahara; Cambodia; Rwanda; Angola; Zaire; and Sierra Leone.

The modern corps transmits, in a secure and timely manner, facsimile, voice, telegraph, and data—it is, in effect, the nervous system of the British army. As of the early twenty-first century, the corps operates three main types of battlefield equipment. The "Clansman" combat net radio system equipment is being replaced by the "Bowman" system, which uses secure voice as the principal means for command and control. Trunk communication in the corps uses "Ptarmigan" and "Euromux" equipment to provide battlefield-area coverage communications. These provide secure mobile telephones across the battlefield, as well as to brigade headquarters and higher. Finally, corps forces also provide facsimile and data and satellite communications. They provide operational theater as well as strategic links back to headquarters. Equipment can range from small man-pack sets to large vehicle-transportable equipment.

With officers and soldiers serving in every British and NATO headquarters, Royal Signals constitutes about 9 percent of the British army with Regular and Territorial Army Regiments (Reserve Component), each generally consisting of between three and up to six squadrons, with between 600 and 1,000 personnel. The strength of Royal Signals as of the early twenty-first century is about 900 officers, 8,200 regular soldiers, and 5,300 territorial soldiers. Royal Signals units are permanently based in Germany, Holland, and Belgium, from where they provide the necessary command-and-control communications and electronic warfare support for both the British army and other NATO forces. Royal Signals units are also based in Cyprus, the Falkland Islands, Belize, Gibraltar, Afghanistan, and Iraq. The size, role, and deployment of Royal Signals units are organized to meet the command-and-control requirements of the formation commanders. Because of this, no two units have the same organization or role. Corps headquarters is at the Royal School of Signals located at Blandford Camp in Dorset.

Danny Johnson

See also Blandford Camp; Boer War Wireless (1899–1902); Defence Communications Service Agency (DCSA); European Late Nineteenth-Century Wars; Falklands Conflict (1982); Golden Arrow Sections; Gulf War (1990–1991); Heliograph and Mirrors; North Atlantic Treaty Organization (NATO) Communications & Information Systems Agency; Signals Research and Development Establishment (SRDE); Suez Crisis (1956); TELCOM Mobile Wireless Units; Telegraph; World War I; World War II

Sources
Adams, R. M. 1970. *Through to 1970: Royal Signals Golden Jubilee*. London: Royal Signals Institution.
British Army. "The Royal Signals: Other Communications Systems." [Online information; retrieved April 2006.] http://www.armedforces.co.uk/army/listings/l0106.html#ARMY%20FIXED%20TELE COMMUNICATIONS%20SYSTEMS.
Lord, Cliff, and Graham Watson. 2003. *The Royal Corps of Signals: Unit Histories of the Corps (1920–2001) and Its Antecedents*. Solihull, UK: Helion.
Nalder, R. F. H. 1953. *The History of British Army Signals in the Second World War*. London: Royal Signals Institution.
Nalder, R. F. H. 1958. *The Royal Corps of Signals: A History of Its Antecedents and Development*. London: Royal Signals Institution.
Royal Corps of Signals. "A Brief History." [Online information; retrieved May 2006.] http://www.army.mod.uk/royalsignals/history.html.
Royal Engineers Museum and Library. "Telegraph and Signals." [Online information; retrieved May 2006.] http://www.remuseum.org.uk/rem_his_special.htm #signals.
Warner, Philip. 1989. *The Vital Link: The Story of Royal Signals 1945–1985*. London: Leo Cooper.

United Kingdom: Royal Navy

The Royal Navy traces its history back a half-millennium. Along with its many other innovations, the British Admiralty has sometimes resisted but more usually embraced improvements in communications.

Days of Sail

The "Navy Royal" of Henry VIII in the early 1500s was the forerunner of the modern Royal Navy, which dates to the mid-seventeenth century. A series of wars against the Dutch and French helped to hone naval practice and ship design. The first naval signal book (with colored drawings of fifteen flags) appeared in 1673 in the midst of these wars. A published and more comprehensive book—though still a private venture—appeared in the early 1700s. As its wartime naval strength increased from 40,000 in the wars of 1739–1748 to 150,000 at the peak of the Napoleonic Wars, the navy required use of notorious "press gangs" to obtain the needed sailors.

In 1776 Admiral Lord Richard Howe tried to reduce the growing number of confusing nonstandard flag signals to create an integrated system, one he further revised in 1782. The Royal Navy adopted a related but more streamlined signal flag system devised by Captain Sir Home Riggs Popham in 1800 (modified in 1803 and 1812). The Popham system proved vital when used by Admiral Horatio Nelson in his victory at the Battle of Trafalgar on 21 October 1805.

For a century, from 1815 to 1914, the Royal Navy generally ruled supreme and greatly aided the expanding empire. Wooden ships gave way to iron and then steel as sails were replaced by paddles and then screw propulsion. Through much of this period, however, naval signaling remained fairly static, using a book of flag signals issued in 1857 and adopted by many other nations over the next three decades. Various night signals of flashing lights were continually being perfected, eventually resulting in the late nineteenth

century in the Aldis lamp, which remained in active service for ship-to-ship communication for nearly a century.

In 1888 the Admiralty announced plans for the first formal training in signaling (heretofore it had been learned on the job), to include the traditional flags, various light signals for nighttime operations, mechanical semaphores, and electric telegraphy, among other modes. Courses were set up at both the Portsmouth and Devonport (and later Chatham) naval bases. Training lasted for two months, about half focused on the theory of signaling overall and the other half devoted to practical training. These became more organized signal schools in the mid 1890s, and became centralized in Portsmouth.

Rise of Radio

At the same time the Royal Navy became a center of early wireless telegraphy experimentation, chiefly by then Captain Henry Jackson. By 1898 the navy had formed an experimental wireless telegraphy department operating on HMS *Defiance* for continuing experiments that achieved increasing transmission distance. Some worried that wireless transmission might threaten a ship's powder magazine. In 1899, however, Marconi apparatus was installed on four ships during fleet exercises and these removed most doubts about both the safety and value of the new technology.

But intership interference was a serious problem (tuning to specific frequencies was not yet being practiced), which limited the value of wireless.

While the Navy cooperated with Guglielmo Marconi and utilized his equipment, by the early 1900s military and commercial needs and equipment began to increasingly diverge. Magnetic detectors of wireless signals replaced the fragile coherers, and antennas (aerials) hung between ships' masts became more common. Radio equipment was now powered by the ship's generators rather than the troublesome batteries used earlier, and wireless capability was increasingly found on ships as small as destroyers. The Wireless Telegraphy Branch was established in 1907 and the signaling schools extended their curriculum accordingly. The Navy soon (1909–1913) developed several dedicated shore wireless stations for fleet communications (parallel to what the U.S. Navy was doing). Signal officers (often admirals' flag lieutenants) now controlled message distribution from origin to reception. Wireless research and experimentation continued, now aboard the three hulks making up HMS *Vernon* moored in Portsmouth (it moved ashore, though retaining the ship designation, in 1923). By World War I, British submarines carried wireless apparatus, though it could generally cover only about 50 miles.

The Royal Navy's first direction-finding equipment arrived with the inception of World War I in 1914. This proved vital in keeping track of the German High Seas Fleet as well as in locating and monitoring German wireless transmitters on both ships and land. Capture of codebooks from the German cruiser *Magdeburg* in 1914 aided the process hugely. The Navy's Room 40 soon became the center of this code-breaking process. Y Service monitoring stations were also soon established. The Admiralty established the Government Code and Cipher School in 1919 (to help break foreign codes while improving the security of British ciphers), which was transferred to the Foreign Office in 1923.

Wireless played an important part in the battles of Coronel, where a German squadron almost wiped out a weaker British force, and the subsequent fight off the Falkland Islands, where the British loss was avenged.

The British squadron steaming to the Falklands observed radio silence to mask its movements. Likewise, monitoring of German wireless traffic provided the Royal Navy's Grand Fleet with advance notice that the Germans were moving into the North Sea at the end of May 1916. But radio played a lesser role in the Battle of Jutland itself, as British commanders relied on traditional flag signals—with varied results. The growing importance of wireless led in 1917 to elevating the Signal Section to a division. Later the same year a committee was established to work out interference between army and navy stations.

After World War I, vacuum tube (valve)–powered equipment began to replace older arc and spark-gap devices. An "empire" chain of high-frequency land stations was established at various points throughout the British colonies to aid in naval communication. After considerable debate, signaling (meaning with flags and lights) and wireless operators were merged as radio experimentation and equipment improvement continued. Increased focus on line telephone links for naval stations also took place.

World War II
During World War II, two Cunard–White Star liners, *Queen Mary* and the new *Queen Elizabeth*, were treated as naval auxiliaries when carrying troops and thus carried and used naval ciphers. They (and several other large liners) were known in the service as "the monsters," as their displacement exceeded any naval fighting ship. Wireless crews were expanded when Prime Minister Winston Churchill was aboard, as he was on several transatlantic occasions for meetings with President Franklin Roosevelt.

Most wartime fleet radio work was in the low and medium frequencies as VHF radio was still experimental. The American TBS ("talk between ships") system was later adopted and used VHF. Telegraphy code was preferred over voice so that a physical copy of orders resulted and because circuits were not designed for clear voice signaling. Most messages were encrypted to discourage enemy listening, and far more went from the Admiralty in London (often by a broadcast system) to ships at sea rather than the other way around. Ships used a random two-letter call to hide their identity from enemy listeners, and transmitters could operate on multiple frequencies, usually at the lowest possible power (again to discourage enemy monitoring).

Radio (and other modes of communication) contributed crucially to several Royal Navy engagements of the war. The sinking of the German *Graf Spee* off Montevideo in December 1939 was aided by radio deception, suggesting the shadowing British cruisers had been more seriously damaged than was the case. The sinking of *Bismarck* early in 1941 was made possible when the German battleship broke radio silence, assisting in giving away her location. Atlantic convoys were shepherded by radio and Aldis lamp, all the time communicating with the Admiralty. HMS *Bulolo* became the Royal Navy's first specially fitted headquarters ship (soon followed by three others, with the design shared with the U.S. Navy), loaded with all means of communication. She was on hand for D-Day (6 June 1944). In March 1945, Royal Navy units joined the American navy for the final months of the Pacific War, integrating communication links and ciphers and codebooks with the larger U.S. force.

Postwar Change

The postwar period saw extensive ship-to-shore radio systems merged with the merchant navy in 1946 in a move to trim costs. High-speed Morse automation replaced hand-operated telegraphy links. Royal Navy use of high-quality voice, radio teletype, and facsimile services was tested aboard HMS *Vanguard* (the service's final battleship) when she served in 1947 as the royal yacht for a visit to Australia. Royal Navy units were involved with United Nations forces in the Korean War, again using American signaling systems and codebooks. In Europe the North Atlantic Treaty Organization (NATO) was taking hold and naval forces were swinging over to use of VHF (while the U.S. Navy was making the transition to UHF). Combined naval exercises helped to test changing modes of communicating. Many were under the auspices of the developing NATO command through its Allied Naval Communications Agency based in London.

By the late 1950s, Royal Navy communications had begun to shift to more automated operation as well as developing early data communication links. Reliable Radio Teletype initiated automated operations in 1955. The first Royal Navy computer, Signal Transmitting Receiving and Distributing equipment, appeared in the Admiralty in 1957. The Integrated Communication System, which entered service in the mid-1960s, incorporated broadband as well as centralized control and monitoring. By 1963, the Royal Navy's radio equipment used single-sideband technology.

As Britain drew down its commitments and forces from "East of Suez," however, demands on naval communication diminished and change came more slowly. Still, by the 1990s, command, control, and communications systems aboard naval vessels allowed a variety of modes of communication, most of it increasingly digital and utilizing communication satellites. The 1982 Falklands War (and the Gulf War eight years later) showed the value of satellite links over great distances from London to the fighting squadron. Electronic countermeasure equipment became more common and effective. As with the U.S. Navy, Royal Navy ships began to employ women in communication roles at sea, in part due to a growing shortage of men. But fewer operators were needed with the increasingly automated, digital, and Internet-based modes of signaling.

Christopher H. Sterling

See also Aldis Lamp; Atlantic, Battle of the (1939–1945); Bletchley Park; Code Breaking; *Defiance*, HMS; Falklands Conflict (1982); Flaghoist; Flags; Government Code & Cipher School (GC&CS, 1919–1946); High-Speed Morse; Jackson, Henry B. (1855–1929); Jutland, Battle of (1916); Marconi, Guglielmo (1874–1937); Napoleonic Wars (1795–1815); Night Signals; North Atlantic Treaty Organization (NATO) Communications & Information Systems Agency; Popham, Home Riggs (1762–1820); Radio Silence; Semaphore (Mechanical Telegraphs); Single Sideband (SSB); Talk Between Ships (TBS); Trafalgar, Battle of (21 October 1805); Ultra; World War I, World War II; Y Service

Sources

Broome, Jack E. 1955. *Make a Signal!* London: Putnam.

Broome, Jack E. 1973. *Make Another Signal: A History of Naval Signals from Salamis to World War II.* London: William Kimber.

Hezlet, Arthur. 1975. *Electronics and Sea Power.* New York: Stein & Day.

Hill, J. R., ed. 1995. *The Oxford Illustrated History of the Royal Navy.* Oxford, UK: Oxford University Press.

Kent, Barrie. 1993. *Signal! A History of Signalling in the Royal Navy.* Clanfield, UK: Hyden House.

Palmer, Michael A. 2006. *Command at Sea: Naval Command and Control Since the Sixteenth Century.* Cambridge, MA: Harvard University Press.

Royal Navy. "History." [Online information; retrieved April 2006.] http://www.royal-navy.mod.uk/server/show/nav.3839.

U.S. Marine Corps

The U.S. Marine Corps, the American military service first formed in 1775 and permanently established in 1798, has always sought modes of communication that work effectively in sea, land, and (as of 1913) air operations. Organizationally, the corps is part of the U.S. Navy, providing its seaborne military strength. The Navy, in turn, supplies many of the support functions for the corps. Marines have been committed to combat in virtually every American military action from the nineteenth century into the twenty-first.

Amphibious warfare techniques were developed in the years between the world wars (the Fleet Marine Force was formed in 1933) and proved invaluable in the Pacific during World War II. Beginning in 1942, the Marine Corps used Native American code talkers for many of its island radio links—and the Japanese never could decipher the messages. By the war's end in 1945, the corps had grown to include six divisions, five air wings, and supporting troops (including communication units)—nearly a half-million Marines. At the outbreak of the Korean War in mid-1950, a much-diminished Marine Corps had no unit of any size deployed in the Far East. After three years of war, however, corps strength ballooned back up to nearly a quarter-million men in June 1953. Marine use of ground-support helicopters in Korea greatly expanded its capabilities and communications.

The corps played a key role in the 1970s' development of the Rapid Deployment Force, a multiservice organization created to ensure a flexible, timely military response around the world. The Maritime Pre-Positioning Ships program was begun in late 1979 to provide three Marine amphibious brigades ready for airlift to potential crisis areas where they would unite with previously positioned ships carrying their equipment (including communications) and supplies. Marine air units averaged 60 percent fixed wing and 40 percent helicopter aircraft able to operate from small carriers at sea or land bases.

By the 1990s, on any given day, about 175,000 Marines were deployed away from their home bases. During the decade, the Marines were "sent in" to some crisis spot more than fifty times—on average, the Marine Corps is called upon once every five weeks. Marine Air-Ground Task Forces formed into four separate Marine Expeditionary Units deploy for six months, each having an average strength of 2,200 Marines and sailors, and their own communications capabilities. Consisting of three to five amphibious assault ships, they move freely across the seas. They represent the United States' most flexible and immediate means of exerting force abroad, one often used by the North Atlantic Treaty Organization (NATO) and in other combined operations.

As of the early twenty-first century, the Marines' Command, Control, Communications and Computers (C4) Branch identifies, analyzes, and introduces new communication and information systems technology for Marine Corps use. The C4 Branch also supports numerous Marine Corps network developmental tasks and interoperability demonstrations. Among its ongoing projects is the Expeditionary Tactical Communications System (ETCS), which is an over-the-horizon/on-the-move system allowing shipboard units to be in contact with dismounted Marines using modified iridium satellite phones providing networked communications with a push-to-talk voice and position location capability. ETCS began to deploy in mid-2006. Network Services pro-

vide a primary node for testing the "last mile" in secure wireless communications for extending bandwidth on the battlefield. They are also used within the Defense Information Systems Agency for meshed Voice over Internet Protocol experimentation and Quality of Service testing. Finally, the On the Move Combat Operations Center is being developed to provide both voice and data communications to the infantry battalion commander for surface and vertical employment during ship-to-objective maneuvers.

Marines also provide defense personnel for American embassies abroad.

Christopher H. Sterling

See also Code Talkers; Communication Satellites; Defense Information Systems Agency (DISA); U.S. Navy

Sources
Bartlett, Merrill L., and Jack Sweetman. 2001. *The U.S. Marine Corps: An Illustrated History*. Annapolis, MD: Naval Institute Press.
Krulak, Victor H. 1984. *First to Fight: An Inside View of the U.S. Marine Corps*. Annapolis, MD: Naval Institute Press.
Marine Corps Warfighting Laboratory. "Command, Control, Communications and Computers Branch." [Online information; retrieved December 2006.] http://www.mcwl.usmc.mil/tech/c4.cfm.

U.S. Military Telegraph Service (USMTS)

During the American Civil War (1861–1865), military leaders recognized that the telegraph had become a major factor in the rapid exchange of news, information, and ideas, making it indispensable for the conduct of military operations. At the outbreak of the war, all the telegraph facilities of both the North and South were in the hands of private individuals. In April 1861, with full cooperation of the telegraph companies in the North, the government assumed control of all telegraph lines leading into Washington DC. Edward S. Sanford, president of the American Telegraph Company, helped organize a small unit in the War Department to operate and control the lines. Following the Union disaster at Bull Run (1861), more effective efforts were made to harness the existing communications structure by establishing the United States Military Telegraph Service (USMTS). USMTS was to be staffed by civilians appointed from the commercial telegraph industry; it led to a unique organization with an outlook that often conflicted with established military norms.

Anson Stager, general superintendent of Western Union, was selected as chief of the service and appointed colonel. He developed a plan for a unified service with telegraph lines going to the headquarters of every major independent command. He recommended that a bureau be established to purchase and distribute all material needed for the construction and operation of the military telegraph lines under the direct control of the secretary of war. Stager's plan was approved and USMTS was established as a civilian bureau attached to the Quartermaster Corps. The civilian operators were given the status of quartermaster civilian employees. The issue of civilian status raised many concerns regarding military control and of those men wounded or killed during operations.

On 31 January 1862 Congress authorized President Abraham Lincoln to take over any telegraph and rail lines needed for national defense. In February, the Union Army took control of all telegraph lines. To ensure security of information, various codes and ciphers were developed to encrypt messages. To the frustration of many commanders, only USMTS men understood the keys and had to take time to encode messages, which often slowed communications. Some commanders were suspicious of the service and were careful about the wording of messages lest Secretary of War Edwin Stanton disapprove of their decisions.

By the end of 1862 there were 3,500 miles of telegraph line in the system. As armies moved, wire had to be put up and taken down as well as repaired, an often dangerous job that resulted in the death or wounding of one in twelve men engaged in that work. However, USMTS did not go much farther beyond major Army headquarters, leaving a communications gap between the frontline units and commanders in the rear. To fill this gap, the U.S. Army Signal Corps, under Colonel Albert J. Myer, had established a small field system using the Beardslee telegraph that did not require skill in Morse code. A field train carried flags, night signals, rockets, the Beardslee telegraph, and ten miles of wire for use in the combat zone (usually a distance of five to eight miles). As Union armies moved forward, the field telegraph was employed to establish forward communications back to the more permanent installations of USMTS.

However, there was much conflict between the Signal Corps under Myer and the civilians under Stager over who should direct the overall system. In 1863 Myer challenged the status of USMTS, arguing that the Signal Corps should have control of all military communications. Stager countered that the reverse should occur. After Myer incurred the wrath of Stanton and was relieved as chief signal officer, Stager was put in charge of all military telegraphy, which by then consisted of more than 950 civilians who operated 5,300 miles of telegraph line.

By 1864 commanders at all levels had grown to depend on the military telegraph in whatever form it took to command and control their armies. USMTS laid its lines without orders to the various headquarters almost before the troops were in position. However, strict control of codes and ciphers persisted and Stanton specifically forbade commanders in the field from interfering with the system. Although USMTS command and control was foreign to military concepts of the day, the system worked and provided instantaneous information regarding military operations from the tactical battlefield to the White House.

Steven J. Rauch

See also American Civil War (1861–1865); Army Signal Corps; Beardslee Telegraph; Bull Run, Battle of (1861); Lincoln in the Telegraph Office; Myer, Albert James (1828–1880); Stager, Anson (1825–1885)

Sources

Bates, David Homer. 1907. *Lincoln in the Telegraph Office*. New York: Century Company.
Markle, Donald E., ed. 2003. *The Telegraph Goes to War*. New York: Edmonston Publishing.
Plum, William R. 1882. *The Military Telegraph During the Civil War in the United States*. Chicago: Jansen, McClurg (reprinted by Arno Press, 1974).
Raines, Rebecca Robbins. 1996. *Getting the Message Through: A Branch History of the US Army Signal Corps*. Washington, DC: U.S. Army Center of Military History.

U.S. Navy

The U.S. Navy built its initial flag-based signaling on that of the Royal Navy, though the two services fought one another during the American Revolution (1776–1783) and again in the War of 1812 (1812–1815). Yet during its more than 200 years of operation, the American Navy's signaling and communication functions have been poorly recorded. Several factors account for this dearth, prime among them that the Navy lacks a separate signals arm. There has also been a prejudice against writing by most senior naval officers, as well as a long-standing Navy predilection to ignore history (the Army, Marine Corps, and Air Force have all done better). More recent is an understandable concern for secrecy. The Navy controls the U.S. Marine Corps, which has always had its own specialized communication needs—these are not included here.

Signals for the Sailing Navy

Early American signaling was largely ad hoc with variance across individual commanders and battles. Well before formation of an American Navy in 1776, flaghoists played a central naval signaling role. While many alphabetic and numeric flag systems were adopted from Britain's Royal Navy (which, in turn, had borrowed from the French), the first American adaptation was that of Thomas Truxton in 1797, which used number flags in a system of nearly 300 signals. This was followed by the Barron signal book of the early 1800s, which was better organized. Modifications appeared over the years.

American naval vessels also employed semaphore signaling. While based on early land-based eighteenth- and nineteenth-century systems, both British and French navies helped develop various means of mechanical and pre-electric telegraph/semaphore systems, used atop ship masts for years. The U.S. Navy used masthead semaphores on ironclad or steel vessels, as well as the ever-handy and versatile two-flag (often simply two-arm) semaphore for many years. The basic arm, or identical two-flag, semaphore system remains in occasional use—albeit perhaps more informally between sailors who know this system and find themselves on adjacent ships. From the mid-1800s to the twentieth century, there were also various "shape" signal systems operated with various levels of success.

The Navy was often innovative and at least attempted use of almost every known means of communicating at sea, including use of single- and multishot pyrotechnics—a field in which Edward Very developed a reputation. (Indeed, flares are still used today but generally for safety, rescue, or clandestine operations rather than signaling.) Another traditional form of signal that was widely used (even after the turn of the twentieth century and introduction of airships and aircraft) was message-carrying pigeons.

The Navy initiated use of telegraphy to tie Washington headquarters to various ports and bases by the late 1840s. The slow adoption of steam propulsion led to further signaling changes, including new signal books for flag systems and initial use of night signal lights. The standard Rogers and Black signaling system also employed some pyrotechnic devices. As the Civil War (1861–1865) began, however, officers siding with the Confederacy took with them existing naval signal books, placing Union Navy signals in jeopardy. Yet Union naval authorities never took sufficient action to eliminate signal confusion with a new signal book, and a number of naval actions were negatively impacted by the persistent signal problem. A signal office was only established in 1869, when a new signal book was issued. While more signalmen were trained, no move was made to establish a separate signaling corps as existed in the Army. By the 1870s, an American edition of the International Code eased communication between naval and merchant vessels. Wig-wag flags as developed by Albert Myer were used between U.S. Army and Navy forces.

"Interior" communication requirements are common to all navies. In the seventeenth and eighteenth centuries, naval forces provided communication via men's voices, speaking trumpets, speaking tubes, megaphones, boatswain's pipes, and trumpets or bugles—as well as drums manned by seagoing marines. In the nineteenth century, alarms (often via bells) were added, along with various physical means to communicate engine requirements from bridge to engine room, including engine order telegraphs, mechanical counters, and other devices. By the twentieth century, the sound-powered telephone had appeared, along with electric telephones, loudspeakers, and the ubiquitous 1-MC system with its classic opening line: "Now hear this!" Redundancy is a feature of all such systems, for command and control must be maintained despite loss of electric power or other battle damage. If the officers and crew of any warship cannot effectively communicate—no matter what may have occurred—that ship is, or soon will be, lost as an effective fighting platform.

Electricity and Wireless at Sea

Experiments with the use of electricity at sea began in the 1870s. In 1888 Bradley Fiske experimented with ship-to-ship communication using conduction. Ardois lights were in use by the early 1890s, replaced by the Telephotos system of light signaling later in the decade. Telegraph connections to even distant ports were in place by the same time, though commanders grumbled about losing control and becoming mere messenger boys for the naval command in Washington.

The Spanish-American War of 1898 pushed naval officials into creating a widespread system of coastal signaling stations.

These were connected by telegraph or telephone lines and could use flags, torches, or signal lights to communicate with nearby ships. As so often happens, however, the system fell into disrepair when the war emergency abated. The operations of Admiral George Dewey in Manila initiated another aspect of naval signals warfare that would see widespread adoption during the world wars—the cutting of an adversary's undersea cable communications. But communication problems were evident in the infamous Admiral Sampson/Commodore Schley controversy that was really the result of naval signal operations. Navy Secretary John Long was not aware that his many orders to Commodore Winfield Schley, though telegraphed instantly to Tampa, Florida, then had to be carried by ship to reach Schley at sea. Long's messages often took days or weeks to arrive. Meanwhile, Long grew frustrated at Schley's failure to respond promptly. No one realized these orders were not received as sent, but were more akin to placing an order in a bottle, corking it, and tossing it out to sea on the Santiago side of Cuba where Schley was seeking the Spanish fleet. A postwar investigation finally brought all this to light—and wiser heads saw realized valuable the new wireless technology might be.

By 1899 a board of naval officers was appointed to examine the potential of wireless. Complaints about loss of an individual commander's control arose again. Initial application of radio was slow and tentative as the Navy experimented with different wireless systems, including those developed in other nations (such as the Slaby-Arco devices from Germany). Samuel Robison's first manual of wireless telegraphy for naval signalers appeared in 1906. Only slowly did the Navy focus on American inventors and equipment.

The scope and breadth of naval radio activity is illustrated by its many applications in the battle fleet (especially during and after the Great White Fleet world cruise of 1908–1909); improvements in the Navy's coastal signal service; development of the Arlington (and soon many other) naval radio stations, which allowed direct contact with distant ships; and research efforts within the Naval Research Laboratory. Soon the Navy was playing a dominant radio role, often serving as the lead agency in federal dealings with regional and worldwide concerns.

During World War I (1914–1918), radio equipment rapidly improved and radio communication with aircraft was developed, including the early use of radio equipment on patrol seaplanes. On U.S. entry into the war (April 1917), the Navy took control of all wireless transmitters in the United States, taking many off the air for the duration. New higher-power (a million watts and more) radio stations were built in Annapolis and on the coast of France to aid increased Atlantic naval communication. The Navy was focused on convoy protection and antisubmarine warfare. Wireless telephone transmitters were mounted on more than a thousand ships and were an instrumental part of the antisubmarine campaign.

Between the two world wars, the U.S. Navy was largely dependent on its own laboratories for radio improvements, as the commercial industry was taken up by demand for consumer radio equipment. That and restricted budgets limited much expansion of naval radio despite more widespread fleet deployments and war games in the 1920s and 1930s.

World War II

The global naval operations of World War II (1939–1945) made naval communications a central aspect of planning and fighting.

American naval forces worked with Royal Navy units in the Battle of the Atlantic antisubmarine campaign even before formal American entry into the war at the end of 1941. The two services maintained extensive detection and communication links ranging from the highly technical to the basic (blinker lights) for talk between ships. The other seven common ship-to-ship methods were loudhailer (voice), semaphore flags, flaghoist, colored lights at night, steam whistles, and both Morse code and voice radio. Air-to-ship signals remained a problem. During much of the war, Navy warships had to hold invaluable information until daylight, as enemy submarines could pick up night signals by light or radio. Demand for Navy signalmen rose sharply.

The North African invasion (Operation TORCH, November 1942) demonstrated the communication challenge when the different U.S. Army and Navy signal systems required coordination for joint amphibious operations. Much standard radio equipment proved unsuitable for amphibious operations, as it was not waterproof, demonstrating the need for an amphibious command-and-control ship. As the war progressed, what had been naval vessels' radar plot (a small darkened space away from other light sources) absorbed other functions and became a terminal for radio, radar, and lookout reports. Information received would be correlated and passed to bridge, gunnery, and other stations as necessary. Ultimately, the radar plot became a combat information center established in large spaces below decks within protected compartments with as many as fifty men in each center. Advanced telephone and teleprinter circuits played a large role in keeping widespread naval units in touch with the Navy Department in Washington, as, by 1944, did new and very high frequency radios. On some occasions, the

absence of at least one kind of communications—as with observing radio silence by a fleet at sea—proved essential for operational surprise and success.

Far more important than in earlier wars was the World War II need for maintaining secure coded communications while breaking into enemy communication links. Thanks to the work of Laurance Safford, among many others, the Navy's OP-20-G, operating out of Nebraska Avenue (Washington DC) and other facilities, was at the forefront of World War II breaking and reading of Japanese codes, including the Magic operation shared with the Army. Code breaking proved of central importance in landmark victories from the mid-1942 Battle of Midway to the end of the war.

Postwar

Since World War II, the U.S. Navy has faced a greater technologic challenge than any other armed forces. It now operates on and under the ocean, over land masses (including the Arctic, Antarctic, rivers, lakes, and inland seas), as well as in both air and space. Merely to survive in these spheres is a continuing challenge, but to conduct warfare and communications at the same time provides a supreme challenge. And there are separate communication needs for the Navy and the related U.S. Marine Corps. What has made today's operations possible is the growing use of digital communication systems including dedicated communications satellite capacity.

The Naval Tactical Data System (NTDS) was a computerized information processing system developed by the Navy in the 1950s, approved for implementation in 1956, and first deployed in the mid-1960s in combat ships. The system evolved as computers and related equipment were improved. Consoles and display units became more capable, as did other components. Its successful operation in combat conditions off Vietnam helped to increase naval reliance on and versatility in electronic communication while reducing use of visual signals. NTDS was the first digital system installed on any American naval vessel, as well as in a number of foreign fleets. Used into the 1990s, NTDS paved the way for greater integration of digital systems throughout American combat vessels.

Secure naval communications for a half-century came under the aegis of the Naval Security Group (NSG), successor to the wartime OP-20-G. Until reorganized under another command in 2005, NSG maintained naval coded communications. As technology advances, higher security classifications of most modern naval communication systems limit publication of historical or descriptive material. Naval communication achievements continue to multiply, however, even if not always evident in general publications.

The Navy and Marine Corps often operate in consort with other forces. In NATO operations, integrated military and naval forces often include several allies speaking different languages. Such operations can involve dozens of major warships, landing and supply vessels, thousands of troops, troop ships, landing craft, V/STOL (vertical/short takeoff and landing) aircraft, helicopters, and naval patrol and fighting aircraft of both the Navy and Marine Corps. Each individual unit needs to communicate with others simultaneously in a clear, secure, two-way fashion.

David L. Woods and Christopher H. Sterling

See also Atlantic, Battle of the (1939–1945); Combat Information Center (CIC); Fiske, Bradley A. (1854–1942); Flaghoist; Flags; Flagship; Hooper, Stanford C. (1884–1955); Magic; Midway, Battle of (3–6 June 1942); Myer, Albert James (1828–1880); Naval Radio Stations/Service; Naval Research Laboratory (NRL); Naval Security Group (NSG); Naval Tactical Data System (NTDS); Nebraska Avenue, Washington DC; Night Signals; North Atlantic Treaty Organization (NATO) Communications & Information Systems Agency; *Ohio*, USS; OP-20-G; Pearl Harbor, Hawaii; Radio Silence; Robison, Samuel Shelburne (1867–1952); Safford, Laurance F. (1890–1973); Semaphore (Mechanical Telegraphs); Signal Book; Signal Rockets; Spanish-American War (1898); Submarine Communications; Talk Between Ships (TBS); Truxton, Thomas (1755–1822); Undersea Cables; U.S. Marine Corps

Sources

Bullard, William H. G. 1915. "The Naval Radio Service: Its Development, Public Service, and Commercial Work. *Proceedings of the Institute of Radio Engineers* 3 (1): 7–28.

Fiske, Bradley C. 1903. "War Signals." *Proceedings of the U. S. Naval Institute* XXXIX (December): 4.

Hooper, Stanford C. 1922. "Keeping the Stars and Stripes in the Ether." *Radio Broadcast* June: 127–132.

Hooper, Stanford C. 1929. "Naval Communications: Radio Washington." *Proceedings of the Institute of Radio Engineers* 17 (September): 1595–1620.

Howeth, L. S., 1963. *The History of Communications-Electronics in the United States Navy.* Washington, DC: Government Printing Office.

Luce, Stephen B. 1877. "Signals and Signaling." *Potter's American Monthly* VIII (64): 297–302.

Niblack, Albert P. 1892. "Naval Signaling." *Proceedings of the U.S. Naval Institute* XVIII: 4; 64: 431–505.

Woods, David L., ed. 1980. *Signaling and Communicating at Sea.* 2 vols. New York: Arno Press.

V

V-Mail

V-mail, or Victory mail, was developed during World War II as a valuable method for allowing the U.S. home front and its military personnel abroad to keep in touch. Utilizing a microfilm mail process that originated in England, V-mail allowed considerable shipping space that might otherwise be taken up with letters to be used instead for needed war materials. A single mail sack of V-mail letters could replace the thirty-seven mail bags required to carry 150,000 regular one-page letters. The weight savings were as dramatic—from 2,575 pounds of normal mail to a mere 45 pounds of V-mail. And V-mail traveled faster, usually being sent by air whereas normal letters usually were sent by sea. From 1942 to the end of the war, close to 1.5 billion messages were sent to and from all theaters of war using this system.

The system of microfilming letters (developed by Kodak Limited) was based on the use of special V-mail letter-sheets, a combination of letter and envelope that were made widely available across the United States and at military facilities abroad, typically in pack-ets of a dozen sheets. The letter-sheets were designed and gummed to fold into a distinctively marked envelope. The user wrote a message in the limited space provided, added the name and address of the recipient, folded the form and mailed the letter. (In keeping with the practice of free mailing privileges for soldiers in combat zones, the V-mail letters sent from military personnel overseas did not require postage stamps.) Such V-mail letters were then reviewed by censors, photographically reduced to thumbnail size on rolls of microfilm, and sent to a processing station overseas located near the addressees. There, individual facsimiles of the letter-sheets were reproduced about one-quarter their original size (about 5 inches by 4 inches) and the miniature mail was then delivered to the recipient.

All this took a while to develop. The first large Army-operated V-mail station overseas was opened on 15 April 1943 at Casablanca in North Africa. Between 15 June 1942 and 1 April 1945, just over a half-billion V-mail letters were sent from the United States to military post offices and about the same number were received from military personnel abroad. Yet in spite of the widely advertised benefits of V-mail (it was touted as patriotic and part of the war effort), most people still sent regular first class letters. In 1944, for instance, Navy personnel alone received 38 million pieces of V-mail—but more than 272 million first class letters.

Christopher H. Sterling

See also Postal Services

Sources
Snyder, E. D. 1944. "V-Mail." *Radio News* U.S. Army Signal Corps Issue (February): 126–127, 428, 430, 432.
Wildenberg, Thomas. 2005. "You've Got V-Mail." *Naval History Magazine* 19 (July): 3.

Vacuum Tube

Invented in 1904, improved in 1906, and fully understood by about 1912, the vacuum tube (or "valve" in British usage) became central to wireless communication from about 1920 until superseded by the transistor in the 1960s. For a half-century fragile vacuum tubes formed the core of most military electronic equipment.

While Thomas Edison had been developing the incandescent lightbulb in the late 1870s, he had noticed that a metal plate inserted in the lightbulb could indicate the presence of an electric current—what became known as the "Edison Effect." Building on that finding was the late 1904 invention of the first vacuum tube (or thermionic valve) in England by John Ambrose Fleming (1849–1944), who was a scientific adviser to the Marconi Company. It was intended as a radio detector or receiver. Two years later, American Lee de Forest (1873–1961) added a third element (a tiny screen or grid) between Fleming's two-element diode to create a triode, or what he called an Audion tube. In 1912, Edwin Howard Armstrong (1890–

1954) described the broad capabilities of the triode, which was by then beginning to replace spark-gap and other modes of wireless transmission. AT&T bought rights to the de Forest Audion and used them as amplifiers to open up the first coast-to-coast telephone circuit in 1915. De Forest's company and Western Electric were the primary American tube producers prior to 1917.

World War I vastly increased demand for production of vacuum tubes for military and naval radio receiving and transmitting equipment. General Electric, Westinghouse, and other firms entered the market to meet new Signal Corps and U.S. Navy orders. The initial Signal Corps order in 1917 was for 80,000 tubes to be delivered at a rate of 500 a week at first, rising to 6,000 tubes a week in six months. Further orders for thousands of standard-design tubes came in 1918 from both the Navy and Signal Corps. In all, well more than a half-million tubes were made during the war and immediate postwar years.

By the early 1920s, triode-powered transmitters and receivers were standard equipment in civil and military applications. The large naval radio station, NAA, near Washington, was based on vacuum tube technology. By 1922 improved means of tube manufacture and cooling led to vastly more powerful tubes. But vacuum tubes, like the lightbulbs they resembled, were fragile, threw off heat, and needed constant replacement. Radio equipment had to "warm up" (its tubes) before being used. Development of four-element vacuum tubes in 1929 was the last fundamental improvement in basic tube technology. By the late 1930s considerable progress had been made in miniaturizing vacuum tubes to develop smaller electrical devices.

In World War II, improved vacuum tubes powered aviation radios, early radar equipment, and the first computers in both Britain and the United States. Tubes were far more robust (some were made of metal rather than glass) and were getting smaller to enable lighter, mobile equipment. Vacuum tubes powered the Semi-Automatic Ground Environment system for the Air Force in the 1950s and are still used in some transmitters and other specialized functions. Manufactured into the 1960s, vacuum tubes were generally and gradually displaced by transistors and then solid state electronics.

Christopher H. Sterling

See also Armstrong, Edwin Howard (1890–1954) ; de Forest, Lee (1873–1961); Edison, Thomas A. (1847–1931); Naval Radio Stations/Service; Radio; Semi-Automatic Ground Environment (SAGE); Solid State Electronics; Transistor

Sources

Fleming, J. A. 1919. *The Thermionic Valve and Its Developments in Radiotelegraphy and Telephony.* London: The Wireless Press.

Institution of Electrical Engineers. 1955. *Thermionic Valves: 1904–1954: The First Fifty Years.* London: Institution of Electrical Engineers.

Stokes, John W. 1982. *70 Years of Radio Tubes and Valves.* Vestal, NY: Vestal Press.

Tyne, Gerald F. 1977. *Saga of the Vacuum Tube.* Indianapolis, IN: Howard W. Sams.

Van Deman, Ralph Henry (1865–1952)

Ralph Van Deman was the father of American military intelligence and played a central role in establishing effective World War I code breaking, laying the groundwork for expanding intelligence operations.

Born in Delaware, Ohio, on 3 September 1865, Van Deman earned a bachelor of arts degree at Harvard University (1888) and a medical degree at a medical school in Cincinnati (1893). He entered the Army as an infantry officer in 1891, and though given leave to complete medical school, evidently never served as an army surgeon. He graduated from the Army's Infantry and Cavalry School at Fort Leavenworth in 1895 and the first Army War College class in 1905. With the map section of the Army's Military Information Division, he served in Cuba and Puerto Rico in 1898. After assignments in the Philippines and China, in 1915 Major Van Deman urged his superiors to form a general staff section focused on intelligence. The next year the Army assigned intelligence officers to its six continental and overseas departments. With America's entry into World War I in 1917, Secretary of War Newton D. Baker established the Military Intelligence Section (MIS) at the War College under Van Deman's direction.

MIS took charge of the supervision and control of military espionage and counterespionage for the duration. Much was borrowed from British and French intelligence; staff organization took time, and only one officer was handling foreign intelligence collection by the end of 1917. As American Expeditionary Force (AEF) intelligence was very active, Van Deman turned to counterintelligence, particularly against the possibility of internal subversion in the United States. Confronted by a shortage of suitable officers for his expanding operations, Van Deman utilized civilian detectives, volunteers, and a corps of (enlisted) intelligence police.

Van Deman created eight numbered subsections, designated MI-1 through MI-8. The Cipher Bureau (MI-8) under Van Deman's direction, saw cryptology become an adjunct of military intelligence. Herbert O. Yardley, a civilian code clerk for the State Department, was placed in charge. Because the War Department's telegraph code of 1915 was designed to promote economy over security,

MI-8 hastily devised a new code, which was compromised almost as soon as it was issued. Though no replacement could be developed until after the 1918 armistice, Yardley's team proved most effective at breaking foreign codes. Seeking qualified personnel, Van Deman accepted assistance from Colonel George Fabyan, director of Riverbank Laboratories in Illinois, which trained three classes of Army cryptographers in 1917–1918. MI-8 later developed its own training course.

Utilizing Signal Corps personnel, Van Deman also established a radio intelligence capability with stations along the Maine coast and the Mexican border to monitor German intelligence and diplomatic transmissions. Because certain of his counterintelligence activities had impinged on the constitutional rights of U.S. citizens, however, now Colonel Van Deman was relieved of his duties in June 1918 and sent to France to assess AEF's intelligence activities. Two months later, his former agency became the War Department's Military Intelligence Division.

Van Deman served as the Army's chief intelligence and counterintelligence officer at the Versailles peace conference. He turned to other duties in 1920, was promoted to brigadier general in 1927, and to major general several months before retiring in September 1929. He resumed his intelligence activities in retirement, establishing his own personal intelligence network and maintaining files on people deemed "subversives." He advised the War Department from 1941 to 1946. Van Deman died in San Diego on 22 January 1952.

Keir B. Sterling

See also Friedman, William F. (1891–1969); Mauborgne, Joseph Oswald (1881–1971); Signals Intelligence (SIGINT); Yardley, Herbert O. (1889–1958)

Sources

Bigelow, Michael E. 1990. "Van Deman." *Military Intelligence* 16 (5): 38–40.

Campbell, Kenneth J. 1987. "Major General Ralph H. Van Deman: Father of Modern American Military Intelligence." *American Intelligence Journal* 8 (Summer): 13–19.

Powe, Marc B. 1975. "American Military Intelligence Comes of Age: A Sketch of a Man and His Times." *Military Review* 55 (12): 17–30.

U.S. Army, Military Intelligence Division. 1918. *Work and Activities of the Military Intelligence Division, General Staff.* Washington, DC: War Department.

Van Deman, Ralph. 1988. *The Final Memorandum of Major General Ralph H. Van Deman, USA, Ret., 1865–1952: Father of US Military Intelligence,* edited by Ralph E. Weber. Wilmington, DE: Scholarly Resources.

Vehicles and Transport

Using land vehicles to carry or transmit military communication dates back at least to Roman times when military roads were maintained for use by, among others, military couriers, some of whom traveled by chariot or coach. For centuries vehicular speeds did not exceed the horse. Only in the mid-nineteenth century did that change with early railways. Thanks to wireless, since about 1920 more vehicles have served less to carry messages than to receive them as commanders coordinate motorized transport and fighting units.

Railways were the first modern vehicles subject to wartime communications. By the mid-nineteenth century in Europe and during the American Civil War (1861–1865), effective railway networks moved not only troops and equipment but, albeit more rarely, the couriers and dispatches that tied armies together—especially where faster telegraph links were unavailable. That the Union had a far more extensive and effective railway network was one factor in its eventual victory. Railroads quickly became essential in carrying heavy cargoes of wire and other telegraph and signaling equipment. By the twentieth-century world wars, railroads were primary land carriers of men and equipment, their routes and schedules often coordinated by use of radio.

At the other end of the weight scale, the bicycle, developed in modern form in the late nineteenth century, appears to have seen its first military application during the Boer War (1899–1902), ridden by messengers over short distances. Light and simple to use, the bicycle is often faster and more agile in urban traffic than are motor vehicles. Though the bicycle had limited military signal value, its history in warfare is long—bikes were widely used by Viet Cong messengers during the Vietnam War in the late 1960s and were common in the Swiss army into the 1990s.

The motorcycle became a very useful means of delivering military messages before and during World War I—until wireless largely subsumed the job. Harley-Davidson motorcycles, for example, were used by the U.S. Army during the Mexican Punitive Expedition of 1916. More than 90,000 Harley motorcycles were produced during World War II, many of them used for signal dispatch. Lighter motor scooters were also used farther behind the front.

As motor vehicles became more robust, the small truck came into widespread military use. During World War II, the jeep often served to get word (and, more often, people and equipment) through as needed. Willys-Overland was one of two firms that responded to an Army quartermaster request for small (quarter-ton four-wheel drive) utility vehicle designs in 1940. In November, the first 1,500 were ordered from Ford, Willys-Overland, and Bantam. Final production by the end of 1945 totaled nearly 615,000 vehicles, most built by Ford and Willys. They remained in service around the world for decades.

Specialized radio facilities built into light trucks were vital to fast-moving Axis and Allied armies, especially in the African and then European theaters of World War II. With transmitters and receivers built and tested to stand rugged treatment over difficult terrain, wide temperature and humidity variation, and constant use, these vehicles were essential to keeping active commanders in touch with fast-changing battle fronts. Multiple spare parts (especially fragile vacuum tubes) were supplied, waterproofing was standard, and antennas were mounted on springs. In addition to transmitting messages, tons of radio, telephone, and telegraph equipment and wire were transported by trucks from logistic centers to front lines.

Robust communication links were vital to the decisive use of armored forces during World War II. Fleets of tanks and personnel carriers were coordinated by central command thanks to growing use of radio communication. U.S. Army vehicles made early use of FM multichannel radio for static-free high-frequency communications, despite many sources of interference within the vehicle itself. Throat and then lip microphones were developed to improve communication in high-noise situations. Virtually all armored vehicles, Allied or Axis, contained at least one form of radio to meld them into an effective mobile force.

Miniaturization and digitization vastly improved mobile radio equipment starting in the 1960s. By the late 1970s cellular mobile communications added further flexibility to the coordinated command of military vehicles of all types. Current combat net radios provide voice and data connectivity and form the basic layer for tactical command and control from division to battalion and company level. Modern systems offer sophisticated communications security (encryption) and frequency hopping for efficient spectrum utilization and electronic counter-countermeasures. Military satellites allow ready communication with mobile units in multiple locations.

Today, emergency mobile command vehicles provide a civilian application of military communication units. Large vans or trucks contain a variety of communication links, terrestrial and satellite, for use in local and regional emergency situations. Medical vehicles (including ambulances) also apply communication lessons often first learned on the battlefield.

Christopher H. Sterling

See also Airplanes; Airships and Balloons; Flagship; Golden Arrow Sections; Intelligence Ships; Mexican Punitive Expedition (1916–1917); Military Roads; Mobile Communications; TELCOM Mobile Wireless Units; Vacuum Tube

Sources
Bishop, Denis, and Chris Ellis. 1979. *Vehicles at War*. Cranbury, NJ: A. S. Barnes.
Conner, W. D. 1917. *Military Railroads*. Army Corps of Engineers, Professional Papers No. 32. Washington, DC: Government Printing Office.
Defense Update. 2005. "Mobile Cellular Networks in Military Use." [Online article; retrieved December 2006.] http://www .defense-update.com/features/.
Fitzpatrick, Jim. 1998. *The Bicycle in Wartime: An Illustrated History*. Dulles, VA: Brassey's.
O'Connell, J. D. 1942. "Development of Vehicular Equipment." *Radio News* Special Signal Corps Issue (November): 106–109, 198–202.
Olive-Drab.com. "Military Vehicle Ownership Guide." [Online information; retrieved December 2006.] http://www.olive-drab .com/od_milveh_guide.php3.
Zaloga, Steven, and Hugh Johnson. 2005. *Jeeps 1941–45*. London: Vanguard.

Vietnam War (1959–1975)

The long Vietnam War (ca. 1959–1975) was strongly impacted by applications of changing communications technology.

Background

The international military conflict in Vietnam during the 1960s and early 1970s had its roots in the post–World War II decision by France to reassert its colonial authority over Indochina, which comprised all of Laos, Cambodia, and Vietnam. The French return was contested by a Communist-led nationalist movement known as the Viet Minh, which was directed by the experienced revolutionary leader Ho Chi Minh. Hostilities erupted in December 1946, spreading through Vietnam. The war dragged on for seven years, culminating in the disastrous defeat of French forces at Dien Bien Phu in 1954. The French withdrew, and Vietnam was partitioned into sectors north and south of the 17th Parallel. In the South, American military and economic aid subsidized the pro-Western government of President Ngo Dinh Diem, while Ho Chi Minh consolidated Communist power in North Vietnam. The Communists had decided to reunify Vietnam by force, and guerrilla attacks, led by southern insurgents and bolstered by arms from North Vietnam, grew in intensity after 1959.

In 1961 President John F. Kennedy decided to increase American aid to South Vietnam and to deploy thousands of military advisers to assist the South's Army of the Republic of Vietnam (ARVN). The Communist insurgency continued to expand, as men and materiel from the North entered South Vietnam via the "Ho Chi Minh Trail," a complex of footpaths, bike routes, and—eventually—improved roads that crisscrossed through the borderlands of Cambodia and Laos. President Lyndon Johnson committed U.S. combat forces to defend South Vietnam in 1965. American military manpower in Vietnam reached more than 540,000 troops in 1969, before President Richard Nixon ordered the phased withdrawal of U.S. forces. In 1973 the United States concluded the Paris Peace Accords with North Vietnam and withdrew all its remaining troops from the South. Two years later the North Vietnam Army (NVA) launched a major offensive against the South, and by the end of April 1975 the South Vietnamese government had collapsed. Vietnam was formally reunified as the Socialist Republic of Vietnam, with its Communist government based at Hanoi.

Communist Communications

The Vietnamese Communists' military efforts during both the Franco-Viet Minh War (1946–1954) and the later American war (1959–1975) were planned, organized, and conducted by four major entities: the so-called Viet Cong (VC), or southern guerrilla apparatus; the NVA; the Vietnam Lao Dong, or Vietnam Workers' Party (VWP), usually referred to as the Communist Party; and the People's Armed Security Forces (PASF), the northern-based internal security police, similar to the Soviet Union's KGB, which was responsible for ensuring the political obedience of NVA units and commanders.

Each of these organizations maintained discrete communications systems. For each, the primary tools for long-distance commu-

nications were paper documents and couriers; open radio broadcasts that carried VWP policy statements; and Chinese- or Soviet-supplied radio transceivers, which usually transmitted enciphered messages produced by relatively simple encoding systems. In 1959 special NVA units, reinforced by PASF political police, began developing networks of communications-logistics posts inside Laos' border with South Vietnam. These posts provided secure rest stops, storage depots, and meeting places for military units and political cadres. Eventually these networks grew into the Ho Chi Minh Trail complex and provided crucial overland transit for couriers and operatives carrying military information to and from North Vietnam.

America's direct entry into the war in 1965 and NVA's big-unit intervention in South Vietnam prompted a reorganization of NVA communications personnel and protocols. Reliance on radio communications with field troops increased, and all NVA division headquarters soon included a signals battalion. Each NVA regiment had a signals company, and specialized communications platoons were also developed for each NVA battalion in the field. NVA regional command staffs included specially trained cryptographers. Nonetheless, U.S. intelligence estimates showed that signals personnel comprised less than 5 percent of total NVA unit strength, compared with up to 20 percent in American ground forces. The scarcity of field-capable radio equipment limited the Communists' radio communications, and both NVA and VC forces used a grab-bag of Chinese, Soviet, and Eastern European as well as captured American and Japanese radio equipment throughout the war.

NVA radiomen used Morse code and, at higher operational levels, encrypted voice transmissions. Security protocols also included use of prearranged transmission times, frequency changes, concise messaging, and one-way communications. Transmission locations were removed from staff headquarters and were changed frequently to thwart enemy direction finders. NVA security policies required that during large operations, minimal use was made of radios. Troops relied instead on couriers, flares, flashlights, whistles, and the like.

The Communists' signals interception and intelligence units were highly successful in penetrating ARVN and U.S. military communications throughout the Vietnam War. Using imitative deception techniques, such units could participate in ARVN/U.S. radio nets, posing as "friendlies." When undetected, they transmitted false information, called for artillery or air strikes on ARVN/U.S. or civilian positions, requested halts to damaging enemy fire, lured ARVN/U.S. units into ambushes, and even called for American "dustoff" helicopters to evacuate VC/NVA wounded to U.S. medical facilities. The fact that both ARVN and U.S. forces routinely used open voice transmissions and predictable frequencies eased the work of intelligence collection.

As early as 1963, the VC began developing special technical reconnaissance (TR) cells that used captured radios to monitor ARVN radio traffic. By 1966 it was estimated that all VC units at the provincial district level had active TR operatives. As the war went on, these units, with their NVA counterparts, exploited parallel message traffic carried on distinct ARVN and U.S. radio networks to break Allied codes. In addition, sophisticated equipment aboard Soviet and Chinese naval vessels allowed these ships to function as floating signals interception platforms. They monitored American naval and aircraft communications and tried to decipher encoded U.S. radio transmissions. These assets provided real-time data on U.S. air operations to North Vietnam's air defense units. After 1973 the Soviet Union and China began providing more sophisticated multichannel transceivers to NVA field units. After American bombing ended in early 1973, telephone wires were placed along main arteries of the Ho Chi Minh Trail, facilitating NVA voice communications with Hanoi.

American and Allied Communications

The Army Signal Corps units first provided communications facilities in Vietnam beginning with American military support for French forces in 1950–1951. U.S. civilian agencies began in 1955 to provide radio equipment and technical assistance to the South Vietnamese government's police and internal security agencies. When President Kennedy increased the American military advisory effort, however, the need for expanded U.S. military communications systems in South Vietnam emerged. Initially U.S. advisers relied on ARVN radios and on their own high-frequency transmitters. In 1962 planning began for a larger system capable of further expansion.

The system that emerged, code-named BACK PORCH, was built by the U.S. Air Force and operated by a U.S. Army Signal Corps battalion. It used long-distance tropospheric scatter radio to link military camps as much as 200 miles apart. Key stations with billboard antennas were located at Phu Lam (near Saigon), Nha Trang, Qui Nhon, Da Nang, Pleiku, and in Ubon, Thailand. At the same time, a parallel microwave-based system, designed for civilian agencies' use in non-VC areas of the Mekong Delta and known as SOUTHERN TOLL, was financed by the U.S. Agency for International Development. As the insurgency spread in the delta, however, SOUTHERN TOLL increasingly carried military and intelligence information. Meanwhile, new stations were added to the BACK PORCH system in 1964, and by 1965 this system was linked to a new Southeast Asia regional communications system based on undersea cables and built by the U.S. Air Force, known as WETWASH. Improvements to communications links with staff commands in Hawaii and the U.S. mainland included capacity upgrades for the experimental satellite ground terminal installed at Phu Lam in 1964. Priority access over all systems was assigned to command-and-control and intelligence users, while logistics, personnel, and other less urgent matters were carried on slower radio-teletype links until the introduction of first-generation digital communications (the Automatic Digital Network) in 1968.

Introduction of American ground forces into South Vietnam in 1965 precipitated special tactical communications problems. The most critical of these centered on the Army's new airmobile tactics, in which ground troops were ferried by helicopter to remote locations to make contact with enemy forces, often traveling great distances from U.S. base camps. Mobile multichannel, voice-capable radios were already the backbone of American ground forces' communications equipment, but these man-packed transceivers were of limited use in the complex terrain, particularly in the Central Highlands and the interior provinces of South Vietnam. Army aviators were deployed to circle over U.S. ground units engaged in field operations, providing airborne message relay platforms between ground troops and rear area commanders. During the Ia Drang Valley battles of October–November 1965, for

example, specially equipped Caribou twin-engine aircraft were on station above the battlefields twenty-four hours a day for twenty-eight consecutive days. The communications link thus permitted Army airmobile forces to call in both medical evacuation units and close air support.

The complexity of South Vietnam's terrain and the varying types of warfare in which U.S. forces were involved—from the Army Special Forces' small-unit counterinsurgency and reconnaissance teams to the intensive bombing missions of the U.S. Air Force and naval aircraft over North Vietnam—made coordination of battlefield communications essential to the U.S. military effort. During the enemy Tet Offensive of early 1968, when VC forces launched simultaneous attacks throughout South Vietnam, communications facilities were particularly hard hit. At Hue, protracted fighting by outnumbered U.S. Marines prevented the principal U.S. station from falling into enemy hands, but communications interruptions did occur at many other locations. In the "mini-Tet" of May 1968, a VC attack on an infantry division's mountaintop signal station at Nui Ba Den, near Tay Ninh, successfully penetrated the site's defensive perimeter and damaged much of the equipment. By the summer of 1968 enemy attacks on U.S. signals installations were averaging eighty per month.

Since VC and NVA ground forces usually operated without radio traffic, American and ARVN radio direction-finding and monitoring equipment were of limited use. However, in air operations over North Vietnam, Vietnamese Communist pilots—flying Soviet-built aircraft—followed Soviet communications protocols that relied on continuous radio interface with ground controllers. Most of these transmissions were monitored by U.S. military agencies and by the U.S. National Security Agency.

Meanwhile, new communications technologies were being adapted to attack VC/NVA logistical operations. The Department of Defense developed battlefield seismic, acoustic, and radio sensors that could detect the movement of vehicles, men, and supplies. Disguised as vegetation and air dropped throughout target areas, including in Laos and Cambodia, the sensors transmitted data to specially adapted monitoring aircraft, while Air Force bases in Thailand processed the data and planned and conducted interdiction air strikes.

The May 1970 American incursion into Cambodia presented different challenges. With little advance notice of the operation, American ground units initially relied solely on FM radio nets and inefficient mobile antennas. Ground operations were stalled by inadequate interface of communications equipment, while logistics commands used telephone and teletype links to their respective headquarters.

Winding Down

Although overall American troop deployments in Vietnam dropped from 544,000 in July 1969 to less than a tenth of that by July 1972, most stationary military communications assets remained in place, ready to meet any military emergency. In March 1970, the U.S. Joint Chiefs of Staff approved a plan for the phased transition of fixed-site communications facilities to ARVN, but military exigencies forced multiple changes to the plan over succeeding years. American advisers, meanwhile, provided training for ARVN and South Vietnamese government technicians. Elsewhere, as American signals units left Vietnam, much of their portable equipment was either transferred to ARVN or shipped to South Korea for American forces stationed there.

After the Paris Peace Accords of January 1973, which mandated the complete withdrawal of American military forces from Vietnam, U.S. and third-country civilian contractors continued providing assistance to ARVN and South Vietnam government agencies. By September 1974 all but a handful of these contractors had withdrawn. Shortages of skilled technicians and spare parts rendered some 40 percent of the American-supplied communications equipment held by ARVN divisions inoperable. As a result, increasing quantities of ARVN's classified material was carried by courier.

Likewise, fuel shortages and maintenance lapses disabled most of ARVN's direction-finding aircraft, just as Communist forces in the field were beginning to rely more heavily on radio communications. During the final spring offensive by Communist forces in March 1975, however, NVA troops again observed radio silence protocols. When ARVN defenses deteriorated more rapidly than expected, NVA commanders found that their subordinates—following pre-set orders and observing radio silence—failed to take the fullest tactical advantage. Nonetheless the Communist commander, NVA General Van Tien Dung, used the Communists' own telephone links to Hanoi for last-minute consultations. Dung's forces seized control of Saigon on 30 April 1975, bringing the war to a close.

Laura M. Calkins

See also Airmobile Communications; Automatic Digital Network (AUTODIN), Couriers; Microwave; Military Affiliate Radio System (MARS), Mobile Communications; Phu Lam, Vietnam (1961–1972); Radio; Radio Silence; Teleprinter/Teletype; Tropospheric Scatter

Sources

Bergen, John D. 1986. *Military Communications: A Test for Technology—The US Army in Vietnam.* Washington, DC: Government Printing Office, U.S. Army Center of Military History.

Conboy, Kenneth, and Dale Andrade. 2000. *Spies & Commandos: How America Lost the Secret War in North Vietnam.* Lawrence: University Press of Kansas.

McCoy, James W. 1992. *Secrets of the Viet Cong.* New York: Hippocrene Books.

Military History Institute of Vietnam. 2002. *Victory in Vietnam: The Official History of the People's Army of Vietnam, 1954–1975,* translated by Merle L. Pribbenow. Lawrence: University Press of Kansas.

Rienzi, Thomas M. 1972. *Communications-Electronics, 1962–1970.* Washington, DC: Government Printing Office, U.S. Department of the Army.

Verrone, Richard Burks, and Laura M. Calkins. 2005. *Voices from Vietnam: Eyewitness Accounts of the War, 1954–75.* London: David & Charles.

Voice over Internet Protocol (VoIP)

Voice over Internet Protocol (VoIP) technology provides enhanced communication over the Internet. VoIP equipment looks like other telephones, but some advanced models have color video displays, emphasizing the converged communications capabilities of such systems.

The Department of Defense (DoD) began experimenting with VoIP capabilities in the late 1990s, seeking to push the benefits of such integrated communications down to small unit and individual soldier levels. Service application began in 2003 in Iraq and Afghanistan, but full application will extend into the 2010s. DoD has adopted the Internet Protocol (IP) as the networking technology for its developing Global Information Grid,

but is also enhancing the current Defense Information System Network to emphasize increased bandwidth. The Defense Information Systems Agency (DISA) sees VoIP as converging its presently separate voice, video, and data networks and began VoIP operations in Falls Church, Virginia, in 2001. DISA initiated pilot networks for the Central and Special Operations commands, and DISA operations in Iraq utilized a secure pilot VoIP system.

At the same time, the individual military services have conducted pilot projects and initial deployments of VoIP technology. The U.S. Marine Corps has been especially active in field implementation of VoIP, using easily transportable command-and-control combat operations centers. These are modular, field-deployable systems normally installed in tents and using computer stations with touch screen displays. VoIP can provide current battlefield information while soldiers are on the way to their destination, eliminating the former information blackout between mission departure and arrival. The system switches to a command-and-control role once troops are in battle. The benefits of converged voice and data are especially evident in medical evacuation operations where a medical helicopter evacuation can be launched in about half the time as previously.

Although battle-area deployment of VoIP technology has received considerable attention from military services and technology developers, permanent force installations are also being readied for eventual VoIP conversion. Within the Air Force, for example, worldwide locations must eventually transition to high-speed, fiber optics–based networks. The Air Force Combat Information Transport System program installs and operates voice and data networks at more than a hundred Air Force, Air Reserve, and regional Air National Guard sites. It was initiated in 1998 to develop improved information transport, network battle management, and network defense. Two-thirds of those sites had been converted to fiber optic capability by the mid-2000s, setting the stage for VoIP implementation, which will involve considerable equipment upgrades. Lackland Air Force Base in Texas and Scott Air Force Base in Illinois were among the first to pilot VoIP operations. Two-thirds of the U.S. Navy's voice communications was VoIP-enabled by the mid-2000s.

Elsewhere, in mid-2005, British Telecom and Nortel announced a plan to provide managed IP services to the British Ministry of Defence, which could result in improved security around emerging VoIP technology. This is part of the Defence Fixed Telecommunications Service to build and manage a coordinated communications infrastructure for some 2,000 locations serving the army, Royal Navy, and Royal Air Force.

Use of military VoIP raises substantial concerns as the technology still suffers fundamental security shortcomings. VoIP services pose a threat because they require some firewall ports to remain open, which can give hackers opportunities to penetrate a network. Thus military VoIP applications can be exposed to security breaches if not implemented carefully and correctly.

Christopher H. Sterling

See also Combat Information Transport System (CITS); Defence Fixed Telecommunications System (DFTS); Defense Information Systems Agency (DISA); Global Information Grid (GIG); Internet

Source

Miller, William L. 2005. "Voice over the Future." [Online article; retrieved March 2006.]

http://www.military-information -technology.com/article.cfm?DocID=914.

Voice Relay

Voice relay has one historical meaning, and another quite different and technically enhanced meaning in recent years. Often overlooked in any survey of military communications is the simple and ready expedient of using the human voice. Probably the oldest such means of signaling, speaking—or shouting—at a distance is perhaps the single means of message relay that stretches across human history from the earliest times to the present. The term "voice relay" can mean this ancient and traditional mode of signaling or much more recent digital developments.

Use of the human voice has always been limited in two important ways. Shouting can carry only so far, depending somewhat on conditions (a shout in a cave will carry farther than in hilly open country, for example) and on the strength of the individual voice. A voice will carry farther in the winter when leaves are off the trees (and thus cannot soak up noise). Thus voice relay is not much use for true distance communication—unless a system is established to have a series of people shout from point to point, thus allowing greater distance to be covered than any single voice could. Presuming optimal conditions, such a relay can in theory cover a good deal of ground in very little time. The other drawback, of course, is that use of the voice automatically shows an enemy where the shouting person is. They can hear and quickly locate the source of a voice.

Traditional voice relay is generally communication "in the clear," that is, not encoded. As typically employed in battle-field conditions, shouting provides warnings or information, but usually in plain language. Presuming an eavesdropper understands the language, he also understands the military message sent. But anyone can listen and learn—secrecy is nearly impossible. While voice relays can be coded (say, using numbers for specific meanings), such a system must be worked out in advance and may be difficult to understand clearly at the limit of voice range.

In recent years, the term "voice relay" has also come to indicate application of digital technologies to relaying voice signals. Voice relay is one form of captioning, which converts spoken language or dialogue to visible print on a video screen (also called closed captioning). It can provide functional equivalency for the hard of hearing, indicate a method of telephone messaging for those who are deaf or hard of hearing, indicate

digital means of transmitting voice signals on the Internet and other transmission systems. The Automatic Voice Relay System is a type of VoIP useful for mobile-to-mobile communications in amateur (ham) and military applications alike.

Christopher H. Sterling

See also Ancient Signals; Human Signaling; Internet; Mobile Communications; Voice over Internet Protocol (VoIP)

Sources

Biran, Gil. "Voice over Frame Relay, IP and ATM: The Case for Cooperative Networking." [Online article; retrieved September 2005.] http://www.protocols.com/papers/voe.htm.

Bruninga, Bob. 2000. "Automatic Voice Relay System." [Online article; retrieved September 2005.] http://web.usna.navy.mil/~bruninga/avrs/avrs2000.htm.

Woods, David L. 1965. *A History of Tactical Communications Techniques.* Orlando, FL: Martin-Marietta.

W

Walkie-Talkie

Walkie-talkie was a term informally applied to several U.S. Army Signal Corps tactical two-way radios during World War II. Based on the analog vacuum tube technology of the time, the portable devices (the first ones using AM, and later models based on FM technology) were bulky and heavy by modern standards.

While the Signal Corps labs at Fort Monmouth, New Jersey, had been experimenting with transceivers (transmitter-receivers) since 1936, they had been based on amplitude modulation (AM) technology. The first Signal Corps' walkie-talkie units (SCR-193, -194, and -195) appeared in 1939. These pack sets transmitted voice signals on frequencies between 27 and 65 MHz but were heavy and inconvenient to carry. Galvin Manufacturing (later Motorola) developed the first handheld two-way AM radio, the "handie-talkie," in 1940. It weighed 2.3 kg and had a range of about one mile. Known as the SCR-536, the devices came to be manufactured at a rate of fifty a day by early 1942 and more

than 130,000 were made by the end of World War II. Physically, the device looked like a long, olive-drab–colored brick (and weighed as much or more) with an antenna sticking out of the top. They were used at the platoon or company level.

Colonel Roger Colton at Fort Monmouth made the important decision to shift these tactical devices to frequency modulation (FM) because it would allow reliable, static-free single channel radio communication, even between moving vehicles. FM inventor Edwin Howard Armstrong donated his time and patents for military equipment. Initial FM military radios were for vehicles, as they were too heavy for man-carry portability. The first portable FM two-way radio for the Signal Corps was designed by Daniel E. Noble (1901–1980), an engineer working for Galvin. Weighing 35 to 40 pounds, the radio became the SCR-300 backpack unit, used channels in the 40–48 MHz spectrum, and offered a range of up to 20 miles. Based on battery power, this was the "real" walkie-talkie, the Army's first handheld portable, two-way FM transceiver. The original version used a

This is the famous World War II "Walkie-Talkie" (SCR-300) portable two-way radio shown in winter use. With the analog tube-based technology of the time, it looks (and it was) heavy and clumsy by modern standards. (U.S. Army Signal Center Command History Office, Fort Gordon, Georgia)

half-duplex channel (only one radio transmits at a time, though any number can listen) and a push-to-talk switch that began transmission. The walkie-talkie's built-in speaker could be heard by the user but also those in his immediate vicinity (a feature sometimes helpful, but often not if enemy forces were nearby). The first walkie-talkie equipment was airlifted to the Mediterranean Theater for use during the early 1944 Allied landings at Anzio, Italy. These devices were used by infantry platoons, companies, and battalions and variations were soon developed for field artillery and tank units. Eventually, Motorola produced nearly 50,000 of these famed SCR-300 walkie-talkie units during the course of the war.

Improving technology after 1945 saw production of smaller and lighter devices with greater capabilities—the first transistorized pocket transmitter appeared in 1960, and a two-way radio followed two years later. This portable technology began to see limited civilian use even during World War II. After the war, the basic walkie-talkie idea quickly expanded into a family of devices, the forbears of later citizen's band radios in the 1970s and the first analog cell phones in the early 1980s.

Christopher H. Sterling

See also Armstrong, Edwin Howard (1890–1954); Fort Monmouth, New Jersey; Mobile Communications; Modulation; Radio

Sources
McElroy, Gil. 2005. "A Short History of the Handheld Transceiver." [Online article; retrieved September 2006.] http://www2 .arrl.org/qst/2005/01/0501047.pdf#search= %22walkie-talkie%20history%22.
Petrakis, Harry Mark. 1965. "The Talkies—Handie and Walkie." In *The Founder's Touch: The Life of Paul Galvin of Motorola*, 144–147. New York: McGraw Hill.
Tasker, Alan D. 2000. "U.S. Military Portable Radios." With rebuttal by Dennis Starks. [Online article; retrieved June 2006.] http://hereford.ampr.org/history/ portable.html.
Thompson, George Raynor, et al. 1957. "Ground Radio and Radio Link or Relay. Transformed by FM." In *The Signal Corps: The Test (December 1941 to July 1943)*. U.S. Army in World War II, The Technical Services, 229–241. Washington, DC: Government Printing Office.
War Department. 1945. *Radio Set SCR-300-A, Technical Manual TM 11–242*. Washington, DC: Government Printing Office.
Woods, David L. 1965. "Tactical Wireless, Radio, and Radiotelephone." In *A History of Tactical Communication Techniques*, 209–239. Orlando, FL: Martin-Marietta (reprinted by Arno Press in *Telecommunications*, 1974).

War Department Radio Net

By the end of World War I, the U.S. Army utilized a variety of radios, both mobile and fixed, yet it lacked a nationwide strategic radio network, let alone one that linked Washington DC with America's overseas territories. In 1920–1922, Colonel Hanson B. Black, working in the Office of the Chief Signal Officer, set out to create just such an integrated strategic network.

There were many reasons for establishing a government-operated strategic communications network. It would reduce dependence on, and the cost of using, the nation's commercial radio and wire services while providing the Army with personnel trained in long-distance communications. In addition, an Army-wide network could aid with any civil disturbances, labor union violence, or natural disasters such as hurricanes.

The Signal Corps also wanted to create a central message center to handle not only radio messages but also War Department messages sent by commercial wire. This proposal caused a struggle within the government because the War Department had controlled its own message center, independent of the Army Signal Corps, since the American Civil War. The Adjutant General Corps also sought to manage the War Department's message center. The post office wanted to add the Army's long-distance radios to its own Air Mail Radio Net. Nevertheless, the Signal Corps beat out its rivals and established its War Department Radio Net in 1922 and the War Department Message Center in 1923. The corps' victory followed logically from the fact that the message center would be intimately connected to the new Radio Net.

In 1922, the Washington DC network control station, WXY, coordinated eighty-nine Army radio stations, which linked all continental corps area headquarters and overseas Army departments, such as Hawaii and the Philippines. By December 1922, the network handled an average of 10,407 messages per day. The savings proved to be enormous, especially because the War Department Message Center and Radio Net handled messages for the State Department and more than forty other governmental agencies. In 1928, WXY's call sign was changed to WVA and then to WAR (which came to stand for "We Are Ready"), demonstrating that, for all its work with nonmilitary agencies, the Signal Corps had not forgotten its mission to make the nation ready for war.

This network enterprise was not without its share of challenges. During the economic boom of the 1920s, many experienced operators left the Army as soon as they could to get better-paying jobs in the private sector. Several technical difficulties, such as summer static, could only be solved by the acquisition of better radios; yet the Army's budget had been cut extensively during that same period. Still, the soldiers who manned the Net, along with some civilian employees, developed a certain esprit de corps, helped along when a trickle of new and improved equipment arrived, in particular transmitters operating at higher frequencies. In 1928, WAR proved its worth during a Florida hurricane when it linked Army radios with a nongovernmental ham (amateur) station. The 1930s Depression initially brought even harsher budget restrictions, but personnel turnover declined as jobs in the private sector became scarce. By the late 1930s, the Army's budget began to increase (especially after 1939, when World War II began in Europe), which meant that the Radio Net could not only erect new stations, such as in Iceland in 1941, but could also begin to devote its facilities almost exclusively to military traffic.

On 7 December 1941, the War Department Message Center gained a brief moment of notoriety when, just before the Japanese attacked Pearl Harbor, the Army sent out a last-minute warning to its commanders in the Philippines, Panama, and Hawaii. The Message Center discovered that static had blocked its circuits to the West Coast—but instead of turning to the Navy, which had a more powerful transmitter in Washington, the Message Center sent the warning by Western Union wire; it reached Hawaii Army headquarters only after the attack had ended. The Radio Net suffered considerable criticism for using Western Union, but it is difficult to see whether any other course would have seriously affected the attack's outcome.

World War II brought a sudden and enormous increase in workload. The network was renamed the Army Command and Administrative Network (ACAN) and had new stations to control in Great Britain, Australia, and elsewhere around the world. The Message Center, now called the War Department Signal Center, had its demand for more personnel met in part by Women's Army Corps (WAC) soldiers, many of whom worked in the code section. By 1944, the Signal Center had 511 enlisted men and 273 WACs, but even that was not enough. Technical improvements, such as semi-automatic tape relay and mechanical enciphering, helped with the workload. On one day, 9 August 1945, ACAN processed more than 50 million words, mostly by radioteletype outside the continental United States and wire facilities within.

At the end of World War II, ACAN and the Signal Center were reduced in size with demobilization. In 1947 the Signal Center was renamed the Army Command and Administrative Communications Agency (ACACA), still under the Signal Corps. ACACA not only controlled the Message Center and WAR but also provided administrative, training, and logistical support to a multitude of Signal Corps agencies, such as the White House Communications Agency and the Military District of Washington. It also coordinated the ham operators who comprised the Military Amateur Radio System (MARS); later, "Amateur" was replaced by "Affiliate."

The Korean War meant more work for ACACA and ACAN—traffic originating in the Pentagon doubled from mid-1950 to early 1951—but even after the end of that conflict they had many Cold War chores, despite a shrinking budget. As one example, ACACA continued giving logistical support to other Signal Corps activities in the Washington DC area, while ACAN communicated with troops still in Germany, Korea, and elsewhere.

During 1957–1958, ACACA was renamed the Army Communications Agency; by this time, it had turned its attention to communications support for the government's evacuation and relocation facilities in case of nuclear attack. The Signal Corps emphasized communications automation and signal security in response to this new task.

In 1962 the Signal Corps and other Army technical branches lost their traditional structure and autonomy in a major reorganization within the Department of the Army. Thus the Radio Net passed out of the control of the Signal Corps, itself no longer an operational entity.

Karl G. Larew

See also Army Signal Corps; Military Affiliate Radio System (MARS); Radio; White House Communications Agency (WHCA)

Sources

French, E. F. 1925. "War Department Radio Net." *Signal Corps Bulletin* 30: 13–16.

Larew, Karl G. 1956. "ACACA History: A History of the Army Command and Administrative Communications Agency, 1899–1956." Washington, DC: Unpublished ms. written for ACACA, now located in the archives of the Military History Institute, Carlisle Barracks, PA, and of the Command Historian, Signal Corps, Fort Gordon, GA.

Office of the Chief of Military History. 1956–1966. *United States Army in World War II: The Technical Services: The Signal Corps.* 3 vols. Washington, DC: Office of the Chief of Military History.

War on Terrorism

The early twenty-first century brought a new American focus on battling terrorists—many of them (but not all) Islamic fundamentalists—who, with the al-Qaeda 11 September 2001 attacks on New York and Washington, brought a new kind of war directly to the United States. Regional wars in the Middle East and elsewhere contributed to a growing sense of "us" versus "them" in cultural as well as military terms. "Terrorist" was taken to mean those, organized or not, who aimed much of their behavior at civilian targets, hoping to cause chaos and thus modify national policies. Modes of communication are central on both sides of this emerging equation.

Communication in any battle is a matter of transmitting appropriate information into the right hands at the correct time. The U.S. military relies on a process of communication and assessment often referred to as the observation-orientation-decision-action (OODA) loop. Military analyst John Boyd developed the OODA loop theory to describe communication within the military bureaucracy and the flow of information necessary to make strategic decisions. This model is both hierarchical and vertical. Decisions are made at high levels and filter to those in the field. In any of the services, strategic planners communicate with operational commanders. Military communication is seen as a systematic process involving many levels—from foot soldier to general. Even with digital information links, such a process can take valuable time.

The attacks on New York and Washington brought a new set of challenges to the decision-making process in the military. These arose from expanding abilities of potential adversaries to communicate effectively and quickly. Terrorists approach warfare from an asymmetrical perspective. Both wars against Iraq along with that in Afghanistan have illustrated that virtually no adversary is able to match the United States in conventional military capabilities. As a result, terrorists with knowledge of the OODA loop seek to take advantage of the slower bureaucracy of the U.S. military to exploit a temporary advantage. For example, the acquisition and use of modern communications allowed many of the pro-Taliban groups in Afghanistan the opportunity to change sides once the order of the battle was established in the early days of American operations there.

Further, few terrorists engage in formal decision making and can thus move quickly. Terrorist organizations are more flexible, being based on dispersed units, which are less reliant on communications during pre-planned attacks. The network terrorist group rarely has a central leadership to attack. The war on terrorism pits these decentralized terror groups against armed forces originally designed to defeat an industrialized and centralized enemy—the Soviet Union. Though the Iraqi insurgency has modified thinking, the U.S. paradigm of warfare is still largely aimed at traditional theater warfare and attrition and its communications reflect this more conventional model of warfare. On the other hand, terrorists hope to cut off military forces and aim at society in general. The terrorist threat demands a reappraisal of communication assets. The challenge is how best to engage terrorists such that the bureaucratic OODA loop helps rather than interferes with a rapid response.

Those who advocate hierarchical systems point to the success of "smart bombs," satellites, and other technology to target a threat accurately while posing the least threat to your own forces. Others call for more use of human resources and intelligence. Put another way, the OODA decision loop needs to remain in the hands of the soldier on the ground. A compelling argument can be made for increased military training to encourage independent thinking and more rapid decisions. In addition, the soldier on the ground must have the necessary ability to correctly orient forces and the agility required to shift from one orientation to another.

Early operations in Afghanistan in 2002 demonstrated the value of agility in orientation and communication. Decisions during the initial phases of ground combat revealed a military very competent to make rapid real-time decisions. Special Forces recognized that the technological advantage enjoyed by U.S. forces also needed supplementing with local methods—horseback, local clothing, beards to reduce the likelihood of being recognized as American, and so forth. Special Forces on the ground understood the intent and goals of commanders at Central Command (CENTCOM) in Tampa, Florida, and made decisions accordingly. Their communications were typically of field

forces updating commanders—and not the more conventional hierarchical model. As more forces became involved, however, reliance on hierarchical communications and decision making increased and successes were less frequent. Too often American forces were handcuffed by the hierarchical and rigid OODA loop that traveled half a world away to CENTCOM for relevant decisions.

Similar bureaucratic concerns affect the battle against terrorism on the domestic front. Formation of the Department of Homeland Security in the aftermath of the 2001 attacks led to years of organizational turf wars and confusion despite huge spending increases. Yet public security agencies including police and fire units continued to complain of radios that could not intercommunicate in emergency situations. Overlaps in responsibility and unwillingness to share information across the military services, the National Security Agency, the Central Intelligence Agency, and the Federal Bureau of Investigation (there are sixteen agencies concerned with national intelligence) slowed the nation's response to natural disaster (Hurricane Katrina in 2005, for example) as well as border security and more specific terrorist threats. There is yet no clear agreement on what vital infrastructure has to be protected, let alone by whom and how. A National Counterterrorism Center was formed in 2005 in an attempt to coordinate across the variety of national and regional security agencies.

The communications dilemma posed by what are really numerous wars on terrorism is quite clear: Communication from the bottom up allows for a more localized understanding of the situation but leaves decisions in the hands of less-senior military forces. Coordination across forces and agencies is vital. The continuing war on terrorism presents a host of challenges.

Matthew Wahlert

See also Gulf War (1990–1991); Iraq War (2003–Present); National Security Agency (NSA); Signals Intelligence (SIGINT)

Sources

Friedman, George, and Meredith Friedman. 1996. *The Future of War: Power, Technology, and American World Dominance in the 21st Century*. New York: Random House.

Hammes, Thomas X. 2004. *The Sling and the Stone: On War in the 21st Century*. St. Paul, MN: Zenith Press.

Peters, Ralph. 1999. *Fighting for the Future: Will America Triumph?* Mechanicsburg, PA: Stackpole Books.

Vandergriff, Donald. 2002. *The Path to Victory*. Novato, CA: Presidio Press.

Wilcox, Greg, and Gary I. Wilson. 2002. "Military Response to Fourth Generation Warfare in Afghanistan." [Online article; retrieved December 2005.] Reprinted at http://www.d-n-i.net/fcs/wilson_wilcox_military_responses.htm.

Warfighter Information Network–Tactical (WIN-T)

The Warfighter Information Network–Tactical (WIN-T) is the U.S. Army's developing tactical telecommunications system. It will consist of communication infrastructure and network components designed to operate from the maneuver battalion on the front line to a war theater's rear boundary.

The WIN-T network is designed to provide and combine command, control, communications, computers, intelligence, surveillance, and reconnaissance support capabilities that are mobile, secure, survivable, seamless, and capable of supporting multimedia tactical information systems within a battle area. WIN-T will allow all Army commanders and other communications network users to exchange information both internal and external to the theater, from wired or wireless telephones, computers (Internet-like capability) or video terminals. WIN-T employs a combination of terrestrial, airborne, and satellite-based communication links to provide robust connectivity. It will also interface with the developing Global Information Grid to allow worldwide connectivity.

The system makes use of highly mobile, high-capacity line-of-sight radios using quick-erect antenna masts, fiber optic cable, and wide-band digital radios that will provide the transmission capacity necessary to communicate information required by modern forces in the field. The radios will provide connectivity to form a backbone transmission network and will replace current low bandwidth radios. For range extension, WIN-T will use unmanned aerial vehicles and satellite systems to connect command posts. Users will be able to view Web pages and place voice and video calls on a handset that will interface with a network of satellite and terrestrial-based sites.

The program will cost $10 billion to develop and put into place. Initial design and testing concluded late in 2005. The first Army unit is scheduled to field WIN-T by 2008, as the system begins to replace the current mobile subscriber unit system. Unlike most current military networks, WIN-T will offer seamless interoperability with other networks, including legacy, joint, coalition, and even commercial networks, utilizing all available links to support Army units anywhere. The system will utilize commercially available elements and will be able to integrate with existing as well as new systems, with dedicated links designed specifically for the military.

Christopher H. Sterling

See also Communication Satellites; Fiber Optics; Future Combat Systems (FCS); Global Information Grid (GIG); Internet; Mobile Communications

Sources

U.S. Army. 1999. *Warfighter Information Network–Tactical (WIN-T) Operational Requirements Document* (November 5). [Online article; retrieved June 2006.] http://www.fas.org/man/.

Wood, Camilla A. 2005. "Warfighter Information Network–Tactical." [Online article; retrieved June 2006.] http://www.highbeam.com/library/docfree.asp?DOCID=1G1:135813080&ctrlInfo=Round 20%3AMode20a%3ADocG%3AResult&ao=.

Warsaw Pact (1955–1991)

The Soviet-directed Warsaw Pact alliance was developed in response to the creation of the North Atlantic Treaty Organization (NATO) in 1949. During much of its existence, the Warsaw Pact (named for the Polish capital where the treaty was signed on 14 May 1955) essentially functioned as a part of the Soviet Ministry of Defense. In its early years, the Warsaw Pact served as one of the Soviet Union's primary mechanisms for keeping its East European allies (Poland, East Germany [as of 1956], Czechoslovakia, Hungary, Romania, Bulgaria, and—until 1962—Albania) under its political and military control. But the Soviets took no steps to integrate the various armies into a multinational force. After uprisings in Poland and Hungary in 1956, however, military exercises with Soviet forces and the allied national armies became the focus of Warsaw Pact military activities.

With the creation of the East German National Peoples Army early in 1956, a Signal Corps (*Nachrichtentruppen*) was formed on 1 March 1956. Training was carried out on the basis of modified programs of the Soviet army. Equipment was of either Soviet or German origin and the technical standard was equivalent to that of the German army at the end of World War II. Between 1957 and 1969, development was characterized by the adaptation of the structures of the Warsaw Treaty Organization to suit the needs of the National Peoples Army. Improvements in education and combat readiness were made within the signal corps. Modernization of communication equipment progressed rapidly.

During the 1970s, responsibility for the electronics of flight safety was absorbed by the corps, which became the Signal and Flight Safety Corps (*Nachrichten und Flugsicherungstruppen*). Independent battalions were responsible for flight safety links on airfield zones and for the radio navigation and aircraft radio communications within the whole of East Germany. Radio, radar, and illumination systems were included under their responsibility. The battalions were attached to joint fighter-wing command posts and the radio technical (radar) troops. The East German signal corps was absorbed into the West German Fernmeldetruppe with reunification in 1990.

In 1968, following the pact's invasion of Czechoslovakia (ending the "Prague Spring" liberalization movement), Romania demanded the withdrawal from its territory of all Soviet troops and advisers. In the 1970s and 1980s, Bulgaria, Czechoslovakia, and East Germany (and sometimes Cuba) became the primary Soviet proxies for transferring arms and military advice and advisers to the Third World. By the 1980s, the Soviet Union provided 73 of the 126 Warsaw Pact tank and motorized rifle divisions. The Warsaw Pact countries provided forward bases, staging areas, and interior lines of communication for the Soviets against NATO. The pact collapsed with the end of the Soviet state in 1991.

Through all of this changing role of the Warsaw Pact, as one might expect, Soviet communications gear and systems connected and controlled the various military services. At first considerable use was made of captured wartime German radio and other equipment, but as that wore out and could not be replaced, Soviet communications equipment became dominant. Some of it was quite good, but much was of an earlier electronic generation or lower standard and thus demonstrated lower capabilities than comparable NATO equipment and systems.

Soviet planning by the 1970s emphasized ensuring the continued operation of the Soviet Union's own command, control, and communications while attacking those of NATO. Its doctrine of radio electronic combat indicated a strong commitment to coordinated use of electronic means to degrade NATO's ability to communicate. Direct attack by Warsaw Pact military forces might take the form of sabotage on existing microwave radio relay sites, satellite earth terminals, and major switching centers. NATO radio equipment in the high-frequency, tropospheric scatter, and microwave realms was considered particularly vulnerable to pact jamming and exploitation. But Warsaw Pact nations never had sufficient budgets to overcome the West's communications leadership.

As the Cold War ended in the early 1990s, the former Soviet satellite nations were saddled with poor and rudimentary modes of communication. When (in March 1999) Poland, the Czech Republic (Slovakia broke off in 1993), and Hungary became members of NATO, a primary and immediate goal was to substantially upgrade their military

communications and to develop interoperability with other member nations. Military spending (as a portion of gross domestic product) increased accordingly in each former pact country, Poland's military being twice the size of the other two nations' combined. The necessary communications links between Warsaw, Prague, and Budapest with NATO headquarters in Brussels were put into place even before the three former Warsaw Pact countries joined NATO. NATO soon funded upgrades and established basic communications links between each country's operations center for air defense and the alliance's air defense system. Several other former pact countries (including Slovakia, Romania, and Bulgaria) joined NATO early in 2004.

Cliff Lord and Christopher H. Sterling

See also Baltic Nations; Eastern Europe; Germany: Army; Russia/Soviet Union: Army

Sources

Cronican, John G., Jr. 1981. "Centralized Control and Decentralized Execution." [Online article; retrieved April 2006.] http://www.airpower.maxwell.af.mil/airchronicles/aureview/1981/jan-feb/cronican.htm.

Library of Congress, Federal Research Division. 1990. "Appendix C: The Warsaw Pact." [Online information; retrieved April 2006.] http://www.country-data.com/frd/cs/soviet_union/su_appnc.html.

Waterloo, Battle of (18 June 1815)

The Battle of Waterloo, fought on 18 June 1815, was the seminal confrontation that finally ended Napoleon's domination of Europe. After a brutal day of fighting and heavy losses, the eventual outcome was decided, in part, by problems of judgment, coordination, and communications on both sides. Weather (it had rained hard the night before) had a deleterious impact on field conditions, making effective communication all the more vital.

This battle relied almost totally for its communications on the use of couriers either on foot or horseback. Sending messages this way meant a delay in instructions being carried out, and there was a high chance of their being intercepted and never arriving. Given the numbers of troops involved and the distances involved, couriers had potentially fatal results if communication failed. Napoleon did not have any system in place (even duplicate couriers) to ensure that his orders had been received. Smoke on the battlefield also made visual signaling difficult.

Centralization of the French command portended trouble if Napoleon's signals and intentions could not be received in the field, for his commanders had learned over the years not to act independently of the emperor's wishes. And those wishes varied, for Napoleon was ill that day and was not making his usual incisive and rapid decisions. Further, his usual communications officer had died at the beginning of the month, and Napoleon appointed a replacement, Marshal Nicolas Soult. Although Soult was a good operations officer, he was inexperienced and lacked foresight in organizing the dissemination of battle orders. Delays in effective communications and orders during the long day of battle would cost the French heavily.

For example, Marshal Michel Ney failed to capture Quatre-Bras because he delayed attack and was waiting for further communication. In command of Napoleon's Old Guard and in the thick of the fighting, Ney could not see the overall battle or observe British troop positions on the ridge above the battlefield. Similarly, comte d'Erlon's corps failed to see real action at either Quatre-Bras or Ligny because of another confusion of orders. Napoleon had sent a single messenger to tell General Emmanuel Grouchy to stop pursuing Marshal Blücher's Prussian force and to return to join the main French force facing the Duke of Wellington's allies. But Grouchy, besides being slow to act, did not even receive this order until 7:00 p.m., well after the battle's outcome had already been established. Thus his 70,000 French troops would not assist when they might have made a substantial difference.

Nor was all well with the allies. For one thing, unlike the French, Wellington's force had to work with multiple languages (German, English, and Dutch—among others) and several armies spread across considerable ground. Coordination and communication with the advancing Prussian force under Gebhard von Blücher (who spoke no English) was, as Winston Churchill later put it, mysteriously defective. For much of the day, Wellington was poorly informed as to where the Prussians were. Only their late afternoon arrival finally turned the tide of battle for Wellington.

Yet at times, signals could be patently simple—as when Wellington appeared on the skyline at the end of the battle and merely waved his large black hat to signal for a general allied pursuit of retreating French troops. By early July, the allied force entered Paris.

Christopher H. Sterling

See also Couriers; Napoleonic Wars (1795–1815)

Sources
Adkin, Mark. 2002. *The Waterloo Companion: The Complete Guide to History's Most Famous Land Battle*. Harrisburg, PA: Stackpole.
Barbero, Allesandro. 2005. *The Battle: A New History of Waterloo*, translated by John Cullen. New York: Walker.

Weapons Data Link Network (WDLN)

The Weapons Data Link Network (WDLN) is a developing American networked system of guided missile control, allowing common two-way communication links between air crews, ground personnel, and the in-flight weapon itself. WDLN is part of the trend toward net-centric military communications in the early 2000s.

Primarily an Air Force and Navy program with some participation by the Army and Marine Corps, WDLN was created as an initial effort to integrate network-enabled weapons into the Global Information Grid. Developing information exchange standards for weapons and their controllers is seen as an important part of increased interoperability.

A series of 140 WDLN flight tests in October–November 2005 demonstrated that air crews and ground controllers could use the same two-way communications links for sending guided weapons to their targets. Inflight updates are a central part of the system, invaluable for seeking moving targets, often a vital part of counterterrorism actions. Ground or air crews can communicate target changes to the weapon and the latter can report their own status.

Development of WDLN is projected to extend into 2008–2010 before full-scale adoption, and essential aspects of it will probably be applied to other weapons systems.

Christopher H. Sterling

See also Airplanes; Global Information Grid (GIG); Information Revolution in Military Affairs (IRMA)

Source

Tuttle, Richard. 2006. "Widening the Net." *Aviation Week*, February 26, 59–61.

Welchman, Gordon (1906–1985)

Gordon Welchman was one of the most important British World War II code breakers at Bletchley Park.

Welchman was born in England on 15 June 1906, son of the archdeacon of Bristol. After studying as a mathematics scholar at Trinity College (part of Cambridge University) from 1925 to 1928, Welchman became a research fellow and then lectured in mathematics at Sidney Sussex College for a decade beginning in 1929.

He joined the Government Code & Cipher School at Bletchley Park in September 1939 and was soon playing a central role in developing its code-breaking process in 1939–1940. He served as head of Hut Six from 1940 to 1943, the section at Bletchley Park responsible for breaking German army and air force Enigma ciphers. Welchman then became Bletchley's assistant director for mechanization (of code breaking).

Welchman made two crucial contributions to the British code-breaking operation. In his first, he designed the organization that would operate on shifts for twenty-four hours a day throughout the war. His second concerned an electromechanical device. In his early code-breaking effort, Welchman developed an enhancement to Alan Turing's design for an electromechanical code-breaking machine, dubbed the "bombe." Welchman's enhancement, the "diagonal board," rendered the bombes more efficient (by dramatically reducing the number of false "stops" they encountered and making it much easier to devise bombe "menus") in helping to break messages enciphered on the Enigma machine. After the first bombe with such a diagonal board was installed at Bletchley Park in August 1940, bombes became a primary tool for helping code breakers solve Enigma "keys" for the remainder of the war. Some 200 were built.

Welchman was one of four Bletchley Park code breakers who broke the line of authority to appeal for more personnel. In a 21 October 1941 letter, hand delivered to 10 Downing Street for Prime Minister Winston Churchill, Welchman and his colleagues indicated that Bletchley needed more staff and resources to get the vital code breaking done. (The others were Alan Turing, Stuart Milner Barry, and Hugh Alexander.) Churchill ordered immediate "Action this Day" to see that Bletchley received all it required on a top-priority basis, and he wanted to know this had been done. Reorganization of Bletchley's leadership and operation was one result.

Welchman moved to the United States in 1948 and began working with computers and information technology, becoming an American citizen. He joined the Mitre Corporation in 1962, working in Bedford, Massachusetts. For the fist time since the war, he was again working on secure and survivable communications systems, this time for the U.S. military. And his focus changed, for now his concern was how to develop secure systems rather than break them.

After his retirement, while still doing some consulting work for the U.S. government, he published *The Hut Six Story* (1982), one of the first "inside" analyses explaining exactly how Bletchley Park code breakers had operated. The last 100 pages detailed his concerns about the status of Cold War secure communications. Though much of the World War II code-breaking process had been declassified, Welchman ran into trouble with the Official Secrets Act given the level of detail included in his book. His security clearance was lifted and he was banned from any detailed discussion of the wartime Enigma machine. Possible further prosecution was deflected by Welchman's death on 8 October 1985.

Christopher H. Sterling

See also Bletchley Park; Code Breaking; Enigma; Government Code & Cipher School (GC&CS, 1919–1946); Signals Intelligence (SIGINT); Turing, Alan Mathison (1912–1954)

Sources
Welchman, Gordon. 1982. *The Hut Six Story: Breaking the Enigma Code.* New York: McGraw-Hill.
West, Nigel. 1988. *The SIGINT Secrets: The Signals Intelligence War, 1900 to Today, Including the Prosecution of Gordon Welchman.* Rev. ed. New York: William Morrow.

White House Communications Agency (WHCA)

The White House Communications Agency (WHCA) was created as the White House Signal Detachment by the War Department on 25 March 1942, early in American participation in World War II. A new radio system had been installed in the White House immediately after the Pearl Harbor attack in December 1941.

The detachment was activated under control of the Military District of Washington to provide normal and emergency communications requirements in support of the president. The detachment provided mobile radio, teletype, telephone, and cryptographic aids in the White House and at the presidential retreat, which President Franklin Roosevelt called Shangri-La, now known as Camp David. In 1954, during the Eisenhower administration, the detachment was reorganized under the Office of the Chief

Signal Officer and renamed the White House Army Signal Agency.

The agency was transferred in 1962 to the auspices of the Defense Communications Agency under operational control of the White House Military Office, and became the White House Communications Agency.

WHCA played significant roles in many historical events during World War II, the Korean War, the Vietnam War, and operations in Panama, Guatemala, the Middle East, and Somalia. WHCA was also a key communication link during the assassination of President John Kennedy in 1963 and the attempts on the lives of Presidents Gerald Ford (1975) and Ronald Reagan (1981). The 11 September 2001 terrorist attacks greatly increased the focus on secure communications by WHCA.

Today, the president, vice president, and their staffs have the use of both secure and nonsecure telephones, as well as data and facsimile systems. WHCA runs the White House signal switchboard, which handles 2,500 calls a day. The audiovisual unit sets up sound systems, microphones, and lighting for the press conferences or other presidential functions such as speeches and state dinners. WHCA sets up and records radio broadcasts for the president from any location around the world. WHCA videotapes presidential movements, processes film from official White House photographers, and makes video recordings for the White House and staff.

For quick trips overseas, a team of at least twenty goes out five days in advance to establish needed communication links— more extended trips require forty-five personnel three weeks in advance.

The agency has evolved over six decades from a small team of thirty-two personnel working out of the basement of the White House to nearly a thousand staff in the self-supporting joint service command. Headquarters for WHCA is at the Anacostia Navy Yard in Washington DC. Agency staff also work at the Washington Radio Network System in downtown Washington and serve in detachments in Maryland and Maine, with communication support teams in Arizona and Texas.

Christopher H. Sterling

See also Defense Information Systems Agency (DISA)

Sources

Hill, Laura. 2003. "White House Communications Agency Transforms to Meet New Challenges." [Online article; retrieved June 2006.] http://www.findarticles.com/p/articles/mi_m0PAA/is_1_28/ai_103992792.

Jacques, March Laree. 1999. "Transformation and Redesign in the White House Communications Agency." *Quality Management Journal* 6 (3).

Sutherland, Don. 1990 "No Busy Signal— Instant Worldwide Communications." *Airman Magazine* (May). [Online article; retrieved June 2006.] http://www.disa .mil/whca/.

Wireless Telegraph Board

Appointed by President Theodore Roosevelt in 1904, this panel, made up primarily of Army and Navy officers, developed the first American policy for wireless communications, assigning most authority to the U.S. Navy. It provided an important boost to both naval and Army radio efforts.

Often called "The Roosevelt Board," the panel of officials was appointed on 24 June 1904 by the president, acting on a recommendation of the secretary of the navy. Three Navy officers, General Adolphus Greely of the Army Signal Corps, and a representative of the weather bureau (then in the Department of Agriculture) were assigned the task of determining the role of radio in the federal government. Despite the recent innovation of wireless, or radio, already evident during the board's proceedings was the jealously guarded territory of several government agencies already experimenting with or applying the technology. Yet the board reached unanimous conclusions, assigning a dominant role to the Navy.

The report of 29 July 1904 concluded that the Navy was to provide coastal communications for government use, including the receipt and transmission of radio messages to and from ships at sea, unless commercial services were able to take on that task. The weather bureau was to turn over its wireless transmitters to the Navy. The Army was granted the right to erect and operate radio stations as needed subject to not interfering with the coastal stations operated by the Navy. Finally, the board recommended that Congress adopt legislation to prevent monopoly in radio and that administration of such concerns—as well as the licensing of private or commercial transmitters—should be assigned to the Department of Commerce and Labor.

The report, merely twenty-four pages long (and eighteen of those were appended documents), had considerable impact on military communications, as virtually all of its recommendations were adopted. The panel concluded that "wireless telegraphy is of paramount interest" to the Army and Navy in both peace and war "and that such use shall be unrestricted." Needs of the military, and especially the Navy, were to be paramount in any consideration of radio's development in the United States.

Christopher H. Sterling

See also Greely, Adolphus W. (1844–1935); Radio

Sources
Howeth, L. N. 1963. "The Roosevelt Board." In *History of Communications-Electronics in the United States Navy*, 76–77. Washington, DC: Government Printing Office.
Wireless Telegraph Board. 1904. *Wireless Telegraphy: Report of the Interdepartmental Board Appointed by the President to Consider the Entire Question of Wireless Telegraphy in the Service of the National Government.* Washington, DC: Government Printing Office.

World War I

At least three factors made the 1914–1918 world war vastly different from earlier conflicts: widely separated battlefronts, rapid improvements in technology, and a growing reliance on fast-changing modes of communication. No prior war had taken place on so many disparate fronts on more different terrain, or with forces on land, at sea, and in the air. While armed forces of both the Central powers (chiefly Germany, Austria-Hungary, and the Ottoman Empire) and the Allies (primarily Britain, France, and Russia, and after 1917, the United States) moved with dispatch from reliance on visual and mechanical signaling to applying electrical communication systems, results were often less than those sought. Military and naval communication varied from the use of flags to messages carried by wire via voice or electric current, including some of the first air-to-ground systems aboard airplanes and dirigibles.

Static trench warfare on the Western Front required widespread use of pyrotechnic signals and whistles to shift troops in or out of trenches, or warn of gas attacks. Much battle terrain was flat, handicapping sending and receiving of visual signals. As General R. Nalder (later head of the Royal Corps of Signals) later noted, visual signaling fell into disfavor at the front because it was conspicuous and placed participants in danger. Artillery smoke made seeing anything difficult. It was more often the messenger, rider (on horseback, bicycle, motorcycle, or small vehicle), dog, or pigeon that actually carried the day. Opposing trenches were so close in some areas that voice commands could be readily overheard.

Telegraphers (not yet part of the British signal arm, they operated as a part of the Royal Engineers) began to take precedence. Telephones were increasingly applied at headquarters level. Wire lines for telegraphy and telephony had to be either strung or buried. That was best done along roadways, but as opposing forces often shelled roads to interdict communications, hand carts were used to string wire cross-country. Wire strung from poles could all too easily be cut by rifle or shell fire. Along front lines, wire had to be laid, buried if conditions permitted, or run along special communication trenches. There seemed no completely safe place for wire—in some African areas, giraffes broke wires and white ants ate cable insulation.

Military radio equipment in 1914 was crude. Antennas were obvious targets, and equipment was fragile, cumbersome, and vulnerable to weather or enemy action. There were few trained operators and never enough radios were available (a U.S. Army division of 20,000 men rarely had more than six radios even in 1918). But radio's biggest drawback was the lack of senior commanders willing to use or trust it in battlefield conditions. Poorly organized at first, Army radio users also suffered from security breaches such as sending vital messages in the clear rather than in code. Wireless equipment on both sides steadily improved with continuous-wave vacuum tube transmitters of 1918, little resembling the cranky spark-

gap devices with which the war began. Allied radio equipment improved more than did that of Germany as devices became standardized over the last two years of the war. On the Western Front after 1916 radio operators also made use of conduction Fullerphones and French systems.

Several key battles, including those of the Marne and Tannenberg (both 1914), were decided in part by which side made the most effective use of communications, including wireless. Radio was more useful away from the trench-bound Western Front (in the Middle East and East Africa, for example) where alternative modes of communication were rare as was the likelihood of signal interference or enemy code breaking.

This varied communication activity soon prompted large increases in personnel assigned to signal duties on both sides. All countries ramped up training programs for radio and wired communication operators. The U.S. Navy supervised a mandatory pooling of private patents "for the duration" to encourage manufacture of the best possible equipment. The U.S. Army established a large Signal Corps research center that became Fort Monmouth, New Jersey, which developed improved transmitters for use on land and in the air.

While the Army Signal Corps in 1917 included but fifty-five officers and 1,600 enlisted men, in just eighteen months, by Armistice Day (11 November 1918) those numbers had grown to 2,700 officers and 53,300 men. The corps built some 1,700 miles of poles to carry 20,700 miles of wire. Another 2,000 miles of poles with 28,000 miles of wire were leased from the French. The corps operated 82,000 miles of wire in France alone, not including wire for 200 telephone exchanges nor wire used by combat units. Millions of telegrams were sent by the Army before 1919.

Naval signaling used both traditional and newer methods. The 1918 Royal Navy *Handbook of Signalling*, for example, described use of nearly twenty different signal systems: flags and pendants via flaghoist, semaphore signs and flags, Morse code (sent in daylight by flag waving, signal lantern, heliograph, or wireless telegraphy; at night using signal lanterns or wireless; and in foggy conditions by sound signals), flag waving, telephone, heliograph, and special means to communicate with the Army. Flaghoisted flags included the twenty-seven flags of the International Code of Signals along with the Navy's sixty-four others—thirty-one flags, nineteen pennants, eleven triangles, and three burgees. Combinations of these allowed for a more sophisticated means of signaling than was often available on land.

At the same time, radio was also used effectively in both the British and German fleets and became an essential element in such large naval battles as Jutland (31 May 1916). Distance, darkness, or smoke all made visual signals questionable. As spark-gap equipment was replaced by better arc (1916–1917) and then vacuum tube–powered equipment (1918), naval radio's value improved further. Radio direction-finding techniques, developed before but vastly improved during the war, made wireless signaling at sea dangerous, as triangulation could readily locate a ship's transmitter thus placing the vessel at risk from submarine attack. Knowing this danger, allied convoys of merchantmen usually maintained radio silence (relying on visual signals), as did most military vessels while on patrol. The German cruiser *Emden*, for example, was successful as a wide-ranging commerce raider for a long period in 1914 largely by keeping radio silence. Electronic jamming of enemy radio signals was often attempted, though usually with little effect.

Early naval actions in 1914–1915 featured attacks on the communications of opposing forces. German and Allied naval actions, for example, included capturing or destroying outlying enemy radio transmitting sites in the Pacific, Africa, and elsewhere. Cutting of German telegraph cable connections between Europe and North America forced German use of radio telegraphy—which could be intercepted by Allied code breakers. Indeed, just such an interception, in this case of the infamous "Zimmermann Telegram" in early 1917, would lead to American entry into the war. World War I witnessed the rapid development of aerial communications. Early aircraft were essentially limited to observation, and like the balloon of fifty years earlier, flying was a function assigned initially to signal corps. Many rather simple systems were devised for communicating with aircraft from the ground below. These included panels of cloth in various shapes, patterns, and colors. Lights were also used. Inventive military minds began to use aircraft to spot and photograph enemy positions. Early signaling from the air was more limited—often to messages dropped to the ground.

Only with the development of effective (and relatively lightweight) ground-to-aircraft radio could the airplane become a more effective fighter, and ultimately a bomber. Radio also contributed to the coordinated use of German Zeppelins as bombers. But as happened on the ground, German leadership in radio at the start of the war had diminished by its end, by which time the Royal Air Force had 600 radio-equipped airplanes and more than 2,000 ground stations. Between 12–15 September 1918, Brigadier General Billy Mitchell led nearly 1,500 aircraft to the St. Mihiel area in the largest bombing effort of the war, foretelling what was to come.

David L. Woods and Christopher H. Sterling

See also Airplanes; Airships and Balloons; Armstrong, Edwin Howard (1890–1954); Army Signal Corps; Ferrié, Gustave-Auguste (1868–1932); Fort Monmouth, New Jersey; Fullerphone; Ground Radio; Hooper, Stanford C. (1884–1955); Jutland, Battle of (1916); Marne, Battle of (September 1914); Naval Radio Stations/Service; Radio Silence; Tannenberg, Battle of (1914); Telegraph; Telephone; Undersea Cables; United Kingdom: Royal Corps of Signals; Vacuum Tube

Sources

Beauchamp, Ken. 2001. *History of Telegraphy*, chaps. 8–10. London: Institution of Electrical Engineers.

Hezlet, Arthur. 1975. *Electronics and Sea Power*, chaps. 4–6. New York: Stein & Day.

Howeth, L. S. 1963. *History of Communications-Electronics in the United States Navy*, chaps. 16–25. Washington, DC: Government Printing Office.

Moreau, Louise. 1991. "The Military Communications Explosion, 1914–1918." *Antique Wireless Association Review* 6: 135–154.

Nalder, R. F. H. 1958. *The Royal Corps of Signals: A History of Its Antecedents and Development*, chaps. IV–XIV. London: Royal Signals Institution.

Report of the Chief Signal Officer to the Secretary of War. 1919. Washington, DC: Government Printing Office (reprinted by Arno Press, 1974).

Schubert, Paul. 1928. "Era of Military Use," in *The Electric Word: The Rise of Radio*, 85–187. New York: Macmillan.

Woods, David L. 1965. *A History of Tactical Communication Techniques*. Orlando, FL: Martin-Marietta (reprinted by Arno Press, 1974).

World War II

By any measure, World War II was the largest conflict in human history. It was fought on virtually ever continent by military forces numbering in the millions. And tens of millions died—far more civilians than uniformed personnel. As with most recent wars, conflict sped up the pace of technological development. And improving modes of communication played a central part in all theaters and for all combatants. As with the prior world war, communication varied from the long traditional (e.g., couriers) to the new and exotic (electric cipher machines). Far more than in the earlier conflict, code breaking and signals intelligence played an important part in the eventual Allied victory in 1945.

The Allied ability to research and develop and then mass produce and apply cutting-edge electronic technology was another key factor in that victory. Germany and Japan lacked the industrial infrastructure (even before sustained Allied bombing reduced that infrastructure further) to sustain such an effort over a long war. Thus Axis countries standardized on 1937–1940 technology-based radios and other electrical equipment and had to rely on them through the war, while Allied nations enjoyed the use of steadily improved radio and other communication technology.

In a global war where air power and ground mobility were dominant factors, every combatant made extensive use of radio, for the need to effectively command and control forces took precedence over the risks of interception. Washington, London, Tokyo, and Berlin were all constantly in touch with their major field commands at home and overseas. Research during the war, especially in the United States, greatly expanded usable spectrum and opened up a variety of new transmission modes. Edwin Armstrong's newly developed FM radio proved valuable for local communication on land and sea, for instance, between merchant ships and their naval escorts in a convoy. Armstrong declined his FM patent royalties for military uses for the duration. By the end of the war, virtually every Allied military vehicle and aircraft carried a transceiver. Relatively small "walkie-talkie" radios allowed infantry to stay in constant communication with local headquarters—one of the first demonstrations of small-scale mobile communications in wartime.

The vital role of effective communications stands out in specific campaigns—in the Atlantic antisubmarine war (especially from 1939 to 1943), the 1940 Battle of Britain, and the Battle of Midway in mid-1942 as the turning point in the Pacific war—and in every case, Allied communications superiority was an essential facet of eventual victory. Sometimes it was a matter of technology—code breaking in the Atlantic war, the Royal Air Force's integrated use of radio and radar in the Battle of Britain—and sometimes a combination of luck and technology, as in correctly reading Japanese intentions at Midway thanks to code breaking melded with aggressive command decisions. In the end, of course, it was a matter of brute industrial and military force that defeated Germany and Japan, though communications surely helped.

The telegraph was of more limited importance in this war (save for widespread use of extensive telex and teleprinter circuits); telephones were far more central than they had been in World War I. Indeed, telephones carried two-thirds of communications within the United States and some overseas sites, though telegraphy remained the more secure long-distance communication mode. In combat theaters, alternative routing helped to ensure communications continuity. While telephone switchboards had changed little since World War I, portable field telephone equipment was vastly better and was widely used.

Dramatically improved communications allowed political and military leaders to micromanage distant battles, a temptation to which Hitler increasingly succumbed as the war turned against Germany. His orders were sent through the huge underground Zossen site near Berlin, all of them coded by the Enigma or German "Fish" codes—and by the end of the war, most were being read in real time (as Ultra) by the Allies. Allied radio and cable links, after plugging some early weak points, generally escaped enemy penetration. The American SIGABA and British Typex cipher equipment—and the SIGSALY system used by Prime Minister Churchill and President Roosevelt to talk by telephone across the Atlantic—each of them perfected during the war, could be operated by hastily trained personnel, yet proved invulnerable to enemy code-breaking efforts.

Although all sides relied on machine encryption to protect their communications, the British Government Code & Cipher School (at Bletchley Park) and American cryptanalysts (mainly at Arlington Hall and Nebraska Avenue) developed techniques to break codes (aided by captured codebooks and coding machines) and eventually were able to read enemy messages almost as quickly as their intended recipients. Alan Turing and others worked at Bletchley Park to develop early analog computers to assist in the growing code-breaking task. Frank Rowlett and others helped to break Japanese codes, especially the difficult Purple naval and diplomatic codes. Careful systems of monitoring of enemy radio transmissions, as well as traffic analysis of those signals, brought vital information to the Allies. The ability to read enemy codes also helped in several highly successful Allied deception efforts to mislead enemy commanders. At the same time, however, Allied code-breaking successes were very closely held and many field commanders did not know the derivation of information provided (which did not help skeptics believe in what they were told).

Essential radio security was sometimes achieved by requiring total radio silence, as with the Japanese fleet sailing to attack Hawaii in December 1941. Another secure approach was American Army use of members of various Native American tribes as "code talkers" communicating messages by simply speaking their own languages, which were totally unknown to the Germans or Japanese. Lonely island-based coast watchers communicated (usually with radio, occasionally with couriers) vital information during the Pacific campaign, keeping Allied forces up to date on Japanese moves, at great risk to themselves.

Battlefronts were not always mobile. Communication links, both wired and wireless, were made a central part of massive defensive fortifications including American coast defenses, the French Maginot Line of the 1930s, and the German-built Atlantic Wall of the early 1940s. These links could not, however, overcome the fatal weaknesses of static defenses in a mobile war.

All sides applied propaganda lessons learned during the first war in the second. Of all the fighting powers, German propaganda was clearly the best synchronized with its military effort. Film and radio (broadcasting was new to this war) helped promote fear of German arms, as did bright poster art and printed media. Psychological operations on the tactical level were first used on a large scale during World War II, and in all theaters, though with varied impact. By late in the war, psychological warfare units often operated even at the small-unit level. The most successful Allied military efforts were carefully designed leaflets intended to lower enemy soldier morale and/or induce his desertion or surrender. They emphasized the decent treatment a prisoner would receive as well as bad conditions back home, and declared that officers were getting better food and shelter than frontline soldiers. These were particularly effective in Europe, less so in the Pacific because of cultural differences. Many millions of leaflets were dropped by aircraft.

As in World War I, though even more so here, growing communication needs again led to extensive programs devoted to training the thousands of radio operators needed on land, at sea, and in the air. The variety of more sophisticated systems (including limited use of television), especially those for air and naval forces, required longer and more specialized training efforts.

World War II could not have been fought without modern communication technologies. Armies and navies (and increasingly air forces)—and the areas over which they fought—were far larger and could move more quickly than traditional means of communicating could have controlled.

Christopher H. Sterling

See also Airplanes; Arlington Hall; Armstrong, Edwin Howard (1890–1954); Army Airways Communications System, Airways and Air Communications Service (AACS, 1938–1961); Army Signal Corps; Atlantic, Battle of the (1939–1945); Atlantic Wall; Bletchley Park; Britain, Battle of (1940); Code Breaking; Code Talkers; Deception; Electric Cipher Machine (ECM Mark II, "SIGABA"); Enigma; German "Fish" Codes; Germany: Air Force; Germany: Army; Germany: Naval Intelligence (*B-Dienst*); Germany: Navy; Government Code & Cipher School (GC&CS, 1919–1946); High-Speed Morse; Identification, Friend or Foe (IFF); Japan: Air Force; Japan: Army; Japan: Navy (*Nippon Teikoku Kaigun*);

Magic; Maginot Line; Midway, Battle of (3–6 June 1942); Mobile Communications; National Research Council (NRC); Nebraska Avenue, Washington DC; Office of Strategic Services (OSS); Propaganda and Psychological Warfare; Radio; Rowlett, Frank B. (1908–1998); SIGSALY; Talk Between Ships (TBS); Telephone; Teleprinter/Teletype; Turing, Alan Mathison (1912–1954); Ultra; United Kingdom: Royal Air Force; United Kingdom: Royal Corps of Signals; United Kingdom: Royal Navy; V-Mail; Y Service; Zossen, Germany

Sources
Beauchamp, Ken. 2001. *History of Telegraphy.* History of Technology Series 26, chaps. 8–10. London: Institution of Electrical Engineers.
Hezlet, Arthur. 1975. *Electronics and Sea Power,* chaps. 8–10. New York: Stein & Day.
Kent, Barrie. 1993. *Signal! A History of Signalling in the Royal Navy,* chaps. 10–13, 21–22. Clanfield, UK: Hyden House.
Nalder, R. F. H. 1953. *The History of British Army Signals in the Second World War.* London: Royal Signals Institution.
Raines, Rebecca Robbins. 1996. *Getting the Message Through: A Branch History of the US Army Signal Corps,* chaps. 7–8. Washington, DC: Office of Military History.
Sexton, Daniel J. 1996. *Signals Intelligence in World War II: A Research Guide.* Westport, CT: Greenwood.
Terrett, Dulany, et al. 1956–1966. *The Signal Corps. U.S. Army in World War II: The Technical Services,* 3 vols. Washington, DC: Government Printing Office.

World Wide Military Command and Control System (WWMCCS)

Operating from 1963 to 1996, the World Wide Military Command and Control System (WWMCCS) was a centralized system to access information and communicate directives to American military forces. Labeled a "loosely knit confederation" of systems, WWMCCS lacked the centralized design, procurement, and operations needed to perform its mission successfully on a consistent basis.

Through the 1950s the U.S. Department of Defense (DoD) operated several command-and-control systems including the National Military Command Center, the Alternate National Military Command Center, and the North American Air Defense Command headquarters, in addition to the Ballistic Missile Early Warning System, Semi-Automatic Ground Environment, and Strategic Air Command (SAC) Automated Command and Control, among others. In May 1960 DoD put these systems under unified control to become the Defense Communications System, managed by the Defense Communications Agency. In October 1962, a concept of operations for WWMCCS sought to integrate all of these systems.

At the same time, automated data processing (ADP) was seen as the best means to handle increasing levels of message traffic. The incompatibility of ADP equipment purchased by the separate services, however, complicated matters. An attempt to correct this problem resulted in the WWMCCS Intercomputer Network, a centrally managed information processing and exchange network. It was this system that DoD relied on to manage the military responses to the crises of the 1970s.

In the early 1980s DoD decided to modernize WWMCCS; by 1983 contracts were awarded to develop an evolutionary upgrade known as the WWMCCS Information System (WIS). In September 1992 DoD terminated the WIS and replaced it with the Global Command and Control System, which became operational in 1996.

WWMCCS performance through the years was inconsistent. Very early on it worked well. When an American plane was shot down in East Germany in 1964, the fact was known in Washington within seven minutes of its occurrence. The messages had been conveyed by WWMCCS. In the following years, however, it failed at critical times. The first major instance was in 1967, when the Israelis fired on a communications ship, the USS *Liberty*. Messages to leave the area had not been passed on to the ship in time. In 1968 a similar problem with communications occurred when another communications vessel, the USS *Pueblo*, was seized by North Korea.

During the Arab-Israeli War of 1973, WWMCCS functioned well, but two years later, its failures complicated the rescue of crew members of the *Mayaguez*. When President Gerald Ford requested information on the availability of carriers in the Pacific, the system crashed.

Though WWMCCS again worked very well in its last conflict (the Gulf War of 1990–1991), it was replaced five years later.

There were several reasons behind the disappointing performance of WWMCCS. First, in this period the technology did not exist to support all of the missions that the Joint Chiefs of Staff wanted to have performed.

Second, it was a collection of systems that had never been designed or built with interoperability in mind: They could often work well individually but not together. Also, the military culture in this period was hostile to interservice cooperation. Service systems were designed and procured at lower levels without consideration of overall requirements, as centralized objectives were seen as secondary.

Robert Stacy

See also Automatic Digital Network (AUTODIN); Automatic Secure Voice Communications (AUTOSEVOCOM); Communication Satellites; Communications Security (COMSEC); Computer; Computer Security (COMPUSEC); DARPANET; Defense Advanced Research Projects Agency (DARPA); Defense Communications Agency (DCA, 1960–1991); Defense Communications System (DCS); Defense Switched Network (DSN); Gulf War (1990–1991); Intelligence Ships; Semi-Automatic Ground Environment (SAGE); Vietnam War (1959–1975)

Source
Pearson, David E. 2000. *The World Wide Military Command and Control System: Evolution and Effectiveness*. Maxwell Air Force Base, AL: Air University Press.

Y Service

The British "Y Service" was made up of radio (or wireless, in British usage) intercept or listening posts located in Britain and abroad before and during World War II. It was carefully coordinated to intercept as much German and Italian (and some other nations') radio traffic as it could, the messages then being passed on to Bletchley Park (or regional centers) for decoding and interpretation.

The groundwork for the establishment of British radio interception stations dates to World War I. Early on in that conflict, by using the new loop aerials for direction finding, British wireless operators could locate enemy transmitter locations. Tracking those locations (later termed "traffic analysis") was extremely valuable in determining where enemy troop concentrations were located even if message content could not be determined. An extensive "listening" program had developed to tune to German telegraph and telephone services from some thirty sites along the Western Front. Results were sent to a central cipher bureau at General Headquarters in St. Omer. Special stations used triangulation to determine the locations of wireless transmission from enemy aircraft and airships, and thus to direct attacks on their flight paths. The Royal Navy set up nearly twenty coastal listening stations to similarly keep track of German navy signaling.

Growing out of all these efforts was Britain's 1919 formation of its Government Code and Cipher School (GC&CS). During the interwar years, the War Office operated similar listening operations at several points in the Middle East and India. When the Royal Navy renewed its interception interest in 1924, the fleet wireless telegraph operators were organized to help as "procedure Y," the derivation of the later designation of the whole service. In 1926 the army opened a continuing listening operation for GC&CS in an abandoned nineteenth-century fort in Chatham, east of London. It would operate there until moved in 1941 to Beaumanor. Finally, the Metropolitan Police got involved, interested in picking up signals from moving transmitters.

Thus the Royal Navy, War Office (army), Air Ministry, and police were all operating, largely independent of one another, by 1927.

A GC&CS "Y" committee provided some coordination of these efforts after 1928. In the late 1930s, new listening posts were set up to tune to the growing wireless use of Germany, Italy, and Japan. Growth in the number of Y stations continued up to and after the inception of World War II in 1939.

By 1941, the War Office had some 400 receivers located in five widespread listening sites. Additional transmitters focused on direction finding for traffic analysis. By the end of the war the Foreign Office had approximately 800 Y staff at various locations. The Foreign Office and each of the three military services maintained their own multiple Y Service sites through the war, which used fixed receiving and direction-finding facilities located around Britain and in the Mediterranean war zone. Britain also maintained extensive Y sites in the Indian subcontinent, Bermuda, East Africa, Iran, and elsewhere. The service-operated sites each focused on the radio traffic of their enemy counterpart. A few of the larger operations also undertook some traffic analysis and decrypting duties to lighten the load at Bletchley Park and speed tactical information to frontline commanders.

As many enemy radio frequencies as could be monitored (sets and operators were always in short supply) were constantly scanned, and a central record was kept of all known (and new) transmitting sites. Intercept operators did not have to speak the language being heard (traffic analysts clearly did), yet soon became used to the jargon and abbreviations regularly used by the various enemy forces. The parallel Radio Security Service listened on some British high frequencies for any possible illicit use of radio by spies. Radio amateurs and other volunteers were soon performing a substantial part of the Y Service operations to free up military personnel. All told, more than 8,000 military and civilian operators, many of them women, were involved, and all of them kept the secret of the Y service for decades after the war.

Naturally the other warring nations maintained similar services, though usually with lesser results as far as breaking Allied codes was concerned. The Germans had a limited listening system in North Africa, for example, and in 1941–1942 when British and U.S. codes (and use of them) were weak, Germany often learned a good deal about Allied plans. The U.S. Navy was operating four or five radio monitoring sites in the Pacific before inception of hostilities late in 1941, and it expanded that network as Allied forces moved toward Japan.

Of course all military services understood that the listening process was ongoing—and that the best defense was the use of absolute radio silence and utilization of other means of military communication.

Christopher H. Sterling

See also Bletchley Park; Code, Codebooks; Code Breaking; Enigma; Germany: Naval Intelligence (*B-Dienst*); Government Code & Cipher School (GC&CS, 1919–1946); OP-20-G; Radio Silence; Signals Intelligence (SIGINT); Ultra

Sources

Clayton, Aileen. 1980. *The Enemy Is Listening.* London: Hutchinson.

Macksey, Kenneth. 2003. *The Searchers: How Radio Interception Changed the Course of Both World Wars.* London: Cassell.

Pether, John. 2000. *Funkers and Sparkers: Origins and Formation of the Y Service.* Bletchley Park Reports No. 17. Bletchley Park, UK: Bletchley Park Reports.

Piekalkiewicz, Janusz. 1992. *Rommel and the Secret War in North Africa, 1941–1943: Secret Intelligence in the North African Campaign.* West Chester, PA: Schiffer.

Skillen, Hugh. 1989. *Spies of the Airwaves.* London: Hugh Skillen.

Yardley, Herbert O. (1889–1958)

Herbert Yardley was the most important American code breaker until 1929 and, while he later became a controversial figure, is often called the father of U.S. government code-breaking efforts.

Born on 13 April 1889 in Worthington, Indiana, Yardley became a railway telegrapher after secondary school, and then took a job as a government telegrapher in 1912. He moved to Washington DC and became a code clerk at the State Department. After American entry into World War I in 1917, Yardley entered the Army as a first lieutenant, assigned to code making and breaking work at the Army War College, where he soon established the country's first communications intelligence operation within the MI-8 division. He hired a staff and even undertook work for the Navy, which then lacked its own such office. One episode of code breaking led to the apprehension and execution of a German spy crossing the Mexican border. Others required a mass attack on many encrypted messages to break a military code. By the end of the war, more than 150 military and civilian workers were employed in Yardley's operation, which had read more than 10,000 messages in some fifty different codes and ciphers.

In 1919 Yardley established the Cipher Bureau (later dubbed the "American Black Chamber"), with support of the State and War departments; New York served as its communications center. There two dozen staffers set to work on the code and cipher systems of foreign nations as reflected in their diplomatic telegrams. A major success, made public in Yardley's later book, was breaking Japanese messages concerning a naval disarmament conference held in Washington in 1921–1922. In 1923 the New York operation was trimmed to a half-dozen workers in a budget-cutting move.

When Henry Stimson became secretary of state early in 1929, and learned that the State Department was helping to support Yardley's operation, he withdrew funding, infamously stating that "Gentlemen do not read each other's mail." The War Department, having established its own code office under William Friedman in Washington, declined in May 1929 to continue Yardley's effort on its own.

Yardley now faced a crisis of income and decided to write about his code-breaking experiences over the past dozen years. The result was publication of *The American Black Chamber* (1931), which became a best seller in several languages. Engagingly written and filled with anecdotes, the book exposed American methods and successes against a number of countries during and after World War I. When he tried to follow this success with another book, however, the government stepped in and confiscated the manuscript.

Yardley's later life was a constant search for a continuing role. He accepted an offer from China to help it establish a code-breaking effort, and was based in Chungking in 1938–1940 (while there, he wrote a book that appeared long after his death). He undertook code breaking for Canada in late 1941 until pressure from the United States got him dropped as a security risk. Always a master poker player, at the end of his life Yardley wrote *Education of a Poker Player*, which became a best seller. But long before the book's commercial success, Yardley died on 7 August 1958 in Silver Spring, Maryland.

Christopher H. Sterling

See also Code Breaking; Friedman, William F. (1891–1969); Mauborgne, Joseph Oswald (1881–1971); Signals Intelligence (SIGINT)

Sources

Kahn, David. 2004. *The Reader of Gentlemen's Mail: Herbert O. Yardley and the Birth of American Codebreaking*. New Haven, CT: Yale University Press.

Yardley, Herbert O. 1931. *The American Black Chamber*. Indianapolis, IN: Bobbs-Merrill.

Yardley, Herbert O. 1983. *The Chinese Black Chamber: An Adventure in Espionage*. Boston: Houghton Mifflin.

Z

Zossen, Germany

Located 25 miles south of Berlin, the Zossen underground complex of bunkers and tunnels served as the protected communications nerve center first for the German armies under Adolph Hitler's command and later for the Russian forces occupying East Germany.

Originally cleared as a firing range and infantry school, by 1914, the 60,000-acre area had become Europe's largest military base, dotted with handsome buildings, some of which survive to this day. Bunker complexes called "Maybach" (a command center) and "Zeppelin" (communications) were built beginning in 1934 by the Nazi regime. The initial communications links constructed in 1934–1935 involved considerable redundancy to better withstand air attack. The Zossen bunker complex was well connected with subterranean links to the military commands in central Berlin, and to a trunk cable ring buried around the city. Priority construction of the Zeppelin bunker in 1937–1939 involved installation of dozens of massive telephone and telegraph switch-boards. Most were operational by August 1939 in time for the German attack on Poland. Radio facilities were also added. Substantial battery backups guaranteed continued operation even with loss of the electric power grid due to air attack. The Allies never discovered the existence of these backups until after the war and bomb damage was largely superficial, indicating that the backups had not been targets.

Fast-moving Soviet forces occupied the virtually intact Zossen bunker facilities on 20 April 1945. Most equipment was dismantled (often quickly and thus badly) and shipped back to the Soviet Union. The two Maybach bunkers were destroyed by 1946, but the Zeppelin communications center was retained, albeit empty of equipment. In the 1950s, new construction reactivated the surviving Zossen bunkers and by 1960 fear of a missile-based European war led to re-equipping of the Zeppelin bunker area as a communications center. It could be totally self-sufficient (including air circulation) for up to a month. At the height of the Cold War between 30,000 and 70,000 Russian soldiers and their dependents were based there in an extensive surface community. All of this was manned for more than three decades, ending only when Russian troops pulled out in 1994.

The long-time military zone was opened for civilian development after the Cold War, and scores of old barrack buildings have since been reconditioned into apartments. Tours are given in some of the surviving bunker sites, some of which retain their Soviet-era equipment.

Christopher H. Sterling

See also Germany: Army; Underground Communication Centers

Sources
Fischer, Jan Otakar. 2000. "Beating Swords into Suburbs in East Germany's Bunker Capital." *New York Times*, March 16, D1, D4.
Kampe, Hans-George. 1996. *The Underground Military Command Bunkers of Zossen, Germany: History of Their Construction and Use by the Wehrmacht and Soviet Army, 1937–1994*. Atglen, PA: Schiffer.

MILITARY COMMUNICATIONS MUSEUMS

International Museums

There are many military communications museums outside of the United States, many on or near military bases. To fully appreciate their content and context, visitors understandably should have some proficiency in a language other than English. Because of security concerns limiting public access, a number of these are best visited online; on-site visits often have to be planned well in advance. Contact information and opening hours are subject to change.

Australia

Royal Australian Army Corps of Signals Museum (Molloy Road, Simpson Barracks, Macleod, Victoria 3085, Australia-03-9450-7874) is presently closed for building upgrades. Collections focus on the Corps of Signals operations in the two world wars.

Britain

Bletchley Park (The Mansion, Bletchley Park, Wilton Avenue, Bletchley, Milton Keynes, MK3 6EB; http://www.bletchleypark.org.uk/page.cfm?pageid=159) is the home of Britain's top secret World War II code-breaking operation known as Ultra. Included on the site is a full-size rebuilt version of the Colossus computer developed and used at Bletchley, and a communications-electronics museum as well as a collection concerning Winston Churchill.

Duxford Radio Society (Buildings 177–178, Duxford Airfield, Cambridge, England; http://www.duxfordradiosociety.org/index.html) operates a two-building museum at the Duxford Airfield museum south of Cambridge that is run by the Imperial War Museum. It is open on Sundays, and often on other days. Displays include Allied and captured military radio equipment from both world wars.

Imperial War Museum (Lambeth Road, London SE1 6HZ, United Kingdom; http://www.iwm.org.uk/) is the premier British museum concerning the nation at war. Housed in the former mental hospital known as "Bedlam," the museum was substantially redesigned in the early 1990s. It is open daily except for three days around Christmas. The IWM also operates the Cabinet War Rooms and Churchill Museum near Parliament, as well as several other sites. Communications figure in many of the exhibitions.

Intelligence Museum at RAF Chicksands (Dorset, United Kingdom— 01462–752341; http://www.army.mod.uk/intelligencecorps/chicksands .htm) is open by prior appointment every weekday. The museum, formed in 2000, outlines the history of British Military Intelligence from the time of Queen Elizabeth I and recounts the story of the Intelligence Corps since its formation in 1914. The Medmenham Collection covers the history of aerial photographic interpretation from World War I up to the present day. There are exhibits on the wartime Royal Air Force and postwar U.S. Air Force signals operations here.

Naval Communications & Radar Museum (HMS Collingwood, Fareham, PO14 1AS; http://www.recelectronics.demon.co.uk/collingrad.htm) can be visited by appointment only, as the museum is on an active military base. The extensive collections focus on twentieth-century equipment from Britain and other nations.

RAF Signals Museum (RAF Henlow, Bedfordshire, England; http://www .geocities.com/raf_signals_museum/) is open by appointment only. It is a relatively new and still developing facility, which includes a recreated Y Service station.

Royal Signals Museum (Blandford Camp, Blandford Forum, Dorset DT11 8RH, England—01258-482248; http://www.army.mod.uk/royalsignals museum/) is the national museum of army communications, and the exhibits and displays show the part that communications have played in the many wars and campaigns of the last 150 years. The museum was founded in Catterick, in North Yorkshire in the mid-1930s, and moved to Blandford Camp in 1967. A refurbished and expanded museum opened on 28 May 1997. The Web site offers a virtual tour.

Canada

Military Communications and Electronics Museum (Box 17000, Station Forces, Kingston ON, Canada K7K 7B4; http://www.c-and-e-museum.org/ about_e1.htm) is open most days of the week. Housed in a handsome purpose-designed building that opened in 1996, the museum offers exhibits relating to the people, technology, and changing times for all of Canada's military forces (which were merged in 1968).

Germany

German Naval Signals Headquarters (St. Jacques, near St. Peter Port, Guernsey, Channel Islands; http://www.showcaves.com/english/gb/misc/German NavalSignals.html) is a museum open from April through October, on Thursday and Saturday afternoons. The facility was established in 1942, though the bunker, now home to the museum, opened in early 1944. While technically in Britain, the focus is on German wartime signaling.

Japan

Yokohama World War II Japanese Radio Museum (045–301-8044; http://www .yokohamaradiomuseum.com/) has a Web site with some English captioning, as well as a map on finding the museum. The museum has an extensive collection of army and naval radios, some dating to World War I.

Netherlands

Royal Netherlands Army Signal Corps Museum (Elias Beeckmankazerne, Nieuwe Kazernelaan 10, PO Box: 9012, 6710 HC EDE; http://www .museumverbindingsdienst.nl/gesvbddeng.html#rnascm) is open Wednesday and Thursday afternoons only. The collection began in 1965, opened to the public four years later, and moved to its present building in 1982. The story of the Royal Netherlands Army Signal Corps, formed in 1874, forms the central part of the collection and the extensive library.

Russia

Military Historical Museum of Artillery, Sappers and Signal Troops (Alexandrovsky Park 7, St. Petersburg, Russia; http://eng.peterout.ru/art/ museums/15/), located opposite the Peter and Paul Fortress, includes about 50,000 items, among them artillery weapons, cold steel arms and firearms, and items of military engineering technology (including signaling). One part of the exposition is demonstrated in the open air. Open Wednesday through Sunday.

RKK Museum (RC&C Ltd., Sushevskaya Str., 9–4, Moscow; http://www .radiomilitari.com/r.html) is an extensive private museum focusing on military communications, especially for the Great Patriotic War (World War II) period, and including Soviet, German, and American equipment. The Web site offers English-language material and is also quite extensive.

South Africa

South African Signal Corps Museum (Wonderboom Military Base, Field Box, Box 1, Pretoria 0106) was established at the Army Gymnasium in Heidelberg (about 30 miles south of Johannesburg) around 1985. The gymnasium was then the home of the School of Signals and 1 Signal Regiment. A decade later, the School of Signals was moved to the Wonderboom Military

Base about 12 miles north of Pretoria (where the South Africa Army Signal Formation was also located) and 1 Signal Regiment was moved to a different base. The museum was subsequently placed in storage. In 2002 volunteers worked to reopen the museum at Wonderboom. All the equipment came out of storage, and the museum was arranged to cover telecommunications from the Boer War (including some very old and valuable Siemans and Marconi equipment dating back to the early 1900s), through the world wars, and up to the Border War/War of Liberation in the 1980s. For the latter, the museum reflects both South African equipment and that used by and captured from the Cubans, Russians, and other forces. Some command-and-control and electronic warfare equipment round out the display. The museum is apparently open to the public.

Sources

Foundation for German Communication and Related Technologies website: http://cdv-and-t.org/.

German Naval Signal Headquarters virtual tour website: http://www.occupied.guernsey.net/naval_sigs_h_q_.htm.

Military Museums and Monuments links: http://www.geocities.com/Pentagon/7087/ukmain04.htm.

Signals Collection, '40-'45 website (a virtual museum covering several countries): http://www.qsl.net/pe1ngz/signalscollection.html.

Worldwide Military Radio links: http://www.qsl.net/ab4oj/1ststeps/links.html.

U.S. Museums

There are a growing number of military communications museums in the United States, most of them on or near military bases. Many other museums include some reference to military communications, but those listed here are the museums that hold collections primarily focusing on that topic. Because of security concerns, many are best seen online, and visits often have to be planned well in advance. Since the 11 September 2001 terrorist attacks, security at all military bases has been sharply increased. Contact information and opening hours are subject to change.

Air Force Communications

AFCA Visitor's Center (Building 1700, Scott AFB, IL—call (618) 229–5690 for information and access; http://www.aacsalumni.com/AFCA%20Visitors%20Center/AFCA%20visitors%20center.html) is located not far from St. Louis, in the Illinois suburbs. It includes information on key communications developments, equipment, and people, and many photos and information are provided on the Web site.

Air Force Museum (1100 Spaatz St., Wright-Patterson AFB, Fairfield, OH 45433—(937) 255–3286; http://www.wpafb.af.mil/museum/) is the world's oldest and largest military aviation museum. Open seven days a week, it is easily accessible and displays some 300 aircraft. Included within the collection are many aspects of aviation communications.

Army Communications

U.S. Army Signal Corps Museum (Conrad Hall, Bldg. 29807, Fort Gordon, GA 30905—(706) 791–2818 or (706) 791–3856; www.gordon.army.mil/ocos/ Museum/) is open Tuesday through Saturday. Located in the southern part of Georgia, the museum includes exhibits about Albert J. Myer, the founder of the corps; American Civil War items such as the Beardslee Electro Magneto; a circa-1870 meteorological office; signaling equipment used in the West, circa 1880; Spanish-American War equipment; the Greely expedition to the Arctic; aviation; World War I "Hello Girls"; trench warfare; a World War II signal message center; pigeons; signals in space; the Cold War; the Vietnam War; and more.

Army Communications and Electronics Museum (Kaplan Hall, Building 275, Fort Monmouth, NJ 07703—(732) 532–1682; www.monmouth.army .mil/C4ISR/services/museum.shtm) is open only with a prior appointment. Located in the northeast corner of New Jersey, Fort Monmouth is "the center of gravity" for the development of the Army's command, control, communications, computers, intelligence, sensors, and reconnaissance systems. Much of the Army's research and development of these high-tech systems is done at Fort Monmouth and is reflected in the museum.

Navy Communications

The Navy Museum (Washington Navy Yard, Building 76, 805 Kidder Breese SE, Washington, DC 20374-5060—(202) 433-4882; www.history.navy.mil/ branches/nhcorg8.htm) is open seven days a week by prior appointment due to security concerns. Its extensive Web site offers a useful preview of the substantial collections, which include electronics and communications, such as a submarine combat information center.

Others

Historical Electronics Museum (1745 Nursery Rd., Linthicum, MD 21090— (410) 765–0230, www.hem-usa.org) is located just outside Baltimore-Washington International Airport. It displays breakthroughs in electronic history in the areas of communications; radar; countermeasures; and electro-optical, underwater, and space electronics. This is a private collection operated with considerable help from Northrop Grumman. Open Monday through Saturday, it also offers an extensive library and archives.

National Cryptologic Museum (Colony Seven Rd, Fort Meade, MD—(301) 688-5849; http://www.nsa.gov/museum/) is the official National Security Agency museum, located in a former motel building on the Baltimore-Washington Parkway, midway between the national capital and Baltimore. It is open weekdays and alternate Saturdays and offers an extensive series of galleries on the history, especially from a U.S. point of view, of cryptography and signals intelligence from the earliest times to the present.

National Museum of American History (Smithsonian Institution, National Mall, Washington, DC; http://americanhistory.si.edu/) offers a huge general collection that includes exhibit galleries on U.S. military history as well as the development of communication.

Sources

A Guide to U.S. Naval Museums. 1993. Washington: Naval Historical Center.
Allen, Jon L. 1975. *Aviation and Space Museums of America.* New York: Arco.
Thompson, Bryce D. 2000. *U.S. Military Museums, Historic Sites & Exhibits,* 2nd ed. Falls Church, VA: Military Living Publications.

MILITARY COMMUNICATIONS CONFERENCES

A large number of conferences and equipment exhibitions, many of them held annually, provide a useful way for military, government, and industry figures to learn about the latest trends in military communications.

A few of the important American examples are noted here, many of which are held in the Washington DC area in order to attract military and government decision makers. Most are commercially sponsored and combine speeches and workshops with exhibitions of the latest equipment and services. Many additional conferences are held in Europe (aimed at the North Atlantic Treaty Organization) as well as within the more important military powers of the world. Some of these include classified briefings, while others are open. Most are highly technical and range in length from part of one day to several days.

The Institute of Electrical and Electronic Engineers (IEEE) Communications Society and the Armed Forces Communications Electronic Association (AFCEA) cosponsor *MILCOM*—the *Military Communications Conference*—which was first held in 1982. *MILCOM* has become the premier international conference for military communications, attracting high-level attendance (upward of 3,000 people) from government, military, industry, and academe from around the world. *MILCOM* provides industry the opportunity to promote communications technologies and services to commanders from all branches of the armed forces, Department of Defense, the U.S. government, and the heads of multinational forces from around the globe. The *Annual Convention of the Armed Forces Communications and Electronic Association*, as well as the more recent annual *AFCEA-West*, are additional interface conferences between military and industrial representatives. IEEE's many societies also hold several conferences in the course of a year, some of them relevant to military communication concerns.

The *Joint Battle Management Conference (JBMC)* concerns total battlespace awareness through transformation of the military into a network-centric force capable of sharing time-sensitive information and using service interoperability to win on the battlefield. Working with the Joint Chiefs of Staff and U.S. Joint Forces Command, the conference contractor has assembled presenters to illuminate the military and industry on the *JBMC* roadmap as well as all current and future system requirements.

Many other meetings are more specific in their focus. The *Annual Conference on Military Radios*, first held in 2001, addresses the needs, initiatives, opportunities, and challenges in developing the next generation of military radios. The *Military Data Links Conference* helps to underscore the centrality of computerized data networks and their security. Numerous meetings centered on space communications or security and communications include military aspects. A trade journal sponsors the annual *Military Sat-Com Forum*. A similarly focused annual meeting has been held in Europe since the late 1990s. *Military Antenna Systems* is another example of a very focused annual conference. Another trade journal sponsors the *Military Technologies Conference*, which ranges beyond communications. Think tanks are also active in this field. The Heritage Foundation, for example, sponsored a *Conference on Defense Transformation*, which included discussion of communication issues.

Naturally many other conferences dealing with telecommunications technologies include sessions of value to—and sometimes specifically directed toward—military users. One example is the annual *Sarnoff Symposium*, held in Princeton, New Jersey, the site of the former RCA research center named after the long-time head of the company. Cosponsored by IEEE, in recent years, these meetings (which have been held for nearly three decades) have included many sessions focused on security and surveillance techniques as well as counterterrorism.

Sources

Annotated conference listing (Harris Corp.): http://www.harris.com/tradeshows.asp.
IEEE Communications Society conferences: http://www.comsoc.org/confs/.
Important conferences: http://mia.ece.uic.edu/~papers/WWW/conference/.
Past MILCOM proceedings (1988–2005): http://ieeexplore.ieee.org/xpl/RecentCon.jsp?punumber=3223.

GLOSSARY OF ACRONYMS

AACS: Army Airways Communications System; later Airways and Air Communications Service

ABCS: Army Battle Command System

ACS: Alaska Communications System

AFB: Air Force Base

AFCA: Air Force Communications Agency

AFCC: Air Force Communications Command

AFCEA: Armed Forces Communications & Electronics Association

AFCS: Air Force Communications Service

AM: amplitude modulation

AUTODIN: Automatic Digital Network

AUTOSEVOCOM: Automatic Secure Voice Communications

AUTOVON: Automatic Voice Network

AWACS: Airborne Warning and Control System

C2: command and control

C3: command, control, and communications

C3I: command, control, communications, and information

C4: command, control, communications, and computers

CIC: combat information center

CITS: Combat Information Transport System

COMCAN: Commonwealth Communications Army Network (UK)

COMSEC: Communications Security

DARPA: Defense Advanced Research Projects Agency

DCA: Defense Communications Agency

DCS: Defense Communications System

DCSA: Defence Communications Service Agency (UK)

DISA: Defense Information Systems Agency

DMS: Defense Message System

DoD: Department of Defense

DSN: Defense Switched Network

ECM: electric cipher machine

ECM/EW: electronic countermeasures/electronic warfare

EHF: extremely high frequency (spectrum)

EMP: electromagnetic pulse

Enigma: German code machine, World War II

Fax: facsimile

FCC: Federal Communications Commission

"Fish": German World War II codes

FM: frequency modulation

Fullerphone: British voice system using telegraph lines, World War I

GC&CS: Government Code and Cipher School (UK)

GHz: gigahertz (spectrum)

GIG: Global Information Grid

GPS: Global Positioning System

Heliograph: mirror device used in visual communications

HF: high frequency (spectrum)

HMS: Her (or His) Majesty's Ship (Royal Navy)

IEE: Institution of Electrical Engineers (UK)

IEEE: Institute of Electrical and Electronic Engineers

IFF: Identification, Friend or Foe

IRAC: Inderdepartment Radio Advisory Committee

IRMA: Information Revolution in Military Affairs

ITU: International Telecommunication Union

Jamming: deliberate transmission of interference to block radio signals

JASCO: Joint Assault Signal Company

JTF-GNO: Joint Task Force–Global Network Operations

JTIDS: Joint Tactical Information Distribution System

JTRS: Joint Tactical Radio System

kHz: kiloHertz (spectrum)

LF: low frequency (spectrum)

Magic: American effort to break Japanese codes, World War II

MARS: Military Affiliate Radio System

MHz: MegaHertz (spectrum)

MOD: Ministry of Defence (UK)

NATO: North Atlantic Treaty Organization

NBS: National Bureau of Standards

NCS: National Communications System

NDRC: National Defense Research Committee

NETCOM: Network Enterprise Technology Command (U.S. Army)

NIST: National Institute of Standards and Technology

NRL: Naval Research Laboratory *or* Navy Radio Laboratory

NRO: National Reconnaissance Office

NSA: National Security Agency

NSG: Naval Security Group

NTDS: Naval Tactical Data System

NTIA: National Telecommunications and Information Administration

OP-20-G: Navy Signals Intelligence

OSS: Office of Strategic Services

PCM: pulse code modulation

RAF: Royal Air Force (UK)

RCS: Royal Corps of Signals (UK)

SAC: Strategic Air Command (U.S. Air Force)

SAGE: Semi-Automatic Ground Environment

Semaphore: physical telegraphy—using flags or wooden devices

SIGINT: signals intelligence

SINCGARS: Single Channel Ground and Airborne Radio System

SIPRNet: Secret Internet Protocol Router Network

SRDE: Signals Research and Development Establishment (UK)

SSA: Signal Security Agency

SSB: single sideband (radio transmission)

STRATCOM: Strategic Communications Command (U.S. Army)

TBS: talk between ships

TRI-TAC: Tri-Service Tactical Communications Program

TV: television

UHF: ultra high frequency (spectrum)

Ultra: British effort to break German Enigma codes, World War II

USS: United States Ship (naval vessel)

VHF: very high frequency (spectrum)

VoIP: Voice over Internet Protocol

WAMCATS: Washington Alaska Military Cable and Telegraph System

WAR: War Department Radio Network; also, "We Are Ready"

WDLN: Weapons Data Link Network

WHCA: White House Communications Agency

Wig-Wag: hand-held semaphore flags

WIN-T: Warfighter Information Network–Tactical

WWMCCS: World Wide Military Command and Control System

FURTHER READING: A BASIC BIBLIOGRAPHY

The following briefly annotated bibliography surveys the major published sources (chiefly books) providing an overview of military communications history. Entries are divided into sections on survey histories, military (army) communications, naval communications, aviation communications, and some useful Web sites.

There are several important limitations to this list. It is restricted to material published in English; it generally excludes the many works dealing with specific wars, services, organizations, or people (which appear in the bibliographic references in relevant entries in the text); and it generally excludes material concerning only one nation *except* Britain and the United States (as they are so central to the story). Citations to material on specific nations appear with relevant entries. Because they change (and disappear) so rapidly, only a few general Web sites are listed separately. Those titles thought to be of central importance are identified as essential books. Readers new to this subject matter might want to begin with those.

Survey Histories

Bridge, Maureen, and John Pegg, eds. 2001. *Call to Arms: A History of Military Communications from the Crimean War to the Present Day.* Tavistock, UK: Focus Publishing.

Largely built around British post office and telecommunications contributions and the British services, this is a very insightful overall survey.

de Arcangelis, Mario. 1985. *Electronic Warfare: From the Battle of Tsushima to the Falklands and Lebanon Conflicts.* Poole, UK: Blackford Press.

A translation from the Italian original, this provides a useful historical survey of twentieth-century applications of "invisible war" technologies from the Russo-Japanese War (1904–1905) to developments in space.

Devereux, Tony. 1991. *Messenger Gods of Battle: Radio, Radar, Sonar, the Story of Electronics in War.* London: Brassey's.

Historical review of the role of electronics in military history, including the development and applications of radio, radar, sonar, and space electronic warfare.

Headrick, Daniel R. 1991. *The Invisible Weapon: Telecommunications and International Politics, 1851–1945.* New York: Oxford University Press.
While focused on international relations and the effects of changing cable and radio technology on the same, there is a good deal of useful military communications comment tucked away in this valuable study, especially in chapters 8 and 9 (World War I) and chapters 12 and 13 (World War II).

Holzmann, Gerard J., and Björn Pehrson. 1995. *The Early History of Data Networks.* Los Alamitos, CA: IEEE Computer Society Press.
Despite its rather odd title, this is a fine history of early (pre-electric) means of communications, many if not most of them military in origin or application. It focuses especially on the semaphore or mechanical telegraph systems of Chappe and Edelcrantz, and includes a translation of the latter's 1796 treatise.

Jane's Military Communications. 1979–Present. Coulsdon, UK: Jane's Information Group, annual.
A now-standard directory to equipment and systems for most countries of the world, it includes sections on tactical communications; ground-based and strategic communications; terrestrial microwave and tropospheric scatter; naval systems and equipment; air force communications; satellite systems and equipment; line and transmission systems; data and text; encryption and security; surveillance and signal analysis; direction finding; jamming; facsimile; audio; and laser, optical, and video systems.

Macksey, Kenneth. 1990. *For Want of a Nail: Impact of War on Logistics and Communications.* London: Brassey's.
While this uses "communications" in the British sense, thus including transport, it does offer a useful assessment of the growth of military logistics and communications since 1850, including the importance of supporting fighting troops with ammunition, food, equipment, and so forth. It covers the impact of railways; logistics support in World War I; the mechanization of 1916–1917; the problem of distance in global warfare; present-day solutions; and what the future holds.

O'Connell, J. D., et al. 1962. "A Summary of Military Communications in the United States—1860 to 1962." *Proceedings of the IRE* 50 (May): 1241–1251.
Broad survey focusing on a century of wired and wireless connection—one of only a handful of such attempts.

Price, Alfred. 1978. *Instruments of Darkness: The History of Electronic Warfare.* 2nd ed. New York: Scribners.

In twelve chapters the author describes the story from World War II through the Vietnam War—much of it ranging well beyond communications to cover radar, electronic countermeasures, etc.

Scheips, Paul J., ed. 1980. *Military Signal Communications. Historical Studies in Telecommunications,* 2 vols. New York: Arno Press.

Invaluable anthology that covers the history of American and British army use of the telegraph, telephone, and other means of electrical communications. Volume 1 includes twenty-seven papers, many covering the Civil War and telegraph eras. Volume 2 includes another twenty-nine covering signaling techniques with semaphore, telegraph, telephone, and radio service. An essential book.

Sexton, Daniel J. 1996. *Signals Intelligence in World War II: A Research Guide.* Westport, CT: Greenwood.

This is a very useful annotated bibliography of SIGINT (including code breaking) in the European and Pacific theaters, with more than 800 citations. As this topic is only briefly included in the present volume, Sexton's reference is especially useful.

Woods, David L. 1965. *A History of Tactical Communication Techniques.* Orlando, FL: Martin-Marietta Corp. (reprinted by Arno Press "History of Telecommunications," 1974).

A pioneering effort, this remains the only survey history of tactical-level military communications ranging across the years from ancient uses of messengers and signal flags up to various electrical means. While not documented, this remains an essential book.

Military (Army) Communications

Adams, M. R. 1970. *Through to 1970: Royal Signal Corps Golden Jubilee.* London: Royal Signals Institution.

A handsomely illustrated album surveying stories of British army signals and the technologies applied. See also Nalder.

Army Times, editors of. 1961. *A History of the United States Signal Corps.* New York: Putnam.

Popular history in twelve chapters from the Civil War to pioneering satellite operations. See also Marshall.

Beauchamp, Ken. 2001. *History of Telegraphy*, "Military Operations [with the Telegraph]," chap. 4; and "[Wireless] at War," chap. 8, 102–133 and 266–307. London: Institution of Electrical Engineers.

Wired telegraph and wireless in several countries' armies from the late nineteenth century to after World War II, including wireless, direction finding, and training functions.

Burton, Laurette. 2002. *The Royal Corps of Signals*. Stroud, UK: Tempus Publishing.

A brief survey that contains more than 200 graphic images of the corps on training, ceremonial, civic, and base duties as well as in action in many theaters from the Western Front of World War I, the Western desert, Far East, and Europe in World War II to Borneo and Northern Ireland in more recent times.

Harfield, Alan, ed. 1989. *Pigeon to Packhorse: The Illustrated Story of Animals in Army Communications*. Chippenham, UK: Picton.

Traces the history of animals in communications from the change brought about by the invention and then use of the electric telegraph during the Crimean War, 1854. Chapters on the telegraph troop, animal transport used in Indian signals, the cable wagon and cart, camels, messenger dogs, horses, the advent of wireless, and the Pigeon Service.

Lord, Cliff, and Graham Watson. 2003. *The Royal Corps of Signals: Unit Histories of the Corps (1920–2001) and Its Antecedents*. Solihull, UK: Helion & Co.

Beginning with the formation of the corps, this provides overviews of the Signals Order of Battle at specific times in history; detailed precis of specialist signal units including commando and para units. Provides the history of thirty-five commonwealth and related corps with scores of unit histories from the 1920s to the present. An essential book.

Lord, Cliff. 2007. *Royal Corps of Signals: Unit Histories of the Corps (1920–2001) and its Antecedents: Supplementary Volume* Solihull, UK: Helion.

Adds more detailed information on Australia, Canada, India, New Zealand, Nigeria, Pakistan, Rhodesia, Singapore, and South Africa. The emphasis is on the six decades since the Second World War. An essential book.

Mallinson, Howard. 2005. *Send It By Semaphore: The Old Telegraphs During the Wars with France*. Ramsbury, UK: Crowood Press.

Developments in France and Britain of mechanical semaphore systems, immediate predecessor of the electric telegraph.

Marshall, Max L., ed. 1965. *The Story of the U.S. Army Signal Corps*. New York: Franklin Watts "The Watts Landpower Library."

An anthology by multiple authors, this is divided into two parts—half historical material and half dealing with the corps at the time of publication. See also *Army Times*.

Nalder, R. F. H. 1958. *The Royal Corps of Signals: A History of Its Antecedents and Development (circa 1800–1955)*. London: Royal Signals Institution.

This is by far the most detailed history of any country's signaling technology. Nalder's book is of the depth and quality of the official histories published in the United Kingdom. An essential book—for more recent period, see Lord and Warner.

Radio News, editors of. 1942. Special U.S. Army Signal Corps Issue, 28 (5).

Offers a good overview of signal corps history in several articles, plus a solid sense of the state of equipment, operations, and training in the first year (for the United States) of the war. The thirty articles are supplemented with numerous illustrations, including some in color.

Radio News, editors of. 1944. Special U.S. Army Signal Corps Issue, 31 (2).

Includes forty well-illustrated articles (with color photography) on American and overseas operations and equipment (including illustrations of German and Japanese captured radios).

Raines, Rebecca Robbins. 1996. *Getting The Message Through: A Branch History of The US Army Signal Corps*. Army Historical Series. Washington, DC: Government Printing Office.

First comprehensive history of the corps, including trends in technology of instruments used. An essential book.

Scriven, George P. 1908. *The Transmission of Military Information*. Governors Island, NY: Journal of the Military Service Institution.

Articles reprinted from the journal on the signal corps and the mobile army and wireless, electrical and visual communication, and relation of signal corps to the coast artillery. Useful for contemporary view as wireless was becoming more widely used.

"Signal Corps Centennial Issue." 1960. *Transactions of the Institute of Radio Engineers* MIL-4 (October): 396–607.

Thirty-five papers on high-frequency communications, radar, and other developments in military electronics, including historical surveys. Photos, references.

The Signal Corps. 1956–1966. *U.S. Army in World War II: The Technical Services.* Washington, DC: Government Printing Office.

This three-volume series offers a well-documented and detailed assessment of both technology development and applications, as well as Signal Corps operations during the war. An essential trilogy, as follows:

1. Terrett, Dulany. 1956. *The Emergency* deals with the period up to the Pearl Harbor attack.
2. Thompson, George Raynor, et al. 1957: *The Test* covers the initial American role in the war, December 1941 to July 1943.
3. Thompson, George Raynor, and Dixie R. Harris. 1966. *The Outcome* completes the story, covering from mid-1943 through 1945.

U.S. War Department, Office of the Chief Signal Officer. 1917. *Manual No. 3: Technical Equipment of the Signal Corps.* Washington, DC: Government Printing Office.

One of the best (and best illustrated) guides to the telegraph, telephone, cable, aerial line, and related equipment used at the time.

Warner, Philip. 1989. *The Vital Link: The Story of Royal Signals 1945–1985.* London: Leo Cooper.

A survey of post–World War II developments, demonstrating the expansion of technological options; Signals roles included maintaining battlefield communications, electronic intelligence, and electronic warfare. The book concentrates on the history of the corps using personal anecdotes. An essential book—for earlier material, see Lord and Nalder.

Wilson, Geoffrey. 1976. *The Old Telegraphs.* London: Phillimore.

Definitive source for pre-electric semaphores, a large proportion of which were built and operated by military services.

Woolliscroft, D. I. 2001. *Roman Military Signalling.* Charleston, SC: Tempus Publishing.

First book on the subject, focusing on activities in Britain and Germany, and offering original research findings.

Naval Communications

Beauchamp, Ken. 2001. "Military Telegraphy at Sea." In *History of Telegraphy*, chap. 9, 308–347. London: Institution of Electrical Engineers.

Radio in several countries' navies from the turn of the twentieth century to after World War II, including shore stations, cable ships and cables, and training.

Boslaugh, David L. 1999. *When Computers Went to Sea: The Digitization of the United States Navy*. Los Alamitos, CA: IEEE Computer Society.

The four-decade development of the Naval Tactical Data System (NTDS) is related, from radar to code breaking to weapons directing to the development of tactical shipboard computers from the 1950s into the 1990s.

Gebhard, Louis A. 1979. *Evolution of Naval Radio-Electronics and Contributions of the Naval Research Laboratory*. Naval Research Laboratory Report 8300. Washington, DC: Government Printing Office.

An important study of the development of improving wireless technology. Includes discussion of radar and electronic countermeasures as well as radio communication. See also Taylor.

Hezlet, Arthur. 1975. *Electronics and Sea Power*. New York: Stein & Day.

The role of wireless and other electronics (including radar and code breaking) in naval warfare from the late nineteenth century into the 1960s.

Howeth, L[inwood] S., 1963. *History of Communications-Electronics in the United States Navy*. Washington, DC: Government Printing Office.

Numerous appendices, photos, notes, bibliography, index. Well-documented history focusing on wireless and radio applications. The forty-two chapters appear in sections on the decade of development (to World War I), the golden age (1914 to the early 1920s), and the age of electronics (through World War II). Very important study that despite its age has not yet been superseded. An essential book.

Kent, Barrie. 1993. *Signal! A History of Signalling in the Royal Navy*. Clanfield, UK: Hyden House.

From signal flags to wireless and on to modern methods—this is the definitive history to date. The first part (seventeen chapters) relates the history chronologically while the second (six chapters) provides an anthology of selections from documents and earlier narratives. An essential book.

Palmer, Michael A. 2005. *Command at Sea: Naval Command and Control Since the Sixteenth Century*. Cambridge, MA: Harvard University Press.

Wide-ranging study, focusing on the days of sail, making clear the impact signaling systems had on naval command and control functions.

Taylor, A. Hoyt. 1949. *Radio Reminiscences: A Half Century*. Washington, DC: U.S. Naval Research Laboratory (republished 1960).

The author's experiences from the turn of the century to World War II, with a host of details on people and technical developments. See also Gebhard.

Woods, David L., ed. 1980. *Signaling and Communicating at Sea* 2 Vols. *Historical Studies in Telecommunications.* New York: Arno Press.

Extensive anthology of contemporary papers and documents—an invaluable collection. Volume 1 includes thirty-one items, most devoted to visual signaling. Volume 2 continues with twenty-seven more that are largely devoted to wireless, including research. An essential set of books.

Aviation Communications

Beauchamp, Ken. 2001. "Military Telegraphy in the Air." In *History of Telegraphy,* chap. 10 , 348–388. London: Institution of Electrical Engineers.

Photos, diagrams. Radio in several countries' air forces from the turn of the twentieth century to after World War II.

Morrison, Larry R. 1997. *From Flares to Satellites: A Brief History of Air Force Communications.* Scott Air Force Base, IL: Air Force Communications Command Office of History.

One of many publications issued for the fiftieth anniversary of the U.S. Air Force, this offers a good brief survey with photos and annotations.

Snyder, Thomas S., gen. ed. 1981. *The Air Force Communications Command: Providing the Reins of Command 1938–1981 [1991].* 3rd ed. Scott Air Force Base, IL: Air Force Communications Command Office of History.

Well-illustrated history of the organization and technology of aircraft communications in the U.S. Army (to 1947) and Air Force. An essential book.

Selected Web Sites

This very brief listing excludes museum Web sites (which are listed under Military Communications Museums). All sites listed were valid as of the fall of 2005. (Many more useful sites are noted after individual entries within the text.)

Military communication links
http://militaryradio.com/links.html

Branch History of Canadian Defence Communications/Electronics
http://www.img.forces.gc.ca/commelec/Brhistory/hisSpla_e.htm (zip file)

Radio Systems Aboard HMCS Haida
(by Jerry Proc, with extensive detailed chapters on Canada)
http://webhome.idirect.com/~jproc/rrp/toc.html

Rongstad's Worldwide Links to Military Communications-Electronics
http://vikingphoenix.com/public/rongstad/military/c4i/commelex.htm

Royal Naval Communications Association
http://www.rnca.info/frameindex.htm

U.S. Air Force Communications Agency History
(includes an extensive survey history)
http://public.afca.af.mil/history_pages/flares1.htm

U.S. Army Communications-Electronics Command
http://www.monmouth.army.mil/cecom/

INDEX

1st Air Force Combat Camera Squadron (United States), 352

4th Wireless Group (United Kingdom), 195

10th Cavalry ("Buffalo Soldiers" [United States]), 164

11th Air Assault Division (United States), 9

55th Army Signal Corps (United States), 352

92nd Infantry Division (United States), 164

93rd Infantry Division (United States), 164

Advanced Research Projects Agency (ARPA), 237–238

Air Force Command, Control, Communications and Computer Agency (AFC4A), 1

Air Force Communications Agency (AFCA), **1–3**
and command, control, communications, computer, intelligence, surveillance, and reconnaissance (C4ISR) capabilities, 2
Field Operating Agency (FOA) of, 1–2

Air Force Communications Command (AFCC), 1

Air Force Communications Service (AFCS), Air Force Communications Command (AFCC), **3–6**

Air Force Frequency Management Center, 1

Air Force Operational Test and Evaluation Center, 1

Air Force Research Laboratory, **6–7**

Airborne Communications Control AN/ASC-5, 9

Airborne Warning and Control System (AWACS), xxxvii, 203, **7–8**

Airmobile communications, **8–10**

Airplanes, **10–13**
and the Airborne Command Post ("Looking Glass"), 12
British, 11
Cold War applications of, 12

drone aircraft, 12
post–World War II, 11–12
pre–World War I, 10
World War I, 10–11
World War II, 11

Airships and balloons, xxvii, **13–15**
British, 14
German Zeppelins, 13–14
U.S., 13, 14 (photo), 15
use of during the American Civil War, 273–274

Airways and Air Communications Service (AACS), 3–4

Alaska Communications System (ACS), 4, **15–17**
Alascom, 16
Washington Alaska Military Cable and Telegraph System (WAMCATS), 15–16, 37
White Alaska Integrated Communications and Electronics (WHITE ALICE), 16, 59, 458

Aldis lamp, **17–18,** 17 (photo)

Alexander, Edward Porter, **18–19,** 20, 68, 102

Allied Submarine Detection Investigating Committee (ASDIC), 43

Alternate Joint Communications Center (AJCC), **413–415**

American Civil War (1861–1985), xxvii, **19–21,** 36, 55–57, 142, 271–272, 395, 401, 429–430
construction of military roads during, 296
establishment of the U.S. Military Telegraph Service (USMTS), 20
photography during, 352
postal services during, 361
railway networks of, 492–493
use of balloons during, 273–274
use of the telegraph during, 441–442
use of the "wig-wag" communications system during, 18, 19–20, 160, 214
See also Bull Run, Battle of; Coston signals

American Institute of Electrical Engineers
(AIEE), 230–231
American Telephone & Telegraph Company
(AT&T), xxviii, xxxi, **21–23,** 58, 59, 448, 449
and the "Bell Battalions," 21
forced breakup of, 23
role of in Korean War communications, 22
role of in World War I communications, 21–22
role of in World War II communications, 22
Western Electric subsidiary of, 21–23
American Teletype Corporation, 448
American wars (to 1860), **23–24**
American Revolution (1776–1781), 23
Mexican War (1846–1848), 24
War of 1812 (1812–1814), 24
Ancient signals/signaling, **24–26**
of Aneas the Tactician, 25
of Cleoxones and Democritus, 25
fire signals, 25
Antheil, George, 267
Appalachian (AGC-1), **26–27**
Ardois light system, **27–28**
Arlington Hall, **28–30,** 29 (photo), 86, 117, 402,
520
Armed Forces Communications & Electronics
Association (AFCEA), **30–31**
Armstrong, Edwin Howard, xxxii, **31–32,** 32
(photo), 37, 111, 369, 372, 490, 503, 519
Army Airways Communications System, Air-
ways and Air Communications Service
(AACS), **32–34**
Army Amateur Radio System (AARS), 292–293
Artillery/gunfire, **40–41**
Association of Old Crows (AOC), xxxviii, **41–42**
Atlantic, Battle of, **42–44**
Atlantic Wall, xxxii, **44–45,** 45 (photo)
Automated Weather Distribution System, 5
Automatic Digital Network (AUTODIN), 4,
47–48, 119, 120, 121, 354
Automatic Secure Voice Communications
(AUTOSEVOCOM), **48–49**
Automatic Voice Network (AUTOVON), 4, 5,
122

Babbage, Charles, 98
Bain, Alexander, **51–52,** 145
Baird, John Logie, 450
Baltic nations, **52–54**
Estonia, 52
Latvia, 52–54
Lithuania, 54

Banker, Grace, **54–55,** 55 (photo)
Baran, Paul, 109
Bardeen, John, 455
Beardslee telegraph, **55–57,** 56 (photo)
Beauregard, P. G. T., 18, 68, 102
Bell, Alexander Graham, xxvii–xxviii, **57–58,** 58
(photo), 148, 230, 444
Bell Telephone Laboratories (BTL), xxxv, **58–60,**
145, 455
Berners-Lee, Tim, 239
Bigbie, E. E., 209
Black, Hanson B., 505
Blair, William Richards, **61–62**
Blake, Gordon, 33
Blandford Camp, **62–63**
Bletchley Park, **63–65,** 405, 520
See also German "Fish" codes; Government
Code and Cipher School (GC&CS [Great
Britain]), Ultra; Welchman, Gordon
Blue Ridge, 27
Boer War (1899–1902), xxvii, xxix, 444, 493
Boer War wireless, **65–66**
signaling during, 160, 308
Bolero Project, 33
Bolton, John, 209
Bonaparte, Napoleon, 511–512
Boyd, John, 434, 507
Brady, Mathew, 352
Brattain, Walter, 455
Britain, Battle of, xxxii, **66–68,** 67 (photo), 138,
372, 446
British School of Military Engineering, 143
Brodie, Alexander, 336
Bull Run, Battle of, **68–69,** 102
Bush, George W., 2
Bush, Vannevar, **69–70,** 98, 316

Cable and Wireless Limited, 439–440
Camp Crowder (Missouri), **71–72**
Canada, **72–75,** 74 (photo)
air force signaling, 74
army signaling, 73–74
merger of all armed forces signal organizations, 75
National Defence Communications System,
74
navy signaling, 74–75
origins of signaling in, 72–73
Canadian Forces Reorganization Act (1968), 75
Canadian Forces Supplementary Radio System
(SRS), 76

Canine, Ralph, 381–382
Carruthers, Bruce, 73
Carty, John J., 37
Caselli, Giovanni, 51, 145
Cassity, James, 392
Caulfield, William, 295
Central Intelligence Agency (CIA), 316–317, 341,
    404
  Underground Facility Analysis Center of,
    466–467
Central Security Service (CSS), 319
Chappe, Claude, xxv, **76–77,** 131, 383, 397
Chappe semaphore system, xxvi, 311, 312, 397–
    398
Chatau, Pierre-Jacques, 383
Cheney, Dick, 414
Cher Ami, and the "Lost Battalion," 31, **77–78**
Chicksands, **78–79**
China (People's Republic of China), **79–82**
  development of computer viruses by, 81
  military communications network in, 80
  modernization of communications in, 80–81
  and the People's Liberation Army (PLA),
    80, 81
  signal corps development in, 80
Churchill, Winston, 42, 64, 463, 478, 520
Ciezki, Maksymilian, 357, 358, 359
Clark, Mark, 464
Coast defense (United States), **82–84**
  and fire control (FC) communication, 82, 83
  importance of radio to, 84
  and the "telautograph," 83
  and the use of telephone communications, 82
Code breaking, xxxiii, xxxix, **86–87,** 182, 253,
    520–521. *See also* Arlington Hall; Bletchley
    Park; Code talkers; Polish code breaking
Code/codebooks, **84–86,** 261
Code talkers, **87–89,** 88 (photo), 406
Colomb, P. H., 157, 209
Color, **89–90**
Colton, Roger, 503
Combat information center (CIC), **90–91,** 90
    (photo)
  primary purpose of, 91
Combat Information Transport System (CITS),
    91–92
Combat Logistics Network (COMLOGNET), 47
Combined Communications-Electronics Board
    (CCEB), 294–295
Commonwealth Communications Army Net-
    work (COMCAN [Great Britain]), **92**

Communication satellites, **92–96**
  growing use of, 94
  origins of, 93
  U.S. military satellites, 94–96
Communications, military, xxiii–xxiv
  between World Wars I and II, xxxii
  during the digital era, xxxvii–xxxviii
  during the Korean and Vietnam Wars, xxxiv–
    xxxvii
  during World War I, xxix–xxxi
  during World War II, xxxii–xxxiv
  pre-electric era, xxiv–xxvi
  telephone and telegraph era, xxvi–xviii
  trends underlying development of, xxxviii–xl
  wireless era, xxviii–xxix
Communications intelligence (COMINT), 404
Communications Security (COMSEC), **96–98**
Communications Security Establishment (CSE
    [Canada]), **75–76**
Computers, **98–101**
  advances in mainframe computers, 99–100
  and computer security (COMPUSEC), 100,
    101–102
  development of Colossus, 98–99, 405
  electronic numerical integrator and computer
    (ENIAC), 99
  and Secret Internet Protocol Router Network
    (SIPRNet), 100, 102
Confederate Air Force, 19
Confederate Army Signal Corps, xxvii, 18, 19,
    102–103
Congreve, William, 401
Cooke, William F., 51, 440
Coston, Benjamin Franklin, 103
Coston, Martha J., 104
Coston signals, **103–104**
Couriers, **105–106**
Cuban Missile Crisis, **106–108,** 107 (photo), 221,
    320, 450
Custer, George A., 148

Daniels, Josephus, 156
DARPANET, xxxvi, 6, **109–110**
da Silva Rondon, Candido Mariano, 260
de Bigot, Sebastian Francisco, 173, 223
Deception, **111–113**
  and the "double-cross" system, 112–113
  during the Korean and Vietnam Wars, 113
  during the Six Day War, 138
  Operation Fortitude, 112
  Operation Mincemeat, 112

Defence Communication Service Agency
(DCSA [Great Britain]), **113–114**
Defence Fixed Telecommunications System
(DFTS [Great Britain]), **114–115**
Defense Advanced Research Projects Agency
(DARPA), 109, 110, **115–116**
major concerns of, 116
Defense Communications Agency (DCA), **117,**
119–120
Defense Communications Board/Board of War
Communications, **117–118**
Defense Communications System (DCS), **118–
119**
Defense Information Systems Agency (DISA),
119–120
Defense Intelligence Agency (DIA), 404
Defense Message System (DMS), 119, **120–121,**
139
Defense Switched Network (DSN), 118–119,
121–122
Defiance, **122–123**
de Forest, Lee, **110–111,** 111 (photo), 369, 437,
490
de la Bourdonnais, Bertrand-François Mahé,
173, 223
de Reynold-Chauvancy, Charles, 223
Dewey, George, 378, 419, 485
Diego Garcia, **123–124**
Distant Early Warning (DEW) Line, 22
Dogs, **124–126,** 125 (photo)
Dogs for Defense, Inc., 125
hearing of, 126
value of, 126
Dom Pedro, 147
Donovan, William ("Wild Bill"), 341, 342
Driscoll, Agnes Meyer, **126–127,** 389

Eardley-Wilmot, A. P., 223
Eastern Europe, **129–130**
Czechoslovakia, 129
Poland, 129–130
Romania, 130
Eberle, E. B., 356
Edelcrantz, Abraham, xxvi, **130–131**
Edgeworth, Richard Lovell, xxv
Edison, Thomas A., **131–132,** 230, 326, 490
Egypt, **132–134**
Egyptian Air Defense Force (ADF), 133
information infrastructure of, 133
military strength of, 132–133
wars of with Israel, 133

Einstein, Albert, 269
Eisenhower, Dwight D., 463–464
Electric cipher machine (ECM Mark II,
"SIGABA"), **134–136,** 135 (photo)
Electromagnetic pulse (EMP), **136–137,**
138–139
Electronic countermeasures/electronic warfare
(ECM/EW), 41–42, **137–139**
in China, 81
Electronic numerical integrator and computer
(ENIAC), 99
Electronics intelligence (ELINT), 138, 404
E-mail systems, **139–140**
Enigma cipher machine, xxxii, **140–142,** 141
(photo)
European wars, late nineteenth-century,
142–143
Crimean War (1854–1856), xxvi, 142, 219, 352,
383, 467
Franco-Prussian War (1870–1871), 142, 442
Everest, George, 209
Ewing, Alfred, 380

Fabyan, George, 126
Facsimile/Fax, **145–146**
Falklands conflict (1982), **146–147,** 373
Fateful Day (25 June 1876), **147–148**
Fenton, Roger, 352
Ferrié, Gustave-Auguste, **148–149**
Fessenden, Reginald A., **149–151,** 150 (photo),
370
Fiber optics, **151–152**
military advantages of, 152
Field, Cyrus, xxvii, **152–153**
Field wire and cable, **153–154**
disadvantages of, 154
military use of, 153–154
types of, 153
Fire/flame/torch signaling, **154–155**
Greek and Roman use of, 154–155
Native American use of, 155
Fiske, Bradley A., **155–156,** 399
Flaghoist signaling, **156–158**
basic flag designs, 156–157
colors of, 157
disadvantages of, 157–158
Flags, **158–161**
army flag telegraphy, 159–160
colors of, 159
European use of, 160
military signaling with, 159

two basic systems of (one-flag and two-flag),
  159
Flagship, **161**
Fleming, John Ambrose, **161–162,** 490
Flowers, T. H., 180
Foreign instrumentation signals intelligence
  (FISINT), 404
FORTEZZA cards, 97, 102, 239
Fort Gordon (Georgia), **163–164**
Fort Huachuca (Arizona), **164–165**
Fort Meade (Maryland), **165–166,** 319
Fort Monmouth (New Jersey), **166–167**
Fort Myer (Virginia), **167–168**
France, 130, 442, 511–512
France, air force communications of, **168–169**
France, army communications of, **169–172**
  army communications units, 171–172
  battle management system of, 171
  Commission for Military Telegraphy, 170
  and information technology, 171
  use of electric telegraph for, 170
  use of semaphore telegraph stations, 170
France, naval communications of, **172–174**
  during the Cold War, 173–174
  during World War II, 173
  tactical communications systems of, 173
  use of numerical flag code by, 173
Franklin, Benjamin, 13
Friedman, William F., xxxii, 86, 134, **174–176**
Fuller, Algernon Clement, 176, 177
Fullerphone, **176–177,** 176 (photo)
Future Combat Systems (FCS), **177–178**

Gauss, Karl, 209
Genghis Khan, xxv, 307, 355
Gerke, Friedrich Clemens, 305
German "Fish" codes, xxxii, **179–181**
German Radio Monitoring Service, 187
Germany, air force communications of, **181–182**
Germany, army communications of, **182–186,**
  442
  during World War I, 183–184
  during World War II, 184–185
  line communications of, 183
  post–World War II to the present, 185–186
Germany, military communications school,
  186–187
Germany, naval communications of, **189–190**
  during World War I, 189
  Naval Communications Research Establish-
    ment, 189

post–World War II to the present, 190
  and submarines, 190
Germany, naval intelligence, **187–189**
  Naval Communications Intelligence Division
    (B-Dienst), 188
Gigot, Felix, 355
Global Command and Control System (GCCS),
  190–192, 241
Global Information Grid (GIG), xxxviii,
  192–193
  and the GIG Bandwidth Extension (GIG-BE),
    192
Global positioning system (GPS), xxxviii,
  193–195, 194(photo), 202, 240, 290
Golden Arrow sections, **195–196**
Goldmark, Peter, 450
Gordon, John B., 163
Government Code and Cipher School (GC&CS
  [Great Britain]), xxxiii, 63, 64, **196–197,**
  402–403, 405, 452, 453, 525, 526
Graf Zeppelin (LZ-130), 14
Grant, Ulysses S., 271
Great Britain. *See* United Kingdom
Great Wall (China), **197–198**
Greece, military communications of,
  198–199
  during World War I, 198
  during World War II, 198–199
  Hellenic Signal Corps, 198
Greely, Adolphus W., **199–200,** 285, 515
Grouchy, Emmanuel, 512
Ground radio, **200–201**
Gulf War (1990–1991), xxxviii, 10, 124, 133,
  201–205, 240, 241, 373, 456, 458
  coalition communications system of, 203
  and the destruction of Iraq's communication
    system, 204
  as a "hyperwar," 202
  and the Joint Surveillance and Target Attack
    Radar System (JSTARS), 202
  Operation Desert Storm Network (ODSNET),
    203–204
  two phases of, 202–203
  use of satellite communication during, 202

Hadrian's Wall (Great Britain), **207–208,**
  208 (photo)
Hale, George Ellery, 318
Hall, Reginald, 380
Hammer ACE, 1, 5
Hebern, Edward, 126

Heliograph and mirrors, **208–211,** 210 (photo)
  decline in use of, 211
  and Morse Code, 209
  range of the heliograph, 210–211
  sources of light for, 208–209
  and the U.S. campaign against Native
    Americans, 210
  use of during colonial wars, 209
"Hello Girls," **211–213,** 212 (photo)
Heraldry/insignia, **213–215,** 214 (table)
  ancient use of, 213–214
  and the Signal Corps device, 214
  use of in sporting events, 215
Hicks, Janet E. A., 39
High-frequency direction finding (HF DF),
    215–217
High-speed Morse code, **217–218**
Hindenburg (LZ-129), 14
Ho Chi Minh, 494
Hooper, Stanford C., **218–219**
Horses/mules, **219–221,** 220 (photo)
  during the Afghan War (1878–1880), 219
  during the Crimean War (1854–1856), 219
  during World War I, 219–220
Hotline/Direct Communications Link (DCL),
    221–222
Howe, Richard, xxv, 159, **222–223,** 477
Human intelligence (HUMINT), 404
Human signaling, **223–224**

Identification, friend or foe (IFF), **225–226,** 471
Imaging intelligence (IMINT), 404
India, **226–228**
  commercial telegraph line in (1857), 226
  Indian Signal Service, 226–227
  and technology, 227
  and tensions with Pakistan, 227
Information Revolution in Human Affairs
    (IRMA), **228–229,** 433–434
Information warfare (IW), 228
Infrared signal systems, **229–230**
  the NANCY HANKS system, 230
Institute of Electrical and Electronic Engineers
    (IEEE), **230–232**
Institute of Radio Engineers (IRE), 231
Institution of Electrical Engineers (IEE),
    232–233
Integrated circuit (IC), 296, 416
Intelligence ships, **233–234,** 233 (photo)
  and AGER vessels, 234
  and SWATH vessels, 233–234

U.S. intelligence ships, 234
Interdepartmental Radio Advisory Committee
    (IRAC), 321–322, 423–424, 425
International Code of Signals (ICS), **234–236**
International Frequency Registration Board
    (IFRB), 237
International Maritime Consultative
    Organization (IMCO), 236
International Telecommunication Union (ITU),
    146, **236–237**
Internet, **237–240**
  and ARPANET, 238, 239
  development of the World Wide Web
    (WWW), 239
  and the Domain Name System, 238
  and TELENET, 238–239
  and the U.S. Defense Advanced Research
    Projects Agency (ARPA), 237–238
  See also Secret Internet Protocol Router Net-
    work (SIPRNet)
Iraq War (2003–present), xxxviii, 10, **240–244,**
    249, 373
  and the Army Battle Command System
    (ABCS), 241
  and the Blue Force Tracking (BFT) system,
    241
  changing communication technology used in,
    240–243
  lessons of, 243
  and the TeleEngineering Kit (TEK), 242
Israel, 81, 133, **244–245**
  and the Israeli Defense Forces (IDF), 244
  and the Mountain Rose system, 245
  and the Six Day War (1967), 138, 234
Iyappa, A. C., 227

Jackson, Andrew, 24
Jackson, Henry B., xxviii–xxix, 123, 143,
    247–248, 477
Jamming, **248–250**
  during the Iraq War, 249
  during World War I, 248
  during World War II, 248–249
Japan, 81
Japan, air force communications of, **250–251**
  during World War II, 250
  lack of communication between army and
    naval air forces, 250–251
Japan, army communications of, **251–254**
  during the Russo-Japanese War (1904–1905),
    252–253

during the Sino-Japanese War (1894–1895), 252
during World War I, 253
during World War II, 253
in the feudal period, 252
modernization of, 251–252
Japan, naval communications of, **254–255**
during World War I, 254
during World War II, 254–255
See also Midway, Battle of
Jenks, Robert W., 223
Johnson, Frances, 352
Johnson, Joseph, 68
Johnson, Lyndon B., 495
Johnston, Philip, 87–88
Joint Assault Signal Company (JASCO), **255–256**
Joint Tactical Information Distribution System (JTIDS), **256–258**
Joint Tactical Radio System (JTRS), **258–259**
Joint Task Force–Global Network Operations (JTF-GNO), **259–260**
"Jungle Telegraph," **260–261**
Jutland, Battle of, **261–262,** 396

Kempenfelt, Richard, 223
Kennedy, John F., 106–107, 430, 494
Khrushchev, Nikita, 107
Kilby, Jack St. Clair, **263–264,** 416
Kimmel, Husband E., 348
Kleinrock, Leonard, 238
Konvalinka, J. V., 223
Korean War (1950–1953), xxxiv, 22, **264–266,** 373, 375, 480
communications problems during, 265
Eighth Army (U.S.) operations in, 264–265
and the Mukden Cable system, 264
and Operation Roll-Up, 264–265
propaganda used during, 365
Korn, Arthur, 145

Lamarr, Hedy, **267–268**
Langer, Gwido, 358, 359
Language translation, **268–269**
Langley, Samuel P., 199–200
Lasers, **269–270**
Lee, Robert E., 19
Lenin, Vladimir, 384
Lights and beacons, **270–271**
Lincoln, Abraham, xxvii
use of the telegraph by, **271–272,** 272 (photo)
Long, John D., 419, 420

Longstreet, James, 19
Lowe, Thaddeus, xxvii, **273–274,** 273 (photo)

Magic, **275–277**
Maginot Line, xxxii, **277–278,** 277 (illustration)
Mance, Henry C., 209
Mandl, Fritz, 257
Maori signaling, **278–279**
Marconi, Guglielmo, xxix, 65, 162, 247, **279–281,** 280 (photo), 369, 477
Marion, Francis, 356
Marne, Battle of, **281–282,** 371–372, 517
Marryat, Frederick, 158, 234–235
six-part signal code system of, 235
Mauborgne, Joseph Oswald, **282–284**
Mauldin, Bill, 41
Maxwell, James Clerk, 162
McClellan, George, 429
McDonald, John, 223
McDowell, Irvin, 68, 69
McPeak, Merill, 202
Meade, George G., 165
Measurement and signatures intelligence (MASINT), 404
Medal of Honor winners, U.S. Signal Corps, **284–286**
Barnes, Will Croft, 284
Greely, Adolphus W., 285
Johnston, Gordon, 285
Kilbourne, Charles E., 285
Lane, Morgan D., 284
Medieval military signaling, **286–287**
Mercury, **287–288**
Meteor burst communications (MBC), **288–289**
Meucci, Antonio, 200
Mexican Punitive Expedition (1916–1917), **289–290,** 299
Microwave, **2901–291**
high-powered microwave (HPM) bombs, 291
Midway, Battle of, **291–292**
Miles, Nelson A., 164, 355–356
Military Affiliate Radio System (MARS), **292–294**
Military Communications-Electronic Board, **294–295**
Military Message Handling System (MMHS), 139
Military roads, **295–296**
British, 295
Roman, 295
U.S., 296

Milligan, James E., 103

Millikan, Robert A., 318

Miniaturization, **296–297**

Missile range communications, **297–298**

Mitchell, Billy, 15–16

Mobile communications, **298–302**
   during the Gulf War, 301
   during World War I, 299
   during World War II, 299–300
   early attempts at, 299
   modern, 300–301
   and radio, 299, 300

Mobile wireless assembly (MWA), 440

Modulation, **302–303**
   amplitude modulation (AM), 302
   frequency modulation (FM), xxix, 302
   phase modulation (PM), 302–303
   and software-defined radio (SDR), 303
   very high frequency (VHF), 302, 372, 373, 479

Moore, Gordon, 416–417

Morse, Samuel F. B., xxvi, 200, 303, **305–306,**
   440–441

Morse Code, 27, **303–305,** 304 (photo)
   International Morse Code, 305

Mount Whitney, 27

Multilingual Automatic Speech-to-Speech
   Translator (MASTOR), 268–269

Murray, Donald, 448

Murray, George, 398

Music signals, **306–308**
   during the Boer War, 308
   Greek and Roman, 307
   use of the drum in, 307
   use of gongs in, 308
   use of in navies, 308
   use of the trumpet in, 307–308

Myer, Albert J., xxvii, 18, 20–21, 35–36, 68–69,
   102, 167, 223, 304, 306, **308–310**
   activities during the American Civil War, 309
   development of the "wig-wag" communications system, 19–20, 159–160, 214
   See also Fort Myer (Virginia)

Nalder, R., 516

Napoleonic Wars (1795–1815), xxv–xxvi,
   311–313
   Peninsular Campaign of, 312
   use of the Chappe semaphore system during,
   311–312
   use of signal flag relay system during, 312
   See also Waterloo, Battle of

Nassar, Gamel Abdel, 432–433

National Bureau of Standards (NBS), **313–314**

National Communications System (NCS),
   314–315

National Defense Research Committee (NDRC),
   315–316

National Electric Signal Company (NESCO),
   150

National Institute of Standards and Technology
   (NIST), **313–314**

National Reconnaissance Office (NRO), **316–318**

National Research Council (NRC), **318–319**

National Security Agency (NSA), xxxvii, 87,
   319–321
   and the Cuban Missile Crisis, 320
   effect of new technology on activities of,
   320–321
   and the *Oxford* SIGINT collection vessel, 320
   and SIGINT, 319, 320
   and the UKUSA network, 320, 403

National Telecommunications and Information
   Administration (NTIA), **321–322,** 424, 425
   Interdepartmental Radio Advisory Commit-
   tee (IRAC) of, 321–322, 423–424

Native American signaling, **322–323.** *See also*
   Code talkers

Naval radio stations, **323–326,** 324 (photo)
   and the Arlington radio station NAA,
   324–325
   stations outside of the United States, 325
   technical equipment used in, 324–325

Naval Research Laboratory (NRL), **326–328,**
   437–438
   bureaucratic changes in, 327
   space research of, 327

Navigation Satellite Timing and Ranging
   (NAVSTAR), 193–194, 202

Nebraska Avenue (Washington, DC), **333–334**

Nelson, Horatio, xxv, 454

Network Enterprise Technology Command
   (NETCOM), **334–336**

Newman, Max, 180

New Zealand. *See* Royal New Zealand Corps of
   Signals

Ney, Michel, 512

Night signals, **337–338**

Noble, Daniel E., 503

North Atlantic Treaty Organization (NATO),
   174, 385, 458, 475, 479, 511

Communications & Information Systems
   Agency (NCSA) of, **338–339**

Northampton (CA-125), 26–27
Norris, William, 102–103
Noyce, Robert, xxxv, **263–264,** 416

Office of Scientific Research and Development
  (OSRD), 316
Office of Strategic Services (OSS), **341–342**
Ohio, **342–343**
The Old Telegraph (G. Wilson), 399
OP-20-G, **343–345,** 487
O'Reilly, Henry, 429
Osman, A. H., 356
Oxford, 106

Palluth, Antoni, 357
Pasley, Charles, 398
Patton, George S., 112, 464
Pearl Harbor, attack on, **347–348,** 375
Pershing, John J., 164, 211, 289
Pheidippides, 105
Philippines, **348–350**
  origins and operations of the Philippine
    Signal Corps, 348–349
Philipps, H. Cranmer, 223
Phonetic alphabet, **350–352,** 351 (table)
Photography (military photography), **352–354,**
  353 (photo)
  combat camera (COMCAM) units of all
    service branches, 352–353
  Joint Combat Camera Center (JCCC) of, 353
Phu Lam (Vietnam), **354–355**
Pierce, John, 455
Pigeons, use of in military signaling, xxvii,
  xxxiv, **355–357,** 356 (photo)
  in ancient times, 355
  in World War I, 356
Polish code breaking, **357–360**
  key personnel of, 359–360
  Project GALE, 357–358
Popham, Home Riggs, xxv, 159, **360–361,**
  398–399, 477
Postal services, **361–363**
  British, 361, 362
  during the American Civil War, 361
  during World War I, 362
  during World War II, 362
  U.S., 362
Powell, Colin, 228
Preece, W. H., 444
Propaganda/psychological warfare, xxxi, xxxiv,
  363–366, 366 (photo)

  during the Korean War, 365
  during the Vietnam War, 365–366
  during World War I, 364
  during World War II, 364–365, 521
  psychological operations (PSYOPS), 363

Quartz crystals, and radio control, **367–368**

Radar, xxxii, 373
  German "crooked leg" system, 67
  ground control approach (GCA) radar units,
    60
Radio, **369–374,** 371 (photo), 493–494
  origins of, 369–370
  post–World War II usage, 373–374
  radio silence, **374–375,** 521
  use of during the Korean War, xxxiv
  use of during World War I, 370–372, 517,
    518
  use of during World War II, 372–373,
    519–520
  and the very high frequency (VHF) spectrum,
    9, 11, 39, 372, 373
  See also Ground radio; Modulation; Quartz
    crystals, and radio control
Radio Corporation of America (RCA), 16, 150
Reber, Samuel, **375–376**
Rejewski, Marian, 357, 359
Renaissance and early modern military signals,
  376–378
  innovations during, 377
  signal fires, 376–377
Richardson, E. H., 124, 125
Robison, Samuel Shelburne, **378–379**
Rochefort, Joseph J., 126, 292, 389–390
Rogers, James Harris, 201, **379–380**
Rojdestvensky, Z. P., 459
Rome Air Development Center (RADC), 6
Ronalds, Francis, 312
Room 40, 261, **380–381**
Roosevelt, Franklin, 17, 520
Roosevelt, Theodore, 260, 515
Rowlett, Frank B., xxxii, 134, **381–382,** 389, 520
Royal Australian Corps of Signals, **45–46**
Royal New Zealand Corps of Signals, **336–337**
  during World War I, 336–337
  during World War II, 337
R?zycki, Jerzy, 357, 359
Rumsfeld, Donald, 113
Russia/Soviet Union, air force communications
  of, **382–383**

Russia/Soviet Union, army communications of, **383–386**
  and the Chechen conflict, 385
  countermeasures of against enemy command and control, 384–385
  during the Cold War, 384
  and "radio-electronic combat" (REC), 384
  telegraph systems, 383
  wireless systems, 383–384
Russia/Soviet Union, navy communications of, **386–387**
  during the Cold War, 387
Russo-Japanese War (1904–1905), 459–460, 468

Safford, Laurence F., 126, 127, **389–390**
Salisbury, J. D., 352
Sampson, William T., 419
Sanford, Edward S., 20
Sarnoff, David, xxxiv
Satellite communications, **390–394,** 469
  and the Air Force Satellite Communications System (AFSATCOM), 94, 392
  and the Communication Moon Relay Project, 390–391
  and the Fleet Satellite Communications (FLTSATCOM) system, 94–95, 392
  and the Global Broadcast System (GBS), 393
  and the Initial Defense Satellite Communications System (IDSCS), 393
  military satellite communications (MILSAT-COM), 94, 391–392
  and the Milstar Satellite Communications System, 95–96, 393–394
  optimum altitude for, 391
  of the Soviet Union, 391
Scherbius, Arthur, 140
Schley, Scott, 419
Scott, Frank, 394
Scott Air Force Base (Illinois), **394–395**
Searchlights/signal blinkers, **395–397,** 396 (photo)
Secret Internet Protocol Router Network (SIPRNet), 100
Semaphore systems, xxvi, 214, 383, **397–399,** 398 (photo). *See also* Chappe semaphore system; Flags
Semi-Automatic Ground Environment (SAGE), xxxvii, 12, **399–400**
Shafter, William R., 419
Shockley, William, 455

Short, Walter C., 348
SIGABA, 390
Signal book, **400–401**
Signal Officer Candidate School (OCS), 163
Signal rockets, **401–402**
  drawbacks of, 402
Signal Security Agency (SSA), xxxvii, **402–404**
Signals intelligence (SIGINT), 76, 106, 107, 319, 320, 403, **404–407**
  during the Cold War, 406–407
  during World War I, 405
  during World War II, 405–406
  origins of, 404–405
Signals Research and Development Establishment (SRDE [Great Britain]), **407–409**
SIGSALY voice communication system, xxxiii, 59, **409–410,** 520
Silicon chip, xxxv, 263–264
Silicon Valley (California), **410–412**
Single Channel Ground and Airborne Radio System (SINCGARS), **412–413**
Single sideband, **413**
Site R. *See* Alternate Joint Communications Center (AJCC)
Six Day War (1967), 138, 234
Slaby, Adolph, xxix, 143, 182
Smoke signals, **415–416**
Society of Wireless and Telegraph Engineers, 231
Solid state electronics, **416–417**
South Africa (and the Boer Republics), **417–418**
  and the Special Signal Services (SSS), 418
Spanish-American War (1898), xxvii, xxviii, **418–420,** 444, 468
  signal flags used during, 419–420
Spectrum frequencies, **420–422,** 421 (chart)
  extremely high frequency (EHF), 422
  extremely low frequency (ELF), 421
  high frequency (HF), 421
  medium frequency (MF), 420
  super high frequency (SHF), 422
  ultra-high frequency (UHF), 420, 422
  very high frequency (VHF), 420, 421–422
Spectrum management, **422–425**
  early nineteenth-century legislation concerning, 422–423
  and the Interdepartmental Radio Advisory Committee (IRAC), 321–322, 423–424, 425
  and the Joint Frequency Panel (JFP), 424–425
  and the U.S. Military Communications-Electronics Board (MCEB), 424

Spencer, Knight, 223
Spies, **425–427**
Spratt, Jack, 223
Spread spectrum technology, 267–268,
    427–428
Squier, George Owen, **428–429**
Stager, Anson, xxvii, 20, 21, **429–430**
Stanton, Edwin M., 21, 36, 429
Strategic Communications Command
    (STRATCOM), **430–431**
The Strategy of Terror (E. Taylor), 364
Stubblefield, Nathan, 200, 201
Submarine communications, **431–432**
Suez Crisis, **432–433**
Sweden, 130
"System of systems," **433–435**
System-of-Systems Common Operating
    Environment (SOSCOE), 177–178

Talk between ships (TBS), **437–438**
Tannenberg, Battle of, 371–372, 383, **438–439,**
    517
Taylor, Edmund, 364
Taylor, Zachary, 24
TELCOM mobile wireless units, **439–440**
Telefunken, 185, 189
Telegraph, **440–444,** 442 (illustration)
    needle telegraph, 440
    use of in the American Civil War, 441–442
    use of in British colonial areas of Africa, 443
    use of in the Crimean War, 441
    use of in Europe, 441
    use of in World War I, 443
Telegraph Automatic Routing Equipment
    (TARE), 449
Telemetry intelligence (TELINT), 404
Telephone, xxvii–xxviii, **444–447,** 445 (photo)
    British use of, 444–445, 446
    "trench" telephones, 445
    use of during World War I, 445
    use of during World War II, 445–446
Teleprinter/teletype, **447–449,** 447 (photo)
    development of, 447–448
Television, **449–451**
Terrorism, war on, **507–509**
    bureaucratic issues concerning, 508
    communications dilemma posed by multiple
        "wars" on terrorism, 508–509
    and the Department of Homeland Security,
        508

flexibility of terrorist organizations regarding
    communications, 507–508
and the observation-orientation-
    decision-action (OODA) loop, 507, 508
operations in Afghanistan, 508
Tesla, Nikola, **451–452**
Tiltman, John Hessell, xxxiii, 179, **452–453**
Trafalgar, Battle of, **453–454**
Transistor, **455–456**
Trexler, James H., 93, 390–391
Tri-Service Tactical Communications Program
    (TRI-TAC), **456–457**
Tropospheric scatter (troposcatter), **457–458**
Truxton, Thomas, **458–459**
Tsushima, Battle of, xxix, **459–460**
Turing, Alan Mathison, xxxiii, **460–461,** 520

Ultra, **463–464**
Underground communication centers, **464–467,**
    465 (photo)
    and the Underground Facility Analysis
        Center, 466–467
    U.S. sites, 466
    use of during the Cold War, 465–466
    use of during World War II, 464–465
Undersea cables, **467–470**
    decline in use of, 469
    drawbacks of, 469
    fiber optic cables, 469–470
United Kingdom, xxiv, xxix, 442
    and the Falklands conflict, 146–147, 479
    and the Suez Crisis, 432–433
    telephone usage by in the Boer War, 444
    See also Britain, Battle of; Y Service
United Kingdom, Royal Air Force (RAF) of,
    66–67, 79, 468, 469, **470–473**
    and Chain Home radio direction finding
        (RDF) stations, 66, 67 (photo)
    and identification, friend or foe (IFF) signals,
        471
    and the No. 90 Signals Group, 471–472
    as the Royal Flying Corps (RFC), 470–471
    Tactical Communications Wing (TCW) of,
        472–473
United Kingdom, Royal Corps of Signals,
    473–476
    origins of, 473–474
    service of in World War I, 474–475
    service of in World War II, 475
    since 1945 to present, 475–476

United Kingdom, Royal Navy of, xxix, **476–480**
   changes of in the post–World War II period,
      479–480
   during early "days of sail," 477
   during World War I, 478
   during World War II, 478–479
   and the rise of radio, 477–478
UNIVAC, 313, 329
U.S. Air Force, xxxv, 16, 151
   and the Ground Electronics Engineering
      Installation Agency (GEEIA), 298
U.S. Army, 416, 424
   Army Airways Communications System, 11
   Army Battle Command System (ABCS),
      xxxviii, **34–35**
   Army Electronics Research and Development
      Laboratories, 9
   Army Security Agency, 28
   Army Signal Intelligence Service (SIS), 28, 86,
      402
   See also U.S. Army Signal Corps
U.S. Army Signal Corps, 10, 11, 21, 22, **35–40**, 38
      (photo), 57, 83, 84, 110, 159, 334–335, 347,
      416, 505
   and aerial communications, 36
   during the Cold War, 38–39
   during the Korean War, xxxiv
   during the Vietnam War, 39
   during World War I, 37
   during World War II, 37–38
   establishment of, 223
   publication of the *Monthly Weather Review*, 36
   and quartz crystal oscillators, 367–368
   use of balloons by, 13
   use of telephones by, 444
   See also Fort Gordon (Georgia); Fort Mon-
      mouth (New Jersey); Medal of Honor win-
      ners, U.S. Signal Corps; Reber, Samuel;
      Tri-Service Tactical Communications (TRI-
      TAC); War Department Radio Net/War
      Department Message Center Program
U.S. Department of Commerce, 321, 423
U.S. Department of Defense (DoD), xxxv, 105,
      139, 192, 316–317, 362, 392, 450, 498, 522
U.S. Marine Corps, 497
   communications of, **480–481**
U.S. Military Telegraph Service (USMTS), 20, 57,
      481–483
U.S. Navy, xxix, 22, 151, 416, 423, 424, 468
   Communication Moon Relay Project
      (CMR), 93

Naval Computer and Telecommunication
      Station (NCTS), 124
Naval Security Group (NSG), **328–329,** 487
Naval Tactical Data System (NTDS), **329–330**
Navy Radio Laboratory, xxix, **332–333**
   See also Naval radio stations; Naval Research
      Laboratory (NRL); OP-20-G ; U.S. Navy,
      communications systems of
U.S. Navy, communications systems of,
      330–332, 483–487
   during World War I, 485
   during World War II, 485–486
   Global Command and Control System–
      Maritime, 331
   Naval Communications Processing and
      Routing System, 330
   Naval Computer and Telecommunications
      Area Master Station (NCTAMS), 331
   Naval Network and Space Operations
      Command (NNSOC), 330
   Naval Network Warfare Command
      (NET-WARCOM), 330–331
   Navy Communications Supplementary
      Annex (NAVCOMMSTA), 334
   Navy/Marine Corps Intranet (NMCI), 331
   Office of Naval Research (ONR), 327
   post–World War II operations, 486–487
   signal use for sailing ships, 483–484
   submarine communications, 431–432
   use of electricity and wireless at sea, 484–485
U.S. Signal Communications by Orbiting Relay
      Equipment (SCORE), 93

Vacuum tubes, xxx–xxxi, xxxii, 162, 280, 437,
      490–491
Vail, Alfred, 166, 200, 303, 306, 441
Van Deman, Ralph Henry, **491–492**
van Trotsenburg, C. K., 65
Vehicles/transport, **492–494**
   bicycles, 493
   motorcycles, 493
   railways, 492–493
   trucks, 493
Vietnam War, xxxvi–xxxvii, 39, 373, 493, **494–499**
   American and Allied communications
      (BACKPORCH and SOUTHERN TOLL),
      496–498
   background of, 494–495
   communist communications, 495–496
   last days of the war, 498
   propaganda used during, 365–366

and the U.S. incursion into Cambodia, 498
See also Airmobile communications; Phu Lam,
    Vietnam
V-mail, **489–490**
Voice over Internet Protocol (VoIP), xxxvii,
    499–500
Voice relay, 500–501
von Arco, George, xxix, 143, 182
von Blücher, Gebhard, 512
von Clausewitz, Carl, 295

Wade, George, 295
Walkie-talkie, **503–504,** 504 (photo)
Warden, John, III, 201–202
War Department Radio Net/War Department
    Message Center, **505–507**
    and the Army Command and Administrative
        Communications Agency (ACACA), 506
    renaming of as the Army Command and
        Administrative Network (ACAN), 506
Warfighter Information Network–Tactical
    (WIN-T), **509–510**
Warfighting Integration (AF/XI), 2, 3
Warsaw Pact, **510–511**
Washington, George, 23
Waterloo, Battle of, **511–512**
Weapons Data Link Network (WDLN), **513**
Welchman, Gordon, xxxiii, **513–514**
Wenger, Joseph, 126, 389
Wheatstone, Charles, 51, 440
White House Communications Agency
    (WHCA), **514–515**
Wilson, Geoffrey, 399
Wilson, Woodrow, 289
Wireless Institute, 231

Wireless Telegraph Board (the "Roosevelt
    Board"), xxix, **515–516**
World War I (1914–1918), xxix–xxxi, **516–519**
    difficulty of using visual signals during,
        516–517
    factors differentiating it from previous wars,
        516
    naval signaling and radio usage during, 518
    propaganda use during, 364
    pyrotechnic signals used during, 516
    radio equipment used during, xxx, 517
    telegraph and telephone use during, 517
    U.S. Signal Corps operations during, 517
    See also Jutland, Battle of; Marne, Battle of;
        Tannenberg, Battle of
World War II (1939–1946), xxxii–xxxiv, 33,
    519–522
    Allied code-breaking success during, 520–521
    Allied technical advantage during, 519
    propaganda use during, 364–365, 521
    radio security and silence during, 521
    telegraph use during, 520
    telephone use during, 520
    See also Midway, Battle of; Pearl Harbor
World Wide Military Command and Control
    System (WWMCCS), xxxv–xxxvi, xxxvii,
    119, **522–523**

Yardley, Herbert O., **527–528**
Y Service, **525–526**

Zimmermann, Arthur, 380
Zossen (Germany), **529–530**
Zygalski, Henryk, 357, 358, 359–360
"Zygalski sheets," 358